THE MINNESOTA MESSENIA EXPEDITION

Reconstructing a Bronze Age Regional Environment

THE MINNESOTA MESSENIA EXPEDITION
Reconstructing a Bronze Age Regional Environment

Edited by
William A. McDonald
and
George R. Rapp, Jr.

THE UNIVERSITY OF MINNESOTA PRESS □ MINNEAPOLIS

Printed in the United States of America
at the North Central Publishing Company, St. Paul.
Published in the United Kingdom and India by the Oxford
University Press, London and Delhi, and in
Canada by the Copp Clark Publishing Co. Limited, Toronto

Library of Congress Catalog Card Number: 75-187168
ISBN 0-8166-0636-6

To the Memory

of

CARL WILLIAM BLEGEN

(1887 - 1971)

◇◇

He loved modern Messenia,
Pioneered in the exploration of its Past,
And inspired others
To follow in his Footsteps

FOREWORD

We should perhaps make a few explanatory remarks about the format of the book. In dealing with subject matter so diverse in time and type, even the arrangement of chapters can pose difficulties. We originally intended a progression along the following lines: mapping – physical setting – archaeological exploration – communications – technical studies – historical development (Late Bronze times to the present). The order finally adopted not only presents the historical material before most of the technical but reverses the historical approach. That is, we begin with the best-known period (the present) and work *backward* through time in the written documents to the target phase in the Late Bronze Age. Only then do we introduce the results of our own archaeological exploration that has been concentrated on the Bronze Age. Following this pivotal chapter (8) in the heart of the book, specialists in the technical fields present evidence that bears directly or indirectly on the target period.

Our intent may be illuminated if we share with readers a title that was proposed by the senior editor (and is still dear to him) but was abandoned by popular demand as too archaic and sentimental. "Messenian Vistas" does suggest the idea behind the revised order of chapters, namely, looking back along the corridors of time to focus on the later second millennium B.C. The basic format might therefore be described as: first, picking up useful insights along the way from later documented conditions; second, presenting the most relevant evidence from the Late Bronze Age itself; and third, using scientific techniques to illuminate various features of the ancient physical environment and human adaptation to it.

A word now about the appendix, footnotes, and bibliography. With the greatest regret we decided that the fundamental data on each of the ancient habitation sites that has been put together over the past decade and systematized in Registers A and B must be relegated to the status of an appendix (pp. 264–321). The individual sites are arranged there and referred to throughout the text according to a system described in Chapter 8, page 123. Ideally, this material ought to be printed after Part I of Chapter 8, since the interpretations in Part III depend so heavily on it. But what really matters is that users of the book realize the basic importance of the information in the Registers not only for Chapter 8 but also for arguments advanced in other chapters and for much future research in the regional environment. On page 322 we provide equations between the site numbers used in the provisional publications (*AJA* 1961, 1964, 1969) and the revised system used throughout this book. With the exception of Chapter 6, footnotes have been practically eliminated, and necessary information on published material referred to in parentheses throughout the text will be found in references at the end of each chapter. This section is much fuller in the case of Chapter 5 because of the special character of the sources (many of them unpublished).

In the spelling of the numerous modern Greek placenames that appear in this volume we have tried first to ascertain the standard popular form in the spoken language (*dhimotikí*) and then to transcribe it phonetically. Our system of transliteration approximates closely that employed in *A Gazetteer of Greece* of the Permanent Committee on Geographical Names for British Official Use (London, 1942). There are two slight differences from the British practice: *ch* instead of *kh* for Greek *chi*, and *i* instead of *oi* for the Greek diphthong *oi*. In the case of certain ancient names in common use today we have, exceptionally, kept the familiar spelling: for example, Pylos, Olympia, and Kyparissia instead of Pílos, Olimbía, and Kiparissía. Other ancient names appear in two forms: for example, Methone and Korone when the context is classical, but Methóni and Koróni when it is medieval and modern. At least in the Site Registers and in the list accompanying the modern reference map, we have taken pains to mark the correct stress on every name. Elsewhere in the volume accent marks are used sparingly. Long ago Leake noted the difficulties the Romans encountered in representing Greek names in Latin. The task of the modern student is more complicated, because of Slavic, Italian, Turkish, and Albanian influences on Greek names and the imposition of unnatural forms of the purist language (*katharévousa*) by official fiat. Though aware of the inconsistencies of spelling that remain in our text, we yet believe we have attained a high degree of accuracy in searching out the genuine popular forms and approximating their sound in roman script.

It is a formidable job to look back over a wide-ranging project that has continued for more than a decade and to single out individuals and groups whose assistance deserves special recognition. In our case the difficulty is compounded by the fact that three digging seasons at Nichoria have already passed as the manuscript goes to press. We had hoped to have this volume ready for publication before the excavation began but we underestimated the problems inherent in multiple authorship. And since the excavation has already produced considerable new information relevant to certain aspects of the surface survey, it would have been arbitrary to exclude it. Hence we must also acknowledge here various acts of generosity and support that are not strictly connected with the main purpose of the book.

Pride of place should without question go to the Louis W. and Maude Hill Family Foundation, its board of directors, and its general secretary (now president), Mr. A. A. Heckman. The first Hill Foundation grant in 1962 recognized the potential in the idea behind the University of Minnesota Messenia Expedition (UMME). Two additional subventions in 1964 and 1967 showed the foundation's continued confidence in the direction we were following and made possible a greatly expanded scope of operations. Along with a grant from the Bollingen Foundation of New York in 1963 and contributions from a number of private individuals, the generosity of the Hill Family Foundation should be credited with a crucial part in the UMME project. Of course, a successful interdisciplinary undertaking of this magnitude must have clear problems to attack, prudent planning, cooperation from the host country, and a carefully chosen staff. But it cannot realize its potential without financial sponsorship that demonstrates respect for its integrity and allows flexibility in the use of the funds provided.

As is made clear in Chapter 1, the original inspiration that led to our surface search for ancient habitation sites in Messenia came from Carl W. Blegen. His support never wavered over seventeen years, and his prestige with both Greek and American colleagues smoothed many a rough spot. For almost the same span of years Spyridon Marinatos has been in positions of responsibility in the Greek Archaeological Service and has directed much of his own research to the reconstruction of Messenian prehistory. Also, Professor Marinatos has been in the forefront among archaeologists working in Greece in the recognition of the actual and potential contributions of "science in archaeology." It would therefore have been particularly appropriate for him to write an introduction to this volume. He was, in fact, invited to do so, but the pressures of other commitments forced him to decline.

We also owe a great deal to two former directors of the Greek Archaeological Service, the late Ioannis Papadimitriou and Ioannis Kondis. The directors of the Service, along with the successive ephors for western Peloponnese, Dr. Nicholas Yalouris, Mr. George Papathanasopoulos, and Miss Theodora Karayeorya, have been responsible for granting us annual permits to work in the region and for supervising our multifarious activities in the field. The epimeletes (assistants) attached to the ephorate with headquarters at Olympia, especially Messrs. Petros Themelis and Angelos Choremis, have also been most helpful.

We acknowledge in addition the assistance of a number of agencies of the Greek government that are not directly concerned with archaeological work, notably the Royal Hellenic Air Force, the Greek Atomic Energy Commission ("Democritos"), the Institute of Geology and Subsurface Research, and the Ministry of Agriculture. In these and many other associations we came to realize that scientists (both native and foreign) working in Greece are uniformly anxious to cooperate with archaeologists. To select just one of many examples, the president of the GAEC, Mr. P. Demopoulos, has not only provided facilities for the research of several of our geochemist and metallurgist colleagues but has also initiated discussions on ways and means to promote closer ties generally between archaeology and relevant scientific studies.

We want, further, to record the support of American administrators. Dr. Henry S. Robinson, director of the American School of Classical Studies in Athens from 1959 to 1969, was always most helpful in negotiations for our archaeological and para-archaeological projects, all of them carried on under the direct or indirect auspices of the School. His successor, Dr. James R. McCredie, continues to demonstrate sincere interest in our work. And Mr. Theodore Wertime, since his appointment as Cultural Attaché in the United States Embassy at Athens in 1969, has proved both by official and personal assistance that he has a strong commitment to this kind of wide-ranging scholarly enterprise.

As for official encouragement at the local level, we are deeply grateful for the interest and assistance of numerous administrators at our own institution, the University of Minnesota. Three presidents, Messrs. Morrill, Wilson, and Moos, have given us far more than routine support. Vice-President Stanley Wenberg helped us to secure initial financial support. Various officials of the University of Minnesota Foundation and the University's Business Office have been generous with time and assistance. The deans of the Graduate School, the late Theodore Blegen (brother of Carl Blegen) and his successor, Bryce L. Crawford, Jr., have been personally interested and officially helpful. Various committees handling research funds, short leaves of absence, and sabbatical leaves were always receptive to ways in which our work could be carried forward. The staff members of the Press have shown admirable patience and skill in handling the preparation of the book. The preliminary typing and checking was capably handled by Mrs. William McDonald and the Misses Corliss Bodley, Ingeborg Westfall, Sue Wachter, and Bronwen Meade.

We feel compelled to make one exception to the principle that the help of UMME colleagues is taken for granted. Professor Loy, in addition to co-authoring two chapters, has assumed responsibility for the production of all plans and maps in a uniform style. Whatever usefulness and comprehensibility the whole enterprise may demonstrate is owed in no small degree to his conscientious work, and that of his University of Oregon student assistants, Steve Anderson, Leon Henderson, and Fred Walker. The drawings of a reconstructed view of the town on Nichoria ridge in the Late Bronze Age on the jacket and title page and the olive tree on pages 1 and 263 are by Lyle Folkstad, who is artist for the Nichoria excavation.

In the case of the less formal assistance of academic colleagues, both at home and abroad, full acknowledgment becomes next to impossible. Literally scores of names occur in the footnotes accompanying the periodic reports that were published in the *American Journal of Archaeology* for 1961, 1964, and 1969. We sincerely hope that the references below will not be misunderstood by others whose generosity is not specifically recorded here.

The editors wish to acknowledge University leaves of absence for the spring 1970 term (Rapp and Cooke), for the fall 1970 term and sabbatical leaves in 1958–59 and 1967–68 with subventions from the Guggenheim Foundation (McDonald). Professor Loy held a fellowship in 1965–66 from Foreign Field Research Program of the Division of Earth Sciences, Natural Research Council; and he received a summer Research Award in 1970 from the Office of Scientific and Scholarly Research, University of Oregon. Dr. Aschenbrenner carried out research contributing to his chapter under a grant from the National Institutes of General Medical Sciences in 1969–70. Professor Topping received grants from the Johnson Fund of the American Philosophical Society (1959) and from the Classics Fund of the University of Cincinnati (1968). He also wishes to thank the staff of the Archivio di Stato, Venice, for help during his visit in 1970 and for permission to reproduce pocket map 5-10. Pocket map 5-9 is based on a map that accompanied Dr. F. Sauerwein's article in *Erdkunde* 23 (1969), which Professor Dr. H. Hahn, editor of *Erdkunde*, has kindly granted permission to use.

Professor Hope Simpson's assistance in fieldwork over the years was made possible in part by grants from the Michael Ventris Memorial Award (1959), the Leverhulme Trust (1963), the Canada Council (1967, 1968), and by the cooperation of the Universities of London, Birmingham, and Queen's University (Kingston, Canada). Dr. Van Wersch wishes to acknowledge the assistance and encouragement received from Professor Philip Raup, who was also instrumental in obtaining funds from the Agricultural Development Council, Inc., for research that proved to be complementary to that done under the auspices of UMME. Professor Wright is especially indebted to the following colleagues: Professors Willem Van Zeist, W. A. Watts, and M. E. D. Poore, as well to field and laboratory assistants Marius Jacobs, Jean C. B. Waddington, T. C. Winter, and Richard F. Wright. Professor Matson wishes to acknowledge the support received from the National Science Foundation (Grant GS-357, 1963), and from the Central Fund for Research of the Pennsylvania State University. He appreciates the field assistance of Eskil Broburg and Roger Howell.

The authors of Chapter 14 have a special debt to a very large number of colleagues who aided their metallurgical and geochemical research: Dr. Paul Fields, Argonne National Laboratory; Professor Richard Ramette, Carleton College; Messrs. Vasilios Spyracos, Nikos Terzakis, and Stavros Vrahamis of GAEC (Democritos); Oskar Kortan, H. Stavrinou, D. M. Pantazis (Cyprus); Dr. Leon Picon, Dr. Rustu Ovalioglou, Dr. Sadrettin Alpan, Dr. Raci Temizer, Professor and Mrs. Tohsin Ozguc, Mr. Donald Hattie (Turkey); Professor Constantine Conophagos, Peter G. Embry, Dr. Allan Johnson, Dr. S. Junghans, Dr. R. Pittioni, Mr. George Parker, Dr. E. Preuschen, Mr. William Phelps, Dr. V. G. Kallipolitis, Dr. Colin Renfrew.

In the geophysical fieldwork the authors had useful help and advice from Dr. Martin Aitken, Dr. E. T. Hall, and Mr. Brian Mitchell. The Wenner-Gren Foundation made a grant to aid Mr. Mitchell's work in 1966.

The authors of Chapter 8 were assisted in different campaigns and for various periods by numerous junior and senior colleagues with a passion for field exploration — among them Mrs. Nancy Wilkie, Miss Nancy Spencer, Mr. James Muhly, Mr. Stuart Thorne, Mr. Eskil Broburg, Mr. Roger Howell, Mr. and Mrs. Julian Whittlesey, Professor Sterling Dow, and Professor Sheila McNally.

There is one further general debt of gratitude that we want to acknowledge — that is to the many hundreds of villagers and townspeople throughout Messenia. They have been uniformly hospitable, generous, helpful, and concerned. Some have volunteered valuable information that we could not have obtained in any other way. All did whatever they could to make our work in their homeland pleasant and productive. Only readers who have themselves experienced the true *philoxenia* (hospitality) of the Greek countryside can fully appreciate the warm feeling in our hearts every time we return to this verdant and lovely part of the world.

Minneapolis
January 1972

LIST OF AUTHORS

Stanley Aschenbrenner, Research Associate, University of Minnesota

John Chadwick, Reader in the Greek Language, University of Cambridge; Fellow of Downing College, Cambridge, England

Strathmore R. B. Cooke, Professor of Metallurgy, Institute of Technology, University of Minnesota

Jesse E. Fant, Associate Professor, Division of Surveying and Photogrammetry, Department of Civil and Mineral Engineering, Institute of Technology, University of Minnesota

Eiler Henrickson, Professor and Head, Department of Geology, Carleton College, Northfield, Minnesota

Richard Hope Simpson, Associate Professor, Department of Classics, Queen's University, Kingston, Ontario, Canada

John F. Lazenby, Senior Lecturer in Ancient History, Department of Classics, University of Newcastle upon Tyne, England

William G. Loy, Assistant Professor, Department of Geography, University of Oregon, Eugene

Fred E. Lukermann, Professor, Department of Geography, University of Minnesota

William A. McDonald, Professor, Department of Classics, and Director, UMME, University of Minnesota

Frederick R. Matson, Research Professor of Archaeology, Department of Anthropology, Pennsylvania State University, University Park

Catherine Nobeli, Research Chemist, Nuclear Research Center "Democritos," Athens, Greece

George R. Rapp, Jr., Associate Professor, Department of Geology and Geophysics, and Associate Director, UMME, University of Minnesota

Peter Topping, Charles Phelps Taft Professor of History and Later Greek Studies, University of Cincinnati

Herman J. Van Wersch, Assistant Professor, Department of Agricultural and Applied Economics, University of Minnesota; Agricultural Economist, University of Minnesota, AID Project, Tunis, Tunisia

H. E. Wright, Jr., Professor, Departments of Geology and Geophysics, and of Ecology and Behavioral Biology, University of Minnesota

N. J. Yassoglou, Professor, University School of Agriculture; Head, Earth Sciences Department, Nuclear Research Center "Democritos," Athens, Greece

LIST OF ABBREVIATIONS

A: Archaic

C: Classical

CEM: cemetery

EH: Early Helladic

FAO: United Nations Food and Agriculture Organization

G: Geometric

H: Hellenistic

HAB: habitation site

LH: Late Helladic

M: Medieval

MH: Middle Helladic

N: Neolithic

NSSG: National Statistical Service of Greece

#: number of site

R: Roman

UMME: University of Minnesota Messenia Expedition

Journals

AAA: *Archaiologika Analekta ex Athenōn*

AJA: *American Journal of Archaeology*

AM: *Athenische Mitteilungen* (Athenische Abteilung des Deutschen Archäologischen Instituts)

AMCM: *Atti e Memorie del Primo Congresso internazionale di Micenologia*

Arch Eph: *Archaiologikē Ephēmeris*

BCH: *Bulletin de Correspondance Hellénique*

BSA: *Annual of the British School of Archaeology at Athens*

Bull Lund: *Bulletin de la Société Royale des Lettres de Lund*

CQ: *Classical Quarterly*

Deltion: *Archaiologikon Deltion*

Ergon: *To Ergon tēs Archaiologikēs Hetaireias*

Hesperia: *Hesperia. Journal of the American School of Classical Studies at Athens*

IG: *Inscriptiones Graecae*

JHS: *Journal of Hellenic Studies*

JHS Arch Reports: *Archaeological Reports* (supplement to *JHS*)

Op Ath: *Opuscula Atheniensia* (Swedish School of Archaeology in Athens)

Praktika: *Praktika tēs en Athēnais Archaiologikēs Hetaireias*

RE: Pauly-Wissowa, *Real-Encyclopädie der klassischen Altertumswissenschaft*

TABLE OF CONTENTS

List of Figures

List of Pocket Maps

List of Plates (between pages 322 and 323)

List of Tables

THE MINNESOTA MESSENIA EXPEDITION
Reconstructing a Bronze Age Regional Environment

1
THE PROBLEMS AND THE PROGRAM

by

William A. McDonald

This introductory chapter has several purposes. In the first place, it provides a brief account of the development, scope, and aims of the project sponsored by the University of Minnesota and called the University of Minnesota Messenia Expedition (UMME). Then the *region* on which we have concentrated attention is defined, and the problem of the areal implications of the Kingdom of Pylos at its acme in the Late Bronze Age is raised (see Fig. 2-1). This is followed by a brief description of the extent and nature of the collaboration among UMME staff members in fieldwork and in the preparation of this book, with a view to placing the project in fair perspective as an *inter*disciplinary versus a *multi*disciplinary effort. A historical sketch of field exploration in the Aegean area shows that our special concern with the interaction between humans and the natural environment has clear precedents, especially in the nineteenth century. Finally, the organization and staffing of three recent projects somewhat comparable with ours (two in the Middle East and one in Meso-America) are traced in some detail, and certain contrasts and similarities are noted between these enterprises and ours.

The Background

Successive developments in UMME's staff and program have been previously reported in considerable detail (McDonald and Hope Simpson 1961, 1964, 1969). Particularly since World War II there has been a growing awareness of the value of "science" in "archaeology." It should be made clear from the start, however, that throughout this book our use of the term "archaeologist" versus "scientist" is purely a matter of convenience. We wish neither to confirm nor to deny the claim that archaeology, in assembling and handling its evidence, is (or is becoming) a discipline that uses methods similar or identical to those followed by general or specific areas of the physical, biological, or social disciplines. UMME's approach did not spring full-grown from the head of anyone who was already convinced that collaboration between the two groups is necessary. The project began with no predetermined design. The current stage is the culmination of a series of specific "felt needs," the search for qualified and interested specialists to fill them, and the availability of funds for the necessary field and laboratory projects.

It is scarcely possible at this distance to identify the original impulse. My interest in surface exploration was stimulated by association with Professor Carl Blegen in 1939. Search around the Bay of Navarino (see Fig. 2-1) was followed by tests on a hill called Epano Englianos, about 9 km north of the bay in the district with which the name Pylos has been associated since antiquity. The trenches revealed the burnt ruins of a palace dating from the thirteenth century B.C., near the end of the *Late Bronze Age* — also termed *Late Helladic* or *Mycenaean Age* in Aegean nomenclature (Blegen and Kourouniotis 1939; McDonald 1942) (see Table 1-1, Chronological Chart).

By 1952 the clay tablets found in the palace archives in 1939 began to yield their secrets to the decipherers. It became clear that the palace had been the major col-

TABLE 1-1. CHRONOLOGICAL CHART

Major Events and General Trends in Messenian History
(Absolute Dates Uncertain before 5th Century B.C.)

Date	Period	Phase	Events and Trends
↑ B.C. 3000, 2900, 2800, 2700	NEOLITHIC		Pottery and artifacts (nearly all "Late Neolithic") from scattered caves and open sites
2600	EARLY HELLADIC	I	Small villages, typically on low ground near coast
2500, 2400		II	Monumental building complex at Akovitika
2300, 2200, 2100, 2000		III	Gray Minyan pottery (northeast Peloponnese); Indo-European dialect (?); Extroverted attitude
1900	MIDDLE HELLADIC	I	Cutting coastal pine forest; Multiple burial mounds
1800		II	Growing population; Introverted attitude (?); Fortified inland hilltop sites
1700		III	"Adriatic" pottery
1600			Matt-painted pottery
1500	LATE HELLADIC (MYCENAEAN)	I	Peristeria grave goods suggest royal wealth and general prosperity
		II	Clusters of tholos tombs suggest numerous small kingdoms
1400		IIIA	Rapidly increasing population and trade
1300		IIIB	Aggressive political unification; Trojan War; Population about 50,000 (?); Destruction of Pylos palace (Linear B tablets)
1200	("Dark Age" begins)	IIIC	Severe depopulation; Traditional date for Dorian invasion and partition of Messenia
1100			
1000	PROTO-GEOMETRIC (SUB-MYCENAEAN)		Poverty and cultural splintering
900	"Dark Age"		New (?) racial stock partly responsible for distinctive ceramic trends
800	GEOMETRIC		Population slowly rising; Homeric poems composed (?)
700	(Spartan Domination begins)		First Messenian War (about 743–23?)
600	ARCHAIC		Second Messenian War (about 670–50?)
500	Spartan Domination		Increasing population
400	CLASSICAL		Revolt? (about 490); Third Messenian War (about 470–60); Peloponnesian War (431–04); Founding of Messenian state with federal capital at Messene (368)
300	HELLENISTIC		Joined Aetolian league (about 213)
200			Joined Achaean league (about 191)
B.C. 100	ROMAN		Roman control imposed (about 146); Messenia made part of Province of Achaea (about 27 B.C.)
BIRTH OF CHRIST			Roman civil wars
A.D. 100			Stability and prosperity under Empire
200			Raids of Heruli (267); fortification around Altis at Olympia
300			Visigoths encamp in Elis (395–96); pillage of Olympia
400			
500	BYZANTINE MEDIEVAL		Raids by German tribes; Severe earthquakes (especially in 522, 551)
600	("Dark Ages" begins)		Bubonic plague (541–44); Large-scale immigration of Slavs
700	"Dark Ages"		Plague (747)
800			Constantinople re-established control of Peloponnese
900			Christianization of Slavic settlers
1000			
1100			Relative prosperity; Breakdown of centralized control, piracy, flight to mountain refuges
1200			
1300	FRANKISH		Relative prosperity
1300			Messenia (Province of Kalamata) part of principality of Achaia or Morea under Frankish control (1205–1432); Serious decline (Black Death)
1400			Large-scale immigration of Albanians
1500	OTTOMAN I		Recovery; population about 45,000; Almost all Messenia under Turkish control (1460–1685)
1600			Depopulation
1700	VENETIAN		Venetian control (1685–1715); population doubled (about 24,000 to about 50,000)
1800	OTTOMAN II		Turkish control (1715–1821); Great destruction in 1770's and 1820's; Prosperity; population nearing 100,000 by 1821
1821 A.D.			Outbreak of Greek Revolution

lection and distribution center in a widespread network of dependent towns and villages, and so it was natural to extend the surface search over a far broader area and to concentrate on reconstructing the settlement pattern contemporary with the palace. From the start, however, the chronological focus was on the whole Late Bronze period (about 1600–1100 B.C.), without neglecting evidence of habitation from neolithic until medieval times. The many place-names mentioned in the Pylos tablets also led to the initiation of a complementary project, a collection of place-names now in use throughout the region (McDonald 1959; Georgacas and McDonald 1969).

In 1958–59 these lines of research were widened in area and sharpened in effectiveness when Hope Simpson (archaeology) and Topping (medieval history) became associated in the fieldwork (Topping 1956; Hope Simpson 1957; McDonald 1960; McDonald and Hope Simpson 1960; Waterhouse and Hope Simpson 1960, 1961). By that time, too, the need for technical assistance on problems of alluviation along the west coast prompted us to bring in as field consultant Dr. Diomedes Haralambous, a member of the department of geology in the University of Athens (Haralambous 1959).

In the 1960 campaign we enlisted Lazenby (Greek history) to aid in the search for prehistoric sites. By this time we were also deeply interested in trying to reconstruct the pattern of land communications, especially to trace the line of the road we interpreted as a Late Bronze Age highway for wheeled traffic joining the Pylos area with the head of the Messenian Gulf (McDonald 1964a; McDonald and Hope Simpson 1964; McDonald 1968; see Ch. 2).

In 1962 UMME was formally organized (insofar as it ever has been), and some financial stability was assured. Each year since then an average of five staff members have spent periods ranging from a few weeks to several months in fieldwork. The archaeologists gradually improved search techniques and familiarized themselves with the modern countryside and inhabitants (McDonald 1964b). But at the same time we became increasingly aware that fieldworkers with our kind of training and experience generally lack the necessary background to follow up important avenues leading to the reconstruction of the ancient situation, as well as to a fuller understanding of the modern (McDonald 1967). It was an obvious move to seek first the advice and then the active help of colleagues who do have the necessary technical competence.

The handiest colleagues were at my own institution, the University of Minnesota, and it is a natural outcome that about half of the present staff are either faculty or were formerly graduate students at the University. At the same time, we can scarcely be accused of parochialism. The chapters that follow were written by staff members at nine different institutions of higher learning, a research institute, and a government department. Eleven of the authors live in the United States, two in Greece, two in England, and one each in Canada and Tunisia. As scientists came to outnumber archaeologists, historians, and philologists, some adjustment seemed indicated at the supervisory level. Rapp (geochemistry and geophysics) became associate director in 1966, and he was later persuaded to join in editing this book.

There is little point here in a detailed account of the gradual increments of research interests and personnel. Wright (geology and palynology), Lukermann (geography), and Fant (civil engineering) joined us in 1962; Matson (ceramic engineering) in 1963; Chadwick (philology) in 1964; Loy (geography and cartography) in 1965; Van Wersch (agricultural economics) and Rapp in 1966; Henrickson (economic geology), Yassoglou (soil chemistry), and Cooke (metallurgy) in 1967; Aschenbrenner (social anthropology) in 1969. It should be emphasized that this publication does not mark the completion of the enterprise. Some individual and joint projects described in succeeding chapters are well along toward completion; others are just getting launched. If a new line of research promises useful light on the natural and/or cultural history of the region, we shall search for a congenial and skilled practitioner. Several projects have already extended far beyond Messenia, and almost all have broader implications in time if not in space.

It is of course true that the larger the staff and the more varied their projects, the more difficult becomes the exchange and coordination of information. But we believe that the potential advantages of the broader approach outweigh the problems it creates. The categories of specialist research that can (at least theoretically) make useful contributions to a basically archaeological and historical study of this kind are so numerous that an organization which tried to include all of them might well become unwieldy. But any project that does not include the basic ancillary disciplines has, in our opinion, compromised its effectiveness.

Figure 1-1 is intended to identify our major concerns both in the regional survey and in the excavation, beginning in 1969, of a Bronze Age and Early Iron Age settlement at Nichoria (#100; see explanation of site numbers used herein on p. 123). The circular format of the chart is borrowed from MacNeish's *Prehistory of the Tehuacan Valley* (1967). Although our reach in terms of the scope and variety of the total project undoubtedly exceeds our grasp in the form of solid evi-

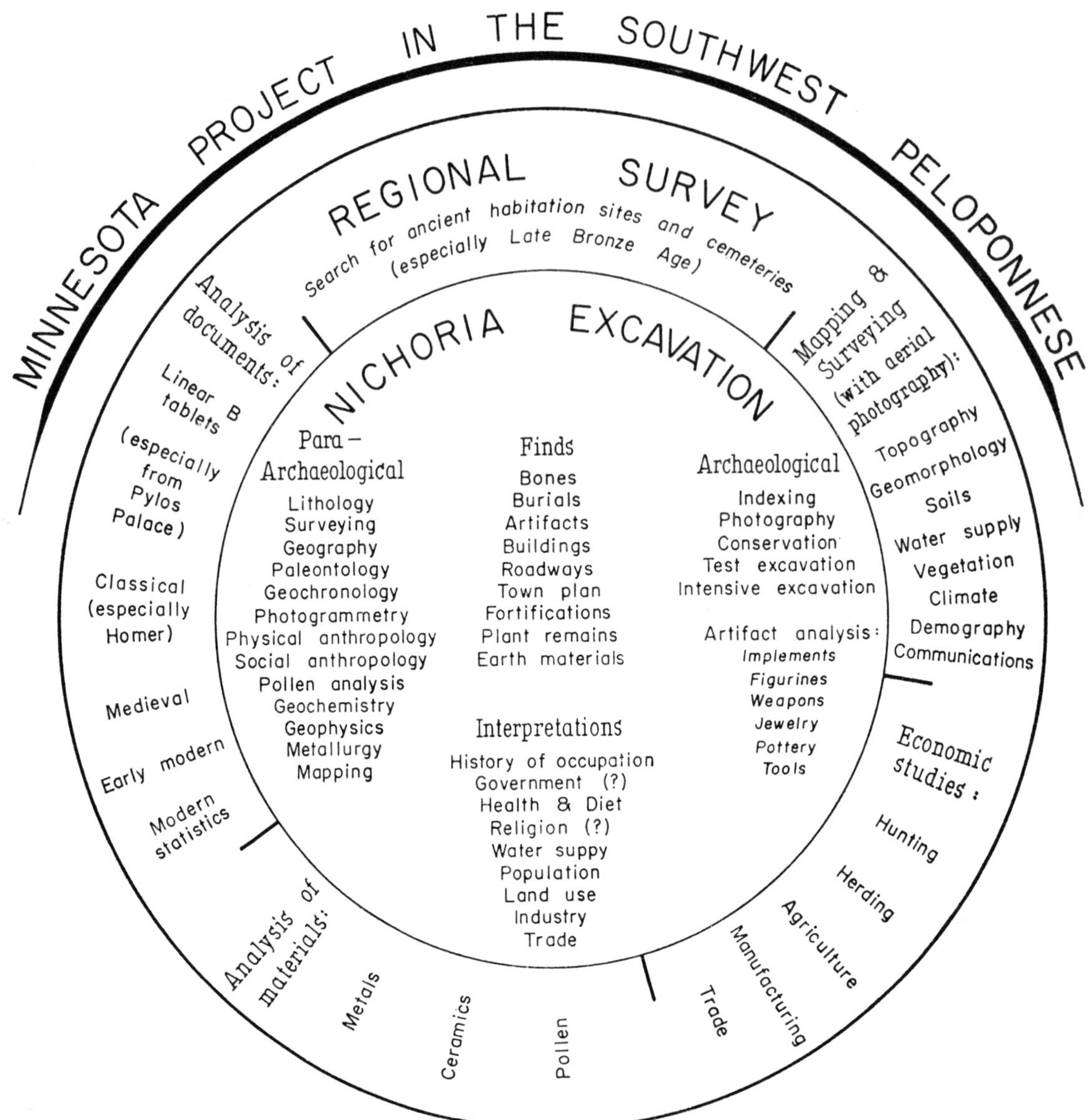

Figure 1-1. UMME approach to the problems

dence to date, every item in the chart is indeed being given serious consideration. Particular attention is invited to the way in which the excavation (mainly in the future) is planned to complement the regional survey (mainly in the past). This sequence is, in our judgment, the proper and logical one, except that a series of limited test excavations at a number of settlements in different subregions and of different periods would have been an extremely useful transitional phase.

But, to return to the first phase, let us try to be more specific about the underlying rationale. What are some of the specific "archaeological" problems to which a group of this size and diversity can be expected to apply itself with more hope of success than archaeologists working alone? Generally speaking, they concern the interaction among humans, other biota, and the physical environment—or, to quote Hawley (1950, p. 72), "the human interdependencies that develop in the action and reaction of a population to its habitat." Man, like other organisms, is of course deeply affected by his immediate environment, but he has also managed to break out of his limiting surroundings or significantly to modify them, purposely or accidentally, by his own activities.

We are concerned with problems of human ecology in a particular historical period (the Late Bronze Age) and in a specific region (extreme southwest Greece). In practice, however, the limits of time and space have to be quite elastic. As mentioned above, some projects have led far beyond the borders of modern or ancient Messenia. In the chronological sense, only one chapter (7) could be said to be exclusively concerned with Mycenaean times, and even there what is known about the human and natural history of the region before and since is broadly relevant. Actually, the period that is stressed most in Chapters 4, 11, and 13 is the present century. For a number of studies the current situation has to form the basis against which is projected what we know or theorize was similar or different in the past. Chapters 5 and 6 provide some guideposts at given intervals between Mycenaean and modern times. Chapters 8, 9, 12, and 15 are concerned to a greater or lesser degree with the totality of elapsed time since humans are known to have first occupied the region. Chapters 3 and 10 (and in a sense 14 as well) include physical processes that may go back eons of time before human history.

Looking back over the record of Greek archaeology, one notes that interest in the Late Bronze Age has remained fairly steady ever since Schliemann's dramatic discovery of the royal shaft graves at Mycenae almost a century ago. In the interval several royal citadels have been fully or partially excavated; and countless tombs have been discovered throughout central and southern Greece, on the islands off both coasts, and even farther afield. We now know a good deal, too, about cultural and trade connections that extended far beyond the Mycenaean sphere of political control. On the other hand, the search for and thorough excavation of small, typical, ordinary habitation sites has been very much more spotty and incomplete.

The decipherment of the Linear B script and consequent light on the contents of the tablets has provided an added impetus for Mycenaean studies and offers absorbing tasks in collating this new documentary evidence with results of exploration, salvage, and excavation (see especially Chs. 7, 8, 16). Since the tablets are mainly concerned with subjects of a social and economic nature, this development has tended to lessen somewhat the traditional emphasis on the "high culture," the art and architecture of the wealthy.

At the same time, useful new quantitative ways of looking at relatively neglected aspects of past cultures have proved their validity in other parts of the world and are now beginning to be exploited in Greek prehistoric and "proto-historic" archaeology. Yet many basic questions about Mycenaean civilization remain unanswered – and usually unasked. Surface exploration can contribute to the solution of some of them. Others will require a whole generation or more of excavators and scientist colleagues who make such problems the focus of their work. And, of course, satisfactory solutions to many problems on which we should like to have information will always elude us.

For instance, what parts of the Aegean world were most heavily populated and what parts were scantily used or essentially unexploited in Mycenaean times? What was a large, average, small area for a Mycenaean village? Did any significant percentage of the population live in year-round individual farmsteads or practice short-distance transhumance in the dry summer season? How many families made up a village of average size? How many individuals composed the average family? What was the typical arrangement of houses within a village? What was the typical arrangement of rooms within a house? Was there any hierarchy among village houses, in size or other characteristics? Were there any "public" buildings? How much land belonged to the average village and what percentage of it was cultivated? How were cultivation and herding organized among the inhabitants? What kind of soil, drainage, exposure did farmers prefer for what crops? Did they use irrigation and, if so, how extensively? Was marshy ground drained for agriculture or was it used for pasture (especially for larger animals)? Was water brought from a distance to supply some villages? Did they normally use dug wells if there was no perennial stream or nearby spring? What were the main factors (in addition to good land and sufficient water) that determined where villages were built? Was the timber cover generally heavier and the run-off of rainfall notably less than at present? What kind of timber did they use for major construction and where did they get it? Is there any truth in the claim that erosion was becoming a problem for Mycenaean agriculture? Is there any evidence of a significant shift in climate during the Mycenaean period? Did they have any local supplies of metals (especially copper) worth exploiting with available technology? What were the sources of imported precious and useful metals? How did they pay for them and who were the carriers? Did Late Bronze Age Greece as a whole and our region in particular produce a surplus of food staples or were imports necessary? How much inter-kingdom or intra-kingdom trade was there in food, raw materials, and manufactured goods? Did kingdoms, districts, or individual villages specialize in certain products like olive oil, hides, wheat, honey, and pottery, and obtain other staples by trade, or did each political division or subdivision or even each village aim to be as self-sufficient as possible? What was the typical diet? Did it include such items as fish, wild game, or olive oil in significant quantities? How were overland and sea communications organized? Was a major share of wealth derived from acting as middlemen in international overseas trade? Did the Mycenaeans construct monumental harbor installations? Were there many roads capable of bearing wheeled traffic, both within and between kingdoms? Is there any evidence for epidemic disease, malnutrition, chronic malaria? What about technical processes for manufacturing bronze weapons and implements, for firing pottery, tanning leather, cutting hard stone, weaving textiles, making paints, dyes, or plaster? What relations can be established between the known distribution of habitation sites and such natural features as relief, soils, microclimate, forest cover, accessibility, and water supply?

At present there are no satisfactory answers to most of these questions, for the Late Bronze Age or any other period in Greek prehistory. Even for literate times, the combined documentary and archaeological evidence is relatively untapped. Nor can any sudden breakthrough be expected, even with revised aims and methods. Some lines of research are very time-consuming and results may be disappointing. But a generation of work that integrated scientifically oriented surface exploration and excavation with study of the modern situation and a review of relevant documents from the literate stages of Greek history (especially the postclassical) could revolutionize our insights into some of these vital aspects of Greek archaeology and history.

The Region

The areal implications of the "Kingdom of Pylos" (which was the provisional title of this book) are admittedly vague. No one can define with confidence its exact limits, even in the last year of the palace when the tablets were inscribed. The relevant evidence will be fully discussed in Chapters 7, 8, and 16, but it is perhaps appropriate to make some brief introductory comments here. Readers are referred to the first few pages of Chapter 3 for an account of the region's major physiographical features. (See also Pocket Maps 3-5 and 3-7.)

It appears that in early Mycenaean times southwest Peloponnese was partitioned into a fair number of small independent kingdoms. One can reasonably infer that the acquisition or loss of territory by these petty kings, through war or diplomacy, was a spasmodic and irregular process. The widespread tholos tombs with contents dating about 1600–1300 B.C. presumably mark the location of their capitals (Marinatos 1952ff.). The building of the older part of the palace discovered by Blegen at Epano Englianos may have signalized the attainment of the first phase of a major expansion of the local kingdom previously centered there. It is certainly tempting to join Blegen in connecting this development with King Neleus, who according to tradition was a newcomer from Thessaly. And the unified palace block that was added a generation or so later might coincide with the widest territorial extent of the Pylian kingdom. This second phase is plausibly linked with a further consolidation of territory by Neleus' son, King Nestor of Homeric fame. Perhaps the boundaries had receded considerably before the royal citadel went up in flames around the end of the thirteenth century B.C. (Blegen and Rawson 1967, pp. 422–23).

As on so many other basic questions, informed and cautious inferences about the size of the Pylian kingdom are as near as we can come to the true situation at present. The available evidence from surface survey and excavation, from the Pylos tablets, and from the Homeric poems and later tradition is vague and sometimes conflicting. But, in sum, we have more information on the extent of the kingdom of Pylos than is available for reconstructing the territory of any other contemporary political unit in Greece.

We may begin by briefly delimiting the area of the *modern* countryside that has been studied. No one, to our knowledge, has successfully defended the proposition that Pylian territory ever extended any appreciable distance north of the Alpheios River or east of the Taygetos Mountains (see Fig. 2-1). These two major features in the topography of southwest Peloponnese constitute the landward boundaries of what we shall refer to throughout as the *region* under study. And nature, in the form of the Ionian Sea and the Messenian Gulf, has decisively set the limits to the west and south.

In terms of modern political geography, this territory includes the *nomós* (province) of Messenia with its four *eparchíes* (counties) of Triphylia, Pylia, Messini, and Kalamata, plus the southernmost *eparchia* of Olympia belonging to the nomos of Elis (see Fig. 2-1 and Pocket Map 1-1); the keys to the modern place-names referred to by number on Pocket Map 1-1, appear on pp. 323ff. Since Messenia never reached as far north as the Alpheios in historical times, it is obvious that this denomination is not strictly applicable to this whole region in either the classical or modern context. But "Messenia" is so convenient a referent that, after this initial explanation, it will be regularly used to designate the total region under discussion. The "Pylos district," on the other hand, has a much more restricted geographical application in the following pages, being confined to the district within a dozen kilometers of the Bay of Navarino. "Triphylia" will regularly be used in the classical (and not the modern) sense of the district between the Nedha and Alpheios rivers. (See Pocket Map 3-5.)

It would be difficult to support our delimitation of this particular region in terms of "uniformity of natural features," "social and cultural homogeneity," or "some kind of structural and functional unit" (Steward 1950, p. 54). In the latitudinal direction the Alpheios River is not necessarily a more logical border than other physical features further north or south. And there are other feasible boundaries west of the Taygetos Mountains. In the cultural sphere, it is not possible to demonstrate that there was uniformity within and diversity beyond the borders we have chosen. Indeed, in the Late Bronze Age there seems to have been striking cultural similarity between one kingdom and another. Finally, we cannot prove that this exact area (neither more nor less) was a distinct political and/or economic unit or subunit at any time in its history. Nevertheless, the area delimited by the Alpheios River and the Taygetos range does have basically clear and logical physical limits, does exhibit reasonably uniform cultural characteristics at all periods, and does form a viable "container" for the *maximum* extent of the kingdom on which we are concentrating.

Methodology and Organization

We have often debated among ourselves and consulted with knowledgeable colleagues outside our group as to whether there is a commonly accepted dividing line between multidisciplinary and interdisciplinary projects. Certainly, no one can criticize the use of the term *multidisciplinary* to describe a program carried out by seventeen specialists in such varied fields as archaeology, geology, paleobotany, social anthropology, civil engineering, ceramic technology, geochemistry, geography, geophysics, agricultural economics, soil chemistry, philology, metallurgy, and history. And yet some of us still cherish the hope (or illusion) that we have taken at least the first uncertain steps toward the cohesiveness and integration of viewpoints that is suggested by such terms as *interdisciplinary* and *cross-disciplinary*.

According to Steward (1950, p. 8), "an interdisciplinary approach requires an adequate conceptualization of area, of interdisciplinary problems, and of method." It has already been stressed that all UMME collaborators share the concentration on a single geographical region and also (to varying degrees) on the reconstruction of the culture and environment of a limited period of time. And we have listed above a series of specific problems on which each of us has searched through his own discipline for evidence that might contribute to a solution. As for our method, several chapters have been co-authored by colleagues in different formal disciplines. We have pondered how relevant evidence from whatever source can be brought to bear on a given problem. Each author was urged to read every chapter in early drafts, to extract information applicable to his own data, and to suggest material in his area that might illuminate or modify a colleague's point. And, finally, seven of us met for three days in November 1970 in an intensive effort to knit individual contributions more closely together. Each of us has tried to visualize readers, not as specialists in his own discipline or subdiscipline, but as first of all UMME colleagues and then as a wider general audience.

Most important of all, every collaborator has spent considerable time in Messenia, and some periods of fieldwork have involved as many as six of us at the same time. Thus, we have quite literally *col-labor*-ated and common problems were discussed over every meal and between every jolt of the Land Rover. The writer and Hope Simpson have worked for days and even weeks in the field with nearly all members of the staff. Although our primary purpose was to introduce them to the region and to assist with language and other practical problems, the reverse benefits were firsthand acquaintance with varied field techniques as well as patient explanation of their theoretical basis. An archaeologist does not thereby become a geographer or a ceramic technologist; but he does learn in a practical way how even limited acquaintance with these disciplines may sometimes illuminate previously obscure points. And, as scientific colleagues see the archaeological evidence with fresh eyes, they may discern new problems or contribute to the solution of long-standing puzzles.

Some Precedents in Aegean Archaeology

To gain a clearer perspective on our own project, it may be worthwhile to glance back over the past century or two for comparable undertakings. We will be concerned mainly, though not exclusively, with field exploration rather than excavation. And we will concentrate on the Aegean area, although there is no doubt that, at least in the present generation, more significant interdisciplinary efforts can be cited in other parts of the world.

In classical archaeology, attention to the natural environment as well as to the works of man is no innovation. The apparent novelty in our generation is in fact the re-emergence of a tradition that was largely abandoned (to our great loss) with the advent of specialization. Even in classical antiquity authors like Herodotos, Strabo, Pliny, and Pausanias, though primarily concerned with man and his monuments, include descriptions of the land and physical phenomena. They quite clearly assume that their readers expect to view the people they are describing in their natural setting. Perhaps "human geography" is the most appropriate modern category for this kind of writing, although it may shade off into "travel literature." The ancients themselves used the term *chorography*, which emphasizes the spatial situation and physical factors without implying a secondary status for the human inhabitants. The surviving bulk of this kind of writing certifies clearly enough to its original popularity (Lukermann 1961).

Strabo, for instance, in his introduction to the *Geographica* holds that the chorographer, like the philosopher, is interested in the "art of life" and seeks to acquire knowledge "both of the heavens [astronomy, meteorology] and of things on land and sea, animals, plants, fruits, and everything else to be seen in the various regions." A work on geography, he says, involves the arts, mathematics, natural science, history, and myth. And he makes a point particularly apposite to our studies when he observes that different places possess different advantages and disadvantages, some the result of nature and some of human activity, and that usefulness or waste results from these varying circumstances.

On a less theoretical level Pausanias (4. 29. 13) introduces his tour of Messenia as a "description of the country and its towns." He tells of the salt spring between Abia and Pharai; of the clean stream of the Pamisos flowing through cultivated land, navigable for ten stades (nearly 2 km) from the sea and frequented by fine fish, especially in the spring of the year; of a great plane tree out of which flows an abundant spring that supplies drinking water to Korone (modern Petalidhi); of the rock called Mothon that lent its name to the town of Mothone (Methoni) and by its underwater projection makes the entrance to the harbor narrow and protects it from heavy seas; of the sandiness of the soil around Pylos and its unsuitability for grazing cattle; of the river Nedha in the valley called Aulon that forms the boundary between Messenia and Elis.

After the classical period, visitors to remote and romantic places continued to report with comparative catholicity on the landscape as well as the people. It is true that early Western travellers to Greece, like Cyriacus of Ancona, Pacifico, Coronelli, Wheler, Chandler, Scrofani, Clarke, Pouqueville, Leake, and Dodwell, usually had an overriding archaeological interest. In the Preface to his *Travels in Morea* [*Peloponnese*] (1830), for instance, Leake writes: "It was almost entirely by connexion with ancient history that Greece, or its inhabitants, or even its natural productions, could long detain the traveller . . . whence arose a continual reference to the Greek and Latin authors, and a frequent necessity for citing even their words, which gives to travels in Greece a *learned aspect*" (p. vi). But explorers like Leake did not confine their reporting to the surviving monuments and the identification of ancient towns. Even if their geographical interest was primarily motivated by the reflection that the natural setting was basically the same as in classical times, they were aware of its relevance at all periods. And although they usually viewed the contemporary inhabitants as nothing more than pitiful survivors of ancient greatness, they often provide a lively account of the contemporary way of life.

In the fourth decade of the nineteenth century the *Expédition* [or *Commission*] *Scientifique de Morée* (Bory et al. 1831–38) is a striking phenomenon that looks both backward and forward, as is clear from its stated purpose "to render homage to the glorious country that the armed might of France has set free." On the one hand, the Expédition reflects the continued intellectual and romantic attachment in the West to ancient Greece and her monuments. At the same time this remarkable scholarly enterprise constituted one phase of a political program that was calculated to demonstrate in the strategic Near East the variety and potency of France's military and scientific prowess. Concentration on Morea (as Peloponnese was then called) as a separable region was not particularly new. The southern part of the Greek peninsula was known to be rich in remains of classical and later times and had often been selected for exclusive attention by travellers. Indeed, chorographic literature is of necessity intensive and regional, even if separate treatment of a number of geographic units adds up to a survey of a whole political entity.

At any rate, for several years following 1829 some of France's best architects and artists ranged the Peloponnese drawing and measuring ancient monuments and rescuing or recording sculpture, inscriptions, and miscellaneous antiquities that were still threatened with destruction even after Greece had won her independence. Of course, this kind of activity had been going on, particularly in and near the larger centers, since the sixteenth century. The novel element was the scale and thoroughness of the Expédition's work.

Nor was the second major emphasis completely unprecedented. Here, however, one is impressed by the varied staff and specialized techniques, as well as by the scale of the operation. A corps of experts, highly trained in several developing sciences, systematically covered the region, mapping the relief, studying the geology, climate, flora, and fauna, and recording practically every significant physical phenomenon amenable to the scientific methods of observation and analysis then known.

What is particularly important for our review is that archaeological and scientific aspects were coordinated and that, in general, participants were knowledgeable about classical antiquity and aware of the historical as well as the contemporary relevance of their work. The financial resources of a national treasury and the talented personnel of a great civil service and military organization were, of course, major elements in the feasibility of the project. But its conception, planning, and the rationale leading to its authorization demonstrate an awareness of the added dimension that organized science offers in cooperative efforts to see the past in the widest possible perspective. Although we are here concerned more with methodology and scope than with the results, Topping has some interesting comments on the latter aspect (Ch. 5; see also the end of Ch. 6).

Of course, one could not expect projects on the scale of the Expédition to be suddenly adopted as standard practice in archaeological fieldwork. But it is disappointing that this great experiment seems to have had relatively little impact on archaeological methodology in the following generation. Able and devoted researchers continued to converge on Greece, from France as well as from other Western nations; but one finds little in their voluminous reports to suggest that they saw useful allies in the developing social and natural sciences.

In this respect as in so many others, Heinrich Schliemann injected a fresh outlook into the archaeological scene in the later decades of the century. His publications refer constantly to expert consultants and laboratory reports by an impressive variety of specialists. Many of the problems on which he sought advice were connected with excavated finds, and in this respect his practice was not unique. Excavations of sorts had preceded his; and those in charge occasionally acknowledge help from the laboratories of geologists, metallurgists, and chemists. But Schliemann's radical departure was to invite experts in various disciplines to join him in the field, and to collaborate in exploration as well as excavation. Again, the availability of ample funds to pay their expenses must have been a contributing factor. But the basic reason was that Schliemann realized that if the archaeologist does not have specialist colleagues on the spot, important evidence is certain to elude him.

Architects, artists, engineers, and above all the general scientist Rudolph Virchow accompanied Schliemann in his expeditions around the Troad and mainland Greece. The atmosphere of those impressively broad-gauged regional explorations is perhaps best suggested in the first chapter of *Ilios: The City and Country of the Trojans* (1880). Here Schliemann attempts to synthesize the varied data gleaned by his own colleagues and by other observers as far back as classical times. The early chapters contain sections on the region's geographical boundaries, relief, hydrology, climatology, zoology, botany, and ethnography. Appendix VI comprises a long "Catalogue of the Plants hither-to known of the Troad, compiled according to the collections of Professor Rudolph Virchow and Dr. Julius Schmidt and from the literary sources by Professor Paul Ascherson of Berlin, Professor Theodor von Heldreich of Athens, and Dr. F. Kurtz of Berlin."

Virchow dug pits to test conflicting theories (concocted in scholarly studies far from the scene) about changes in the local drainage system caused by later alluviation. A chart of local wind direction and weather is reproduced from P. De Tchihatcheff's *Asie Mineure: Climatologie et zoologie*; and the companion volume, *Description physique, statistique et archéologique* is frequently quoted or paraphrased. Schliemann also consulted such works as P. Barker Wells' *Topography of Ancient and Modern Troy*, P. W. Forschhammer's *Topographische und physiographische Beschreibung der Ebene von Troia*, and Virchow's own *Beiträge zur Landeskunde der Troas.* It is quite clear that these and other physical scientists had bestowed unusual care on the environs of Troy, and no doubt their interest derived in part from this region's historical-mythological connections. They could be included in Schliemann's category of "travellers, who beside their principal archaeological, geological or geographical objects of study, paid also attention to the ever-attractive children of Flora."

Virchow, a famous pathologist as well as political theorist, social organizer, geologist, ethnographer, and general scientist, spent months with Schliemann in the field and they kept up a voluminous correspondence when Virchow was at home in Germany. In this same chapter Schliemann publishes an analysis, originally presented by Virchow to a learned society in Berlin, of the *Conchylia* collected in the excavations and in excursions throughout the Troad. Schliemann's work at Troy is perhaps the most striking example in the annals of Greek archaeology of a temperament and a time when "a man with eyes to see could look upon an organ, a plant, an animal, a land form, a human custom or a constellation and describe what he saw without worrying about whether or not he had committed an interdisciplinary indiscretion" (Hine 1967).

Schliemann seems nevertheless to recognize that he does not measure up to the ideal he had set for himself. For instance, he begins the section on the flora of the Troad with the admission that "not being a botanist myself, I think I can do no better than quote here . . ." It is as if in his mind a thoroughly rounded intellectual should be able to take in his stride one more science (like one more language). But if archaeologists of such versatility had ever existed, they had disappeared before 1900. And the general scientist, one of whose major interests was archaeology, had also become a much less common phenomenon. Perhaps the main inhibiting factor that was beginning to operate at that time (and has gathered force ever since) was a kind of defensiveness referred to above. Scholars came to be afraid of venturing an observation or hypothesis in an area of knowledge where they might betray a lack of control over all the known evidence.

Pressure toward specialization was mounting rapidly. Researchers like Philippson (1892) are describing primarily the physical setting; others like Frazer (1898) emphasize the strictly archaeological lore of monuments and ancient literary authorities. Yet the synthesizing instinct is still there. The physiographic description does not totally eliminate people, ancient or modern; and the emphasis on ancient cultural phenomena does not always rule out consideration of the natural environment and the modern inhabitants. Indeed, Frazer was one of the pioneers in what is now called comparative anthropology.

The trend toward specialization was no doubt inevitable as knowledge grew in bulk and complexity. At any rate, twentieth-century scholars who are interested primarily in archaeology have seldom had the competence (or concern or courage) to write about the physical environment, and vice versa. A few, like Kirsten (1959), who carried on Philippson's work, have attempted to bridge the widening gap. Most authors of archaeological publications, however, after some perfunctory opening remarks about "local topography," leave the impression that the ancient cultural remains are their only concern.

By 1900 the synthesis of cultural and environmental factors had apparently transcended the capacity or eluded the concern of individual scholars. Hence, the only realistic approach lay in collaboration by two or more experts whose specialties complemented one another. But throughout the first half of the twentieth century, at least in Greek studies, progress in this direction was limited and tentative. Since World War II, however, there are indications that cooperative efforts are making some headway.

For the sake of clarity, rapprochements between specialists in other disciplines and archaeologists working in Greece may be divided into several categories (granting that both categories and examples may be somewhat arbitrary):

1. Individual archaeologists have occasionally taken much more than a casual or amateur interest in various phenomena of the physical and biological environment and/or the modern way of life (e.g., Dawkins in folklore; Catling in geochemistry).

2. Individual scientists have rather more frequently conducted an investigation of some specialized aspect of natural or human resources and attempted to relate their results to archaeological and/or literary evidence (e.g., Davies in metallurgy; several members of the Institut Polonais d'Histoire de la Culture Matérielle in agriculture; Forbes in a varied series of technological studies).

3. Through such involvements as the second category, certain scientists have become widely recognized authorities in a special field, and excavators frequently call on them for expert assistance. Depending on circumstances, they may spend a longer or shorter time at the site and/or process samples in their laboratories. Although their work still tends to be regarded as an "archaeological sideline," they may eventually establish wide and important correlations (e.g., Angel and Charles in physical anthropology; Haelbeck and Hopf in botany; Gejvall and Boessneck in zoology; Van Zeist and Wright in palynology; Caley in the chemistry of ancient metals).

4. An archaeologist and one or more scientists have sometimes attempted a cooperative approach to a limited problem that holds special interest for both fields (e.g., Cook and Belshé in paleo-magnetism; Pritchett, Higgins, Burdon, and Kraicsovits in the topography of ancient battlefields; Marinatos, Edgerton, and Mavor in seismic geology).

5. Archaeologists normally do a fair amount of searching before selecting a new excavation site. Some very encouraging recent developments may perhaps be classed as an extension of interdisciplinary practice in this context. A team of archaeologists and scientists first surveys a region with some specific problem(s) in mind. The site or sites finally selected for excavation are thus, in the combined judgments of the experts, those most likely to shed light on the problem(s) (e.g., Higgs' group in northwest Greece, Rodden's in Macedonia, Renfrew's in the Cyclades and Thrace).

6. Excavators have occasionally attached scientists to their staff, perhaps part-time but at least in an organic, long-range association (e.g., Farnsworth in the Athenian Agora).

In the context of the last category, no excavation director would deny in principle the desirability of selecting staff members with a wide range of competence. Yet until recently the tendency has been to staff excavations with mature scholars and younger apprentices who share almost identical backgrounds in the humanistic areas of classical languages, history, and art. Of course, each staff member will probably have to develop some special skills and competencies on the job. But the fact remains that, insofar as one's previous academic training prepares one to be an excavator or a member of a field expedition, nearly all are cast in much the same mold. The standard exception has been the staff architect (and occasionally an artist) who nowadays is almost never classically educated and who is almost always the only member of the staff who is paid a salary.

Perhaps a perennial dearth of funds is as basic a reason as ingrained attitude to explain this situation. Well-trained scientists are accustomed to being remunerated for their time and expertise. It is no accident that the recent interdisciplinary projects that we are about to describe had considerable backing from major foundations. But it is also true that the importance of evidence yielded by environmental studies has often been minimized or ignored by archaeologists trained to deal in a traditional context with relatively well-known and literate cultures. Archaeologists working in the Aegean area tend to show more awareness of the value of collaboration with historians, epigraphers, and recently with experts in linguistics (especially onomatology); but such scholars rarely become regular collaborators in the field.

UMME in the Perspective of Recent Team Approaches to Archaeological Exploration

It is a healthy sign that the long-established tradition of archaeological field exploration in the Aegean area has been gaining momentum through the twentieth century (Hope Simpson 1969; Hope Simpson and Lazenby 1970). This is work of the greatest importance, particularly in our own time when modern agricultural and earth-moving machinery is rapidly destroying surface indications that have survived for millennia and when farmers and shepherds are abandoning marginal land and allowing it to revert to impenetrable maquis. The more or less systematic area surveys of an impressive number of scholars cannot be praised too highly. Their work represents a great reservoir of vital information; but there are disturbing problems and frustrations. It is not so much a question of the harvest being ready and the laborers few, as that the laborers have no over-all organization and consequently the fruits of their labor are being dissipated. The critical need is for a master plan that will direct and encourage further efforts and sponsor a comprehensive publication of all the known evidence. Then, of course, an extensive program of protection and salvage would have a chance of success (McDonald 1967).

Yet the record will show that extremely few field projects in Greece have been as intensive as the UMME survey in southwest Peloponnese and that scholars from other disciplines have rarely been involved in active, long-range participation. When we seek the closest recent parallels (as well as instructive contrasts) to UMME's interdisciplinary regional exploration, we must look outside the Aegean area. In several parts of Europe, especially Britain and Scandinavia, this has been recognized for generations as a useful approach to antiquity. More recently the idea has spread to additional parts of Europe, the Near East, and the Western Hemisphere. A check of published results and considerable discussion with knowledgeable colleagues reveals a striking rise in such projects, especially in the Americas. Three examples have been selected as particularly instructive models. There is always, of course, room for disagreement in choices of this sort, but these three would surely have to be included in any thorough survey.*

The three projects in question can properly be classed as regional paleoecological studies in the sense discussed above. Sponsors are the Department of Anthropology and the Oriental Institute of the University of Chicago for the first two, and the Department of Anthropology of Pennsylvania State University for the third. The first has been directed by Robert Braidwood and Bruce Howe (1960), the second by Robert Adams (1965), and the third (in preliminary form) by William Sanders (1965). I shall outline as briefly as possible the scope, organization, and methods — but not the results — of each in turn.

Professor Braidwood's Prehistoric Project may be the most comprehensive enterprise of its kind anywhere to date. The work in northern Iraq (1947–1955) has been followed by further campaigns in west central Iran (1959, 1960) and in southeastern Turkey (since 1963). Braidwood and his team have now tentatively explored a huge sector of the inner arc of the "fertile crescent" that stretches from the eastern end of the Mediterranean Sea to the east side of the Persian Gulf. I shall use the

* Among other interdisciplinary undertakings, the following perhaps call for special mention: (1) the Oaxaca Valley Project directed by K. V. Flannery and sponsored by the Smithsonian Institution; (2) the Virú Valley Project directed by G. R. Willey and sponsored by the Smithsonian Institution; (3) the Soviet Project in the lower Amu Darya and Syr Darya in Central Asia directed by S. P. Tolstov; (4) the Tehuacan Project directed by R. S. MacNeish and sponsored by the Robert S. Peabody Foundation; (5) the San Lorenzo Expedition directed by D. Coe and sponsored by Yale University; (6) the Cases Grandes Project directed by C. DiPeso and sponsored by the Amerind Foundation; (7) the Glen Canyon Project directed by J. Jennings and sponsored by the University of Utah. I claim no detailed knowledge of the methods or results of most of these ambitious undertakings, and in any case they could not all be discussed at length here. It might be added that the staff of the first group includes three archaeologist-anthropologists, a geographer, a geomorphologist, an ethnologist, two botanists, and a specialist in prehistoric textiles; and that of the second group comprises eight archaeologist-anthropologists, two ethnologists, and a cultural geographer.

1960 report on the Iraq portion to explore Braidwood's basic focus and methodology. Yet the subsequent shifts in geographical concentration (dictated in part by political realities) and in staff (no doubt for financial reasons as well as varying commitments and new sources of information) illustrate a point previously made, namely, that such long-range and complex projects cannot be planned definitively in advance.

The focus in time has consistently been on the emergence of the settled village farming community out of the age-old hunting and gathering economy. The absolute limits of the quest have been gradually shifting backward to somewhere in the neighborhood of eleven thousand years or even longer before the present. In addition to senior and junior archaeologist-anthropologists, the field staff has included at various times a geologist, three zoologists, a paleoethnobotanist, a limnologist, and experts in agronomy and plant genetics, pollen analysis, ceramic technology, and dental paleontology. The expedition's work has included considerable testing and excavation of selected sites as well as widespread surface exploration. Four of the associated specialists wrote individual chapters in the 1960 publication.

Braidwood's team set as its goal the attempt to establish interrelationships among a whole set of factors: intensive exploitation of a given piece of terrain by food-collectors; their increasing tendency to dwell in the open rather than in caves; the domestication of plants; the domestication of animals. Basic questions include: How significant are the known early village sites that can be plotted on a distribution map? Were the climate pattern and general ecological situation of the region roughly similar to or radically different from those of more recent historical and modern times? Is it safe to project the present-day observations of the naturalists back some ten thousand years?

Braidwood calls for an "idea archaeology" where the archaeologist, working with natural scientists in the field, "can place the presently imponderable factors of the ancient environment and a culture's utilization of its natural resources in their proper perspective" (p. 7). He says frankly that "the presence of our natural science colleagues on the staff has prevented us from committing a considerable number of nonsensical generalizations to print, on subjects in which we are naive" (p. 175). He observes, for instance, that the natural scientists with whom he is associated tend to be cautious in viewing cultural changes as climatically or environmentally induced (but see Wright 1968). This is, of course, simply a caveat against sweeping theories of geographic determinism – a very different matter from ignoring or misunderstanding the important part environment has played in the history of culture. Braidwood also feels that archaeologists will have to come to realize more clearly the potential contributions of ethnologists and cultural anthropologists who have carefully studied contemporary peoples at approximately comparable cultural levels and living in similar natural environments.

In the Diyala Basin Archaeological Project, Professor Adams concentrated on a much smaller region (about 8,000 sq. km) in the marginal irrigated country east of the Tigris above Baghdad. On the other hand, the continuum in time is somewhat longer (about 4000 B.C. to A.D. 1900) and the cultural complexity much greater than in Braidwood's Prehistoric Project. The major field reconnaissance was carried out in a single year (1957–58), and the staff was limited to two archaeologist-anthropologists. Adams was responsible for putting together the entire publication. The focus of the project included "both textual investigations of a wide spectrum of problems concerning ancient Mesopotamian agricultural history [to be published by Thorkild Jacobsen], and archaeological field investigations of the remains of early settlement and irrigation in a particular area" (p. vii).

Thus, Adams' work neatly supplements Braidwood's. Interest centered on the development of intensive agriculture, beginning at a stage when city-states were forming and in an area where farmers had come to depend on irrigation rather than seasonal rainfall for the maturing of their crops. The study of the Diyala Basin also had the advantage of available texts to supplement the archaeological evidence. Both studies, however, are aptly described in Adams' words as concerned with "long-range problems of human interaction with the environment," and especially with the "slowly changing relation of man to land" and the "patterns of human adaptation to, and exploitation of, a highly specialized natural setting" (pp. vii, viii).

Adams' first section, "The Contemporary Setting," discusses the climate, flora and fauna, land and water, basic patterns of agricultural subsistence, and recent settlement trends in the region. For a single scholar to attempt such an assignment recalls the virtuoso performances of a century and more ago, and the author is aware of the challenge. "The problem imposed by such an objective is, of course, that it must draw from a number of highly specialized fields – with the attendant risk of being insufficiently well-grounded in most of them. Particularly in fields more distant from the author's own primary training in anthropology and Near Eastern archaeology, it has been necessary to rely heavily upon secondary works . . . Even greater reliance has been placed on advice freely given by many colleagues, both during the initial intensive fieldwork and in the frequently interrupted years of study since."

The strictly archaeological phase included not only highly sophisticated and effective research in the settlement pattern but also a series of limited test excavations. The results are summarized in a section called "The Changing Patterns of Ancient Occupance" that comprises studies of the agricultural situation in five successive historical periods. A concluding chapter reviews the "Configurations of Change in Irrigation and Settlement." Three appendixes describe the methods of archaeological field survey (in which aerial photographs played a major role), the ceramic basis for assigning sites to one or more of sixteen chronological phases, and a site register. The total number of sites is an impressive 867, of which Jacobsen had discovered 119 in a preliminary survey in 1936–37. For each site the register specifies a number keyed to the maps, a local placename, an estimate of size, and the period(s) of proved habitation.

The Teotihuacán Valley Project in Meso-America exhibits basically similar goals but somewhat different scale and organization. The fieldwork extended from 1960 to 1964 and comprised a program of excavation as well as exploration. Senior staff members included two archaeologist-anthropologists and a plant ecologist-palynologist. Much of the actual survey was carried out by undergraduate and graduate students. Several of the latter, as well as senior staff, provided supervision and continuity throughout the project. The area under study is about 1,400 sq. km. The preliminary report was written entirely by the director.

This is one segment of a coordinated series of surveys that are planned eventually to cover the whole Basin of Mexico. Professor Sanders lists specific overall objectives as follows: tracing the development of agriculture with special focus on irrigation, terracing, and other patterns of land use; establishing the history of rural and urban community types; constructing at least a relative profile of population history; and exploring functional relationships among such phenomena as settlement patterns, agricultural techniques, and demography.

One chapter stresses available evidence on the natural environment – topography, hydrology, climate, soils, and history of vegetation. A second outlines the modern culture-induced situation – domesticated animals and plants, irrigation, land use, demography. Then these factors are projected back into the sixteenth century (with the help of written texts), and finally to pre-Hispanic times. Dr. Sanders holds that "the culture of a given people can be considered essentially as a complex of adaptive techniques to the problems of survival in a particular geographic region – a means by which humans successfully compete with other animals and with plants" (p. 192).

The archaeological survey involved careful surface search (with the aid of aerial photographs) and coordinated test excavations. Approximately 600 sites were discovered in this relatively small area. For the 350 that were intensively studied, blow-ups of airphotos were made and the most relevant physiographic, archaeological, and modern features of land use were entered on detailed individual topographic maps. The pottery from each site was first classed in four major groupings, and these units were then subdivided. Excavation was undertaken to clarify the functions of several architectural types observable above ground and to check and refine the ceramic sequences.

Contrasts and similarities in individual features between these team projects and that conducted by UMME will become obvious in the chapters to follow. But it may be useful here to attempt a brief over-all appraisal so as to see the UMME undertaking in some kind of initial perspective.

We might begin by noting that the four enterprises exhibit close parallels in certain specific questions to which they seek an answer. That is, in the current phraseology, they are problem-oriented. All four lay great stress on investigating the natural environment, beginning with the contemporary situation and working backward through time. All attempt to learn as much as possible about the ways in which human beings have altered the environment, especially in their most vital of all activities, agriculture. All have concentrated on sophisticated surface exploration and the study of the pottery and other surface finds to reconstruct past population distribution and density.

In additional respects, too, they show substantial similarities. All are regional projects, concentrating on a limited area. But the size of the area varies tremendously and not necessarily in proportion to the size of the staff or the length of the study. Thus, Braidwood's search is by far the most extensive, and Sanders' the most intensive. The same point is borne out by another observation. Braidwood nowhere (to our knowledge) specifies the total number of sites discovered, but they will naturally be widely scattered. Sanders' region, on the other hand, has produced the highest number of sites in relation to area, approximately one site per 2.3 sq. km (cf. Adams' approximately one site per 9.2 sq. km and UMME's approximately one site per 13 sq. km). We assume that their totals, like ours, include sites discovered by other explorers. Although the intensiveness of search will be likely to correspond roughly to the size of the region and the man-hours of search, other factors must also be taken into account. For instance, Sanders' and Adams' regions are basically oriented to irrigation agriculture, where a relatively dense pattern of population is to be expected. Braidwood's region and early period essentially rule out irrigation, and irrigation was probably practiced much less intensively (and we cannot definitely prove that it was used at all) in the UMME region. Another important variable is the contrasting patterns of relief, i.e., the much lower percentage of the land surface amenable to agriculture of any kind in Braidwood's and the UMME areas.

The most obvious over-all contrast is that UMME has been able to carry out so far only very limited test excavations of selected habitation sites to supplement the surface exploration. In 1959 Dr. Nicholas Yalouris, then ephor of the Greek Archaeological Service in charge of Western Peloponnese, and I briefly tested two sites (#'s 100, 107). Ten years later UMME began a major excavation at one of these, called Nichoria (#100) and, after two seasons of work, we now have considerable evidence on the history of occupation there and on the sequence of local pottery. But it is dangerous to generalize about the history of a region from a single site, no matter how important. It is true that systematic excavations were carried on within our region at two other major sites in the Bronze Age, by Blegen at Epano Englianos (#1) and by Valmin at Malthi (#222). But the usefulness of the former for our purposes is limited by the excavator's understandable concentration on the evidence from the latest (palace) phase, and Valmin's results cannot be uncritically accepted (see Ch. 8). Marinatos and others have also excavated at several sites, but they have concentrated on cemeteries, which do not provide the stratigraphic evidence on which ceramic sequences depend. (See Fig. 8-1, Pocket Map 8-14.)

In terms of textual supplement to field archaeology, there are of course no contemporary texts to consult for Braidwood's horizon. The evidence from written documents is probably most vital in Adams' case. Sanders can use this kind of documentation only for the later part of his time span, and the usefulness of the Linear B texts from UMME's focal period is limited by the tentative state of our understanding of their content (see Ch. 7). Over-all, however, the relevant historical evidence is definitely richer for Adams' and the UMME regions.

The Braidwood and UMME projects contrast with the others in at least two rather obvious respects – size and diversity of staff, and concentration on a single period of time. It is true that in practice Braidwood's specific temporal focus is still so loosely pinned down that he must seek evidence over a very long span. But theoretically he is not closely concerned with what preceded or followed the period of incipient domestication of plants and animals in his region. The same could perhaps be said in a still looser sense about UMME's focus on the situation in the Late Bronze Age, although many of our inferences are based on information from later, historical times. On the other hand, Sanders and Adams are interested in a continuum extending to modern times.

As to staffing, the limited range of Sanders' senior staff may have been at least partly balanced by a relatively large number of students who had a wider variety of background. Adams, however, is wary both in principle and practice of the large and diverse team approach. He confides (by letter) that he admires such ambitious undertakings, but "preferably from a distance and in the hands of others." His point of view is thus in direct opposition to that of Braidwood who (no doubt justifiably) asserts that the Prehistoric Project represents "a greater effort in a cross-disciplinary sense than has ever been attempted in southwestern Asia." The issue reaches quite deeply and affects not only the feasible range of first-hand fieldwork but also the end product, the publication. We thus return, finally, to a point already made – that it would be desirable if archaeologists could reach agreement on the use of such terms as *multidisciplinary*, *cross-disciplinary*, and *interdisciplinary* to define quite varied methodological approaches.

There is no argument – at least among scholars like Adams and Braidwood – about the importance of obtaining all relevant information about the natural environment as well as the cultural features of the target region. The real nub is *how* best to collect the information, digest it, and present it in integrated form. It is virtually ruled out that one archaeologist, no matter how versatile, would have the time and training to assemble the varied types of information first-hand. To multiply archaeologists in the field might eliminate the problem of lack of time, but not lack of training.

If, however, the information has already been collected and published by reliable specialists with the latest techniques, and if the archaeologist has the time and ability to assimilate their evidence and to discuss specific problems with them or with equally able colleagues, then it is difficult to see how this process differs vitally in basic methodology from the same archaeologist inviting the same scientists to join him in the field. In this sense, perhaps Adams' operation might also be called interdisciplinary. But it is extremely unlikely that all of the conditions just outlined would be satisfactorily met very often. And as pointed out above, there are many real, if sometimes subtle, gains in long-term collaboration in the field and in later stages of the attempted synthesis.

On the other hand, it has to be admitted that a large, diverse and shifting group of specialists poses serious logistic problems both in the field and in the publication. This kind of operation, no matter what the intention, is likely to end up closer to the multidisciplinary concept. The crucial checkpoints are, of course, in the original formulation of the problem(s) and procedures, in the actual fieldwork, and in the publication – particularly the latter two stages. If no real integration results from working and writing together, then Adams' methodological approach has at least as good a chance of achieving some measure of interdisciplinary success.

Given a relatively large staff such as the Braidwood or UMME teams, there are theoretically three methods of organizing the publication. One is for the director or some other individual to do all of the final writing; a second is to assign a section to each specialist; and the third is to find some workable compromise between these two procedures. The Braidwood and Howe publication and the present UMME report have both sought such a compromise. More individual staff members have assumed a share in our case, and more chapters are the result of collaboration between two staff members. But in spite of every counteracting effort and advantage, such a publication will inevitably lack some of the unity and cohesiveness of a "monograph" like those written by Adams and Sanders.

REFERENCES

Adams, R. 1965. *Land Behind Baghdad: A History of Settlement in the Diyala Plains.* Chicago and London.

Blegen, C. W., and Kourouniotis, K. 1939. "Excavations at Pylos, 1939," *AJA* 43:557–76.

Blegen, C. W., and Rawson, M. 1967. *The Palace of Nestor at Pylos in Western Messenia.* 2 vols. Princeton, N.J.

Bory de Saint-Vincent, J. B. G. M., et al. 1831–38. *Commission Scientifique de Morée: Section des Sciences Physiques.* 4 vols. Relation, Géographie, Géologie, et Mineralogie, Zoologie, Botanique. *Atlas.* Cf. also Puillon de Boblaye, *Recherches géographiques sur les ruines de Morée.* Paris, 1836.

Braidwood, R. J., and Howe, B. 1960. *Prehistoric Investigations in Iraqi Kurdistan.* (University of Chicago Studies in Ancient Civilization, No. 31). For a more popular account, cf. Braidwood's "Biography of a Research Project," in *Chicago Today,* 1960, Vol. 2, No. 3.

Frazer, J. G. 1898. *Pausanias' Description of Greece.* 4 vols. London.

Georgacas, D. J., and McDonald, W. A. 1969. *The Place Names of Southwestern Peloponnesus.* Athens and Minneapolis.

Haralambous, D. 1959. "Geomorphologische Untersuchungen in der Bucht von Navarino," *Praktika of the Athenian Academy* 34:92–96.

Hawley, A. 1950. *Human Ecology: A Theory of Community Structure.* New York.

Hine, V. 1967. "From Oikos to Oikumene," unpublished seminar report, University of Minnesota.

Hope Simpson, R. 1957. "Identifying a Mycenaean Site," *BSA* 52:231–59.

———. 1969. *A Gazetteer and Atlas of Mycenaean Sites.* Bulletin of the Institute of Classical Studies, University of London, Suppl. No. 16.

Hope Simpson, R., and Lazenby, J. 1970. *The Catalogue of Ships in Homer's Iliad.* Oxford.

Leake, W. M. 1830. *Travels in Morea.* 3 vols. London.

Loy, W. G. 1970. *The Land of Nestor: A Physical Geography of the Southwest Peloponnese.* National Academy of Sciences, Office of Naval Research, Report No. 34. Washington, D.C.

Lukermann, F. 1961. "The Concept of Location in Classical Geography," *Annals of the Association of American Geographers* 51:194–210.

MacNeish, R. S., et al. 1967. *The Prehistory of the Tehuacan Valley,* Vol. 1. *Environment and Subsistence.* Austin and London.

Marinatos, Sp. 1952ff. Annual reports of excavations in the *Proceedings* (*Praktika*) and *Work* (*Ergon*) of the Greek Archaeological Service.

McDonald, W. A. 1942. "Where Did Nestor Live?" *AJA* 46:538–45.

———. 1958. "Early Greek Attitude toward Environment as Indicated in the Place-Names," *Names: Journal of the American Name Society* 6:208–16.

———. 1960. "Deuro- and Peran-Ankalaia," *Minos: Revista de Filologia Egea* 6:1–7.

———. 1964a. "Overland Communications in Greece during LHIII, with Special Reference to Southwest Peloponnese," *Mycenaean Studies: Proceedings of the Third International Colloquium* pp. 217–40. Madison.

———. 1964b. "Archaeological Prospecting in Greek Lands," *Archaeology* 17:112–21.

———. 1967. "Some Observations on Directions and a Modest Proposal," *Hesperia* 25:413–18.

———. 1968. "Exploration in Messenia: 1964–1967," *AMCM* 1:101–7.

McDonald, W. A., and Hope Simpson, R. 1960. "Where a Whole Mycenaean World Awaits the Spade —," *Illustrated London News* April 30, pp. 740–41.

———. 1961. "Prehistoric Habitation in Southwestern Peloponnese," *AJA* 65:221–60.

———. 1964. "Further Explorations in Southwestern Peloponnese: 1962–1963," *AJA* 68:229–45.

———. 1969. "Further Explorations in Southwestern Peloponnese: 1964–1968," *AJA* 73:123–77.

Pausanias. 2nd century A.D. *Description of Greece.*

Philippson, A. 1892. *Der Peloponnes. Versuch einer Landeskunde auf geologischer Grundlage nach Ergebnissen eigener Reisen.* Berlin.

———. 1959. *Die griechischen Landschaften,* 2nd ed. Vol. 3, Pt. 2, pp. 319–523. *Der Peloponnes: Der Westen und Süden der Halbinsel.* Ed. E. Kirsten. Frankfurt.

Sanders, W. T. 1965. *The Cultural Ecology of the Teotihuacán Valley.* Pennsylvania State University. Mimeographed paper.

Schliemann, H. 1880. *Ilios: The City and Country of the Trojans.* London.

Steward, J. 1950. *Area Research: Theory and Practice.* Social Science Research Council Bulletin, No. 63. New York.

Strabo. Beginning of Christian era. *Geographica.*

Topping, P. 1956. "Le Régime agraire dans le Péloponnèse latin au XIVe siècle," *L'Hellénisme Contemporain* 10:255–95.

Waterhouse, H., and Hope Simpson, R. 1960. "Prehistoric Laconia I," *BSA* 55:67–107.

———. 1961. "Prehistoric Laconia II," *BSA* 56:114–75.

Wright, H. E., Jr. 1968. "Natural Environment of Early Food Production North of Mesopotamia," *Science* 161:334–39.

2
SURVEYING AND MAPPING

by

Jesse E. Fant and William G. Loy

Some archaeologists have begun asking new questions that require the assistance of engineers and geographers. For example: What relationships can be established between the known distribution of habitation sites of various periods (including the present) and such natural features as relief, soils, microclimate, forestation, accessibility, water supply? How were overland and sea communications organized? What were the main factors (in addition to good land and sufficient water) that determined where villages were built? How were buildings constructed and what was their relation to other buildings? These are spatial questions that involve the locations of points and the delineation of areas. They demand adequate mapping of the phenomena being considered.

In addition to assistance in seeking answers to such questions, certain services are required in an archaeological area study. Some of them are basic to the general questions and some are in the realm of technical assistance. Since the basic questions rely on accurate information concerning the physical patterns of relief, soils, microclimate, location, and so forth, the first order of business is to acquire these data and to map them at the same scale for ease of comparison. When there are no existing maps or they are unsuitable, the formidable tasks of original compilation of usable maps cannot be sidestepped.

Technical assistance includes the creation of systems of locational control at various scales. Archaeological sites once found must not be lost, and a notation that the place is 20 minutes' walk north of village X in Messenia is technically inadequate. A much more exact geographic position is needed. At a more detailed scale, the locations of phenomena within the neighborhood of a single site (say a five-kilometer radius) are of interest because this is probably the approximate area that once belonged to that site. At yet a more detailed scale, it is desirable to map a site and its immediate environs; hence a base map must allow the presentation of facts such as irrigable river terraces and the topographic configuration of the site itself. At a still more detailed scale, a plan of the actual site is needed so that one can plot to an accuracy of a few centimeters the exact position of features such as the positions of walls recorded in pre-excavation surveys or test trenches. Finally, the precise positions, in three dimensions and with an accuracy of perhaps two centimeters, of finds within a specific trench are needed during excavation.

Scale is to an engineer or a cartographer as proportion is to an artist or tempo to a musician. It must be right. To put it in more practical terms, the scale of a map determines the detail that can be presented on it and, at the same time, closely defines the effort that will be required to compile the map. The map scale must be matched to the problem. If too much of the earth is shown on one sheet, the data presented will either be inaccurate or illegible; if the map is too detailed and large, the costs and labor needed to produce it will be excessive.

The map scale is chosen by weighing the definition required by the subject to be mapped against the practical dimensions of the map worksheet that the cartographer wishes to handle. Assume that your pencil is as sharp as the next fellow's, and that you can be accurate to within 1 mm (one twenty-fifth of an inch) if you work on a dimensionally stable material such as mylar plastic. Your error in position of a point or line could be, to give some examples, 200 m at 1:200,000 (1 m equals 200,000 m at the map scale), 50 m at 1:50,000, 2 m at 1:2,000, and 2 cm at 1:200 scale. The other variable, worksheet size, is based on convenience and is influenced by the shape of the area being studied and the proportions of the final printed page. To be practical, the maximum dimension of a worksheet should not exceed one meter.

The map making in support of various UMME projects commenced in 1962, and the maps of the basic physical patterns were compiled in 1965 and 1966. Fant provided locational control surveys for a variety of projects over several seasons, including one site map by traditional stadia means and later (when aerial photographs became available) by photogrammetry. Loy studied the whole region systematically by air-photo interpretation. The aerial photographs, generously provided by the Royal Hellenic Air Force, facilitated a careful hill-by-hill stereoscopic scrutiny of the surface which incidentally identified probable Mycenaean sites during the geomorphological classification of the land.

We have decided against describing serially each of the kinds of mapping support as they were developed to meet emerging needs of the Expedition. Instead, we shall concentrate on the problem of selecting proper scales, proceeding from the most general to the most detailed scale employed. Examples will be given from each of the classes of scales along with practical suggestions and references to more detailed explanations of procedures used.

For the problems encountered in regional archaeological studies such as the Messenia project, encompassing a total area of more than three thousand square kilometers but also requiring detailed information on areas a few meters on a side, we have found that four map scales are needed: (1) regional, 1:500,000 to 1:100,000 (optimum 1:200,000); (2) micro-regional, 1:100,000 to 1:25,000 (optimum 1:50,000); (3) site, 1:25,000 to 1:200 (optimum 1:2,000); and (4) micro-site, 1:200 to 1:1 (optimum 1:20). The relative area that can be accommodated on a single map at the first three of these scales is illustrated in Figure 2-1, a location map for southwest Peloponnese. The total area shown is the region under study; the area delineated by the dashed line is a "neighborhood" mapped at the micro-regional scale. The site map areas are shown by fine dots. A micro-site area, however, cannot be shown at the printed scale of this location map because its total extent would be covered by a dot of the size used to represent villages.

Regional Maps. The scale for the regional mapping is 1:200,000, or approximately three miles to the inch. This scale was chosen because it is the most detailed scale that portrays the total study area on one sheet of convenient size, approximately 50 by 70 cm. In addition, a good base map already existed at this scale on the same projection as the more detailed topographic maps. A base map of larger dimensions would not have been desirable because it might have led to over-reduction. Reductions in excess of 50 percent of original often result in a cartographic catastrophe, filled-in symbols and broken fine lines. Publication of the maps compiled at 1:200,000 at a final border-to-border size of 25 by 35 cm required folded maps placed in the pocket inside the back cover.

Several of the regional maps were compiled from secondary sources such as previous maps or government statistics; however, the location maps of archaeological evidence were made primarily from information collected during several field seasons by UMME members (see Pocket Maps 8-11 to 8-18). The geomorphology map (Pocket Map 3-7) was constructed by the interpretation of several hundred aerial photographs, although such one-man assaults on governmental-scale tasks are not recommended. When planning regional mapping, one must carefully assess informational needs and sources of secondary data if the task is to be kept under control in terms of man-hours.

The positions of archaeological data such as habitation sites or tomb locations are mapped at the regional scale to show distribution patterns and to facilitate the analysis of the communication routes between points. Dense patterns of points (more than one per square kilometer) cannot be shown at the regional scale because of the appreciable map area covered by the locational symbol. If the pattern is too crowded, an inset map of a scale that will carry a greater informational load is required. Routes may be shown in their approximate locations, but since the width of the line on the map equals more than 200 m on the ground, precise route locations are not possible on regional scale maps.

The regional scale location is adequate to show the relative positions of places for purposes of regionalization, but it is not adequate to serve as their locational archive. In addition to the usual association of a place with a local toponym and nearby village, a site's position should be preserved by an accurate determination of the latitude and longitude of the place by the best means available, usually careful scaling from a detailed topographic map. A location thus defined is permanent

Pirgos
Katakalo
Olympia
OLYMPIA
Zacharo
Andhritsaina
Kakovatos
GULF OF KYPARISSIA
ELIS
MESSENIA
Parapoungi
Vasiliko
Kokla
Malthi
Derveni pass
Kyparissia
TRIPHYLIA
MESSINI
Filiatra
Aristodhimion
Gargaliani
Thouria
Proti
Chora
Messini
Kalamata
Palace of Nestor
Rizomilo
KALAMATA
Petalidhi
Kambos
Sphaktiria
GULF OF
Pylos
Bay of Navarino
PYLIA
Kardhamili
IONIAN SEA
MESSENIA
Methoni
Koroni
Sapientza
Skhiza
Cape Akritas
Venetiko
LEGEND
Nomos boundary
Eparchy boundary
Commune boundary
Principal roads
ELIS = NOMOS
Scale in Kilometers
0
10
20
N
Area of site-scale map
Neighborhood map

Figure 2-1. Modern location map

and usable on any map that has coordinates. Ideally, the position should be further fixed by locating it on aerial photographs by pinholing the spot and annotating the reverse of the photograph itself.

The regional resource analysis was based on several maps, all of which were compiled or changed by photographic means to a common scale of 1:200,000. They were either prepared on translucent dimensionally stable mylar or printed on photosensitive translucent mylar for ease of comparison by overlay.

Although all of the resource elements were compared at 1:200,000, most of their patterns were not of sufficient quality or significance to warrant publishing 1:200,000. For example, a geology map was compiled from a Greek Department of Geology and Subsurface Research map at 1:500,000 and a United Nations map at 1:300,000, plus field checking (Loy 1970). Because map enlargement is poor practice, the geology pattern was ultimately reduced, drafted, and reduced further for publication in Loy's study of the physical geography at a scale of approximately 1: 600,000. The soils map that appears in the same study was handled similarly.

The maps of the vegetation pattern and the climatic elements mapped and published in Loy (1970) were not drafted at 1:200,000 for other reasons. The base information of tree cover at 1:100,000 was adequate for detailed mapping, but the paucity of forested land did not warrant the effort. The number of stations for which rainfall data were available did not justify drafting at 1:200,000. These maps, therefore, were constructed at approximately 1:300,000 for publication at approximately 1:400,000. The vegetation map was supplemented by vegetational cross-sections, and the rainfall map was supplemented by Thornthwaite water-balance diagrams (Fig. 3-1), wind roses, and tabular data (Loy 1970).

The patterns of geomorphology (Pocket Map 3-7) and hydrology (Pocket Map 3-6) were compiled and drafted at the full 1:200,000 scale. Special emphasis was given to these patterns because land and water are the basic resources of the region at all periods. Compilation of the geomorphology map began with detailed photo interpretation of a set of 1:30,000 aerial photographs coupled with extensive field checking. Special care was taken to differentiate between farmland which is good now owing to modern public works and land which was probably unproductive in the Late Bronze Age. This information was later transferred to 1:50,000 worksheets by reflecting projector and reduced to 1:200,000 for drafting. This map (Pocket Map 3-7) is discussed in Chapter 3.

The locations of all water sources now used for gravity irrigation were plotted on 1:50,000 worksheets from information provided by Ministry of Agriculture personnel, air-photo interpretation, and field checking. Irrigation by pumping was omitted. These data were transferred to the 1:200,000 base map for drafting and comparison with the geomorphology map.

Micro-Regional (Neighborhood) Maps. Intermediate in scale between the regional and the site maps are the micro-regional maps at 1:50,000, or approximately one inch to the mile. This scale is an awkward one. It is too detailed to show a large area on one sheet, yet not detailed enough to present information where accuracy within a few meters is desired. In the Messenian research the micro-regional scale was used for neighborhood maps to show the setting of a site in the texture of the topography and in relation to its most probable access routes. Agricultural or grazing hinterlands could also be shown at this scale. The neighborhood of Nichoria (#100) near the northwestern corner of the Messenian Gulf is shown in Figure 2-2 (see also Fig. 4-1).

Micro-regional maps of areas of 100 to 400 sq. km can be transformed graphically to illustrate the environs of a site through the techniques of isometric or perspective drawings (Stacy 1958). If a site is in suitable topographic position, ideally at the foot of a slope or on a small hill, these means of map-like presentation at the micro-regional scale can give an excellent feeling for the situation of the site (see Fig. 2-3). They are not of constant scale, however, and measurements cannot be taken from these illustrations. Oblique photographs taken from low-flying aircraft or a vantagepoint on the ground may also serve as a basis for a perspective illustration (Bolton and Newbury 1967).

Site Maps. As one narrows his area of interest from the region to the neighborhood to the environs of a particular site, the amount of detail to be portrayed and the accuracy of its mapping increases tremendously. Within the square kilometer or two surrounding the site, one wishes the exact location, dimensions, and elevation of archaeological data such as tombs, roads, habitation areas, structures, and artifacts. Also needed are the positions of springs, water channels, houses, and power lines. Areal data to be delimited include surficial materials or soil, bedrock, and vegetation patterns. One also hopes to be able to calculate the angles of slopes and elevations from the site map and to use them to locate accurately the outlines of excavation trenches or geophysical traverses.

To satisfy these demands specially designed surveys at various scales are required. From the discussion above it is obvious that the site map at 1:2,000, with its error factor of perhaps two meters, is sufficient only to de-

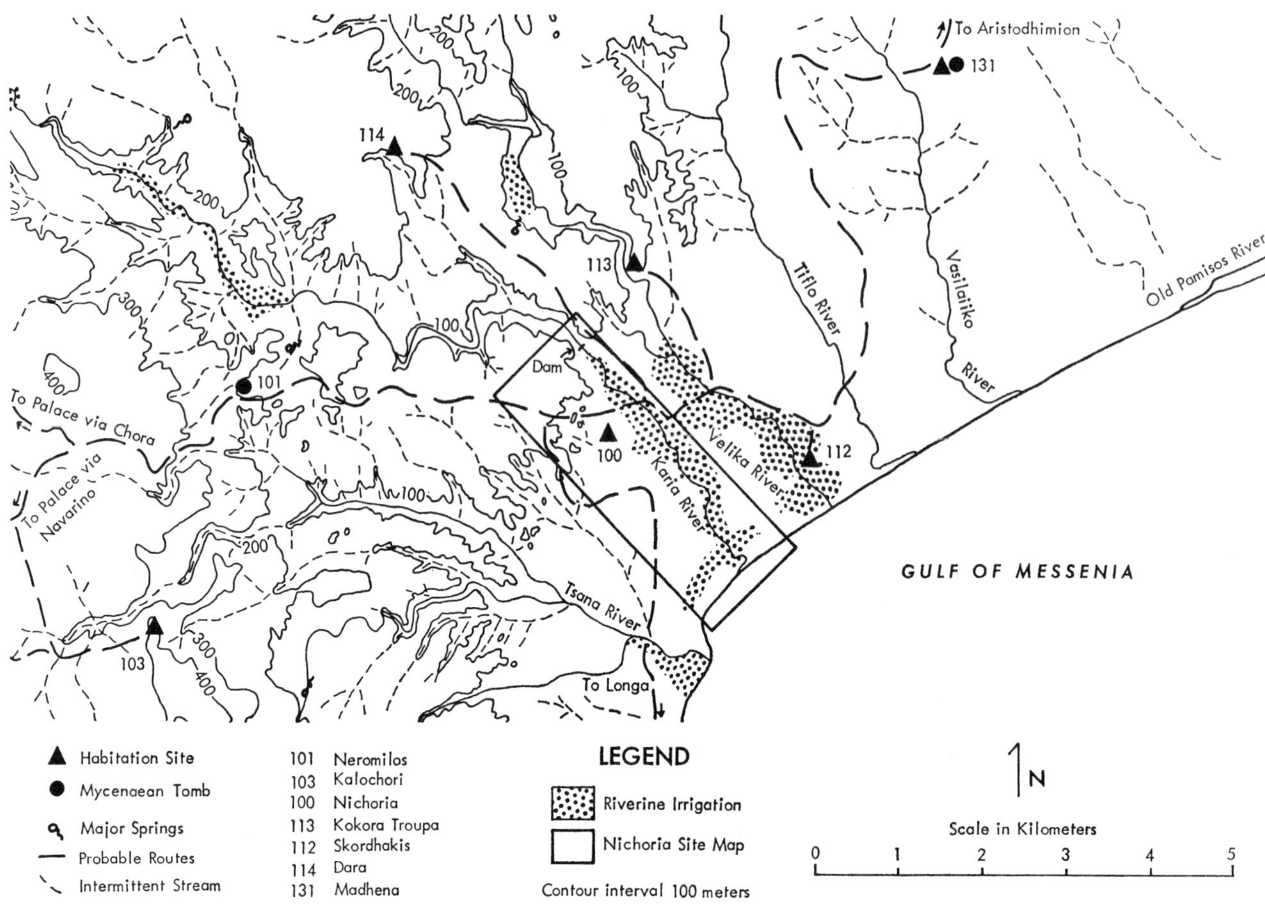

Figure 2-2. Late Bronze Age neighborhood of Nichoria

lineate such items as habitation areas, property boundary lines, large structures, and agricultural information. For more exacting work, such as the locational control of individual traverses within a geophysical survey, a working scale of perhaps 1:200 is needed. In order to locate artifacts within an individual trench, scales of 1:20 may be utilized.

Before discussing these special surveys, a word of caution on the use of aerial photographs as maps is in order. The temptation to use aerial photographs as substitutes for maps must be resisted because, except in the case of high quality photography over a level plain, the changes of scale across an aerial photograph are too great to allow measurements of even minimal accuracy. We do not intend to deny the considerable utility of the aerial photograph as a basis from which to construct site maps or on which to maintain field orientation, but only to caution that aerial photographs may have considerable scale variations. One set of photographs for a village in Messenia showed the same field on two prints with an area variation of two times. Aerial photographs used correctly are a tremendous aid. Writing directly on the photograph with a china marking pencil, the fieldworker can mark the location of tombs, trace water channels, or delineate vegetation boundaries. These annotations can later be transferred from the photographs to base maps, either by inspection or by the use of a reflecting projector.

A serious problem arises when one attempts to provide examples of site and micro-site mapping in a book of this type owing to the size limitation on what may be printed. If these detailed maps are reduced to page size or if only part of the map is shown, the net effect is lost. A compromise solution has been to reproduce some maps in their entirety or nearly so at compilation scale or only slightly reduced (Pocket Maps 2-2, 2-3, 2-4 and Figs. 2-8, 2-12). In some cases, such as the stadia site map, no example is shown as attempts to draft a suitable illustration resulted in failure.

Site maps are made by stadia or plane table (the traditional means employing an instrument man and a rod man) or by photogrammetry, which utilizes stereoscopic pairs of specially taken aerial photographs, some ground surveying, and a stereoplotting instrument. In Messenia all surveying before 1965 was done by stadia owing to the unavailability of aerial photographs; thereafter, photogrammetric methods were used.

The hill of Kafirio (#107), near Longa, was surveyed in 1962 (see Pocket Map 2-4. The original survey is printed here with only slight trimming and at full scale.). The survey provided a map of a small area where McDonald and Yalouris conducted trial trenching in 1959 and is typical of a site map needed for reporting archaeological exploration. The survey of 8 hectares (19 acres) required six instrument positions, 105 stadia observations, and one field day. The equipment used was a tape, stadia rod, and a Wild T-O compass theodolite.

The top of the acropolis is approximately 150 by 95 m, oriented with the long dimension in a north-south direction. The average slope of the steep bank near the top of the hill is about 60 percent (6 m vertical to 10 m horizontal). This bank is much too steep to climb except by pulling oneself up by grabbing the bushes. Below this was another terrace 20 to 50 m wide. An additional drop of 5 m places one, on the south, on a long, rather uniform slope to the sea. To the northwest one crosses a saddle and then goes up a ridge to higher ground. The only productive trial pits, #'s 5 and 6, are shown at the northeast side of this ridge.

The mapped area was planted in vines, grain, figs, and olives, with the steep banks between terraces covered with brush and weeds. To make the map, points A, B, C, D, E, and F on the map were occupied as instrument stations; 32, 9, 10, 20, 27, and 7 stadia ob-

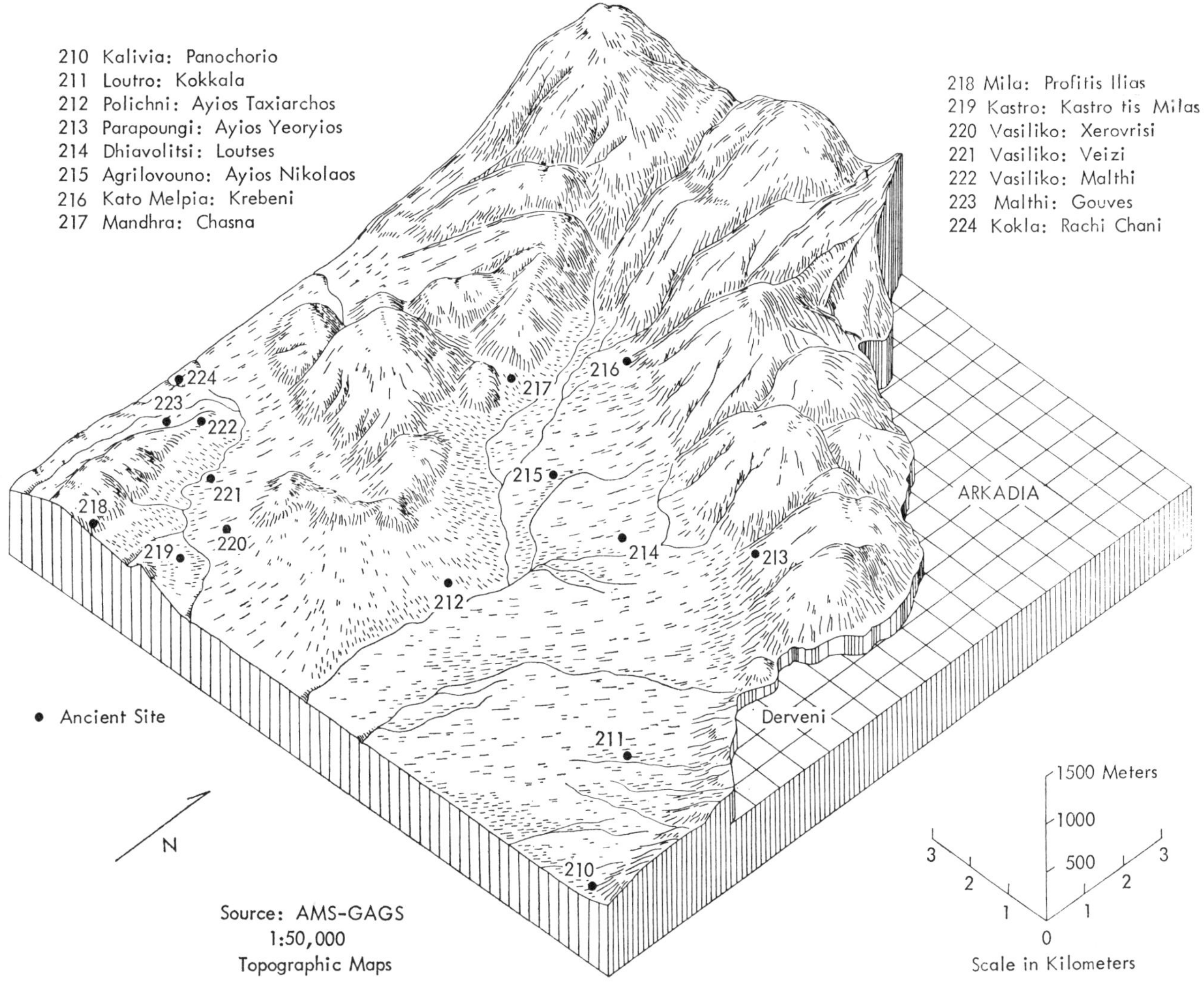

Figure 2-3. Upper Messenian Plain

servations were taken at each station respectively. The frequency of instrument positions and stadia shots was dictated primarily by visibility (trees and vines or topography). An area of this size could normally be mapped from one or two instrument positions, but the steepness of slope and other factors made six necessary. To show detail such as drying beds for currants (minimum of two stadia readings), trees (one stadia reading per tree) and field lines (at least one stadia reading per 30 m) would have required much more field time. As a comparison of the detail which could be shown if an infinite number of stadia shots were taken, compare the Kafirio Survey map with the photogrammetric map of Parapoungi (Pocket Map 2-3. The printed map is reduced in extent and scale approximately one-fourth from the original.). For the purpose of this map, however, these additional details were not needed.

The Kafirio map is typical of stadia maps in that it shows true directions, true elevations and slopes, true areas, true locations of buildings and other features, and it gives a feeling of the general character of the area. Names of property owners, churches, the nearest village, and local place-names may be obtained and shown on the map. This represents, in our opinion, the minimum acceptable standards for a site map, either for study purposes or for publication.

The largest mapping project accomplished in 1962 was a stadia map of 150 hectares (about 370 acres) in the vicinity of Nichoria (#100) near Rizomilo. This map covered about twenty times the area of the Kafirio survey and, since the same field procedures were used, took approximately twenty times longer. The map scale chosen was 1:2,000 because of the size of the area and method used; a contour interval of 5 m was chosen because of the excessive range (about 120 m) in elevation.

This map was used for the same purpose as the Kafirio survey — namely, to show the location and environs of trial trenches, tombs, roads, and concentrations of artifacts for illustrative purposes in a preliminary publication. Although it was reasonably successful and valuable, it was decided that larger and more detailed site maps were needed by the geomorphologist, geographer, and agricultural economist for their site studies not only at Nichoria but at Aristodhimion (#123), Parapoungi (#213), and Malthi (#222). Because of the time and labor involved, these maps would have been impossible to make by stadia; therefore photogrammetric methods were studied and implemented.

In March 1965, the Royal Hellenic Air Force made special mapping flights over six sites at a height of about 1,100 m. The photographs were taken with a six-inch focal length precision camera, and each photograph overlapped the next by about 60 percent in the direction of flight to provide stereo-pairs.

The scale of vertical aerial photographs (see Fig. 2-4) can be roughly determined by the simple relation $ab/AB = f/H$, where ab = length on photograph, AB = length on ground, f = focal length, and H = flight height (see Fig. 2-4). Given that $f = 6$ in. $= 0.152$ m and $H = 1100$ m, the scale of these photographs can be determined as follows:

$$ab/AB = 0.152 \text{ m}/1100 \text{ m} = 1/7200$$

This equation can be used in two ways: first, the flight altitude can be predetermined for a desired photographic scale, and second, the scale of photography and flight height can be determined by measuring on a photograph between two image points for which the ground distance is known.

These computations are only approximate since difference in elevation between the two points and the tilt of the camera during exposure complicate the simple relationship. Nevertheless, it is necessary to know the approximate scale when studying and using aerial photographs. To map from aerial photographs in stereoplotting instruments, it is necessary to know the distance between two points visible in the stereo model and the elevations of four points in the corners of the stereo model. A ground control survey consisting of a traverse and a level net is required to obtain this information. The ground control surveys for the 1965 photography were made in the summer of 1966, and the maps were compiled in a stereoplotter during the academic year 1966–67 in the photogrammetry laboratory at the University of Minnesota. The maps were compiled at a scale of 1:1,500 and reduced to a scale of 1:3,000 for use in the field. A study of Pocket Map 2-3 shows the great detail that can be recorded by this method. The contours represent more accurately than from stadia methods the true physical shape of the land (no interpolating of finitely spaced readings is necessary), all buildings are correctly shown as to orientation and size, and field and terrace lines are shown in correct horizontal position and elevation. At the compiling scale, crops can be shown and kinds and numbers of trees plotted since they are easily distinguished in the stereo model. From an engineer's viewpoint, photography and photogrammetrically prepared maps are essential tools of archaeological and geographic studies. Such maps have been used in the construction of all of the site maps for the UMME project.

A further advantage of the photogrammetric method is the inventory of information contained in the photographs. As additional data are needed, the diapositive

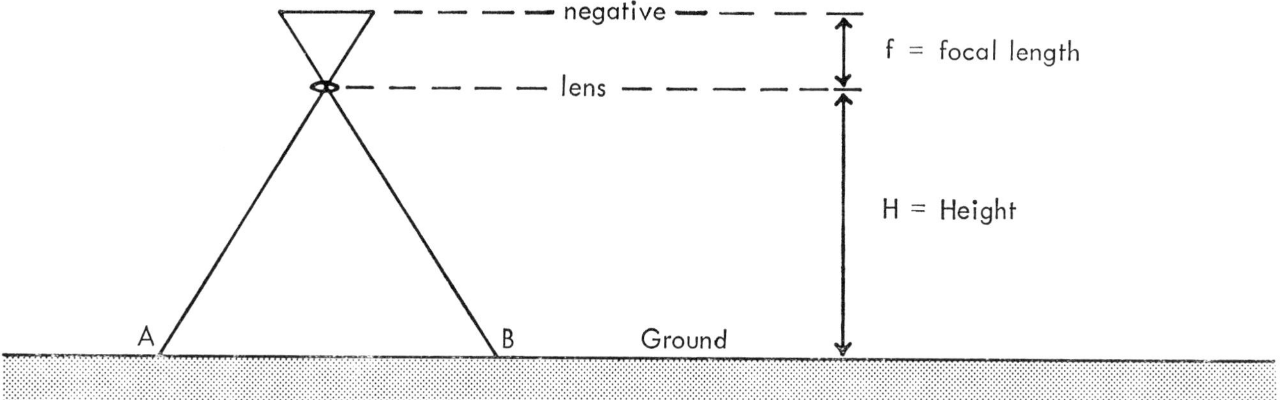

Figure 2-4. Scale relationship diagram

plates need only be reoriented in the plotter and the additional information compiled. These factors led us to use stereo photography from the start for the excavation at Nichoria. This program will be discussed later in the chapter.

The preferred survey method – plane table, stadia, or photogrammetry – for any situation is dependent on equipment available and on properties of the terrain. The photogrammetric method gives better over-all accuracy in terms of contour, road, and stream locations because the plotter operator can follow the small changes in alignment that are not possible with stadia or plane table. However, photogrammetric methods are not suitable for flat or heavily wooded sites, and the complications of securing photo coverage and a plotter for small projects in foreign countries might dictate the stadia or the plane-table method. As the areas become larger, the photogrammetric method becomes cheaper than stadia or other methods, and worth the effort. On the other hand, as the area becomes smaller or less complicated, the photogrammetric method becomes more expensive than stadia. Certain types of site surveys can be done well by ground methods, since the interpretation of the results requires close field inspection, study, and measurement. However prepared, these special-purpose maps provide the filing system for the features being studied.

Route Surveys. The locations of ancient routes or actual road lines are of great value in archaeological, historical, and geographical studies of a region. The analysis of curve radius, slope, alignment, and location at a site provides information as to the use, age, and type of road. Route surveys were made in 1962 and 1964, one in Messenia and one on Crete. These maps were made at scales of 1:2,000 and 1:1,000, respectively.

The knowledge that chariots were used in the Late Bronze Age and that, according to Homer, Telemachos, Odysseus' son, was driven in a chariot from Pylos to Sparta spurred McDonald's and Hope Simpson's interest in roads for wheeled traffic and in road patterns. They discovered in the Neromilos-Kazarma area a spot where elevation changes rapidly and where several roads, parallel to and following the alignment of the modern Kalamata-Pylos highway, indicate progressive highway development over a long period (McDonald and Hope Simpson 1964). They therefore asked Fant to make a map and a thorough study of this area and its roads.

Before starting this mapping in Messenia, Fant inspected the well-known Late Bronze Age road leading north from Mycenae toward Corinth to acquaint himself with the details of a known chariot road. The Mycenae road, starting about one kilometer beyond Perseia Spring, is visible for two or more kilometers. It has very gentle grades, an absence of cuts (or only low cuts) on the uphill side and built-up terrace walls on the downhill side. The road could be classified as being made with fill rather than "cut and fill," though the latter characterizes most sidehill construction. The most striking characteristic is the profusion of drainage channels (culverts), spaced about three to six meters apart and with low corbelled openings under the roadway.

Drainage is, of course, a major factor in maintaining a good smooth roadbed on graveled and unpaved roads. Modern construction uses ditches parallel to the roadway, combined with culverts where necessary to carry the water under the highway. Without ditches, the cross-drains must be closely spaced to achieve good results. There is a major bridge where the Mycenae road crosses a narrow intermittent streambed. The opening is an inverted V about 0.8 m wide at the bottom, 1.8 to 2.0 m

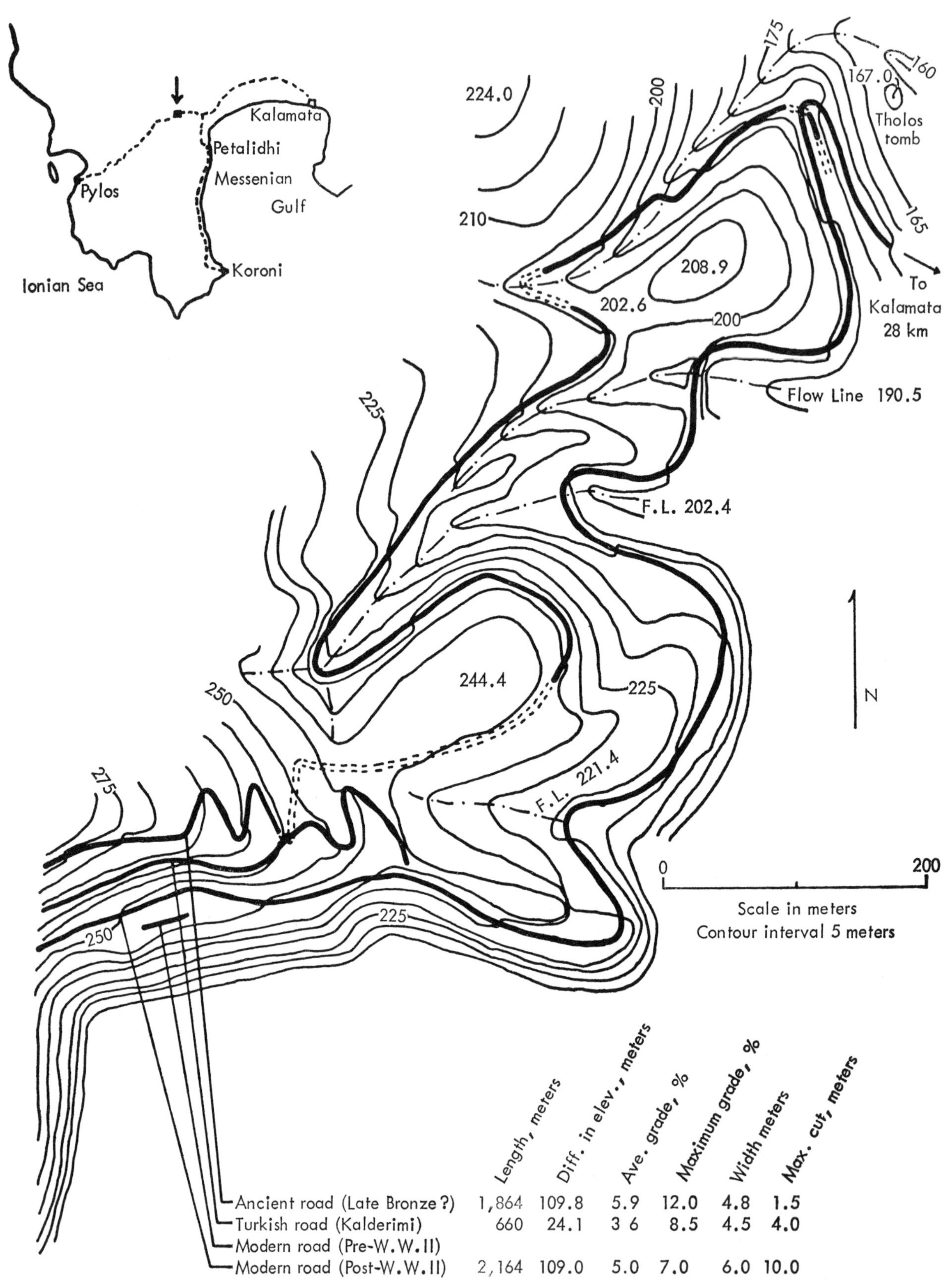

	Length, meters	Diff. in elev., meters	Ave. grade, %	Maximum grade, %	Width meters	Max. cut, meters
Ancient road (Late Bronze ?)	1,864	109.8	5.9	12.0	4.8	1.5
Turkish road (Kalderimi)	660	24.1	3 6	8.5	4.5	4.0
Modern road (Pre-W.W.II)						
Modern road (Post-W.W.II)	2,164	109.0	5.0	7.0	6.0	10.0

Figure 2-5. Kazarma-Neromilos highway survey

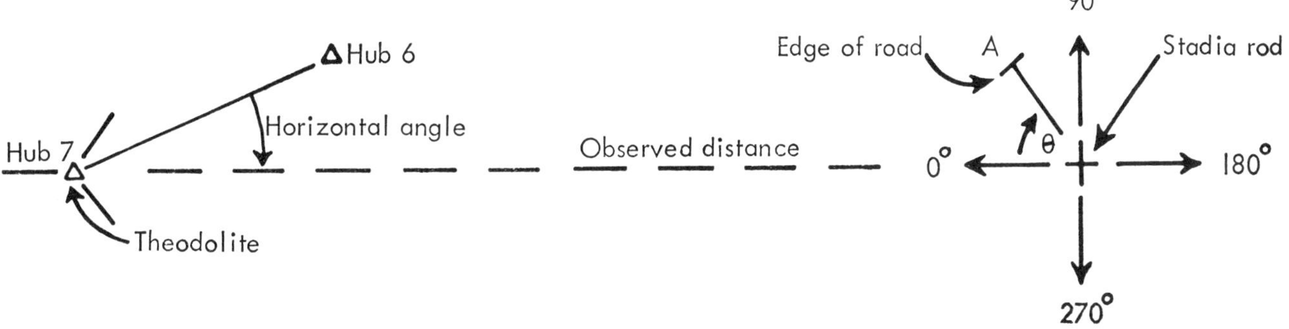

Figure 2-6. Stadia shot

high and open for a depth of 5.7 m. The bridge was made of boulders laid to form a corbelled arch similar to the bridge over the Chaos ravine at Mycenae, the arches at Tiryns, and the bridge just north of the highway on the road to Epidauros. Although no levels for grade or other measurements were made on the Mycenae road, superficial inspection provided a good understanding of the construction.

The mapping of the highway system in the Kazarma-Neromilos area of Messenia was made by stadia methods. The basic problem was to map the four different roads that are visible, one above another, on the north side of a deep ravine. Traverses were run down the highest and presumably earliest road and along the modern highway (see Fig. 2-5, which depicts the northeast two-thirds of the area surveyed). Additional observations were taken to interpolate contours where the road shots were insufficient for this purpose. The survey involved 200 hectares, 17 instrument positions, 303 stadia observations, and three field days. The total length of the area mapped was about 2,000 m.

The modern paved highway is characterized by ditches, catch basins, and culverts typical of any new road. The maximum cut is 10 m and the maximum grade 7 percent. The pre–World War II gravel road was practically obliterated by the modern construction, but it could be described as narrower with sharper curves. The medieval or Turkish road (*kalderimi*) had a cobblestone surface (Pl. 4-3), and some attempt was made to provide a sufficient radius at curves for ease and safety in ascent and descent. This road is shown on Figure 2-5; at the switchback the three radii of the road are about 10 to 12 m. The radius of curve on the modern highway at the low end of the pass is 11 m, which is close to the minimum radius of curvature for automobiles. There is at least one preserved drainage structure crossing under the kalderimi, but no drainage ditches are visible along its course. The cobblestones would provide a surface which would not erode if water flowed across the surface. It is clear, because of its roughness and narrowness, that this road was for pedestrians, pack animals, and riders and not for wheeled vehicles (cf. Pl. 3-2). The cuts were lower, the grades steeper, and the width less than for the modern highway. This indicates that it was not designed as a rapid, convenient road for vehicles.

The highest road (Pl. 3-4), in which UMME is particularly interested, is characterized by greater variation in slopes (a maximum of 12 percent), lower cuts (a maximum of 1.5 m), and sharper curves on the switchback (about 4-m radius). Obviously, this road was not built for modern transportation. The present surface appears to be the exposed cut, with a little gravel covering the rock face. There is relatively little terrace wall construction of the monumental kind seen at Mycenae, and no cross drains of any kind were found. The drainage would presumably have been across the road, which suggests that a relatively smooth surface for chariot travel would be very difficult to maintain.

Fant's conclusion is that, if a Late Bronze Age road ran between Kalamata and Pylos, it would logically fall in this location, that is, a pass between two plains of about 115 m difference in elevation. The tholos (?) tomb (#101) at the eastern foot of the ravine provides added evidence that the highway line should have been here. There is no evidence in connection with the road itself to indicate the date of construction. Possibly in the future selected trial trenches across the roadway could uncover some ceramic evidence to suggest the date of construction.

The further question, Was there a chariot road between ancient Pharai (Kalamata) and Sparta? remains unanswered. However, noting the difficulty of highway construction at the present time through the Taygetos Mountains, and assuming that the details of construction for a chariot road would have some relation to the basic requirements of modern construction as to grade and radius, there is real doubt that such a road could have been built. Although it is evident that a good chariot road between the Gulf of Argos and Corinth would have great commercial and military value to justify the construction, the same reasoning is not so compelling in the case of a road over the Taygetos Mountains.

Another stadia survey, at a scale of 1:1,000, was made in 1964 where an alleged Minoan road leads up out of the eastern end of the Lasithi Plain of Crete in the vicinity of the chapel of Ayia Pelayia (Evans 1928, p. 63). Although several methods could theoretically be used for such a survey (photogrammetric, grid and elevations, cross sections), the only practical method was to make a stadia survey combined with taped measurements for details.

The explanation of this survey might be rather detailed and technical for some readers, but it illustrates how two surveying techniques can be combined to produce data capable of being analyzed at two levels of accuracy. Amplified discussions of the techniques described below and detailed explanations of surveying procedures mentioned elsewhere in this chapter may be found in surveying texts (e.g., Kissam 1947).

The stadia measurements gave the necessary information of horizontal position and elevation for the control points, alignment, direction, and elevation of the centerline of the roadway. Direct measurements gave the necessary information on widths of road, radius of curvature, building and fence details. Fourteen control points were established along the road, and centerline stadia shots were taken at frequent intervals. Widths of road were recorded at many of the stadia shot locations, and at curves additional information was taken by recording the distances to the edge of the road and referencing them by angle as shown in Figure 2-6.

The theodolite is at Hub 7 on the control traverse and oriented with respect to Hub 6. The rodman takes the stadia rod to a desired point where the horizontal angle and observed distance are read. If the rod is on the center of the road, the rodman measures the width and this is recorded. Where the width alone will not provide sufficient information, additional measurements are made at an angle with respect to the line back to the theodolite. This angle (θ) and the measurements are recorded. The complete notes for one curve on this survey are given in Table 2-1.

Points A, B, C, D, and E are plotted on the map by the use of a compass rose oriented to grid north of the map. These points are plotted as crosses on Figure 2-7. The auxiliary information under the "notes" column is plotted, and each "bit" is plotted as a small circle. As

Table 2-1. Stadia Field Notes[a]

Shot	Horizontal Angle	Vertical Angle	Observed Distance (in m)	Horizontal Distance (in m)	Difference in Elevation (in m)	Elevation (in m)	Notes
Hub 6	0°00′						
A	105°42′	−3°43′	71	70.6	−4.59	818.73	On centerline, width 2.8 m
B	106°00′	−1°50′	54	54.0	−1.73	821.59	On centerline, width 3.1 m
C	95°10′	+4°40′	30	29.8	+2.43	825.75	On centerline, for θ angles of 0°, 3.4 m to edge; 90°, 5.6 m to edge; 180°, 2.6 m to edge; 270°, 6.0 m to edge
D	77°05′	+8°22′	53	51.9	+7.63	830.95	On centerline, width 3.0 m
E	70°00′	+9°12′	82	79.9	+12.92	836.24	On centerline, width 3.2 m

[a] Theodolite at Hub 7; height instrument = 1.60 m; elev. = 832.32 m.

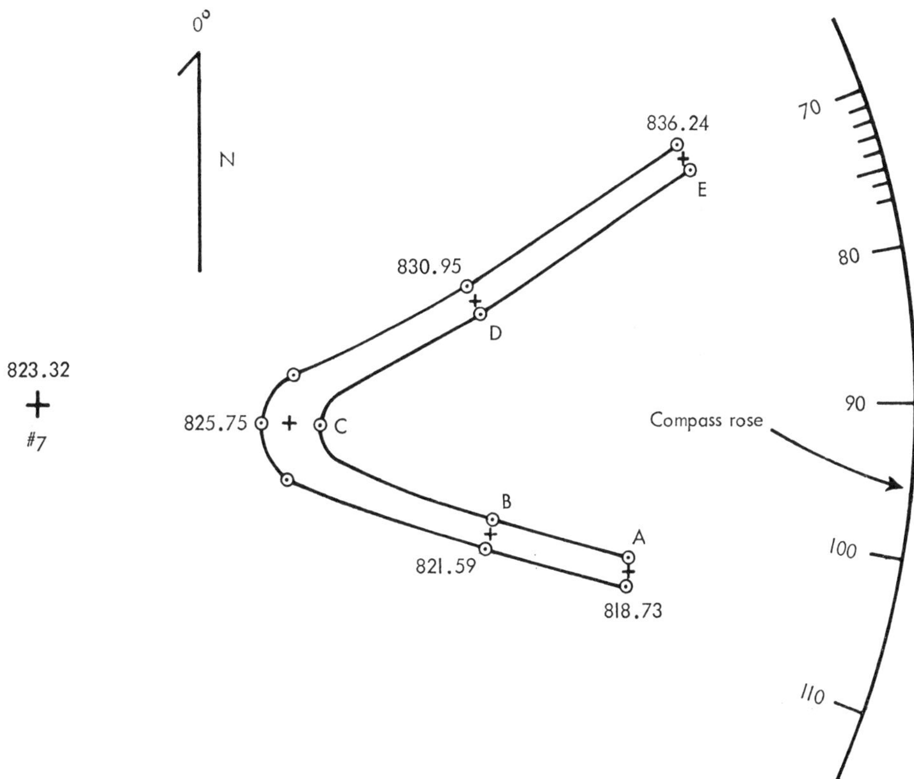

Figure 2-7. Curve plotting

can be seen, the five stadia points are supplemented by twelve additional points, making it rather easy to plot the road through the curve. From the map, radii and grades can be computed. For curve illustrated in Figure 2-7, the radius can be scaled approximately and the slopes computed between stadia shots (see Table 2-2).

Table 2-2. Curve Analysis

Point	Distance (in m)	Elevation	Difference in Elevation	Slope
A		818.73		
A to B	16.8		+2.86	17.0%
B		821.59		
B to C	27		+4.16	15.4
C		825.75		
C to D	26		+5.20	20.0
D		830.95		
D to E	29		+5.29	18.2
E		836.24		
Average				17.7%

All curves were surveyed in like manner. Figure 2-8 illustrates a section of the road mapped. The sharpest radius of curvature was 1.1 m on six of the curves; eleven more had radii under 1.6 meters. The width of the road varied from 2.6 to 3.8 m with an average width of 3.0. The road from the plain to the top of the pass is 1,736 m long, with a rise of 309 m, giving an average 17.8 percent grade. The grade on much of the road is approximately 20 percent, with short stretches of 24 percent grade. There are no drainage structures visible in the entire length of the road, although there are some rather large retaining walls on the lower side.

The Ayia Pelayia road probably was not a chariot road because the grades are too steep, the curves are too sharp, and no drainage structures have been provided to help maintain a smooth surface. The steps now found in the roadway, unless added later, would indicate that the road was not originally designed for wheeled vehicles. There is no evidence of consistent engineering design.

Special Purpose Site Maps. Another form of site map is the control survey which accurately preserves the location of scientific data of investigations. This is a technical service that is needed by various members of the UMME team. In 1966 surveys were made at five locations in the Nichoria area and on the sand bar between Navarino Bay and Osmanaga Lagoon (Pl. 16-3). The surveying details will be reported here, but the interpretation of these results will appear in Chapters 12 and 15. At Osmanaga Lagoon (Pl. 5-2), for example, our palynologist needed the horizontal position and elevation of pollen core samples taken from the lagoon and profiles of the sand dunes near Voïdhokilia Bay (Fig. 2-9). This information was necessary for the study of the vegetational history of the area and for the attempt to reconstruct the geomorphology of the harbor and nearby coast.

More detailed site surveys were provided for the geophysicists' work on Nichoria. The magnetometer, which

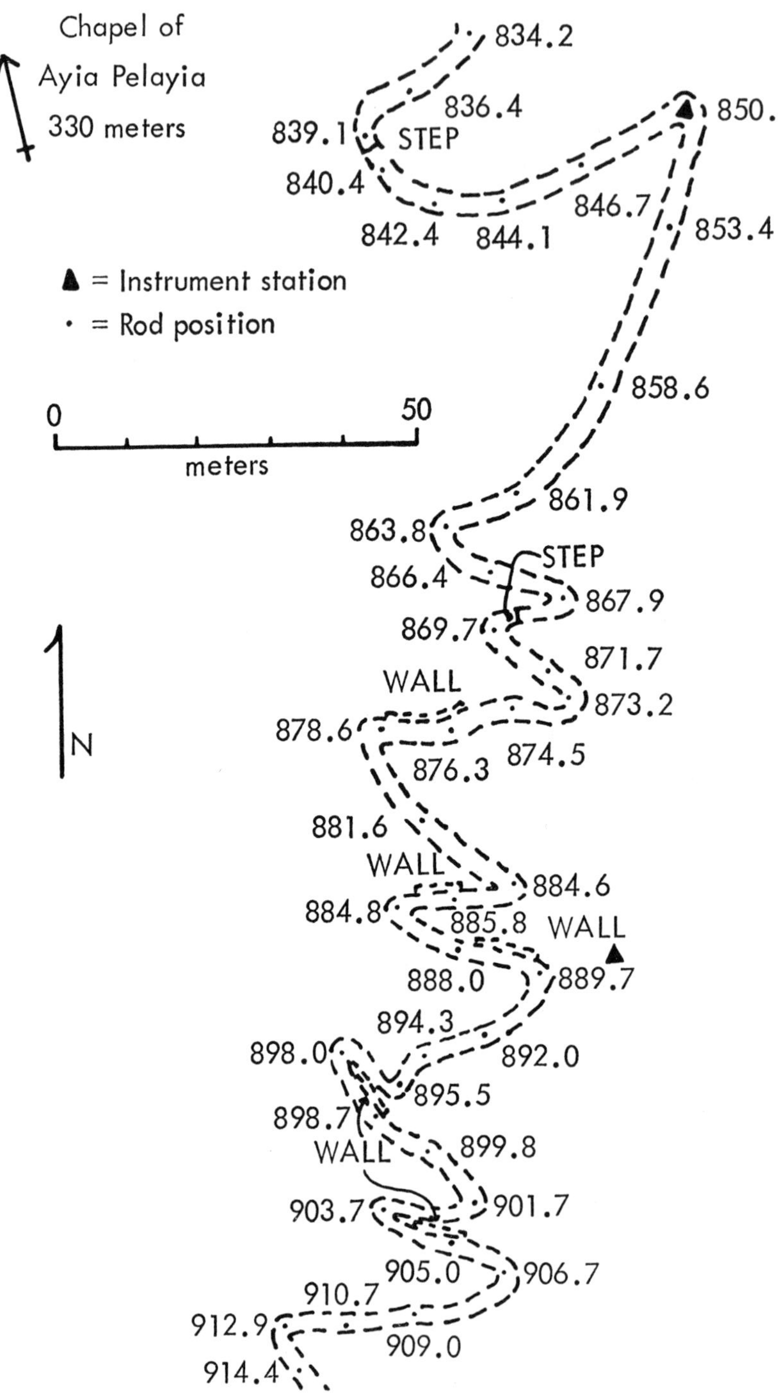

Figure 2-8. Crete: Ayia Pelayia road survey map, printed here at full scale. This represents the central third of the original map (Fant 1964)

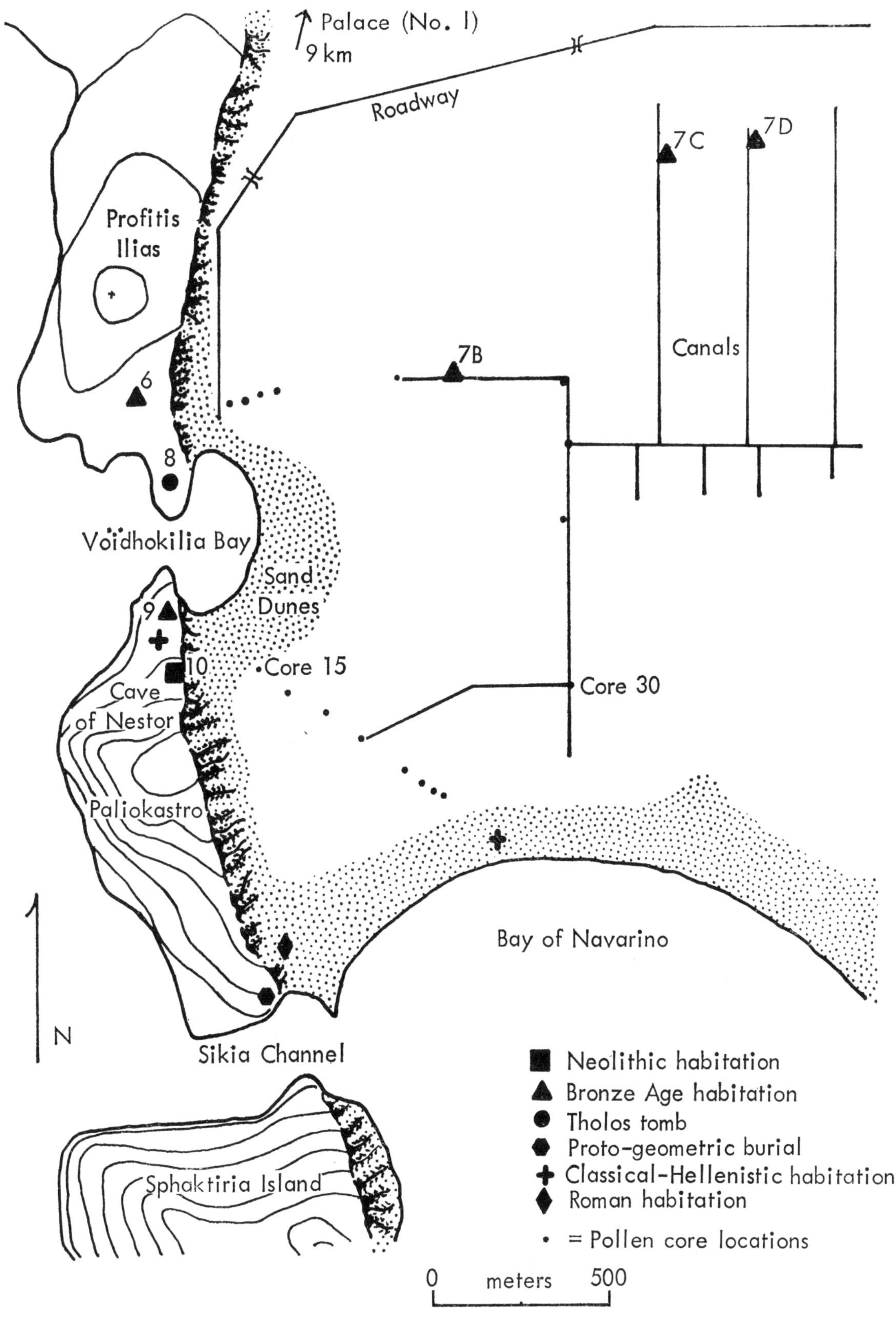
Palace (No. I)
9 km
Roadway
7C
7D
Profitis
Ilias
Canals
7B
6
8
Voidhokilia Bay
Sand
Dunes
9
10
Core 15
Core 30
Cave
of Nestor
Paliokastro
Bay of Navarino
N
Sikia Channel
Sphaktiria Island
Neolithic habitation
Bronze Age habitation
Tholos tomb
Proto-geometric burial
Classical-Hellenistic habitation
Roman habitation
• = Pollen core locations
0
meters
500

Figure 2-9. Control survey: Osmanaga

detects changes in the magnetic field that may indicate underground walls, pottery, and/or artifacts, must be read at close intervals in a grid pattern in order to obtain the values from which magnetic contours may be plotted (Pls. 16-1, 16-2). To establish a grid, ropes were tied into a 6- by 10-m "fishnet" with a 1-m grid. This rope grid was laid on the ground and magnetometer readings taken at the corner of each section in the grid. After all readings were taken, stakes were placed at the corners of the 6- by 10-m area and the rope moved to the next area to be tested. All grids were numbered in the notes. The location work required surveying in all of the corner stakes, providing the proper orientation, and locating enough "landmarks" so that each net, grid point, and anomaly can be relocated for later test excavation.

As can be seen on Pocket Map 2-4, the orientation is determined with respect to astronomic north, magnetic north, and from the major control point (the stump of an olive tree). Angles were read from this point to other control points and to a visible guard post on the highway about 500 m to the northwest. The original survey drawing is reproduced here at full scale in redrafted form.

The grid stakes and trees were located by measurement and angle from three control points: *number one*, *number three*, and *stump*. The terraces were located as well as the outlines of the cultivated areas, so that the area mapped can easily be related to the over-all map of Nichoria. It was difficult to lay the rope grid in proper position because of the numerous trees and irregularities of the ground; however, by the use of the accompanying map, each reading could be re-established to within 50 cm of its true position on the ground. The control points can be re-established accurately to within 1 cm, and the orientation to 1 min. of angle if another astronomic observation is taken or the guard post is used as a backsight. An anomaly can be relocated by measurements to the nearest trees (scaled distances) or by an angle and distance from a control point. Mapping was essential because it would be most unwise to mark these points on the ground. Also, with reliable maps, the operator of the magnetometer does not need to take elaborate notes to identify and locate his grids for future use, and the location of the grids can easily be re-established.

Two general conclusions can be drawn from these site maps at the scale 1:1,000 to 1:2,000. If the archaeologist needs a map to show the physical settings of cemeteries, habitation sites, excavation trenches, or for a special project, a stadia or ground survey is sufficient. Not much of the present landscape detail is shown, however, since such information adds nothing for the purpose intended. On the other hand, if there are to be extensive studies of the present man-land relationships such as cultivation patterns, land use, and so on, then it is absolutely essential that a map be made photogrammetrically showing all possible detail.

Micro-Site Maps 1:200 to 1:1. The considerations of using ground or aerial methods for detailed scale or small-area maps change somewhat in that the previously discussed methods — stadia and standard photogrammetry (airborne exposed photographs) — do not provide adequate accuracy or detail. At micro-site scales the archaeologist needs (at least potentially) details on *everything* within the mapping limits. The principal method of making such surveys is by a grid system. In the grid survey a series of stakes are placed at grid points throughout the area by use of a theodolite and tape; elevations are obtained for each of the grid points by a level. Objects can then be located accurately with respect to the grid points; the spatial position of any point or object is given by its x, y, and z coordinates. The main dis-

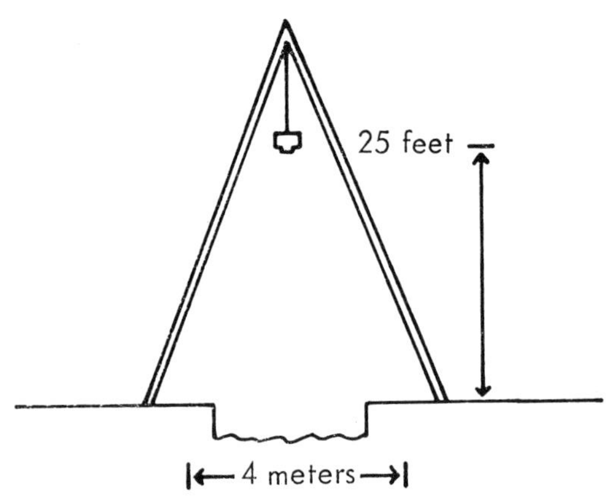

Figure 2-10. Stereo photography: one-camera system

advantage of this system is the slow, tedious work involved in measuring and transferring data to field books and then to maps or plans. It is also difficult to properly map curved surfaces such as pottery and stone walls, and extensive sketching is necessary. For these reasons photogrammetric methods have notable advantages for micro-site surveys. The surveyor-engineer-photogrammetrist can assist the archaeologist in efficiently mapping the site, and tiresome hours of measuring, sketching, and recording can be eliminated. Also, with photographic recording a complete record is obtained, permitting future reference and study.

Research in photogrammetric micro-site mapping was initiated at Nichoria in 1969 and continued in 1970. Before explaining the development of the photography and photogrammetric methods, two points should be made clear. First, photogrammetric procedures and equipment exist but are little used mainly because the terrestrial stereo cameras and the plotters to compile the maps are expensive, and, second, they are not readily accessible to the archaeologist. We make no claim that the methods we have developed can compete in accuracy with commercially available techniques such as those advertised in photogrammetric journals. Our primary goal is to develop techniques, at a reasonable cost, which can be used by the archaeologist in his work.

In the 1969 trial excavation season an 80-mm focal length, 2¼ by 3¼ inch camera with interchangeable roll film backs was purchased. In addition, Julian Whittlesey brought to the site several cameras, one radio controlled for balloon suspension, and the equipment needed to pursue his method of low-altitude photography by the use of bipod and balloon suspension systems (Whittlesey 1966).

The radio-controlled, balloon-supported camera provided us with photographs from various heights and taken with a variety of films: color, infrared color, and black and white. Various filters were used to isolate certain portions of the electromagnetic spectrum. Aerial remote-sensing methods to detect buried objects were part of the over-all research, which also included magnetic and electrical methods on the ground. The aerial photographs did not reveal outlines of buried structures. This was not unexpected since the site was very dry and difference in moisture content is a strong sensing parameter. Also, plowed ground provided a very rough surface and much of the hilltop is obscured by trees. The balloon photographs did provide good photographic coverage of all trial excavations and an excellent total-site photograph when, on a calm day, the balloon carried the camera to an altitude of 500 meters.

Since stereophotographic recording and mapping were planned for the 1970 season, when the major excavation was to begin, some experimenting was done in 1969 both with the balloon and with a bipod arrangement that Whittlesey had used successfully elsewhere. We found it impossible to hold the balloon steady at low altitudes and therefore turned to the bipod method. Experimental procedures were tried in camera suspension, altitude, separation of camera positions, and mapping instrumentation. Ideally, we wanted two photographs oriented in the same direction with an overlap of about 60 percent and taken from the same elevation.

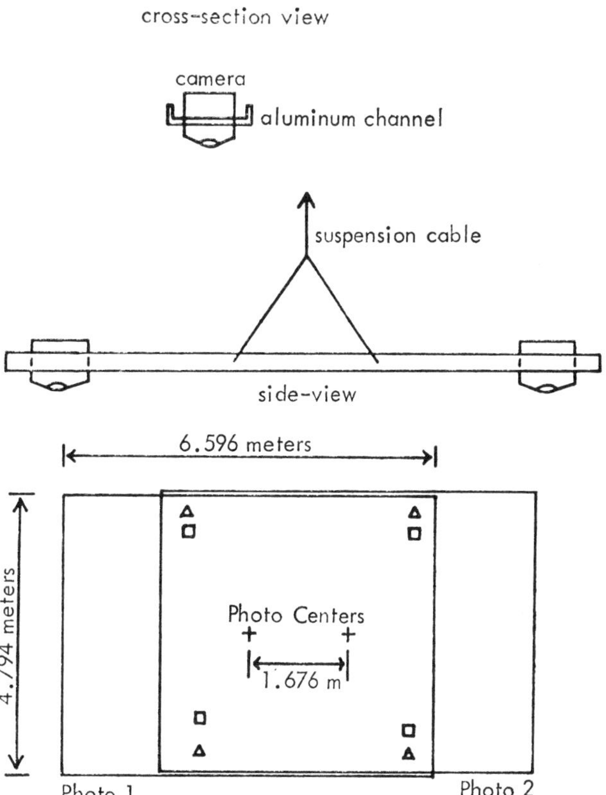

Figure 2-11. Stereo photography: twin-camera system

The best platform for stereophotography at low altitudes seems to be a bipod arrangement from which the camera is suspended over the excavation to be photographed (see Fig. 2-10). In 1969 a bipod was built from local materials, and trench photographs were taken with the 2¼ by 3¼ inch camera. To obtain stereophotographs one picture was taken, and the bipod was then leaned to the second picture position. Since the camera was hung from a rope, it was difficult to take both photographs with the same orientation. Rotation and swing because of wind made it difficult to get good stereopho-

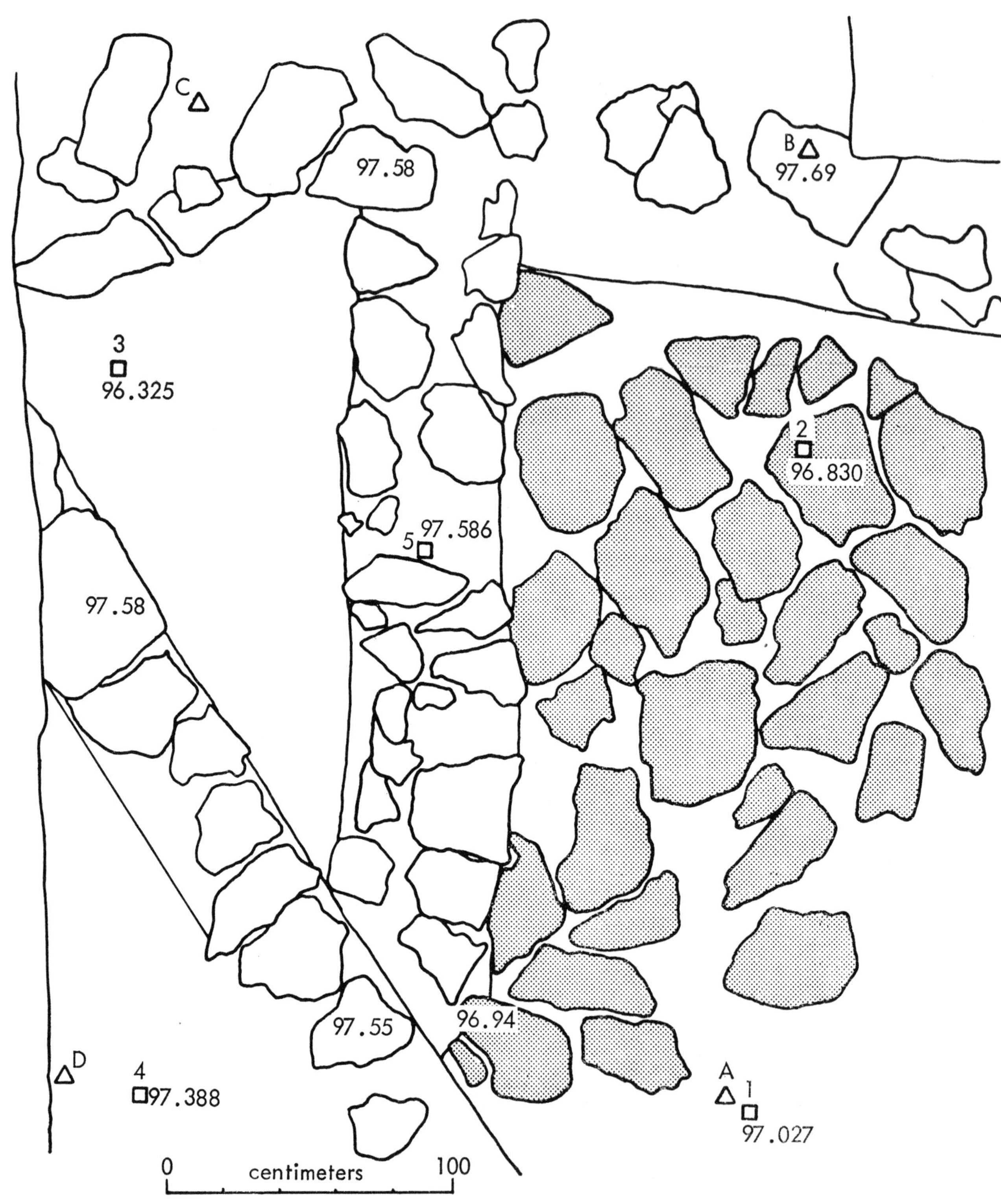

Figure 2-12. Micro-Site map, scale of 1:20, printed here at full size. Triangles represent horizontal control points; squares, vertical control points. Compare Plate 1-1

tographs. However, the idea was sound, and the photographs obtained gave a satisfactory low-altitude record of many of the trenches dug in the 1969 season.

A better system was devised for the 1970 expedition to provide stereo coverage of 4 by 4 m grids. A 7.6 m bipod was built of 2-inch aluminum tubing in 1.5 m sections for easy assembly. The tubing had sufficient strength so that it could be erected by two men and held in a vertical position by two guy-ropes fastened to the top. A pulley arrangement at the top of the bipod permitted the cameras to be raised to the photographic position, about 6.7 m.

Two cameras were mounted on a rigid aluminum channel section 1.67 m apart with parallel axes (Fig. 2-11). This use of two cameras permitted good and consistent stereo-overlap. Further, the pictures were taken simultaneously by air-bulb synchronization.

For the design altitude and camera spacing, the photographic scale (using the equation from p. 24 and an 80-mm focal length) is 1:84; each photograph covers 4.794 by 6.596 m; and the stereo overlap is about 75 percent, an area 4.8 by 4.8 m. A typical stereo-pair from this bipod camera arrangement is shown in Plate 1-1.

Viewing this stereo-pair with a stereoscope shows the excellent detail and record that can be obtained. The small triangular and square targets in the photographs are the horizontal and vertical control points, respectively, necessary for orientation in the stereoplotting instrument. Four horizontal and five vertical points are required for each photo pair. These points were located near the corners and the center of the overlap area (see Figs. 2-11, 2-12). The values shown in Figure 2-12 are elevations.

In the field the survey data are recorded, and some information is obtained on wall elevations. The photographs are developed in the laboratory of the excavation house and contact prints made for the archaeologist in charge of the excavation, the photogrammetrist, and the record. These contact prints are further annotated and indexed. The final mapping is done in the photogrammetry laboratory at the University of Minnesota.

Diapositives are made on 24 by 24 cm plates from the negative in an enlarger. The negatives were enlarged about 2.7 times during the diapositive making process and 5.0 times through projection in the Kelsh plotter. The final plotting scale for the maps is about 1:6. This scale is quite large and calls for a reduction to the 1:20 scale used by the archaeologists. Figure 2-12 is a full-scale portion of the completed map for the grid of photographs in Plate 1-1.

This map represents one grid among many being dug during the excavation now in progress. The map shows walls and floor (patterned) of a Late Bronze Age building, but detailed archaeological analysis is not a part of this chapter. It should be noted that, with the stereophotographs and the 1:20 scale map of a total excavation site, the archaeologist has the complete areal information needed to make his analysis. Moreover, if any doubts should arise over measurements or identifications, the photographic record can be re-examined.

Micro-site surveys become very detailed and specialized. The methods used must, in many cases, be imaginative and original to solve unusual problems efficiently and economically. To make efficient use of one discipline – mapping – by other disciplines requires close cooperation and communication between the participants in the project.

REFERENCES

Bolton, T., and Newbury, P. A. 1967. *Geography through Fieldwork*. London.

Evans, A. J. 1928. *The Palace of Minos at Cnossos*, Vol. 2, Pt. 1. London.

Kissam, Philip. 1947. *Surveying*. New York.

Loy, W. G. 1970. *The Land of Nestor: A Physical Geography of the Southwest Peloponnese*. National Academy of Sciences, Office of Naval Research, Report No. 34. Washington, D.C.

McDonald, W. A., and Hope Simpson, R. 1964. "Further Explorations in Southwestern Peloponnese: 1962–63," *AJA* 68:229–45.

Stacy, John R. 1958. "Terrain Diagrams in Isometric Projection — Simplified," *Annals of the Association of American Geographers* 48:232–36.

Whittlesey, J. 1966. "Photogrammetry for the Excavator," *Archaeology* 19:273.

3

THE PHYSICAL SETTING

by

William G. Loy and H. E. Wright, Jr.

The area of southwestern Peloponnese with which we are concerned has already been delimited – from the Alpheios River on the north to the Messenian Gulf on the south, and from the Taygetos Mountains on the east to the Ionian Sea on the west. It covers about 3,800 sq. km (1,400 sq. mi), with a maximum length of 100 km (62 mi) from north to south and maximum breadth of 50 km (31 mi). With the exception of a narrow coastal plain and the broad Pamisos Valley north of the Messenian Gulf, the terrain is mostly mountainous, or at the least a hilly upland. The most prominent topographic features are shown on Pocket Map 3-5.

In the north, the dissected hill lands of the Alpheios River Valley are bordered on the south by the Minthis and Tetrazi mountains, which are separated by the Nedha River. The Kyparissia River makes another break, and then come the Kyparissia Mountains, which project southward in the Aigaleon ridge and other fingers that reflect the differential erosional resistance of steeply inclined sedimentary beds. Mt. Ithomi is the easternmost of the ridges. These fingers lead southward to the plateau (kampos) east of Pylos, and this continues to the end of the Messenian peninsula, punctuated by deep valleys and by mountains such as Ayios Nikolaos, Likodhimos, and Tzarnaoura.

East of the Kyparissia Mountains is the Messenian Plain, which is essentially a northward projection of the Gulf of Messenia. This is the traditionally rich agricultural heartland of Messenia. A series of low hills (the Skala ridge) east of Mt. Ithomi serves to divide this lowland into a lower plain (the Pamisos Valley) and an upper plain (the Steniklarian Valley). The latter extends to the west as the Soulima Valley. The entire plain is drained southward to the Gulf of Messenia. The Pamisos River proper rises in the northeastern corner of the lower plain at the huge springs of Ayios Floros and terminates in a vast marsh separated from the sea by beach sand. The wetlands are now drained for agriculture (Sauerwein 1968).

East of the Messenian Plain lie the rugged Taygetos Mountains, which reach an elevation more than 2,000 m above sea level and comprise the core of the Mani peninsula. Formed dominantly of limestone, they present a precipitous front to the west, cut by a few deep gorges like that of the Nedhon River east of Kalamata. They provide a natural boundary for our region on the east.

The considerable diversity in regional topography throughout the area produces corresponding contrasts in such aspects of the human environment as microclimate, soils, water supply, and vegetation. Although not severe enough to impede seriously the free exchange of people and ideas, the topographic diversity is enough to encourage local autonomy and specialized subsistence patterns. The early inhabitants must have learned to take maximum advantage of local resources, and in so doing they may have developed at least some degree of agricultural specialization. This diversity may in turn be expected to have played a significant role in Messenian history, particularly in the gradual political unification of the Late Bronze Age.

In gross estimate, 40 percent of the modern land surface of the region is classed as arable, 42 percent pasture, and 15 percent forest. Because agriculture has always been the basis of the Greek economy and because the average proportion of arable land in Greece as a whole is only 28 percent, this one statistic goes far to explain the relative prosperity and attractiveness of southwest Peloponnese. At present the most common crops are grain, olives, grapes, currants, and figs. The present population is about 250,000. The biggest town is Kalamata, with about 40,000 people. It is the capital of the nomos of Messenia, but it is quite eccentrically located near the southeast corner of the province on the gulf, where it has an artificial deep-water harbor. The largest concentrations of population outside of Kalamata are elsewhere in the Pamisos Valley and in a few towns near the west-central coast between Kyparissia and Chora. Smaller towns and villages are scattered densely on the edges of alluvial river valleys, on the coastal plains, and on the more fertile upland plains (see Pocket Map 1-1). Hamlets can be found in all but the most forbidding and rugged areas. Families prefer to live in groups, however small, and year-round individual farmsteads are practically nonexistent.

The climate is typically "Mediterranean," with long hot dry summers and short cool rainy winters. Messenia's position on the windward side of the higher mountains accounts for an unusually heavy rainfall from October to April. The total annual average is from 800 mm on the coast to over 1,000 mm on the higher slopes, and anything over 500 mm is classed as "humid" in this part of the world. In addition, Messenia has a geologic structure generally favorable for springs, with limestone, sandstone, and conglomerate interbedded with impervious slate. The tremendous catch basins in the mountains result in exceptionally numerous and abundant springs at lower elevations. Most rivers flow only seasonally, so that the springs lessen the damaging effects of the summer drought. In addition to providing water for practically all the towns and villages, the springs feed irrigation systems that water at least 6,000 hectares (15,000 acres) of fruit, vegetables, and forage crops (see Pocket Map 3-6). A further fortunate circumstance is that almost anywhere groundwater can be tapped by shallow wells ranging in depth from 3 to 10 m. Although the climate is in general hospitable for human habitation, minor variations in the annual rainfall pattern render somewhat precarious the agricultural use of much of the available land. This underlines the crucial importance of the perennial rivers and natural springs and the land that can be irrigated from them. The control and allocation of local water resources must always have played a major part in the economic and social development of the region.

The swampy ground, especially in the Pamisos Valley, provides relatively abundant forage for the larger domesticated animals. Smaller ruminants can do well in the rough and barren areas and on the higher mountain slopes. Continuous forest, now largely confined to high and rough areas in the Taygetos range, must have provided earlier inhabitants with abundant timber and fuel, and it must have sheltered plentiful wildlife as well. Seafood is in moderate supply. Perhaps Messenia's greatest handicap for economic development is an almost total lack of useful metal deposits, but this is by no means an exceptional feature in Greece.

The combination of unusually abundant water, a relatively high percentage of arable land, and moderate climate explains Messenia's dense agricultural population now as well as its past reputation for productivity, according to the ancient sources. A fragment from one of Euripides' lost plays testifies eloquently to the favorable "image" that this region enjoyed in the fifth century B.C.: "rich in produce, watered with countless streams, furnished with good pasture for both cattle and sheep, not cold in the blast of winter nor again too hot in summer, with fertility greater than words can express." It is probable, however, that until the nineteenth century A.D. these natural advantages were seldom, if ever, more intensively exploited than in the Late Bronze Age, which is our particular focus in time.

Climate

The dry aspect of the Greek climate has been overemphasized, partly because most tourists come to Greece in the summer for sunshine and dry weather, and partly because the climatological record for Athens is used to characterize the entire country – and Athens is on the dry side of the peninsula. In contrast to the stereotype of an arid land of blazing sun, southwest Peloponnese can better be thought of as an area of two contrasting seasons, one cool and wet and the other warm and dry. In midwinter the cold can be cutting and the rainy periods persistent. By February, stainless steel razor blades rust in Kalamata, and the unimproved roads in the Kyparissia Mountains turn into slimy, deeply rutted trails that challenge a Land Rover to its utmost.

The climatic regime of Peloponnese is similar in general to that of the entire Mediterranean basin. The mild, cloudy, and rainy conditions of winter are followed by a summer of drought, dominated by a hot sun burning down from a cloudless sky. Violent weather, with tornadoes, hurricanes, or other windstorms, is either lacking or rare.

The seasonal contrasts are related to the annual migrations of the Subpolar and Subtropical jet streams. In the winter the sinuous Subpolar jet stream, which travels eastward as fast as 500 km per hour at elevations of 5,000 to 12,000 m, guides outbreaks of moist maritime polar air from the North Atlantic across France and into the Mediterranean. During the summer it migrates northward to the latitudes of Scandinavia, and the Subtropical jet stream moves northward from the Sahara and aligns itself with the Pyrenees Mountains, effectively isolating the Mediterranean from the stormy influence of the Subpolar jet stream.

To this dynamic hemispheric circulation one must add the influence of topography in relation to the prevailing winds, a factor that is most important in this region in the winter, when the upper-air conditions often severely limit the height to which surface weather systems can develop. Topography has little effect during the summer, when there is no moisture-laden air mass and when the entire air column is dry and stable (Hare 1962, p. 173).

The summer drought lasts from late May to early September throughout most of the Mediterranean area. At this season Greece is under the influence of the eastern limb of the Azores high-pressure cell. Air that is forced aloft as far west as the American Midwest descends over Greece, warming as its pressure increases and thereby increasing by many times its ability to hold water. There is no strong circulation pattern in the lower atmosphere, and, except for the cool northeastern trade winds (called meltemi) that spin off from the Asiatic high and enter the Aegean, the winds are sluggish and variable. The drought in Greece may be broken by occasional thunderstorms caused by local heating from the ground, but these are rare in our region.

In September, the dominance of the Azores high-pressure cell lessens, and rains become more frequent. Eventually a cold front dips southeastward across France to break the heat and drought with cool west winds and showers. In October and November these outbreaks of maritime polar air increase in frequency to several per month.

More important at this season than the extension of North Atlantic storms, however, are the cyclonic depressions that form or are deepened in the lee of the Alps. As the westerlies force their way over the Alps, an eddy is formed over Genoa and the Po Valley (Hare 1962, p. 82). The resulting storm center brings rain to the Dalmatian coast of Yugoslavia and the west coast of Greece before continuing on to the Levant.

By May the westerlies have again shifted north of the Alps, and the Subtropical jet stream returns to the latitude of the Pyrenees, causing the end of the rains.

Thus the climate of southwest Peloponnese cannot be considered arid. Although the lowlands experience five to six months and the uplands three to four months of weather when evaporation exceeds precipitation, the excess of moisture in the winter makes the climate basically humid. The regime of rainfall is such that the three winter months from December to February contribute half of the total rainfall, and the spring and fall bring the other half, with the summer months from June to August being almost devoid of precipitation (see Fig. 3-1).

Because the moisture-bearing winds come from the sea on the west, the amount of precipitation in Greece increases with elevation but decreases inland, especially on the eastern sides of uplands. The windward west coast of our region receives 80 cm of rainfall annually, the same amount as Minneapolis, Minnesota. The hill land and upland plains (kampos) of the central Messenian peninsula receive more than 100 cm of rainfall annually, and the higher mountains may receive more than 150 cm.

On the east side of this upland mass, in the plains, the annual rainfall is reduced to only 60–70 cm, because the eastward-travelling moist air masses lose some of their moisture on the windward slopes. Much of the rainfall may be concentrated at the east edge of the plains, near Kalamata, where shallow, weak cold fronts may be trapped by the Taygetos Mountains. These fronts stagnate and produce the solid overcast and frequent showers, lasting three to four days, that characterize the local weather in winter.

The winds of the Ionian Sea and the Messenian Gulf are best termed light and variable, as seen from records for Pirgos, Kyparissia, Methoni, and Kalamata. Methoni records the most constant winds, west and northwest in the summer. The other stations record winds channeled by nearby valleys, such as the northeast winter winds of Kalamata that must reflect cold-air drainage down the Nedhon River Valley.

Low-velocity winds are the rule except for Methoni, where winds of more than 20 km per hour occur nearly one-half of the winter, and where gales blow 5 percent of the time during January and February. The winter rains come with some wind, but the strong rush of wind associated with passage of lows in the American Midwest, for instance, is absent. In the summer, the common cause of gentle breezes is the differential heating of land and water. The land heats more quickly in the morning, causing the air over the land to rise. By late morning the local pressure gradient is sufficient to cause a cool sea breeze to blow several kilometers inland, ameliorating the heat. The wind abates in late afternoon. At night the process is reversed, and a land breeze blows out to sea.

Although frost is rare in the lowlands, snow can be seen capping Taygetos for much of the winter. The lowest temperature ever recorded at Kalamata is 26°F. For the coastal stations of Kalamata, Kyparissia, Methoni,

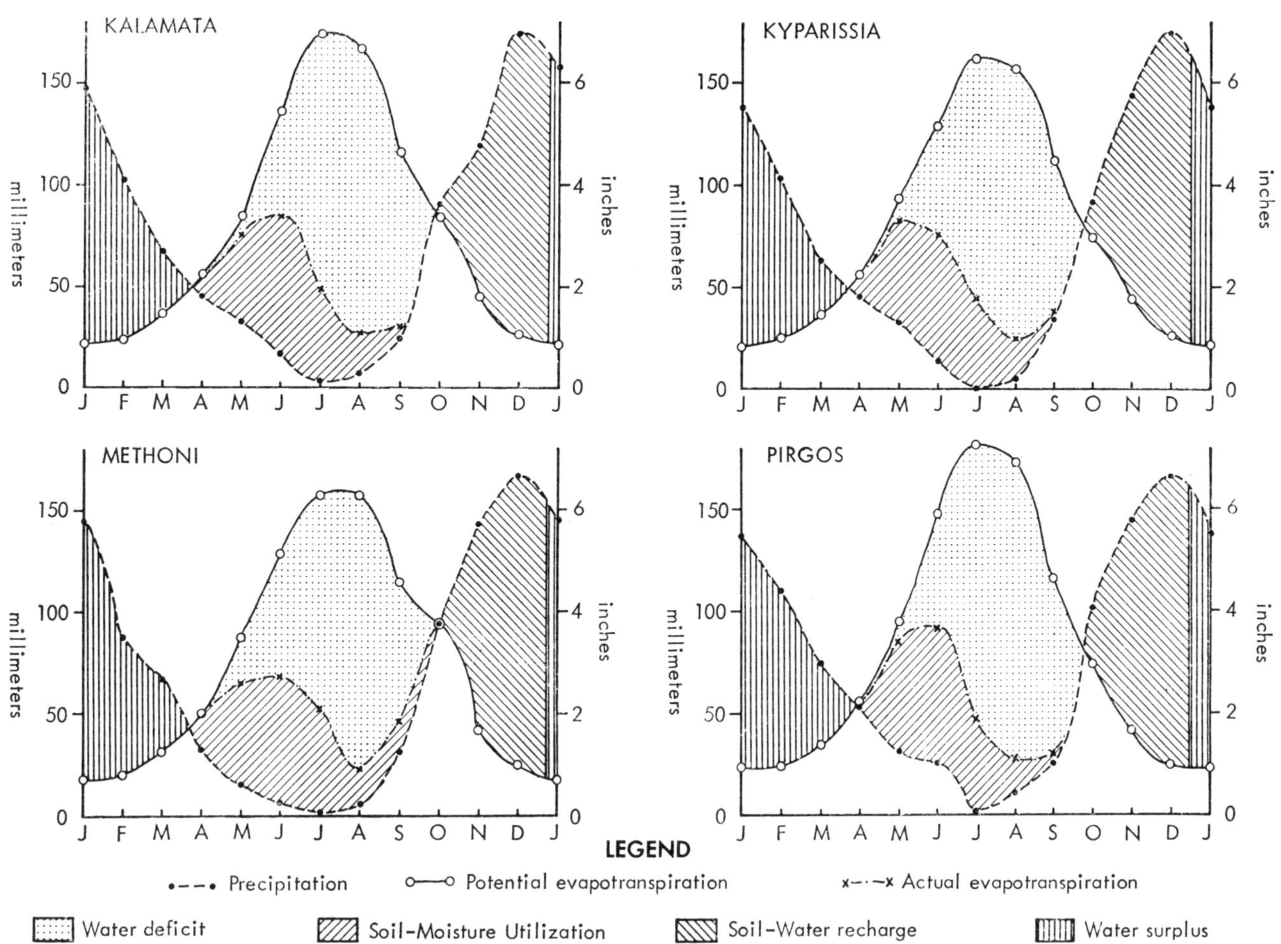

Figure 3-1. Thornthwaite water-balance diagrams for four localities in the UMME region

and Pirgos, the mean temperature for January and February is 52°F and the mean July and August temperatures 80°F, an annual range of only 28°F. The diurnal range is very small, often only two or three degrees. Although the stations for which data are available show a uniform temperature picture throughout the area, it must be remembered that all these stations are near the sea. Higher stations have an average decrease in mean temperature of 1°F per 100 m increase in elevation (Mariolopoulos 1961, p. 18). This decrease gives the mountain villages a noticeably cooler climate.

Data on the minor climatic elements are available only for the four major stations mentioned above. The relative humidity at these coastal stations averages about 75 percent winter and summer, except for Kalamata, where the summer relative humidity drops to 55 percent. It decreases to the south and inland, becoming low enough to dry crops in the summer sun. The weather is cloudy or partly cloudy 35–40 percent of the year (Mariolopoulos 1961, p. 24). At Methoni, one day in three is overcast during the winter, and only three days a month are relatively clear; in summer there are still one or two cloudy days and up to ten partly cloudy days per month. Haze is seldom heavy, but its occurrence is widespread.

During the winter there is an ample water supply but by the end of March the rapidly increasing potential evapotranspiration value exceeds the amount of precipitation (see Fig. 3-1). During April, water stored in the soil is drawn upon, and by May the need outstrips the supply, creating a large deficit. All stations but Methoni indicate an exhaustion of soil moisture by the first week of September. Within three to four weeks the rains come in substantial amounts, and soil recharge begins in the first week of October. The soil is fully recharged by mid-December, and the remainder of the rain is available for runoff.

The diagrams in Figure 3-1 illustrate the inequality of supply and demand of moisture in a Mediterranean climate. They also illustrate the precarious nature of the climate. The four months of drought, from late May to mid-September, can extend into October or November if the rains arrive late. This delay would triple the severity of complete soil-moisture depletion, perhaps in extreme cases killing all but the most drought-resistant upland vegetation and those plant communities near springs. It is apparent from the sayings of farmers, however, that they view the absence of spring rains with more alarm than the late coming of the fall moisture. For example, "When it doesn't rain during the first week of January, but it does during Eastertime, then the farmer who has sown much will be happy," and, "If it rains twice in March and once in April, then the farmer who has sown much will be happy." Also, "When it rains at Eastertime, the purse will be full." Although they seem concerned for several rains during the cereal-growing period, the farmers also want good ripening conditions, for they say, "It always rains in May upon a cursed place."

It appears that climatic changes during historic times have been minor. A careful analysis of the geographical factors related by Thucydides in the *History of the Peloponnesian War* indicates that the climate has changed little since then (Meigs 1961). The voluminous ancient literature has been studied by Mariolopoulos, who concludes that "The temperature and hygrometrical character of the country have not changed, while the winds and rains have today the same distribution and frequency as they had during the classical times" (1961, p. 51). Although an attempt was made by Carpenter (1966) to attribute to climatic change all kinds of puzzling historical events, such as the collapse of the Mycenaean kingdoms (see also Bell, 1971), scientific evidence for such relations is poor indeed (Wright 1968). More will be said on this subject in the discussion of vegetational history (Ch. 12).

Landforms and Geologic History

The landforms of Messenia, outlined in the introduction to this chapter, reflect three major stages in the geologic history of the region. The rocks composing the mountains consist primarily of limestones formed in widespread seas ranging in age from Triassic (200 million years ago) through Cretaceous (70 million years ago). These relatively pure carbonate rocks, gray and dense, form the jagged peaks of the high mountains and the precipitous cliffs that characterize the Greek landscape.

The limestones grade upward to shales, sandstones, and conglomerates. These rocks were formed as sediments when the rising mountains were eroded and reduced to mineral particles, which were then carried to the shallowing seas during the early Tertiary (to about 30 million years ago). The conglomerates in this series are visible in nearly vertical beds as the road from Kalamata to Pylos rises onto the plateau west of Rizomilo. We can visualize for this time mountains as high and rugged as those of the present. Gravel, sand, and silt were spread onto vast alluvial plains and thence into the remnants of once-extensive seas, which periodically spread over the alluvial plains to deposit the marine shales and limestones that are interbedded with the terrestrial sediments.

By middle Tertiary time the pace of mountain building reached its culmination, as a manifestation of the great Alpine geologic revolution which affected the entire region from the Pyrenees to the Himalayas and beyond. In Greece it produced a series of tight north-south folds traceable to the Dinaric Alps and northwestern Yugoslavia. The linear mountain ridges that reflect the differential erosional resistance of the folded rocks are discontinuous in places because of great faults that caused displacement of thick rock units.

The epoch of deformation continued into the late Tertiary. It is still going on to a limited extent, as is indicated by the frequent earthquakes. By Pliocene (late Tertiary) time the mountains had been eroded to nearly their present form, and the plains bounding them had been etched in softer rocks. A remnant of such an erosional plain now exists as the smooth plateau (kampos) south of the Kyparissia massif. These lowlands graded down to the sea level of the day. Their outer edges may even have been planed by waves.

Further geologic events affected principally the coastal areas and the major rivers as a result of the fall in sea level (or, more likely the reciprocal movement of the land). The coastal lowlands just mentioned were lifted 300 m above the sea. The streams that flowed to the sea across these lowlands were rejuvenated in their lower reaches, as they plunged to the lowered sea level, and they eroded deep valleys. The broad valley of the Pamisos River between the Taygetos Mountains and the kampos was excavated at this time. Also, sea cliffs were eroded by the waves.

This uplift of the land was followed by the reverse movement, and the rejuvenated valleys were deeply flooded by the sea. The Pamisos Valley became a broad bay, of which the Gulf of Messenia is the remnant. On the east the bay was bounded by steep sea cliffs leading up to limestone mountains, and on the west it lapped up onto the eroded edge of the kampos. The west coast of the Peloponnese was broadly inundated at this time, and estuaries extended far inland along the Alpheios and the Nedha rivers. Southwest Peloponnese was largely restricted to the Taygetos, Kyparissia, and smaller mountain masses and to the plains (kampos) at their bases. The inundated areas were partially filled with marine silts eroded from the remaining land areas. Next to the old limestone sea cliffs east of the Pamisos Valley are oyster beds and beach gravels. Some are now visible hundreds of meters above sea level on the ridges east of modern Thouria, buried in light brown silts and sands. The intricate shoreline of the day can be traced around limestone promontories and inlets by the remnants of silt and oyster-bearing gravels plastered on the bedrock. The same can be found on the west coast of Peloponnese near the Alpheios River, where thick masses of light brown silt, now deeply dissected, are transected by the highway and the railroad.

The prehistoric site of Nichoria (#100) is underlain by such Pliocene marine silts, which here lap onto the edge of the kampos. They reach to over 300 m above present sea level. Where deeply dissected by subsequent erosion, they show steep but smooth brush-covered slopes, with no rock outcrops.

This great epoch of Pliocene marine submergence was followed by an uplift of the land totaling about 300 m, so that the oyster beds and marine silts are now found far above modern sea level. The great bays and estuaries became stream valleys once again, and much of the still unconsolidated marine sediment was eroded, leaving patches plastered on cliff indentations. Some large areas of marine silts remain essentially undissected, however, and they now form extensions of the kampos, only locally cut to steep-sided, flat-floored valleys. Along the coasts, this most recent land uplift resulted in erosion of the sea cliffs once again, thus restoring the rugged coastal relief.

Since the last major land uplifts, coastal processes have smoothed the shoreline by building bars across bays, eroding headlands, and filling in re-entrants. Along the west coast, from Pylos to Pirgos, longshore bars of sand have formed slightly offshore, thereby enclosing lagoons behind them (Pls. 5-1, 5-2). The lagoons are gradually filling with sediment brought by coastal streams, which themselves have formed alluvial fans at the base of the mountains or hills. This final epoch of local coastal erosion and deposition has probably not been simple, for during this period the Mediterranean sea level is known to have fluctuated as a response to continental glaciation in north-temperate latitudes. The sea levels of the glacial periods were below those of today, so their record is largely submerged. But those of interglacial times were slightly higher than those of today – at least according to evidence elsewhere in the Mediterranean. In Greece itself the contemporaneous land movements seem to have obscured any possible pattern of marine terraces resulting from absolute changes in sea level.

Regional Physiography

This geologic history of marine deposition, land uplift, erosion, and alluviation has resulted in the development of several distinctive landform units, conveniently grouped into three broad categories – mountains, inland plains and hill lands, and coastal plains (Pocket Map 3-7).

The mountain group includes principally Taygetos, with its core of high, sharp ridges running zigzag between steep-sided gorges, all in resistant limestone. On the western flank, benches or shoulders occur that may be either structural or erosional. In addition there are rocky ridges, of which the Kyparissia mountain group is the most important; these are controlled by the structure of the limestone.

The inland plains and hill lands include five subtypes. The kampos is the broad Pliocene erosion surface that is cut across tilted bedrock west of the Pamisos Valley. Located at the base of the Kyparissia Mountains, which project above it, the kampos has an elevation of about 500 m, and it slopes gently away to 300 m, where it merges with the plain of onlapping sands and gravels and marine silts – the remnant of the Pliocene terrace. Where the kampos is eroded to less than half its original extent, it is mapped separately as dissected kampos. Where the Pliocene terrace has been dissected to less than half its extent, it is mapped separately as hill land. Where the Pliocene sediments of the lower Kyparissia Valley are cemented gravels, they are mapped as ridges.

The third group of landforms, the lowland plains, include alluvial slopes (such as alluvial fans and mountain-valley bottoms) and alluvial and coastal plains. Many of these are still forming today, and their recent history encompasses the Mycenaean era, so their characteristics and manner of formation are of particular interest.

The hill-slope erosion that produces alluvial sediments is controlled by the nature of the vegetation cover, which in turn is a manifestation of climate. At the same time, direct climatic factors such as intensity and amount of rainfall also control erosion of hill slopes. Together these and other direct and indirect climatic factors determine the tendencies toward cutting or filling along the valley floors. Furthermore, in a stream close to the sea, the vertical movements of sea level and land level may affect the erosional or depositional tendencies in the lower reaches of the stream. Because of the complex interaction of these factors, it is extremely difficult to decipher the thin and irregular stratigraphic record of coastal streams, although in alluvial valleys of other Mediterranean countries attempts have been made to work out a consistent sequence of erosion and deposition, with dating made possible by radiocarbon dates and by artifacts found in the sediments (Judson 1963; Vita-Finzi 1969). In southwest Peloponnese, the alluvial fills of most mountain streams carry little record of interest. The great alluvial plain in the delta of the Pamisos River, which was recently drained for agricultural development, terminates southward in a complex of sandbars produced by the waves of the Messenian Gulf.

At Akovitika (#155), on the east side of the alluvial plain just inside the sandbars, an important complex of Early Helladic buildings was found at a depth of at least 60 cm in the black alluvial muck (see Ch. 8). This is a measure of the amount of deposition that has occurred during the last 4,500 years.

Groundwater

Any summer traveller to Greece will attest to the high quality of its water, supplied by springs and wells that deliver clear, cold refreshment when it is most needed. Abundant supply of groundwater reflects a favorable geologic structure and landform pattern, as well as relatively high annual rainfall. Although approximately two-thirds of the annual rainfall in southwest Peloponnese is dissipated by evapotranspiration (FAO 1966, p. 13) or is lost to runoff and to undersea springs, the remainder infiltrates to recharge the groundwater and supply the perennial springs.

Two geologic elements are necessary for a spring: an aquifer (a water-bearing stratum) and a barrier to movement. In our region the best aquifers are Tertiary conglomerates and limestones, Quaternary gravels, and Mesozoic limestones. Barriers include Tertiary shales, massive Pliocene silts, and the Quaternary clays of the bottomlands. Most aquifers permit the passage of water through the porous structure found in granular rocks or along fractures or bedding planes in limestones.

A spring occurs where an aquifer is blocked by a barrier near the ground surface. The largest springs in the entire area are at Ayios Floros and Pidhima, respectively 19 km and 15 km north of Kalamata at the west base of the Taygetos Mountains (Pocket Map 3-6). The Cretaceous and Eocene dolomitic limestones in the mountains have an extensive honeycomb of solution channels that may even draw water from beyond the topographic watershed (Burdon and Papakis 1963, p. 169). The water-conducting system of the mountain limestones abuts the barrier formed by the Pamisos Valley alluvium. Ayios Floros, whose source zone extends so deeply that some of its waters have been described as being "lukewarm and stale" (Philippson 1959, p. 403), is perhaps the most evenly flowing spring system in the whole region. Its flow ranges from 4.5 to 5.5 m^3/sec. The flow of Pidhima ranges from 1.0 to 1.5 m^3/sec. The highest flows occur between February and May, the lowest in September (FAO 1966, p. 100). The water in the Ayios Floros system probably takes several months or even years to complete a cycle, and therefore it is not affected by one or two dry years. The perennial marshes below these springs indicate strong flow the year round. On most maps, the spring of Ayios Floros is indicated as constituting the primary source of the Pamisos River, which waters the lower Messenian Plain.

The dozens of lesser springs scattered through the region do not have such stable water sources (Pocket Map 3-6). Most of them exit from local aquifers with limited rainfall catchment areas. There are thousands of small seeps that dry up by August and cannot properly be called springs. The most regular water sources tap extensive formations of limestone or conglomerate, which are interrupted by a barrier that concentrates the water and forces it to flow out a single exit.

Areas that are composed entirely of limestone are poor in springs. Few springs or permanent streams are found in the Taygetos Mountains, and it appears that all of the water of the central Taygetos is funneled to Ayios Floros or Pidhima (see Pocket Map 3-6). Farther south, the lack of an appropriate barrier appears to be the reason for the paucity of springs on the east side of the Messenian Gulf. The few springs that do occur are located at the contact of the Cretaceous limestone and older partly metamorphosed limestones or along major faults. Most of the groundwater is probably dissipated in undersea springs.

Few springs occur in the plateaus (kampos) of the Messenian peninsula, either because the areas of pure limestone have no barriers to concentrate the water outflow or because the shales and siltstones do not allow enough infiltration. The Kyparissia Mountains to the north, however, are rich in springs (Pocket Map 3-6), which occur in an area of complex geologic structure exhibiting tight alternations of folded limestone and shale sheared by thrust faults. Strong springs rise on the west coast at the thrust fault along the western side of the Kyparissia Mountains. Other springs rise on the northern perimeter of the Kyparissian massif, where the folded rocks meet the Pliocene terrace near Kyparissia. Most springs occur in zones along the north-south bands of upturned sedimentary rocks, especially south of the transverse valley which extends west from the Soulima Valley.

An inventory of the significant springs is mapped on Pocket Map 3-6. Few have been measured, but their relative sizes may be estimated from the calculation that each irrigated hectare (2.5 acres) uses 7,000 cubic meters of water per year (FAO 1966, v. 2, p. 15). All springs that irrigate areas more than two hectares have been included, so it is unlikely that many significant water sources have been omitted, although the data for the eparchy of Olympia are less detailed than those for the other eparchies.

Although groundwater per se is of principal interest, some spring water is not used near its source but is allowed to flow some distance in a natural channel. This water is used during the summer in the 26 small riverine irrigation projects that are shown in parentheses on Pocket Map 3-6. The works required for such stream irrigation systems are very simple. An earth dam a meter or less high and generally less than 10 m long is constructed across the channel, and the water is led off on one or both sides into simple troughs cut by hoe in the easily worked yet impervious alluvial silt. By this means the water is kept above the lowland on the valley side, and it can be tapped by simply notching the outer lip of the channel to release some of the flow. When the irrigation is complete, a mud plug stops the flow. In view of the proven engineering ability of the Mycenaeans, it appears likely that these small river systems could have been used by the Late Bronze Age farmers with approximately the same efficiency as they are used today, and therefore they should be considered as part of the natural water resource.

In southwest Peloponnese there are now about 4,000 hectares of spring-irrigated land and almost 2,000 hectares watered by small river projects, a total of 6,000 hectares (15,000 acres) under gravity-water irrigation. Today a similar amount of land is being irrigated by water pumped from wells. A perennial supply of well water is not difficult to obtain if one can dig down to a sufficiently large water-bearing stratum. The shallowest available aquifer is usually a layer of gravel in stream bottoms. Above the gravels is generally a clayey alluvium that is still accumulating under present climatic conditions at an estimated rate of a few centimeters per century.

There are perhaps ten thousand wells in our region. Those dug in the alluvium near a valley head often dry up in August as the groundwater percolates into the major valley systems and is not replenished, but wells in the large valleys, like the lower Pamisos, produce water from a depth of 5–8 m all summer. In the Messini commune, for example, eight hundred wells draw water from an average depth of 6 m. On the flanks of the Messenian Gulf the alluvium is less deep. Longa has fifteen wells with water at a depth of 3 m, and Loutro across the gulf has twenty wells at a similar depth. The upland areas do not have similar tabular aquifers, but well water can usually be obtained at a depth of 6 to 9 m, especially downhill from a spring line. Pumped wells irrigate less than a hectare per well. Some wells occur in the most improbable places: there is a well, for instance, within 20 m of the top of Mt. Ithomi.

Well water is not difficult to obtain, except in the Mani. There is no evidence that the Mycenaeans dug wells for irrigation in a fashion similar to that of the modern inhabitants, but certainly they could have made wells in the alluvial bottomland for drinking water. In fact, well water would have been somewhat easier for the Mycenaeans to obtain in the valley bottoms because the depth to the gravel aquifers would have been less. In the absence of well pumping it is also probable that the water table was higher and that some streams that are now intermittent were then permanent.

This extrapolation assumes that the climate and other controlling hydrologic conditions were the same in the Late Bronze Age as today. Studies of vegetational history (Ch. 12) imply that the rainfall has not significantly changed, but the heavier forest cover may have resulted in greater infiltration and less runoff. So groundwater conditions were probably at least as favorable as those of today, and the springs of 3,000 years ago were thus similar in size and position. The vagaries of underground cavern development and collapse might change the location of the exit or close off a channel, or the earth movements manifested by earthquakes might close some springs and open others, but three millennia is a short geologic time for many major changes in the groundwater system.

Coastal Landforms

In any country that has always looked to the sea for some of its food and for much of its trade, communications, and political security, the coastal landforms take on a special importance. Geologically, the coastal areas are the most dynamic of any part of the region, in two respects. First, erosion and deposition by coastal waves and currents have produced far more noticeable changes during the time with which we are particularly concerned (the last 4,000 years) than have stream erosion and deposition and other gradational processes in the interior. Second, the deleveling or other crustal disruptions manifested by earthquakes can produce their most notable effects along the coast, where the levels of land and sea are critical to landform development as well as to human activity.

Along the west coast between Pylos and Pirgos, longshore currents driven by waves striking the shore obliquely have built up sandbars in front of old sea cliffs or across bays, thus tending to smooth out the shoreline. The limestone headland at Klidhi (#302) near the modern spa of Kaiafa anchors a series of dune-covered coastal bars to north and south. Where a bar develops slightly offshore, a lagoon may form behind it (Pl. 5-1). The bars and lagoons may block the egress of streams from the hill lands, and the load of stream sediment may accordingly be dumped locally as fans or deltas into the lagoons, which thereby may be partitioned and eventually filled. Lagoons in various stages of filling occur in the Pirgos-Kyparissia segment of the west coast. The largest fan is that of the Alpheios River, which in fact may have originally been a delta into the open sea, protruding enough to supply sandy sediment necessary for bar development to north and south. The long lagoon that extends southward from the Alpheios fan to the headland at Kaiafa has an irregular northward end because of the fringes of deposition extending into it from the Alpheios fan, and it has an irregular inner margin because of the entrance of small fans from the sandy foothills to the east. Gradually the entire lagoon is being filled by these fans, and eventually it will become a smooth plain. Near Kaiafa about 3 m of organic sediment has been deposited since the lagoon formed about A.D. 250, according to radiocarbon dates of the lagoon sediment (see Ch. 12).

The water levels in the lagoons fluctuate between winter, when rains bring strong inflow from the land, and summer, when evaporation makes the water brackish and may temporarily lower the water surface below sea level. In some cases the winter inflow from streams may be large enough to produce an overflow through the coastal bar, but the damage is repaired during the rest of the year by the persistent longshore drift of sand, so that gaps are usually ephemeral. Even the Alpheios River has difficulty in penetrating the drifted sandbars during the seasons of low river flow.

South of the Kaiafa headland, where the railroad and highway cross from the coastal bar to the mainland, only a single lagoon remains, because along this stretch of steep limestone cliff no sandy streams enter to partition it. But south from this cliff to Kyparissia the coastal upland is formed once again of Pliocene sandy sediment, and a series of alluvial fans from the upland have completely filled the lagoon and converted it to an arable alluvial plain, bounded seaward by a smooth coastal bar, a situation essentially similar to that for the alluvial plain of the lower Pamisos River at the head of the Messenian Gulf.

Osmanaga Lagoon

Perhaps the most interesting — and historically the most significant — of the coastal plain segments with associated lagoon and beach is located north of the Bay of Navarino (Pl. 5-2, Fig. 2-9). After the period of Tertiary mountain building, a large lowland nearly parallel to the coast was etched there in soft rocks between a coastal ridge of hard limestone (including Paliokastro) and the upland. It was then partly filled with Pliocene sediments and then re-excavated — the remnants can be seen on the east flank of the lowland along the highway that descends to Pylos from the upland. The Pliocene sediments may once have completely covered Paliokastro and other limestone ridges west of the lowland.

The last major rise of sea level left the lowland largely submerged, in the form of the Bay of Navarino. But after sea level became stable, the northern end of the bay was cut off by deposition of sand that had its origin along the gentle east side of the bay and was shifted northward by waves entering the bay from the main opening on the southwest. The long bar thus formed across the north end of the bay is attached at its west end at a point just north of a second but much smaller inlet to the bay, namely Sikia Channel. Waves bring sand also through Sikia Channel, and a small cusp has formed in the bar at the point where the opposing longshore sand drifts from east and west meet. The cusp extends southward across the Sikia inlet as a submerged shoal. The water flow through this inlet, however, is probably great enough to keep the shoal submerged and the inlet open to the sea, although it was artificially blocked to large ships by the Turks when they abandoned Paliokastro.

Behind the main bar is Osmanaga Lagoon (see Pl. 5-2). Previous to the current reclamation efforts, the lagoon held almost a meter of brackish water, although during summers the level was considerably lower as a result of evaporation. In the winter the lagoon is subject to flooding from stream flow, and at the same time, when strong storm waves enter the bay, to inwash across low spots in the bar where the usual low sand dunes have not formed.

An outlet through the bar was formerly kept open artificially for fish-raising operations in the lagoon. Such an outlet could also be maintained to allow the lagoon to serve as a harbor for shallow-draft boats. For the historical problems at hand, it is important to determine whether the water in the lagoon was deeper in the past, before the sediments had accumulated to their present thickness of about 6 m.

The lagoon has been partly filled from the north end by alluvial deposits brought by streams from the upland. Winter inflow has now been largely halted by the construction of a semicircular dike and a canal which conducts the incoming streams around the toe of the alluvial fan to outlets directly to the sea through the coastal bars. It is planned that water accumulating from winter rains on the lagoon itself will be withdrawn by a system of canals to a main terminus midway along the inside of the bounding bar, where a pumping station is to be constructed.

A peculiar feature of the west side of Osmanaga Lagoon is Voïdhokilia Bay and its fringe of sand dunes that protrudes into the lagoon. The bay occurs at a narrow break in the limestone ridge that bounds the lowland on the west – a break that is shorter and slightly thinner than Sikia Channel. Winter waves move strongly into this bay, which has a straight fetch from the northwest, and a steep semicircular beach capped by very high sand dunes has formed. At one point in the very center of the arc the winter waves have locally overflowed the rugged dune ridge, but this point can hardly be considered an inlet to the lagoon. At the sheltered northwest corner of this small bay, where a canal has recently been cut across the dunes to lead the northern alluvial waters past the lagoon and into the sea, the remains of what may have been stone foundations seem to record some type of port activities in the past. Possibly a shallow canal was dug at this point in the Late Bronze Age so that small boats could be brought from Voïdhokilia Bay into the lagoon.

The history of Osmanaga Lagoon and its associated features can be partly determined from its sediment and the objects it contains. Borings at several points across the lagoon (see Fig. 2-9) indicate that the clayey sediment is generally at least 4 m thick, although it is more than 7 m thick in the north toward the alluvial fan that was its primary source. The clayey sediment thins to the south as it approaches the sandbar that separates the lagoon from Navarino Bay. It seems clear therefore that this sandbar was built first and that the lagoon's sediments accumulated behind it, starting about 2000 B.C., according to a radiocarbon date at the base of the sedimentary fill (Ch. 12). Voïdhokilia Bay, on the other hand, developed later – at least its fringe of sand dunes is encroaching on the lagoon, for the sand at the toe of the dunes rests sharply on lagoonal clays. The dunes are so high that the bay, although an excellent small harbor itself, could never have been used as a natural entrance to the lagoon, although an artificial cut could have been made next to the rock wall, as suggested above.

The formation of the Navarino sandbar and Osmanaga Lagoon about the end of the third millennium B.C. is probably related to the attainment of a nearly stable sea level at approximately that time. Sea level had been much lower during the glacial period, and it rapidly rose in early postglacial time as the continental ice sheets melted. Study along various stable coastlines of the world indicates that sea level reached to within a few meters of its present level 3,000 to 6,000 years ago and that subsequent changes have been relatively slight. Greece is not necessarily stable, of course, for earthquakes are common even today, and slight vertical movements of the land might be expected during the last few thousand years. However, beach sands occur on the coast a few kilometers north of Osmanaga Lagoon with shells of the marine snail *Strombus bubonius*, an index fossil of the last interglacial period. The elevation of these sands is about 5 m above present sea level – an entirely expectable height for undisturbed beach deposits of the last interglacial interval. Land movements must therefore not have been great since that time.

The water level of the lagoon generally equals sea level, because water seeps through the sandbars separating it from the sea. But during winter floods the level may be temporarily higher, and after the long summer drought it may be lower because of evaporation. If sea level were the same about 2000 B.C. as it is today, the depth of the lagoon would have been at least 4 m more than at present. The lagoon therefore may have been more suitable as a harbor at that time. By these calculations, the water depth during the Late Bronze Age, after an estimated 1 m of sedimentation, would have been about 3 m, as contrasted with 1 m at present.

On the other hand, we cannot be certain that sea level has been constant since 2000 B.C. In fact, discovery of various archaeological objects both in the lagoonal deposits and in the southern sandbar indicates that sea level was lower at certain times in antiquity. Hellenistic structures, now slightly submerged by the waters of the bay, are reported by Pritchett (1965) near the west end of the sandbar, and a Hellenistic cemetery has been partly excavated on the north side of the sandbar, within the area normally covered by the lagoon. In the northwestern part of the lagoon we collected many potsherds and other objects from the clays thrown up in the excavation of the drainage ditches (see Ch. 8). They can be referred to the Early and Late Bronze Age, and at least some of these objects imply habitation sites and thus dry ground. Radiocarbon dating of the lagoon sediments indicates that the Mycenaean level is buried in the sediment almost 3 m below the present water surface in the lagoon. Because the water level in the lagoon is generally about the same as sea level, this implies that sea level was lower. For Hellenistic times the figure is about 1.5 m. It thus appears that the lagoon must at times have been as shallow or shallower than it is today.

These conclusions, coupled with indications that longshore drift of sand on the outer face of the bar tends to close any breaches through the bar, imply that Osmanaga Lagoon was probably not a much better harbor in antiquity than it is today. The harbor entrance would be difficult to keep open for deep-draft boats, and the lagoon would be shallow. The little outlet that shows on old maps was used until recent years in association with fish weirs constructed at the southern edge of the lagoon, but it probably had to be dredged periodically on the bay side even for this purpose. On the other hand, the Mycenaean labor supply was abundant enough that such dredging was probably a minor impediment to port maintenance if in fact the lagoon was deep enough to be useful.

In any case, Osmanaga Lagoon has been in existence in approximately its present form since about 2000 B.C., essentially shut off from the Bay of Navarino as well as from Voïdhokilia Bay. Pritchett's evaluation of the topographic situation of the area described by Thucydides (Bk. IV) is thus confirmed for a much longer time period—that is, that the sandbar was in existence and that the lagoon was not a major harbor for deep-draft boats. It seems simplest to assume that sea level rose from its last low stand to within 3 m of its present level in the Early Bronze Age, and that the closing off of Osmanaga Lagoon by the construction of the Navarino sandbar began about that time. In subsequent time, the bar has built up at the same slow rate as sea level has risen. At the same time and at about the same rate, the lagoon has been filling with sediment, so it has remained shallow. The major changes have been the encroachment of the Voïdhokilia dunes at the northwest side of the lagoon, and the advance of the alluvial fans on the northern and eastern sides. Otherwise, the lagoon probably had much the same general form in Mycenaean time as it does today, and its serviceability as a harbor was probably restricted to small boats, and even then with appreciable dredging and other maintenance to keep it serviceable.

Even though the evidence seems good that sea level was lower in the area of the Bay of Navarino between the Early Bronze Age and Roman times, this may not have been the pattern for all of the Peloponnese, because the proven tectonic instability of Greece (Galanopoulos 1964) might result in purely local vertical movements of the land. A careful examination of ancient coastal sites in the western Mediterranean (Fleming 1969) leads to the conclusion that all instances of sea level change in that region can be attributed to tectonic activity. In the Aegean area, the seismograph record for 1904–52 shows even more earthquakes than in the western Mediterranean.

On the other hand, studies in stable coastal regions such as Florida indicate that worldwide sea level was 1–3 m lower in about 2000 B.C., and that it has gradually risen since then. The evidence from Osmanaga Lagoon and the Bay of Navarino is therefore consistent with this picture, so the tectonic instability may not have affected relative sea level in this area.

REFERENCES

Bell, Barbara. 1971. "The Dark Ages in Ancient History. I. The First Dark Age in Egypt," *AJA* 75:1–26.

Burdon, D. J., and Papakis, Nicolas. 1963. *Handbook of Karst Hydrogeology, with Special Reference to the Carbonate Aquifers to the Mediterranean Region.* Athens, Institute for Geology and Subsurface Research.

Carpenter, Rhys. 1966. *Discontinuity in Greek Civilization.* Cambridge.

FAO. 1966. *Economic Survey of the Western Peloponnesus, Greece.* Rome, United Nations, FAO.

Fleming, N.C. 1969. *Archaeological Evidence for Eustatic Change of Sea Level and Earth Movements in the Western Mediterranean during the Last 2000 Years.* Geological Society of America, special paper 109.

Galanopoulos, Angelos. 1964. "Seismic Geography of the Peloponnese," *Peloponnisiaki Protochronia,* 49–53. In Greek. Athens.

Hare, F. K. 1962. *The Restless Atmosphere.* London.

Judson, Sheldon. 1963. "Erosion and Deposition of Italian Stream Valleys during Historic Time," *Science* 140:898–99.

Mariolopoulos, E. G. 1961. *An Outline of the Climate of Greece.* Athens, University of Athens Meteorological Institute.

Meigs, Peveril. 1961. "Some Geographical Factors in the Peloponnesian War," *Geographical Review* 51:370–80.

Philippson, A. 1959. *Die griechischen Landschaften,* 2nd ed. Vol. 3, Pt. 2, pp. 319–523. *Der Peloponnese: Der Westen und Süden der Halbinsel.* Ed. E. Kirsten. Frankfurt.

Pritchett, W. K. 1965. *Studies in Ancient Greek Topography,* Vol. 1. Berkeley.

Sauerwein, Friedrich. 1968. *Landschaft, Siedlung u. Wirtschaft Innermesseniens (Griechenland).* Frankfurter Wirtschafts- und Sozialgeographische Schriften, Vol. 4. Frankfurt.

Vita-Finzi, Claudio. 1966. "The New Elysian Fields," *AJA* 70:175–78.

———. 1969. *The Mediterranean Valleys: Geological Changes in Historical Times.* New York.

Wright, H. E., Jr. 1968. "Climatic Change in Mycenaean Greece," *Antiquity* 42:123–27.

4
A CONTEMPORARY COMMUNITY

by

Stanley Aschenbrenner

To aid archaeological interpretation, this chapter describes a single farming village of Messenia in which the author resided from June 1969 through July 1970. Certain aspects, rather than the economic system as a whole, are treated here because the latter is probably quite different from what existed in earlier times and especially in the Bronze Age. Yet it is equally probable that some features of the modern village economy may be projected back in time, or can at the least guide such projection. Furthermore, when relationships among factors are being projected backward and when archaeological evidence reveals data for only one (or some) of the factors, those without relevant archaeological evidence may be inferred by virtue of the relationship obtaining among them all. Thus, for example, when jars for the storage of olive oil or wine are excavated or when Linear B tablets refer to amounts of these commodities, we may calculate some range of values for area of land planted in such crops or for labor expended in their production. The basis for the inference is the known relationships in a contemporary community among yield of oil or wine, area cultivated, and labor.

Because the data presented below are derived from a particular community and its land, they pertain most directly to the ethnographic reconstruction of the Middle Bronze to Early Iron Age community (Nichoria #100) located in the same area where excavation is currently proceeding. However, it is the author's hope and intention to present data, relationships, and findings relevant to a general understanding of rural life in earlier periods.

General Description

The contemporary Messenian community of Karpofora (a politically defined unit of local government as well as that unit's territory and population) is 2 km inland from the northwestern corner of the Messenian Gulf (see Fig. 4-1). Some 10 km to the east is Messini; further east another 12 km is Kalamata (the capital of the province or nomós); and 5 km to the south is the little coastal town of Petalidhi. Following prevailing Mediterranean custom the people of this area have a strong inclination to a nuclear residential area, set like a hub in the midst of their surrounding fields (see Fig. 4-1). But the community now has two residential areas – the new one, Rizomilo, developed in the valley of the Karia River after the construction of the modern highway, and the original village 1.5 km toward the upland. Local practice designates the old residential area as Karpofora (Pl. 12-1). The expression "the community" refers to the totality (the combined population, the two habitation areas, and the surrounding fields and land).

Areally the community consists of 630 hectares (1 hectare = 2.47 acres) with a roughly rectangular outline. Three major categories of terrain occur within these limits: (1) alluvial valley bottoms, (2) valley slopes, and (3) relatively flat hilltops. Most of the valley bottoms surround the Karia River, whose perennial flow allows irrigation of most of the plain. On the west side of the Karia Valley is a flat-topped ridge with the local toponym Nichoria (site #100). Here we found the surficial cultural remains of occupation in the Bronze Age (and afterward) that UMME is now investigating through excavation. West of this scene of ancient habitation is another smaller valley, Vathirema, opening at its southeast end into the Karia Valley. In the northwest the Vathirema slopes upward to the flat country. Just west of Vathirema, on the opposite side of Nichoria, is Karpofora, the old residential area. Karpofora is also

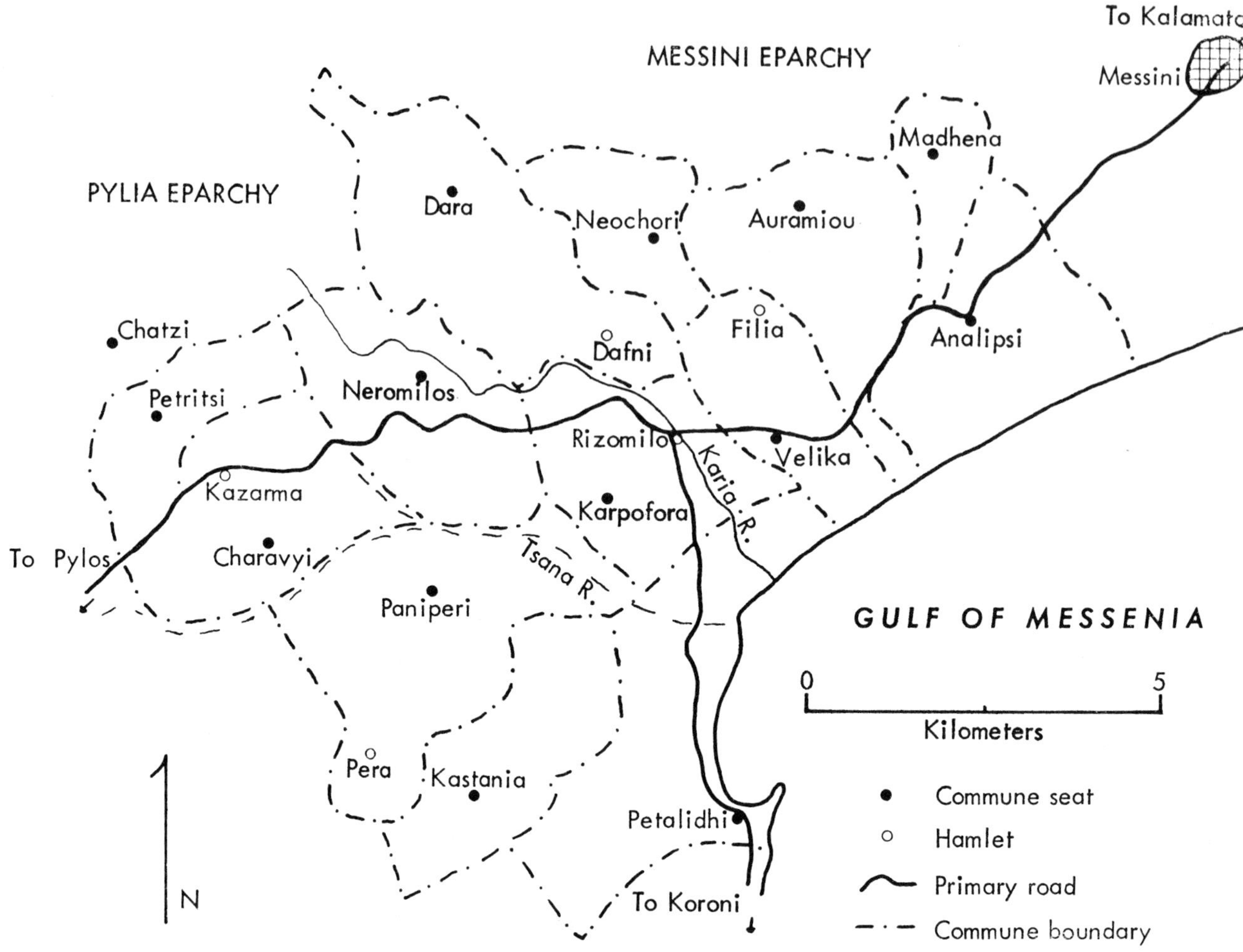

Figure 4-1. Neighborhood of Karpofora

located on a flat-topped ridge, although it is much larger and has in general easier slopes than Nichoria. West of Karpofora is another narrow valley, like Vathirema, and on the top of its western slope is the boundary of the community. The elevation above sea level of the valley bottoms is from 20 m sloping up to 35 m in the northwest; the elevation of the ridges and flat hills between the valleys is from 70 to 95 m, again with the upward slope to the northwest.

According to the National Statistical Service of Greece census of 1961 (to be referred to as NSSG 1962a, 1962b, 1964 – see References), the basic division of village area is: 400 hectares in all types of agricultural land use, 200 ha in brush or wild grazing land, and 30 ha in residential area (NSSG 1962a, p. 94). Although the use of agricultural land is taken up in a later section of this chapter, some general points will be presented here. Tree crops (mainly figs, olives, and citrus) occupy 239 ha, vines (grapes and currants) 32 ha, and annual crops 93.5 ha. "Grazing land" seems to include not only all the low brush areas found mainly on the steeper valley slopes and in a few scattered areas of the flat upland, but also the river course and the beds for the paved, graveled, and dirt roads (NSSG 1962a, p. 94; 1964, p. 41).

During 1969–70 the steady population was 353, with 111 in Karpofora and 242 in Rizomilo. This is down from the high of 471 in 1961, when Karpofora had 201 and Rizomilo had 270 (NSSG 1962b, p. 143).

Despite modernizing changes, population mobility, and contemporary systems of communication, the community remains fundamentally agricultural in character. Every household farms or tends sheep. Some households, however, have heads who pursue other occupations as well (shopkeeper, carpenter, plasterer, construction laborer, painter, etc.) and some have sons wholly employed in such nonagricultural pursuits. The agricultural economy is relatively diversified (trees, vines, grain, fodder, shepherding, and livestock — listed in Table 4-1). Although participation in the cash-oriented national economy is strongly increasing, there is a very notable subsistence basis to the community economy.

A brief review of the modern history of the community from agricultural and demographic standpoints reveals something of the range of possibilities and potentialities to be used in reconstructing the economies of earlier communities that once used essentially the same natural resources.

Until about 1880 the village seems to have had a diversified but fundamentally family-subsistence economy with only very weak participation in a larger market or cash-oriented economy. Wheat and barley were produced and mainly processed at home. Wine and table grapes were grown. But a major use of land and a significant occupation of families was the grazing of small herds of sheep and goats. Direct evidence for the extent of tree crops is meager, but, along with indirect evidence, indicates that beyond subsistence usage tree crops were minor. For instance, Poucqueville (1827, pp. 61–62) includes the village in the area without olives and raising only grain. The total population during this period seems to have been relatively stable; Poucqueville lists 30 families (probably between 120 and 150 persons) in 1815; Rangavis (1853, vol. II, 578) gives 30 families and 136 persons circa 1849; and the census of 1870 gives 194 persons. Yet underlying this semblance of steady growth lies much change in the historical continuity of the population. Without exception, the present families now refer to their ancestors settling in the village after 1830 and having come from the Steniklarian Plain, from near Megalopolis in Arkadia, and so on.

The year 1880 seems to mark a watershed in the economy and demography of the village. The economy begins to be linked to the larger economy by the production of crops for cash in the marketplace, and the population begins a steady growth both through its own births and the addition of new families. This growth manifests itself despite some loss through emigration to the United States and numerous deaths in the influenza epidemic of 1918–19.

Beginning in 1880 currants were being planted both in newly cleared land and also in fields where grains were previously grown. Then, about 1890, the fig became an attractive cash crop and more land was cleared. It is difficult to determine the use previously made of the fertile valley floor of the Karia River, but soon virtually all of it was planted in figs. The first mill for grains was built on the west side of the Karia in 1880 by an entrepreneur from the city of Kalamata. By about 1900 another flour mill was built on the east side of the river. The appearance of these two mills is significant not only for possible suggestion of increased grain crops or for a shift from home grinding but also because they introduced the two dams and ditch networks that soon evolved into the irrigation system for the river valley.

Olive oil production in the village (on any but a household scale) seems to date from about 1895 when the flour mill on the west side was converted to an oil mill. And by 1909 an oil mill was built within the upper village area (still the only settlement at this period).

Clearing of land for new fig plantations continued to 1940. Grafting of olives and gradually the planting of cuttings continued as well, but the olive was still only a small part of the total yield, and much of the increased production seems to have gone toward local consumption as the diet improved. By 1920 the village showed its new ties with the market economy in new secondary occupations of merchants for importing wheat and flour, and for the sale of cloth yard goods. Also, the village became the residence of a collector of agricultural taxes.

But it was the construction in 1925 of an all-season road, one that for the first time was of sufficient width for a wagon, that formed the tie of the village to its region. One could now cross the Karia River by bridge instead of ford. The road from Messini in the east to Pylos on the west coast was joined with that to Koroni in the south, and the junction on the west bank of the river became a strategic point. At once the development of a new settlement area (Rizomilo) began at this junction, as some new families, but mainly families from the old settlement, built here on the edge of the rich and irrigated river valley. Soon some of this watered land was planted with oranges and lemons — another move to crops for the cash market. In 1928 the flour mill on the east bank of the river took advantage of the new road and bridge connections and added the processing of oil olives to its milling operation. As if to show that the pre-1880 activity of tending flocks had not been abandoned in the midst of the new pursuits, a milk merchant set up operation shortly at the new settlement of Rizomilo to collect milk and cheese to be sent off to the little city of Messini. By 1940 the permanent population had increased to 396, double the 1879 population, and there were 50 or more transient agricultural workers.

The changes attendant on the war years of the 1940's and the two decades since are largely responses to the behavior of the world economy. During the war the village reverted to a subsistence basis. More wheat was planted, often where vine crops had been, since the currant market was weak and the crucial materials for spraying the vines were not available. Olives and animals were continued, but the sheep and goat population decreased steadily during the war years. These animals were often requisitioned by the Italian or German soldiers or by the guerillas; and owners often had to slaughter them for food. Postwar herds have not risen beyond a quarter of their 1940 size. After the war the price of figs and currants remained much lower, but the market for olive oil grew and the price remained good. Hence, the farmers set about planting olives both in new land and also in place of figs and currants. So by the late 1960's oil production was already ten times its 1940 level, and in another ten years it is believed the current production will quadruple. This reveals how rapid has been the shift to the planting of olives. In the postwar period, too, the irrigated area has increased as most cultivation in the river valley has changed from figs to a different range of cash crops (citrus, potatoes, maize, apricots, alfalfa).

The contemporary village is approximately 50 percent self-subsistent for food. Oil, wine, fruits, potatoes, cheese, meat, and garden vegetables are produced by most families in sufficient quantity for their consumption. Most families purchase some flour or bread, and all depend on outside sources for fish, macaroni, sugar, salt, and coffee. The cash from crops buys some foods, but it goes mainly toward clothing, bedding, house construction, luxury goods, ceremonial life, transportation, dowry, farm tractors, fertilizer, and education of children.

The foregoing historical sketch describes the shift in bases, or at least emphases, of the village economy. It thus shows a range of possible forms of the economies of the prehistoric villages. At one end of the range is a family subsistence economy based on grains, grazing of sheep and goats, with some vine and tree crops. At the other end is an economy with a good measure of family food subsistence but producing and selling a large surplus of raisins, olive oil, dried figs, and the produce from irrigated mixed crops. Furthermore, figs, olives, and vines have been grown in virtually every part of the terrain — from river bottoms to upland slopes and plateaus.

Calendar of Work Activities

A description of the distribution of the modern villager's work activities according to crop, month, type of work, and climatic regime provides much of the data needed to reconstruct a possible work calendar for the Bronze Age communities in the same territory.

Figure 4-2 presents basic activities for the kinds of crops that might have been in cultivation in the Bronze Age. The data for this calendar derive from the author's observations during fourteen months' residence in the village. The exact timing of many of the activities in the spring and fall is regulated by the incidence, frequency, and intensity of rainfall locally. Since rainfall may vary from the single year of observation, two precautions have been taken to enhance the generality of the calendar. First, the time for each activity is long enough to cover the earliest and the latest instance of the activity rather than merely the period of widespread and intense activity. Second, the calendar was compared with one prepared by Van Wersch (1969, personal communication) after he observed the regime in four Messenian villages in 1966–67 (see Ch. 11). There was essential agreement between the two calendars.

The regulative action and influence of the rainfall regime on the work schedule deserves some elaboration (see also Ch. 3 and Fig. 3-1 for related discussion). Figure 4-2 gives the average monthly rainfall from the nearest reporting weather station, which is at Messini, only 10 km to the east. The rainy season begins with a few scattered days of rain in October, separated by several clear days. The fall work of plowing must await the occurrence of two such soaking rains to soften the ground. Fall clean-up by burning now starts. In November the frequency of rainy days increases, until by late November plowing must stop because the ground is saturated and remains muddy and soft even on clear days.

In December and January rain is virtually an everyday occurrence, and the farmer worries whether he can complete olive harvest. Finally, in late February breaks in the rain are long enough to permit well-drained areas to dry sufficiently for plowing. Through March the intervals without rain increase, and more of the land dries out enough for plowing. Now there is concern that rains abate long enough for low-lying, poorly drained, and river-plain fields to be plowed in time for planting of field crops (potatoes, maize, garden vegetables) or before the vines send out tender buds, easily broken in cultivation. By late April the intervals between rains are greater and the days of drying are longer, so some of the better-drained fields become too dry for plowing until just after a rain. By early May plowing must stop because the earth has become too hard. The dry season has arrived, and although showers might aid the vine and tree crops, at least until mid-July, they would injure the ripening grain. In August and early September, when rain can spoil the production from fig trees and vines, rains are rare and greatly feared. From mid-September

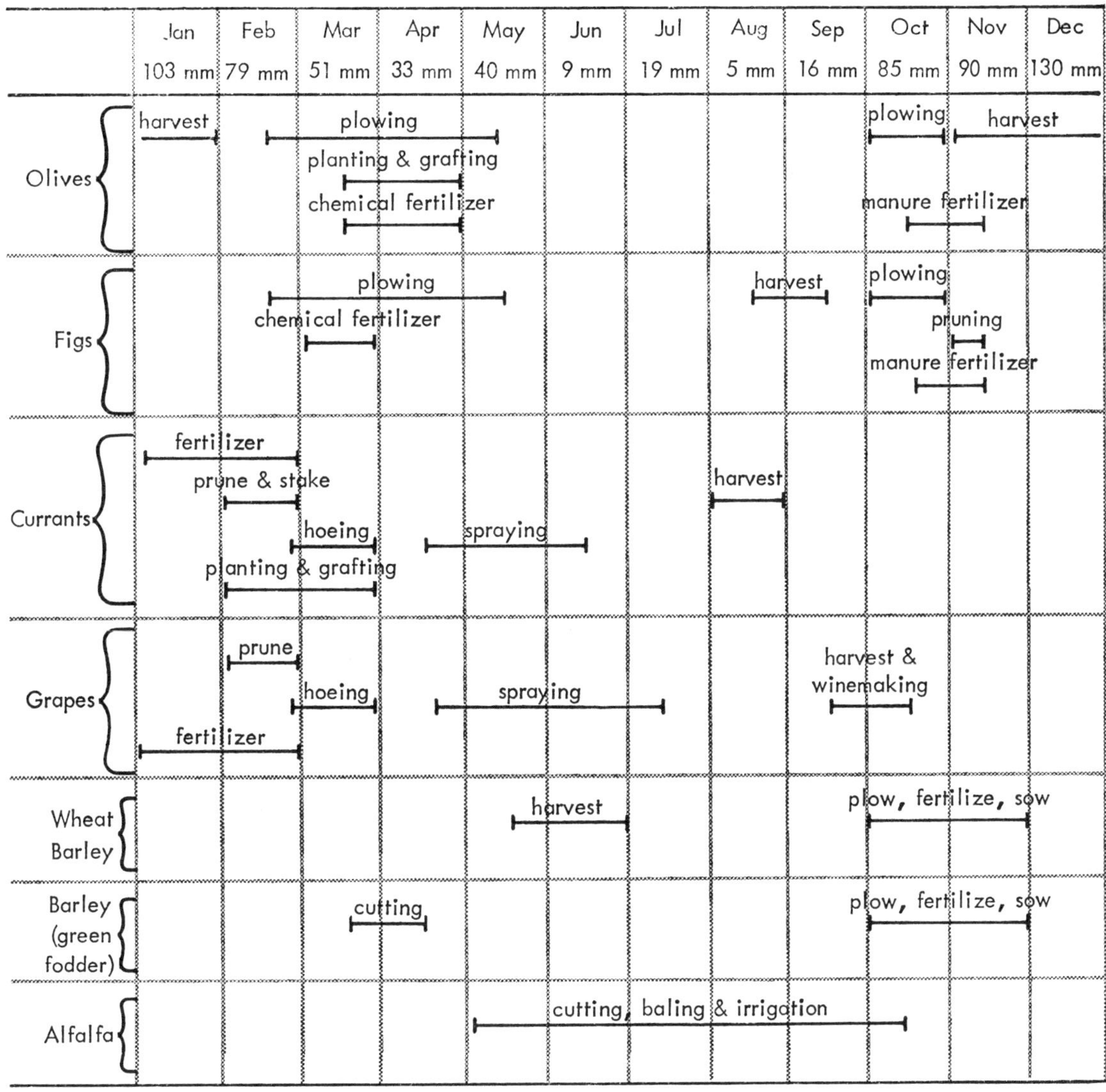

Figure 4-2. Calendar of crop activities, correlated with mean monthly rainfall for Messini as reported in Loy (1970, p. 36)

on, the earth is parched, and the olive crop as well as all young, newly planted trees need the soaking of a rainy day.

In summary, the onset and termination of the two plowing periods is controlled by rains, just as the patterning of days with and without rain control what fields can be plowed. The days for harvesting oil olives are governed by the rains. The sowing of cereals must be delayed far enough into the fall to minimize the danger that heavy rains in early spring would beat down the stalks. Whether newly planted or young vines and trees survive the dry season hinges on the incidence of the first rains of fall.

The synoptic view given by Figure 4-2 also suggests certain periods when agricultural work demands are low and hence when labor is available for other activities, such as house building, construction of roads and ditches, land clearing, corvée labor projects, or craft occupation. One such period is the six weeks from the end of wheat harvest until the onset of fig harvest. Currant harvest occurs in early August, but it is mainly accomplished in three to five days. A second period of low work extends from mid-September to nearly mid-October or whenever rains permit most fields to be plowed. Wine-making intervenes here, but it is a one- to three-day activity. The third such period is the month of January, when most have finished olive harvest and the fertilizing of vines is quickly done. Finally, during all the days of rain, the press of agricultural tasks is relieved and indoor crafts can be pursued.

It remains to comment briefly on a few activities variously distributed over the calendar. A continuing, daily task of each farm family is that of providing feed and water for oxen (including cows, which are also used for plowing), horses, donkeys, and goats. During the heart of the rainy season – from late November to early February – these animals are usually kept in stables on rainy days and are fed baled alfalfa or wild grass or branches of shrubs. When it is not actually raining, they are staked out to graze. At this time watering animals is easy. During the rest of the year the animals are regularly let out to graze, but increasingly as spring develops there is need for special trips to watering places or the transporting of well water for animal use. The task of provisioning the bread oven and kitchen fire with small branches and, in winter time, the fireplace with large pieces of wood goes on throughout the year, but with a peak of intensity in the early fall. All the clipped shoots of vines and the mass of prunings from olive harvest are saved for such use, but in addition brush is gathered. In the middle of both fall and spring there is field clean-up by the burning of plant stalks and the ever-encroaching brush along field boundaries.

Table 4-1. Use of Crops and Livestock

Tree	
olive, oil: subsistence and cash	apricots: new, intended for cash
olive, eating: subsistence	peaches: subsistence
fig: mostly cash	apples: subsistence
mulberry: animal fodder, some silk	pears: subsistence
cypress: subsistence and cash	quince: subsistence
oranges: subsistence and cash	almonds: subsistence and cash
lemons: subsistence and cash	walnuts: subsistence and cash
pomegranate: subsistence	poplars: new, intended for cash
kalami (a reed): subsistence and cash	plums: subsistence
Field	
wheat: mostly subsistence	maize: subsistence, green and cereal fodder
barley: subsistence, green fodder	potato: subsistence and cash
oats: subsistence, fodder	tomato: subsistence and cash
alfalfa: subsistence and cash	cucumber: subsistence and cash
Faba bean: mainly cash	egg plant: subsistence and cash
sweet pea: cash	cabbage: subsistence and fodder
string beans: subsistence and cash	kitchen garden: subsistence
squash: subsistence and cash	
Vines	
grapes, eating: subsistence	currants: cash, some subsistence
grapes, wine: subsistence and cash	
Livestock	
chickens: subsistence	goats: subsistence
donkeys: transport	sheep: subsistence, mostly cash
horses: transport and plowing	lambs: mostly cash
pigs: subsistence, some cash	cows: plowing, raising calves for cash
oxen: plowing	
bull calves: cash	

Crops and Livestock

The following discussion is mostly concerned with a few of the present-day crops that were also important in the Late Bronze Age economy. The range of crops and animals found in the modern community appears in Table 4-1, with a categorization of their roles in the economy. The table suggests the fruitfulness of the land and the diversity of production that is possible. This diversity results both from the family-subsistence character of the economy and the more recent move to production for cash. The latter has led to shifts in the volume of various products as well as to the adoption of new ones. The relative importance of crops in 1969, as determined by the area devoted to them, is shown in the accompanying tabulation (1 stremma = 0.1 hectare = 0.25 acre).

	Stremmata
olives (oil and eating)	1,300
fig	1,000
citrus (irrigated)	400
currants	250
grapes	50
wheat	200
alfalfa (irrigated)	300
other irrigated crops	800

The phenomenon of increasing fragmentation of land holdings with each generation during the past 150 years is due to the dowry and inheritance customs. All sons inherit equally, and daughters often have fields given in their dowries. Probably the fragmentation has not greatly enhanced the over-all diversity of the community. In 1961 the average farmer had 5.5 separate, noncontiguous fields (NSSG 1964, p. 59). But it has greatly increased the distribution of this diversity over the landscape of the community, because in each succeeding generation sons have sought to retain their father's diversity of products but on ever more finely divided fields.

Listed in Table 4-1 are many of the items on Chadwick's botanical list derived from the Pylos tablets (see Ch. 7). Especially, the "main food-plants" (wheat, barley, olive, vine, and fig) are or have been the chief crops of the contemporary community. A description of these crops based on modern data may aid in developing a sharper picture of the Bronze Age community that also produced them in the same environment. Only olives, vines, and figs will be considered. The justification for the exclusion of wheat and barley is first that the extent of these grain crops has declined greatly and therefore production data are limited, and second that the technology and practice used now is so modernized as to greatly minimize any guidelines to be gained for archaeological interpretation (but see Van Wersch's discussion in Ch. 11). Also, olives, vines, and figs have some features as crops that warrant special consideration.

These three crops, in contrast to the grains or even animals, involve a long interval (10–25 years) between planting and grafting and the return of full harvests. During this lead time to production the farmer must continue to provide some minimal care for the plants. There is no quick return a few months or seasons later to reward the decision for these crops and the initial seasons of effort expended for them. These are the crops of a stable community; once the commitment to them is made, the awareness of the lead time and the effort invested constitute a strong deterrent to moving to a new location.

Olives. Both eating and oil olives are cultivated. Although there are few trees of eating olives (150 perhaps), over 15,000 oil olives cover 130 hectares. Much of the discussion that follows applies to both, but it will be well to differentiate the two from the outset.

Eating olives are normally harvested when fully ripe in late October, in contrast with oil olives, which ripen a month or more later. The harvest season for eating olives is brief because the trees are few, and the technique involves no severe pruning (as with oil olives) but rather a combination of picking and some beating of the tree with long sticks. Perhaps as a result of this difference in technique, the yield of eating olives seems not to vary greatly from one season to another.

As a crop, olives have characteristics rich with economic and social implications. Trees and vines as a group share the feature of a lag of several years between regular planting and the first harvests, to say nothing of full yields. But the olive stands out in the group as having an even longer lag. Conversely, the olive compensates by having a very long productive life that villagers consider to be virtually indefinite if a minimum of continuing care is provided.

A second characteristic is the pronounced tendency of the yield to alternate every other year. Oddly enough, this fluctuation, typically 50 percent or more, is not on a tree-by-tree basis but regularly on a scale involving whole regions. Van Wersch advises in a personal communication that this is thought to be "due to (a) accidental causes, such as frost, hail, sirocco, drought, parasites; or (b) permanent lack of nutrients. The tree generally lacks sufficient reserves to give a good crop every year." No doubt the practice of severe pruning in heavy harvest years greatly reinforces the effect of these factors. Suffice it here to give some description and examples. First a local example. In 1969 Karpofora and the immediately surrounding area had a heavy harvest from the oil olives, whereas in the neighboring districts, especially to the west, the harvest was small. This was the "on" year here while 1968 was the "off" year, and the opposite relationship prevailed in the neighboring districts. Without fail, questions put to local farmers elicited the reply that such is the rule, namely, a regularly occurring pattern of inter-regional variation and heavy yields in alternating years.

A second example of this fluctuation comes from the statistics for Greece *as a whole.* The accompanying tabulation was compiled from data reported in Sweet-Escott's valuable economic survey (1954, pp. 120, 180).

	Thousands of Metric Tons
1946	80
1947	145
1948	46.7
1949	224.6
1950	38
1951	140
1952	70

Thus, the same striking alternate-year fluctuation in production owing to natural causes occurs on the national scale. Pansiot and Rebour also find this on a world scale in FAO statistics (1961, pp. 10, 11). This phenomenon and its nearly predictable occurrence, when coupled with the storability of olive oil, provide the modern speculator and hoarder with a great opportunity. In a Bronze Age kingdom with the redistributive economy suggested by Ventris and Chadwick (1956; Ch. 9) it probably meant something else. But it is a phenomenon to which interpretative thinking must give heed.

A third characteristic is the striking adaptability of the olive to a wide variety of growing conditions — terrain, quality of soil, amount of ground moisture. Although it is not tolerant of areas where average temperature falls below 10° C, the olive has great survival power in drought conditions, especially after reaching twenty years of age. As a partial consequence of this but also as a result of the widespread dependence (until recently) on grafting onto wild trees, many productive trees (perhaps one-fifth of the total) are found outside orchards or groves. Olives are intercropped with cereals, with vines, and with field crops. Many are near habitations, in yards, and along field boundaries and roads.

Fourth, eating olives and especially the oil are readily stored, and the storage period easily covers the alternate years of low yield. Indeed, in the modern local market, last year's oil normally commands a slightly higher price than the oil of the new harvest.

Fifth, the harvest season from November to mid-January occurs at a time of low labor demand or relative inactivity. Hence where agricultural diversification is present, cultivation of the olive aids a uniform distribution of agricultural labor, or it can be added to the schedule of other crops with a minimum of interference. This characteristic must tend to compensate for the long lead time. However, for plowing, in contrast with harvesting, the olive competes directly with other crops calling for cultivation. As already noted, it is often difficult to get the required plowing completed in the intervals when the rains and ground conditions permit it.

The heavy pruning of oil olives during harvest affords three useful by-products. The prunings are hauled to the stables and areas where animals are tied, nearly always near the houses. The leaves serve as fodder for oxen, donkeys, sheep, and goats. The branches, large and small, are then used for kitchen fires, baking ovens, and fireplaces. Some of the prunings are burned green soon after pruning, but most remain to dry and are used through spring, summer, and the next fall. Finally, appropriate cuttings are stored in sand beds until spring, when they are planted. At present this is the most common propagating technique. Yet one can still observe the formerly common bark graft in which the wild stock is cut off, three or four small downward slits made in its bark from the top of the stump, wedge-shaped scions inserted in the slits, a string tied about the stump and a mud seal applied.

Most of the data concerning the production of olive oil in the community lend themselves to concise presentation as shown in Table 4-2. But some amplification and qualitative description will aid the reader in checking their applicability to Bronze Age communities.

The technology and practice employed in cultivating, harvesting, and processing are simple. All plowing is done by animal, mostly with a pair of oxen but occasionally with a single horse. The plow has a steel share, with single moldboard or, for rocky soil, a symmetrically pointed share. Until fifteen or twenty years ago the plows were all wooden with only a steel point on the share. The farmer's major aim in plowing is to control the growth of weeds and grass that develop from October through March.

The harvesting crew typically consists of one man and two or three women. Great strips of burlap or canvas (10 by 2 m) are spread out under the tree, each piece overlapping the other so as to cover the area under the tree and extending for one or two meters out beyond the ends of the branches. The man climbs up the tree with hatchet and small saw and begins to prune off the branches. If the tree is loaded, the pruning is very severe and several large limbs (as much as 8 to 10 cm in diameter) are cut off, as well as many smaller ones. The women below pick up the branches in one hand and beat them with a meter-long stick held in the other. The larger limbs are first cut up by the women to facilitate manipulation. The blow of the beating stick snaps the olives loose and they fall upon the cloth. After he has finished pruning, the man aloft is handed a longer beating stick with which the highest, central olives are snapped free. Then he descends and from the ground with a long pole beats off the few olives remaining on the lower branches.

Table 4-2. Data for Olive Oil Production

- Calendar of major activities
  - Harvest: Nov. 1 to Jan. 15
  - Plowing: Feb. 15 to May 15
  - Planting: Mar. 15 to May 1 (grafting, cuttings, and balled plants)
  - Fertilization: Mar. 15 to May 1
- Planting density
  - 9 trees/stremma (avg.), older grafted trees
  - 12 trees/stremma (avg.), newer trees from cuttings and balled plants
- Oil yield (in heavy harvest year)
  - By tree and age
    - Large mature tree: 50 kg
    - Medium (30–40 yr) tree: 15–20 kg
    - Small (15–30 yr) tree: 7–15 kg
  - By weight of fruit: 4–6 kg fruit normally produce 1 kg oil
  - By area (for 1,300 stremmata, total area of community with olives)
    - 1968: 54.8 kg/stremma
    - 1969: 115 kg/stremma
  - Total for community
    - Pre-1940 heavy harvest year: 12,000 kg
    - 1968 light harvest year: 70,000 kg
    - 1969 heavy harvest year: 150,000 kg
- Labor (male and female)
  - Plowing (M): 1 man-day/4 stremmata
  - Harvesting (M&F): 1 man-day/20 kg oil
  - Pressing (M): 1 man-day/70 kg oil (using only human and animal power)

After each branch is free of olives the women toss it on a pile beyond the burlap covering the ground. When all cut branches have been beaten and the man has finished beating with the long pole, the burlap strips are carefully emptied one into another until a single one holds the heap. Now while one woman culls out twigs and leaves and puts the olives into a burlap sack, the others move the strips to the next tree. A large, heavily loaded tree requires two or three hours to harvest. This description applies to the harvest for a fully laden tree (i.e., in the alternate productive season). The following year, when the recently denuded tree has but little fruit and has spent its energy mainly in recouping the loss of evergreen leaves and putting forth new branches, the harvesting involves little pruning. For many trees there is no pruning and at most only a few heavily laden branches will be cut; the chief activity is the beating of branches on the tree with poles.

Oil pressing is the facet of production in which modern technology has recently been introduced. Until 1956 the village had an oil mill operating with only animal and human power, and hence data concerning its operation are still available. Its capacity was 500 kilograms of oil in a full twenty-four hours of operation. Nowadays a similar quantity of oil can be pressed in three to four hours. Nonetheless, efficiency of the extractive process with the old technology is nearly the same. The process is in three steps: (1) crushing olives, (2) pressing off the mixture of oil and juice, and (3) separating oil from juice. The old mill in Karpofora crushed olives by a rotating millstone turned by a horse pulling a horizontal beam attached to the vertical axle of the mill. Two other mills in Rizomilo used water from the Karia River as power for this rotary motion. Initially, the mill in Karpofora crushed olives using a horse to raise a block of wood which would then fall on the olives. Pressing off the liquid was done by a screw press turned down by men pulling on a bar attached to the screw. Later a hand-operated winch was used to screw down the press even more tightly. Separation of the oil was attained by simple gravity. The liquid was put in a tank and allowed to settle. The oil then rose to the surface, where it was carefully skimmed off.

Vines. The vine crops of the community are grapes (both for table and for wine) and currants. With the exception of two or three types grown on overhead arbors, little distinction is made between table and wine grapes. Several types are used interchangeably. The currants grown here and in the surrounding region are deep purple and bear seed. Both currants and grapes are readily grafted onto each other and the history of crop changes of individual fields is replete with shifts from one to the other as market conditions for each have changed.

Although a new vine begins to bear in four to five years, it is not until about the tenth year that the crop is significant, and fifteen to twenty years are required for full yields. Farmers say that after fifty years the plant yield begins to decline, though there are few examples of vineyards of this age. In modern practice farmers find spraying and dusting five or six times in the spring and early summer to be essential. During World War II when the spraying material was unavailable because of copper shortage, vine yield was so low that most cultivation ceased.

Although farmers have tried vines in most locations of the village land (a matter much encouraged by the continuing fragmentation of land), slopes and drained areas seem to be preferred. In the spring it is crucial for the ground to drain enough to permit hoeing before the fragile buds have set. Modern cultivation is often by small motorized tillers. Rains just before harvest when the fruit is well developed can greatly reduce the yield.

The remainder of this discussion concentrates on grapes because the Pylos tablets refer only to wine, not to currants. Nonetheless it may be well to note briefly the unique feature of currant culture in order to provide a complete treatment. The trunk of the currant plant seems to remain unable to support the loaded plant, even when the plant is mature. Thus the practice of tying the trunk to a stake or two is always used for currants, whereas this is necessary only for young grapevines. Currant harvest occurs in early August, that of grapes in late September. After being cut, the clusters of currants are spread out on open drying floors where they are turned several times during a ten-day period. The dried fruit then requires the removal of the stems before being stored for local consumption or shipped to the market.

Table 4-3. Data for Wine Production

Calendar of activities
- Harvest and wine making: Sept. 20 to Oct. 5
- Pruning vines: Feb. 5 to Mar. 1
- Hoeing and cultivation: Feb. 20 to Apr. 1
- Fertilizing: Feb. 20 to Mar. 15
- Spraying: Apr. 20 to Jun. 20 (4–6 times)

Planting density: 100–115 vines/stremma
- Wine Yield
  - 1,400–1,700 kg/stremma of mature vines in good year
  - Total for commune
    - Pre-1940: 64,000 kg
    - Present: 45,000 kg, but 25 percent is sold as grapes

Labor (male and female)
- Pruning (M) and collecting cuttings (F): 1 man-day/stremma
- Hoeing (M): 2 man-days/stremma
- Staking (M) and tying (F): 1½ man-days/stremma (new plants only)
- Spraying (M): 2 man-days/stremma
- Fertilizing (M): 1 man-day/stremma
- Harvest and transport (M&F): 6 man-days/stremma
- Wine making (M&F): 2 man-days/stremma

The technology of wine production remains rather simple (Table 4-3). Pruning is performed with modern steel clippers. Hoe cultivation is rapidly giving way to use of a motorized rotary tiller. Olive branches or stout reeds (kalamia) are used for stakes and a piece of dry grass for tying. Spraying, however, involves not only modern chemicals but also a hand-operated tank and pump carried on the back. Chemical fertilizers have now largely replaced manure. Harvesting, which is the only work carried out by a crew rather than an individual man or his wife, involves cutting clusters with a small knife, then carrying baskets of these on the shoulder to load the larger pair of baskets which a donkey will transport to the village or field house where the wine is made.

In wine making, a man stamps the grapes with bare feet in one of three kinds of enclosures – a square masonry pit with plastered sides, a movable wooden box with a floor of slats through which the juice flows, or a huge round basket of wicker construction that stands above a plastered basin. The juice runs off into a large kettle which is frequently emptied into barrels in a nearby storeroom. No yeast is added, but farmers now often take a sample of the juice to town to be tested for sugar content. If the sugar is insufficient for 12 percent alcohol, currants are added. Pine resin is added to provide the characteristic flavor of Greek wine. With the passage of six or seven weeks, the still unclear and slightly sweet young wine is tapped from the barrel, where it is stored for drawing off the daily ration. All colors and types of grapes are mixed, so that the wine usually has a pinkish hue.

Figs. Compared with oil olives and even eating olives, fig production is simpler in technology, more stable in yield, and much earlier in reaching full value after planting. It is thus a happy complement and aids diversification of the crop schedule.

The domesticated fig usually begins to yield a notable harvest ten years after planting. However, it has a limited life-span and after fifty to sixty years it dies. In modern times and under the impetus of cash production, the village farmers have tried figs in virtually every available terrain and always with some success. But though figs are well adapted to the long dry season, rainfall has two notable effects on yield. First, the sugar content of the fruit is considerably increased if there has been a soaking rain in June or July. Secondly, the occurrence of rain during the harvest season greatly hampers drying and proper storage of the fruit (see description below).

Table 4-4. Data for Fig Production

Calendar of activities
Plowing: Feb. 15 to May 5
Fertilization: Mar. 1 to Apr. 1
Pollination with caprifigs: Jun. 15 to Jun. 20
Harvest: Aug. 10 to Sep. 15
Planting density: 10–12 trees/stremma
Yield
By tree: 25 kg/mature tree (avg.)
By area: 250 kg/stremma
Labor (male and female)
Plowing (M): 1 man-day/4 stremmata; .25 md/stremma
Fertilization (M): a man-day/10 stremmata; .1 md/stremma
Pollination with caprifigs (F): 1 man-day/10 stremmata; .1 md/stremma
Harvest (M&F): 1 man-day/.22 stremma; 4.5 md/stremma; a man-day/55 kg

Data for fig production appear in Table 4-4. A fuller description of the production practice may well begin with plowing. Plowing may occur in either the fall or spring, the farmer's choice of time probably being largely a function of his total plowing schedule. When possible, spring plowing is preferred, for it reduces the luxuriant winter growth of grass and weeds that will impede picking the fallen fruit during harvest. Spring plowing also seems to have the advantage of opening the soil to absorb the maximum amount of early summer rains, which enhance the sugar content of the fruit.

Fertilization in the past few years has increasingly been chemical. But the older practice was to haul stable manure in a pair of huge baskets tied on a freight saddle carried by a horse, mule, or donkey. Formerly, when more sheep and goats grazed on the grass under the trees, villagers say deliberate fertilization was not so essential.

Successful production of dried figs requires pollination from another kind of fig, the caprifig. Without human aid, this pollination would occur in only a limited way and few figs would mature. For this reason each farmer seeks to maintain two or three caprifigs for the essential pollen. In mid-June for four or five days small insects (like gnats or fruit flies) enter the caprifig "fruit" and transfer the pollen to the immature ordinary figs. A fig "fruit" is really a syncarp or fleshy receptacle inside which are both male and female flowers (Taylor, 1961, p. 397). To assure pollination, farmers gather the caprifig "fruits" during the critical period and string them like beads to form a loop. Two or three such loops are then hung on branches of each ordinary fig tree.

For harvesting figs, a crew consisting of one man and one or two women is usual. By mid-August some of the fruit of the domesticated trees has turned golden and dropped to the ground. The women now gather the fallen figs into large, heavy aprons, which they periodically empty into baskets. The man loads the baskets on a donkey to haul them to a drying floor, which is usually near the village or a field house. Here the figs are laid out on flat racks made with wooden frames and reed floors. The figs remain on the racks to dry in the sun for five days or so, being turned several times. In lieu of racks, large sheets of heavy paper or plastic may be used, but these lack the feature of being easily stacked and covered should the weather bring the feared rainstorm or a heavy dew. Since each day more figs ripen to gold and then drop, the above activities continue daily for a month. When by mid-September most figs have fallen naturally and those stubborn ones that remain hanging have ripened, the crew uses poles to strike the branches and snap the late ones loose. The dried figs are removed from the drying floor and sorted to exclude broken-skinned ones, which become pig fodder. The remainder are ready for storage and consumption by the villagers. The fruit for cash and export markets is sent off for fumigation, sorting, and packaging.

The fig tree requires little pruning, so that it is not a regular source of fuel. However, the wood of the fig is nearly always used to make ox yokes, for when dry it combines the features of light weight with toughness. Formerly, when the village had more animals, fig leaves were picked in early fall for use as fodder, since in this season just before the rains revive the wild grass there is the greatest shortage of fodder.

Reeds. In most places where it is permitted to develop in the valley floor of the Karia River one sees the large bamboo-like common reed *Arundo donax* (called *kalami* in the Greek vernacular). It reaches a height of 3 to 5 m in a year and will continue to produce canes or bamboo-like stalks each year. The reeds are cut in early February and provide the villagers with material for diverse uses. So great is the demand for the reed now that a farmer having a surplus can sell it at 3 cents per stalk.

The most frequent and continuing use is for stakes to support plants (young grapes, all currants, tomatoes, cucumbers, green beans, etc.). For the bottom or floor of the shallow frames for drying figs the reed serves admirably. Reeds are also laid over roof rafters to support the tiles. They form interior walls of either a plain lath type or the base on which to plaster. Small temporary sun shelters as well as chicken coops to protect young chicks from snakes are also constructed of reeds.

Livestock. As a ready reference, the accompanying tabulation lists the kinds and populations of livestock recorded in 1961 (NSSG 1964, p. 59) and in the fall of 1969. The decrease in horses, donkeys, and cattle during the eight-year interval probably reflects (1) the population decrease from 471 to 353 persons, (2) the introduction of tractors for both cultivation and transport, and (3) the increasing reliance on motorized transportation (buses, motorcycles, and trucks of all sizes). Yet the real significance of these enumerations for our interpretative task lies not in the change but in what we learn of continuing community requirements for animals to plow and transport commodities. Changes in the other kinds of livestock do not show a clear pattern but probably reflect the mounting tendency of farmers to find ways of converting labor and resources to cash or to employ these to minimize cash expenditures for food.

Every household in the village maintains a donkey for transporting both freight and persons. The donkey is admirably suited to such tasks in this terrain with its steep slopes, narrow terraces, and space-conserving paths. The donkey's hauling capacity of about 150 kg is most often put to loads of figs, currants, green olives, grapes, water, brush, bales of hay, and bundles of fresh fodder.

Horses now serve only a dozen households that use them for general hauling, but less commonly than the donkey. The real purpose of the horse is plowing, which is always done by a single animal. The horse has enough strength for this task and the advantage of being only one mouth to feed, whereas oxen and cows must be used in pairs. But the horse lacks the slower and steadier pace and pull of the team of oxen or cows needed in the rockier or heavier soils of the area. Use of the horse for drawing carts and wagons has remained remarkably low in modern times. Thus, oral histories reveal no permanent use of carts before 1925, when the main road was improved, and after 1935 a single cart served the needs of all. This fact shows the virtually exclusive reliance on packs for transport.

	1961	*1969*
Horses	21	12
Mules	1	0
Donkeys	96	80
Cattle (oxen, cows, calves, heifers)	100	22 oxen & cows; 40 calves & heifers
Sheep	166	190
Goats	101	106
Pigs	81	100
Poultry	1,183	800

Plowing by oxen or cows is the more common mode, despite the disadvantage of being unable to use them for general transport. Most farmers prefer the cow, since it yields a calf per year for cash sale as some return for the long periods of feeding and watering without any use in plowing. The cost and trouble of keeping cattle is such that in 1969 only four households kept a pair for plowing. Another fourteen families with a single animal arranged a sharing relationship, usually with just one other household that had a single cow, so that on an alternating basis each could have a full team.

The 12 horses and 22 oxen and cattle (11 teams) provide the community with twenty-three plowing units. A plowing unit can cover between .3 and .4 hectares per day, depending on terrain, thickness of weeds or stubble, and soil condition. The figure of .3 hectares is closer to personal observation and safer to use. The community has 240 hectares in cultivation, of which about 30 are in vines cultivated by hoe (or nowadays by small rotary tiller). Hence, there are about 210 hectares which require 30 days of plowing by twenty-three units, each operating at .3 hectares per day. A second plowing, or harrowing, proceeds a bit faster, perhaps .4 hectares per day. In the spring of 1970, some plowing units occasionally went to other communities to plow for cash, but correspondingly, there was some plowing by tractor. So the two may cancel each other. The observed difficulty that some farmers had in finding enough days for plowing when it was not raining and the soil moisture was suitable, plus the common lack of a second plowing, suggest that the twenty-three units are probably a minimum for the area under cultivation.

Every household keeps some productive livestock. The typical complement is one or two milking goats, one or two pigs, and chickens. The goats are bred each year to produce a pair of kids for slaughter in the spring. Perhaps half the households raise a calf to be sold to urban slaughterhouses. Virtually all the sheep are kept by four households, who specialize mainly in shepherding. In the spring lambing season the number increases by roughly 100. The rich growth of winter grass in the orchards and especially the valley bottom continues to attract outside shepherds who bring flocks here from Arkadia, though this practice has greatly diminished since World War II. (The role of these non-Messenian transhumants on the Messenian scene is a matter to be kept in view but, regrettably, it cannot be taken up here.)

An adequate estimate of the community's land for supporting sheep and goats must not rely merely on data from the contemporary situation. Many records for the pre–World War II period were destroyed in that terrible decade of occupation and civil war, but the well-confirmed conclusion from local oral histories is that in the 1930's there were no fewer than 1,000 head of sheep and goats kept by the households of the community. Most households herded small flocks of 25 to 50. A milk and cheese merchant began operation in 1934 in Rizomilo shortly after the opening of the new road, further confirming the considerable size of the flocks. Less well authenticated accounts suggest that the number was considerably above 1,000 before the 1930's. At that time far more than the 1961 total (200 ha) was in brushy grazing land, but the community was already planting tree and vine crops heavily. A value of 1,300 head may be a likely year-round total, although in the noncritical winter and spring when fodder is abundant, the number was swelled by the transhumant flocks.

This decline in sheep and goats after 1940 is correlated with the shift to chemical fertilizers for crops. Before that time small herds were kept in rude temporary folds located in fields, remaining in each for four to five days. Gradually, the fields were thus fertilized; in addition, manure was deliberately hauled for trees.

Table 4-5. Main Items of Diet and Their Source (in Percentages)

Food	Produced by Consuming Household	Produced within Village but by Another Farmer	Purchased from outside Village
Olive oil	100		
Eating olives	100		
Fresh fruit	80	10	10
Wine	80	20	
Potatoes	50	30	20
Rice			100
Macaroni and similar products	30		70
Bread	30		70
Flour	40		60
Vegetables, including wild greens	60	20	20
Fish (fresh and preserved)			100
Meat			
Chicken	100		
Pork	80	20	
Beef		5	95
Mutton		50	50
Kid	80	10	10
Game birds and pigeons and doves	60	30	10
Eggs	80	10	10
Cheese	80	10	10
Sugar and honey			100
Salt			100
Yogurt		10	90

Diet

The source of the main items of diet in the community affords a significant perspective on its economy. Table 4-5 presents a rough estimate based on my field observations.

Since diet items do not occur with equal frequency or quantity in meals, some weighting is essential to estimate the degree of food subsistence, to grasp the importance of crops with a subsistence surplus, etc. The staples of a day's meals are: olive oil (always) and table olives (very often); soft cheese; bread (always); potatoes, rice, or some macaroni products (always); a garden or wild vegetable; wine (less common for women); and some snack-size servings of meat, chicken, or fish. Equally regularly a part of daily food intake, but most often taken between meals are: the local fruit of the season; sweetened coffee (less common for women); a sweet pastry or fruit preserve; and alcoholic beverages of beer, wine, or liqueur.

We may now try to estimate the relative amount or importance of these items. The conspicuous item of olive oil seems to have a consumption rate that varies considerably – from 30 to 125 kg per person per year. The author always found oil amply present when taking meals unexpectedly with families, even those on the low end of the range of prosperity. This confirms the impression that oil is the principal source of fat and of much caloric value to all persons of the community. Bread is not merely an indispensable accompaniment to every meal, but is consumed in large amounts. The 80 households purchase an average of 75 one-kilo loaves per day; 10 households bake virtually all their bread; 40 households still bake irregularly. Thus, at a conservative estimate, 110 kg of bread are consumed daily, which equals .31 kg per capita per day and 110 kg per capita per year. The rest of the starches in a starch-heavy diet come from a main dish consisting largely of potatoes, boiled rice, or a macaroni product. Such dishes average better than one per day. Thus, though self-sufficient in oil, the community is less than 50 percent self-sufficient in its heavy starch intake.

In meat, dairy, and poultry products, patterns are less clear, and consumption varies among families. Cheese, however, is consumed daily by nearly all families at an average rate of half a kilogram per day. Chicken is the most regularly used meat, with fish in some form next. Mutton or kid and the far less common beef and pork tend to be served on Sundays and holidays and for guests. For some families winter game birds or domesticated pigeons are reasonably common in the diet. Over-all, it is probably safe to estimate that the community is about 60 percent self-sufficient in meats and related foods.

Two of the major crops of the community, figs and currants, are remarkably minor items in the diet, especially in stored form. Although the eating of green figs is insignificant, dried figs are eaten during harvest to the extent of reducing regular meal taking. Most families store no figs at all for later consumption, although some store as much as 20 kg for winter snacks. Fresh currants are eaten by many in amounts to make regular meals shrink, but virtually no dried currants are stored for later use.

Water

Water is such an essential factor in the existence of man, other animals, and plants that its availability always demands attention. But in Messenia its importance is intensified by the long dry season, the nature of the sources, and its salient interest to the people of the community.

Water comes from five sources: rain, springs, wells, rivers, and piped systems. The monthly average rainfall (Fig. 4-2) shows the winter wet season that soaks the community for a few months and the long dry season, though its average nature tends to mask how late into the fall the dry season often extends. Springs, though minor in this community, show the adaptation to the dry season. One small perennial spring is located in the old road pass just below and north of the Nichoria ridge. During most of the year the seepage into a clayey basin 50 cm in diameter and 4 cm deep is sufficient only to refill the basin in two hours. But the spring flows all year and was several times seen to be the destination of women leading oxen or goats during September and October. Northwest of Karpofora and at the head of the deep, narrow valley to the west is a surface seepage of water that continues into July and allows the cultivation of a small kitchen garden some 1,000 m from the village. Farther northwest is another seepage that irrigates new trees and a kitchen garden until late in the summer.

Wells, the third source, supplied nearly all of the water for household uses until early 1969, when the transition to a system of piped-in water commenced (see below). All of the wells are located in valleys. The two oldest wells served the Karpofora habitation site. One of these is in the deep valley west of the Karpofora ridge, and the other is located to the southeast, where Vathirema Valley fans out into the Karia Valley bottom. The depth of the latter is about 15 m. Five dug wells in the Karia Valley provided water for the Rizomilo habitation area. Since World War II three wells of driven steel pipe with hand pumps have been added to serve the Rizomilo population.

The Karia River, a fourth source, flows all year, providing the adjacent community with water to irrigate more than 80 hectares. The present system of ditches and dams gradually evolved from that built by private initiative about 1880 to operate two flour mills, one on each side of the river. The irrigation system is now maintained and operated by the community. From its simple construction, except for a few recent improvements, one can see how easily earlier farmers could have used irrigation to exploit this rich valley.

Finally, in the last two years the principal source of household water is rapidly shifting to the seven-village system that brings water through pipes from a large spring 15 km north, near the village of Vlasi. Although the new system is of the greatest importance for the life of the contemporary community, we may properly ignore it and concentrate on the older sources. Fortunately for my observations, the new system was not complete until the summer of 1970, and in 1969 the flow of piped water was sporadic so that reliance on wells was still the rule.

Before 1935 when only the Karpofora habitation site existed, the main source of household water was the two wells described above. The trip to the western and nearer well (some 400 m away) involves a final very steep descent of 60 m to the tiny valley bottom. The well to the southeast is 1,000 m away and at about the same elevation, but the grade is more gradual.

To one or the other of these wells a woman from a family of five had to go each day with her donkey and two open-topped wooden tubs, plus a small barrel or a clay jar, in order to fetch the 25 gallons of water needed. This amount suffices for drinking, kitchen use, limited bathing, and perhaps a bit left for a very limited washing of small clothing. A round trip averages about 45 minutes for the western well and an hour for the eastern well. Additional trips were made for such uses as a full clothes washing, watering of animals, and watering of kitchen garden or ornamental flowers. The trip to the well is bearable in the cool of dawn or dusk of a summer day, but becomes an ordeal if often repeated in hot weather. A final complication was that the western well sometimes dries up toward the end of the summer season.

Several modes of adaptation to the water-poor character of the upland habitation site were regularly employed. For washing clothes, most women made the trip of 2 km down to the plentiful water in the lower Karia River. The women set off in the early morning with a donkey loaded with large copper cauldron, soiled clothes, bedding, rugs, and so on. By afternoon, wind and sun dried the wash draped over bushes. Gardens are often located in more irrigable bottoms, and animals were taken down for the day to the lusher bottoms where they could graze and be watered before the return at dusk.

For the last sixty years and more, over half of the families of the village have regularly coped with the dry-season water problem in a different way. It should be noted that the practice to be described began well before any families lived year-round in the new settlement at Rizomilo. Since all families had fields in several locations and the old settlement of Karpofora is located on the western side of the village land, it follows that most families had fields located closer to the river and often on the river valley floor. So if they moved to one of these fields during the summer and fall, they might be more conveniently located for working such fields, some of which are irrigable. And they surely would be closer to the river water and to wells that could be dug to tap the groundwater of the valley floor. Families did build houses in their lower fields, equipping them with baking ovens and cooking areas, and they often dug wells. So prevalent was this practice that the normal settlement is reported to have been nearly deserted and summer coffeeshops were set up to serve in the new location. Though this "mini-transhumance" has virtually ceased, some twenty-seven of the houses built in fields still survive, often as storehouses.

When one asks farmers why they made this seasonal shift they cite convenience to water (for household, garden, animals, and crop irrigation), to their fields, and to fodder for animals. These factors are also what farmers cite when asked why they later moved permanently to the new settlement area of Rizomilo. Both the seasonal transhumance and the permanent move to Rizomilo indicate the importance of a water supply in the dry season. The transhumance also suggests to us an adaptation that could have been used by earlier Bronze Age communities who had their permanent village on the adjacent ridge (Nichoria), which seems to have been similarly lacking in a good source of water in the dry season.

In the rainy season fetching water from the wells is more difficult owing to the slippery, muddy paths as well as the rain itself. Yet the amount of water needed from this source drops to no more than drinking and kitchen use, for most people save rain water and roof runoff for washing clothes and for the animals. I found no instances of rainwater used for drinking.

Locational and Spatial Aspects of the Community

Keeping in mind the foregoing description of the community's terrain, crops, water resources, and recent developments, we may now make some observations on its locational and spatial aspects. We should also recall that the Bronze Age community in this area had its village site on Nichoria ridge, which is but a 10-minute walk from Karpofora on the opposite (eastern) side of Vathirema Valley (see Pocket Map 10-19).

The area of the modern community encloses the Karia and its plain out to where these meet with the coastal flat (Fig. 4-1). Today this riverine feature is an important asset — agriculturally because of the diversified irrigated crops it sustains, and residentially because of its convenience to fields, water, and communications. But in the rather recent past the river had a different significance. Then river floods were "especially feared," as noted in a nineteenth-century topographical account nearly devoid of human responses (Philippson, 2nd ed., 1959, p. 402); the account accords well with the descriptions of older villagers. This problem was gradually solved with the deepening of the channel as gravel was hauled away for the construction of roads. It is no surprise, then, to learn from local accounts how in those days the bridgeless stream halted winter travel and that one chose among several fords according to river condition. The impression seems clear that the river was a boundary. The two flour mills on either side of the river and close by one another witness both to its divisive effect and to its use.

In this period before the modern road network with its T-shaped intersection in Rizomilo at the Karia bridge, the community area had a different orientation to the prevailing routes. A coastal route from the Pamisos Plain to Pylos ran near the northern community boundary, just as it does now, although the old route ascended out of the valley via a pass immediately north of the Bronze Age site of Nichoria. The branch to Petalidhi remained on the east of the Karia until nearer the sea where there was a ford followed by an ascent to some low hills. A third route in the vicinity was a cutoff running roughly southeast from Neromilo to near the mouth of the Tsane River, where it joined the coastal route to Petalidhi and Koroni. Thus the three route segments enclosed the community in a triangle (see Ch. 9).

Until about 1950 the making of clay tiles continued in Rizomilo. Philippson (1959, p. 404) noted at the end of the nineteenth century that "in the area of the Skarias River mouth, brick clay is found on the slopes and is made into roof tiles." The most recent kilns were located on the western valley floor and near the water necessary for mixing; the clay was taken from a slope 0.5 km to the south. The discovery of ancient sherds precisely here suggests that this resource has been important for a considerable time. A similar and contemporary industry, kilns to convert limestone to lime, was located along the old Pylos road just as it ascends north of Nichoria ridge and near the great limestone outcrop.

The significance of the community's location so near the seacoast is difficult to assess. For today's villager, the sea does not even represent an opportunity to swim, and it may be no more than a "barometer" believed to indicate the onset of rain through changes in its roar. In the period before 1925 the community's tie to sea traffic was mainly mediated by Petalidhi where (as informants recall) steamers and caiques picked up figs and currants or unloaded livestock from the Mani. But that sea contact could exist near the mouth of the Karia is attested by two examples. During the 1920's lignite, mined at Dhafni and transported in little wagons travelling along a suspended line extending the length of the valley, was loaded in boats and barges near the river mouth. Also in this period caiques stopped here with flour and wheat consigned to local merchants who distributed it to several inland villages.

The emergence of the new residential area of Rizomilo occurred in the prewar period and seems to be largely due to the construction of the new road with its bridge, increasing irrigational use of the runoff water from the two mills, a desire for more dependable sources for household water, and possibly, the conquest of malaria in Greece during the 1930's. We cannot similarly explain the emergence of the old residential area, since its existence predates current historical data; but we can comment on its locational characteristics and compare them with those of the nearby Bronze Age habitation on Nichoria ridge. Nearly all of the contemporary villagers consider the Karpofora residential area to have a climate superior to that of Rizomilo – cooler in the summer, less damp in the winter, and without mosquitoes. Countering these is the salient disadvantage of its inconvenient and unreliable wells. On all of these counts Karpofora and Nichoria are the same, and they are virtually alike in having a panoramic view and in their proximity to the only nearby source of limestone for construction of buildings. Nichoria has readier access to the valley plain and a genuine command overlooking the older road as it ascends to the uplands and on to Pylos, whereas Karpofora is more centrally placed to the former livestock grazing areas in the west, the former grain-growing areas of the uplands, and generally to arable land (see Fig. 4-1). Such a sketch is perhaps as much as we can note in advance of the careful reconnaissance planned for the area.

We may complete a view of the contemporary community by turning to the Karpofora residential area. Figure 4-3 gives the plan of the village's stone-walled houses approximately as they were in 1928 when all of them were in use. Then the village population was 372 persons (NSSG 1928) dwelling in 71 houses, or 5.2 persons per house. The plan also shows nonresidential structures: oil mill, church, school, as well as some of the smaller structures which served variously as stables, kitchens, and storage areas. Of the latter three kinds of structure, there were undoubtedly more than those shown in the plan. The built-up area is approximately 4 hectares, yielding a density of 93 persons per hectare. This is low when compared with the 112 persons per hectare found to be the average for a sample of ten modern Messenian villages (see Ch. 8).

The terrain within the habitation area slopes gradually upward toward the west, the difference in elevation between the eastern and western thirds of the area being about 3 m. This higher, western third has the oldest houses. Expansion of the residential area as the population increased was almost entirely downslope to the east and then to the north. But a more detailed look at

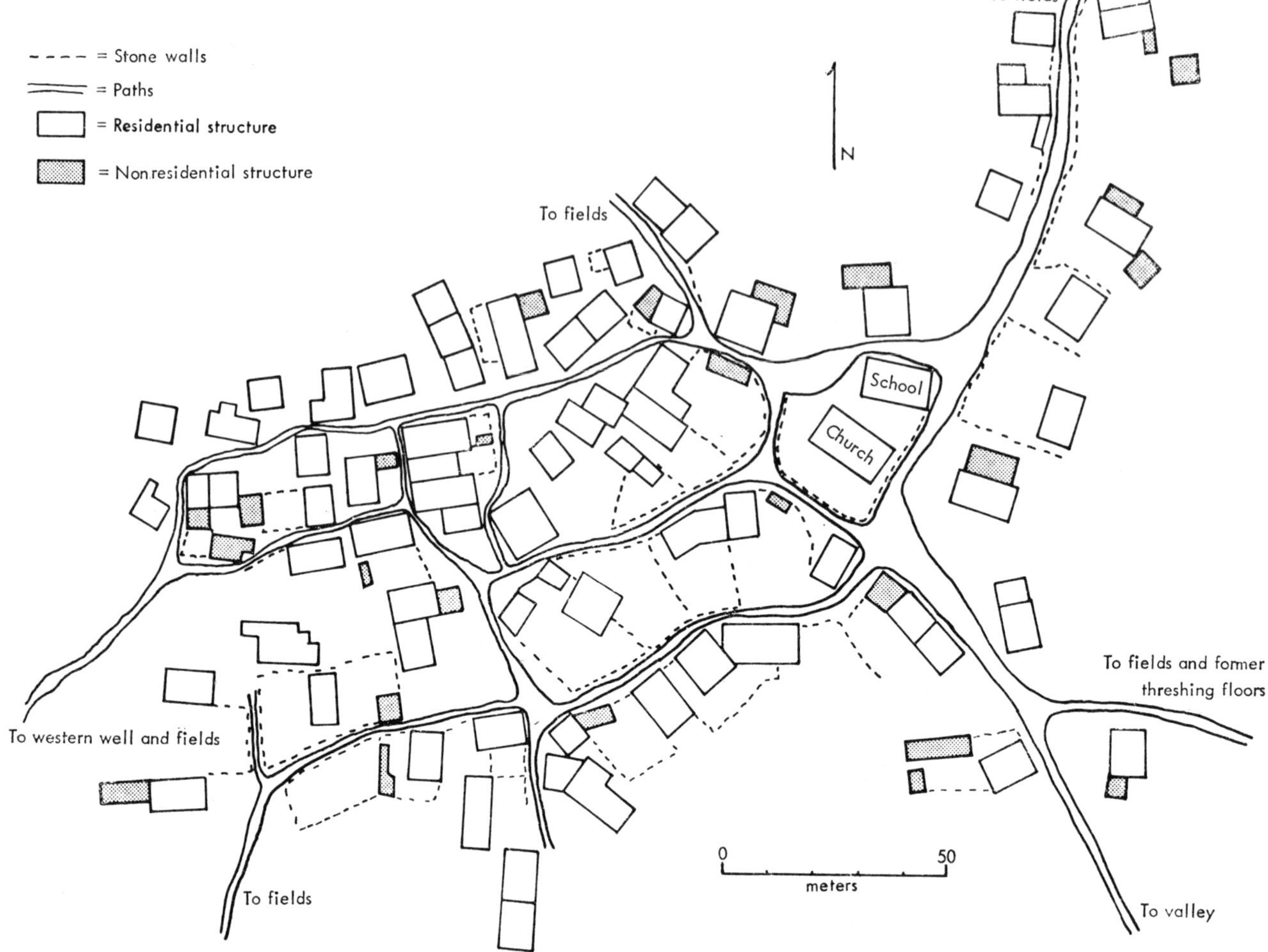

Figure 4-3. Sketch plan of Karpofora village about 1928

the history of the structures reveals another, earlier trend in the use of space, that of increasing density as the population rose. Only subsequently was the total built-up area expanded. This resulted, as the many contiguous houses and their dates of construction indicate, from the practice of sons building adjacent to their fathers, or younger brothers next to elder brothers. Not surprisingly then, the subareas of the village were mainly occupied by elementary families, all of the same family line or lineage.

The plan also shows (by the dotted lines representing stone walls, usually some 2 m in height) that there was a notable tendency to enclose the yards of the houses. Nearly always such enclosing walls are found with the houses that held the richer families. Typically, one small building in the yard served as a kitchen and another building was a winter stable; but in other cases a single larger out-structure housed both functions. Somewhere in the yard is the bread oven, freestanding or adjoining another structure. In some yards there are masonry vats for the crushing of wine grapes. In any case, wine making is an activity that occurs in the yard, just as does the drying of grain, sorting of dried figs and currants, butchering, and some weaving. The yard is also home for many animals: chickens peck about, and donkeys, horses, cattle, and goats are all tethered there at night. Piles of brush, prunings, and wood are stacked in the yard to fire the kitchen hearth, the bread oven, and, more recently, the fireplace.

Every household uses some indoor space for storage of food supplies. Containers for wine and oil compose the greater share, but sacks of grain and potatoes, crocks of eating olives, salted pork, and cheese require considerable area. About 33 of the 71 houses had two stories, and in these the ground floor was the storage area. In the remaining houses some portion of the single floor was devoted to storage, or in a few cases a detached building so served. But since single-story houses tended mostly to be those of the less wealthy, we may assume they had less to store in what surely is a considerably smaller area.

Conclusions

How does the preceding view of a particular contemporary community inform a reconstruction of human activity on the prehistoric scene of Messenia? Something like an upper limit on the productive capability for ancient communities can be estimated by using the production of modern communities as a base. The data presented begin to provide this base. The sequence of changes in the productive and demographic characteristics of Karpofora during the past century—from a mostly subsistence-level economy based on grains and livestock to an economy developing exchangeable surpluses of tree and vine crops, and the accompanying steady rise in population under peaceful conditions—must have been repeated many times in Messenian communities of the past, as later chapters suggest. But in particular, this may be the sequence we should assume for the Late Bronze Age, because it culminates in the economy of the Pylian kingdom with the exchange of surpluses indicated in the tablets.

The modern crops of olives, figs, and vines were also important in the Bronze Age. Hence the particular attention given to the relationships of land, yield, labor, and schedule of activities for these crops provides a guide to estimates for Bronze Age communities. This guide, for example, when coupled with the estimated population for the Late Bronze Age peak (both the individual sites in Register A and also the regional estimate in Ch. 8) makes possible some calculation of the production in Messenia in that period. Beyond this, the tree and vine crops involve a noteworthy lag between their planting and full harvests. Such crops thus imply a more stable community than one with a grain- and livestock-based economy. This observation affords us a start in grappling with the problem of assessing the probability of continuous occupation through intervals shorter than can be discriminated by current pottery chronology, especially at sites known chiefly by surface sherds. Finally, there is the rather predictable tendency for olive yield to fluctuate from year to year in one area, between areas, and also in the whole Mediterranean basin. This phenomenon coupled with an easily stored commodity such as olive oil could have been the impetus for an oil trade among the areas within the Pylian kingdom as well as in the wider ancient world.

Also, the construction of the modern irrigation system suggests how easily irrigation might have been used by earlier villagers to exploit the valley plain during the dry season. Finally, the summer shift of families from the upland habitation area to houses nearer the river could well have been the seasonal habit of earlier communities, both here and in similar locations.

REFERENCES

Loy, W. G. 1970. *The Land of Nestor: A Physical Geography of the Southwest Peloponnese.* National Academy of Sciences, Office of Naval Research Report No. 34. Washington, D.C.

NSSG. 1962a. *Division of the Area of Land According to the Basic Categories of Use.* In Greek. Athens.

———. 1962b. *Population of Greece: From the Census of 19 March 1961.* In Greek and French. Athens.

———. 1964. *Results of the Census of Agriculture-Livestock of March 1961*, Vol. 1, Sec. 3. *Peloponnese.* In Greek and French. Athens.

Pansiot, F. P., and Rebour, H. 1961. *Improvement in Olive Cultivation*, FAO Agricultural Studies No. 50. Rome.

Philippson, A. 1959. *Die griechischen Landschaften*, 2nd ed. Vol. 3, Pt. 2, pp. 319–523. *Der Peloponnes: Der Westen und Süden der Halbinsel.* Ed. E. Kirsten. Frankfurt.

Poucqueville, F. C. H. L. 1827. *Voyage de la Grèce*, 2nd ed. Vol. 6. Paris.

Rangavis, Iakovos R. 1853. *Hellenica*, viz., *Geographical, Historical, Archaeological, and Statistical Description of Ancient and Modern Greece*, Vol. 2. Athens.

Sweet-Escott, Bickham. 1954. *Greece: A Political and Economic Survey 1939–1953.* Royal Institute of International Affairs. London and New York.

Taylor, Norman, ed. 1961. *Taylor's Encyclopedia of Gardening*, 4th ed. Boston.

Ventris, M., and Chadwick, J. 1956. *Documents in Mycenaean Greek.* Cambridge.

5
THE POST-CLASSICAL DOCUMENTS

by
Peter Topping

The Period A.D. 330–900. We know little about the Peloponnese as a Byzantine province. The few data at our disposal reflect the obscurity and isolation of the "lands down under" (*ta katōtika merē*), an expression often synonymous with the peninsula in Byzantine usage. ("Morea" as a name for the Peloponnese became widely current only after the Frankish conquest.) Remote from Constantinople and far to the south of the great Via Egnatia, the peninsula received scant attention from the chroniclers and historians of the capital. In this chapter I must often make generalizations about the Peloponnese as a whole because of our ignorance of specific conditions in its southwestern region. For the Byzantine province a number of my remarks derive from the fine monograph of Antoine Bon, *Le Péloponnèse byzantin* (1951).

Strabo, a contemporary of the emperor Augustus, describes Lakonia and Messenia as a "mostly" deserted area of Greece. This remark of his should not be taken literally. In any case, districts as fertile as Messenia and Elis can hardly have remained depopulated during the long Pax Romana. It is impossible to estimate the number of inhabitants in southwest Peloponnese at this or any other time during the middle ages. The disorders of the third century in the empire seem not to have affected the region greatly except at Olympia. A fortification wall built to protect the central area of the Altis, formerly attributed to the fifth or sixth century, has been shown to belong to the second half of the third century (Kunze 1955). Almost certainly its erection was connected with the invasion of Greece by the Heruli, which is reported by late Greek historians. This Germanic people, after wreaking great destruction in Athens (267), and sacking Corinth, Sparta, and Argos, evidently reached Olympia. The fourth century was on the whole relatively peaceful until its closing years, when the Visigoths led by Alaric invaded the Peloponnese. They remained in the peninsula for more than a year. They pillaged the temples at Olympia, but the extent of the destruction they wrought there and elsewhere in Elis has probably been exaggerated.

More barbarian attacks on Greece came in the fifth century. The Vandals of Africa and Sicily posed the greatest threat to the Peloponnese, through their landings on the west coast and the Ionian Islands in 467 and 477. The security of the entire Balkan peninsula was seriously affected in the sixth century by Turkic and Slavic tribes who crossed the Danube and penetrated deeply into Greece. Until the death of Justinian (565) the wall across the Isthmus of Corinth effectively protected the Peloponnese. However, a series of natural catastrophes struck Greece and the Mediterranean world in Justinian's era. Severe earthquakes in 522 shook the entire east, from Dyrrhachium to Cilicia; among other cities Corinth was leveled. It was probably now that the monuments of the Altis at Olympia were destroyed, rather than in the great shocks of 551, which together with a tidal wave devastated the shores of the gulfs of Patras and Corinth. A greater calamity than the earthquakes was the "pandemic" of bubonic plague in the Levant and Europe in 541–43. This pestilence returned at least five times between 555 and 608. No trustworthy figures are available for the toll in human lives. But from the parallel course of the bubonic plague of the fourteenth century (Russell 1958) the loss of a fifth or a fourth of the population is a plausible inference.

By the late sixth century the Peloponnese had no doubt suffered a real decline from its material and demographic level in the second or third centuries A.D. However serious the decline, we do not believe it can be attributed to drought and famine caused by a drastic climatic change such as Carpenter (1966) hypothesizes in order to support his explanation for the fall of the Mycenaean civilization and the coming of the Dorians (see Wright 1968). Rather, it is more likely that the Peloponnese, and Greece as a whole, had gradually declined since the second century owing to the excessive fiscal demands of the imperial governments and the cumulative effects of earthquakes, pestilence, and barbarian inroads. Although, during these centuries, several hundred basilicas were constructed throughout Greece, including those at Filiatra and Pheidias' studio at Olympia, their number and splendor are out of proportion to the human and economic resources of the country. They were built mainly on the coasts and islands and quite often on the sites of pagan worship that the Church was eager to take over (Zakythinos 1966).

If the period we have thus far considered is obscure, that of the seventh and eighth centuries is truly a "Dark Age." But there can be small doubt that in this period – and in any event not later than the eighth century – large numbers of Slavs infiltrated the peninsula and settled in it permanently. The Byzantine naval command maintained control on the eastern coast from Corinth to Cape Malea. But the intruders must have occupied almost all of the interior and western regions of the peninsula (Lemerle 1963). Elis and Messenia have preserved a significant number of Slavic place-names, including Navarino, "place of maples" (Vasmer 1941). Recently published documents of the fourteenth century reveal more names of Slavic origin in these districts and also record a "village of Slavs" (Sclavoforo = Sklavochóri) near the bay of Navarino (Longnon and Topping 1969). It can hardly be questioned that Slavs settled at many points in the region.

On the other hand the number of Greek names recorded in medieval sources shows that it is unlikely that the native population completely disappeared. Some of these names have had a continuous life since antiquity in more or less the same location, often evolving into more popular forms – for example, Olena, Alpheios, Methone, Korone, Kardamyle, Halmyros and Leuktron. Other names, though derived from ancient Greek, were bestowed on new settlements at an apparently early date – for example, Mandínia and Arkadhiá. It is a plausible explanation that Greeks from Arkadia retreating before incoming Slavs gave this name to the castle and site of ancient Kyparissia. The largest group of Greek place-names is found in sources of the thirteenth and fourteenth centuries. Some examples are Aëtos, Romanou, Platanos, Kremmidhi, Kinigou, Petalidhi, Charokopio, and Pidhima. In any event, the vast majority of the peasants in the fourteenth century were Greek: this is evident from the baptismal and family names of several hundred serfs recorded in the fiscal censuses drawn up for Frankish landlords of Elis and Messenia (Longnon and Topping 1969).

In the early ninth century, Byzantine military and ecclesiastical authority was re-established in most parts of the peninsula. The success of the missionary effort to convert and hellenize the Slavs must have owed much to the presence of a Greek population (Charanis 1970). The Byzantine strategos or governor (who combined military and civil authority) invited back, at this time, a certain number of Greeks from abroad. Such, for example, were the inhabitants of Rhegion (Reggio) in Calabria whose fathers had fled from Patras before the Slavs.

The assimilation of the Slavic population was largely accomplished, at least in the plains, by the tenth century. An enclave of Slavs continued to exist until the end of the middle ages on the western slopes of Taygetos, east of Kalamata, and farther south into the Mani peninsula. Methoni and Koroni became suffragan sees of the metropolis of Patras early in the ninth century. Saint Athanasios, bishop of Methoni under the emperor Basil I (867–86), presumably evangelized Messenia. His *Life*, unfortunately, gives no details on the condition of the country. We cannot know, for example, what were the short- or long-range effects in our region of the plague that was rampant in the empire in 747–48. It may have been especially severe in the Peloponnese, having come to Greece from Italy and spreading to the Near East through the port of Monemvasia.

The Period A.D. 900–1204. In the tenth to twelfth centuries the Peloponnese again enjoyed a period of relative security and prosperity. The archbishopric of Christianoupolis (Christianou) in western Messenia was created before the end of the eleventh century. The handsome cathedral there, which collapsed in the great earthquake of 1886 and was restored in the 1950's, was constructed in the second half of the eleventh century. It and other churches of the eleventh and twelfth centuries in our region, as at Kalamata and Samarina (near Andhrousa; Pl. 11-2), are evidence of a more advanced material and cultural level. We know, however, extremely little about the military, social, and economic organization in this period. Methoni and Koroni were ports of call on the trade routes between Italy and the Levant. The English pilgrim Benedict of Peterborough makes an almost unique reference to the agriculture of southwest Peloponnese at this time: he found the district of Koroni to have the most abundant production of olives in the world. On the condition of the rural population we have no direct testimony, such as archbishop Michael Choniates of Athens provides for Attica about 1200. But we may plausibly suppose that the same factors of rapid decline were present in the Peloponnese as in the empire as a whole on the eve of the Fourth Crusade: fiscal tyranny, the revival of piracy, and the growth of large estates. Much of the population of the coastal plains and towns must have abandoned their fields and workshops to seek refuge in the mountains. The treaty of 1204 that divided the Byzantine territories among Venice and the crusaders refers to lands in western Peloponnese held by members of the Kantakouzenos and Vranas families, by Irene, daughter of Alexius III Angelus, and by Constantinopolitan monasteries – all of these being absentee proprietors. We do not know the precise location of these estates, nor their extent.

Principality of Achaia (Morea). For the Frankish period (1205–1432) we are well informed on the diplomatic and political history of the principality of Achaia or Morea, whose most important provinces were Elis and Messenia. The most recent account is in the first part of Bon's *La Morée franque* (1969). The second part of Bon's monumental study represents a great advance in our knowledge of the topography and historical geography of Frankish Peloponnese. New evidence on the land regime of the principality is now available in the documents edited by Longnon and Topping. They consist mainly of fiscal censuses of serfs and other properties in some forty villages of Messenia and ancient Triphylia (the present eparchy of Olympia, nome of Elis). Though limited in quantity, this evidence sheds some light on the demography and rural economy of the principality. Half or more of these villages can be identified with certainty or given approximate locations. Pocket Map 5-8 shows all the settlements mentioned in medieval sources (to about 1500) that we have been able to locate. There are several dozen more villages named in the sources but of unknown location; and we can assume that still other settlements were never recorded. The map includes northwestern Mani. The grant of a fief to Niccolò Acciaiuoli in 1336 that consisted of six villages in whole or in part, from Almiros to Tzimova (now Areopolis), indicates that the Byzantine despots of Mistra did not always control this district. Neither Franks nor Byzantines effectively controlled the Slavs of Yiannitsa (Pl. 10-1), who briefly held the castle of Kalamata in the 1290's.

Almost all of the names on Pocket Map 5-8 are attested in sources written before 1500, in medieval Greek, French, Latin, and Italian. A few are found on the map of Agnese of 1554; these are assumed to have been in use before 1500.

There was an unusual number of fortifications in southwest Peloponnese in the thirteenth to fifteenth centuries – on isolated strategic points and in towns and villages. This was owing to the feudal system imported by the Franks, which involved a fragmentation of governmental authority, and to the need to defend against attacks from pirates and the Byzantine power centered at Mistra. The map shows many of the castles but undoubtedly there were more than those shown. More often than not, there were settlements beneath or around the castles, sometimes considerable ones, as at Kalamata, Andhrousa, and Arkadhiá. On the other hand, points like Navarino, Archangelos, and Gardhiki apparently had garrisons only, without permanent settlements. Certain settlements are known to have had defense towers in Frankish times, for example, Krestena and Agoulinitsa.

There are at least forty villages mentioned in the Western and Greek medieval sources which cannot be identified, though the general location of some of them is certain. The sources also record a still larger number of names of natural features or small cultivated districts which lay within the territories of villages. It is nearly always impossible to identify these, and none is shown on the map. Finally, in the case of many villages mentioned in sources since 1500 and not appearing on the map, it is a reasonable assumption that they had medieval predecessors that have not been recorded in the surviving scanty source material.

Andrimoni
Aradiani
Archie
Armenikó
Aspra villa
Áyios Ioánnis
Canali
Caraveniza
Castrum Francum
Castrum Leonis
Chortichina
Cincirnicza
Clisivia
Crusuna
Draghani
Euriachi
Glikí
Gricij
Janina
Kósmina
Lákki
Likochorió
Macona
Maniatochóri
Molíni
Mostenítsa
Munista
Parthenada
Petoni
Prinítsa
Próti
Rubenichi
Sklavochóri
Spanochóri
Valiza
Xereni
Xiromiliá
Zagórena
Zaramate
Zivali

Most of the unidentified medieval settlements (p. 66) are referred to as villages, a few as castles. The majority were in Messenia, the rest in northwest Mani and the lower Alpheios Valley. The approximate location of a number of them is known; for example, Maniatochori and Gliki were close to the Bay of Navarino (Topping 1966). The Spanochori here is in the "district of Koroni"; thus it can hardly be the village of this name near Meligala. (Italics indicate the spelling in the sources; roman type when we are sure of the correct form.)

The Franks said "province of Kalamata" to denote approximately the area of Messenia. "Castellany of Kalamata" designated a more restricted area that included lands in the Pamisos Valley and near the Bay of Navarino. Andhrousa, always part of the princely domain, was the seat of the captain of the castellany (Pl. 10-2). Nisi (now Messini) was founded during the Frankish period, in the plain of the lower Pamisos, on the edge of a terrace surrounded by the Pamisos and by a smaller stream, hence the name Nēsí ("island"). In the later history of the principality, Andhrousa and Nisi were more important than Kalamata as administrative centers. The Franks called the Steniklarian Plain *Val de Calamy* or *Lacchi* (for Greek Lakkoi). Their control in northeastern Messenia did not extend as far as Mt. Elenítsa. Southwest of this peak, at the strategic position of Kokkala commanding the routes from Arkadia and Lakonia (see Valmin 1930, pp. 74ff.), the Greeks of Mistra built a fortress after 1264. This was the Gardhiki of the *Chronicle of Morea*, a name which Buchon found still in use in 1841. The name is also recorded in a document of 1354 (Longnon and Topping, p. 103, line 14; #211 in Register A, p. 294). To protect the villages between the Steniklarian Plain and Arkadhiá against the Greeks of Gardhiki, princess Isabella constructed the fortress of Chastelneuf at the end of the thirteenth century. This is perhaps to be identified with the ruined castle of Mila (Valmin 1930, p. 117; #219 in Register A, p. 294).

Rural Economy. As we see from the inventories of the estates of Acciaiuoli and other feudal lords, the chief crops were grain, the vine, and the olive. The grains were wheat, barley, oats, millet, and a vetch (*róvi*) for cattle. Other products were silk, various legumes, honey and wax, figs, nuts, oranges, acorns, cotton, flax, and valonia and galls for tanning and dyeing. There are several mentions of fishponds, including one at Mikromani and one "below" Pila; the latter may well have been in the Osmanaga Lagoon, still referred to by inhabitants around it by the name Dhivári (from Latin *vivarium* through Byzantine Greek *βιβάρι*), since fish were bred in it until the drainage operations of recent years. The production of salt was of some importance. Salines are recorded at the Bay of Navarino, near Grizi, on the shore near Vounaria or Longa, and at Almiros. An inventory of 1354 reveals that Acciaiuoli held two forests of Aleppo pines valued for their resin (Longnon and Topping 1969, p. 71). Both were near Krestena, possibly on the very site of the existing pine forest along the Agoulinitsa Lagoon.

Agricultural productivity probably was low, as the following figures from a document of 1379 suggest (Longnon and Topping 1969, pp. 201f.). From Acciaiuoli's lands at Krestena: 40 measures of wheat, less 8 for seed; 9 measures of oats, less 7½ for seed; and 20 measures of barley, less 12 for seed. From the village of Kremmidhi: 35½ measures of wheat, less 8 for seed; 13 of barley, less 6 for seed; but only 15 measures of oats from 33 of seed.

It may be doubted that Frankish Morea was a land from which its exploiters derived much wealth. In late 1360 an agent of the consort of the Neapolitan prince of Achaia visited her extensive Greek estates to collect whatever revenues he could find. Early in 1361 he composed a detailed report (document VIII in Longnon and Topping) which is a vivid description of the political anarchy and economic difficulties prevailing in the principality. He finally put together in silver coin the equivalent of 2,000 ducats; he could not, however, at the port of Clarence convert so much as half of this quantity of silver into gold. He reported that the grain crop of the princess' lands at Kalamata, Maïna (Mikromani), Andhrousa, and Pila was small because of bad weather in 1360; little wine was produced, for the same cause. He ordered the serfs of two villages in southern Messenia to plant vines on land considered too poor for grain. Other serfs complained that they raised only enough grain for seed on a farm of the princess' at Pila.

Population: 1205–1460. Any estimate of the total population of the region under the Franks would be conjectural. At most we can speak of certain trends in the region as a whole, and present a few findings that bear on the density of the rural population.

The conquest of western Peloponnese by the Franks (1205) was swift and easy, and their rule until 1262 was firm and beneficent. It is reasonable to infer that the population increased during these decades, both in the country and in the fortresses and towns. As fertile provinces facing the West, Elis and Messenia attracted Italian merchants, Latin clerics, and knights and brides from France. The French founded a new port, Clarence (Glarentza), at the northwestern extremity of Elis, probably on the site of ancient Kyllene; it thus lay somewhat outside the northern limits of the UMME region. A busy port, much frequented by Venetian merchants and having its own system of weights and measures, it was the only true urban settlement in western Peloponnese under the Franks.

The re-establishment of Byzantine authority at Mistra in 1262 began a long period of insecurity in the region that ended only with the Turkish conquest two centuries later (1460). Even apart from the overwhelming calamity of the Black Death (1347–48), which carried off a quarter or more of the population, the land was scourged by a series of afflictions – wars with the Byzantines, civil fighting and growing anarchy, landings of Catalan and Turkish pirates, and destructive raids by the Ottoman Turks, such as that which reached Methoni and Koroni in 1387–88. Nevertheless, we believe that there was no serious decline in population before the Black Death. The sources refer to periods of peace and economic plenty in the last third of the thirteenth century. The gains in population earlier in this century were probably maintained, and perhaps there was no net loss in the decades preceding the Black Death. However, there is no doubt that the conditions of insecurity of the fourteenth century caused the flight of many inhabitants to inland villages and safer locations in the highlands.

The inventories of the estates of Acciaiuoli and another Neapolitan courtier drawn up in 1354 and 1357 furnish evidence on the size of five Messenian villages. Although not true censuses, these documents record all of the peasant hearths, whether occupied or not, that owed the basic dues. In addition, they sometimes record peasants of an inferior or more privileged status than those in the main list. Using a hearth-multiplier of four, and counting these added households, we obtain the following figures:

1. Kremmidhi (now Ano and Kato Kremmidhi, eparchy of Pylia): 57 hearths in the main list (a minimum count; the maximum possible is 63) or 228 persons; 21 deserted hearths or 84 persons. Thus, at a time not long before 1354 the village should have had about 312 persons.

2. Grizi (now Akritochori, eparchy of Pylia): 60 hearths in the main list or 240 persons; seven families exempted of the main dues or 28 persons. Since no deserted hearths are recorded, the total is 268 persons.

3. Kósmina (unidentified; near Longa): 49 hearths in the main list or 196 persons; 17 deserted hearths or 68 persons. To these should be added 8 occupied hearths and 5 deserted ones belonging to another lord. Thus we have a possible total of 312 persons before 1357, the date of the chief census.

4. Voulkano (unidentified; on or near Mt. Voulkano, i.e., Ithome): to the main list of 23 hearths can be added 21 hearths of archers, 14 deserted households, and 3 deserted units that had been planted in vines for the lord. Thus the village might have had 61 households, or 244 persons before 1354.

5. *Petoni* (unidentified; in a high location above the northern plain): after the main list of 54 occupied hearths we find recorded one family of precarious tenure, 14 deserted households, and 7 hearths – both occupied and not – assigned to support petty feudatories. The total is 76 hearths, or 304 persons. Such a figure would have been valid, perhaps, only for a date a decade or two before 1354; for already in an incomplete inventory of Petoni of 1338 there are 2 deserted hearths which are still recorded as such in the census of 1354.

Unfortunately, we can deduce little if anything from the size of these villages about the population density of southwest Peloponnese. For any period of Greek history before the late nineteenth century they are sizable settlements. But it is most difficult to estimate how numerous villages of this size were in medieval times. Presumably they were among the most populous and fertile in the principality; high personages at the Neapolitan court would not have been granted poor lands. Acciaiuoli, as proprietor of Petoni, provided in his will (1358) that its income should help to endow a Benedictine monastery in its district. The inventory of 1354 records about forty local names in Petoni's territory. There were probably more, since the entries of the deserted households omit such names. This number suggests that the lands of the village covered a large area. From the names themselves we can tell that the lands included hilly and forested stretches, recent clearings, fields in the plain, a mountain, and watercourses. If Petoni's territory was extensive, perhaps the larger district to which it belonged – the northern plain of Messenia – was thinly populated in the fourteenth century. At best, this can only be a cautious inference.

The high proportion – roughly one-third – of deserted hearths in our villages (Grizi excepted) is striking. The occupants of many of these must have perished in the Black Death; to be sure, a certain number had fled because of the always harsh conditions of serfdom. Some of the fugitives entered the Venetian colony of Methoni and Koroni; it too had been ravaged by the plague and its castellans were seeking labor for its estates.

The insecurity that prevailed in the principality at the end of the fourteenth century is evident in the hearth-counts in a list of 34 places that was prepared in 1391 for an Italian claimant to the princely title (Bon 1969, p. 691). Whereas the ports of Clarence and Kalamata had 300 hearths each, two of the most inaccessible fortresses, Santameri in eastern Elis and Crèvecoeur near Andhritsena, had 500 and 400 hearths respectively—the highest totals in the list. The compiler qualified his figures with *environ* (approximately), and perhaps those for Clarence and Kalamata were based on a fiscal census that did not include burgesses and foreigners in those ports. The high totals for Santameri, Crèvecoeur, and other interior fortresses suggest that these places served as centers of sizable rural districts: unfortified villages within these districts offered too little security to the rural population.

The Venetian colony of Methoni and Koroni (Pl. 11-1) probably had a greater density of population than the Frankish principality in the thirteenth and fourteenth centuries. We know that the home government ordered censuses of the colony to be taken—for example, in 1312 and 1416. These were apparently true population counts, but they have not as yet been found in the Venetian archives. The following calculation, however, suggests a considerable density of the rural population in 1361–62. The "villains of the Commune" were required collectively to furnish gratis 600 bundles of straw every year in each of the two castellanies of Methoni and Koroni. Since each hearth owed a half bundle, each castellany must have had about 1,200 families of these state serfs. Using a multiplier of four, there is a total of 9,600 souls for this class. These would have been the majority of the population in the country districts that adjoined Methoni and Koroni; the serfs on the estates of the Latin church and of private lay lords were few.

A peasantry of about 10,000 or more within the limited extent of the castellanies in 1361–62 would have been a numerous one indeed. But there is no doubt that the population declined both in the principality and in Venetian Messenia in the second half of the fourteenth century. We learn from a document of 1401 that the castle of Koroni (P 33) and the adjacent settlements—called the "old" *burgus* and the *burgus* of St. John—had only 380 persons, of whom 80 were Latins. The castellans were instructed to build a wall around the two settlements to provide protection against the Turks for the inhabitants of both Koroni and Charokopio (Carocopi), the latter described as being two Venetian miles from the castle (1 Venetian mile = 1.08 English miles).

Sure evidence of depopulation in the Peloponnesian peninsula in the later fourteenth and the fifteenth centuries is the large immigration of Albanians. The Greek despots hired them first as mercenaries and soon invited entire clans to settle with their flocks in vacant lands. By the early 1400's they had reached Elis and Messenia and were raiding the districts of Methoni and Koroni. A document of the Venetian Senate (30 August 1410), summarized here, is illuminating: "Our subjects of the district of Koroni have suffered damages from Turkish and Albanian raids, their crops having been left in open places. Now the castle of Castrifranchi and other fortified places offer security to all our villains of the district of Longa and of many other villages nearby. When villains and their possessions are secure from raids of Turks and others, they will prosper more, and our revenues will increase. Let the castellans of Koroni and Methoni proclaim that the population of the Koroni district should transport its products through the month of November to Castrifranchi and other fortified places. Fines will be levied on the wheat, barley, oats, wine, oil, olives, and other products that are kept concealed in the houses of villains." (Sathas 1881, pp. 251–52.) The exact location of Castrifranchi is uncertain (see Longnon and Topping, pp. 251f.).

In 1425 two Albanian chiefs in command of 5,500 mounted men sought permission to settle in the Venetian colony and to aid in its defence. The figure may be a precise one, and it is very possible the men were admitted. A Venetian chronicler (Stefano Magno) records that "30,000 Albanian inhabitants in the mountains" of Peloponnese rose against the despot Thomas in 1453. In 1455 the Signory authorized the settlement of more Albanians in its Messenian colony. It is beyond dispute that this people was a major demographic and military factor in Morea at the time of the Turkish conquest. Stadtmüller (1944) suggests that they constituted more than one-third of the population. It should be noted, however, that Byzantine Peloponnese in the fourteenth and fifteenth centuries received many refugees from other Greek lands as these fell to the Turks and others; this topic, like that of the Albanian influx, needs more investigation.

The Venetian Colony in the Fifteenth Century. The document of 1410 shows that the Venetians were taking energetic measures for the security of their colony. A few years later the hitherto separate districts of Methoni and Koroni were connected by land through the acquisition of Grizi and other villages between the ports. At the same time, the colony was probably extended northward on the east coast of the Messenian peninsula beyond Longa, and certainly on the west coast when the castle of Port-de-Jonc and other places were acquired. Port-de-Jonc—later more familiar as Navarino—had been built by the Franks about 1290. Venice also held Avramiou, a little N/NE of Nichoria (#100 in Register A, p. 280); though somewhat distant from Koroni, the Venetians had acquired this place early, perhaps in the thirteenth century.

It was an essential feature of Venetian policy to improve cultivation and production in the colonies in "Romania," as the Greek lands were called. We may assume that there was some supervision of irrigation in the Messenian colony, for we know that in Crete and Euboea there was much concern with irrigation and its possibilities. There may have been a counterpart in Messenia to the salaried official, called *potamarcho*, who supervised irrigation in the Lelantine Plain of Euboea. The breeding of cattle, sheep, and chickens was encouraged, and animal pastures were regulated. We learn of limitations on the cutting of trees, not only to assure the supply of timber for ships but also to preserve the soil. The Venetians valued the plain of Methoni especially as grassland for fodder. The demand for fodder was great, and the castellans had instructions to compensate the peasants if they required them to seed their own fields for fodder or if they wanted lumber. The Messenian colony was often deficient in cereals and olive oil; the deficit was usually made up from the production of Crete. This deficiency must have been due to the demands of the metropolis for the products of the Greek colonies, as well as to the requirements of the many ships that called at the two ports. Venice had an estimated 80,000 inhabitants at the end of the fourteenth century. The imports from Greece included wheat, olive oil, wine, table grapes, currants, honey, wax, and cheese. The Venetians were not interested in the production of fruits other than the olive (Thiriet 1959).

We cannot credit the Venetians with any technical improvements in agriculture. The only way they knew to increase production was to attract more hands. The authorities were seriously concerned to keep up the size of the rural population, which in the best of times was in danger of being reduced by earthquakes, plagues, and the ubiquitous Turkish and Catalan pirates in search of slaves. As late as the 1330's the Slavs of Yiannitsa had piratical craft in the Gulf of Messenia. The Senate instructed the castellans of Methoni and Koroni to treat with their lord, the "Great" Zassi.

First Turkish Occupation: 1460–1685. From 1460 to 1685 all of Morea was under Turkish rule except for four ports in Venetian hands: Methoni and Koroni, which fell to the Turks in 1500, and Navplion and Monemvasia, which fell to them in 1540. The Venetians conquered the entire peninsula in 1685–88 and held it until 1715. The second period of Ottoman rule lasted till the outbreak of the Greek Revolution in 1821. There is abundant evidence on the Ottoman and Venetian dominations in the archives of Istanbul and Venice; there are also important Greek materials. Ranke used mainly the reports (*relazioni*) of the Venetian *proveditors* or governors for his monograph (1835), in which he gave some attention to demographic and economic matters. Sakellariou (1939) made full use of the Greek sources and the accounts of travellers in describing landholding, taxation, population, and agricultural productivity in the final century of Turkish rule. From Ottoman sources, only a few demographic data on Greece have thus far been published, by Barkan and Gökbilgin. Alexander and Petropulos are preparing studies on taxation in the early Ottoman period and on the economy and demography of the eighteenth century. The census of 1716 being studied by Petropulos provides, among other data, information on the abandonment of villages and changes from medieval to Turkish place-names. In the present state of knowledge I can present tentative findings on population, land use, and productivity based chiefly on Venetian and Greek materials.

For the first Ottoman occupation (1460–1685) we can at most point to certain trends in population and cite figures from the census taken about 1530. The campaign of conquest of 1460 and the Turco-Venetian war of 1463–79 caused large losses through deaths and deportations. The population of the peninsula may well have been at one of its lowest points about 1480. In 1502–03 Sultan Bayazid II ordered the transfer of heretic Turkomans from Anatolia to Methoni and Koroni. Their number was probably quite small. In general, the Muslim element was never numerous in the Peloponnese; it reached about 10 percent of the population only in the eighteenth century. It is reasonable to suppose that in the half-century 1480–1530 there was some economic recovery and increase in population in Morea under the firm rule that marked the Ottoman Empire at that time.

The census made early (about 1530) in the reign of Suleiman the Magnificent (1520–66) gives us an apparently accurate count of the hearths in the peninsula. Barkan established the following figures according to sects: 1,065 Muslim hearths, 49,412 Christian, and 464 Jewish, or a total of 50,941. Barkan's suggested hearth-coefficient of five is, I believe, too high. Using a multiplier of four, indicated by the Venetian statistics (Addendum, p. 78), the total population would be slightly more than 200,000. The figures presented below for the Venetian period justify assuming that southwest Peloponnese had at least one-fifth of this total, or 40,000 to 45,000.

A century and a half later, on the eve of the Venetian conquest, the Peloponnese was severely depopulated. The statements of travellers along with the earliest Venetian census attest to this fact. A prolonged decline of the Ottoman Empire set in after Suleiman's death and affected every region. Tiepolo, the Venetian ambassador at Constantinople in 1573–76, reported to the Senate that the forced tribute of Christian youths to the Ottoman court and army, along with other exactions, was causing the flight of the inhabitants of provinces like Epirus and Morea that lay near Venetian possessions. The military estates (timars) of Morea lay uncultivated for lack of hands.

Besides the periodical tribute of boys – attested for Morea at least as late as 1667 (Codex Mertzios, p. 61) – the occasional recruiting of foot soldiers for the Venetians in Morea was another drain on its male population. Further losses occurred in abortive revolts of the Moreot Greeks and through migrations, such as those of the Greco-Albanians to Italy and that of the Maniates to Corsica in the 1670's. The Venetian governor of Zante (Zakynthos) in 1646 reported the sultan's order that one male be conscripted for the galleys from every seven houses in the peninsula (Codex Mertzios, p. 48). The exploitation of Morea for the needs of the long war with Venice over Crete (1645–69) was undoubtedly harsh. The governor of Zante in 1658 transmitted information from the French consul at Patras that 800,000 reals for one year had been exacted by the Porte and that the inhabitants were in a state of despair (Codex Mertzios, p. 57). We may compare this with the total income of 536,528 reals from Morea reported for almost the last year (1713–14) of the Venetian occupation (Codex Mertzios, p. 180). It is true that Turkish Morea often supplied Zante with grain, especially from Elis, whose rich plain of Gastouni the Turks were to call "Little Egypt." But it was a submerged peasantry that produced cereals in exportable amounts, to the profit of Turkish landlords and the officials who arranged the transactions.

We would suppose, then, that in the century and more preceding the Venetian conquest there was a serious decline in the population of Morea. This generalization will be confirmed or modified when more data come to light from the Istanbul archives. We know, for example, of a census of Morea in 1642; according to a Venetian dispatch from Zante it was carried out with much skill by a certain Faik Bey (Codex Mertzios, p. 35).

Venetian Rule: 1685–1715; Population Data: 1685–1861. The Venetians took a great interest in their "kingdom" (*regno*) of Morea, which compensated them for the bitter loss of Crete. They did much, naturally, to restore and strengthen its defenses – as at Methoni and Koroni (Andrews 1953). The Venetian officials drew up numerous reports on the actual and potential resources of the country, anticipating in this respect the surveys made by American and international teams in the present kingdom of Greece since 1945. The Senate ordered population counts, a comprehensive cadaster, and the compilation of detailed records of concessions and leases of public lands. Most of these materials exist today in the State Archives of Venice and are a mine of data on the Venetian administration and the condition of the country.

The serious depopulation that we believe already existed before 1685 was intensified by the Venetian conquest (1685–88), which was attended by serious outbreaks of the plague and the flight of many inhabitants. Patras offers an example of the severe destruction. Of its prewar population (one Venetian estimate is an improbable 25,000) only 1,615 persons and 1,452 houses remained in 1688. The first total we have for the peninsula is that of Corner (1691), apparently based on the earliest census, taken or completed in 1689; the figure is 86,468, excluding the district of Corinth and all of Mani. In his report of the same year, no doubt referring to the same census, Michiel records a total of 97,118, excluding only Mani, whose inhabitants refused to reveal their numbers. If we total the figures he gives separately for the provinces and districts, the result is a little higher, namely, 98,885. His estimate of an additional 16,000 to 18,000 for Mani is surely too high. Gradenigo (1692) gives a total of "about 116,000" for the entire peninsula, a number, he comments, too slight for its size and fertility. We assume this figure is still based on the first census. By 1700 the population had reached a total of 176,844, stated by Grimani (1701a) in his relation and also found in the archives. During the 1690's the Venetians invited thousands of Greeks from Athens, Euboea, Crete, Chios, Livadhia, Thebes, and still other districts of central Greece to settle on vacant lands in the Peloponnese. A quarter in Methoni was named Chiótes after the Chiot silkworkers. After the peace of Karlowitz (1699) Naupaktians were invited. This policy, at least as much as any natural increase, accounted for the sizable growth. Grimani considered 200,000 to be closer to the actual total; he blamed the "incredible superstition" of the natives for the concealment of the true figures. We may doubt that the population had really reached 200,000 in 1700. The next census – about 1702 – resulted in a total close to Grimani's estimate: 190,653. The number of families was 48,207. The summary of this census, including the subtotals for the 24 districts into which Morea was then divided, was published by Ranke. I have checked his figures against the manuscript he used and another copy (see Addendum, p. 78). The total thus established for southwest Peloponnese – 44,737 – is about 23.5 percent of 190,653. This total is roughly the same as the figure suggested for about 1530 (p. 70). That the peninsula had not yet returned to a normal state is shown by the fact that 302 destroyed villages were counted, or one-sixth of the total of 1,800 inhabited places.

A portion of the first Venetian census of Morea – that of 1689 – was discovered and published by Lampros (1885). It is of particular interest to us because it is an apparently complete count of the inhabitants of the fiscal province of Methoni on the morrow of the Venetian conquest. This province was one of seven divisions of Morea made at the beginning of the Venetian regime for fiscal purposes (Michiel 1691). These fiscal circumscriptions are distinct from the four large administrative provinces of Venetian Morea (see inset of Pocket Map 5-9). That of Methoni had its treasury (*camera*) in the town of Methoni, and it comprised the districts (*territorii*) of Fanari, Arkadhiá, the two Navarinos ("old" and "new"), and Methoni itself. The total population of the province was only 11,202. Michiel recorded the same figure in his report. Unfortunately, the part of the census of 1689 that covered the fiscal province of Koroni has not come to light. But Michiel's total of 17,122 for this province is without doubt the very figure of the census. (The census was done under Michiel and his colleague Gritti as directors of the census and cadaster.) The province of Koroni embraced the districts of Karitena, Leondari, Kalamata, Andhrousa, and Koroni. Since Karitena, in its entirety, and Leondari, in its greater part, lay outside of our region, we must reduce the figure of 17,122 somewhat to arrive at the total population of southwestern Peloponnese in 1689. If to 11,202 we add about 12,000 for the districts of Kalamata, Andhrousa, and Koroni, and if we add further about a thousand for northwestern Mani, we get a total of some 24,000 for the UMME region. Thus its population increased by about 20,000, or 83⅓ percent, between 1689 and 1702.

Emo (1709) reported a total of 250,000 for the entire peninsula as a result of "calculating the number of villages and families." Sakellariou's figure for 1715, on the eve of the Turkish reconquest, is 270,000. He estimates that 25,000 inhabitants lost their lives in the campaign. From these figures we may infer that in 1715 the population of southwest Peloponnese numbered 50,000 or more.

The century 1715–1821 was on the whole a period of growth and prosperity. Sakellariou estimates that the population of the peninsula in 1770, on the eve of the abortive insurrection against the Turks, was 330,000 (including 30,000 Turks), and in 1820, on the eve of the great rising of 1821, 440,000. An estimated 35,000 lives were lost in the rising of 1770 and from the ravages of the Muslim Albanians throughout the 1770's. Messenia was hardest hit at this time. Besides the heavy loss in lives, the destruction of vines, olives, and mulberries was extensive, and was not yet made up by 1821, as travellers observed.

The war of independence (1821–29) is possibly the most destructive conflict in Greek history. Count Kapodistrias, the president of Greece (1828–31), cooperated with the French Expedition in making a census of the population in 1829. There is some ambiguity in the Expedition's use of the geographical names Upper and Lower Messenia. If we add to the former the eparchy of Fanari (the approximate equivalent of the later eparchy of Olympia), which the French placed under the province of Arkadia, and if we exclude from Lower Messenia the districts of Leondari and western Sparta, we get a total of 57,686. We may increase this to 60,000 or a little more if we add a few hundreds for the Messenian villages included in Leondari and a few thousands for southern Elis and northwest Mani. The figure 57,686 is about 17 percent of the total of 336,366 that the French arrived at for all of the Peloponnese. Messenia was more severely depopulated in 1829 than the interior regions, in part because of the devastation by Ibrahim's Turco-Egyptian army, which was based at Methoni, Koroni, and Navarino.

In 1838, in official figures according to the new nomes, Messenia had 69,737 persons (Mansolas 1867). It is uncertain if the eparchy of Olympia was included. In 1851, in the figures published by Rangavis (II 1853) and obtained from official sources, Messenia without Olympia had 76,492 souls. If we add Rangavis' figure of 21,878 for Olympia, the total for southwestern Peloponnesus is 98,370, or at least 100,000 with northwestern Mani. Finally, in 1861 the nome of Messenia, which now officially included the eparchy of Olympia, had a population of 117,181 (Mansolas). This represented 20.2 percent of the population of the peninsula. This percentage would be a bit larger if we included the population of northwest Mani, bringing us close to the 23.5 percent of about 1702. Thus the population of southwest Peloponnese had doubled between 1829 and 1861. The region grew more in population than any other of the peninsula. Internal migration was an important factor in this increase. Many families in Messenia today trace their origin to ancestors who as shepherds and peasants descended from Arkadian mountain villages to fertile but empty lands there, during the first few decades of the new kingdom (see Ch. 4).

Settlement Patterns under Turks and Venetians. In

1834 Colonel Bory de Saint-Vincent, the head of the French scientific commission to Morea, published an instructive table based on the population of eleven eparchies of Peloponnese in 1829. It shows that the average size of families went up as one ascended in altitude – for example, 4.28 around Nisi, the next-to-the lowest, to 5.34 around Kalavrita, the highest. The French took this as a statistical indication that the lower or plains villages had been more exposed to the ravages of invasion and to disease induced by climate. However, Messenia had so far recovered by 1861 that it had the highest density, except for the islands, in the kingdom of Greece: 36.895 inhabitants per square kilometer (in an area of 3,176 sq. km).

I have noted, for the waning Frankish period (p. 69), an apparent movement of the population to mountainous locations in the interior. Such a movement on a much larger scale – and taking in peninsulas (e.g., Mani) as well – became characteristic of Greece as a whole during the centuries of Ottoman rule. Many hundreds of new settlements thus arose in upland districts. Vakalopoulos (1964) is certain that the determining factor in the process of retreat was political – the desire for freedom from the restrictions and burdens imposed by the Turks; he regards the factors of climate and soil as insignificant. The Turks settled mainly in the plains and towns. Suleiman's census, as interpreted by Barkan, shows that they prevailed numerically over the Greeks in many cities and towns.

The dread of pirates likewise stimulated the movement toward the interior, helping to give the coasts of Morea the deserted appearance that is so often mentioned in the sources. Grimani advocated a system of towers along the coasts that would have communicated by means of *mascoli* (cannons). He saw no limits to the benefits of such a system: intimidating pirates; enabling peasants to till vast stretches of land; stopping contraband and promoting coastal trade; and protecting public health through more effective control of travellers, who might be bearers of the plague.

Outbreaks of the plague in Morea are recorded with such frequency from the time of the Black Death until the end of the eighteenth century that we may regard the disease as endemic in the peninsula for five centuries. The plague must have limited population as much as any single factor. Many healthy peasants who in moments of panic moved to mountain locations to escape the contagion no doubt failed to return to their villages in lower altitudes. The scourge was to reappear during the terrible years of the war of independence.

The historical geography from 1460 to 1821 is too little known as yet to permit illustrating the stages of withdrawal to higher altitudes by a series of maps covering the period, especially its first two centuries. New data from Turkish sources may sometime make this possible. For the end of the Turkish period we have long had the invaluable map of the French Expedition. We now have also the map of Sauerwein (1969), showing the pattern of settlements in Peloponnese about 1700. It uses the list of nearly 1500 villages published by Pacifico (1704). Pocket Map 5-9, showing southwest Peloponnese of this date, is based on Sauerwein's. We have, however, replaced his numbering system with one ordered from south to north within the various districts (*territorii*). Our numbers refer to the lists of phonetically transcribed names printed in Table 5-1. (These numbers, of course, are unrelated to the site numbers used throughout this volume.) No differentiation as to size of settlements has been attempted on Sauerwein's map or ours. Such discrimination will be possible only after the publication of the cadasters of Morea completed under Grimani and other officials (see below).

Certain inferences, however, are possible from Pocket Map 5-9. It shows relatively few settlements on the coasts. The density of villages in the Pamisos Valley and Steniklarian Plain is evident. Turkish place-names –

Table 5–1. Key to Pocket Map 5-9, Settlements about 1700

	Koróni (KR)	
11. Aïdhíni	17. Góna	19. Mistráki
24. Anázogli	41. Ismaïlou	3. Mousoulí
7. Armenií	26. Kakórema	37. Panipéri
42. Avramioú	12. Kandirógli	45. Pelekanádha
14. Ayiandhriádhes	15. Kapláni	36. Péra
6. Áyios Dhimítrios	38. Karakasíli	13. Petriádhes
5. Bótou	34. Kastánia	35. Polistári
30. Chaïkáli	8. Katiniádhes	21. Potamiá
10. Charokopió	22. Klisoúra	33. Romíri
44. Chástemi	4. Koróni	2. Saratsá
43. Chatzalí	9. Kortzógli	25. Soúmbali
16. Chomateró	23. Koutsoumádhi	32. Trípi
29. Dhránga	31. Léfka	20. Váltouka
40. Filippáki	27. Likísa	1. Vasilítsi
28. Gambriá	46. Loï	18. Vounária
	39. Míska	
	Methóni (M)	
3. Agatzíki	21. Kandiliskéri	32. Milióti
19. Apáno Mináyia	18. Káto Mináyia	17. Milítsa
28. Arnaoútali	20. Kinigoú	35. Poléna
26. Chalambréza	34. Kondogóni	1. Pórto-Lóngo
38. Chalvátsou	39. Kouloukádha	36. Poulítsi
25. Chandhrinoú	7. Krivitsá	37. Rádhou
5. Chiótes	6. Lachanádhes	22. Soulinári
15. Chomatádha	8. Lendína	11. Spaï
9. Daoúti	33. Maryéli	40. Tripíla
10. Dhiavatiní	29. Mataránga	30. Vlachópoulo
2. Grízi	14. Mesochóri	31. Vlási
27. Groústesi	16. Memerízi	13. Vrísi
23. Kambási	4. Methóni	12. Zeré
	24. Miliotáki	

Table 5-1. (continued)

6. Polianí	28. Soulári	41. Tsapóga
33. Roútsi	19. Soúli	3. Tsernítsa
30. Samará	38. Stála	10. Vromóvrisi
42. Siálesi	16. Tóskesi	32. Zaïmi
5. Sítsova	13. Tourkoléka	46. Zounáti

Navaríno (N)

17. Agorélitsa	16. Mouzoústa	3. Píla
11. Chasánaga	1. Neókastro (New Navaríno)	10. Pisáski
20. Flóka	8. Níklena	14. Pispísia
15. Kavalariá	5. Palaiókastro (Old Navaríno)	13. Plátanos
6. Koukounára	12. Papoúlia	9. Roustémaga
2. Koúrbeï	7. Petrochóri	19. Skárminga
18. Ligoúdhista		4. Zaïmoglou

Andhroúsa (AN)

56. Agrilóvouno	33. Kinigoú	6. Nisí
17. Aïdhíni	55. Konstandíni	60. Parapoúngi
48. Alitoúri	14. Koukkoráchi	10. Piperítsa
16. Alitselepí	54. Koúrtaga	28. Pondiá
23. Aloupochóri	11. Koúrtali	52. Sandháni
21. Andhroúsa	20. Koutífari	29. Siámari
50. Boúga	30. Lézi	35. Símiza
26. Bournázi	5. Likótrafo	39. Skála
25. Chasámbasa	62. Likoúresi	45. Souláki
2. Dára	53. Málta	12. Spitáli
59. Dhesíla	31. Manganiakó	3. Stréfi
57. Dhiavolítsi	51. Mantzári	58. Trífa
27. Dhraïna	7. Mavromáti	36. Tzeferemíni
19. Dhrongári	37. Mavromáti (Ithome)	1. Tzitzóri
24. Dhroumoúsi	44. Meligalá	13. Vasiládha
8. Gaïdhourochóri	47. Milókastro	15. Vromóvrisi
63. Garántza	4. Misirlí	34. Xerokási
38. Golémi	61. Monastiráki	32. Zagárena
9. Karteróli	46. Moústa	41. Zerbísia
43. Katsaroú	18. Moustafámbasa	42. Zéza
40. Kefalinoú	22. Nazíri	49. Zevgolatió

Kalamáta (KL)

8. Aslánaga	10. Farmísi	6. Kamári
2. Asprócho ma	5. Fourtsála	4. Kourtsaoúsi
9. Baliága	15. Gaïdhourochóri	5a. Mikrománi
18. Básta	17. Gliáta	12. Palaiókastro
13. Bisbárdhi	16. Gortsógli	19. Pídhima
7. Delímemi	1. Kalamáta	11. Veïzaga
	3. Kalámi	14. Vrachátaga

Zarnáta (Z)

9. Árba	3. Liasínova	15. Sélitsa
12. Bíliova	4. Málta	6. Varoúsia
13. Brínda	14. Mikrí Mandínia	17. Yiánnitsa
8. Kámbos	1. Miléa	16. Yiannitsánika
5. Káto Dholí	11. Nerínda	7. Zarnáta
2. Leptíni	10. Orová	

Leondári (L)

17. Alitselepí	45. Dhóriza	2. Ladhá Koutsavá
11. Áno Yiannéï	15. Gardhíki	31. Leondári
7. Arfará	36. Ísari	18. Loutró
9. Bála	14. Kalívia of Tourkoléka	44. Mánari
21. Boúra	12. Káto Yiannéï	24. Memí
20. Chirádhes	43. Kerastári	4. Mikrí Anastásova
23. Chóndalou	27. Klimateró	34. Neochóri
29. Chránou	26. Koúrtaga	25. Panaïti
35. Chroúsa	1. Koutsavá Karvéli	22. Petrína
37. Dhedhémbeï	40. Krambovós	
39. Dherboúni		
8. Dhirráchi		

Arkadhiá (AK)

42. Agalianí	41. Klísoura	21. Raftópoulo
66. Álvena	19. Kloní	45. Rípesi
28. Arkadhiá	56. Koúvela	5. Sapríki
25. Armenií	47. Lápi	31. Sarakinádha
37. Artíki	24. Lendekádha	23. Selá
18. Asoútena	22. Lesovíti	44. Sidherókastro
26. Áyios Ioánnis	20. Likoudhési	52. Sírtzi
65. Bártzeli	10. Mákrena	59. Smarlína
34. Bondiá	27. Maleníti	39. Soúli
14. Chalazóni	17. Máli	48. Soulimá
33. Chrísova	36. Malíki	61. Strovítsi
12. Christiánou	57. Mavromáti	63. Triánda (?)
51. Dhimándhra	11. Mórena	3. Válta
13. Filiatrá	4. Mouzáki	43. Vanádha
60. Gárdhitsa	58. Pávlitsa	32. Varibópi
1. Gargaliáno	6. Pedheménou	7. Veristiá
40. Gliáta	2. Pírgos	35. Vidhísova
64. Golémi	46. Pitsá	49. Vláka
54. Kalítsena	55. Platánia	9. Voútena
15. Kanaloupoú	29. Plemeniánou	67. Vrestó
53. Karamoústafa	16. Podhogorá	30. Vríses
38. Katsoúra	8. Potamiá	62. Zoúrtsa
	50. Psári	

Fanári (F)

48. Agoulinítsa	42. Kalivákia	28. Platiána
47. Aloupochóri	18. Kármi	34. Psathiá
31. Ambária	13. Kopánitsa	46. Rása
8. Ambelióna	27. Koumouthékla	39. Rísovo
16. Andhrítsena	30. Koútsi	17. Róvia
10. Áyios Sóstis	36. Koutsochéra	9. Skliroú
32. Bártzi	44. Kréstena	24. Sklíva
20. Beloúsi	19. Lávdha	1. Stasími
7. Bérekla	5. Linístena	25. Troúpes
33. Bisbárdhi	26. Longó	22. Tzorvatzí
35. Broumázi	45. Makrísia	49. Volántza
6. Dhélga	2. Marína	38. Vrína
4. Dhragóï	21. Mátesi	23. Xerochóri
15. Fanári	41. Mázi	12. Xerokarítena
37. Gréka	40. Moúndritsa	29. Zácha
3. Kakalétri	11. Palátou	14. Zeléchova
	43. Paliofánaro	

Gastoúni (G)

34. Alpochóri	16. Kolíri	11. Plátanos
29. Arvaníti	8. Koúkoura	13. Pournári
20. Áyios Yeóryios	12. Krekoúki	37. Retendoú
27. Básta	1. Lagátoura	30. Rómesi
14. Broúma	24. Lála	19. Skafidhiá
23. Chelidhóni	17. Lambéti	18. Skourochóri
25. Dhoúka	21. Lánthi	10. Smíla
4. Flóka	22. Lantzóï	36. Sópi
39. Goúmero	2. Likoúresi	15. Stravokéfalo
28. Kaloletsí	26. Miliés	9. Stréfi
35. Karátoula	3. Miráka	31. Tzóyia
5. Katákolo	38. Ólena	7. Varvásena
32. Katsaroú	40. Pérsena	33. Xilokéra
	6. Pírgos	

usually derived from the names of the landholders – are more frequent in these fertile plains than in the highlands. At the same time we are impressed by the large number of settlements in the mountainous areas. The pastoral Albanians would have naturally tended to settle in the highlands. The surviving Albanian-speaking villages of our area are in the mountains of the eparchy of Triphylia. The most important of these was Soulima, whose intractable inhabitants maintained a certain independence against the Turks (Michiel). In other highlands – such as those of the eparchy of Olympia – surviving Albanian place-names attest to the presence of former speakers of Albanian (Georgacas and McDonald 1967). But the ubiquitous Albanians were also located in lowlands: thus, Michiel speaks of a sprinkling of their villages in the Steniklarian Plain.

Venetian Land Registers. Besides a census of the population, the Venetians on the morrow of their conquest began a register – a *catastico ordinario* – of the lands of the entire peninsula. The dynamic Grimani (1701a) apparently completed the vast effort during his proveditorship. Various parts of this cadaster are known to exist in Venice and Athens. We have copied from the original in the Venetian archives the portions for the districts of Fanari (completed in 1698) and Kalamata (not dated). Accompanying the latter is a map of the district by the surveyor Francesco Fabretti (see Pocket Map 5-10).

From the Fanari survey Professor Sophia Antoniadis (1966) published in Greek translation the data for three villages, including Agoulinitsa. The Addendum contains the translated text of the description of Agoulinitsa. It consists of the following elements: the limits (*confine*) of the territory of the village; the extent of its arable land, pasture, fishery, and vineyards; the inventory of its churches, houses covered with tiles (*copi*) or thatch (*paglia*), and water sources; and the number of families. The extent of the fields, pasture, fishponds, and vines is expressed in the *campo padovano*, a measure of Padua (see p. 78, col. 2, n. a). The area belonging to Agoulinitsa is described with the help of some fifteen place-names. These designate adjacent villages (Volantza, Zagourouni, Aloupochori), a neighboring district (Gastouni), the Alpheios River, a height (Chondroliyia), a source, a fortification, a ravine, a forest, a threshing floor, and the vineyard of a certain Goumas. A few of these place-names survive today and would help us reconstitute the seventeenth-century boundaries of Agoulinitsa (see Addendum, p. 78).

The village of Zagourouni is recorded as destroyed in the register of 1698. It seems not to have been resettled since, but the name has survived. The large majority of the houses in the Fanari district were covered with thatch. Those covered with tiles were very few. Some fifteen villages, however, had *case coperte di plache*, notably Andhritsena, whose 100 families made it by far the largest village in the district. *Plache* is probably from Greek *plaka* and must have designated plates or slates of local material that are still used to roof houses in mountain villages in the area of Andhritsena. It is notable that Andhritsena had twice as much pastureland (4,107 Paduan *campi*) as arable (2,050 *campi*); it also had large vineyards, 2,100 mulberries, and 30 springs.

Also reproduced in the Addendum is the description, in translation, of the boundaries and lands of the village or town of Kalamata in the 1690's. Unfortunately, the number of families and certain other data were omitted from this text. A valuable datum in this description, also confirmed by the map of the entire Kalamata district, is the existence of a sizable forest of poplars around the delta of the Nedhon (named *fiume Calamatianò* on the map). The inhabitants of Kalamata had a very large territory at their disposal: it extended to the boundaries of Mani and the Leondari district on the east and northeast and included an area of mountain pasture even larger than its extensive arable fields in the plain. Only a small proportion of the houses in the entire Kalamata district were thatched; all the rest were covered with tiles. In the description of Pidhima nine mills are recorded at the point where the Magnaticò River issued. This stream, now named the river of Aris (formerly Aslanaga), is here called after the village of Mikromani. The map, too, records the mills of Pidhima. In the description of the villages of Gliata, Basta, and Chortzogli a large pasture in the swampy plain was recorded: this is marked on the Venetian map as *loco paludoso*, lying between these villages and the Ayios Floros sources. This swamp was exploited in more recent times by the inhabitants of Basta (now Plati), Skala, Tzeferemini (now Valira), and the modern village of Ayios Floros. Buffaloes (*vouvália*) used to be brought from Elis in the late spring each year to trample on the plants of the swamp and thereby make the water from it overflow into the Pamisos River.

Grimani (1701b) considered the original cadaster not sufficiently detailed. He wanted a register of individual holdings to determine what public lands had been usurped. With the approval of the home authorities he began a more detailed survey – a *catastico particolare* – and reported completing the portions for the district of Vostitsa (now Aiyion) and for two-thirds of that of Tripolitsa (now Tripolis). He likewise ordered the new survey for the districts of Navarino, Arkadhiá, and Methoni. We do not know if his successors brought this to completion.

The Land and Its Products: 1685–1715. In the absence of more information from the land registers of southwest Peloponnese we must search the *relazioni* and other printed sources for details on the appearance of the land and on its use. Thus Michiel mentions the forest of pines on the coast near Kaïafa and that of oaks in the border area of the districts of Koroni and Andhrousa. The latter is also noted by Pacifico as a "large forest" called after the village of Miska (now Neromilos) in its midst. Grimani sent home special dispatches on the forests. A forester at his order marked about 70,000 trees in the peninsula for the use of the Arsenal. Grimani laid down many regulations for the sound management of the forests and had an expert set up saws run by waterpower to cut boards for the fleet. Gradenigo stressed the unsuitability of the timber of Morea for manufacture and believed the smallness of the boards limited the size of rooms and houses. He pointed out that very little firewood could be transported on the appalling roads; in some places the inhabitants used the dung of oxen and buffaloes for fuel. He urged the introduction of wagons – once a few passable roads had been built – to move the baggage and provisions of Venetian civil and military servants, in order to relieve the peasants and their pack animals of an onerous service. Grimani speaks of timber for construction in Methoni coming by sea from the "nearby" forest of Kaïafa. No doubt such transport was much easier than bringing out lumber from the roadless interior of the Messenian peninsula.

The relation of Michiel furnishes other interesting details. He records a forest of oaks at Katakolo five Venetian miles in length and two in width. He reports that it was leased and that wood from it was sent to Zante to be made into boxes for currants. A remnant of this forest exists today near the monastery of Skafidhia. The Steniklarian Plain, for all its fertility, was only half cultivated. The Pamisos Plain was flooded every winter, doing great damage; there was a large fishery at its mouth. The fishery of the Osmanaga Lagoon was in wretched state, and the salt pans of Methoni were only partly exploited. Michiel listed the following products: cereals (including maize), olive oil, wine, flax, linseed, wool, cotton, cheese, honey, wax, valonia, cochineal, cordovan leathers, large and small cattle, silk, figs, and tobacco. Andhrousa and Nisi had the finest wines. The plain of Nisi also produced cotton. Gradenigo recommended the planting of rice in this plain; he thus anticipated the cultivation of rice here in recent years. Grimani cautioned that valonia oaks should not be cut down, so as not to lose the duty collected on the exported acorns.

Stoianovich (1962, 1966) and Kremmidas (1969) have considered the question of the "arrival" of maize in the Balkans, including Peloponnese. Evidence in Venetian documents persuades me that it was introduced into Morea, in one or more varieties, sometime before the Venetian conquest, perhaps as early as the sixteenth century. The practice of planting it on inundated land, in the midsummer after the water has finally drained itself away, may go back to the early Turkish period. This was done, for example, in the marsh of Aslanaga (now Aris) till recently. Referring to the plain of Tripolitsa, Leake remarked that maize cultivation was the cause of flooded land being allowed to remain under water for many months.

The Venetians were disappointed in their hopes of increasing agricultural production significantly through generous distribution of the vast uncultivated public lands. Emo stressed that by uncultivated lands (*campagne d'incolti*) he did not mean mountains, flooded areas, forests, and swamps that could be redeemed only with much time and expense; rather they were extensive lands that for years had not produced simply for lack of hands to work them. Grimani believed that the recipients of such lands should have been required, under severe penalties, to plant vines, olives, and mulberries. Instead, they exhausted the lands for quick gain, presumably by raising exportable cereals. A notable increase in the production of currants and wine was brought about, thanks to the introduction of vines from abroad and the imposition of a heavy duty on imported wines.

If the Venetians had considerable success in repeopling the peninsula and in certain agricultural sectors, like viticulture, in other respects their economic policies were a failure. The proveditors themselves condemn the trade monopoly enjoyed by the Venetian merchants, contrasting their government's mercantilist restrictions with the freer trade allowed by the Turks. There was also the exhausting burden on the peasantry of maintaining the dragoons and their horses. Much meadowland, like that of Kalamata, was kept in grass for the horses. Villages throughout Peloponnese were assessed quotas of barley for the dragoons' mounts. Emo describes the peasants as having bodies badly afflicted and weak from long infirmity. He urged cancellation of their debts, to save the land from possible depopulation. Emo likewise describes the Albanians as a wretched people huddled with their families in mountainous recesses in mean hovels. In 1805 Leake still found the inhabitants of Mavromati (Ithome) living in huts.

Çiftlik Regime. Yield Ratios. The agricultural potential of Morea – on which the Venetians so often remarked – was not to be realized before the twentieth century. In technique the Moreots were still very backward at the end of the eighteenth century, as Scrofani observed. Allowing fields to lie fallow was their entire science of cultivation. Fertilizer was used for currants alone. Yet Scrofani was impressed by the "grande prédilection pour les eaux" of both Greeks and Turks. "The Moreots can with skill and without losing any part of it conduct, make level and distribute the water in a space of eight, ten, and even twenty miles." A likely example of such a complex construction is the irrigation system – about 8,500 m long – that waters the plain of Pila. Oral tradition ascribes this work to the Turkish period. The cementing of sections of it in recent years has prolonged its utility.

In general, under the regime of exploitation by means of the large agricultural estate – the *çiftlik* – in the Balkans between the end of the sixteenth and the beginning of the nineteenth century, garden cultivation and an irrigation economy were more widely diffused. The *çiftlik* regime stimulated more widespread planting of rice, cotton, and maize (Stoianovich 1953). In regard to the availability of water in Messenia almost three centuries ago, we note a detail from Locatelli's history of Morosini's campaigns (1691). In June 1685, as the fleet was on its way to attack Koroni, just having passed Sapientza, it stopped at the Lecamada River, five Venetian miles from Methoni, to take on supplies of water. This was without any doubt the river of Lachanadha.

Scrofani reported a yield ratio for wheat of seven to one and between four and five to one in the case of other cereals; he was generalizing about Peloponnese. Leake recorded the following ratios, all for wheat: three or four to one in the highest villages of Taygetos; ten to one in most of the fertile parts of Mani; ten to one – a common yield – in the best lands of Messenia, sometimes twenty to one and with irrigation even more. These are higher ratios than those of the fourteenth century (above, p. 67) in the Acciaiuoli villages. Together with the high yield of the newer crop, maize – for example, thirty or forty to one in Elis (Leake) – they help to explain the greater density of population in the late eighteenth and the beginning of the nineteenth century.

Effects of Human Occupation. Almost a century and a half ago, Emile Le Puillon de Boblaye (1833) remarked on the profound effects of man's action on the Peloponnesian landscape. The changes wrought by man since remote antiquity deeply impressed this member of the French scientific mission to Morea, a skilled surveyor and geologist as well as a learned historical geographer. The surface layer of the soil, he observed, had become a veritable human product after three millennia of cultivation. Ceramic debris and the remains of men and animals had become constituent parts of the soil. The denuding of the uplands had long been a scourge. De Boblaye saw the industrious Maniates of the Zarnata district struggle, through terraces, to hold back on their steep hillsides the remnant of the soil. Far more earth had been washed into the gulfs of Morea since the age of man began than had come down throughout the rest of the present geologic era.

De Boblaye deplored the shepherds' "barbarous" practice of burning trees and bushes on mountains to provide pasture for their flocks. He would not believe that this had been allowed in a more civilized ancient Greece. With the destruction of the forest cover, springs had dried up and torrents had devastated much of the plains. Certain direct changes made by man – tombs cut into the rock and enormous limestone quarries, like those near Methoni – were ineffaceable. But de Boblaye was truly awed by the thought of the "indestructible testimonies" buried in the seas. "What a mass of human remains and of the debris of the industry of all the ages," he exclaimed, "has not the roadstead of Navarino alone . . . swallowed up over the last thirty centuries!" If a natural upheaval, he concluded, were to lift up from the sea the remains of man and his works, veritable archives of the history of his species would be revealed.

Summary. For the long period treated herein it is evident that southwest Peloponnese experienced many fluctuations in the numbers of its inhabitants along with slow but profound change in its land surface. The area was bound to be affected by the over-all decline in population in the Roman Empire after the third century, the barbarian invasions, and the catastrophic plague that began in A.D. 541. Yet the Slav invaders must have made up part of the loss in population. The province knew a measure of prosperity when the Byzantine Empire was at its strongest in the ninth to eleventh centuries, and again in the first century of Frankish rule. But decline soon set in again. The fiscal censuses of five Messenian villages reflect the ravages of the Black Death in the region. The depopulation of the fourteenth and fifteenth centuries in Morea in general was partly made up by numerous Albanian settlers. I am inclined to believe that the estimate of 40,000 to 45,000 inhabitants about 1530 is as high a total as the area ever reached from late antiquity until the eighteenth century. Although the increase in both population and productivity has been severalfold from 1715 to the present, the risings of 1770 and 1821, both of which brought vast destruction upon Messenia, illustrate how vulnerable this naturally rich but exposed area has been throughout history.

Addendum. Materials from Venetian Documents

The Population of Morea about 1702

SOURCE: Codice Cicogna, Biblioteca Civico Museo Correr, no. 3248. The table published by Ranke at the end of *Die Venezianer in Morea* is identical, except for minor discrepancies. This census has a connection with the data in Pacifico (1704): he prints the same figures for the number of villages by district.

Summary of the Four Provinces of the Kingdom of Morea

Provinces	Districts (*territorii*)	Villages	Destroyed Villages	Families	No. of People
Romania	5	255	80	9,557	40,829
Achaia	4	419	100	11,445	49,491
Messenia	9	564	72	13,438	54,073
Laconia	6	260	50	11,717	46,260
Totals	24	1,498	302	46,157	190,653

The Nine Districts of Venetian Messenia

District	Villages	Families	No. of People
Navarin	25	512	2,068
Modon	51	664	2,679
Coron	62	1,127	4,295
Andrussa	66	1,600	6,642
Calamata	24	1,228	4,801
Leondari	60	1,257	4,891
Caritena	124	3,030	12,271
Fanari	64	1,458	6,268
Arcadia (= Kyparissia)	88	2,562	10,222
Totals	564	13,438	54,137

Calculation of Population of Southwest Peloponnese

District	People	District	People
Navarin	2,068	Caritena[a]	...
Modon	2,679	Fanari	6,268
Coron	4,295	Arcadia	10,222
Andrussa	6,642	Gastuni[b]	3,940
Calamata	4,801	Zarnata[c]	3,166
Leondari[d]	656	Total	44,737

[a] Caritena is entirely outside southwest Peloponnese as defined by UMME.

[b] Forty villages of Gastuni are in the UMME portion of Elis; the average size of a village is 98.5 inhabitants; 40 × 98.5 = 3,940.

[c] Sixteen (half) of the Zarnata villages are in the UMME portion of Mani. Zarnata district total in Codice Cicogna: 6,332.

[d] Only eight of the 60 villages of Leondari belong to what is now Messenia; the average size of a village is 82 inhabitants; 8 × 82 = 656.

Description of Agoulinitsa

SOURCE: Archivio di Stato, Venice, Archivio Grimani, busta 51, fasc. 144.

The village of Agoulinítsa [consists of] arable fields in the plain, pasture lands in wooded hills and in a forest called Sendoúki, a fishery, and a vineyard. Its limits on the east are: the village of Volántza at the ravine of Bousalá, the mountain of Chondroliyiá, the source of Áyios Yeóryios, Yiftókastro, and a *luro* which falls into the Alfiós river; on the north, the river Alfiós and district of Gastoúni; on the west, the sea; on the south, the ruined village of Zagouroúni, the village of Aloupochóri at the point Bósi, a boundary stone placed above the fishery, the ruined village of Zagouroúni and the said boundary stone and Longofrázeri, *Licori*, Paliálona, Goúmas' vineyard, and the ravine of Bousalá.

Arable land in the plain	4,560	campi,[a]	220 tavole[b]
Pasture lands in wooded hills	693	campi,	140 tavole
Pasture lands and forest Sendoúki	313¼	campi,	170 tavole
Fishery	790½	campi,	180 tavole
Vineyards: 95 zapade[c] and 36 tavole making	17½	campi,	156 tavole
Sound churches	4		
Ruined churches	8		
Houses with tiles	3		
Houses of thatch	41		
Families	44		
Sources	2		
Well	1		

[a] *campi*, i.e., *campi padovani*, pl. of *campo padovano*, 1,710 sq. m in extent, or 42.25 percent of an acre. We have calculated its extent from the following data. The stremma, the basic Greek surface measure, is generally assumed to have consisted of 1,270 sq. m in the Venetian and Turkish periods. From the statistics given in Grimani's relation (1701a, p. 500) it is clear that the stremma constituted 74.4 or 74.5 percent of a campo. (The "new" stremma of the modern Greek kingdom = 1,000 sq. m.)

[b] *tavola* (sing.), unit of measure of Padua. 840 sq. tavole made up one campo padovano.

[c] *zapada* (sing.) denoted the area of a vineyard that a person could hoe in a day (*zapa* or *zappa* = hoe). The Venetian surveyor, G. Mattiazzi, in the Gastouni district in 1689, defined the zapada as consisting of 266 sq. tavole. This is the equivalent of 542 sq. m, or 13.4 percent of an acre. We note, however, that by this definition the 95 zapade and 36 tavole of Agoulinitsa should have amounted to about 30 campi, not the 17½ campi and 156 tavole stated here. A smaller zapada in the Fanari district, to which Agoulinitsa belonged, is not to be excluded. In Elis and Messenia today a laborer can hoe about half of a new stremma or a little more, i.e., 500 to 550 sq. m. (Mattiazzi's definition of the zapada is found in a description he drew up of the land measures used in the district of Gastouni. It is in volume 863 (860), entitled Lettere dei Commissari del Regno di Morea Sindici Catasticatori Domenico Gritti, Michiel Marin, Girol. Renier 3 lug. 1688–12 marz. 1691, in the series Provveditori da Terra e da Mar no. 321, Archivio di Stato, Venice.)

Description of Kalamata

SOURCE: Archivio di Stato, Venice, Archivio Grimani, busta 51, fasc. 146.

Kalamáta [consists of] arable fields in the plain, rocky and wooded mountain-pastures, a forest of poplars in the plain, and vineyards. On the east it borders on Máni and the village of Polianí of the district of Leondári, on the valley of the Xeropótamos, and the public road; and Áyioi Pándes borders on Máni, and from the aforesaid Áyioi Pándes the monastery of Áyios Ilías *lifero*; and the mountain of Kiriákos borders on the village of Polianí. On the north it borders on the aforesaid village of Polianí, from the aforesaid mountain of Kiriákos. On the west it borders on the villages of Kourtsaoúsi, Aïzaga, Kalamáki and Aspróchoma, at the aforesaid mountain of Kiriákos, Katovounó, Mavrospiliá; and the public road borders on the villages of Kourtsaoúsi, Aïzaga and Kalamáki, and from the aforesaid public road the church of Áyios Yeóryios; the church of Áyia Kiriakí borders on the village of Aspróchoma. On the south it has the sea.

Arable lands in the plain	6,000 campi
Rocky and wooded mountain-pastures	7,000¾ campi, 30 tavole
Forest of poplars in the plain	1,651¼ campi, 90 tavole

Zapade of vineyards, olive orchards, mulberries, sound churches, houses with tiles, families, oil presses: [numbers blank].

REFERENCES

NOTE: This list includes a few publications not specifically cited in Ch. 5 — e.g., certain of the relations of proveditors. It is not, however, meant to be a complete bibliography.

Archival Sources (Venice)

Archivio di Stato. Archivio Grimani busta 51, fascicoli 144 and 146.

Biblioteca Civico Museo Correr. Codice Cicogna, No. 3248.

Biblioteca Nazionale Marciana. MS. it. VII, 656 (= 7791), fol. 57–71.

Archivio di Stato and other collections. "Codex Mertzios." This label covers about 300 pages of typewritten data compiled in 1957 by K. D. Mertzios of Venice, corresponding member of the Academy of Athens, at the request of the mayor of Patras. Cf. K. N. Triandafillou, *Historikon lexikon tōn Patrōn* (Patras, 1959), *passim*. The material relates particularly to Patras, also to Achaia, Elis, the Ionian Islands, and occasionally Messenia, during 1595–1794. Available in the public library of Patras and on microfilm in the Gennadeion at Athens.

Published Documents, Books, and Articles

Andrews, Kevin. 1953. *Castles of the Morea.* Gennadeion Monographs No. 4. American School of Classical Studies at Athens, Princeton, N.J.

Antoniadis, Sophia A. 1966. "Symbolē stēn historian tēs Peloponnēsou kata ton 17on aiōna. To archeion Grimani" (Contribution to the History of Peloponnesus in the Seventeenth Century. The Grimani Archive). *Charistērion eis Anastasion K. Orlandon*, 3:153–65 (Athens).

Antoniadis-Bibicou, Hélène. 1966. "Villages désertés en Grèce. Un bilan provisoire." *Villages désertés et histoire économique XIe–XVIIIe siècle*, pp. 343–417. École pratique des hautes études, VIe sect. Les Hommes et la Terre, XI. Paris: S.E.V.P.E.N.

Barkan, Ö. L. 1957. "Essai sur les données statistiques des registres de recensement dans l'Empire Ottoman aux XVe et XVIe siècles." *Journal of the Economic and Social History of the Orient* 1:9–36.

de Boblaye, Emile le Puillon, and Virlet, Théodore. 1833. *Expedition scientifique de Morée. Section des sciences physiques*, Vol. 2, Pt. 2. *Géologie et minéralogie.* Paris. Pp. 372–75, summarized above (p. 77), are by de Boblaye.

Bon, Antoine. 1951. *Le Péloponnèse byzantin jusqu'en 1204.* Paris.

———. 1969. *La Morée franque. Recherches historiques, topographiques et archéologiques sur la principauté d'Achaïe (1205–1430).* 2 vols., text and album. Paris.

Bory de Saint-Vincent, J. B. G. M. 1834. *Expédition scientifique de Morée. Section des sciences physiques*, Vol. 2, Pt. 1. *Géographie. Paris.* The reference above (p. 73) is to p. 61 of this work, based on the data of de Boblaye.

Carpenter, Rhys. 1966. *Discontinuity in Greek Civilization.* Cambridge. Paperback ed. with afterword, New York: Norton Library, 1968.

Charanis, Peter. 1970. "Observations on the History of Greece during the Early Middle Ages." *Balkan Studies* 11:1–34. Thessaloniki.

Chronicle of Morea. 1904. *To Chronikon tou Moreōs. A History in Political Verse . . .* , ed. John Schmitt. London.

Georgacas, D. J., and McDonald, W. A. 1967. *Place Names of Southwest Peloponnesus. Register and Indexes.* Athens and Minneapolis.

Gökbilgin, M. Tayyib. 1956. "Kanuni Sultan Süleyman devri başlarinda Rumeli eyaleti, livalari, şehir ve kasabalari." *Belleten Türk Tarih Kurumu* 20:247–85. French summary, 287–94.

Kremmidas, V. 1969. "Eisagogē kai diadosē tēs kalliergeias tou arabositou stēn Peloponnēson" (Introduction and Spread of Maize Cultivation in Peloponnesus). *Hellēnika* 22:389–98.

Kunze, E. 1955. "Die Ausgrabungen in Olympia im Winter 1954/55." *Gnomon* 27:220–24.

Lampros, Spyridon P. 1884. "Ta archeia tēs Benetias kai hē peri Peloponnēsou ekthesis tou Marinou Mikiel" (The Archives of Venice and Marin Michiel's Relation on Peloponnesus). In his *Historika meletēmata*, pp. 173–220. Athens.

———. 1885. "Apographē tou nomou Methonēs epi Benetōn" (Census of the Province of Methone under the Venetians). *Deltion tēs Historikēs kai Ethnologikēs Hetairias tēs Hellados* 2:686–710, and map.

Leake, W. M. 1830. *Travels in Morea.* 3 vols. London.

Lemerle, Paul. 1963. "La chronique improprement dite de Monemvasie: le contexte historique et légendaire." *Revue des Études Byzantines* 21:5–49.

Locatelli, Alessandro. 1691. *Racconto historico della Veneta Guerra in Levante diretta dal valore del Serenissimo Principe Francesco Morosini . . . dall' anno 1684 fino all' anno 1690. Con li adornamenti delle piante del P. M. Vincenzo Coronelli.* Cologne. 2 pts. in 1 vol.

Longnon, Jean, and Topping, Peter. 1969. *Documents sur le régime des terres dans la principauté de Morée au XIVe siècle.* Documents et recherches sur l'économie des pays byzantins, islamiques et slaves . . . , IX. École pratique des hautes études, VIe section. Paris and The Hague.

Magno, Stefano. 1873. *Annali veneti.* In *Chroniques gréco-romanes inédites ou peu connues*, ed. Charles Hopf, pp. 179–209. Berlin.

Mansolas, Alexandros. 1867. *Politeiographikai plērophoriai peri Hellados* (Socioeconomic data on Greece). Athens.

Pacifico, Pier' Antonio. 1704. *Breve descrizzione corografica del Peloponneso o Morea . . . estratta dal volume di D. Pier' Antonio Pacifico.* Venice.

Rangavis, I. R. 1853. *Ta hellēnika, ētoi perigraphē geographikē, historikē, archaiologikē, kai statistikē tēs archaias kai neas Hellados* (Hellenica, viz., Geographical, Historical, Archaeological, and Statistical Description of Ancient and Modern Greece), Vol. 2. 3 vols. Athens, 1853–54.

Ranke, Leopold. 1835. *Die Venezianer in Morea 1685–1715. Historisch-politische Zeitschrift*, Vol. 2, Pt. 3, pp. 405–501, statistical table, p. 502. Berlin.

Relations or reports (relazioni) read in the Senate of Venice at the end of service in Morea by governors (proveditori) and other officials. Place and date of composition, when known, are given here, otherwise the date read.

Michiel. 1691. Marin Michiel, sindico catasticator in Morea, 1688–91. Dated at Coron, 12 May 1691. Edited by S. P. Lampros, *Historika meletēmata*, Athens, 1884, 199–220.

Corner. 1691. Giacomo Corner, proveditor general in Morea, 1688–90. Dated at Lazareto Vecchio, 23 Jan. 1690 (= 1691). Edited by S. P. Lampros, *Deltion tēs historikēs kai ethnologikēs hetairias tēs Hellados* 2 (1885):293–317. Athens.

Gritti. 1691. Domenico Gritti, sindico catasticator in Morea, 1688–91. Read in the Senate "in the year 1691." Published in Greek translation by P. Chiotis, *Philistor* 2 (1862):219–30. Athens. The translation is defective. Original in Biblioteca Nazionale Marciana, MS. it. VII, 656 (= 7791), fol. 57–71.

Gradenigo. 1692. Tadio Gradenigo, proveditor estraordinario in Morea, 1690–92. Dated at Venice, 8 March 1692. Edited by Lampros, *Deltion tēs historikēs kai ethnologikēs hetairias tēs Hellados* 5 (1900):230–51.

Molin. 1693. Antonio Molin, proveditor estraordinario in Morea, 1692–93. (Molin is also called proveditor general.) Read on 30 May 1693. Ed. Lampros, *ibid.*, 429–47.

Grimani. 1701a. Francesco Grimani, proveditor general dell' armi in Morea, 1698–1701. Dated without place, 6 Sept. 1701. Ed. Lampros, *ibid.*, 448–532.

———. 1701b. Informatione written to Giacomo da Mosto, prov. gen. dell' armi in Morea. Dated Modon, 19 Jan. 1708 [sic in printed text; = 1701]. Ed. Lampros, *ibid.*, 533–61.

Da Mosto. 1703. Giacomo da Mosto, prov. gen. dell' armi in Morea, 1700–1703. Lacks title and date. Ed. Lampros, *ibid.*, 561–67.

Emo. 1709. Angelo Emo, prov. gen. in Morea, 1705–1708. Dated Venice, 18 Jan. 1708 (= 1709). Ed. Lampros, *ibid.*, 644–706.

Loredan. 1711a. Informatione written by Marco Loredan, prov. gen. dell' armi in Morea, 1708–1711, to his successor, Antonio Loredan. Dated at Modon, 20 Sept. 1711. Ed. Lampros, *ibid.*, 715–35.

———. 1711b. Marco Loredan, prov. gen. dell' armi in Morea, 1708–1711. Dated at Venice, 11 Dec. 1711. Ed. Lampros, *ibid.*, 707–14.

Sagredo. 1714. Agostino Sagredo, prov. gen. da mar, 1712(?)–14. Dated at Venice, 20 Nov. 1714. Ed. Lampros, *ibid.*, 736–65.

Russell, J. C. 1958. "Late Ancient and Medieval Population." *Transactions of the American Philosophical Society* n.s. Vol. 48, Pt. 3. Philadelphia, June 1958.

Sakellariou, Michael B. 1939. *Hē Peloponnēsos kata tēn deuteran Tourkokratian (1715–1821).* (Peloponnesus during the Second Turkish Domination.) Texte und Forschungen zur byzantinisch-neugriechischen Philologie, No. 33. Athens: Byzantinisch-Neugriechischen Jahrbücher.

Sathas, C. N., ed. 1881. *Documents inédits relatifs à l'histoire de la Grèce au moyen âge*, Vol. 2. 9 vols. Paris, 1880–90.

Sauerwein, Friedrich. 1969. "Das Siedlungsbild der Peloponnes um das Jahr 1700. Mit einer Karte und einem Ortsverzeichnis." *Erdkunde* 23:237–44, and Ortsverzeichnis, [11] pp.

Scrofani, Xavier. 1801. *Voyage en Grèce de Xavier Scrofani, Sicilien, fait en 1794 et 1795.* Translated from Italian. 3 vols. Paris and Strasbourg.

Stadtmüller, Georg. 1944. Chapter, "Die Geschichte," in *Der Peloponnes. Landschaft, Geschichte, Kunststätten.* Von Soldaten für Soldaten. Hrsg. v. einem Generalkommando. Pp. 42–158. Athens.

Stoianovich, Traian. 1953. "Land Tenure and Related Sectors of the Balkan Economy, 1600–1800." *Journal of Economic History* 13:398–411.

———. 1962. "Le maïs arrive dans les Balkans" (Pt. A). *Annales (Économies, Sociétés, Civilisations)* 17:84–87.

———. 1966. "Le maïs dans les Balkans." *Ibid.* 21:1026–40.

Thiriet, Freddy. 1959. *La Romanie vénitienne au moyen âge. Le développement et l'exploitation du domaine colonial vénitien (XIIe–XVe siècles).* Bibliothèque des Écoles Françaises d'Athènes et de Rome, fasc. 193. Paris.

Tiepolo, Antonio. 1576. Bailo in Constantinople, 1573–76. Relation read in Senate, 9 June 1576. Ed. by Eugenio Albèri. *Relazioni degli ambasciatori veneti al Senato*, Ser. III^a, Vol. II°. Florence, 1844.

Topping, Peter. 1966. "A Frankish Estate near the Bay of Navarino." *Hesperia* 35:427–36.

Vakalopoulos, Apostolos. 1964. *Historia tou neou hellēnismou* (History of the Modern Greek People), Vol. 2. 3 vols. to date. Thessaloniki, 1961, 1964, 1968.

Valmin, M. N. 1930. *Études topographiques sur la Messénie ancienne.* Lund.

Vasmer, Max. 1941. *Die Slaven in Griechenland. Mit einer Karte.* Abhandlungen der Preussischen Akademie der Wissenschaften Jahrgang 1941. Phil.-hist. Klasse. No. 12. Berlin.

Wright, H. E., Jr. 1968. "Climatic Change in Mycenaean Greece." *Antiquity* 42:123–27.

Zakythinos, D. A. 1953. *Le despotat grec de Morée*, Vol. 1, *Histoire politique* (Paris, 1932), Vol. 2, *Vie et institutions* (Athens, 1953).

———. 1966. "La grande brèche dans la tradition historique de l'hellénisme du septième au neuvième siècle." *Charistērion eis Anastasion K. Orlandon* 3:300–27. Athens.

Research in Progress

Alexander, John, Ph.D. candidate in history, Columbia University. Thesis on Ottoman taxation in the area approximately of present-day Greece, late fifteenth to early seventeenth century. Investigation based mainly on the codes (*kānūnnāmes*) of the provincial detailed registers (*sancak mufassal defters*).

Petropulos, John, professor of history, Amherst College. Investigation of Ottoman fiscal censuses of Morea, of the period preceding the Venetian occupation of 1685–1715 and, in particular, of the year 1716. These detailed registers (*mufassal defters*) provide, besides tax data, precise information on agricultural production.

6

GRECO-ROMAN TIMES: LITERARY TRADITION AND TOPOGRAPHICAL COMMENTARY

by

John Francis Lazenby and Richard Hope Simpson

The sources for the history of southwest Peloponnese between the end of the Mycenaean Age and the beginning of the Byzantine era (roughly, from the eleventh century B.C. to the fourth century A.D.) consist mainly of passing references by ancient writers and sporadic inscriptions. To these must be added the archaeological evidence (summarized in Ch. 8 and in Register B, Appendix, p. 310). But attempts at the reconstruction of the basic economy of the area within this period are limited by the following considerations. Firstly, we lack even the kind of incomplete records available for both the Mycenaean and medieval periods regarding agricultural produce and organization. Secondly, the archaeological surveys carried out in the region are incomplete for this period; and many of the sites, being actually in the plains and thus often hidden beneath alluvium, cannot always be detected, let alone correctly assessed, by surface indications alone. Thus, the archaeological evidence, if taken by itself, might yield a partially distorted picture. Thirdly, the ancient historians are mainly concerned with *political* history, and not primarily with economic matters, or indeed with the history of Southwest Peloponnese at all.

For these reasons, it is not possible to present a balanced picture of the ecology and demography of the area during this period. An attempt will, however, be made to systematize our knowledge of Messenia in relation to the main historical events of the period, and to comment on the distribution and topography of the known settlements in the subperiods concerned (Protogeometric to Roman).

THE LITERARY TRADITION (BY J. F. L.)

The surviving literary evidence for the history of Messenia before the fourth century B.C. is extremely scanty. What the ancients knew or thought they knew about it is most systematically set out in the fourth book of Pausanias' *Description of Greece*, written in the second century A.D., but it is doubtful how much reliance can be placed upon this account, both because there is so little earlier evidence by which to check it and because, where there is other evidence, Pausanias often seems to have made mistakes. Earlier than Pausanias, there are scattered references in Strabo's *Geography*, written at the time of Augustus; in the history of Diodoros the Sicilian, who wrote a little before Strabo; in the works of Herodotus and Thucydides of the fifth century B.C.; and in the fragments of the poems of Tyrtaios, the Spartan poet of the seventh century B.C. And that is about all.

The reason is quite simple. To begin with, we have very little evidence for the history of Greece as a whole before the sixth century, and by that time Messenia had passed under Spartan control. Thus, in effect, Messenia had ceased to have a history of her own before the Greeks had really begun to inquire into their own past. But, in addition, the Spartans were extremely reticent and secretive, not to say downright mendacious, even about their own affairs, and this naturally applied, to a greater degree, to the subject peoples over whom they ruled. Thus it was only when the Messenians were in revolt that the rest of the Greek world really heard anything about them; and even then, as we can see in the case of the alleged revolt of about 490 B.C. (see below, pp. 86–87), there is much doubt about the truth.

But about 370 B.C. the picture gradually changes: the Messenians were freed from Spartan control, and we know much more about them and their affairs thereafter until Messenia, like the rest of Greece, came under the rule of Rome. For this period we have the *Hellenica* of Xenophon, the much more detailed references of Diodoros, the relevant biographies of Plutarch, and above all, from 220 B.C. onwards, the invaluable testimony of Polybius who wrote during the second century B.C. From these and other sources, including inscriptions, a detailed and trustworthy account of Messenian history can be worked out; and this has been ably done by C. A. Roebuck (1941) in his *History of Messenia from 369 to 146 B.C.* After 146 B.C. Messenia, together with the rest of Greece, in effect came under Roman control, and there is very little information about it thereafter, although the writings of Strabo and Pausanias tell us something about it in the reign of Augustus and in the second century A.D., respectively.

It must be borne in mind, then, that almost anything that is said about the history of Messenia before 370 B.C. is seriously open to question, and so scanty and untrustworthy is our evidence that it might not seem worthwhile to attempt the task at all. Nevertheless, there is some point in at least seeing what ancient writers have to say about the early history of Messenia, and this is what this chapter sets out to do. When we come to the period after 370 B.C., however, we shall merely summarize what is generally known, emphasizing certain factors that emerge.

The earliest references to Messenia in Greek literature occur, of course, in the Homeric poems, but the picture they present is, unfortunately, very unclear (see Fig. 6-1). In the west, according to the "Catalogue of the Ships" (*Iliad* 2. 591–602), Nestor ruled a kingdom stretching from the River Alpheios in the north to Pylos in the south, with its eastern frontier not necessarily further east than Dorion (Malthi). Around the Gulf of Messenia lay the Seven Cities which Agamemnon offered to Achilles (*Iliad* 9. 149f., cf. 291f.), and which are therefore implied to have come under his authority in some sense, though the *Odyssey* (3. 488–90) rather implies that they formed an independent kingdom ruled by Diokles of Pherai (Kalamata). This evidently puzzled ancient writers, and thus Strabo (8. 358) says that at the time of the Trojan War, Messenia, or "Messene" as it was then called—presumably the Pamisos Valley is meant—was under Menelaus, Agamemnon's brother, but that it passed into the control of Nestor's descendants after the Trojan War. Diodoros on the other hand says (15. 66) that the descendants of Neleus and Nestor held Messenia up to the time of the Trojan War, and *thereafter* Orestes, son of Agamemnon, until the "Return of the Heraklidai." Pausanias apparently knew nothing of any control of Messenia by Agamemnon, Menelaus, or Orestes, and says simply that the descendants of Nestor continued to rule Messenia for two generations after the Trojan War, until "the expedition of the Dorians and the return of the Heraklidai" drove them out.

There was, however, a clear tradition about the end of Achaean rule in Messenia, whether this was latterly exercised by a descendant of Nestor or by someone else. According to this tradition,[1] the Heraklidai, the descendants of Herakles, led the Dorians to the conquest of the Peloponnese and then divided it up among themselves, Messenia falling to the lot of Kresphontes. This event was dated about two generations after the Trojan War, as we have seen—about eighty years after it, according to Thucydides (1. 12. 3). Thus the Greeks believed that at some time during the twelfth century B.C., the Dorians established themselves in both Lakonia and Messenia. Unfortunately, these ancient traditions about the coming of the Dorians are not borne out by the archaeological evidence, and the circumstances of the end of Mycenaean civilization in Messenia are as obscure as they are elsewhere.[2] Nevertheless, it does seem probable that people speaking an ancestor of the Doric dialect did establish themselves in Messenia, though perhaps not until about 1000 B.C.[3] The Doric dialect of Messenia in later times could be due to the Spartan conquest,[4] but it seems unlikely that there were ever enough Spartans actually settled in Messenia to impose their dialect on the helot population; and that the Messenian helots did speak Doric, at any rate in the fifth century B.C., is sufficiently indicated by Thucydides' remarks (3. 112. 4, 4. 30. 3, and 4. 31. 2) about the Messenian soldiers of Demosthenes in 426 and 425 B.C. Moreover, one wonders whether Messenian tradition would have insisted on their Dorian descent, in view of their hatred of the Spartans, unless they had some reason to do so.[5]

According to this tradition, when Kresphontes obtained Messenia as his share of the Peloponnese, he established his capital in the Stenyklaros Plain, and sent subordinate chieftains to rule the rest of the country, now divided into five districts—Stenyklaros itself, Pylos, Rhion, Mesola, and Hyameitis (Strabo 8. 361). The

Figure 6-1. Peloponnesian location map in Greek and Roman times

pre-Dorian inhabitants were admitted to terms of equality, and when the Dorians objected, Kresphontes gathered them all in Stenyklaros. Though we should not, perhaps, treat this tradition too seriously, there is nothing intrinsically improbable in the Dorians mainly occupying the richest agricultural land, at least to begin with, and leaving the rest to their predecessors. The names of the other four districts – Pylos, Rhion, Mesola, and Hyameitis – if they are historical, suggest that the pre-Dorian inhabitants still controlled much of the west and south of Messenia: Hyameitis has been placed on the slopes of the hills west of the Pamisos, and Mesola in the northeast angle of the Messenian Gulf.[6] Rhion was either the peninsula ending in Cape Akritas[7] or possibly a town on the site of the later Asine.[8]

Pausanias (4. 3. 7f.) records the names of six of Kresphontes' descendants who ruled after him, before the outbreak of the first war between Messenia and Sparta. The dynasty, however, was called the "Aipytidai," after Aipytos, the son of Kresphontes by Merope, daughter of the King of Arkadia, according to Pausanias.[9] Whether or not these early kings of Messenia are historical characters, it is really impossible to say, but it is at least possible that Phintas, the last of the six, is historical, for Pausanias (4. 4. 1) records the interesting tradition that it was in his time that the Messenians first sent a sacrifice and a chorus of men to the festival of Apollo on Delos, and that it was Eumelos, the Corinthian poet, who composed their hymn.[10]

According to Pausanias, it was also in the time of Phintas that the first dispute arose between Messenia and Sparta, leading to the death of Teleklos, King of Sparta. Already, before his death, Teleklos may have been active in the district at the head of the Messenian Gulf: Strabo (8. 360) records that he colonized Poiaessa, Echeai, and Tragion from a place called Nedon, and although the locations of these places are uncertain, they presumably all lay near the River Nedon. Kalamata itself, the ancient Pherai, may also have come under Spartan control at this time, for it was later said to be a Spartan colony.[11] If this activity of Teleklos is historical, he may have been threatening the country to the north when he died, because he is said to have been killed at the shrine of Artemis at Limnai.[12]

It was, however, in the time of Antiochos and Androkles, sons of Phintas, that, according to Pausanias (4. 4. 4f.), the real quarrel broke out between Messenia and Sparta, arising out of a dispute between the Messenian Polychares, Olympic victor in 764 B.C., and the Spartan Euaiphnos. Faced with a Spartan ultimatum, Antiochos and Androkles themselves quarreled, and Androkles – who considered that Polychares should be surrendered to Sparta – was killed. Tradition thus clearly held that the Messenians were not united among themselves, and this tradition is borne out by the fact that some Messenians, rather than fight the Spartans, apparently went into exile and settled at Rhegion, where their descendants later formed the aristocracy of the city (Strabo 6. 257). Thus pro-Spartan Messenians were welcomed by a colony of Chalkis, a city on friendly terms with Corinth, the ally of Sparta.[13] Perhaps the continued existence of considerable numbers of pre-Dorians in Messenia accounts for the disunity among the Messenians at this time.

The duration of the First Messenian War is as certain as anything can be in this early period of Greek history, for Tyrtaios[14] (frag. 4, Diehl) says that it lasted nineteen years and that in the twentieth the Messenians fled from Mt. Ithome. Pausanias (4. 5. 10) states that it broke out in 743 B.C., which would mean that it lasted until 723 B.C., and there is no particular reason to doubt these dates; but the coincidence that the last recorded Messenian victory at Olympia occurs in 736 B.C., and the first recorded Spartan in 716 B.C., has suggested a slightly later date.[15] Pausanias' account of the war drew heavily on the work of Myron of Priene, and even Pausanias rejected Myron's view that the Messenian hero, Aristomenes, fought in *this* war (4. 6. 2–5). But in broad outline Pausanias' narrative seems plausible enough. The first important incident in the war was the taking of Ampheia by Alkamenes, son of Teleklos, and if this is historical, it would suggest that Sparta was seeking to round off her conquest of the Kalamata area by cutting the Messenians off from their allies in Arkadia, for Ampheia lay in northeast Messenia.[16] There is nothing intrinsically improbable in the tradition (Pausanias 4. 10–11) that the Messenians were aided by the Arkadians, for the Arkadians themselves probably had cause to fear Spartan aggression: according to Pausanias (3. 2. 5), the Spartans had taken Aigys on the southern borders of Arkadia in the previous generation, and it was perhaps at the same time that they made allies of the men of Skiritis. Nor need we doubt the tradition that volunteers from Argos and Sikyon fought on the Messenian side: Argos was probably at war with Sparta at the time over the Helos Plain,[17] and Sikyon may have supported Messenia out of enmity for the Corinthian allies of Sparta.[18] In fact, the struggle in Messenia formed part of the widespread conflict known as the Lelantine War, which, as Thucydides records (1. 15. 3), split the Greek world into two camps.[19]

After Alkamenes' capture of Ampheia, Pausanias says, the Spartans continually raided Messenian territory but failed to take the towns, while the Messenians retaliated by raiding the coasts of Lakonia and the Spartans' farms on Taygetos (i.e., presumably, in the lower Mani). These raids were interspersed with a number of pitched battles in one of which Sparta was defeated. Gradually, however, the Messenians were forced to concentrate on Ithome, where Euphaes, who had succeeded Antiochos at the beginning of the war, died of his wounds, and was succeeded in turn by Aristodemos. Eventually Aristodemos committed suicide, and the Messenians abandoned Mt. Ithome.

It is possible that the Spartans were distracted from the struggle in Messenia by their operations in southern Lakonia,[20] and thus it was not until Theopompos had come to the throne that success finally crowned their efforts. Prominent Messenians fled for refuge to Sikyon, Argos, Arkadia, and even Eleusis, and the Spartans were left to deal with the conquered territory as they willed. The descendants of the murdered king Androkles, who had fled to Sparta, were rewarded by being allowed to live in the Hyameitis (Pausanias 4. 14. 3), and the people of Asine who had been driven from their homes by the Argives, were settled at a new Asine on the Messenian Gulf.[21] Probably the Pylos district remained independent too.[22] Thus the area of the Spartan conquest mainly comprised the Stenyklaros Plain and the lower plain west of the Pamisos. Eventually this area was carved up into *kleroi* (land-lots) and distributed among Spartan citizens, and there was a strong tradition which connected this distribution with King Polydoros, the younger contemporary of Theopompos, who probably reigned from about 700 to about 665 B.C.[23] Thus Plutarch (*Lycurgus* 8) says that some held that Polydoros added 3,000 new land-lots to an existing 6,000, some that the number was actually doubled. The size of each *kleros*, according to Plutarch, was such as to produce 70 *medimnoi* of barley for the Spartan owner, 12 for his wife, and measures of liquids in proportion, while Pausanias (4. 14. 4–5, cf. Tyrtaios fr. 5 Diehl) says that the Messenians, who actually farmed the land, had to give half their produce to their Spartan masters. If these two traditions are to be treated seriously, it would mean that each *kleros* produced roughly 164 *medimnoi* of barley each year.[24]

But the conquest of the new land in Messenia and the consequent increase in the number of landed Spartans seems to have had serious repercussions in Sparta itself,[25] and it was possibly partly because Sparta was rent by internal dissensions, partly because she suffered a disastrous defeat at the hands of Argos in 669 B.C., [26] that in the second generation after their conquest the Messenians were encouraged to revolt.[27]

Pausanias' account of this Second Messenian War is largely taken up by the exploits of the Messenian hero, Aristomenes, and it is clear that even if he was a historical figure and really was one of the Messenian leaders in this seventh-century revolt,[28] much of his story is pure folktale. Thus it is once again uncertain how far Pausanias' narrative is to be trusted here, although there may well be at least a grain of truth in the story of the battle of the "Great Trench" (Pausanias 4. 17. 2–9), since the trench appears to have been mentioned by Tyrtaios.[29] Pausanias may also be right to see the rebellion as mainly centered in and around the Stenyklaros Plain, in northern Messenia: Aristomenes himself is said to have come from Andania (Pausanias 4. 14. 7), at least one of the battles of the war is supposed to have taken place in the Stenyklaros (Pausanias 4. 15. 7–8), and eventually Aristomenes persuaded the Messenians to take refuge on Mt. Eira, a stronghold in the hills south of the Neda Valley.[30] On the other hand, Pausanias believed that Phintas and Androkles, the descendants of the murdered king Androkles, still presumably ruling the Hyameitis,[31] took part in the revolt (4. 15. 7, 16. 2, and 17. 9), and also the people of Pylos and Mothone (4. 18. 1), who had probably never yet been conquered by Sparta.[32]

According to Strabo (8. 362), the Messenians were also aided by the Eleans, Arkadians, Argives, and Pisatai, of whom the Arkadians and the Pisatai were led by Aristokrates of Orchomenos or Trapezous,[33] and Pantaleon of Pisa, respectively. Pausanias (4. 15. 7–8) says that the Eleans, Arkadians, and contingents from Argos and Sikyon were allies of the Messenians, and that the Corinthians and some of the people of Lepreon sided with Sparta. There is, again, nothing improbable in the Arkadians helping the Messenians, although the story of Aristokrates' treachery and the downfall of his house may be unhistorical.[34] The alliance of Argos with Messenia is also likely enough in view of the Battle of Hysiai, and it is possible that it was Argos which drew Pantaleon of Pisa to the Messenian side. Despite the doubts about the date of Pheidon of Argos,[35] he most probably reigned during the first half of the seventh century, and it was probably in 668 B.C. that he performed his most famous exploit – the usurpation of the Olympic Games.[36] Pausanias (6. 22. 2) says that this occurred in the Eighth Olympiad (748–45 B.C.), but it is doubtful whether the Olympic festival had anything more than a purely local significance at that early date, and Strabo (8. 355) knew of no interruption in the control of the festival by Elis until after the Twenty-Sixth Olympiad (676–73 B.C.). Strabo says that after this Olympiad, the people of Pisa seized control of the festival and maintained it until, after the reduction of the Messenians, the Spartans aided the Eleans to regain control. This makes good sense and suggests that Pantaleon of Pisa was a nationalist leader helped to power by Pheidon of Argos, Pisa being the district in which Olympia lay. Possibly too, the tradition that the Pisatai fought as allies of the Messenians explains why Strabo and Pausanias included the Eleans among Messenia's allies, whereas the probability is that they were allies of Sparta, as Strabo himself implies in the passage about the control of the Olympic Games.[37] The inclusion of Sikyonians among Messenia's allies, finally, need occasion no surprise.

It is further possible that it was the death of Pheidon of Argos which broke up this anti-Spartan coalition. Pheidon's influence had extended, as we have seen, right across the northern Peloponnese to Olympia, and can be gauged by the existence of a system of weights and measures which went by his name (Herodotus 6. 127). Now Nicolaus of Damascus (*FGrHist* 90 F 35) states that he was killed fighting on behalf of friends in a civil war in Corinth, and it may be that this is to be connected with Kypselos' seizure of power about 657 B.C. If this is the case, Pheidon was presumably seeking to overthrow the Bacchiadai, the friends of Sparta. By 657 too, the Spartans may have succeeded in cutting the Messenians off from the Arkadians, for, according to Pausanias (8. 39. 3), they took Phigaleia in 659 B.C. Thus, deprived of the help of Argos after Pheidon's death, and perhaps of that of Sikyon by the seizure of power there by Orthagoras about 656 B.C., and cut off from the Arkadians and Pisatai by the Spartan capture of Phigaleia and the adherence of Lepreon to their side, the Messenians in the north were doomed. The end came for them with the capture of Eira, perhaps about 650 B.C.

Elsewhere there may have been resistance as late as about 600 B.C., for Plutarch (*Moralia* 194b) quotes the Theban general Epameinondas as declaring, in 370 B.C., that it was then some 230 years since the Messenians had been enslaved. It was possibly, then, only in the latter half of the seventh century that Sparta finally conquered the west and southwest,[38] and this area seems to have been treated differently from other parts of Messenia. The people of Nauplia, expelled by the Argives like the people of Asine previously, were settled at Mothone, its former inhabitants having presumably been driven out or enslaved (Pausanias 4. 35. 2); and the vicinity of Koryphasion itself seems to have been left largely deserted.[39]

From about 600 B.C. at latest, then, the whole of Messenia came under Spartan control, and we hear little or nothing about it before the fourth century. It seems to have been divided between Spartan lands worked by helots and a number of perioecic towns. The Stenyklaros Plain, the lower plain west of the Pamisos, and the district at the base of the Akritas peninsula seem to have been Spartan territory, and these lands in Messenia provided a considerable part of the economic resources of Sparta:[40] their conquest undoubtedly set Sparta on the road to becoming the greatest power in the Peloponnese, and indeed in Greece. But one should not imagine that the whole of Messenia was given over to farms worked by helots for absentee Spartan landlords. East of the River Pamisos there were two perioecic towns, at least in the fifth century, Thouria and Aithaia (Thucydides 1. 101. 2), though the precise location of the latter of these places is not certain.[41] At the southern and northern ends of the west coast, too, and along the shores of the Messenian Gulf, the Spartan lands were ringed with perioecic towns. Towards the southern end of the Akritas peninsula lay Mothone, which was to be attacked by the Athenian fleet under Tolmides in 454 B.C. (Diodoros 11. 84. 6), and again in the first year of the Peloponnesian War, when Brasidas "won his spurs" (Thucydides 2. 25. 1–2). North of Pylos lay Kyparissia and Aulon, both probably perioecic.[42] Along the shores of the Messenian Gulf lay Asine, which had a Spartan garrison in the fourth century,[43] and Pherai (Kalamata), which was apparently a Spartan colony.[44] Probably Kardamyle and perhaps other small towns of the northern Mani were also perioecic.[45] Thus, although the inhabitants of Asine and Mothone were ultimately of Argive descent, and the people of Pherai perhaps Lakonians, it is clear that elsewhere there were still free Messenians living in Messenia after the Spartan conquest, and of these the people of Thouria and Aithaia at least were to join in the great revolt of the 460's. There were undoubtedly also people of Messenian descent living in freedom abroad, and some Messenians evidently still contrived to escape, for, perhaps as a result of their alliance with Sparta in the mid-sixth century, the Tegeates undertook not to harbour Messenian refugees.[46]

It was not, however, until the fifth century that large-scale rebellions occurred. The first was almost certainly in about 490 B.C., though because it is not mentioned by Herodotus, or for that matter by Thucydides, this has often been doubted. Plato states explicitly in the *Laws* (3. 698e) that the Spartans arrived one day late for the Battle of Marathon "because of the war against Messene taking place at the time, and perhaps for some other reason – we do not know the full story." Plato is, admittedly, hardly a respectable authority in historical matters, but his statement is supported by other evidence. In the first place, Strabo (8. 362) lists four wars between the Spartans and the Messenians: the first was fought in the time of Tyrtaios' grandfather, the second in the time of Tyrtaios himself; "and, they say," he goes on, "a third and a fourth war broke out, in the last of which the Messenians were suppressed." Presumably this last war is the revolt which ended about 460 B.C., and thus Strabo's sources told of a third war between the time of Tyrtaios and about 460. Secondly, Pausanias (4. 23. 3–5) says that after the Second Messenian War, Anaxilas, tyrant of Rhegion, offered to present Zankle in Sicily to the Messenian refugees if they would help him to take it, and that the city was renamed "Messene" after its capture. Now although Pausanias has clearly made a mistake in the date, since Anaxilas lived in the fifth century, there is no reason at all to doubt that Messenians played a part in the capture of Zankle, if only because it certainly was renamed Messene; and we can probably date this capture closely to 489 or 488 B.C., on the basis of certain coin-types.[47] Finally, the dedication by the Spartans at Olympia for victory over the Messenians "in their second revolt" (*IG* V i 1962), is probably to be dated near the beginning of the fifth century by its letter-forms, and can hardly be as late as about 460, while the bronze tripod by Kalon of Aigina which Pausanias saw in the temple of Apollo at Amyklai (4. 14. 2 and 3. 18. 7–8), and which he says had been dedicated for victory over the Messenians, should belong to between about 500 and about 480 B.C., in view of the literary references connecting Kalon with other artists of the Archaic period; the base bearing his signature (*IG* I ii 501) from the acropolis at Athens should probably be dated to about 500 B.C.[48]

In short, the evidence is overwhelming that there was a revolt of the Messenians about 490 B.C., and Herodotus may have omitted it from his account of the Marathon campaign because his Spartan informants preferred to keep silent about it. For it is clear that much of what they told him about Kleomenes, the King of Sparta at the time, was grossly distorted,[49] and it is very likely that if there was a revolt in Messenia about 490 B.C., it was connected with Kleomenes' desperate efforts to secure his return from exile, which included rousing the Arkadians, the ancient allies of the Messenians, against Sparta itself.[50] But apart from these suppositions, we know nothing about the origins, course, or duration of this Messenian rebellion, though it was presumably more or less over by the time the Messenian refugees helped Anaxilas of Rhegion to seize Zankle in 489 or 488 B.C. We certainly hear of no trouble with the helots during the Persian invasion of Greece in 480/79 B.C., and some idea of the size of the helot population of Lakonia and Messenia at that time can be gauged from Herodotus' statement (9. 10. 28 and 29) that there were 35,000 helot light-armed troops at the Battle of Plataea in 479 B.C., seven for each Spartan hoplite.

There was considerable hostility toward Sparta among her Peloponnesian allies, both during and after the Persian invasion,[51] and eventually, in the 460's, the helots once again seized the opportunity to revolt. Unfortunately, Thucydides, who provides the best evidence for this revolt, is equivocal on the question of the date of its outbreak. In one place (1. 101. 2) he connects it quite clearly with the earthquake which laid Sparta in ruins about 465 B.C.;[52] yet in another (1. 103. 1) he apparently says the revolt ended "in the tenth year," ("δεκάτῳ ἔτει"), and although it is not clear which year precisely he thought it ended, it can hardly be later than about 460 B.C. The simplest solution to this contradiction is to emend "tenth" (δεκάτῳ) to some other figure,[53] but it is possible that "tenth" *is* what Thucydides wrote,[54] and that the revolt did in fact break out about 470 B.C. The explanation of the fact that Thucydides does not mention the revolt until he reaches about 465 B.C. in his narrative could possibly be that it did not reach serious proportions until the earthquake at about that time, and hence that he did not think it worth mentioning until it really began to affect Spartan policy – according to him it prevented Sparta from aiding Thasos in her rebellion from Athens. If the helots had in fact been in revolt since about 470 B.C., it would then be possible to connect their activities with the machinations of the Spartan prince, Pausanias, who was accused of tampering with the loyalty of the helots (Thucydides 1. 132. 4), and who certainly seems to have been alive at least until 470 B.C., if not a year or two later.[55] Indeed, even if Thucydides has correctly dated the outbreak of the revolt to about 465 B.C., it still seems likely that Pausanias had something to do with it. It is suspicious that there was a tradition (Pausanias 4. 24. 2) that the earthquake was the punishment inflicted on the Spartans by Poseidon for their violation of the right of sanctuary at his shrine at Tainaron, for Pausanias had been a suppliant at this shrine shortly before he finally took refuge in the Temple of Athena Chalkioikos at Sparta (Thucydides 1. 133).

But, whatever the truth about the date of the beginnings of the revolt, it seems clear that it did not become serious until the earthquake, and this, on the authority of Thucydides, must be dated to about 465 B.C. – at latest to 464/63 B.C. where Pausanias puts it (4. 24. 2). Of the course of the revolt Thucydides (1. 101. 2) says merely that as a result of the earthquake the helots and the *perioikoi* of Thouria and Aithaia revolted and took refuge on Mt. Ithome. He adds the interesting remark that most of the helots were descendants of Messenians enslaved in the past, and that hence all the rebels were called "Messenians." Diodoros (11. 63–64) adds details about the earthquake and the loss of life that resulted from it (the figure he gives is 20,000!), and says the rebels originally intended to attack Sparta itself, but were deterred by the resolute action of the Spartan king, Archidamos. Plutarch (*Kimon* 16) has much the same story, and adds the detail that only five houses were left standing in Sparta after the earthquake. Herodotus (9. 64. 2) records a battle "in Stenyklaros" in which Aeimnestos, the Spartan who had killed Mardonius at Plataea, was himself slain with the 300 men he commanded, and elsewhere (9. 35) mentions a fight at a place called "the Isthmus."[56]

In general, however, the evidence suggests that the revolt turned into a siege of the Messenian stronghold on Mt. Ithome, and it was because of their alleged skill in siege craft that the Athenians were asked for their help.[57] Other help came to Sparta from Aegina, Mantineia, and Plataea.[58] But despite all the efforts of the Spartans and their allies the Messenians managed to hold out, and eventually they forced the Spartans to grant them terms: they were to be allowed to leave the Peloponnese on condition of never setting foot in it again; if they did, they were to become the slaves of the man who took them.[59]

The Messenians who thus escaped were settled, with their wives and families, at Naupaktos on the Gulf of Corinth, by the Athenians (Thucydides 1. 103. 3), who were now pursuing a policy hostile to Sparta. But the Messenians of Naupaktos continued to regard themselves as Messenians first and foremost, and made dedications as such at Olympia and Delphi.[60] During the Peloponnesian War, too, they performed sterling services for their benefactors. In 431 B.C. Messenian soldiers served with the naval forces raiding the Peloponnese, and after Brasidas had successfully beaten off the attack on Mothone, it was the Messenians who captured Pheia on the coast of Elis (Thucydides 2. 25. 4). Two years later, they helped Phormio in his second sea fight in the Gulf of Corinth, some rushing into the sea, in full armour, to capture enemy ships (Thucydides 2. 90. 3–6); and later 400 Messenian hoplites took part in a campaign in Akarnania (Thucydides 2. 102. 1). In 428 B.C. 500 Messenian hoplites went with the Athenian general, Nikostratos, to Corcyra to aid the pro-Athenian democratic party (Thucydides 3. 75. 1, and 81. 2), and in 426 B.C. Messenian soldiers accompanied Demosthenes on his campaign in Aetolia—indeed, according to Thucydides (3. 94. 3, cf. 97), the campaign was largely their idea. Despite the failure of this campaign, Demosthenes evidently thought so highly of the qualities of Messenian hoplites that later in the same year, at Olpai, he stationed them under his own command on the right wing, opposite Eurylochos and his Spartans (Thucydides 3. 107. 4), and at Idomene shortly afterwards the Messenians led the attack on the Ambraciot outposts, so that their Doric dialect might confuse the enemy (Thucydides 3. 112. 4).

But it was perhaps at Pylos in 425 B.C. that the Messenians really came into their own. Demosthenes originally chose the promontory of Koryphasion for his fort with the idea of garrisoning it with Messenians, considering that they "being the inhabitants of the place of old, and speaking the same dialect as the Spartans, would do the most harm if they used it as a base for raids" (Thucydides 4. 3. 3). Later he was joined by 40 Messenian hoplites from two small pirate vessels (Thucydides 4. 9. 1), and these took part in the assault on Sphakteria (Thucydides 4. 32. 2), their commander (called Komon according to Pausanias 4. 26. 2) led a section of archers and light-armed troops up behind the final Spartan position, by a route the Spartans had thought unclimbable (Thucydides 4. 36. 1f.). After the victory on Sphakteria, Koryphasion was garrisoned by Messenian troops (Thucydides 4. 41. 2), until they and the helots who had joined them were removed at the request of the Spartans after the conclusion of peace in 421 B.C. They were, however, replaced at the request of Argos in 418 B.C. (Thucydides 5. 35. 6–7), and only finally withdrew in 409 or 408 B.C., by agreement with the Spartans (Xenophon *Hellenica* 1. 2. 18). Demosthenes, too, remembered the qualities of Messenian soldiers, and on his way to Sicily in 413 B.C. requested that some Messenian troops be sent with him (Thucydides 7. 31. 2).[61] After the war was over, however, the Spartans expelled the Messenians from Naupaktos and Cephallenia, and they fled for refuge to Sicily and Cyrene (Diodoros 14. 34. 2–3, 78. 5–6).

Despite these activities of Messenians on the Athenian side, and the flight of many helots, particularly after the establishment of the Athenian fort at Koryphasion, the Peloponnesian War saw the first signs of a more liberal Spartan attitude toward the helots, and presumably this meant toward the Messenians too, since, as we have seen, by the fifth century these formed the bulk of the helot population (cf. Thucydides 1. 101. 2). The helots who undertook to swim out to Sphakteria with provisions for the Spartan troops trapped on the island were promised their freedom as a reward (Thucydides 4. 26. 5–6), and although many helots subsequently fled to Koryphasion (Thucydides 4. 41. 3), those who had fought with Brasidas in Thrace were freed in 421 B.C. and settled at Lepreon (Thucydides 5. 34. 1). The helot hoplites sent to Sicily in 413 B.C. (Thucydides 7. 19. 3) were also presumably free men, and in the fourth century emancipated helot soldiers are often referred to by Xenophon:[62] the majority of these were probably from Lakonia, but some must surely have been from

Messenia. The reason for this more liberal attitude, it seems clear, was the declining manpower of Sparta at a time when her military commitments were growing even greater.[63]

It seems clear, too, that although the helots were serfs and were always liable to be treated with savage severity when the Spartans became suspicious of them,[64] some of them were reasonably well off. This is suggested by the constant references to Messenian hoplites by Thucydides, for we can hardly suppose that the Athenians provided equipment for them. The numbers involved also give some idea of the size of the Messenian population at Naupaktos: for example, when 500 Messenian hoplites accompanied Nikostratos to Corcyra in 428 B.C. (Thucydides 3. 75. 1), these cannot have been all the hoplites that were available in Naupaktos, and this suggests that the Messenian population was as large as that of Plataea or Epidauros, for instance, in 479 B.C. (cf. Herodotus 9. 28). The Messenians who were left in Messenia after 460 B.C. were presumably at least as numerous as those who went to Naupaktos, and some of them too must have been relatively prosperous: Thucydides' account of the operations around Koryphasion and Sphakteria, for example, indicates that some of them owned boats.[65] Thus, both at home and abroad, when the day of liberation came, the Messenians had preserved their national feeling, and leaders were available for the new nation.

Freedom returned to Messenia when the Theban general Epameinondas, having defeated the Spartans at the Battle of Leuktra in 371 B.C., invaded the Peloponnese in the following year. He did not dare to attack Sparta herself, but after ravaging Lakonia, he moved on into Messenia and decided to found a city there to act as a center for the new state he was in effect creating. The site he chose was at Ithome, which was not only the traditional center of Messenian resistance, but was also the strongest natural fortress in the country and strategically placed to control it. By creating an independent state in Messenia, Epameinondas hoped to cut Sparta off from the area upon which her economy largely depended, and with the aid of his Argive and Arkadian allies, to hem her into Lakonia. The final step in this plan was the founding of Megalopolis in Arkadia in the summer of 369 B.C. Work was probably begun at Ithome in the spring of the same year, and the Argives and Arkadians played a large part in it, as was only fitting in view of their help to the Messenians in the past. Indeed, if Pausanias (4. 26. 7) is to be believed, it was the Argive general, Epiteles, who was nominally in charge of the project, though Epameinondas himself was regarded as the founder (οἰκιστής) of the new city, and was worshipped there as a hero (Pausanias 9. 14. 5, 4. 31. 10, and 4. 32. 1).

The new city was built on the west side of Mt. Ithome, incorporating the mountain as its acropolis, and land-allotments were made to settlers (Diodoros 15. 66. 1). Presumably the majority of these would have been helots from the surrounding area, but they included also *perioikoi* who had joined the Thebans, land-hungry Greeks from other states, and a number of Messenians from Sicily and Africa, including members of the old priestly families. Some Messenian cults had been kept alive by the helots, particularly that of Zeus Ithomatas: in the oaths of the new state his name appears first, and the Messenians later dated their years by the name of his priest.[66] Their earliest coins, moreover, depict his cult-statue made by Ageladas and presumably brought back by the returning exiles.[67] At least until the end of the fourth century the new city seems to have been called "Ithome," but later the name "Messene" became normal.

The territory of the new state seems originally to have comprised only the old Spartan lands, since a number of the perioecic towns at least remained loyal to Sparta and were only later incorporated into the Messenian state. Thus, for example, it was not until 365 B.C. that the Arkadians captured Kyparissia and Koryphasion and handed them over to Messenia.[68] To protect themselves and their communications with Arkadia, the Messenians not only fortified their city but also seem to have built a number of small forts and towers at other strategic points,[69] while possibly in order to isolate Asine and Mothone, which remained loyal to Sparta, Korone and, perhaps, Kolonides were founded on the east coast of the Akritas peninsula (Pausanias 4. 34. 5 and 8). But, at least in the early years, the Messenians would have had to rely heavily on the Arkadians, Argives, and Thebans, and it is probable that they concluded formal alliances with these states, thus in effect securing recognition in the Greek diplomatic world. However, it was not until after the Battle of Mantinea in 362 B.C. that the new state was finally accepted by the other Greek powers, with the exception of Sparta.[70] This meant that, from then on, Messenia could make alliances with other states and thus protect herself by diplomacy as well as by force of arms. Thus, in 356 B.C., an alliance was concluded with Athens, guaranteeing Messenia against Spartan aggression (Demosthenes 16. 9).

For some time Messenia was left to develop in peace, but later in the fourth century she became in effect a pawn in the game Philip II of Macedonia was playing in the affairs of Greece. He supported Messenia and her allies against Sparta, and this led to the despatch of an Athenian embassy to Messene, led by Demosthenes, in an attempt to counteract Philip's growing influence in the Peloponnese (Demosthenes 6. 19). But the Messenians rejected Athens' overtures, and by the time Demosthenes delivered his *Second Philippic* they had probably concluded an alliance with Macedonia, Argos, and Megalopolis. The Messenians clearly did not want to become involved in squabbles which were not directly their concern, and when, as in this situation, they had to declare for one side or the other, they preferred the more remote. This "isolationist" attitude was to prove a constant feature of Messenian policy for over a century, and is readily understandable when one remembers that the Messenians had only emerged from slavery a generation before. They were, naturally enough, extremely reluctant to imperil their new-won freedom by embarking on a vigorous foreign policy, and it was hardly possible for them even to contemplate seeking the friendship of the Spartans, though these were, both in geographical terms and in terms of the political situation in Greece, often their natural allies. Thus, on this occasion, even when the Athenian seizure of the Megarian forts in 343 B.C. cut Philip off from the Peloponnese, although in response to a second embassy, including Demosthenes again, they became allies of Athens (Demosthenes 9. 72), they refused to join Athens' "Hellenic League" against Philip, and remained neutral at the time of the Battle of Chaironeia in 338 B.C.

After Philip's victory, Messenia was thus in a position to bring pressure to bear upon Sparta in order to secure control of parts of Messenia still in Spartan hands, and, probably as a result of arbitration by Philip's Hellenic League, she received the Ager Denthaliatis and the coastal area along the eastern shore of the Messenian Gulf, as far as the Little Pamisos.[71] Probably Asine, Mothone, and Thouria also passed into Messenian control at this time, so that, with Kyparissia and Pylos in their hands since 365 B.C., the Messenians now controlled the whole area bounded by the River Neda and the mountains of Phigaleia in the north, and by the Taygetos Mountains in the east.

It is clear that the whole of this territory formed a single state until Messene itself and the other towns of Messenia were incorporated into the Achaean League as separate entities in the early years of the second century B.C. There is no mention, either in the literary sources or in inscriptions, of treaties or other dealings with separate Messenian towns before this, and the Messenians as a whole are constantly referred to as though they constituted a single state. Yet there is evidence for a certain amount of local autonomy, for example, at Kyparissia, Thouria, Korone, and Mothone. It seems probable, then, that the Messenians formed a federal league, though with Messene itself as the dominant member, and it is perhaps significant that two of the states which shared in the founding of Messene, namely Boeotia and Arkadia, were organized on federal lines.[72]

Thus, by the time of Alexander, Messenia had become a viable state economically, strategically, and diplomatically. Yet by that time it was very difficult for any small state to be genuinely independent in the face, first, of Alexander and his successors, and later of the Aetolian and Achaean Leagues, and the history of Messenia is the story of one long attempt to remain outside the diplomatic and military manoeuvers of the great powers, without antagonizing them too far. But in this new and dangerous age Messene itself was becoming a fortress of great strategic significance, as Philip V of Macedonia was to be vividly reminded toward the end of the third century when he was advised (Polybius 7. 11) to "seize the ox by the horns" (i.e., to secure control of the Peloponnese by the seizure of Akrocorinth [above Corinth] and Ithome [above Messene]). Thus Messenia's "freedom" was seriously impaired from time to time after 318 B.C. by the presence of Macedonian garrisons in Messene itself, although after his victory in the Chremonidian War (266–62 B.C.), the then king of Macedonia, Antigonos Gonatas, appears to have acquiesced in Messenia's isolation.

By that time, however, the growth of the Achaean League presented a new threat to Messenia's independence. At first the rival Aetolian League appeared to offer some protection against the nearer danger, and probably about 244 B.C. an alliance was concluded between the Messenians and the Aetolians. But Aetolian preoccupation in central and western Greece left Messenia a prey to the Achaean League which, by the incorporation of Megalopolis in 235 B.C., gained a frontier with Messenia, and by 220 B.C. at latest (Polybius 4. 25. 4), had begun encroaching upon Messenia by incorporating Pylos. Yet Messenia's traditional hostility toward Sparta made cooperation with Kleomenes III impossible in his attempt to curtail the growth of the Achaean League, even if the predominantly oligarchic leaders of Messenia had not been out of sympathy with his revolutionary program.

It was not, however, until two years after Kleomenes' defeat at Sellasia in 222 B.C. that the Messenians were finally compelled to abandon the isolationist policy they had pursued with considerable success for some 150 years. The death of Antigonos Doson and the accession of the young Philip V to the throne of Macedonia clearly seemed to the Aetolians to provide an opportunity for renewed interference in the Peloponnese, and accordingly, in 220 B.C., after a campaign of deliberate provocation had forced the Messenian government into taking official action against the Aetolian officer commanding in Phigaleia, an Aetolian army invaded Messenia. The Messenians were virtually compelled to appeal to the Achaean League for help, and their appeal met with a vigorous response: Aratos, the Strategos of the League, demanded that the Aetolians withdraw, and this they did, despite defeating Aratos himself at Kaphyai. At the time, however, Messenia was not permitted to join the Achaean League since this would have contravened the terms of the League's treaty with Macedonia, but shortly afterwards a Messenian application to join Philip V's Hellenic League was accepted. Yet even then the Messenians did not immediately become involved in Philip's activities, using the continued presence of Aetolian troops in Phigaleia as an excuse; and it is not until 218 B.C. that we find Messenian soldiers actually serving with Philip's forces at his unsuccessful siege of Palos on Kephallenia (Polybius 5. 4. 4–5).

Meanwhile, Messenia had itself been invaded by Spartan forces, and although they withdrew without achieving anything permanent, the Messenians naturally responded to Philip's call for an invasion of Lakonia. But the Messenian forces, arriving late and seeking to enter Lakonia by a different route from the one followed by Philip's main army, were turned back near a place called Glympeis in the Kynouria (Polybius 5. 20). In 217 B.C. Messenia was again invaded, this time from north and east, by the Aetolian general Pyrrhias from Elis and by Spartan forces from Lakonia. But although the latter took Kalamai (Yiannitsa?),[73] both invasions were eventually beaten off by the Messenians themselves, and in the autumn of 217 B.C. hostilities were brought to an end by the Peace of Naupaktos, after Agelaos of Naupaktos had dramatically warned delegates at the peace conference (Polybius 5. 104) of "the clouds now rising in the west" (i.e., the threat to Greece presented by the power of Rome and Carthage, then engaged in the life-and-death struggle of the Second Punic War). Messenia had not yet joined the Achaean League, but she had incurred a definite obligation to it by asking for help and by becoming a member of the Hellenic League on Achaea's recommendation. A treaty of alliance had also probably been concluded between Messenia and the League, and Messenia thus passed definitely into the League's sphere of influence.

But the war had evidently exacerbated class feelings in Messenia, and when open civil war broke out in 215/14 B.C. Philip V of Macedonia saw fit to intervene. Despite the attempts of Aratos to restrain him, he twice attempted to take the fortress of Messene and ravaged Messenia when he failed the second time. This blatant aggression against one of his own allies inevitably drove the Messenians into the Aetolian camp, and, probably in 213 B.C., they concluded an alliance with the Aetolian League, although since they are not referred to in the treaty of alliance between Aetolia and Rome (Livy 26. 24. 9), concluded in 212 or 211 B.C., it is possible that their alliance with Aetolia was only concluded after this treaty. At all events, when serious hostilities broke out in 211 B.C. between Rome and Philip who had foolishly allied himself with Hannibal after his great victory at Cannae in 216 B.C., Messenia found herself on the side of Rome. The only recorded actions of the Messenians during this First Macedonian War, however, are the sending of two detachments of troops to hold Delphi when the Aetolians were hard pressed, and they presumably shared in the peace concluded between Philip and the Aetolian League in 206 B.C. By then Messenia had almost certainly become an ally of Rome too, and although there is considerable controversy about it, Livy is probably right to include Messene among the allies of Rome "adscripted" to the Peace of Phoenice between Rome and Philip in 205 B.C. (Livy 29. 12. 14).

Messenia had, as usual, contrived to steer clear of any real involvement in the First Macedonian War, and she took no part in the second. This however put her at a disadvantage as against the Achaean League when, after the Roman victory over Philip at Cynoscephalae in 197 B.C., the Senate appointed ten *legati* to assist the proconsul, T. Quinctius Flamininus, in settling the affairs of Greece. The Messenians claimed the restoration of Pylos and Asine from the Achaeans, but the Roman commissioners naturally preferred the claims of an ally which had given Rome sterling support against Philip. Messenia nevertheless took part in the war against Nabis of Sparta which immediately followed the Second Macedonian War: Nabis had invaded Messenia in 201 B.C. and captured Messene (though not the acropolis) before hurriedly withdrawing at the advance of Philopoemen and troops of the Achaean League. Now, by the treaty which concluded the war between Nabis and Rome and her allies, Messenia recovered the booty Nabis had carried off in 201 B.C. (Livy 34. 35. 6).

Messenia's growing fear of the Achaean League, however, prompted by increasing encroachments — as we have seen, the League apparently controlled Pylos and even Asine by 196 B.C. — probably led her to declare in support of the Aetolian League when it invited Antiochus of Syria to intervene in the affairs of Greece. Thus, after Roman forces under M'. Acilius Glabrio had defeated Antiochus at Thermopylae in April of 191 B.C. and had begun to subdue Aetolia, the Achaeans, as Rome's most active allies, were encouraged to take the final step of coercing Messenia into joining the League. Messenia rejected an ultimatum and prepared to fight (Livy 36. 31. 1–4), but when the Achaean army invaded Messenia and laid siege to Messene, there was little the Messenians could do. They appealed to Flamininus who was then in Greece as a legate to secure the loyalty of the Greeks against Antiochus, but although he ordered the Achaean army to withdraw from Messenia, he nevertheless instructed Messenia to join the League and the Messenians had no alternative but to obey (Livy 36. 31. 9).

The terms under which Messenia now finally joined the Achaean League were inevitably harsh: the towns of Mothone, Kolonides, Korone, and Kyparissia were probably made "independent" and joined the League as separate entities, so that, with the loss of Pylos and Asine previously, the Messenians were cut off from the west coast and from their best ports on the Messenian Gulf. An attempt was made to influence the Senate and then Flamininus on their behalf, but Rome was unwilling to antagonize one of the most powerful states in Greece, and in 183 B.C. the resentment of Messenia burst into open revolt. Hostilities broke out toward the end of that year, but despite the capture and death of Philopoemen, Messenia was soon obliged to surrender on even harsher terms: a garrison of Achaean soldiers occupied Ithome (Polybius 23. 16. 6–13), and the towns of Abia, Thouria, and Pherai became independent and joined the League separately (Polybius 23. 17. 1–2). Moreover, although Polybius does not say so, it seems that Messene lost Andania and most of the Stenyklaros Plain at this time also.[74]

Messene and the other, smaller towns of Messenia thus became regular members of the Achaean League, but they remained hostile to it, and when war broke out with Rome in 146 B.C., sent no troops to its aid. What the position was in Messenia after the defeat and breakup the League is not at all clear. Messene itself apparently regained control of Andania and the Stenyklaros Plain,[75] and retained control of the Ager Dentheliatis by the Milesian decision of about 140 B.C. (Dittenberger *Sylloge* 683), but it is not possible to determine the relationship between Messene and the other towns of Messenia. From now on, however, Messenia as a whole would in effect, like the rest of Greece, have come under Roman control. Pausanias (7. 16. 9–10) implies the creation of a separate province of Achaea after the sack of Corinth by Mummius in 146 B.C., but a number of inscriptions[76] testify to the frequent and probably regular interference in the affairs of Greece by the proconsul of Macedonia. Those Greek states which had not taken an active part against Rome, among which the towns of Messenia should probably be numbered, were theoretically "free," and thus the proconsul, Q. Fabius Maximus, in his letter to Dyme in Achaea (Dittenberger *Sylloge* 684), could refer to "the freedom granted in general to the Greeks." But at the same time Greece south of Macedonia could be referred to in terms which implied that it was part of the province of Macedonia, as in the arbitration between Sparta and Messenia referred to above (Dittenberger *Sylloge* 683) or in the law of about 100 B.C. concerning piracy (*SEG* III 378). Similarly, some states at least which had taken sides against Rome certainly paid taxes to her later,[77] but equally certainly other states which had not fought against her – for example, Sparta (Strabo 8. 365) – were exempt, and presumably Messenia was in the latter category. But although, for example, in Cicero's letters and speeches we hear constantly of the "freedom" of Greek states,[78] it is clear that this "freedom" was very much subject to the will of the Senate and of individual governors. Thus gradually freedom and immunity from taxation were whittled away, so that under the Empire we find grants of freedom and immunity to communities which had, in theory, never lost them. In the case of Messenia, a number of inscriptions relating to the collection of taxes[79] indicate the sort of "voluntary contributions" to which a theoretically "free" city like Messene was liable, possibly in connection with M. Antonius' operations against the pirates of Cilicia in 102 B.C.

These inscriptions, however, together with the one regulating the Mysteries at Andania (Dittenberger *Sylloge* 736) in 91 B.C.,[80] indicate a considerable degree of prosperity in Messenia at this period. For example, the Andania inscription lays down one talent as the minimum property qualification for the five officials who supervised the finances of the Mysteries, and this must mean that fortunes of one talent or more were not uncommon. Some of the other regulations also imply a high standard of living, such as that women must not wear *himatia* worth more than 100 drachmas. The prosperity of Messenia was probably founded upon agriculture, for it appears that even Romans found it worth their while to acquire estates there,[81] and it must be remembered that Messenia had not been so badly affected by warfare as other parts of Greece.

Nevertheless, Messenia, like the rest of Greece, must have suffered increasingly severely from exactions like those implied by the taxation inscriptions referred to above, particularly during the civil wars of the first century B.C. Some idea of what this could mean to Messenia is given by the statement of Appian (*Civil Wars* 4. 74) that during the campaign which culminated at Philippi in 42 B.C. a detachment of the Republican fleet made Tainaron its rendezvous after gathering all the booty it could from the Peloponnese. Still worse probably followed when, after promising to surrender the Peloponnese to Sextus Pompeius in 39 B.C., Antony exacted as much as he could from the area first, though he never in fact handed it over.[82] But Messenia probably suffered worst of all in the campaign which culminated off Actium in September, 31 B.C.: large forces of both Antony and Octavian gathered in Greece, and Antony in particular must have had to live off the country once Octavian's fleet had cut his communications with Egypt. On at least one occasion, indeed, Messenia saw actual fighting when Agrippa attacked Mothone (Strabo 8. 359), and after the war Kardamyle, Pherai, and Thouria were handed over to Sparta, according to Pausanias (3. 26. 7, 4. 30. 2, and 4. 31. 1), because the Messenians had sided with Antony.

After Antony's defeat, Greece continued at first to be administered by the proconsul of Macedonia, but in 27 B.C. Macedonia and Achaea may at last have become separate provinces, both controlled by the Senate. This state of affairs continued until A.D. 15, when in response to complaints from the provincials themselves, Tiberius combined Macedonia and Achaea with Moesia into one vast Balkan province governed by an imperial legate. In A.D. 44, however, Claudius separated them again, and they continued to be governed separately thereafter. In theory this may have made little difference to the status of individual communities, such as those of Messenia, but in practice it appears that, for example, the "contributions" exacted during the civil wars, perhaps particularly by Antony, hardened in effect into regular taxes. Thus when we find the tiny island of Gyaros appealing to Octavian in 29 B.C. to have its tax of 150 drachmas reduced (Strabo 10. 485), we must surely assume that few Greek communities escaped some form of Roman taxation. By the time of Vespasian, regular taxes like the "tax on land" (*tributum soli*) and the "tax on persons" (*tributum capitis*) were probably being paid by the Messenians, as well as indirect taxes like the inheritance tax (*vicesima hereditatium*) paid only by Roman citizens: for the collection of the latter from Achaea there is the evidence of an inscription of the time of Claudius (*ILS* 1546). That the towns of Messenia also declined in status is indicated by the grant of "freedom" to Mothone by Trajan (Pausanias 4. 35. 3), though Mothone may have been specifically punished for siding with Antony since, as we saw above, it was attacked by Agrippa in 31 B.C. But it may be that the Messenians were able, partially at least, to reconstitute the unified state which had existed before 191 B.C., for Tacitus, for example, talks of "the Messenians" claiming the shrine of Artemis at Limnai in a dispute with "the Spartans" in A.D. 25 (*Annals* 4. 43).

Messenia must also have benefited, like the rest of the Roman world, from the general peace which followed the end of the civil wars in 30 B.C., and from the increasing efficiency and honesty of Roman imperial administration.[83] Evidence from Messenia itself is largely lacking, but there is no reason to doubt that this area shared in the prosperity of the first and second centuries A.D. Strabo, admittedly, declares (8. 362) that the greater part of Messenia was deserted in his day, but Pausanias' description of Messenia in the second century A.D. (4. 30–36) certainly does not give the impression that the country was deserted then: Messene, Pherai, Thouria, Korone, Kolonides, Asine, Mothone, Pylos, and Kyparissia evidently still existed as towns, even though Pausanias does talk of the "ruins" of Andania and Dorion (4. 33. 6 and 7). Nor need the civil wars or the barbarian invasions of the third century A.D. have affected Messenia directly, until the raids of the Heruli in A.D. 267 penetrated right down into the Peloponnese. But the story of Messenia from this point onward is covered in Chapter 5.

A TOPOGRAPHICAL COMMENTARY (BY R. H. S.)

The archaeological evidence for the historical period is very incomplete, and any attempt to synthesize what information we have with that from the literary sources cannot, at this stage of our knowledge, lead to definitive conclusions. These notes, therefore, are merely intended to supplement the historical discussion above and, as far as is possible, relate the archaeological evidence to *other* data concerning the topography of the area in the relevant subperiods.[84] Reference should also be made to Figure 6-2, to the corresponding archaeological summaries in Chapter 8, to Register B (p. 310), and to the distribution maps (Pocket Maps 8-15 to 8-18).

Protogeometric and Geometric (about 1050–700 B.C.). Our evidence for the early part of the period is, as has been said, incomplete and unreliable. For instance, the division of Messenia into five districts under Kresphontes can be neither dated accurately nor corroborated by the archaeological record. In any case, we have no means of locating accurately Stenyklaros,[85] Mesola,[86] or Hyameitis.[87] Pylos and Rhion[88] may be easier to place approximately, but their exact extent is quite uncertain.

For the latter part of the period, evidence from the literary sources is reasonably specific, especially regarding the importance of Ampheia[89] and Ithome[90] in the First Messenian War. And the agricultural importance of the Pamisos Valley and surrounding areas at this time is, of course, abundantly clear, since these were the lands for which the Spartans fought. The Messenian raids on the Lakonian coast and the lands "around Taygetus"

(Pausanias 4. 7. 2) seem to imply considerable occupation of the east coast of the Messenian Gulf, where the foothills of Mt. Taygetos begin, with few exceptions, almost from the shore itself. And after the war, a new foundation, Asine, on the west coast of the gulf, housed refugees from Asine in the Argolid.[91] But, apart from these clues, we have little direct evidence concerning the density of habitation, and still less for the size of the individual settlements.

The Archaic Period (about 700–500 B.C.). There is still considerable uncertainty as to the locations of some Messenian centers in the early part of this period. Messenian resistance in the Second Messenian War was concentrated in the Stenyklaros Plain, and in particular at Andania.[92] The refuge fortress on Mt. Eira (Pl. 9-2) at the northern border of Messenia has been convincingly located.[93] Several "perioecic" Messenian towns, in particular Thouria,[94] Aithaia,[95] and Mothone,[96] may have been founded or re-founded in this period, as also seems to be the case of certain hill towns in Triphylia,[97] especially Lepreon[98] and Samikon.[99] In general, there appears to have been a population increase in all areas, although the settlements themselves may have been rather small. Indeed, the Second Messenian War, resulting in Spartan control of much of eastern Messenia, may have curtailed the size of the individual settlements in this area, as a result of the limitations imposed on local autonomy. This would be expected particularly in the areas closely controlled, in the Pamisos Valley and surrounding regions. The only places likely to have been allowed a continued free expansion are those in northern Mani (particularly Pherai, which was apparently a Spartan colony later[100]), and probably also Asine, as well as the more remote areas such as Pylos and Kyparissia.

The Classical Period (about 500–323 B.C.). For this period we can at last be sure of the locations of most of the main towns (see Fig. 6-2). But several of the smaller places mentioned in the ancient literature have not yet been definitively identified although their general vicinity is known (e.g., Aulon,[101] Erana,[102] Polichni,[103] Kalamai,[104] Gerenia, and Alagonia[105] in Messenia; and in Triphylia Epion,[106] Tympaneai,[107] Pteleai,[108] and Hypana[109]). Conversely, there are now a few fairly large classical sites for which we have no certainly or probably attributable names (e.g., #'s 600, 604, and 727, Register B), as well as many smaller settlements, which we should not, perhaps, expect to be mentioned in the sources.

There was at the time evidently a considerable expansion throughout the region,[110] although Spartan domination in the first part of the fifth century B.C. may have continued to restrict autonomy, at least in eastern Messenia. In this connection, the date of the walls of ancient Thouria[111] (Pl. 9-4, cf. Pl. 4-2) could be significant. The account of the revolt of the perioeci of Thouria and Aithaia (Thucydides 1. 101. 2) might be considered to imply that these places had become to some extent independent at this time. But the very fact that the insurgents took refuge on Mt. Ithome[112] might perhaps rather indicate a *lack* of walls of their own.

During the latter part of the fifth and the early part of the fourth century B.C., the Messenians gradually freed themselves of the Spartan yoke,[113] and in the process several Messenian towns became in varying degrees independent of Sparta.[114] These included Kyparissia (Pl. 8-3), Thouria, Kardamyle, Mothone, Asine, and Pylos (Koryphasion), as well as Lepreon and Samikon in Triphylia. Further north, at Skillous, Xenophon was able to enjoy a leisurely retirement, including the hunting of hares, deer, and wild boar.[115]

Subsequently, the founding of Messene in 369 B.C. (Pl. 9-3) and the consequent shift of the focus of settlement farther toward the interior of Messenia may have resulted in the exploitation of some land barely, if at all, cultivated since the Mycenaean period (though this argument *e silentio* might be considered hazardous). But, in any case, as argued above,[116] the full economic effects of the shift may not have been felt until the Hellenistic period.

The Hellenistic Period (about 323–146 B.C.). Apart from the immediate local situation, particularly the new freedom, and the security afforded by the new capital of Messene, there was a general tendency in mainland Greece at this time to move down from the fortified hill towns into the plains. The proliferation of small forts, both in the area of Messene[117] and elsewhere (e.g., Stilari,[118] Yiannitsa [Pl. 10-1], Vounaki, and the later fort at Eira[119]) does not indicate the use of these as refuge centers but rather as guard posts along routes, especially on or near the frontiers. The defense was also facilitated by the new road system.[120] On the other hand, the new towns on the coast were equipped with extensive fortifications (e.g., Mothone,[121] Korone,[122] and Kyparissia[123]), presumably intended mainly for security against seaborne raiders. Pherai[124] and Korone were considerably expanded, and indeed Korone and Kolonides[125] may have been only recently created.

From the latter part of the fourth century until about 222 B.C., the Messenians appear to have enjoyed as great prosperity as was ever known in the Greece of the historical period. And Polybius (4. 73) reports a fairly large rural population in Elis at the end of the third century B.C., as is testified by the amount of booty[126] that fell into the hands of Philip V shortly after. But at the turn of the century, and in the early years of the second century

Figure 6-2. Messenian location map in Greek and Roman times

B.C., political upheavals and invasions resulted in the curtailment of Messenian territory[127] until the time of the settlement imposed by Rome.

The Roman Period (about 146 B.C.–A.D. 330). Under Roman administration, Messenia was apparently prosperous, especially after about 30 B.C.[128] Records of the boundaries between Messenia and Lakonia as certified in A.D. 78,[129] and other inscriptions[130] testify to Roman official interest in the area, which was profitable enough to induce some Romans to acquire estates here.[131] And Roman influence was presumably responsible for the numerous villas (as exemplified by the Trypha and Ayia Triadha mosaics, and by the remains of bath-buildings at Kandirogli, Zaïmoglou,[132] and Grizi[133]). The main coastal towns like Korone, Asine, Mothone, Kyparissia, and Pherai now became even more prominent. The process of abandonment of the fortified hill sites was virtually complete, and settlements were established at the foot of old citadels like Thouria[134] and Kardamyle.[135] In general, however, apart from the towns named above plus Messene and Olympia, the settlements in the area seem to have been rather small (perhaps mainly villas and farms). Yet Pausanias' account shows that although the area may have been a "backwater," it had a romantic appeal to cultured Romans.

NOTES

1. Plato *Laws* 3. 683c; Isocrates *Archidamos* 17–33; Nicolaus of Damascus *FGrHist* 90 F 31; Strabo 8. 359f.; Diodorus Siculus 15. 66; Apollodorus 2. 8. 4–5; Hyginus *Fabulae* 137; Pausanias 4. 3. 3f.
2. Cf. V. R. d'A. Desborough, *The Last Mycenaeans and Their Successors* (Oxford, 1964) esp. pp. 93–97 and 244–57.
3. Cf. for the date *ibid.*, esp. p. 252.
4. Cf. *ibid.*, p. 245; Andrewes, *The Greek Tyrants* pp. 63–64.
5. For example, after the liberation of Messenia in 370/69 B.C., the population of Messene itself was divided into five tribes named after the Heraklidai; cf. *IG* V i 1433; Roebuck (1941) pp. 113–14, n. 25.
6. See nn. 86 and 87 below.
7. G. L. Huxley, *Early Sparta* (London, 1962) n. 176 on pp. 112–13.
8. See n. 88 below.
9. Similarly, the Spartan Royal Houses traced their descent, not from the twin sons of Aristodemos, who with his brothers, Temenos and Kresphontes, had led the Heraklidai back to the Peloponnese, but from *their* sons, Agis and Euryphron. Huxley (*Early Sparta* p. 32 and n. 177 on p. 113) thinks the Aipytidai claimed descent from the Arkadian hero Aipytos, mentioned by Homer (*Iliad* 2. 604): cf. Nicolaus of Damascus *FGrHist* 90 F 31. Andrewes (*The Greek Tyrants* p. 64) thinks that the name of their Royal House is an indication that the Messenians were *not* Dorians.
10. Eumelos was the court poet of the Bacchiadai, the aristocracy of Corinth. For his date see Dunbabin *JHS* 68 (1948): 67. Again Andrewes (*The Greek Tyrants* p. 64) argues that Dorians would have been unlikely to send a sacrifice and chorus to an Ionian god, but Eumelos himself was presumably a Dorian, and after all, he composed the hymn.
11. Cornelius Nepos *Conon* 1. 1; cf. Xenophon *Hellenica* 4. 8. 7.
12. For the location of this shrine see Roebuck (1941) Appendix I, pp. 118–21; *BSA* 61 (1966):115–16, and cf. n. 104 below.
13. Cf. W. G. Forrest, *Historia* 6 (1957):160–75.
14. Quoted by Strabo 6. 279.
15. Cf. Huxley, *Early Sparta* p. 34 and n. 190 on p. 113.
16. See Frazer *Pausanias* III p. 410, and n. 89 below.
17. Cf. Huxley, *Early Sparta* pp. 26–27, 30–31, and 35.
18. Cf. Pausanias 4. 11. 1.
19. Cf. the article cited in n. 13 above.
20. Huxley, *Early Sparta* p. 35.
21. Pausanias 4. 14. 3; see n. 88 below.
22. Huxley, *Early Sparta* pp. 32–33.
23. Cf. W. G. Forrest, *A History of Sparta* (London, 1968) pp. 19–22.
24. By the constitution of Solon, the Athenian *Zeugitai* (i.e., roughly the hoplite class) had to own land producing 200 *medimnoi* of grain, oil, or wine each year (Aristotle *Constitution of Athens* 7).
25. Cf. Huxley, *Early Sparta* pp. 37–52; Forrest, *History of Sparta* pp. 61–68.
26. At the Battle of Hysiai: Pausanias 2. 24. 8.
27. Pausanias (4. 15. 1) dates the outbreak of the second war to 685 B.C., but it is possible that this date, like his date for the beginning of the first war, is slightly too early: although no ancient source connects the two, the hour of Sparta's weakness after Hysiai would have been a likely time for the Messenians to attempt to throw off the Spartan yoke (Huxley, *Early Sparta* pp. 56–57; Forrest, *History of Sparta* p. 69), and if we are right to date the first war from about 735 to about 715 B.C., Tyrtaios' statement (fr. 4 Diehl) that it took place in "our fathers' fathers'" time, would fit a date about 660 B.C. for the outbreak of the second war, fought in his own time.
28. Pausanias drew on the epic of Rhianos of Biene, and it is possible that Rhianos himself believed that Aristomenes lived in the time of the Spartan king Leotychidas II, at the beginning of the fifth century. Cf. Pausanias 4. 15. 2 and Jacoby *FGrHist* Vol. IIIA, p. 136f. (commentary on 265 F 38–46).
29. Huxley, *Early Sparta* p. 58 and n. 380 on p. 130.
30. For the location of Eira see n. 93 below; for the view that the Second Messenian War revolved mainly around the Stenyklaros Plain see Forrest, *History of Sparta* pp. 70–71.
31. Cf. Huxley, *Early Sparta* p. 56.
32. Cf. *ibid.*, pp. 59–60.
33. Pausanias 4. 17. 2.
34. Huxley, *Early Sparta* p. 58 and nn. 381–83 on p. 130.
35. See especially *ibid.*, pp. 28–30 and *BCH* 82 (1958) pp. 588ff.
36. Herodotus 6. 127. For the seventh-century date of Pheidon see, e.g., Andrewes, *The Greek Tyrants* p. 41.
37. Forrest, *History of Sparta*, pp. 69–70. Huxley, however (*Early Sparta* p. 57 and n. 366 on p. 129), believes that Elis did side with Messenia, at least in the earlier part of the war.
38. Cf. F. Kiechle, *Messenische Studien* (Kallmünz, 1959) pp. 34–38; Huxley, *Early Sparta* pp. 59–60. Forrest, however (*History of Sparta* p. 69), thinks that the date about 600 B.C. for the end of Messenian freedom rests merely on a confusion.
39. Cf. Thucydides' description of Koryphasion (4. 3. 2).
40. Cf. Diodorus 15. 66. 1; Plutarch *Agesilaus* 34.
41. Cf. n. 95 below.
42. C. A. Roebuck, *A History of Messenia from 369 to 146 B.C.* (Private Edition, University of Chicago Libraries,

1941) p. 30 and nn. 12 and 13. For the location of Aulon, see n. 101 below.

43. Roebuck *ibid.* and n. 14. For the location of Asine see n. 91 below.
44. Cf. n. 11 above.
45. Roebuck, *History of Messenia* p. 30 and n. 17 on pp. 30–31.
46. Cf. Aristotle fr. 592 (Rose) ap. Plutarch *Moralia* 292b, cf. 277b–c; Jacoby *CQ* 38 (1944) p. 15; Kiechle, *Messenische Studien* pp. 16–18.
47. E. S. G. Robinson, *JHS* 66 (1946):13–21. Thucydides (6. 4. 6) says that Anaxilas renamed Zankle "Messene" after his *own* country of origin.
48. L. H. Jeffery, *JHS* 69 (1949):26–30.
49. E.g., that Kleomenes did not reign for very long (Herodotus 5. 48); in fact, Kleomenes seems to have reigned from at least about 520 to about 490 B.C.
50. Cf. W. P. Wallace, *JHS* 74 (1954):32–36.
51. Cf. W. G. Forrest, *CQ* 10 (1961):221ff.
52. For the date see Gomme, *A Historical Commentary on Thucydides* I pp. 401–2.
53. Perhaps the most plausible emendation is "ἕκτῳ" for "δεκάτῳ" (*ibid.*, I p. 404). Did Thucydides in fact write "οἱ ἐν Ἰθωμῇ δ'ἕκτῳ ἔτει"? If so, the unusual position of the particle "δὲ" might account for the corruption. For "δὲ" occurring later than the second word in a sentence see Denniston, *The Greek Particles* pp. 185–89.
54. As Gomme points out (*Historical Commentary* I p. 403), all the other authorities, beginning with Ephoros, say that the war lasted nine or ten years, and of these Diodoros (11. 63) dates its beginning to the year 469/68 B.C., and Philochoros apparently dated it to 468/67 B.C. (ap. Schol. to Aristophanes *Lysistrata* 1144).
55. See M. E. White, *JHS* 84 (1964):140f.
56. The manuscripts of Herodotus have "Ἰσθμῷ" and Valmin, *Études topographiques sur la Messénie Ancienne* (Lund, 1930) pp. 64–65, identifies this "isthmus" with the Skala hills dividing the Stenyklaros Plain from the lower plain. Others emend "Ἰσθμῷ" to "Ἰθωμῇ."
57. Cf. Thucydides 1. 102. 2; Aristophanes *Lysistrata* 1134–44; Diodoros 11. 64. 2; Pausanias 4. 24. 6; Plutarch *Kimon* 16–17.
58. Aegina (Thucydides 2. 27. 2); Mantinea (Xenophon *Hellenica* 5. 2. 3); Plataea (Thucydides 3. 54. 5).
59. Thucydides 1. 103. 1. As Gomme points out (*Historical Commentary* I p. 303), the terms were lenient except in that a helot who returned would become the personal slave of the man who took him, i.e., would not even have the comparatively privileged status of a helot.
60. Dittenberger *Sylloge* (3rd ed., Leipzig 1915–23) 80–81; *Fouilles de Delphes* III, No. 1.
61. Messene in Sicily, however, did not side with Athens (Thucydides 6. 50. 1).
62. See, e.g., *Hellenica* 3. 4. 20, 5. 2. 24, 6. 5. 24.
63. Thus, when Epameinondas invaded Lakonia in 370 B.C., no fewer than 6,000 helots were enlisted as soldiers by the Spartans, on promise of their freedom (Xenophon *Hellenica* 6. 5. 28–29).
64. For example, the Spartans massacred 2,000 of them in 424 B.C. (Thucydides 4. 80).
65. Thucydides 4. 26. 6–7. Thucydides also gives us some idea of the produce of Messenia at the time: the rations of the Spartan troops on Sphakteria, either allowed by the original truce or later ferried to them by helots in boats or swimming, included "ready-kneaded dough" (σῖτος μεμαγμένος), "barley-groats" (ἄλφιτον), wine, meat, cheese, poppy seed mixed with honey (μήκων μεμελιτωμένη) and linseed (λίνου σπέρμα). Presumably all or most of these were locally obtainable (Thucydides 4. 16. 1, 4. 26. 5, and 4. 26. 8).
66. *IG* V ii 419. 23; *IG* V i 1468. 4–6.
67. Head, *Historia Nummorum* (2nd ed.) p. 341; Pausanias 4. 33. 2. For the mystery cult at Andania see Roebuck, *History of Messenia* pp. 35–37.
68. Diodoros 15. 77. 4; Roebuck, *History of Messenia* p. 38 and n. 62 on pp. 38–39.
69. See n. 117 below.
70. Roebuck, *History of Messenia* pp. 41–46.
71. Tacitus *Annals* 4. 43. 3; Strabo 8. 316; Roebuck, *History of Messenia* pp. 54–57.
72. Roebuck, *History of Messenia* pp. 109–17.
73. See n. 104 below.
74. Roebuck, *History of Messenia* p. 102 and n. 167 on pp. 102–3.
75. Dittenberger *Sylloge* 736.
76. Dittenberger *Sylloge* 826, 705, 684; *SEG* III 378; cf. Plutarch *Kimon* 1–2; *IGRR* I 118.
77. E.g., Euboea (*IGRR* I 118), Boeotia (Dittenberger *Sylloge* 747, cf. Cicero *de Natura Deorum* 3. 49), and Phocis (Pausanias 10. 34. 2).
78. E.g., *ad Atticum* 1. 19. 9, *de Domo* 23, *in Pisonem* 37, *de Provinciis Consularibus* 6.
79. *IG* V i 1432 and 1433; see nn. 130 and 131 below.
80. Cf. n. 131 below.
81. *IG* V i 1433. 26, 1434.
82. Appian *Civil Wars* 5. 77; Cassius Dio 48. 39. 1 and 46. 1.
83. Cf. Tacitus *Annals* 1. 2.
84. The commentary in the notes which follow here is based mainly on the works of Valmin, *Études topographiques*, and Roebuck, *History of Messenia*, which are indispensable for Messenian topography of the historical period.
85. Valmin, index *s.v.* Stenyklaros, esp. pp. 82ff., located Stenyklaros in the western half of the Upper Pamisos Plain; and this is consistent with his arguments for locating Andania there (see n. 92 below). His conjecture that the Kastro of Tsoukaleïka might represent the center of Stenyklaros was discarded in the light of his own later investigations (*Bull Lund* [1933–34] p. 12, cf. Roebuck, *History of Messenia* p. 4 n. 7 and p. 13 n. 35) from which he concluded that the walls at Tsoukaleïka are comparatively modern, built possibly in the Greek War of Independence.
86. Valmin, *Études topographiques* p. 23 and pp. 207f. places Mesola in the northeast angle of the Messenian Gulf, i.e., comprising mainly the territory of Thouria and Pherai.
87. By process of elimination, Hyameitis would have comprised the district on the west side of the Pamisos in the Lower Plain (cf. Valmin, *ibid.* p. 24).
88. Strabo 8. 4. 5 (360), cf. 8. 4. 7 (361), says that Rhion was "opposite Tainaron." This would place it somewhere in the region of the later Asine (cf. Valmin, *Études topographiques* p. 169, and *BSA* 61 [1966]:127 n. 11).
89. See p. 84 above. Valmin, *ibid.* p. 13 and pp. 74ff. comments on the proposed location of Ampheia at Kokkala (#211). He maintains that, although this site is strategic and conforms more or less with Pausanias' description (4. 5. 9), it lies too far from the main route into Messenia (i.e., the Leondari gorge). Valmin accordingly places Ampheia at Helleniko near Desylla (#608), where others have placed Andania (see n. 89 below). But, as Roebuck remarks, *History of Messenia* p. 9 and n. 20, the walls of the Helleniko fort are similar in construction to those of Messene (see n. 117 below), whereas Pausanias (*loc. cit.*) refers to Ampheia "in the past tense." Roebuck (*loc. cit.*) also points out that there may be a reference to Ampheia in *IG* V, 1, 1426 (cf. Valmin p. 62 n. 14).
90. Ithome at this time presumably consisted only of the mountaintop fortress (cf. above p. 85 and n. 14, p. 84 and n. 57).
91. Roebuck, *History of Messenia* pp. 19–22 dispels the doubts raised by Valmin, *Études topographiques* pp. 64ff. and *Bull*

Lund (1934–35) pp. 44–46 concerning the locations of ancient Asine and Korone, at modern Korone (#512) and Petalidhi (#502), respectively. The compelling arguments are firstly the *order* of Pausanias' account (4. 34. 4–12) and secondly the description of Korone as "under Mount Mathia" (i.e., below the modern Lykodimo, a conspicuous landmark). The earliest find from modern Koroni is a sherd of early Archaic Protocorinthian ware (cf. Valmin, *ibid.* p. 178 and *BSA* 52 [1957]:249).

92. Valmin, *Études topographiques* pp. 92ff. (cf. Roebuck, *History of Messenia* pp. 4ff.) identifies the Karnasion Grove and Andania with the remains near Polichni (#607). The main argument is that this area is the provenance of the inscription (*IG* V 1 1390) which describes the regulation of the Andanian Mysteries. The location accords well with Pausanias' description (4. 33. 3–6) of the Upper Pamisos Valley, in which Andania is apparently at the crossroads of the routes from Messene to Megalopolis and from Messene to Kyparissia. The former location of Andania (by F. Hiller von Gaertringen and H. Lattermann, *Hira und Andania* 71 *Berl. Winkelmannsfeste* (1911) pp. 31–37) at Elliniko near Desylla (#608) must now be rejected (see n. 89 above and n. 117 below).

93. This is #611, described by Hiller von Gaertringen and Lattermann, *Hira und Andania* pp. 13–30 (cf. Valmin, *Études topographiques* index *s.v.* Eira, and Roebuck, *History of Messenia* pp. 11–12). Remains were found of a fort of the Archaic period, and of another belonging to the period after the foundation of Messene (for this later fort, see n. 119 below).

94. Although no certain Archaic finds have been made here, it is clear from the activities of the Thourians in the early part of the fifth century B.C. that Thouria was occupied at least in the latter part of the sixth century. It is, in fact, likely that the site was occupied continuously from the Protogeometric period onward.

95. For various guesses as to the position of Aithaia, see Valmin, *Études topographiques* p. 62 (and cf. Roebuck, *History of Messenia* pp. 30–31 and p. 7 n. 16).

96. This is #412. As well as the tradition (see p. 86 above) that refugees from Nauplia were settled at Mothone at this time, we now have archaeological evidence of Late Archaic habitation there (*Deltion* 21 [1966] B′1, p. 164).

97. See #'s 701, 707 (Samikon), 708, 709, 715, and 245 (Lepreon).

98. J. Sperling, *AJA* 46 (1942):83.

99. *Ibid.*, pp. 85 and 87. H. L. Bisbee, *Hesperia* 6 (1937):525–38, described the walls of Samikon, and attributed one section to the Archaic period; but Sperling recorded that only one sherd which might possibly be Archaic was found. Meyer (1957) 34f., 68, 76f.

100. See p. 91 and n. 11 above. For the towns south of Pherai (Kalamata) on the east side of the Messenian Gulf, see Valmin, *Études topographiques* pp. 181ff., Roebuck, *History of Messenia* pp. 15–16, *BSA* 52 (1957):232–39, and *BSA* 61 (1966):113–16. The only definite evidence of Archaic habitation was found at ancient Thalamai (#150, modern Koutifari), in the course of a minor excavation (*BSA* 11 [1904–5]:124–36). But Kardamyle (#147) and Leuktra (#148) at least must have been occupied at this time. Kardamyle is also mentioned by Herodotus (8. 73. 2) and early Doric column capitals have recently been found there (*Deltion* 22 [1967] B′1, p. 206).

101. The first mention of Aulon comes from the early fourth century B.C. (Xenophon *Hellenica* 3. 2. 25). Roebuck, *History of Messenia* pp. 25–26 points out that, according to Xenophon, Aulon was a district rather than a town (cf. Strabo 8. 3. 25 [350] and Pausanias 4. 36. 7). The fort at Vounaki (#601) seems to belong to the late Hellenistic period (Valmin, *Études topographiques* pp. 107ff., and *Bull Lund* (1933–34) p. 11; Roebuck, *History of Messenia* pp. 25–26 and p. 65 n. 28). Thus, although this site *may* have been occupied earlier, and may have been within the district of Aulon, it is by no means certain that it represents a *town* of Aulon in the fourth century B.C. Also interesting in this connection is the fairly extensive classical and Hellenistic site at Ayios Ilias (#602), which commands a good view over the route down the west coast into Messenia.

102. Conjecturally located by Valmin, *Études topographiques* pp. 136–41 at Marathoupolis (#406).

103. The location at Stilari (#233), proposed by Valmin, *ibid.* pp. 79ff. and pp. 102ff., is not contested, although Roebuck, *History of Messenia* p. 12 comments on the difficulty of identifying the ancient place-names in the Soulima Valley.

104. Cf. n. 12 and p. 84 above. Roebuck, *History of Messenia* pp. 122ff. argues convincingly that Kalamai should be placed at Yiannitsa (#537) or at Ayios Vasilios (#536) nearby. The arguments are based on good epigraphical evidence (cf. also *BSA* 61 [1966]:119 and n. 27) and supersede Valmin's suggested location at Pidhima (Valmin, *Études topographiques* pp. 53ff.). The question is connected with that of the locations of Limnai and the Temple of Artemis Limnatis (cf. Valmin pp. 53 and 190ff., and Roebuck pp. 118–21). The location of the Temple at Volimnos (#138) suggested by Roebuck (*loc. cit.*) best suits both the epigraphical and the literary evidence (cf. *BSA* 61 [1966]:115–16).

105. Since the remains at Kitries (#546) are both late and insignificant, it follows that the locations proposed by Valmin, *Études topographiques* pp. 182ff. and others for Gerenia at Kambos (#146) and for Alagonia at Brinda (#548) must be correct. Inscriptions dated to the fifth century B.C. (*IG* V 1 1337–38) have been found at Kambos.

106. Epion is placed by Xenophon *Hellenica* 3. 2. 30 between Heraia and Makistos. Meyer (1957) pp. 68f.

107. The site at Platiana (#705) has been suggested as either ancient Epion or ancient Tympaneai. Cf. Meyer (1957) 22f., 61f., 68n.5.

108. Possibly represented by the site at Vrestos (#701). Cf. Meyer (1957) 55f., 62, 71f.

109. This may be the site at Grilos (#708). Cf. Meyer (1957) 43f., 61f.

110. Sperling, *AJA* 46 (1942):88 comments on the proliferation of hill fortresses in Triphylia (southern Elis) in "this turbulent period in Elean life." But he admits that most of the inhabitants of Elis lived in "fertile low-lying regions" at this time (e.g., Lepreon and Samikon and #'s 700, 701, 705, and 732).

111. In *BSA* 61 (1966):123–24 it is suggested, on the basis of similar walling elsewhere, that the walls of Thouria may be of the late fourth or early third century B.C.

112. See pp. 86–88 above.

113. See pp. 88–89 above.

114. Conversely, Pherai was now apparently a Spartan colony (see n. 11 above).

115. Cf. Pausanias 5. 6. 4–6 and Xenophon *On Hunting*, esp. 2. 2f., 9. 1f., 9. 11, and 10. 1f., and Xenophon *Anabasis* 5. 3.

116. Pp. 89–92 above.

117. See #529. Valmin, *Études topographiques* pp. 67ff. described small subsidiary forts at Psoriari to southwest of Messene, and also to north of Ithome at a place near the gorge of the Sphendamos, a tributary of the Valira River. He also noted the similarity of the latter to the triple bridge over the Mavrozoumenos (see p. 87 above and Pl. 4-1), and to the fort at Stilari (#233). Roebuck, *History of Messenia* pp. 39ff., and esp. 39–40 n. 68, links the construction of the forts of Elliniko (#608), Tzorota

(#614) and Psoriari (where Hellenistic sherds were found, Valmin, p. 69), as well as of the Mavrozoumenos bridge, chronologically with the fortifications of Messene (see p. 87 above). The fortifications on the island of Proti (#407) may also belong to this period, as Roebuck suggests. A full description and discussion of the Mavrozoumenos bridge has been given by Roebuck in *Studies Presented to David M. Robinson* I, 351–355.

118. See nn. 103 and 117 above. Stilari controlled the route from the west coast via the Soulima Valley (cf. Roebuck, *History of Messenia* p. 40).

119. Roebuck, *ibid.* pp. 64f. groups together the construction of the forts at Vounaki (#610, cf. n. 101 above), "New" Hira (#611, cf. n. 93 above), and Yiannitsa (#537, cf. n. 104 above). He suggests that these were part of a frontier defense system set up by Messene in response to threats in the early third century B.C. If Yiannitsa is indeed the site of ancient Kalamai, this would be the fort taken by Lycurgus in 217 B.C. (Roebuck, pp. 59–60 and 122–24, and see p. 91 above).

120. As evidenced in particular by the three gates of Messene, leading north, east, and south, and by the Mavrozoumenos bridge (see n. 117 above).

121. See #412. The exact date of the extant remains is, however, not completely certain, especially in this case; and the argument therefore depends largely on the literary evidence (see pp. 89, 90 above).

122. See #502. For the location of Korone at Petalidhi, see n. 91 above. Valmin, *Études topographiques* pp. 177–79 comments on the remains of the city walls, which were at least 2 km in circumference and about 1.50 m thick.

123. See #72. Valmin pp. 131f. describes the extent of the enceinte walls.

124. See #142. Considerable expansion must be presupposed, to judge from the remains so far uncovered.

125. As is argued above (p. 89), it is probable that Kolonides, together with Korone, was founded after about 365 B.C. Kolonides has usually been placed at Kastelia-Vounaria (#507), a pair of hillocks just above the shore, on the southern edge of the Longa plain (Valmin, *Études topographiques* p. 172 fig. 32). But the known remains here are mainly, if not entirely, from tombs. In *BSA* 61 (1966):125 it is suggested that Kolonides may have been on the seaward slope of the hill of Kafirio (#107) near Longa, in a far better position and with a finer water supply. There is evidence of a fairly large Roman settlement here, and earlier occupation in the vicinity is suggested by the Temple of Apollo Korynthos at Ayios Andhreas (#504). Pausanias' description (4. 34. 8) of Kolonides as being on a high place a short distance from the sea, seems to contradict the location at Kastelia and Vounaria, which are better described as *on* the coast.

126. Cf. Roebuck, *Classical Philology* 40 (1945):152 and n. 27. In the Aetolian raids of 221 B.C. animals were the main booty (Polybius IV 3. 9–10, and cf. IV 4. 1 concerning the raid on Chiron's large ranching estate).

127. See pp. 91, 92 above.

128. See p. 92 above.

129. *IG* V 1 1431. Roebuck, *History of Messenia* pp. 13f. and n. 7 and pp. 118–21, comments on this inscription and on the related boundary markers (*IG* V 1 1371 a–c and 1372 a–b) found by Kolbe and Ross high up on the Taygetos range (cf. Kolbe *AM* 29 [1904]:364–78 and Bölte in Pauly-Wissowa IIIA 1312–15). Three further markers, found by N. A. Giannokopoulos, are discussed by him in relation to the previous evidence in *Platon* (1953) pp. 1–16. He points out that the surveyor T. Flavius Monomitos, a freedman of the emperor Vespasian, was merely inspecting and confirming boundaries laid out previously. These *may* have been set up in the time of Tiberius (cf. Tacitus *Annals* 4. 43), as Giannokopoulos assumes (apparently from Pausanias 4. 1. 1 — but Pausanias does not here say *which* emperor was responsible). In any case, the boundary from A.D. 78 was recognized as the Choireios gorge (the modern Sandava) on the south and Mt. Taygetos on the east.

130. E.g., those dealing with taxation (see pp. 92, 93 and n. 79 above).

131. See p. 93 and n. 81 above. Roebuck, *Classical Philology* 40 (1945): esp. pp. 149 and 157–65, commented on the evidence, particularly that of the Andania inscription (Dittenberger *Sylloge*[3] 736, and of *IG* V 1 1432–33) for Messenian prosperity at this time. But, as he says, the value of the inscriptions "is impaired by the uncertainty whether they refer to all of Messenia or only to the city of Messene and its particular district." That they refer to the latter (as Roebuck surmised) seems to be supported by the inscription (*IG* V 1 1379, "dated vaguely in the second or first century B.C." – Roebuck, p. 153) regulating the grain supply of the town of Thouria. As Roebuck says, "the inscription gives no hint of a shortage of grain but is concerned with disposing the surplus with as much profit to the city as possible, presumably to citizens of its own district. It is to be noted that Thouria, at least for the period of this inscription, had full control over its own grain supply and was not subject to the authority of Messene".

Roebuck (*ibid.*) also tried to estimate the total population of Messenia at this time, on the basis of the area of cultivable land available. He may have underestimated the importance of grain cultivation on hill terraces (i.e., on land categorized by Loy and by Van Wersch in Ch. 11 as "Class II" and "Class III"), his calculations being based mainly on the premise of the paramount importance of the fertile but often poorly drained alluvium of the Pamisos Valley. Several other quite extensive tracts of Messenia are also fertile – for instance, the rolling hill country (now abundant in horses) west of the Pamisos Valley, which presumably constituted the ancient Hyameitis. In addition to the Pylos district itself, there is also a fertile tract on the extensive plateau centered on Mesopotamos, which forms the watershed on the road from Rizomilo to Pylos (see Ch. 11).

132. See #'s 609 and 505.

133. See #'s 508, 519, and 417.

134. See #137. Pausanias (4. 31. 2) speaks of the descent to the plain. Valmin, *Études topographiques* pp. 56ff., remarks that, as Pausanias implies, there was still apparently some settlement on the acropolis of Thouria in the Roman period, to judge from the archaeological evidence, although Pausanias also states that the walls were in ruins.

135. #147; cf. Valmin, *ibid.* pp. 119–202, and *BSA* 52 (1957): 234–36.

BIBLIOGRAPHY

Forrest, W. G. 1968. *A History of Sparta.* London.

Huxley, G. L. 1962. *Early Sparta.* London.

Roebuck, C. A. 1941. *A History of Messenia from 369 to 146 B.C.* Private Ed., University of Chicago Libraries.

———. 1945. "A Note on Messenian Economy and Population." *Classical Philology* 40:149–65.

Sperling, J. 1942. "Explorations in Elis," in *AJA* 46:77–89.

Valmin, M. N. 1930. *Études topographiques sur la Messénie ancienne.* Lund.

7

THE MYCENAEAN DOCUMENTS

by

John Chadwick

The excavation of the Mycenaean palace of Epano Englianos yielded some 1,200 odd clay tablets written in the Greek language and the Linear B script. These were found mainly in a single area, now known as the Archive Room, just inside the main entrance (Blegen and Rawson 1966). They constitute the administrative records of the palace during the last days before its destruction, for none appear to go back more than one year. It is probable that the clay tablets were used for temporary records, and more permanent records, if any existed, must have been kept on perishable material. What we have is a number of documents referring to agricultural production, livestock, bronzesmiths, etc., together with some inventories of the palace storerooms. Many documents were written in the form of "sets" of small tablets, each containing a single entry, rather like a card-index file. Many tablets are broken and damaged, so that few documents are complete, and allowance has constantly to be made for what can be presumed to be missing. None of the documents is historical; they contain nothing but bald lists and accounts.

Naturally enough, in such material words which can be identified as place-names are common. But no document contains a geographical account of the kingdom, much less a map; and their interpretation is therefore exceedingly difficult. None the less, some progress has been made in reconstructing the political geography of the kingdom, and the main purpose of this chapter is briefly to review the evidence and to attempt, with due caution, to compare this with the physical geography of southwest Peloponnese.

It is of prime importance to begin such an investigation without prejudices and preconceived notions. All too often writers on this subject (and I do not except myself) have succumbed to the temptation of trying to reconcile, at all costs, the data in the tablets with Homer's account of the area, imprecise and dubious as it is. Whatever attitude is adopted toward the historicity of Homer, it cannot be doubted that on important points his testimony is inconsistent, and can sometimes be demonstrated to be inaccurate. Thus we must resolutely close our minds to seductive titles like "The Palace of Nestor"; we have no evidence for the name of the Mycenaean ruler of Messenia, whose palace was burnt at the end of the Late Helladic III B period (about 1200 B.C.). In our documents he is simply referred to as *wanax*, "the king." Nor have we any means of dating precisely the events which Homer purports to describe. The destruction of Troy VIIA may or may not correspond to the Trojan War of the Greek tradition; but even if the equation is accepted, it is still impossible to give precise relative dating to the destructions of Troy VIIA and the palace at Englianos. If, as is not improbable, the Homeric tradition contains a kernel of truth, we shall not be able to discern it until we have established the historical facts from other sources.

The Linear B script of the tablets is, like any writing system, an imprecise notation of the spoken form, leaving much to be supplied by the reader; however, in view of the limited nature of the documents there is no reason to think that those who wrote the tablets would have had any difficulty in reading back their notes. As in the case of any shorthand system, they would have presented some problems to literate contemporaries unfamiliar with the subject matter. It is astonishing that we have been so successful in interpreting the tablets, and the frequent gaps and uncertainties in our renderings must be attributed as much to the cryptic nature of the originals as to our inability to read them correctly.

The signs are of three types: The first is syllabic signs,

which are used to spell out the words; these are transcribed alphabetically by groups of letters which give the approximate phonetic value of the sign: e.g., *a*, *ka*, *pte*, *ti*, *wo*, *su*. Transcriptions of Linear B words are written with hyphens between each of the letter-groups representing a sign, thus: *pu-ro*, *di-pte-ra-po-ro*. The second is ideograms—that is, single signs representing persons, animals, artifacts, commodities, etc.; some syllabic signs are also used ideographically as abbreviations. After some variation in practice, ideograms are now transcribed by Latin words appropriate to their meaning, where known; in a few cases a numerical code is used instead. Thus VIR = man, MULIER (abbreviated MUL) = woman, OVIS = sheep, SUS = pig, AMPH(ORA) = two-handled jar, ROTA = wheel, GRA(NUM) = grain, VIN(UM) = wine, OLE(UM) = olive oil, and so on. The third type, numerals, presents no problems, provided they are clearly legible, and are transcribed as ordinary numbers. Square brackets are used to show where the text is incomplete as the result of damage to the tablet. Individual words were normally separated by a small vertical stroke, represented in transcription by a comma.

Alongside the straight transcriptions it is necessary to set a reconstructed phonetic form. Thus, the name of the site at Englianos is spelled with two Linear B signs: *pu-ro*. By a series of rules deduced from Mycenaean practice, we can restore the phonetic shape of this word as *Pulos*, since the sign transcribed *ro* equally does duty for *lo*, and final *-s* is not written. Thus we have the Mycenaean form of the name *Pylos*, where *y* represents a Latin transcription of the later sound of the Greek *u*, which had by then become *ü*. Reconstructed forms will be given in italics *without hyphens*, so that they can be easily distinguished from transcriptions. Since we shall be discussing problems of identification, it is important to get these conventions clear.

We must begin with a study of the place-names on the Linear B tablets. But it must be stated at the outset that the criteria which enable us to determine whether or not a word is a place-name are all too often lacking; there is no device like a capital letter to denote a proper name, nor are words referring to places in any way differentiated in the script. Nonetheless, a variety of indications exist which permit us securely to identify a few words as place-names, and then other words can be shown to belong to the same class.

Greek place-names normally exist in two forms: a simple form such as *Athēnai*, *Korinthos*, and a derivative adjective known as ethnic, *Athēnaios*, *Korinthios*. There are a number of words in the tablets which show derivative forms of this type in *-ios*: for example, *me-ta-pa*, *me-ta-pi-jo* (= *Metapa*, *Metapios*); *ko-ri-to*, *ko-ri-si-jo* (= *Korinthos*, *Korinsios*). Such cases are relatively rare in the material available; for the most part only the simple form occurs, and in some cases only the ethnic. Moreover there are adjectival derivatives in *-ios* which are plainly not ethnic, so that this cannot serve as an exclusive criterion; nonetheless, the existence of adjectival forms of this type is a powerful argument in favor of identifying these words as place-names.

A little more satisfactory is the existence of words with a suffix *-de*, which represents a suffix of the same form found in classical Greek; this is attached to the accusative case and means "toward"; thus, *Pulon-de*, "to Pylos." Any word showing this suffix is therefore a place-name or a substitute for one, such as *woikon-de* "homeward." Unfortunately, here too difficulties arise, because there is another word *de* in Greek, meaning "but" or "and," and since the Linear B script does not allow monosyllables to be written with a single sign, this too is tacked on to the end of the preceding word; *ma-te-de* alongside *ma-te* on the tablet identified as Pylos An 607 is not to be taken as a place-name, but its context plainly shows that it is *mātēr de* "but the mother"; another group of words ending in *-de* is represented by *to-so-de* = *tosonde* or *tosoide* "so much" or "so many." But these cases are fairly easy to distinguish, and the existence of forms with and without suffixed *-de* is a strong indication in favor of a place-name. Where the accusative has a different spelling from the nominative, this assists the diagnosis: *pa-ki-ja-ne*, a nominative plural place-name in *-ānes*, has its accusative with *-de* written *pa-ki-ja-na-de* = *-ānas-de*; the correct transcription of the stem of this word is unknown.

Some place-names identified by this method also possess ethnic adjectives in *-ios*, so that in these cases the agreement of two criteria makes identification doubly sure. *pa-ki-ja-ni-jo* is clearly the adjective to *pa-ki-ja-ne*; *e-ra-te-i-jo* to *e-ra-to(-de)*. There is also one case of a list of words (Vn 20), all of which have suffixed *-de*:

o-a$_2$, e-pi-de-da-to	
pa-ra-we-wo, wo-no	
pi-*82-de	50
me-ta-pa-de	50
pe-to-no-de	100
pa-ki-ja-na-de	35
a-pu$_2$-de	35
a-ke-re-wa-de	30
e-ra-to-de	50
ka-ra-do-ro-de	40
ri-jo-de	20

This appears to be a list recording the distribution (*e-pi-de-da-to* = *epidedastoi* "has been distributed") of wine (*wo-no* = *woinos*?) to nine towns. The same list is repeated on another tablet (Cn 608) but in this case the suffixed *-de* is omitted, and in three cases the form of the name is modified to express the dative-locative case: *pa-ki-ja-si*, *a-pu$_2$-we*, *e-ra-te-i*. A fragmentary version of the same list occurs again in Vn 19, where *pa-ki-ja-ne* shows that the case is here nominative; and again on the large tablet Jn 829, where there are some discrepancies, since *ro-*[*u*]*-so* takes the place of *e-ra-to*, and the list is immediately followed by a further seven entries of the same type. In all cases the names follow in the same order.

Thus, it is easy to establish sixteen words (or seventeen including the variant name) as place-names; and this can serve as the starting point for the identification of many more. The use of suffixed *-de* indicates *me-te-to*, *ne-do-wo-ta*, *o-pi-ke-ri-jo*, *pe-re-u-ro-na* and *ti-no* as place-names. Then with those firmly identified we can see that the Na series of tablets, a group of about a hundred small tablets with entries of a commodity expressed by an ideographic use of a sign, has regularly a place name as the first entry on each. This at once enables us to build a long list of place-names, and the same principle may be applied elsewhere to complete the list. Unfortunately, Mycenaean scribes are not so regular in their habits that it is sufficient to identify a few words in a list as place-names to be able to infer that all others fall into the same class. At times place-names are mixed up with titles, personal names, and so on, in a way which was no doubt clear enough to the writers, but can cause us much confusion. I believe that some words have consequently been wrongly identified as place-names, and the total has thus been inflated (Chadwick 1969).

My estimate of the number of words on the Pylos tablets which can be identified as certain or possible place-names is about 185. For comparison, the number of words in the glossary of L. R. Palmer's *Interpretation of Mycenaean Greek Texts* (1963) which are classified on a similar definition as geographical terms is 256. If, as I believe, this figure is somewhat inflated, my own is probably somewhat conservative, and most scholars would be satisfied with a total around 200.

But before we try to match this figure against the numbers of sites known archaeologically, we must take two other facts into account. Places which lie outside the borders of the kingdom may be mentioned on the tablets. This is especially true of names occurring with the suffix *-de* "toward," and the *eretai Pleurōnade iontes* "rowers who are to go to Pleuron" of An 1 are perhaps being sent to a town in another state. Not that all place-names with the suffix fall into this class, for, as shown above, it is used with towns which are certainly part of the kingdom. The problem also arises in the case of ethnic adjectives which are not represented also by the simple place-name; natives of a town may retain their local appellation even when moved to a distant region. This I believe is true of the ethnics which are used to describe the women on the Aa and Ab tablets, some of which are identical with the names of classical sites on the east of the Aegean; only one, *ti-nwa-si-ja*, appears to belong to the Pylian kingdom, for there is a *ti-nwa-si-jo ko-re-te* "the local official of T" mentioned on Jo 438, and we know his name: *te-po-se-u*. He appears again on On 300, at the end of the paragraph dealing with the Further Province (see below), so perhaps this is a small border state owing allegiance to Pylos, but not directly controlled by the king.

Secondly, it is likely that some geographic names are alternatives. I do not count here alternative forms, such as *pa-ki-ja-ne* and *pa-ki-ja-ni-ja*, *pu-ro ra-u-ra-ti-jo* and *ra-wa-ra-ti-ja*, but entirely different names applied to the same place. This can occur in two ways; places are from time to time given new names, which are thenceforward used in official documents, but the old name often survives in use alongside the new one, at least for some time; historical examples are St. Petersburg/Leningrad, Edo/Tokyo, Constantinople/Istanbul. It is also possible for a native and a foreign name to be used side by side (Ireland/Eire, Siam/Thailand), but this situation is unlikely in the Pylos tablets. The other way in which names can alternate is by overlapping, as when one name refers to the principal town and the other to the whole district (e.g., Exeter/Devonshire, Providence/Rhode Island); and this may occur also on a small scale, as when parts of a large city have separate names. One certain case of an alternative name can be proved on the Pylos tablets: *e-ra-to* is sometimes replaced in a standard list of towns by *ro-u-so*, and since there is a *ro-u-si-jo a-ko-ro* = *Lousios agros* "territory of Lousos" mentioned elsewhere, we may suspect that *ro-u-so* is used to denominate the area in which *e-ra-to* is the principal town.

It follows therefore that the figure of 200 geographical names does not necessarily imply 200 inhabited settlements within the border of the Pylian kingdom. Perhaps 150 would be a cautious estimate, and even so it must be remembered that some of these were probably no more than small villages. This may be compared with the 168 certain Late Bronze habitation sites listed in Chapter 8 in southwest Peloponnese, but the area covered there is the extreme limits conceivable for the kingdom, and the true figure is probably somewhat less. It is also possible that some of these sites which are very close might share a name. It is perhaps reasonable to guess that about half the sites mentioned on the tablets have been discovered by surface search, but there is little basis at present for identifying more than a handful of the names.

Certain types appear to be common among the words certainly or probably identified as place-names:

1. A group of seven apparently compound names ending in *-wo-wo*, plus three with the ending *-wo-wi-ja*, and one ending *-wo-wo-pi*. The words preceding these endings seem to be all masculine personal names in the genitive case, e.g., *ke-ra-ti-jo-jo* = *Kerastioio*. It seems likely that *-wo-wo* therefore represents *worwos* (Classical Greek *horos*) "boundary"; compare the frequent English place names ending in *-bourn(e)*. This type does not appear on the Cretan records from Knossos.

2. Seven place names end in *-e-wa*: *a-ke-re-wa*, *a-no-ke-wa*, *a-pi-te-wa*, *i-te-re-wa*, *na-pe-re-wa*, *si-re-wa*, *wo-no-qe-wa*. This type may be compared with Classical Greek names in *-ea* or plural *-eai* (e.g. *Tegeā*, *Maleā*, *Krokeai*), but since *w* is lost in Classical Greek this cannot be proved. This too is a type absent from the Knossos records. Thus, there would seem to be grounds for supposing underlying differences in the structure of place-names between Crete and the mainland. The first type will represent a Greek type; but the second does not appear to be Greek and its absence from Crete may indicate the presence of another language at the period when the names were given. Those who postulate a single language spoken throughout the Aegean before the coming of the Greeks ought at least to reflect on this fact; analogies suggest that there may have been several languages spoken in these parts in earlier times.

3. Another important group is that of place-names with the nominative plural ending *-a-ne* which can hardly be anything but the type known in Greek as *-ānes*. It must be in origin an ethnic (type *Akarnānes* from which is formed a derivative in *-iā* (type *Akarnaniā*, sc. *ge* "land"). This type in classical Greek has been identified as Dorian (Hammond 1932), but its presence on the Pylos tablets is certain, and unless we are prepared to admit the existence of Dorian settlements in Messenia before the end of the Mycenaean period, any attempt to regard the type as Doric must be abandoned.

The evidence of the tablets shows the following examples:

a-pu₂-ka-ne. An 656.13, An 657.13. An ethnic adjective (although remarkably similar to the place-name *a-pu₂*, it does not appear to be derived from it, since the velar would be unexplained in derivation from a *u*-stem), its nominative singular *a-pu₂-ka* occurs on An 656.20.

i-na-ne. An 18.7. Instrumental *i-na-pi* An 5.8; cf. *i-na-ni-ja* Ae 8, Ae 72, An 18.3.

me-za-ne. Fn 50.4, *me-za-na* Cn 3.1, Sh 736. Possibly not a place-name; very obscure. It seems impossible to link it directly with *Messānā* (*Messēnē*).

pa-ki-ja-ne. Vn 19.4, Xc 113.1. Accusative *pa-ki-ja-na(-de)* Fn 187.4, Vn 20.6, Fr 1209, etc.; dative *pa-ki-ja-si* An 18.11, Cn 608.6, etc.; instrumental *pa-ki-ja-pi* Jn 829.7, Ma 221.1; adjective *pa-ki-ja-ni-jo* Fr 1236, etc. Feminine variant *pa-ki-ja-ni-ja* En 609.1, On 300.3. There is also another form *pa-ki-ja-na* (not accusative) Eb 409.1, Eb 1176.1, En 609.16, etc.

re-ka-ta-ne. An 207. 6,7,8.

te-ta-ra-ne. An 1.5, An 610.9.

wo-tu-wa-ne. Cn 4.8.

If we accept forms in *-a-na* as belonging to this type, which *pa-ki-ja-na* and possibly *me-za-na* suggest, we might add *e-pi-jo-ta-na* with a variant *e-pi-ja-ta-ni-ja*, *pi-ka-na*, *ta-mi-ta-na*; and there are other forms which might belong here but cannot be proved to do so, such as *pa-na-pi*, *ri-sa-pi* and *u-wa-si*.

The type in *-a-na* is hard to separate from the classical names in *-ānā*, *-ānai* (Ionic *-ēnē*, *-ēnai*), which is certainly a pre-Greek type. If so, this is a further reason for rejecting the suggestion that the names in *-ānes* have a Dorian origin.

There are two ways of identifying a Mycenaean place-name with a known site. One is by equating its name with an ancient historical name; the other is by finding internal evidence in the documents which will indicate enough of its features to allow a secure identification. No more than one name can be firmly identified by the second method, though it can contribute valuable clues in many other cases. The certain name is *pu-ro*, which occupies such a predominant role on the tablets that the conclusion that it is the name of the principal site and location of the tablets themselves is irresistible. Fortunately, this can also be identified with the historical name *Pulos* (*Pylos*), which is given by Homer to the capital of Nestor's kingdom in western Peloponnese, and is known in historical times to have been situated at the north of the bay of Navarino. An ancient geographer records the tradition that the name had been transferred thither from another site "under Mt. Aigaleon," and we may suppose that this is reminiscent of a Mycenaean Pylos at Epano Englianos, some 9 km north of the bay. The name *Pulos* was not uncommon in antiquity, and the tablets contain evidence for one and possibly two other towns of the same name: *pu-ro ra-u-ra-ti-jo*, which can be shown to be distant from Englianos, and *ma-to-ro-pu-ro*, if this is to be interpreted as *Matropulos* "Mother-Pylos."

Because so few satisfactory equations can be established by such methodology, attention has been concentrated on formal resemblance to classical names. But although it is in some cases possible to restore the phonetic form of the name with fair certainty, it is hardly ever possible to equate this name with a known location.

The strongest candidate is a place-name]-*pa-ri-so* which may be restored as [*ku*]-*pa-ri-so* on the evidence of the ethnic ku-pa-ri-si-jo. This will answer to *Kuparissos*, the Greek word for the cypress tree (though of non-Greek origin); and a town with a name derived from this word has existed in this area since antiquity. It is now named *Kyparissía*, and in Homer there is a place-name *Kuparissēeis*. There seems little reason to doubt that these are one and the same, and it is therefore tempting to locate the Mycenaean towns on or near the site of the modern one (#70; a naturally strategic position). The area is still notable for its cypresses, though they are common enough elsewhere.

More often a Mycenaean name can be equated with a classical one, but there is no reason to assume that it refers to the same site. Thus *re-u-ko-to-ro* must be the classical name *Leuktron*, but of a number of towns bearing this name (or the plural form *Leuktra*) none is nearer to Pylos than the east coast of the Messenian gulf, and there are good reasons for rejecting that identification. Similarly *ko-ri-to*, with its ethnic *ko-ri-si-jo*, is likely to be *Korinthos* (the Mycenaean ethnic of which would be *Korinsios*, not classical *Korinthios*); but it is absurd to suppose that Pylos controlled the Isthmus of Corinth. Even more doubtful are the place-names which have a meaning in Greek: *ri-jo* = *Rhion*, "the headland"; *ka-ra-do-ro* = *Kharadros*, "the gully." It should be recognized that formal resemblance is useless, unless it can be supported by other strong clues, and our attention ought therefore to be concentrated on discovering as much as possible about the places named in the tablets.

A number of documents prove that the kingdom of Pylos was divided for administrative purposes into two provinces. This emerges most clearly from the two tablets (Ng) attached to the Na series, which list contributions from a large number of towns and villages of a commodity, probably flax, designated by the syllabic sign SA. These tablets, ignoring the second line which is the same in both tablets except for a missing numeral, read:

Ng 319	*de-we-ro-a*$_3$*-ko-ra-i-ja*	SA	1239
Ng 332	*pe-ra*$_3$*-ko-ra-i-ja*	SA	200[

The figure in the second is broken off and 200 is a minimum, 800 a maximum, plus of course some tens and units which have been completely lost. From this it is evident that these are the totals for two areas; the total number of units of SA on the surviving Na tablets is over 1,400, the calculation being rendered complicated by the presence of subsidiary entries corresponding to the second lines of the Ng tablets. Since we have doubtless lost a number of pieces bearing figures, it would be reasonable to guess at a total of around 1,800, and the two Ng tablets together must make up the sum of all the Na tablets. These were presumably divided into two groups corresponding to their totals. Thus, for administrative purposes, the country was divided into two areas.

The names of these two provinces each contain the same second element: -*a*$_3$*-ko-ra-i-ja*, for *ra*$_3$ contains the same diphthong as *a*$_3$: *ai*. The element *de-we-ro-* bears a close resemblance to Greek *deuro*, "hither," since *we* seems at times to be used for u. And *pe-ra*$_3$-, also spelled *pe-ra-a-*, must contain Greek *pera*, "beyond." The two provinces therefore will have been designated as "On this side of —" and "Beyond —," very much as the Romans had provinces called *Gallia Cisalpina*, "Gaul this side of the Alps," and *Galiia Transalpina*, "Gaul beyond the Alps."

The identification of the frontier between the two provinces has caused a great deal of argument. It is my belief that anyone standing on the site of the palace at Englianos cannot fail to notice that Messenia falls into two halves, the western coast, a wide sweep of which is visible from the palace, and the valley at the head of the Messenian Gulf, which is totally concealed by a range of mountains. A few kilometers to the north this range rises to the striking peak now called Ayá (1,218 m). It seemed therefore natural to identify the frontier with this mountain range, and the theory received some confirmation from the resemblance between *a*$_3$*-ko-r-*, which must stand for something like *Aigol-*, and the classical name of this range, *Aigaleon*. Even so, the resemblance is not so close as to be compelling, and a rival theory of L. R. Palmer's proposed that a seamark rather than a landmark ought to be the boundary. If so, the obvious one is Cape Akritas, the southernmost tip of the peninsula. This would have no real effect on the location of the land frontier, since Akritas is the southern tip of the high ground running down the middle of the peninsula. The choice of a seamark results from the supposition that communication between the provinces would be mainly by sea; but now that the existence of a Mycenaean road across the plateau between Pylos and Kalamata (Homeric Pherai) has been demonstrated (see Ch. 2), the arguments against a landmark are much weakened. (See Fig. 7-1.)

Now that we have established the names of the two provinces and identified what seems to have been the line of the frontier, we can proceed to examine the allocation of places between them. It is most unfortunate that the Na tablets were not found divided into two lots, for there can be little doubt that they were contained in separate files or baskets corresponding to the two totalling documents; but they must have been adjacent on the shelves and in the destruction of the Archive Room they ended up in a mixed heap on the floor. Nor does there seem to be any other method of separating the two series, since all were written by the same scribe and have a similar appearance. As we shall see later, in at least one parallel case the documents from the Further Province can be distinguished by the fact that they were written by a different scribe.

The chief evidence for the location of the principal towns comes from a mutilated document (On 300). It is divided into two paragraphs, the heading to the first of which is lost; the second states that it relates to *pe-ra-a-ko-ra-i-ja*, the Further Province. Thus it is reasonable to assume that the first paragraph relates to the Hither Province; but only two place-names from it survive: *pa-ki-ja-ni-ja* which is a variant feminine form of the name *pa-ki-ja-ne*, and *e-ra-te-i-jo*, the ethnic adjective from *e-ra-to*. Both of these figure, in the same order, in the list of towns given in Vn 20 (see above, p. 101), and it is clear that this standard list of nine towns represents the principal centers of the Hither Province. Thus, we can locate the towns in the second paragraph of On 300 in the Further Province, and this shows that the long list of sixteen towns in Jn 829 is

Table 7-1. The Sixteen Towns of Pylos, Listed by Source

Jn 829 Tablet	Ma Tablets[a]	On 300 Tablet[b]	Cn 608 Tablets[c]
pi-*82	pi-*82		pi-*82
me-ta-pa	me-ta-pa		me-ta-pa
pe-to-no	pe-to-no		pe-to-no
pa-ki-ja-pi	pa-ki-ja-pi	pa-ki-ja-ni-ja	pa-ki-ja-si
a-pu$_2$-we	a-pu$_2$-we		a-pu$_2$-we
a-ke-re-wa	a-ke-re-wa		a-ke-re-wa
ro-[u]-so	ro-u-so	e-ra-te-i-jo	e-ra-te-i
ka-ra-do-ro	ka-ra-do-ro		ka-ra-do-ro
[ri]-jo	ri-jo		ri-jo
[ti]-mi-to a-ke-e	ti-mi-to-a-ke-e	te-mi-ti-ja	
[ra]-wa-ra-ta$_2$	ra-wa-ra-ta$_2$	ra-u-ra-ti-ja	
[sa]-ma-ra	sa-ma-ra	sa-ma-[ra]	
a-si-ja-ti-ja	a-[.]-ta$_2$	a-si-ja-ti-ja	
e-ra-te-re-wa-pi	e-ra-te-re-we	e-[ra-te]-re-wa-o	
za-ma-e-wi-ja	za-ma-e-wi-ja		
e-re-i			
	e-sa-re-wi-ja	e-sa-re-wi-ja	
	a-te-re-wi-ja		

[a] The names on the 17 Ma tablets are arranged in the order of Jn 829.

[b] On 300 is fragmentary; if complete, the names would probably match even better.

[c] Cn 608 is one of several lists of the nine towns of the Hither Province alone.

the nine of the Hither Province followed by the seven of the Further Province. The equation is not quite exact, for one name, *e-sa-re-wi-ja*, appears in On 300 and is not on the other list. But the Jn 829 list includes *za-ma-e-wi-ja*, which is absent from On 300 (since it is too long to fit the lacuna in line 12), but is coupled with *e-sa-re-wi-ja* in Vn 493.4.

The list of sixteen towns is shown in Table 7-1. Jn 829 is a list of contributions of bronze made by two officials in each town. The heading gives no fewer than six official titles for the contributors, but in each town contributions are listed only under the titles *ko-re-te* and *po-ro-ko-re-te*, the second contributing not more than a quarter of the contribution of the *ko-re-te*. It is clear therefore that *po-ro-* here equals *pro-* in the sense of "vice-" or "assistant." The identification of the root of *ko-re-te* is disputed, but it is plainly an agent noun in *-ter*, and it may be provisionally translated "mayor," so long as we bear in mind that we know nothing of his functions or mode of appointment. He might equally be a kind of local baron or chieftain. Officials with the same titles are listed on On 300.

Another very important document for this purpose is Jo 438, which is a list of named persons and officials with a weight of gold against each. Since the heading is missing, we cannot be sure whether these are contributions or receipts, but the former is more likely because the names are in the nominative case. If this document were without lacunas, we might be able to make more deductions about the local administration, but it does not appear to follow any standard order. It jumps from one province to the other, and it frequently substitutes names for titles, only rarely giving both. Thus, Jo 438 refers to a man by his name *au-ke-wa*, whereas On 300 has a reference to *da-mo-ko-ro* followed by a lacuna. Fortunately, another tablet (Ta 711) tells us that the king appointed *au-ke-wa* to be *da-mo-ko-ro*. Other connections of the same kind can be traced. For instance, a man's name, *te-po-se-u*, occupies the same position at the end of the second paragraph of On 300 as *da-mo-ko-ro* does at the end of the first paragraph; it is therefore tempting to regard the *da-mo-ko-ro* as an official responsible for the Hither Province. But Jo 438 informs us that *te-po-se-u* was the *ko-re-te* ("mayor") of **ti-nwa-to*, a town otherwise not mentioned except as the origin of a group of women. Possibly therefore **ti-nwa-to* was a distant possession (colony or island?) which was administratively attached to the Further Province, and the parallel with *da-mo-ko-ro* is not significant.

Another important source of geographical information is the so-called "coastguard" tablets, a set of five tablets (An 657, 654, 519, 656, 661) which can be

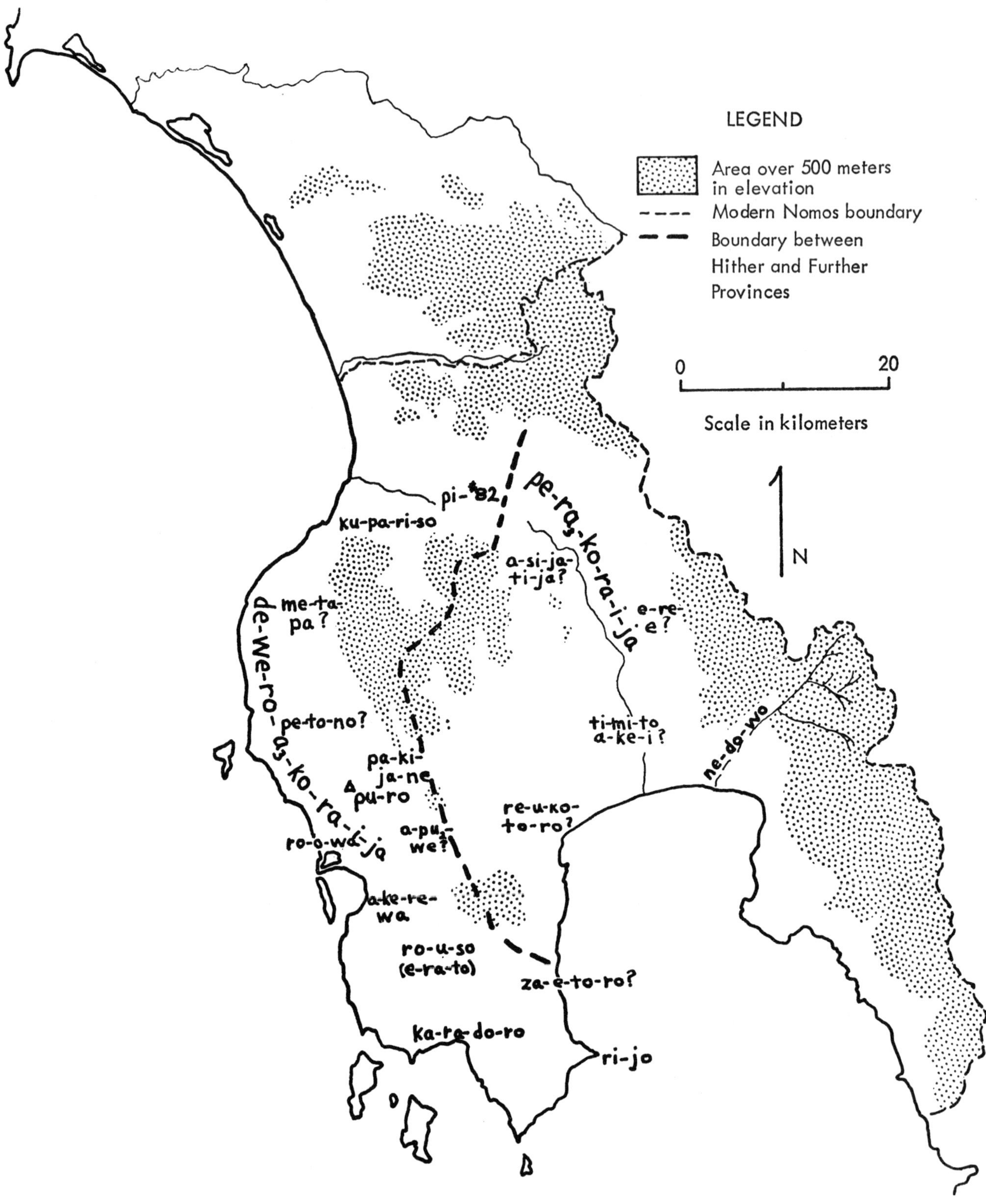

Figure 7-1. Approximate location of two provinces and certain major "tablet" towns. All identifications except *pu-ro* are only very approximate. Larger lettering indicates provinces; smaller, places or rivers.

treated as a single document. Moreover, we can restore these to their correct order, apart from the uncertainty of whether 654 or 519 comes immediately after 657.

Unfortunately, the formula used throughout the set is not entirely consistent, and it is therefore impossible to be sure whether some words not found elsewhere are places or persons. Generally, however, the following pattern is observable: (a) man's name in genitive followed by *o-ka*; (b) place-name (sometimes omitted); (c) group of men's names in nominative; (d) place-name, description of men, *x* men, where *x* is a number between 10 and 110. The heading which introduces the set on An 657 translates quite certainly as "Thus the watchers are guarding the coastal regions." The *o-ka* is almost certainly a word meaning "command," and the preceding name is that of the commanding officer; entry *b* shows the location of the headquarters. Entry *c* is best understood as a list of subordinate officers, and entry *d* apparently gives the force at their disposal and its location.

Now since we are specifically told that the places mentioned are "coastal regions," we can be sure that all the names given are on or very near the coast. Moreover, it is clear that the order of the names on the tablets must follow the coastline, and since the Further Province is represented only in the second half of An 661 the list must begin at the other end of the kingdom, that is, at the northernmost point on the west coast. This can be confirmed by matching the coastguard list with that of the sixteen towns (Jn 829). Those that appear in both (*a-ke-re-wa, ka-ra-do-ro, ti-mi-to a-ke-e*) follow the same order; and there is another link in the ethnic *me-ta-pi-jo* which answers to *me-ta-pa*, the second of the nine. The boundary between the two provinces lies between *ka-ra-do-ro* (eighth of the nine) and *ti-mi-to a-ke-e* (first of the seven); therefore all the places before *ka-ra-do-ro* belong to the Hither Province. The only other place-name in the Further Province is *ne-do-wo-ta(-de)*, which can be given a geographical location in the Kalamata area (see below p. 110 and Fig. 7-1).

Still another valuable clue to the distribution of place names between the two provinces is found in the Aa series of tablets. These are short tablets listing women and children and giving their location. Since I have discussed the details elsewhere (Chadwick and Killen, in preparation), I shall here state briefly the relevant conclusions. E. L. Bennett in 1956 demonstrated that the Aa series was divided into two sets, distinct both in their physical location in the Archive Room and in the handwriting. The two sets are unequal in size; the major one includes Pylos and clearly refers to the Hither Province, the minor one to the Further Province. Thus the place-names on these tablets can be certainly assigned to the correct administrative division.

It now appears that the women listed in these sets are menial workers, very probably slaves, some of whom are employed on domestic chores, but more on textile production (spinning, weaving, finishing, etc.). The majority in the Hither Province are located at Pylos itself, with an important subsidiary center at *ro-u-so*. Correspondingly, in the Further Province the majority are concentrated at *re-u-ko-to-ro* (Leuktron), which is therefore likely to be the main royal establishment of that province. It should be noted that just as Pylos is excluded from the nine towns of the Hither Province, so Leuktron is excluded from the seven of the Further Province; in other words, the royal seats are exempt from the contributions required of other population centers.

Given the information from these three sources, the standard list of nine and seven, the coastguard documents, and the distribution of women workers, we are able to classify a number of the place-names according to province. But it is then possible to go a stage further by observing the company these names keep in other tablets. Here caution is necessary, since some lists plainly mix names belonging to different areas (e.g., Jo 438, see p. 105 above). But it is a reasonable assumption that a name which occurs several times in company with places that can be assigned to one province, and never with any known to belong to the other, is to be located in the same area as those it accompanies in the lists. Study of all the relevant information produces the

Hither Province

A-KE-RE-WA	i-te-re-wa?	pi-ru-te
a-pi-no-e-wi-jo?	KA-RA-DO-RO	PI-*82
a-pi-te-wa?	ke-re-za (at Pylos)	po-ra-i
a-po-ne-we?	ko-tu-we?	pu-ro
A-PU$_2$-WE	[ku]-pa-ri-so	RI-JO
a$_2$-ra-tu-wa	ME-TA-PA	ro-o-wa
a$_2$-ru-wo-te	ne-wo-ki-to wo-wi-ja	RO-U-SO
a$_3$-ta-re-u-si	ne-wo-pe-o	(= E-RA-TO)
e-na-po-ro	o-ru-ma-to	sa-ri-nu-wo-te?
E-RA-TO (= RO-U-SO)	o-wi-to-no	te-ta-ra-ne
e-ri-no-wo?	PA-KI-JA-PI	u-wa-si
e-u-de-we-ro	PE-TO-NO	za-e-to-ro

Further Province

A-SI-JA-TI-JA	ne-do-wo-ta
da-mi-ni-ja	po-to-ra-wa-pi
e-pi-jo-ta-na	RA-U-RA-TI-JA
e-pi-ko-e	re-u-ko-to-ro
E-RA-TE-RE-WA-PI	SA-MA-RA
E-RE-E	TI-MI-TO A-KE-E
e-sa-re-wi-ja	*ti-nwa-to
e-wi-ri-pi-ja	(ti-nwa-t/si-jo)
ke-i-jo (ke-e)	u-pa-ra-ki-ri-ja?
ko-ri-to	ZA-MA-E-WI-JA

accompanying list, in which the nine and seven towns are shown in capitals.

The extra length of the list for the Hither Province probably represents its proximity to the administrative center, rather than its superior size or population. Relative productivity can be tested by reference to the Ma series of tablets, since this is a record of contributions assessed for and paid by the seventeen major centers (one of the sixteen centers seems for this purpose to have been divided into two areas; see above p. 102). The commodities for which the assessment is made are abbreviated and cannot be clearly interpreted, but they seem to include some sort of textile (ideogram **146*) and hides. Since the figures are all roughly proportional, the assessment for **146* will serve as an index of productivity; the total for the Hither Province is 209 units, for the Further Province 281 units. Thus for this purpose at least the Further Province appears to be about one-third more productive than the Hither Province. But for flax production the totals given by the Ng tablets (see above, p. 104) seem to reverse this picture, since the damaged total for the Further Province cannot be restored as more than about three-quarters of the total for the Hither Province, and may be much less. Reference to a map showing the present areas of flax production (Loy 1970, p. 27) confirms that relatively less flax is grown in the lowlands of the Messenian valley and the favored areas are scattered widely over the more westerly areas of the peninsula.

We can now proceed to discuss the location of individual places within the two provinces. Here a major clue is the existence of the standard list, the regular order of which may be assumed to imply a geographical relationship of some kind. It is certainly not an order based upon spelling (quasi-alphabetical) nor in accordance with relative importance. It has usually been taken for granted that the order of the nine towns is from north to south, largely because the last name on the list (*ri-jo*) is a Greek word meaning "cape" "promontory" and the obvious cape in the region is Akritas, the southernmost point of the Messenian peninsula. But before we jump to the conclusion that the beginning of the list must be on the northern frontier, we ought to consider the arrangement likely to be adopted by a scribe with no geographical training who has never seen a map.

This is a state of mind hard to grasp for those to whom maps of one sort or another are everyday objects. But I would suggest that if, having no access to a map, I were asked to list the most important towns surrounding a given point, I would choose one of the main roads radiating from the reference point and list the towns on or near it, and then proceed to the next road, and so forth. This would offer little help, if it were not for the position of our point of reference, the palace at Epano Englianos. The narrow coastal plain to the west of the mountain barrier runs north and south; therefore, the main routes radiating from it will inevitably, in antiquity as today, run parallel with the mountain range (see Ch. 9). There is unlikely to have been more than one main route to the north. To the south there will have been a southeasterly road leading to the easy route over the plateau and thence to the Pamisos Valley; but only the section on the west side of the watershed will have fallen in the Hither Province. A second southern route must have led directly south running close to the coast and communicating with the settlements in the lower western part of the peninsula.

Thus, the north-south order is, in general, likely to be justified even on this assumption; but it calls attention to the plain fact that towns do not usually lie in a single-dimensional line, but scattered about a two-dimensional area. It also suggests that the beginning of the list may in fact be reversed and the first name may therefore belong to the first important center north of the palace. We can find the center of the list fairly easily, for a tablet recording some kind of religious festival seems to place *pa-ki-ja-si* under the general rubric of *pu-ro*, and other references too indicate that this name refers to an important religious center close to Pylos itself.

Consequently *pi-*82*, *me-ta-pa*, and *pe-to-no* must be located north of the palace, but not necessarily from north to south. Here we must refer to the curious fact that these names are absent from the northern sectors of the coastguard tablets, except that men of *me-ta-pa* are deployed there. This seems to indicate that the major centers were not on the coast, but inland. The headquarters of the most northerly coastguard sector is at *o-wi-to-no*, and it may be significant that in An 218 *me-ta-pa* stands in the next line to *o-wi-to-no*. The only other useful information about this trio of towns is that *pi-*82* is the home of an unusually large number of sheep and goats.

Those who, following Homer, wish to put the northern frontier of Pylos on or beyond the Alpheios are inclined to identify *pi-*82* with *Pheiai* (Palmer) or *Pisa* (Ruipérez, Pugliese Carratelli). The value of sign **82* is still very uncertain, but I am tempted to support those who give it the value of sa_2, with the suggestion that the true value is probably *swa*; for although there is no direct evidence for the *w* in the name of *Pisa*, an earlier **Piswa* would account for the long *i* of the classical form and the rare variant *Pĭsa*. But there is no reason whatever to assume that the Mycenaean *Piswa* was on the site of the famous *Pisa* near Olympia on the Alpheios. As in so many other cases, a name which was doubtless descriptive in a pre-Greek language (cf. Homeric *pīsea*, "meadows") will have been attached to many sites.

Attempts to relate *pe-to-no* to a classical *Pephnos* are not only phonetically difficult, but the classical site lies on the far side of the Messenian Gulf and consequently in the Further Province. The third name, *me-ta-pa*, is certainly to be identified with the classical form *Metapa*, but no site of this name is known in the Peloponnese; there is only an inscription from Olympia which refers to the *Metapioi* "the people of Metapa" and records their treaty with another otherwise unknown people, *Anaitoi*. It has been inferred from this inscription that there was a town called *Metapa* in Elis or Triphylia, but the treaties recorded on inscriptions at Olympia refer to towns as far distant as southern Italy, so that it is dangerous to press this evidence too far.

A consideration of the geography of the west coast of the Peloponnese and the disposition of known Mycenaean archaeological sites may help to decide this problem (see Ch. 8). North of the palace at Englianos there is no break in the continuity of sites, now that recent fieldwork has filled the gaps, until we reach Kyparissia; nor is there any natural boundary. But a short way further north the character of the country changes. The Kyparissia River valley is wide, with minor valleys extending north and south, and eventually leads east via Malthi to the upper Messenian Valley (Steniklarian Plain). This area too is rich in Mycenaean remains. But the next valley to the north, that of the river Nedha, leads into wild, mountainous country which effectively limits access to the Kyparissia Valley from the north, except by way of the coast. Those who have seen this territory can have little doubt that this is a natural frontier region. Moreover, known Mycenaean sites are scarce here, though they become more frequent as we approach the Alpheios.

If the Nedha-Kyparissia area is not the frontier of the Pylian kingdom, we must go a long way to the north to find another strategic boundary. The Alpheios itself is a formidable barrier, for it is a large river by Greek standards, and in winter at least an obstacle to communications. But Mycenaean sites lie close to one another on either side of the river, and it is not easy to believe that it was a political frontier as Homer's account of the cattle-raid into Elis (*Iliad* 11. 711–12) suggests. The main argument against it must be its distance from Englianos.

The attempts that have been made to confirm the Homeric frontier by identifying *pi-*82* as *Pheiai* or *Pisa* are in fact an embarrassment, for both these sites lie to the north of the Alpheios: it would thus be necessary to seek another frontier still farther north. And the farther north the frontier, the less plausible does the siting of the capital at Englianos become.

An argument in favor of a more southerly frontier, near the Nedha, can be drawn from the beginning of the coastguard document (see pp. 105, 106). The second sector is manned by men of Kyparissos, a name which, as we have seen, is probably to be located in the area of modern Kyparissia. Palmer has called attention to the fact that the commander of this sector is *Nedwatas*, a name derived from *Nedwa*, which is likely to be the Mycenaean form of the river name. Thus the general probability lies in favor of the more southerly frontier, and the names which might belong north of it are not sufficiently convincing to outweigh this probability. There are too many cases of the duplication of the same name in different parts of Greece for isolated examples to carry much weight.

It is tempting to locate *pa-ki-ja-ne* near modern Chora. We know that it was close to the palace and the extensive cemetery at Volimidhia (#20) just north of Chora proves the existence of an important settlement nearby. We know, too, that in the geometric period some cult continued in the Volimidhia tombs, which might be a reminiscence of the religious associations of Mycenaean *pa-ki-ja-ne*. (See Fig. 7-1 and Pocket Map 1-1.)

The remainder of the nine towns are *a-pu*$_2$*-we*, *a-ke-re-wa*, *ro-u-so* (*e-ra-to*), *ka-ra-do-ro*, and *ri-jo*. Since *a-ke-re-wa* is on the coast, it cannot represent the southeastern route across the hills, and *ka-ra-do-ro* and *ri-jo* are also coastal. Hence this group must lie along the coast as far as, and perhaps even beyond, Cape Akritas.

It used to be thought that *a-pu*$_2$ (the nominative is not recorded, but can be certainly reconstructed from the cases which occur) might be identified with *Aipu*, "the Steep," which is mentioned by Homer as an important place in Nestor's kingdom. But now that we understand the Mycenaean script better, it is clear that this would demand a spelling *a*$_3$*-pu*, and the equation must be rejected. *A-pu*$_2$ corresponds more likely to a form such as *Aphu*, *Alphu*, *Arphu*, *Asphu*. This town probably lies away from the coast and a short distance south of the palace. It might be tempting to think of Koukounara (#65) for this name.

Coming to the important coastal town of *a-ke-re-wa*, we must notice that it lies south of another port, *ro-o-wa*, which is not on the list of the nine. The importance of *ro-o-wa* is indicated by its mention in connection with the *lawagetas* (a very high official, second only to the king) and other important persons (An 724). It is a flax-producing area (Nn 228), but since the name is missing from the main flax records (Na), it is tempting to restore [*ro-o*]-*wa* in Na 568. If so, it is the location of shipwrights (*naudomoi*). These facts have led us to suggest that it is the principal port of Pylos, and geography would incline us to place this at Voïdhokilia, just north of the Bay of Navarino, or on the Osmanaga Lagoon (see Ch. 3). The settlement (#9) appears to have been on the rocky hill commanding the entrance to both these harbors at Paliokastro (classical Koryphasion, a name certainly absent from the tablets). If then Paliokastro is *ro-o-wa*, *a-ke-re-wa* must lie further south, either near modern Pylos or perhaps as far south as Methoni. There cannot have been any harbor along the steep cliffs between these ports. Since it has wheat land as well as sheep pasture, it cannot be the barren island of Sphakteria. Alternatively, if *a-ke-re-wa* is Paliokastro, *ro-o-wa* would lie farther north, probably at a site not yet found.

It was suggested above that *e-ra-to* was the name of the chief settlement in the area known as *ro-u-so*. The latter is almost certainly to be identified as *Lousos*, a name later known in the plural form *Lousoi* in Arkadia, though such a remote spot cannot be the Pylian *ro-u-so*. The name is certainly pre-Greek and has nothing to do with the Greek word for washing (*louō*). *Ro-u-so* does not seem to have been highly productive agriculturally, but possessed large numbers of sheep and goats. It had a royal establishment, containing 86 female slaves and 7 smiths, and was a religious center. Its territory supplied timber (Vn 10). This area must be located away from the coast, probably toward the center of the peninsula.

Ka-ra-do-ro (= *Kharadros*, "the gully") is the name of such a frequent feature of the Greek landscape that it might seem desperate to search for it. But we know it must lie in the southern part of Messenia, not far from the boundary of the Further Province. The description does not fit Methoni, which is on a small promontory; but it does seem very apt for Finikous (#79), the next known Mycenaean coastal site to the east. Surface exploration has proved the existence of an important settlement here; and the site is dominated by mountains cleft by two enormous ravines. Since the number of the Mycenaean name cannot be determined, the spelling might represent a plural, or perhaps a dual, "the two gullies," which would be an attractive description of Finikous.

Ri-jo (= *Rhion*, "the promontory") is the last of the nine and therefore presumably closest to *ti-mi-to a-ke-e*, the first of the seven towns of the Further Province. But the coastguard document mentions only this one of the seven, and thus we might infer that the Further Province had a short coastline. If the whole stretch from Cape Akritas to the river Nedhon (Kalamata) had to be covered by this one sector, it would be much larger than the rest, yet there appear to be only thirty men available for it. Thus I am forced to conclude that the western shore of the Messenian Gulf must have been included in the Hither Province. The first paragraph of An 661 therefore will cover the whole of the peninsula south of the Pylos-Kalamata road. The names listed there are *e-na-po-ro* [.]-*o-ri-jo*,* *ka-ra-do-ro*, *za-e-to-ro*. The obvious location for *ri-jo*, if *ka-ra-do-ro* is at Finikous, is near modern Koroni. It is an astonishing coincidence that an ancient geographer gives Rhion as an old name for Asine, the classical name of this site. Its omission from the coastguard list would be intelligible if *za-e-to-ro* is part of the territory of *ri-jo* and lies farther north, thus better placed for communications with Englianos. The most important Mycenaean settlement in this area is Kafirio (#107), a few kilometers north of Koroni and a little way inland. This would be a convenient headquarters for the detachment of twenty men watching this stretch of coast; and communications to Finikous, if this is *ka-ra-do-ro*, would pass through or close to it.

Passing now to the Further Province, we observe that the coastguard tablets, where the Further Province occupies one sector out of ten, seems to have had a very short coastline. The two place-names given here are *ti-mi-to a-ke-e*, one of the Seven, and *ne-do-wo-ta-de* = *Nedwonta-de* "toward Nedwon." There can be little doubt that *Nedwon* is the same name as *Nedon* (now Nedhon), the name of the river on which Kalamata stands. This forms the natural frontier at the southeastern end of the Messenian Valley; and the fact that guards are being sent to it (as the form indicates) may be taken as confirmation that it is a frontier region. The only other mention of this name (Cn 4.6) is in connection with seven sheep.

It seems therefore clear that the east coast of the Messenian Gulf cannot be included in the kingdom of Pylos, and the implications of this for the evidence of Homer must be considered later (see p. 113). But if the river Nedhon is the frontier, *ti-mi-to a-ke-e* can hardly stand on it, since a force of thirty men is to be moved from it to Nedhon. But it is the seat of the headquarters con-

* The reading of the first sign is too doubtful to allow more than guesses; it might be tempting to regard this name as a compound of *ri-jo* and take it as a fuller form of the name; but since it stands before *ka-ra-do-ro*, this would imply a departure from topographical order.

trolling the sector, and although therefore close to the coast, it need not be on the sea itself.

There are two possible sites so far known archaeologically to be large enough to merit consideration. But before discussing them we must examine the evidence for a royal palace in the Further Province. L. R. Palmer has pointed out that the name *re-u-ko-to-ro*, *Leuktron*, occupies a prominent position in this area, in some ways parallel to that of Pylos in the Hither Province. In the records of female workers (Aa) the majority of those in the Hither Province are at Pylos; the majority in the Further Province are at Leuktron. In fact 67, and possibly as many as 89, women are known to have been employed there. This strongly suggests that a minor royal establishment, with women engaged in textile production, existed at this site. It was apparently not to be compared with the main palace at Pylos, where the number of women workers was over 450, but was nonetheless a fair size.

Two sites worth consideration in this connection are Nichoria (#100) at the southwestern corner of the Pamisos Valley and Ellenika (#137; classical Thouria) about 10 km north of Kalamata. Both were big towns. Nichoria stands in a strategic position midway on the southern road linking the two provinces and is well placed to control the rich bottomland of two river valleys. For these reasons Nichoria could be Leuktron. If so, Ellenika might be regarded as a possible identification for *ti-mi-to a-ke-e*. But these suggestions are still tentative, and it is not inconceivable that they need to be reversed.

The problem of the location of the main towns of the Further Province has been set in a new light by a paper read by Miss Cynthia Shelmerdine to the Mycenaean Seminar at Cambridge, England, in 1971. Her latest research is now in the process of being published. She has demonstrated convincingly that the division of this area into four regions for administrative purposes, which was first suggested by W. F. Wyatt, Jr. (1962), is the only possible arrangement, and therefore likely to represent a physical grouping of the towns. The details must be discussed elsewhere together with the full argumentation, but the results may be briefly summarized here.

The area is first divided into two halves along a roughly north to south line: this frontier is clear from a map, for it can only be the main river of the Messenian Valley, the Pamisos, and its extension northward along the Mavrozoumenos. Each of these halves is further divided into two regions, which must therefore be separated by an east-west line dividing the valley into two parts. Although this is hard to see on a map, it is clear enough to an observer on the ground: a low range of hills, known as the Skala range, forms a nearly continuous ridge across the valley from Mount Ithomi to the slopes of Taygetos.

If we accept that these intersecting natural features correspond to the boundaries of the four regions distinguished by Wyatt and Shelmerdine, it remains only to identify them with the Mycenaean place-names. *Ti-mi-to-a-ke-e* is on the evidence of Jn 829 the most southerly town; hence it must lie either in the southwest, in which case Nichoria is a possible candidate for the name; or in the southeast, in which case it might be Ellenika. For various reasons I think the southwest is more likely, and therefore *Ra-wa-ra-ta*$_2$ is the chief town of the southeast quarter. The northeast quarter contains *Za-ma-e-wi-ja* and probably *E-re-i* (*Helos* "the Marsh"); the northwest *A-te-re-wi-ja* and *E-ra-te-re-we*, names which appear to have connections with towns at the northern end of the Hither Province. This too agrees well with the geography, which allows easy communication via the Kyparissia River valley. This agreement between the administrative grouping and the facts of physical geography offers a persuasive means of identifying the approximate location of these towns.

Thus, few firm conclusions are yet possible, and only excavation is likely to reveal much more about the nature of the towns mentioned in the Pylos tablets. It may be hoped that the excavation at Nichoria will produce tablets; if so, this will confirm its importance and make its identification as a provincial capital highly probable, even if the tablets do not give us the name of the site. But no parallel site has yet been excavated, and it may be that the keeping of archives of clay tablets was restricted to central capitals. Thus, failure to find tablets, even if the conditions for their preservation are met, would not prove that it was not Leuktron.

It would be of the greatest interest if we could form an estimate, however approximate, of the population of the kingdom of Pylos. The number of known settlements and place-names offers some sort of guide, but it is hazardous to judge whether some of the minor sites and names represented a hamlet of two or three families or a substantial village. At the present stage of our researches no dependable over-all estimate can be made, although the authors of Chapter 8 believe that 50,000 may be a reasonable minimum figure for the whole of southwest Peloponnese in LHIIIB.

It may be useful to suggest here some facts from the tablets which may help to form an opinion about population density. The Aa tablets as preserved show a total of 639 slave-women; since the same groups are listed in the Ab set and referred to by the Ad set, we can estimate the true figure when the archive was complete as around

750 women, with approximately the same number of children. Of these about 450 women were accommodated in the area known as Pylos. It is at once evident from this that the population of the entity known to the Mycenaeans as *pu-ro* cannot be judged by the excavated remains of the palace; the lower ground surrounding the hill must have been occupied by a large town. The lower classes probably lived mainly in rough huts which would leave no easily identifiable archaeological trace, but we cannot exclude the possibility of more substantial houses occupied by senior officials and serving also as stores and workshops, like those discovered by A. J. B. Wace outside the citadel at Mycenae. Indeed, Blegen's trenches at the west foot of the acropolis revealed foundations of substantial buildings. I should be inclined to put the total population of the capital of the kingdom at a mimimum of 3,000, and it could well have been much higher.

The figures for assessment of contributions by other towns in the kingdom ought to provide some means of estimating their size and population. We can of course measure the relative size of the sixteen principal towns by comparing their contributions in the Ma set. But it is hard to find any method of turning these into real numbers. The following suggestion is put forward with some hesitation, and in full awareness of the fragility of such evidence; it may perhaps be better than nothing, but it should not be accepted as more than a very tentative proposal.

The Ma series of tablets gives the assessments and contributions of seventeen towns (see above, p. 108) in terms of six commodities. These are referred to by abbreviations and most of them cannot be identified, but they appear to be agricultural products of some kind; some are counted, others weighed. Ma 124 records the contributions of *a-pu*$_2$*-we*, and has a note attached which states that the smiths do not contribute certain quantities. It would appear that these figures, which occur on a number of these tablets, represent a rebate given to certain classes. The figures for the last commodity (abbreviated ME) are assessment 500, rebate 20. Thus we can deduce that the rebate is 1/25 of the total; and this squares with the figures for the other commodities, since a rough proportion is observed among them. Two show figures of 23 with a rebate of 1; one 7, rebate 0; one 10, rebate 1. The last rebate, which is much above the 1/25 given by ME, is probably in a commodity (skins?) which can only be handled in whole units, and is a compensation for the lack of a rebate in the other case.

Now it happens that the records of bronze distributed to the smiths to work on include a section (Jn 693.5ff.) which relates to this same town of *a-pu*$_2$*-we*. This tablet informs us that there were in all nine smiths at this place, two of whom received no allocation of bronze. If, however, we assume, as is reasonable, that the smiths who were allowed a rebate on the Ma assessment were the nine recorded by name on Jn 693, then we can draw the further inference that nine represents 1/25 of the total labor force of the town, since the total assessment must have been based upon the productive capacity of the town as a whole. On this assumption the total labor force would number approximately $9 \times 25 = 225$. Furthermore, we know that *a-pu*$_2$*-we* contributes about 1/10 of the total production of the nine towns of the Hither Province; therefore, the total labor force for the nine towns would be on the order of 2,250.

A somewhat similar calculation is possible for a minor town, *po-wi-te-ja.* Na 923 records the payment from this town for flax as 29 units, with a rebate of 2 units for the smiths. In this series it is evident that the rebates must be added to the first figure, which is presumably the payment, in order to obtain the assessment, since the addition frequently discloses a round figure, often 30. The figure of 31 is somewhat unusual. But it seems reasonable to deduce that the number of smiths at *po-wi-te-ja* amounts to roughly 2/31 of the work force. Jn 601, which gives the list of smiths at this place, is unfortunately damaged; but 13 are listed as having an allocation of bronze, and no fewer than 6 names can have stood in the subsequent paragraph giving the names of those without an allocation. Thus if 19 (or slightly more) smiths represent 2/31 of the total labor force, there would be not less than 294 in all.

The proportion of smiths in the population will not, of course, be constant, since the tablets show that they are concentrated into small communities, often located at places of which we know nothing else. But it may be significant that at the two places where we can estimate the relation of the number of smiths to the total work force, this emerges as a figure between two and three hundred men. If now we allow an average of three others (women, children, and old men) for each working man, the total population of one of these towns might be in the range of 800 to 1,200.

To convert this into an estimate of the total population of the kingdom of Pylos would be hazardous in the extreme. Not all the 200 or so place-names will have been separate economic units, and some were doubtless small farms, upland pasture stations, and the like, with a very small population. Still, the figure of 95 tablets or fragments of tablets of the Na (flax) series argues a total of at least 80 flax-producing areas (since some of the fragments probably belong to the same tablet), and there were doubtless some settlements which did not produce any; so a figure of at least 100 settlements of reasonable size is probable, giving a total population in the range of 80,000 to 120,000.

It is interesting to observe that Carl A. Roebuck (1945) made a rough estimate of the population of *classical* Messenia, on the assumption that all available areas were cultivated in grains, and this came out at 112,500 persons. Perhaps we may use the figure of 100,000 as a very rough guide in estimating the size and importance of the Late Mycenaean kingdom; but it must be remembered that the evidence is extremely fragile, and the multiplication involved in such an extrapolation will have magnified enormously any errors in basic assumptions.

Now that we have achieved a rough outline of the Pylian kingdom as revealed by the Linear B tablets at a date around 1200 B.C., we can turn to Homer and see how his picture fits ours. The key passage is the description of Nestor's kingdom in the so-called "Catalogue of Ships." It is placed between the descriptions of Lakedaimon (Lakonia) and Arkadia and is followed by Elis; so there can be no doubt that it refers to the southwestern quarter of the Peloponnese. The passage runs as follows, omitting a parenthetic story: "Those who inhabited Pylos and lovely Arene, and Thryon, the ford of Alpheios, and well-built Aipy, and dwelt in Kyparisseeis and Amphigeneia and Pteleon and Helos and Dorion, where the Muses met Thamyris the Thracian, and put a stop to his singing, as he came from Oikhalia from the house of Eurytos the Oikhalian . . . Of these the leader was Nestor the Gerenian knight; he had ninety ships drawn up in rows." (*Iliad* 2. 591–602.)

There are no names on the Pylos tablets which could correspond to *Arene*, *Thryon*, *Alpheios*, *Aipy* (on *a-pu*$_2$, see p. 109), *Pteleon*, or *Dorion*. *Kyparisseeis* may correspond to [*ku*]-*pa-ri-so* of the tablets. The word *a-pi-ke-ne-a* occurs on a fragment with no indication how it is to be identified, but a name closely resembling *Amphigeneia* could at need be read into it. *Helos*, "the Marsh," is the name of one of the seven towns of the Further Province; but there is no evidence by which to locate the Homeric town, and the name must have been in use in many parts of Greece: there is another in Lakonia. A word *o-ka-ra* or *o-ka-ra*$_3$ is used on the coastguard tablets as a description of a class of men, and some have seen in this a reference to *Oikhalia*, a town identified as the later Andania, but this is unconvincing in view of the form.

The account given by Nestor of the cattle-raid into Elis (*Iliad* 11. 668–761) seems to confirm the Alpheios as the northern boundary of the kingdom, and Thryon, which the Catalogue places at its crossing, is here called *Thryoessa* and described as on the frontier. But this passage does not add any more names which can be recognized in the Pylos tablets.

Similarly, the Embassy to Achilles recites the names of seven citadels which Agamemnon is prepared to cede to him (*Iliad* 11. 149–53, 291–95). They are described as being near the sea, on the frontiers of "sandy Pylos," in this case apparently the southeastern frontier. The names are *Kardamyle*, *Enope*, *Hire*, *Pherai*, *Antheia*, *Aipeia* and *Pedasos*. None of them can be identified in the available texts. It is possible that they lay outside the area covered by the Pylos tablets, but they must then be confined to the eastern shore of the Messenian Gulf, if the frontier was at the river Nedhon (Hope Simpson 1957).

In the Odyssey Telemakhos travels by ship from Ithaka (to be placed in the Ionian Islands, whatever the local confusions) to Pylos, apparently without calling at any port en route. He arrived at "Pylos, the well-built citadel of Neleus" (3. 4), thus implying that the poet was unaware of the name of the port of Pylos, where Telemakhos found Nestor sacrificing to Poseidon. It cannot, however, have been far from the palace, since when Telemakhos wished to return to his ship, Nestor insisted on his coming to the palace as his guest, and led the way thither, although it was already after sunset. The distance in fact cannot have been less than several miles.

The journey of Telemakhos overland from Pylos to Sparta, and equally the return journey in Book 15, is treated in summary fashion. We are told that they travelled by chariot, and that it took two days with an overnight stop at Pherai, the home of Diokles. The only other piece of information to be gleaned here is that between Pherai and Sparta they came to "a wheat-bearing plain." It has been believed from antiquity that Pherai occupied the site of modern Kalamata. If so, the principal geographical feature between this and Sparta is the Taygetos range of mountains, which rises to more than 2,400 m. It is remarkable that a road suitable for chariots should have crossed it, and even more so that Homer does not consider it worth a mention (see Ch. 2). On the other hand there is no obvious candidate for the "wheat-bearing plain" until the Eurotas Valley is reached, but this is described by Homer (4. 1) as their point of arrival, "hollow Lacedaemon"; a plain in the valley of the river Xeropotamos is hardly large enough to deserve mention. There is no name on the Pylos tablets which could correspond in form to Pherai. This passage also refers to Pylos as a "steep (or high) citadel," whereas the hill on which the palace of Englianos stands hardly merits such an epithet. It is difficult to believe that the poet of the *Odyssey* knew much about the geography of Messenia.

To sum up, there are major discrepancies in detail between the place-names of the Pylos tablets and the kingdom attributed by Homer to Nestor. This does not of course prove that any part of the Homeric poems did not ultimately derive from a Mycenaean source, and the over-all picture is a reasonable match for the known extent of Mycenaean civilization. But we must conclude that on matters of geographical detail Homer's information was either incorrect or anachronistic. Perhaps the simplest explanation is that poetry can be made out of lists of names, suitably embellished, and it does not really matter whether the names corresponded to contemporary sites. No one in Homer's time would have been bothered by names then unknown, for thousands of Mycenaean names probably failed to survive the Dark Age. The difficulties only begin, as in many other points too, when we insist on regarding Homer as an historian instead of a poet.*

Our reconstruction of Messenia in the Late Bronze Age ought therefore to be based upon the tablets and archaeology; only when information from these sources coincides with that provided by Homer can we feel justified in using the epics at all, and where there is a conflict we ought to hold fast to the tablets and archaeology, whatever Homer says. Further information about conditions in the Late Bronze Age, such as the vegetation pattern, road network, and the identification of settlements will assist the interpretation of the Mycenaean documents. But at present too much of the information the tablets contain is unusable owing to our inability to equate names with sites. Whether any significant progress in this task is possible remains to be seen.

The extraction of other kinds of information from the Pylos tablets is far from complete. Attention has been concentrated in this chapter upon the geography because it seemed the most important contribution this study could make to the book as a whole. The paragraphs that follow are therefore only an adumbration of some of the topics which might be discussed. The reader is referred to the bibliography for further information.

Botany. There are numerous references in the tablets to plants, many of which were clearly local crops; but others may figure prominently there precisely because they had to be imported. Thus the presence of any plant name is no guarantee that it was grown in Greece at that time, though staple products like wheat, barley, olive oil, and wine are present in quantities great enough to demand home production. The botanical information can of course be extended by reference to Linear B tablets from other sites, principally Knossos in Crete and Mycenae in northeast Peloponnese. How far this holds good also for Pylos is open to conjecture; but we can assume that the same plants and their products were known throughout the Mycenaean world. A further difficulty arises over the identification of plant names; we can only assume that the name referred to the same species as in classical Greece, and even this is sometimes in doubt. Even where the species is identified, the variety is of course unknown.

The tablets give long lists of rations for dependents of the palace. Some of these are no doubt the actual food eaten; others may describe payments in foodstuffs which might then be used by the recipient for his family as well as himself or exchanged for other goods. Two signs are repeatedly used to describe these rations, accompanied by units of dry measure, and in view of the archaeological evidence and classical parallels it seemed obvious that they were wheat and barley, though to begin with we were uncertain which was which. Both signs are associated with the word *sitos* "grain," but neither with a more specific word, though the word for barley (*kritha*) appears to occur elsewhere. Thus, although the choice between the possibilities for the signs was not easy, a number of factors have contributed to the solution.

The signs are in origin pictographic, but as known to us they are formalized symbols rather than true pictures. Fortunately we can trace them back to the earlier Cretan script, Linear A, where they are a little more naturalistic. The sign for what we believe to be barley has there a fringe of strokes representing the characteristic "beard"; but the other sign still bears little resemblance to an ear of wheat. However, there is a significant difference between the ration scales applied to the two grains, and barley is allocated in larger quantities than wheat. In one case there may be a conversion sum, giving in barley almost exactly double the quantity of wheat; other evidence suggests a barley : wheat ratio of 15:8.

* I regret that I cannot share the views of two of my fellow authors, R. Hope Simpson and J. F. Lazenby, who in their book *The Catalogue of the Ships in Homer's Iliad* (1970) and elsewhere have taken a much more optimistic view of Homer's accuracy. This is not the place to pursue the argument, but the difficulties in the way of accepting the Catalogue as true seem to me insuperable, quite apart from the flat contradiction we encounter at the only point where we can compare it with the tablets. I must admit that the Cretan section is a little more accurate than the Pylian one: three of Homer's seven Cretan cities (in the Catalogue) do appear on the Knossos tablets; and here of course it is easy to argue that the Catalogue represents a kingdom of Late Minoan III date, not the Late Minoan II of the tablets. I would add only two points. No one, I think, will take seriously the exact figures given for the ships of the different contingents, and if these are incorrect, why should the geography be any better? The Catalogue is so constructed that it has little organic unity; thus it would be very easy for later poets to insert or delete passages at will. That it is a poetic invention emerges clearly from the gusto with which it launches into a list of twenty-nine places in Boeotia, and tails off in a series of petty and more or less unidentifiable kingdoms in Thessaly, which are added in a kind of appendix after the logical conclusion of the list in the Dodecannese.

This is in accordance with classical practice, where barley is given about half the value of wheat. The reason is perhaps because the measurements are by volume, not weight, and if not husked the barley grain will weigh lighter for a given volume. This is strong confirmation of the assignment of values to these signs. However, the use of wheat as a main ration is surprising, since in early classical times wheat was much less common than barley, and only later does wheat overtake it. As suggested above, the rations may not have been issued in the nominal form recorded on the tablets, but it is perhaps not impossible that at this period wheat was grown in greater quantities than barley (see Ch. 11).

The wheat ideogram was also used in a series of tablets which refer to land. "So much seed" followed by a volume of wheat is the regular formula to specify the size of a plot of land. Obviously area could be measured in this way, if there were a constant factor relating it to the quantity of seed needed for sowing. But in fact the system has an advantage over a straight measurement of surface area. The rate of sowing will depend upon the fertility of the soil: a flat field on rich alluvial land will be seeded at a much higher rate than a rocky slope. Thus this system is able to compare differing plots of land in terms of their productivity, and it is easy to estimate the quantity of seed used in the light of experience, whereas a great deal of work is needed to calculate superficial area in default of maps.

There is of course no evidence from the tablets to determine the kind of wheat meant; in the Near East emmer was distinguished from wheat. Here the evidence of paleobotany would be valuable.

Olive oil is amply attested on the tablets (Bennett 1955), and there is some evidence to suggest that olives were also used as food. In some cases small quantities of olive oil are qualified by epithets which indicate that it was perfumed; cyperus, rose, and especially sage were used to give it an agreeable scent. Other expressions show that in some cases an ointment was made from olive oil; in classical times too it was the practice of the rich to smear themselves with scented ointment. But the Mycenaean documents suggest that much of this scented oil was for religious purposes, though in what way it was used remains a matter for conjecture. If there were wooden statues of deities, these might have been painted with oil to preserve them; but the only surviving statues are of terracotta, and these are still extremely rare.

The word for fig tree is found on a tablet from Knossos, and this helps to establish the value of the ideographic sign for figs which is found also at Pylos. The rations of the women at Pylos consist of equal quantities (measured by volume) of wheat and figs. Figs are known as rations from classical Greece as well as the Near East; but the quantity is a little surprising. We have no means of telling whether the figs were fresh or dried; if fresh, they must have been issued only during certain months, so if a constant ration is intended they must have been dried.

Wine is directly attested by the storehouse on the palace site at Pylos, in which were found large jars and also sealings bearing the Linear B ideogram for wine. One of these has the word meaning "honeyed" written across it. One tablet seems to record the distribution of wine to the nine towns of the Hither Province, probably some special vintage; but there is room for doubt since the ideogram is here omitted and we rely on the identification of the word *wo-no* as *woinos* "wine." This word occurs certainly in compounds; oxen are called "wine-coloured." At Knossos there is a reference to "sweet new wine." There is no useful information about the vine.

There are a number of spices or condiments mentioned on the tablets, at Pylos notably coriander and cyperus. The exact kind of cyperus cannot be established, but it is used to perfume olive oil. At other sites more spices are named: cardamon, celery, cumin, mint, rush, safflower, saffron, and sesame. Some of these were probably imported.

Another important crop was flax. There has been some debate about the nature of the crop, but references to women as "flax-workers" and to linen cloth strongly suggest that the flax was grown mainly for its fiber, though linseed may also have been in use. This conclusion is borne out by modern practice; a high proportion of the flax now grown for fiber in Greece comes from southwest Peloponnese. The reason must be the relatively damp climate; flax requires running water to prepare the fibers, and this is not something in plentiful supply in Greece. There are requisitions of flax from about a hundred separate places in the kingdom, and the records here seem to show less local grouping than for other products. Since Messenia is very likely to have specialized in linen production in Mycenaean times, some of it was probably exported.

There are references to timber, and among the trees specifically mentioned are box, cypress, "cytisus" (probably *Laburnum vulgare*), elm, willow. There is a probable mention of a palm, but only as depicted in ivory inlay on furniture. Woodcutters are mentioned in the area of *ro-u-so* in connection with supplies to the wheelwrights' shop.

Livestock. The principal domestic animal must have been the sheep, though it did not apparently play so predominant a role in the economy of Pylos as it did at Knossos. There is reason to believe, however, that the organization of flocks at Pylos was similar to what has been established for Crete (Killen 1964). The main flocks raised for wool production were castrated males, and these were kept up to strength by separate breeding flocks.

Flocks of goats are also frequently mentioned, and goatherds are among the occupational terms describing men. Cattle are much more rarely listed, but references to large numbers of oxherds prove the existence of considerable numbers of cattle; they were no doubt used for ploughing and heavy transport. Pigs are mentioned, and there is a special list showing small numbers of pigs being fattened up at the nine towns of the Hither Province.

There are no lists of horses, but sufficient incidental references to guarantee their presence in large numbers. There are lists of chariot wheels, which naturally imply chariots and horses to draw them; but there was perhaps a separate archive, so far undiscovered, in which the horses and chariot bodies were listed. The horses of the period seem to have been small, and this may be why they were not normally used for riding.

The deer is the only wild animal listed on the tablets. The animal is not named, but the ideogram picturing its horned head is instantly recognizable. The skins of oxen, sheep, goats, pigs, and deer are all mentioned as used for leather goods.

Industry. The sheep mentioned above imply the spinning and weaving of woolen cloth, and the apparent linen industry has been mentioned. It is, of course, very difficult to judge whether production was on a scale sufficient to permit exports, since we have at Pylos almost no records of finished cloth. Yet the number of women who are listed under occupational terms connected with spinning and weaving suggests that this was an important part of the economy.

There is one sector in which we can fairly confidently detect an exporting industry. We can establish the presence in the Pylian kingdom of about 400 bronzesmiths (Lejeune 1961). The amount of bronze goods these men would have been able to produce in a year can only be guessed; but if they were reasonably well occupied, they must have made far more goods than the kingdom would have used, since bronze was always a relatively scarce and expensive material. Hence it is almost certain that some of their production was exported. There were apparently no local sources for copper ore (see Ch. 14), so we must assume that the raw materials were mainly imported. The copper probably came from Cyprus, the tin perhaps from the west; if so, the location of the industry in southern Greece where the two trade routes met may be explained. It is possible that it had been transferred there from Crete after the Minoan collapse; tripod cauldrons are described on the Pylos tablets as "of Cretan workmanship," but this does not mean that they were made in Crete. The smiths would also have required abundant fuel, and this may be why they appear to have worked in small communities outside the main centers of population.

Whether the luxury goods that are listed at Pylos are local products or imports cannot be judged. Ivory must have come from Syria or even Africa. Gold is unlikely to have been found in workable quantities in the area; but a mention of four goldsmiths shows that there were local craftsmen. The raw materials at least are likely to have been obtained in exchange for products such as finished bronze goods, textiles, and perhaps scented oil.

REFERENCES

Bennett, E. L. 1955. *The Olive Oil Tablets of Pylos.* Salamanca. (Supplement to Minos.)

Blegen, C. W., and Rawson, M. 1966ff. *The Palace of Nestor.* Princeton, N.J.

Chadwick, J. 1963. "The Two Provinces of Pylos," *Minos* 7:125–41.

———. 1967. *The Decipherment of Linear B,* 2nd ed. Cambridge.

———. 1969. "*Mycenaean te-ko-to-na-pe*," *SMEA* 4:23–33.

——— and Killen, J. T. In preparation. *A Mycenaean Industry.* Cambridge.

Gallavotti, C., and Sacconi, A. 1961. *Inscriptiones Pyliae.* Rome.

Gray, D. H. F. 1959. *Bulletin of the London Institute of Classical Studies* pp. 44–57.

Hammond, N. 1932. "Prehistoric Epirus and the Dorian Invasion," *BSA* 32:131ff.

Hope Simpson, R. 1957. "Identifying a Mycenaean State," *BSA* 52:231–59.

Killen, J. T. 1964. "The Wool Industry of Crete in the Late Bronze Age," *BSA* 59:1–15.

Lejeune, M. 1961. "Les forgerons de Pylos," *Historia* 10:409–34.

Loy, W. G. 1970. *The Land of Nestor: A Physical Geography of the Southwest Peloponnese.* National Academy of Sciences, Office of Naval Research, Report No. 34. Washington, D.C.

Palmer, L. R. 1963. *The Interpretation of Mycenaean Greek Texts.* Oxford.

———. 1965. *Mycenaeans and Minoans,* 2nd ed. London.

Roebuck, C. A. 1945. "A Note on Messenian Economy and Population," *Classical Philology* 40:149–65.

Ventris, M., and Cradwick, J. 1956. *Documents in Mycenaean Greek.* Cambridge.

Wyatt, W. F., Jr. 1962. "The Ma Tablets from Pylos," *AJA* 66:21–41.

8

ARCHAEOLOGICAL EXPLORATION

by

William A. McDonald and Richard Hope Simpson

The focus of the UMME project in both time and space was explained in Chapter 1. We should insist that every chapter in the book has archaeological relevance – and sometimes major archaeological significance. The purpose of this chapter, however, is to present and evaluate the kind of evidence that is traditionally associated with archaeology and that has accumulated – through excavation, exploration, and chance finds – over the past century and more. Naturally, we are particularly concerned with the results of our own surface reconnaissance, which has been concentrated on the remains of the Late Bronze Age. But we include every important discovery known to us of material from any period of human occupation through medieval times.

The most vital specific information on individual sites is presented in tabular form (Registers A and B) in the Appendix (p. 263) and the formulation is explained on pages 123–28. Although meant only for reference, the Registers and the maps of site distribution contain the basic data on which many extrapolations in this and other chapters depend. Finally, we have attempted in Part III to provide an overview of what seem to us reasonable historical implications of the evidence presently available from every epoch through Roman times, though reserving the most thorough analysis for the Mycenaean.

PART I. THE BACKGROUND

The Situation in 1938

In the first century of the existence of the Greek Archaeological Society (1837–1937), Messenia was a relatively neglected region. The centennial publication of the Society (Oikonomos 1938) has nine relevant entries, of which three (#'s 5, 11, 146) belong to prehistoric horizons. These and other sites referred to on the following pages can be located on the distribution maps, Pocket Maps 8-11 through 8-18. It is to be noted, of course, that Oikonomos' publication records only the results of archaeological work by Greek nationals. But Messenia was equally peripheral to the interest of most foreign field explorers and excavators.

The reasons are fairly obvious. Until the 1870's archaeologists were almost exclusively concerned with the remains of the classical period and later. During the dramatic spurt of interest in the Late Bronze Age initiated in the last third of the century by Schliemann, Dörpfeld, Tsountas, and their colleagues, only one discovery suggested that southwest Peloponnese might become important to prehistorians. That was the fine tholos tomb at Kambos (#146), southeast of Kalamata (Tsountas 1891; Pl. 1-2). Then in the first decade of the present century Dörpfeld excavated three rich tholoi and examined much less thoroughly the nearby acropolis at Kakovatos (#300). The site lies midway up the west coast and Dörpfeld identified it as Nestor's capital, and so "Homeric" Pylos (Dörpfeld 1907, 1908, 1913; Müller 1909). For a generation thereafter scholars took relatively little interest in exploration of this remote corner of the peninsula. Attention had generally swung back to the classical focus. Messenia, because of its subservient position to Sparta in archaic and classical times, could scarcely be expected to rival in promise the many other areas that beckoned the traditionally oriented archaeologist.

In classical horizons, sporadic excavation was carried on at the federal capital of Messene (#529) – and there only – in the late nineteenth and early twentieth centuries (Sophoulis 1895; Oikonomos 1909, 1925–26).

Few additional sites of the Hellenistic or Roman period attracted attention (Kyparissis 1911; Skias 1911). Indeed, Messenia seems to have been a somewhat peripheral area even in later Greco-Roman times, as it was until very recently in the modern period. For example, no railroad comes closer to modern Pylos than Kyparissia on the north and modern Messini (Nisi) on the east. As late as 1939 there was no all-weather automobile road from Kyparissia north to Pirgos, and it was not uncommon for buses to be repeatedly bogged down on the "highway" from Kalamata to Pylos. Winter torrents also took a toll of road surfaces and flimsy bridges, even on main routes.

Only four isolated discoveries and one major program of field research stirred Messenia from the archaeological doldrums that still prevailed throughout the first third of the twentieth century. The sanctuary of Apollo Korynthos (#504), noted by Pausanias (4. 34. 7) on the west side of the Messenian Gulf, was identified and excavated (Versakis 1916); and a second sanctuary (#530), attributed to the river god Pamisos (Pausanias 4. 3. 10; 4. 31. 4), was uncovered near Ayios Floros at the headsprings of the Pamisos (Valmin 1938, Pt. II). In the prehistoric context, a tholos tomb that had continued in use into the early Iron Age was discovered at Tragana (#11) just north of the Bay of Navarino (Skias 1909; Kourouniotis 1914). This was the first dependable archaeological evidence that there had presumably been a royal citadel of Late Bronze Age times in the general vicinity of classical Pylos; and the probability was reinforced a few years later when a second tholos (#5) was excavated not far away near the modern village of Korifasion (Kourouniotis 1925–26). The strong tradition in classical sources that Nestor's Pylos was in the Navarino area thus became theoretically tenable again, but few experts wavered in the firm belief that Dörpfeld had settled that problem in favor of Kakovatos.

There were also occasional attempts to connect specific physical remains with other "cities" described in Homeric and later literature. Perhaps most notable were those of Dörpfeld and his colleagues in Triphylia just before World War I (Dörpfeld 1913). They proposed equating Salmoni : Paliopirgo (#308) with Thryon/ Thryoessa, and Kato Samikon : Klidhi (#302) with Arene (for our system of "double" names, see the explanation of Category B below, p. 123). Dörpfeld also carried out a small excavation at Miraka : Oinomaos (#323), which he connected with ancient Pisa; and he was aware of other spots such as Epitalion : Ayios Yeoryios (#303) where prehistoric pottery was strewn over the surface. Dörpfeld's publication is enhanced by the excellent map of Triphylia drawn by Konrad Graefinghoff. In addition, a few scholars were concerned with inscriptions and other relics of the historic period (Wilhelm 1891; Tod 1905), and there were attempts (Weil 1882; Kolbe 1904; Bolte 1911) to use epigraphical as well as literary evidence to fix the boundaries between Messenia and her neighbors in classical or later times.

The first really extensive and systematic surface exploration, however, was carried out by Natan Svensson-Valmin, beginning in 1925. He concentrated on the Soulima Valley (Valmin 1926–27, 1927–28) and discovered or confirmed the following sites in our Register A: #'s 70, 209, 211, 212, 220, 222, 223, 226, 232, 233, and 234. In 1933 Valmin began at Malthi (#222) the only "total" excavation of a prehistoric settlement that has ever been attempted in this whole region and one of few anywhere else in Greece. The settlement was built on a prominent and strategic hilltop near the modern village of Vasiliko, and Valmin identified it as Homeric Dorion (Valmin 1938). In its immediate environs and in the nearby countryside he discovered a number of tholos tombs (#'s 220, 234) and excavated five (Valmin 1926–27; 1927–28; 1938). He also travelled extensively throughout Messenia and published a review of his own results (including the identification of prehistoric sites #'s 79, 128, 137) together with the discoveries and topographical theories of others as far back as classical antiquity (Valmin 1930).

In 1938 and 1939 Carl A. Roebuck spent several months in Messenia and later published in limited edition the major results (Roebuck 1941). His comments on topographical, literary, and historical problems are always illuminating, although the focus of interest is on the historical situation in the fourth to second centuries B.C.

Some idea of the pre–World War II situation may perhaps be gained by noting that the section devoted to Messenia in the authoritative article on Mycenaean culture in the Pauly-Wissowa encyclopedia lists twenty-two prehistoric sites (Karo 1935). Of these at least two are doubtful, and the majority of the others had recently been discovered by Valmin in one quite limited sector of the whole region (see Fig. 8-1).

The Palace at Epano Englianos

Blegen and Kourouniotis had never been convinced by Dörpfeld's identification of Kakovatos as Nestor's Pylos. In 1939, Blegen and his colleagues explored the area around the Bay of Navarino (where the capital had traditionally been located), and they identified prehistoric occupation at the following places in Register A: #'s 1, 3, 4, 37, 44, 101. It was the discovery of the ruins of a royal administration center at Epano Englianos (#1)

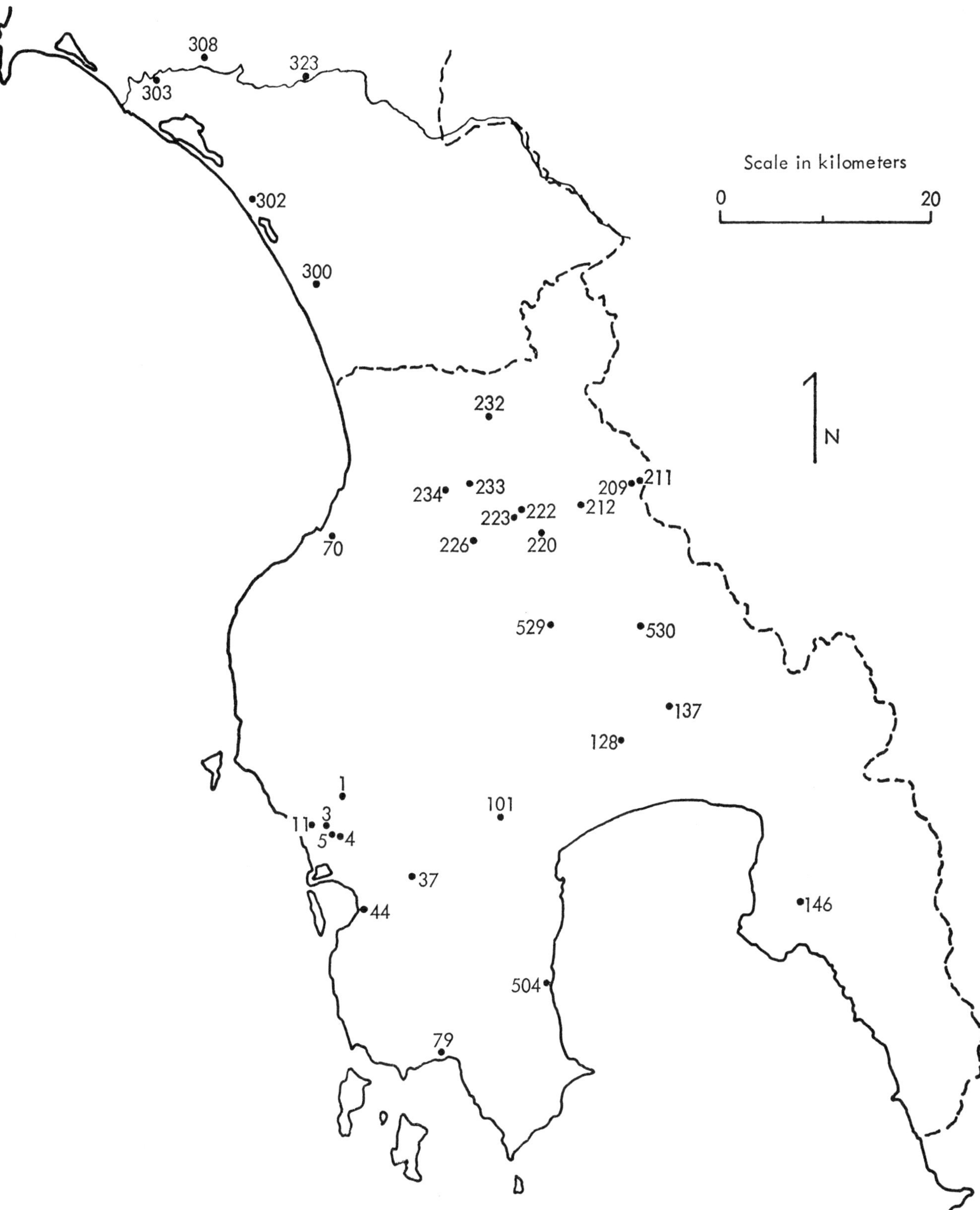

Figure 8-1. Major archaeological sites known in 1940

about 9 km north-northeast of the Bay of Navarino that marked the turning point in the attention paid to Messenia by prehistorians (Blegen and Kourouniotis 1939). As soon as possible after World War II the volume of exploration and excavation quickened dramatically. The Englianos complex was soon being called the palace of Nestor, although there were some dissenting opinions. With the decipherment in 1952 of the Linear B tablets found in its ruins and the prominence in them of the place-name *pu-ro* (Pylos), most of the doubters were convinced. Since then the careful excavation of the relatively well-preserved remains, the exploration of the environs, the recovery of additional texts, and the study of their contents and context have proceeded fairly rapidly, if not always hand in hand. The progress of the excavation has been methodically reported in successive issues of the *American Journal of Archaeology* and is now being summed up in a major series of volumes (Blegen and Rawson 1966; Lang 1968). The Pylos tablets are being studied by many scholars, and in Chapter 7 Chadwick reviews certain aspects of their work and presents some insights and theories of his own. We shall try here to sketch other significant developments.

Excavation and Exploration since 1952

After the death of Blegen's colleague, Dr. Kourouniotis, the Greek Archaeological Service appointed Professor Spyridon Marinatos to direct the Greek share of the joint enterprise in western Messenia. Beginning in 1952, Marinatos has carried on an almost annual program of excavation, chiefly of burial mounds, tholoi, and chamber tombs. The numerous sites discovered and/or excavated by him include the following items in Register A: #'s 4, 8, 9, 11, 12, 20, 21, 25, 29, 32, 35, 36, 46, 52, 53, 54, 109, 200, 201, and 401. The results of these excavations have been provisionally reported in successive issues of the periodicals (Marinatos 1952 and following), and specific references are provided in the Registers. Special attention may be directed to what are probably the highlights, namely, the discovery of a practically intact tholos burial at Routsi (#54) and a magnificent early Mycenaean tholos as well as an earlier burial complex (contemporary with Schliemann's Mycenae shaft graves) at Peristeria (#200). Professor Marinatos has also published wider syntheses suggesting connections between the Late Bronze Age situation in Messenia and the rest of the contemporary Mediterranean world, as well as between the known Late Bronze Age situation and conditions described in the Homeric poems (Marinatos 1962).

Others who have been active excavators in recent years include the successive ephors for western Peloponnese, Dr. Nicholas Yalouris (until 1966), Mr. George Papathanasopoulos (until 1970), Miss Theodora Karayeorya, and their assistants (epimeletes), especially Messrs. Angelos Choremis and Petros Themelis. In addition to planned excavation, these officials with headquarters at Olympia must attempt to cope with a steadily increasing volume of salvage operations. Large-scale road building, drainage, and construction projects, as well as chance finds by farmers and some illegal pillaging, are placing a great strain on the local authorities. A significant proportion of the new sites recorded in the Registers can be credited to their prompt dealing with the evidence, usually under difficult and hurried conditions (Yalouris 1960ff.; Papathanasopoulos 1962ff.; Choremis 1968ff.; Themelis 1966ff.). One of our major concerns has been to try to keep abreast of this flood of material which they have generously shared with us, and to attempt to set it in the perspective of an over-all regional synthesis.

In addition to obligations north of the Alpheios Valley and so outside our region, Dr. Yalouris and his assistants were in charge of salvage operations or more extensive excavations at the following sites: #'s 70, 100, 107, 142, 224, 302, 304, 309, 310, 311, 313, 314, 316, 317, 318, 319, 321, 322, 324, 325, 326, 327, 328, 331, 708, 709, 710, 712, 713, 714, 715, 717, 718, 719, 722, and 733. Specific references to his published reports are provided in the Registers. It will be noted that his activities have been concentrated in the Alpheios area. There were also scattered operations in the rest of the ephorate, except for the Pylos district where Professor Marinatos usually directed salvage work.

Mr. Papathanasopoulos and his assistants were in charge of exploration, excavation and salvage operations at the following sites: #'s 55, 70, 80, 100, 122, 131, 214, 303, 309, 312, 402, 403, 404, 412, 518, 540, 602, 723, and 729. Again, the Registers provide references to his preliminary reports and record the most significant results.

It is worth noting – and may provide a hint of historical priorities – that the program of excavation and salvage outlined above has been mainly in the prehistoric context. The major exceptions are the classical site at Pheia (#304); the temple site at Scillous : Babes (#314); the rich Hellenistic burial mound at Tsopani Rachi (#403); the Hellenistic remains underneath modern Kalamata (#142); a series of Roman buildings at Kyparissia (#70); and a Hellenistic cemetery on the sandspit between the Bay of Navarino and Osmanaga Lagoon (#401). Specific references are provided in Register B.

In addition, interest in historic periods has been maintained by the continuing large-scale excavations of the German Institute at Olympia (#315) on the northern border of the region and of Professor Orlandos in Hellenistic and Roman Messene (#529). Their results are regularly reported in the periodicals and are too well known to require documentation or description here.

With the exception of the University of Cincinnati excavation under Blegen's direction at Epano Englianos, the only excavation site involving a foreign scholar since Valmin's time is Nichoria (#100), an extensive ridge immediately above the village of Rizomilo. In spring 1959, Yalouris and McDonald conducted a short trial excavation there and at a second newly discovered site (#107). Since then, the ephorate has carried out both salvage and planned excavation in the extensive cemeteries around Nichoria. References to the interim reports are provided in Register A. In 1969, UMME began excavations on the Nichoria acropolis, while the ephorate continues to work in the cemeteries.

Having sketched the excavation and salvage operations since 1938, we must now mention two programs of systematic surface exploration. Dr. Jerome Sperling carried out a brief search in an area north of the Nedha River and eastward to the Arkadian boundary (Sperling 1942). Among his discoveries or major confirmations are the following entries in the Registers: #'s 245, 304, 305, 329, 332, 726, 727. Also, Professor Ernst Meyer, continuing his earlier topographic studies in Arkadia and Achaia, ranged southward from Olympia into Triphylia (Meyer 1957). His main concern (like Valmin's on the whole) was with the topography of the classical period. The following discoveries or detailed information referred to in the Registers are owed to him: #'s 312, 313, 330, 717, 718, 730, 732, 734 and 735.

UMME Program of Search

It should be clear from the preceding survey that the considerable documentation now at hand for the pattern of ancient habitation in Messenia is the result of the efforts of a significant number of scholars. Three subregions that seem to have particularly appealed to settlers of all periods have benefited from search by colleagues working before or contemporaneously with UMME's program: the Alpheios Valley, most notably by Yalouris; the Soulima Valley by Valmin; and the Pylos district by Marinatos. Indeed, something like 40 percent of the sites in the Registers were identified by researchers who have had no direct affiliation with UMME and, incidentally, neither they nor we have had notable success in the case of the lush and elusive Pamisos Valley, the rolling upland country west of the Pamisos Valley, or interior Triphylia.

We have tried to develop our own role as a threefold one: first, to bring together the discoveries of other scholars, previously scattered in various publications; second, to check their observations and to supplement their coverage so as to ensure that all parts of the region receive at least a modicum of attention; and third, to coordinate and systematize all the available data and put forward some hypotheses based on all the relevant evidence that we have been able to gather. Although a brief general account of organization, methods and goals was given in Chapter 1 (and further details can be found in our three preliminary publications of 1961, 1964, 1969), we shall begin here with a few remarks on techniques of search.

McDonald came to the task in 1955 with the benefit of Blegen's tutelage. Hope Simpson, after training in Britain and later in Greece under Wace and fresh from a series of explorations in Lakonia (Waterhouse and Hope Simpson 1960, 1961), joined the Messenia project in 1958. It is probably due to the conviction of veterans like Blegen and Wace about the value of surface exploration that we had first become interested in this kind of fieldwork. Certainly, their concern with reconstituting prehistoric habitation patterns influenced our decision to concentrate on the evidence from early periods. The choice of southwest Peloponnese as our target region stems from several considerations – among them McDonald's participation in the Pylos campaigns of 1939 and 1953, the relative lack of systematic exploration there when we began our work, and the hope that the results of a thorough examination could be meaningfully linked with the evidence on the kingdom of Pylos that is provided (albeit rather cryptically) in the tablets found in the ruins of the palace.

Naturally, our methods of search were modeled on those of Blegen and Wace. They are sound methods, tested and improved over a half century (McDonald 1964). The basis is the typological study of the surface pottery; but, of course, one must first locate the sites on which pottery may be found. To do this successfully it is essential to have a firm grasp of the ancient topographical sources and to build on it a thorough familiarity with the modern countryside. One must learn the location of the best agricultural land and most abundant sources of water, what constitutes a good defensive location, healthful orientation, good drainage, easy communication. A knowledge of the present-day language and good rapport with local farmers and officials is also important. So are patience, a dependable and rugged method of transportation, and above all experience and sound instinct gained by trial and error over several seasons. The last mentioned item is probably the main reason for the fact that each succeeding campaign of our search has turned out to be more productive than its predecessor.

Yet as early as 1961 we had come to the conclusion that we must supplement the traditional methods with new means of getting the job done with greater precision and speed. The most obvious need was for aerial photographs and for expert assistance in their interpretation. This technique had never (to our knowledge) been used systematically for surface search in Greece, although it had been producing spectacular results in other parts of the world for more than a generation. When we found the opportunity to state our case to the responsible authorities in the Royal Hellenic Air Force, they were remarkably helpful. They provided a set of photographs for the whole region at a scale of 1 : 30,000 and they arranged special flights over selected sites to provide us with air-cover from much lower altitudes. The aerial photographs soon became indispensable tools to speed up the search for new sites and to see known ones in new perspective, both individually and in relation to one another. Professor Fant (and later Professor Loy) provided expert instruction in using the photographs. A detailed account of our gradual acquisition and utilization of this know-how (still in progress) would be out of place here. Description of some of the techniques is provided in Chapter 2. It may be worth recording, however, that in recent campaigns our ratio of "hits" to "misses" has risen to well above 50 percent. This kind of precision is in startling contrast to a decade before when we had no alternative to climbing every likely looking hill and counted ourselves fortunate if we "scored" on 10 percent of them.

A more fundamentally revised approach, however, resulted from the dawning realization that archaeological exploration can (and ought to) involve far more than simply locating ancient sites. The major thrust of this whole book is to begin to explore some of these wider perspectives. But even in the matter of locating ancient sites there are practical advantages for the field archaeologist in working closely with geologists, geographers, soil scientists, and agricultural economists. One is helped, for instance, to distinguish Pliocene terraces from alluvial fill, and one finds that early farmers liked to set their villages on the former but cultivate the latter; hence, the border zones are likely places to search. One is shown how theories of communications networks and economic nuclei may be applied to specific situations, and again there are practical gains in narrowing down the search. One finds that there are comparatively simple methods of distinguishing a natural formation from an artificial mound or fill. And one begins to understand why a given valley can or could support far more inhabitants than its larger neighbor and why a particular spot was chosen for an ancient and/or modern village.

In other chapters the experts themselves explain the practical application of their own specialty to archaeology. Such techniques (as well as others that science will surely provide) have the potential to make archaeological reconnaissance and excavation much more effective. Even when (or if) archaeologists are better trained in the fundamentals of science and technology, they will need the expert's help in the field as well as in the laboratory. Yet, in both excavation and exploration, the archaeologists of the future will still have their own appropriate ways of going about their job. In fact, both exploration and excavation provide ideal situations for the practical application of interdisciplinary techniques.

PART II. FORMULATION OF THE SITE REGISTERS

In preliminary publications (McDonald and Hope Simpson 1961, 1964, 1969) we described in considerable detail all of the sites then known to us where the ceramic record proves habitation in prehistoric times. The scheme of presentation seemed to be reasonably satisfactory. At any rate, it is endorsed and followed very largely in the parallel publication on prehistoric Euboea (Sackett et al. 1966). It was clear, however, that the repetition of such a bulk of material here would throw the whole book out of balance. Hence, we decided, rather reluctantly, that the raw data in the Registers must be printed as an appendix (see p. 263) rather than as an integral part of this chapter.

In the Site Registers, we have done our best to abbreviate, standardize, and simplify the most essential information on individual sites. We and other explorers see a definite need to agree on the most practicable method of publishing this kind of evidence. A standard formulation may thus emerge for the eventual preparation of a much-needed coordinated survey of Greek lands (McDonald 1966). The risk in such a codification, of course, is that economy may result in obscurity. Hence, we provide here a point-by-point explanation of the formulation. Readers may still find it useful (or even necessary) to refer back to the much fuller details in our previous articles and in other publications cited.

Most categories in the Prehistoric Register (A) comprise the kind of data that is regularly recorded in traditional archaeological search. The others fit into the broader environmental framework outlined in Chapter 1. These data are drawn upon and sometimes expanded elsewhere, but it is convenient to use the tabular form of the Register to bring together as much as possible of the disparate evidence.

A separate Post-Mycenaean Register (B) records the settlements, sanctuaries, and tombs so far discovered where the present ceramic record indicates that habitation *began* in the geometric period or later (up to medieval times). That is, we do not repeat in Register B the evidence already provided in A for later habitation of sites that are proved to have been occupied also in prehistoric times. On the other hand, sites occupied in both prehistoric and post-Mycenaean times will, of course, appear in the distribution maps for the appropriate individual periods (Pocket Maps 8-11 through 8-18). The numbering system will identify foundations with prehistoric associations (1–399) versus those that seem to have been occupied only in later times (400–799). It should be re-emphasized, however, that prehistoric sites numbered 1–399 may also have been occupied in later antiquity.

Since the focus of this study and of our earlier publications has been consistently on the earlier material, Register B is much less detailed than Register A. In fact, we have as a rule included in B only seven of the sixteen categories of information provided in Register A. Also, it is quite probable that at least a few known sites that ought to be included in Register B have been overlooked, although we have checked our own field notes and the published literature as thoroughly as time permitted.

Categories of Information

A. Site Number. Each site is assigned a number that serves to identify it in discussion throughout the book and in the distribution maps. The numbering system used in our 1961 publication for the prehistoric sites then known was consecutive for the whole region, beginning at the northwest and ending at the southeast. New discoveries reported in succeeding publications were assigned the same number as the nearest original site, with an added capital letter (25A and 25B ought to be near 25, etc.). But as the proportion of additions approached and finally exceeded the original sites it was clear that the system was becoming unwieldy. Furthermore, the inclusion here for the first time of settlements that were apparently not occupied until post-Mycenaean date made imperative the adoption of a more flexible means of identification.

Although we were not able to borrow or invent a perfectly satisfactory substitute, we have adopted a scheme that (though rather complicated) does adequately identify sites now known and will accommodate future discoveries, unless they are far more numerous than we can now anticipate. The whole region is divided more or less arbitrarily into four subregions: southwest, southeast, center, north (see Fig. 8-2). Each subregion is assigned a sequence of 100 numbers to identify the prehistoric sites and a second sequence of 100 numbers for the post-Mycenaean settlements. Since the southwest was clearly the heartland in the period with which we are most concerned, the prehistoric sites there are numbered 1 to 99 and the later ancient sites 400–499. Similarly, the prehistoric sites in the southeast subregion are numbered 100–199 and the later ancient sites 500–599, the center subregion 200–299 and 600–699, and the north subregion 300–399 and 700–799.

We claim no very precise rationale for the progression of numbers *within* each subregion, but no one should quarrel with the decision to assign the #1 position in the southwest to the palace site at Epano Englianos. In the case of the prehistoric settlements (Register A) the new numbers are followed in parentheses by those previously used to identify each site, so that checking back with our earlier publications should not be unduly confusing (see also Conversion Table, p. 322).

B. Site Name. The name of each site serves, of course, as the major means of identification. Here too we have altered the scheme employed previously for the prehistoric entries and thereby brought our usage into line with the recent Euboea publication. The change consists simply in reversing the position of the local toponym and the name of the modern village or *kinotis* (community under a unified local government). Hence we identify the administrative unit within whose territory (if our informants, maps, and available statistical material were dependable) the ancient site is now located. This unit is usually, but not necessarily, the nearest inhabited place. Although most readers will be familiar with neither name, the order here adopted is nevertheless more logical than that in our previous publications. Anyone who wishes to locate one of these sites, either on the ground or on a map, will almost necessarily start with the modern village. So, for example, when we designate the site of the palace as "1 Chora: Epano Englianos," the numeral shows that it is located in the southwestern subregion, so that the modern village of Chora can be more easily located on the ground or in maps. And one knows that the land occupied by the ancient site (now called Epano Englianos) belongs to Chora and should be familiar to the villagers there. (See Pocket Map 1-1 for modern villages.)

The place-names are generally written to conform with present local phonetic usage and a serious attempt has been made to standardize and simplify spelling (see the statement in the Foreword). The only intentional exceptions are where a break with the established learned usage would be jarring and perhaps pretentious (e.g.,

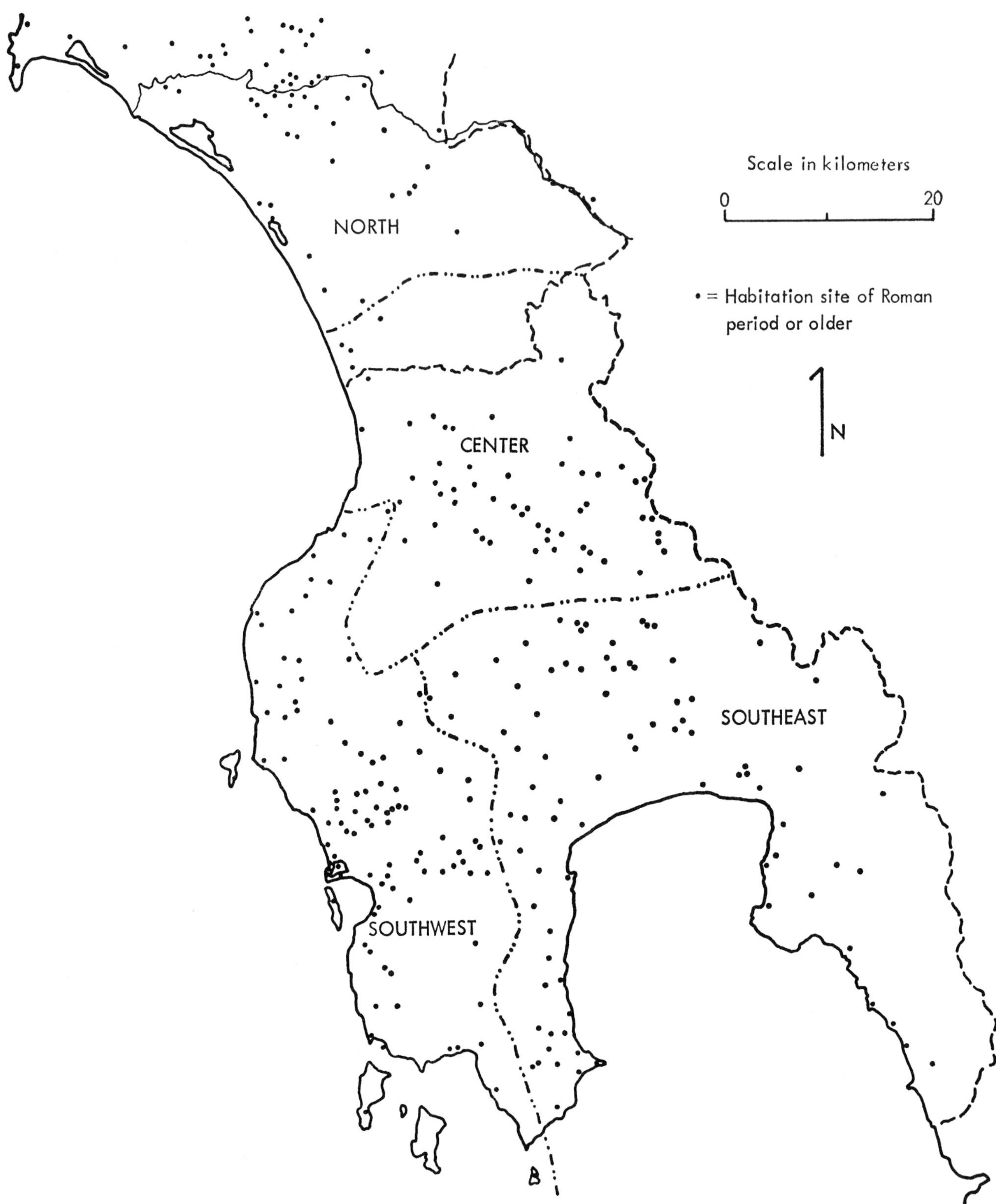

Figure 8-2. Location map of subregions

Pilos for Pylos or Olimbia for Olympia). We have also indicated the stressed syllable in each case – an indispensable bit of information for anyone asking directions in the field.

In the case of sites that have been equated certainly or tentatively with towns whose ancient names are known from historical sources, we have included this information (with or without an interrogation mark) in brackets following the regular compound identification. Thus, the full designation of the palace site evacuated by Blegen is "1 Chóra:Epáno Englianós (Mycenaean [and Homeric?] Pylos)."

C. Bibliography. We cite in chronological order the major references known to us that record the discovery, exploration, and excavation (if any) of each site. Fuller bibliographies and discussions in our own previous publications are also noted. In general, if ours are the only publications referred to, the site was discovered by us. On the other hand, we first identified a fair number of sites on which others have since commented in print, and we have previously published comments on many sites discovered by others.

D. Site Location. In previous articles on the prehistoric settlements and in our field notes and maps, we have used various means to record exact location. The most precise, of course, is to identify the spot on the best available large-scale maps and to cite exact latitude and longitude. But without access to unusually detailed standard maps, these coordinates can scarcely be of much practical value to the average researcher. We have also advocated and generally followed the practice of providing compass bearings from the site to at least two obvious landmarks. But we realize that this method too has serious limitations in terms of communicating practical information.

It is probably true that, for the person who wants to visit a particular site or to locate it reasonably closely on a conventional map, the most realistic procedure is to provide standard directions (as in the Euboea publication and others). Since we cannot reproduce here the painstaking descriptions in the preliminary articles, we have decided to give a careful calculation from the aerial photographs of the *approximate* distance and direction as the crow flies *from* an easily identifiable point (unless otherwise specified, the village to which the site belongs). Thus, Epano Englianos is located "3 km S-SW" (of Chora). If the distance is less than 1 km, 100-m intervals are given; beyond 1 km an estimate is made to the nearest half kilometer. Direction is indicated by E, SE, E-SE, and so forth. Brief additional information about a still nearer local landmark or helpful method of pinpointing a place is also provided when feasible. So we specify that Epano Englianos lies "beside main highway."

With such directions a traveller *who makes Chora his starting point* should have relatively little trouble in finding the palace site even if the identifying sign and the metal roof were to disappear. Luckily, too, one can nearly always find in Greek villages a generous resident who will act as guide to any spot in the vicinity, if the local toponym is known by the traveller and correctly pronounced.

Using these brief data and the best available maps, the scholar working in his study should usually be able to locate a given site reasonably accurately. And maps are now in existence that provide as good an idea of the local relief as one can achieve in any but the most painstaking verbal directions.

E. Physical Description. Here particularly the capsule type of reporting is inevitably incomplete and imprecise. In the preliminary articles we included detailed descriptions, although we also realized that good photographs and sketches are likely to be much more effective. The consistent use of neither method has been possible here, but we have included views of a few important and typical sites. Approximate elevations (e.g., of a plateau or mountain) are sometimes specified in particular situations, but the elevation of each site *above sea level* is not given.

Instead of providing any or all of the above, we decided to confine the description to one of a number of simple standardized rubrics such as "top of high hill," "top and E slope of medium hill," "S and E slopes of low hill," "N end of low ridge," "medium spur projecting W," "low mound," "valley floor." The "high-medium-low" designations here denote *approximate local relief* – that is, "more than 50 m," "50–30 m," "less than 30 m" above the nearest river bottom or valley floor (and *not* above sea level). Such a statistic does have real significance in important factors like defensibility, distance from good land and water, and the like.

F. Archaeological Description. In the distribution maps a solid triangle indicates a habitation site only; a solid circle records a grave, cemetery, or cemeteries only; a solid triangle within a circle shows that there is evidence *both* of habitation *and* of burials. In the Registers the abbreviations HAB(itation), CEM(etery) and HAB + CEM serve the same purpose. When a burial is suspected but has not been certified or when surface pottery is extremely scarce over a limited area, we use an outlined circle or triangle as a symbol in the maps, and an interrogation mark after the abbreviation in the Registers.

In the case of cemeteries we have specified whenever

possible the type of grave ("tholos," "chamber tomb," "multiple burial mound," "cist") and the approximate number so far known. We have also attempted to provide an idea of their relation to the associated settlement, if its location is known.

In addition, we note foundations of house walls or fortifications that are visible above ground, "foreign stones" (i.e., transported to the spot from elsewhere) that were presumably used in such structures, artifacts such as blades and cores of obsidian, stone implements, and tiles. For excavated and salvage sites, we provide the briefest possible characterization of the results, including the various categories of finds.

G. Analysis of Pottery. This is, of course, the focus of provisional dating in traditional surface exploration. It offers the best hope of making a fairly rapid and reasonably dependable estimate of shifting habitation patterns over long periods of time. Scrupulous excavation and comparative studies are making possible the classification of Greek pottery types with increasing precision. But for Messenian prehistory at least, the scarcity of firm stratigraphic results means that conclusions from the surface pottery (mostly very fragmentary and undecorated; rare painted pieces usually in poor shape) are still open to considerable doubt (McDonald and Hope Simpson 1969, p. 172). Also, it is sometimes difficult to be sure whether we have correctly diagnosed scanty and worn surface remains that we tentatively assign to post-Mycenaean times.

Since considerations of space preclude the repetition of our previous painstaking descriptions of the more distinctive bits of prehistoric pottery found on individual sites, we have decided to print here only the bare results of the analyses, and not the basis for them. Hence, category G in Register A generally duplicates the chronological data recorded in the "Summary List of Sites" in the latest preliminary article (McDonald and Hope Simpson 1969). The same series of symbols (N = Neolithic; EH = Early Helladic, etc.) has been retained, with the addition of M = medieval or Byzantine. The M designation is particularly vague, since it covers at least a millennium, and we lack the background to more closely identify the pottery with any assurance. In one chronological division only, the target period in Late Helladic, a fair number of closely datable excavated groups (mostly from tombs) have been discovered in our region, and we have ourselves sometimes felt that we got sufficient diagnostic surface sherds to suggest further subdivisions (LHI; LHII; LHIIIA-B-C).

A notation in parentheses indicates that surface pottery was "heavy," "medium," or "sparse" when we visited the particular site. One must remember, however, that such information can be misleading. Badly eroded sites may show more surface pottery than others with deep stratification. Also, conditions vary at different seasons. We have frequently found that there were notably more or less sherds in sight on a second visit to a spot, but we have very rarely had to change our estimate of the periods involved.

H. Extent of Habitation. In category F the approximate number of known graves is recorded. A cemetery may occasionally give some idea of the size (as well as of the prosperity) of the associated settlement, although such inferences should be regarded with extreme caution unless there is other supporting evidence. For the habitation site itself, however, we have adopted what we regard as a considerably more dependable index, an estimate of the size (and orientation) of the area strewn with surface pottery and other habitation debris. Sometimes the darker color of the soil of a previously inhabited area supplies a further clue. The equivalent in hectares or fractions thereof is added within brackets (1 ha = 10,000 sq. m or 2.471 acres).

Again, we are fully aware of how cautiously such calculations must be regarded. As already mentioned, erosion and wash versus deep earth cover, the season and state of cultivation when the collection was made, the history and use of the site, and various other factors might make such observations meaningless or even misleading. Yet, in sum, individual discrepancies may largely cancel one another out. In any case, in the absence of precise and extensive excavations there seems to be no other equally promising basis for a tentative estimate of the over-all size of unexcavated village sites.

I. Communications. We employ here the terms "crossroads," "mainline," "secondary," and "isolated" to designate relative accessibility to the regional communications network (see Ch. 9). The natural lines of overland travel have apparently been basically the same from prehistoric times to the present. It is true, however, that in the last generation or two a few highways have been built and many tracks have been widened and straightened and grades eased to accommodate wheeled traffic.

As for communications by sea, settlements are labeled "on," "within easy reach" of, and "distant" from the coast, and *present* natural conditions for sheltering small shallow-draft ships are rated as "excellent," "fair," or "poor." Of course, there have been local coastal changes since ancient times, some of them perhaps fairly drastic (see Ch. 3). The "on," "within easy reach," and "distant" categories are defined, respectively, as "1 km or less," "1–5 km," and "more than 5 km" from the *nearest point on the coast.* We have included an estimate to the nearest kilometer of the distance as the crow flies.

This may provide a bit more specific information, especially in the case of "distant" places. But the distance by road or path would always have been more, and many stretches of coast are devoid of usable harbors.

Not enough is known about the possibility of river traffic in prehistoric times to warrant speculation along these lines.

J. Strategic Features. Military control, defensibility, position vis-à-vis the road network, and similar factors must have been major determinants in the original siting and especially in the relative growth of many settlements. Terms such as "strong defensive position," "route intersection," "control of pass," "exceptionally wide view" represent an attempt to assess such criteria. We have tried to limit entries in this category to cases where these characteristics seem to be unusually striking.

K. Water Supply. The availability of a good supply of fresh water (as well as good land) is absolutely vital for a thriving village, whether ancient or modern; but to assess the relative quality and quantity of water resources is a laborious and risky undertaking (see Ch. 3). Available recent statistics are spotty and sometimes undependable. There are sharp seasonal anomalies in places. Personal judgment and memory are fallible, and notes taken on the ground and the testimony of local informants are seldom complete or fully accurate. It is obvious, too, that modern statistics and conditions cannot be projected indiscriminately into various periods of the past. Yet we believe that the information assembled from fieldwork, aerial photographs, and government statistics (1961) is too valuable to be omitted.

Since the smaller rivers are now dry for several months of the year, most villages rely directly or indirectly on water from natural springs. We therefore record in Register A the approximate distance and direction of the most accessible spring(s) from each site, and we estimate the flow as "copious," "fair," or "poor." If surplus spring water is used for irrigation, that information is included in category N.

There are two other potentially useful kinds of data that have not yet been treated exhaustively. We have calculated in most cases the approximate distance and direction of sites from an accessible river or stream (if any), and we note cases where the flow is perennial. Also, if our information indicates that the nearest modern village or the agricultural area surrounding the ancient site depends on wells or on water piped in from a distance, this fact is noted, but the situation is changing nowadays with bewildering rapidity.

L. Total Land. We assume that the inhabitants of ancient settlements controlled a fixed amount of land, both cultivated and unimproved. It is not at issue here whether the land was "owned" in small parcels by individual farmers (as is generally true today), by the village collectively, by a relatively few landlords, by religious establishments, or by the king. The cryptic references in the Pylos tablets suggest that the system at that time was complicated and perhaps rather unstable. Our aim, however, has been to find a workable basis on which to estimate the amount of land that might have been utilized by the inhabitants of each known ancient settlement.

Even if we had discovered the exact location of every settlement that existed at some point in the past (which is certainly not the case), their exact territorial boundaries would still be problematical. And there must have been minor shifts, if not major ones, at frequent intervals and for various reasons. Yet, given the density of the known habitation pattern in the Middle and Late Bronze Age and the relative thoroughness of the search, objective calculations with some theoretical validity may be attainable.

We have measured the distance from each MH-LH settlement (see Part III of this chapter for their remarkable continuity) to its nearest neighbors in three different directions. Using modern practice as a guide, the outside limit for any measurement was set at 5 km (an hour's walk); but in fact remarkably few of the known ancient sites were so isolated. We then used the three measurements to obtain an *average radius* for each site. This figure is given in Register A, together with a close approximation of the equivalent in hectares (1 ha = 10,000 sq. m or 2.471 acres).

In estimates attempted in this and later categories of Register A, we see no way at present to handle the tricky factor of precise contemporaneity (see Part III of this chapter). That is to say, there may have been much bigger gaps between inhabited places at various points in the total MH-LH span, with much of the intervening land unclaimed and unused. Therefore, although all sites here included were settled as early as MH times, it is no doubt safer to view some of these estimates as applicable particularly to the most heavily populated prehistoric phase (LHIIIB).

M. Cultivated Land. We have extracted from the aerial photographs the percentage of the total land in category L that is *now* cultivated (see Ch. 11). "Cultivated land" is defined as all land being currently cropped or harvested or in recent fallow. The estimate is given to the nearest 10 percent and the approximate equivalent in hectares is also supplied. Extensive ground checking suggests that the estimate from the aerial photographs is quite reliable. Naturally, the modern pattern of land use in a particular area will differ (perhaps drastically in some cases) from that in various epochs of the past. One can sometimes see evidence of fairly recent abandonment of once-cultivated land, and the exploitation of available land must have varied tremendously over the centuries. But we have found no more reliable method of calculating the approximate area that was at least available for use by communities known to have existed in the Late Bronze Age. In any case, there is surely relevance in recording the percentage of land under cultivation within exactly the same total territory at another epoch of dense population and intensive exploitation, namely, the present.

A further parameter that will be discussed in Chapter 16 as a possible rough check on ancient population is to estimate how many inhabitants (on the average) this amount of cultivated land will now maintain.

The uncultivated portion within the predetermined radius would presumably have been used then (as now) mainly for grazing and fuel, although we believe it likely that much more of it was in forest (see Ch. 16). The potential resources of a given settlement (ancient or modern) for herding animals are difficult to calculate because flocks may range long distances for pasturage, particularly in the summer season. And animals seem to have formed a relatively more important part of the economic resources of many ancient communities than is true at present.

N. Irrigated Land. Here we record the number of hectares of land now intensively cultivated with the aid of irrigation from nearby springs and/or perennial streams. The statistics are those reported for 1961, and we have done our best to distribute these figures among the ancient settlements in accordance with category L. Actually, a careful study is needed of the whole problem of the status of technical knowledge in prehistoric Greece and its application to irrigation and to hydraulic engineering in general. The meager evidence now available is discussed in Chapters 3, 11, and 16. But we here record our belief that in the Late Bronze Age irrigation may well have been used as intensively as nowadays, proportionate (of course) to population in the two eras.

O. Population. From the estimated area of the ancient settlements (category H) we provide in Register A a calculation of the approximate number of inhabitants. The basis for arriving at the formula used (1 ha = 130 persons) and its relative reliability will be more fully discussed in Chapter 16 in the context of general population trends on a regional basis.

We will simply mention here that we have attempted a preliminary estimate of the modern situation in Messenia by plotting from aerial photographs (1965) the settlement area of ten representative villages and using the largest population figures in recent official census data (usually those reported for 1928, before large-scale movement to the big towns and abroad had left many houses vacant). This calculation suggests that the average relationship is about 112 persons per hectare (see Table 8-1). On the basis of meager evidence from Messenia and elsewhere in Greece, it seems reasonable to believe that prehistoric villages were somewhat more densely built up than at present. Hence our estimate of 130 persons per hectare is probably within reasonable range of the true average.

P. Special Features. This category is a miscellaneous one where essential information that does not fall naturally into any of the earlier classes can be recorded. It includes a brief notice of any excavation carried on at the site, as well as particularly striking aspects of what might be called microclimate or local environment (orientation, protection from cold winds, availability of summer breezes, drainage).

Table 8-1. Population Density of Representative Modern Villages

		Population by Census Year				Density
Village	Area	1928	1940	1951	1961	per Ha.
Parapoungi	5.6 ha	389	*411*	324	212	75.5
Mavromati	7.2	578	*792*[a]	499	432	110
Korifasion	7.6	699	. . .[b]	843	*926*	121.8
Ellinoeklisia . . .	5.2	338	353	424	*510*	98
Dhesilla	8.7	*944*	917	658	660	108.5
Pila	3.7	209	*373*	321	281	100.8
Plati	7.7	*1,082*	1,110	1,031	272	140.5
Anemomilos . . .	2.34	*353*	322	284	191	150.7
Arsinoë	3.8	374	372	*436*	385	114.7
Karpofora	4.0	390				97.5
Average						111.8

[a] May include residents of nearby monastery.
[b] The census figure of 1,568 includes all of *kinotis* and other settlements.

PART III. COMMENTARY ON THE SITE REGISTERS

As in the case of the data reproduced in Register A, we have tried here to avoid unnecessary repetition of observations and theories already published in the three preliminary articles (McDonald and Hope Simpson 1961, 1964, 1969). But since the major theme in both cases is the analysis of population distribution in southwest Peloponnese throughout prehistoric times, some plowing of the same ground is inevitable. In addition, the strictly "archaeological" evidence will be combined with some relevant information from other chapters; but only in the final chapter shall we attempt a synthesis.

In Messenia during the past decade we have been groping toward a concept that has recently been discussed in a series of thought-provoking essays under the title *Settlement Archaeology* (Chang et al. 1968). In Chapter V of that publication, Bruce C. Trigger proposes to look at settlement patterns in terms of three levels: the individual structures; the arrangement of structures within a settlement; and the distribution of settlements over the landscape. He points out that at present there is little in the way of systematic understanding of settlement patterns to guide the archaeologists, and he sensibly suggests that the initial approach should be the study of similar phenomena in living societies.

It is clear, then, that the data really needed before writing the following pages would include much more of the kind of research Aschenbrenner reports in Chapter 4 and a reasonable number of fully excavated settlements from various periods in the past. We hope that in time these desiderata can be realized in Messenia. The distribution of contemporary settlements and case studies of a selected number constitute a large but perfectly manageable research project for a team of geographers and anthropologists. Fully excavated ancient settlements, however, are quite another matter. There are numerous historical and practical reasons to explain our present ignorance in this respect. Throughout the whole Bronze Age in the Aegean area only two sites immediately come to mind. One is Mrs. Boyd-Hawes' excavation at Gournia in Crete, the other Valmin's at Malthi (#222). Perhaps this coincidence explains Valmin's repeated observation that the village plan at Malthi resembles that of Gournia. Furthermore, surface indicators in the Aegean are relatively meager, compared (for example) with Meso-America. One can rarely find outlines of structures above ground from which to infer anything definite about individual buildings or settlement plan before excavation.

Excluding Malthi, excavation at Messenian prehistoric sites has concentrated almost entirely on tombs and on the major buildings at the royal citadel at Epano Englianos (#1). Hence, we have very little quantitative evidence in the first two of Trigger's categories, normative individual structures (houses) and comprehensive plans of individual settlements. It will require a generation or more of concentration – in Messenia as well as elsewhere in Greece – just to begin to redress the balance.

Meanwhile, we must focus our attention on the very considerable evidence bearing on Trigger's third category, the distribution of ancient settlements over the landscape. Register A and Pocket Maps 8-11 through 8-15 show that Messenia is in a particularly favorable position here (vis-à-vis other regions in the Aegean) for prehistoric times. In later periods, the evidence is probably no more complete than average, but the Messenian material has at least been brought together now in Register B and Pocket Maps 8-16 through 8-18 and can be conveniently reviewed and compared (using the overlays) with earlier patterns as well as with the medieval (Pocket Map 5-8), early modern (Pocket Map 5-9), and contemporary situation (Pocket Map 1-1) and with the basic patterns of geomorphology (Pocket Map 3-7), soils (Pocket Map 11-21), and water supply (Pocket Map 3-6).

It is thus clear that a firm basis exists for studying the distribution of settlements over the Messenian landscape. But these in themselves are simply the raw data. An attempt to understand and explain the pattern within a given period or the variations in successive phases is a still more challenging task. To quote Trigger again, "If we conceive of the settlement pattern as an outcome of the adjustment a society makes to a series of determinants that vary both in importance and in the kinds of demands they make on the society, we must consider not merely the range of factors affecting settlement patterns but also the manner in which different factors interact with one another to influence a particular pattern. Factors vary in importance according to both the local situation and the temporal relationship that they have to one another" (pp. 70, 71). And he further warns that a number of different solutions are possible to the same problem.

Perhaps the most logical starting point is the definition of the region included in our study and the rationale for setting the boundaries that were briefly explained in Chapter 1 (see Fig. 2-1). We shall begin by quoting Gordon Willey's "Appraisal" of the various articles in the publication referred to above (Chang et al. 1968). "The total landscape distribution," he writes, "is the most difficult of all to comprehend. For one thing, it can be brought into focus only after considerable archaeological research has been carried out in a zone, region, or area, and after conclusions have been reached about the size and borders of the territorial unit under consideration" (p. 216).

Of Willey's two conditions, we have certainly fulfilled the first; but our decision on the limits of the region to be studied rests on a weaker foundation. In Chapter 1 it was pointed out that, in the present state of knowledge about local cultural characteristics, it would be very difficult if not impossible to distinguish self-contained units differing notably from one another in terms of their artifact assemblages. The so-called koinê (common culture) – in language, architecture, weaponry, political and social institutions as well as in ceramics – seems to be a well-established characteristic of the Mycenaean kingdoms.

Cultural as well as physical isolation must have been much more marked in earlier epochs, but we have not yet reached the stage where such distinctions can be safely drawn. The decision as to how far to cast our net had to be based on other factors. Broadly speaking, they may be classed as physiographic and historical.

The seacoast leaves no doubt about western and southern boundaries. On the east, the Taygetos range represents a vast and formidable natural barrier. It usually served as the essential political boundary between Messenia and Lakonia as far back as Greek history is recorded, although it did not prevent the Spartans from invading and eventually dominating Messenia in archaic and classical times.

The northern limit is not nearly so clear. In Chapter 7 Chadwick infers from the tablets that at the time of the destruction of the palace the border was no farther north than the Nedha. Our surface exploration has admittedly been much less thorough in the heavily dissected area between the Kyparissia and Alpheios valleys, but our strong impression is that the known Mycenaean settlements there were sparse, isolated, and "provincial." Thus, this territory may have constituted a kind of buffer zone (as Chadwick believes) beyond the political unit with the capital at Epano Englianos. But it seems equally possible to the authors of this chapter that in the most dynamic phase of Pylian expansion there was a major push to the north and that regular communications with the Alpheios Valley were maintained by coastal road and shipping. When one is dealing with pre-Mycenaean times, it can be questioned whether the very concept of a "northern boundary" of the aggregate "region" makes much sense. Certainly the social units (however organized) were very much smaller, and the network of separate parcels of land to which each laid formal claim (if they did so at all) must have been a veritable maze.

In any case, we have through the years been collecting evidence on the prehistoric habitation in the lower Alpheios Valley and in Triphylia; and it would be arbitrary to ignore these data now because we cannot prove that this northern territory ever belonged to the kingdom of Pylos. Even if it did not, the Alpheios Valley is a reasonable physiographic marker for the northern limit of the region that we define as southwest Peloponnese.

We shall begin the discussion of the settlement pattern by reviewing the evidence marshalled in the *American Journal of Archaeology* (1969) for the successive prehistoric phases and adding some further observations of our own as well as information supplied by our colleagues. Then we shall make some parallel but less detailed observations about post-Mycenaean developments. The account will be easier to follow if the information in the Registers (see Appendix) and in the accompanying distribution charts (Pocket Maps 8-11 through 8-18) is frequently consulted. The charts include both "certain" and "probable or possible" sites (see legends) and in a sense tell their own story.

Register A (Prehistoric)

Paleolithic. There is as yet practically no authenticated Paleolithic habitation in the southwest, although its eventual discovery can be confidently predicted in view of developing evidence elsewhere in Greece—particularly on and near the west coast of Elis and Epiros.

For the record, it may be mentioned here that site #67 deserves expert examination. Also, in the spring of 1969 Roger Howell picked up on the terraces above the beach near Nichoria (#100) two stone implements that may be of Paleolithic date, and in the fall of 1970 he and Lukermann noted several more specimens on a similar terrace site to the northeast, below the village of Velika. We also understand that the Greek Archaeological Service undertook in the summer of 1970 further examination of a large cave near Areopolis in the Mani (actually beyond the SE border of our region). Here a group of speliologists claimed some years ago to have discovered Paleolithic artifacts.

Neolithic. (Local chronology has not yet been firmly established; probably beginning considerably later than the sixth millennium date presently indicated for northeastern Greece; and probably petering out in the early third millennium B.C.) Known Neolithic habitation is so far quite meager and scattered (see Pocket Map 8-11). There are seven sites where diagnostic sherds or other artifacts demonstrate habitation, plus eleven others in the probable or possible category (Pl. 2-2). Four of the certain and four of the possible sites are caves, widely scattered over the southwest and southeast subregions (see Fig. 8-2 for the internal subdivisions we designate as southwest, southeast, center, and north). The two caches of celts (see legend, Pocket Map 8-11) cannot be proved to have been associated with habitation sites. The two isolated celts (#'s 28, 239) presumably indicate that there was Neolithic habitation somewhere in the area of each find-spot.

Only one certain site (#304) seems to have been an open settlement on a prominent acropolis; and this is also the only authenticated habitation site north of the Kyparissia River. All five of the possible open sites are on high hills. Valmin (1938) identified a small quantity of pottery from his excavation on the Malthi hilltop (#222) as Neolithic and he thought some of it similar to wares from Orchomenos and therefore probably imported. But it is now impossible to check typologically most of the material he recovered and the stratification claimed at Malthi must be viewed with reserve, although the N figurine is unquestioned.

About one-third of the total are situated on or very close to the coast (Pl. 6-2). A more typical situation seems to have been in rather remote and isolated gorges, in most cases above what are now perennial rivers. There is literary (#10) and archaeological (especially #117) evidence that some of the caves had later cult use. The only cave site even partially excavated is the so-called cave of Nestor (#10) and the results have not been published. Mr. William Phelps examined our meager collected material and noted only a few sherds from one site (#113) that are clearly earlier than "Late Neolithic" (fourth millennium B.C.?).

It is unprofitable to try to make even the most tentative statements about the Paleolithic and Neolithic horizons of human habitation in Messenia until experts have made a much more thorough surface search and followed it with test excavations.

Early Helladic. (Local chronology has not yet been firmly established; probably ending about 2000 B.C.) The data are still scanty for occupation in the Early Bronze Age (see Pocket Map 8-12). There are 22 certain and 13 probable or possible settlements. Locations vary from free-standing acropolis (Pl. 7-2) to ridge top, terrace, and perhaps the occasional cave. The most distinctive type, however, comprising slightly over one-half (57 percent) of the total, is a low natural knoll or artificial mound (Pl. 7-1). In the case of the certain examples, the percentage rises to two-thirds.

The sites so far discernible may also reveal something substantive about the over-all settlement pattern. By far the most noticeable concentration is on the Pliocene slopes just above the alluvium in the Pamisos and Steniklarian plains. Over one-third of the known sites ring this great valley, which has been the agricultural heartland of Messenia ever since. We believe that the marshy land both in the lower valley southwest of the copious Ayios Floros springs and especially in the delta (Valtos) near the mouth of the Pamisos may have been too wet for agriculture, though perhaps useful for pasture in the dry season (see Chs. 3 and 16). Certainly, one would not expect such low marshy ground to be chosen for settlements. Yet at Akovitika (#151), deep in the delta and close to the present coast, Mr. Petros Themelis began in 1969 the excavation of the foundations of a large and well-built structure that is reminiscent of the "House of the Tiles" at Lerna and probably of approximately the same EHII date (Themelis 1970). In 1970 the main building was further cleared under the direction of Miss Theodora Karageorga, and it was discovered that a second major structure of somewhat similar plan abutted it at right angles, and that there were smaller detached components belonging to the complex.

In addition, one can perhaps distinguish two minor concentrations of population in the north and in the southwest. In the Alpheios district there appears to have been a little cluster of habitation around Olympia and another just north of the Alpheios estuary; and several sites have been identified at the north and south edge of the coastal plain in the Pylos vicinity. It would appear, too, that a village or villages (#7B-C) occupied very low ground in the northwest sector of the Osmanaga Lagoon (see Ch. 3). A few additional sites were scattered along the sea, particularly on the west coast between the Alpheios and Pylos districts.

One quite striking phenomenon is that, like their contemporaries elsewhere in Greece, the inhabitants of Messenia in the Early Bronze Age seem to have preferred to live on or near the sea (Pl. 7-3). Of the known sites 31 percent are situated directly on the coast (often at river mouths) or within a kilometer of the present coast; and 45 percent are within relatively easy reach of the sea, 5 km (an hour's walk) or less. This factor argues for a way of life strongly oriented to seafaring, fishing, and trade, as well as for a political situation in which small unprotected coastal villages were not seriously threatened by casual pirates or more highly organized sea marauders.

Since it appears that practically all of the obsidian found at sites in the southern mainland originated on the island of Melos (Renfrew et al. 1965), this would prove direct or indirect trade between Messenia and the Aegean, presumably by sea around the peninsula. The chance find of a couple of marble figurines of Cycladic types at Ayios Andhreas (#304) supports the existence of such contact. Furthermore, most of the inland settlements are on or very near rivers, particularly the great Alpheios and Pamisos that still have a perennial flow. It is an attractive hypothesis that these communities, too, may have derived their livelihood in part from fishing and commerce, using small river boats. Again, a chance find of a Cycladic figurine deep in the interior, north of Olympia, might point in that direction. Finally, the fine ceramic wares found on the surface of a number of sites (notably #'s 124, 137, 245, 246 – of which only one is coastal) indicate that they were in close touch with other and better-known regions of the Greek mainland (Pl. 2-3).

There can be no doubt, however, that agriculture and herding formed the main economic basis of the Early Helladic settlements. It is noticeable that they are in general contiguous to light fertile soils, usually on easy well-drained slopes. In nearly every case the inhabitants would have found plentiful pasture for their flocks in the lower and wetter areas nearby so that exploitation of distant pasturage would probably have been unnecessary (and perhaps dangerous).

The startling new evidence from Akovitika (#151) demands a reassessment of what we had previously inferred about certain aspects of the Early Helladic situation in Messenia (Themelis 1970). But, to defer its consideration for the moment, it is reasonably sure that the other known EH settlements were all small. Indeed, some of them may have been just farmsteads sheltering one large family, and there is at present no proof that they were occupied year-round. No hierarchy of graduated size is indicated by the surface remains. Since almost all were occupied later in the Bronze Age, one can form no reliable idea of their precise extent in EH times. In the case of the two reasonably certain one-phase settlements (#'s 124, 246 – excluding Akovitika), the area strewn with pottery would suggest a maximum population of about 100 * and 50 respectively. If one inferred from this an average population of 75 individuals or 15 families (averaging 5 per family), the population of the certain settlements in the whole region might have been about 1,600. If we include the possible or probable sites, the number rises to 2,600. Since EH mound sites are likely to be plowed down and are particularly difficult to spot on the ground or in the aerial photographs, it may be presumed that a larger than average proportion of settlements from this period has escaped detection. Therefore, a minimum over-all estimate might be in the range of 3,000 to 4,000 souls.

Of course, a solid basis for even the most carefully hedged estimates of prehistoric population in Messenia does not yet exist. Some of our colleagues have therefore pressed us to avoid absolute numbers entirely, since it is so easy for the most cautious estimates to become accepted facts. Perhaps we should have heeded their advice. The general discussion (Ch. 16) on demographic trends throughout Messenian history will perhaps put our evidence in truer perspective. But we should emphasize here that we believe a beginning on prehistoric population trends has to be made now with the available data. Naturally, there are major unknowns that make it a perilous attempt. For example, we see no alternative at present to using the working hypothesis in the EH and later extrapolations that the intrasettlement population remained relatively stable during major phases of the Bronze Age. But, in fact, there must have been sharp, even drastic peaks and troughs over such long periods of time that we cannot yet document at all precisely (e.g., sites #124 and 246, singled out above, certainly seem to have flourished particularly when the EHII ceramic style was in vogue). Indeed, it is perfectly possible that at least some sites that we date EH, MH, and so forth were totally deserted for varying periods within major phases.

Again excluding Akovitika, the only excavated site where significant EH settlement has been claimed is Malthi (#222). It is disagreeable to be obliged to question the conclusions of such an indefatigable and conscientious excavator, but it is becoming increasingly difficult to accept some of Valmin's attributions of pottery types, and particularly his stratigraphic claims. He believed that the earliest recognizable village was abruptly destroyed and that above an ash layer a fortified Middle Bronze settlement with curvilinear houses was built. The lofty and steep Malthi hilltop is, as we shall see, a canonical setting for a Middle Helladic settlement, but it is quite atypical for Early Helladic. The more recently discovered village site (#224), on a low hill beside the copious Kokla spring and only 1 km west of the Malthi acropolis, was apparently occupied all through the Bronze Age, and it is a much likelier candidate for the major EH settlement in the immediate vicinity.

It is unwise at this point to try to arrive at any serious evaluation of the recent evidence from Akovitika (#151). The excavators themselves must have the first authoritative word. Yet their discovery constitutes by far the most important evidence to date bearing on Messenian history in the Early Bronze period, and it cannot be completely ignored here. The buildings have massive and well-preserved stone foundations whose very existence, at a considerable distance from the nearest source of material, proves that a social and political organization of considerable size and sophistication already existed in the southeast corner of the Pamisos delta. One immediately begins to speculate how widely its control of economic resources and manpower extended. The site itself is as eccentric geographically to Messenia as is the modern capital at nearby Kalamata. It would appear (see Ch. 3) that the area was then (as it is now in spite of recent major drainage operations) swampy, unhealthful, and difficult to cultivate. The major factor in the choice of site seems to have been commercial considerations. This must have been a particularly usable harbor

* Our original estimate of the extent of site #124 was "ca. 120 m E-W and 70 m N-S in minimum dimensions" (McDonald and Hope Simpson 1964, p. 235). Another ground check prompted us to change "minimum" to "maximum" in Register A of this volume. Anyhow, it appears to have been an unusually large site by local EH standards, and averaging it with the only other one-phase EH site has probably skewed the "average population" factor considerably too high. This is an example of the slenderness of the available evidence, particularly at this early period.

in the river delta, perhaps protected by an intricate approach through the swamps.

Middle Helladic. (Local chronology has not yet been firmly established; probably ending 1600–1500 B.C.) In this period there was a pronounced population increase in areas already occupied, and a noticeable movement into areas that seem to have been previously uninhabited (see Pocket Map 8-13). Register A contains 58 certain and 49 probable or possible settlements or cemeteries. In the first category (certain), 44 (or 76 percent) appear to be new foundations; in the second (probable), 38 (81 percent). These statistics in themselves would suggest either the advent of outsiders or a relatively rapid increase among the indigenous population (or possibly both).

If a few of the sites occupied in both EH and MH times were carefully excavated, it might be possible to learn whether (a) there is evidence of destruction and dislocation in the latest EH phase (as Valmin originally claimed at Malthi), or whether (b) there is reason to believe that the latest EH inhabitants simply disappeared and the site lay unoccupied for some time before the earliest MH occupation, or (c) that there was an apparently peaceful and gradual transition to the earliest MH level. Surface exploration can perhaps furnish some relevant data. Ten of the twenty-two certain EH sites continued in use (or were reoccupied) in MH times; three certain EH sites were probably occupied in the MH period. Of the thirteen EH sites in the possible or probable category, two were certainly occupied in MH times and six may have been. One possibly significant phenomenon is that only one of the seven certain EH sites in the southeast subregion shows evidence of MH occupation. For some reason – perhaps because it was farthest from their point of origin (see below) and/or because much of the land used by EH people tended to be near low ground – there were also fewer new MH foundations here than in the other subregions.

In any case, it would be extremely dangerous to argue that, because at nine (or 41 percent) of the certain EH sites there is no surface evidence for MH habitation, a ruthless invading group had wiped out a sizable segment of the people who had formerly occupied the region. Definite information will probably have to await a coordinated excavation program, but the old answers are not necessarily the right ones.

For example, site #246 on the north bank of the Nedha River and very near the coast falls in this category, but an apparently new and somewhat larger MH settlement (#243) was built on the opposite bank, a few meters higher and about a kilometer farther inland. One justifiable inference would be that newcomers destroyed the EH site (or found it abandoned) and continued to cultivate its land, but that for some reason – possibly danger of flood or desire for a more sheltered situation – they relocated the village site. On the other hand, it is by no means impossible that descendants of the earlier villagers decided to relocate their settlement and thereafter learned the new (MH) style of pottery making, either from travelling potters or from an admixture of newcomers who joined them peacefully (Pls. 2-3, 2-5).

In the current excavations on the acropolis of Nichoria (#100) a bit of evidence has appeared that may have relevance in this context. The earliest MH residents of Nichoria, as of Lerna, drilled holes in EH sherds (particularly bases of sauceboats) and used them, probably for spindle whorls. This presumably indicates that an abandoned EH site somewhere nearby was known to the later inhabitants. So far there is no clue to its location, but it may very well have been at a lower elevation and nearer the best agricultural land in the river valley to the southeast of the acropolis.

A possibly instructive situation occurs, too, in the case of three low-lying EH sites (#'s 122, 124, 129) in a north-south line near the west bank of the Pamisos River and a fourth EH settlement (#132) beside the Ayios Floros marshes. None of them shows any sign of occupation during MH, but all four were again inhabited in LH times (#124 on a slightly higher site numbered 123 in the immediate vicinity). Although this could be pure coincidence, one is tempted to infer that there was some kind of causal relationship. Newcomers to the area in MH times may have been used to a different agricultural regime and lacked experience in methods of draining and farming low ground. Of course, a period of consistently higher groundwater could have forced old (or new) inhabitants to move. Or such sites may have seemed too exposed and vulnerable for the conditions prevalent in a less peaceful era.

As for the type of site occupied by MH people, the statistics from Register A apparently bear out the generalizations attempted in our latest article (McDonald and Hope Simpson 1969). Not only do they seem to have preferred isolated inland locations, but their villages were most often perched on the top or slope of high hills, spurs, or ridges (Pls. 7-4, 8-1, 8-3). About 45 percent of the certain MH sites were "high," 32 percent "medium," and 20 percent "low." Thus, the sites lent themselves to defense because of the difficulty of access, whether or not they were artificially fortified.

Valmin's association of the fortifications around the hilltop site of Malthi with the MH habitation phase seems to be correct. This might suggest that it was already important to ensure by military means control of certain strategic positions, because this isolated mass dominates the west end of the narrow pass between the Steniklarian Plain and the Soulima Valley. The Malthi walls had been so completely leveled that only excavation demonstrated the existence of their foundations. From surface indications we have very little evidence as to whether other MH hilltop sites were fortified. The most likely case is #231, where we are reasonably sure there was a surrounding wall in prehistoric times; but it is not clear whether it belonged to the certain LH phase or to a probable MH phase (or both). Moreover, even if fortification was the rule in this period, one need not necessarily infer that it was a time of violence. Fortifications might be explained as protection of humans and flocks against depredations by wild animals and casual robbers, rather than for strictly military purposes.

When we examine the distribution of MH settlements, it would appear that the great eastern valley, which had the most obvious concentration in EH times, gained relatively little and may even have lost population in the southern part (Pocket Maps 8-12, 8-13). This development is probably significant in view of the generally much heavier population in the region as a whole. One possible explanation, as previously suggested, is that MH farmers did not find it easy to cope with land in which the water table was high. Also, they may have preferred less open and vulnerable country.

One of the two areas of minor EH concentration, the lower Alpheios Valley, gained marginally in MH times. The second, the immediate Pylos vicinity, seems to have approximately doubled in population.

On the other hand, there were at least three new areas of major MH concentration. One was a wider area that we have called the Pylos district, lying north and east of the Bay of Navarino. In this connection, Wright's earliest paleobotanical evidence from Osmanaga Lagoon is probably relevant (see Ch. 12). The rapid drop in the predominance of pine pollen in the early second millennium B.C. suggests extensive destruction of the forest cover by man. The obvious reason would be to clear land for agriculture, although there would also be a growing demand for timber in construction. The second new area comprised the high rolling country (very difficult to search) west of the Pamisos Valley. The third was the valley of the Kyparissia River and its continuation east of the watershed into the Soulima Valley.

Adding to these a scattering of new sites along the west coast between the Pylos district and Kyparissia, we see that a strong beginning was made in MH times toward intensive occupation of the "great rectangle" that became the nucleus of population in LH times. To define this great rectangle briefly, it practically surrounds the rugged Kyparissia, Aigaleon, and Kondovounia mountain mass. Its east-west arms stretch inland from Kyparissia to the Steniklarian Plain and from the Bay of Navarino to the northwest corner of the Messenian Gulf. Its north-south arms parallel the west coast and the west side of the Pamisos Valley. About 42 percent of all the certain MH sites and 28 percent in the probable category form a wide, concentrated "rim" around this great rectangle.

It would also appear that there was a very modest increase in the string of coastal sites between Kyparissia and the mouth of the Alpheios River, and the lower Messenian peninsula was now attracting a few settlers. On the other hand, there is not a single certain MH site on the east coast of the Messenian Gulf.

When we compare MH and EH sites with respect to accessibility to the sea, another striking contrast appears. Whereas about one-third (31 percent) of the EH sites were on the coast, the ratio drops to less than one-sixth (15 percent) in MH times. One notes also that surface exploration reveals little MH pottery which appears to be imported. Indeed, all indications point to the conclusion that these people were fundamentally uninterested in trade and other outside contacts. The majority seem to have preferred to cultivate their fields and pasture their flocks in small communities that may have had relatively little contact even among themselves. Of known MH villages 62 percent are situated more than 5 km (an hour's walk) from the coast, compared with 45 percent in EH times. This psychological attitude (if the inference is dependable) constitutes what is probably the strongest argument for the proposition that the MH period saw an influx of new people with a quite different tradition from that of the EH inhabitants. The alternative (much less likely in our opinion) would be that threats from outside had forced an essentially peaceable and extroverted people to adopt a radical change in life style.

A couple of further culture traits reinforce the above impression, and it may turn out that these phenomena – Adriatic ware and multiple burial mounds – were associated. Valmin first recognized at Malthi a distinctive class of coarse gray or brown incised pottery (cf. Pl. 3-1). He later professed to see a close similarity between it and pottery recovered from sites extending over much of Greece (particularly the west), the Ionian Islands, and all the way around the Adriatic Sea to southeast Italy and Sicily (Valmin 1939). For this reason he called it "Adriatic ware," and he constructed an ambitious and rather imprecise hypothesis about the impact on Greek prehistory of the people who made and used it.

We cannot follow his argument here in detail, and it appears not to have had a favorable reception from Greek or Italian prehistorians. In his reports during and immediately after the Malthi excavation (Valmin 1934–35) he regarded the incised ware as "a special ware of Middle Helladic, side by side with the two other types" [gray Minyan and matt-painted]; but by the time of the final publication he had radically revised his opinion. "It was everywhere in the majority and seemed to be, from the beginning to the end of the history of the acropolis, almost of the same quality. During this long period, roughly speaking about one thousand five hundred years at least, it seemed to have been made and used without being essentially and radically changed or developed . . . Such a pottery must be proof of continuity of populations" (Valmin 1938, p. 240).

His latest relevant publication, as mentioned above, develops the thesis of an "Adriatic" culture complex characterized especially by this type of ceramics but with other less distinctive features of settlement location and domestic architecture (Valmin 1939). Although most obvious around the Adriatic, he claimed that it had connections with west, central, and east Europe on the one side, and with Aegean culture on the other. It is at present quite impossible, he said, to fit the Adriatic culture into Aegean chronological and typological schemes.

Valmin's earlier impression of the incised ware as a new phenomenon of the MH occupation at Malthi was almost certainly correct. And the best indication that it had disappeared at Malthi in LH (at least in LHIIIB) is that later on he found scarcely a single fragment in excavating a section of the LH site (#223) at the western foot of the Malthi hill (Valmin 1960). Yet his thesis that the incised ware represents the presence of people with northwestern (Adriatic) connections is not necessarily invalidated because the chronological limits have to be drastically reduced. We have found identical pottery on the surface of a fair number of sites, notably in the northern and western parts of the region; and it seems quite consistently to be associated with other pottery in the recognizable MH tradition. It occurs in greatest quantity at site #213 at the northeast edge of the Steniklarian Plain and is also represented as far north as #303, as far south as #80, and as far southeast as #206. Preliminary study of the material from the 1969 and 1970 excavations at Nichoria (#100) suggests that modest amounts of Adriatic ware are stratified in MHII levels. So the appearance of the incised ware does seem to be an important indication of a new and distinctive culture tradition that reached Messenia in the MH time range.

There is a second phenomenon, namely the multiple burial mound, that may be new at about the same time. The mound that has been most carefully investigated so far is #52, in the heart of the Pylos district (see the relevant bibliography in Register A). Marinatos found here that the earth had been heaped over an outer circular socle of stone slabs about 14 m in diameter. A sizable number of huge pithoi, lying on their sides and facing outward, were set into the stone socle at regular intervals. They had contained inhumation burials with practically no funerary gifts. In the center was a horseshoe-shaped chamber containing no signs of burial.

An impressive number of apparently similar tumuli, identifiable by the associated stone slabs and bone and pithos fragments, are now known (see Pl. 1-4). Marinatos mentions 12 in the vicinity of #52 and at least twice that number in western Messenia. Our Register A lists 27 tumuli at 12 sites (all of them except #200 clustered in the Pylos district) where the attribution is sure or probable. And it is a fair inference that a good many more await discovery or have been completely destroyed.

It is of utmost importance to date these distinctive monuments as closely as possible and to determine the provenience of this burial custom (unless it evolved locally). Marinatos is inclined to assign them to the very end of EH or to MH times. It is unfortunate that diagnostic pottery has not yet been found associated with them. The late EH vase from the vicinity of his site #52 was apparently a chance find and not definitely from the mound itself. When evidence from carefully excavated EH and MH habitation sites is available, it should be possible to crossdate the pithoi. In the meantime, we can only record our strong impression that the tumuli began to be built in the earlier part of the MH phase in Messenia. And it is probably more than coincidence that they appear to have been concentrated in the Pylos district, which became the political heartland of Messenia in the LH phase (at least, in LHIIIB).

Indeed, it seems to us a likely and intriguing inference that there is a close connection between an earlier phase in the use of Blegen's palace site (#1) and the impressive group of these tumuli (#'s 13, 14) on top of the high parallel ridge to the northwest. We suggest that these tumuli represent a cemetery connected with the MH habitation phase that is certified in the lower levels below the palace itself. In a few deep soundings Blegen recovered both gray Minyan and MH matt-painted pottery. This level may represent the earliest occupation on the hill, and associated with the certifiable MH material were sherds of incised Adriatic ware.

As to the origin of the Messenian tumuli, we may at least mention the recent claim (Hammond 1967) that rather similar burial structures might suggest a direct connection between the funerary architecture of the "Kurgan" people who came into Macedonia from the

Danube region in the Late Neolithic period, certain Early and Middle Bronze structures in Albania and Levkas, and eventually the grave circles and shaft graves of Mycenae. The circular stone foundation and the central "chamber" in Marinatos' tumulus (#52) seem reasonably analogous, and round enclosures with pithos burials in pits are well known from Levkas. Hammond may have pushed the theory too far, but his evidence does provide a possible lineage for the Messenia tumuli, as does Valmin's for the incised pottery. It looks as if we must seriously consider the possibility that the beginning of what we call the Middle Helladic period in Messenia is signaled by the appearance of these important culture traits (and presumably the people to whom they were familiar), and that they reached Messenia from farther up the west coast.

We have already stressed that settlements were much more numerous and widespread in MH than in EH times. The raw statistics (58 compared with 22 certain; 49 versus 13 probable) suggest that the number of villages had approximately tripled. In addition, it is a safe assumption that, on the average, MH settlements were considerably larger; but it is very difficult in the present state of our evidence to estimate how much larger. We shall later cite somewhat more detailed evidence for the size and population of LHIIIB communities, but since both MH and LH pottery occurs on the surface of most sites, it is virtually impossible to estimate how much individual settlements had grown (or possibly shrunk) from the one major phase to the next, or during a major phase.

A striking proof of continuity between MH and LH is that (excluding tombs) there is just one settlement (#106)—and it is a poor and inconclusive example—that was definitely inhabited in MH and that shows no evidence of habitation in LH. If we take the average extent of the handful of MH settlements on which LH habitation is uncertain, the figure is 8,400 sq. m or 0.8 hectares. Applying the formula developed for Category O in the Register, the average population of an MH village would be approximately 100 persons (20 families), an increase of about 20 percent over the size calculated for EH sites. Then, by multiplying this average village population by the number of certain MH sites (58), we arrive at a minimum MH regional population of approximately 6,000. There is no way at present to estimate rationally the population of the 49 known sites that were probably or possibly inhabited in MH times. We may postulate, however, that there were 100 MH villages in the region (surely no exaggeration) and that the average size was about that suggested above. We would then arrive at a total regional population of about 10,000 souls, an approximate threefold increase over the EH projection.

Again, the only MH settlement that has been systematically excavated is Malthi (Valmin's Dorion III and IV). We see no reason to doubt his attribution to MH times of the earliest fortification system with its several gates and "towers," or his contention that the village had a larger population in MH times than either before or after that period. For whatever it is worth, he reports that of a total of about 320 "rooms" in the closely packed labyrinthine structures within the walls, MH pottery was found without contamination in 99 rooms and MH mixed with pottery from other periods in 210 rooms. Our formula would suggest that, since there were about 1.1 ha within the walls, the population was about 140 (28 families). This would mean that the houses contained an average of over two rooms per inhabitant. The average house sheltering the average family of five would have consisted of at least ten rooms. It would be rather surprising if the MH inhabitants of Malthi really had such commodious accommodations. Possibly they crowded considerably more than 140 inside these walls; but it is quite unlikely that Valmin's 320 "rooms" were all in use at any one time.

At any rate, in comparison with the suggested mean population for MH settlements, Malthi was somewhat larger than average. House walls were both rectilinear and curvilinear, but it was impossible in most cases to distinguish one house from another. Occasional graves with contracted single burials were found within the walls. Valmin is emphatic that the evidence suggested an "almost imperceptible transformation" from MH times (Dorion IV) to the settlement of Mycenaean times (Dorion V). The MH settlement was, according to his reading of the evidence, definitely a country town, populated mainly by farmers and shepherds. But he saw it also as a modest commercial and manufacturing center serving the people who cultivated somewhat less fertile areas surrounding Malthi's own fine, well-watered territory. In this connection he points to a row of storerooms built against the fortification wall.

There are innumerable questions that immediately come to mind in connection with economic, social, and political conditions in and around MH Malthi – questions for which a completely excavated settlement might be expected to provide at least some tentative evidence. Valmin was more aware of the potential than most excavators of his generation and did his valiant best with the resources and methods at his disposal. Still, the results are disappointing, and it is often difficult even to be sure whether he is referring to the MH or LH situation. Since our own focus in this book is on the latter, we will defer further discussion of the Malthi material.

Late Helladic or Mycenaean. (Local chronology has

not yet been firmly established; ending about 1100 B.C.) The half-millennium from about 1600 to 1100 B.C. is the target phase for this chapter and indeed for the whole book. It is fortunate that, compared with earlier prehistoric times and with the immediate post-Mycenaean centuries, a considerably broader range of evidence is available for this particular era. In the first place, there is far more material of a strictly archaeological nature, both from excavation and from surface exploration. In addition there is a small corpus of contemporary written documents. They come from one site and are strictly relevant only to the time around 1200 B.C. But since that site was the capital of a whole kingdom, and the administrative machinery in use in its final year certainly required several generations to reach that stage, the Pylos Linear B tablets have much broader relevance in both time and space. Even in the difficult initial stages of their decipherment, they have illuminated many aspects of the local Mycenaean culture where purely archaeological evidence could never offer more than hints. The documentary evidence is treated by Chadwick in Chapter 7, but the problem of making at least a start on correlating the content of the tablets with the archaeological data is ours as well as his. In general, however, coordinated attempts along these lines will be reserved for the final chapter.

Again, although Hope Simpson and Lazenby systematically examine in Chapter 6 the evidence on Messenia preserved in classical documents, we cannot afford to ignore here possible correlations of a specific kind between the archaeological data and later Greek literature and tradition, especially the Homeric poems. This is a notoriously tricky area in which expert opinion ranges all the way from those who hold that later "evidence" has practically no basis in fact to those who confidently follow it and correspondingly downgrade or ignore the archaeological results. In this chapter and especially in the final one, we have tried to chart a middle course (McDonald 1967, *passim*). On the question of the northern frontier, for example, some critics will feel that we should have placed no credence in Homer's admittedly confusing testimony concerning the Alpheios, whereas others will be disappointed that we refused to go all the way with Homer by shifting the nucleus of the whole kingdom to Triphylia.

Finally, there is the category of "scientific" evidence bearing on the natural environment in Mycenaean times. Our colleagues have been urged from the start to seek for solid facts and to construct reasonable hypotheses along these lines. As in the case of the literary documentation, however, we shall borrow from them in this chapter only such data as bear on the specific archaeological problem under discussion.

Compared with the Messenian evidence available for later Mycenaean times (roughly equivalent to the subphase LHIIIB in northeast Peloponnese), what we now know about the earlier Mycenaean era (roughly equivalent to the normative subphases LHI, LHII, and LHIIIA) is highly unsatisfactory. In the first place, it is only the later phase of the occupation on the Epano Englianos acropolis that is relatively well-preserved, painstakingly excavated, and published in final form. There is no equally reliable account from the only other fully excavated acropolis, that of Malthi, where in any case the LH phases seem to have seen a steady loss of population from the hilltop to lower sites in the immediate vicinity. Indeed, not only for Messenia but for the whole Mycenaean world, there is a serious dearth of published evidence on both the royal establishments and the towns around them in earlier Mycenaean times. However, in other parts of Greece (particularly northeast Peloponnese) several reliably stratified settlements have been painstakingly tested and the general ceramic sequence is reasonably well established. As with earlier periods (and later also), we must for the time being assume that the same over-all diagnostic criteria apply to Messenia, although it may turn out that there were notable lags and/or local peculiarities (Pl. 3-3).

Pocket Map 8-14 shows the sites for which occupation in LHI through LHIIIB is certain or probable. We had considered including a map showing the certifiable sites occupied in the Late Bronze Age *before* phase IIIB; but we concluded that the present evidence (provided in Category G of Register A) is so scrappy that a separate distribution map might actually be misleading. For what it is worth, the present total of LHI–IIIA sites is 60, of which about 27 percent are known from tombs alone and another 35 percent have tombs associated with a habitation site. Most of the tombs, especially the remarkably numerous tholoi, are in western Messenia and have been excavated in a wide-ranging program conducted by Professor Marinatos. Others, especially a concentration in the lower Alpheios Valley, were discovered by chance and the contents salvaged by the ephorate. Thus, it is clear that the "accidents" of excavation and chance finds play an unusually large role in the data here discussed. Nevertheless, considerable raw material is already available for a detailed study of earlier local Mycenaean fine wares and other typical grave goods. We shall not attempt anything of the kind here, but we have provided in Register A the major references to excavation, salvage, and preliminary discussion of the relevant material.

Of the 50 sites where occupation is certain in both MH and LH, just under one-half (23) are included in the above-mentioned group where LHI–IIIA material has been certified. But it is natural to assume* that practically every site in the "MH–LH" category was occupied in the interim between MH and LHIIIB. Thus we can posit a *minimum* of sorts for total sites inhabited in early Mycenaean times – the 60 for which there is evidence of LHI–IIIA occupation multiplied by two, or 120. This figure would suggest that there was at least a modest increase in the number of early Mycenaean settlements compared with the 100 or so estimated for MH.

As for population distribution in the early Mycenaean period, it would appear that (keeping in mind the caveat about arbitrary and accidental excavation and salvage sites) there was remarkable continuity between MH and LH in terms of the areas where settlements were concentrated, as well as where they seem to have been scattered or altogether missing. Such new sites as we can now detect do not essentially change the over-all picture. This consideration, in itself, argues powerfully for continuity in the makeup of the people.

When we try to establish the size (and inferred population) of the early Mycenaean settlements, there is no trustworthy basis on which to compare them with their predecessors in MH and successors in LHIIIB. We shall see in a moment that a steep increase over the MH figures, in both number of settlements and total population, is certain in LHIIIB. Was this increase basically a phenomenon of the later period only or did the change occur much more gradually over the intervening centuries? We inclined to the first alternative in the short preliminary discussion in our last journal article (McDonald and Hope Simpson 1969), but we may have been unduly influenced by the natural predominance of "late" sherds in the surface collections, that is, from what seems to have been the final occupation period on many sites. The very sparse available data (LHI certain at 19 sites; LHII at 22; LHIIIA at 33) could be said to hint at gradual growth. At any rate (excluding post-Roman developments), surface exploration has reinforced a widely shared assumption that it was in late Mycenaean times (when tradition records a unification by the Neleid dynasty) that this region reached its acme of power and population.

The numerous tholos tombs (Pls. 1-2, 1-3, 2-4) excavated by Tsountas, Dörpfeld, Kourouniotis, Valmin, Blegen, and especially by Marinatos were almost without exception built before LHIIIB – most of them long before. The rich grave goods from Peristeria (#200) now suggest that there was already notable royal wealth in Messenia in the sixteenth century, at about the same time that the burials were being made in the shaft graves of Mycenae. Royal wealth and monumental tomb architecture are fairly sure indicators of a flourishing economy and a broad base on which rulers could levy taxes, tribute, and forced labor. Cemeteries of chamber tombs (Pl. 2-1) probably belonged to court retainers, royal relatives, and perhaps to the most prosperous commoners. For us at least, it is difficult to imagine that families of "ordinary citizens" possessed the wealth needed to construct and equip them. Successive burials in the same tombs usually occurred for at least one generation and often (perhaps usually) over several generations and even centuries. Although many continued in use into LHIIIB, it appears that, as with the large tholoi, relatively fewer chamber tombs were actually constructed after the fourteenth century. The Alpheios subdistrict may form an exception here, to judge by several recent accidental discoveries of cemeteries of chamber tombs dating to LHIIIB and even LHIIIC.

In any case, if one were to estimate prosperity on the basis of present information about tombs and their contents, it would appear that the late Mycenaean period has less claim to pre-eminence than the earlier centuries. As a curious corollary, we have as yet little reliable evidence from early Mycenaean times (in Messenia or elsewhere) about the dwellings of kings, courtiers, and commoners. Messenian sites like #'s 35, 100, and 200 may eventually help to fill this crucial gap when they have been more fully excavated and published. The 1969 and 1970 excavations at Nichoria (#100) suggest that early Mycenaean levels (particularly LHII) are relatively well preserved and that the population on the acropolis may have been heaviest then. But it is at least possible to theorize now that toward the end of the Mycenaean period the major state (i.e., royal) expenditures shifted from an earlier emphasis on tombs and tomb furniture to buildings for the living, fortifications to protect people and possessions, large road-building and drainage projects, and the like.

There are at present, however, no reliable indications that the average early Mycenaean settlement was much larger than its MH predecessor. If we were arbitrarily to increase the size by the same 20 percent projected earlier for the increase in number of sites, the average village size would be one hectare. So the average population per village would be 130, and the total population in early

* As mentioned above, continuity of habitation is a tricky matter to prove even in the case of an excavated site. And exact contemporaneity of two or more sites is often just as difficult to demonstrate. As a matter of fact, we cannot prove that the sites on which pottery assigned to the thirteenth century B.C. occurs were occupied *at the very same time*. But there are strong arguments for viewing these people as essentially attached to the same land over the generations and not shifting frequently from place to place (see Ch. 16).

Mycenaean times would be about 16,000. This is certainly a conservative, and probably a minimal estimate. It may later become clear that the population had increased far more rapidly in early Mycenaean times.

Turning now to LHIIIB, even a superficial comparison of Pocket Maps 8-13 and 8-14 shows that there was a sizable increase in the number of LH versus MH settlements. We must always keep in mind that an unknown percentage of the new foundations were earlier than IIIB, but there is every reason to believe that practically all of them continued in use in IIIB. The total is 195, of which 168 are certain. Although 28 of these are known only from cemeteries, we assume that in practically every case the associated village site was not far away. New foundations show a significant reversal when compared with the kind of sites chosen by MH people. Of the certain MH settlements, 45 percent were "high," 32 percent "medium," and 20 percent "low" (or flat). In contradistinction, of the 60 LH settlements where there is no hint of MH occupation, 52 percent are "low," 28 percent "medium," and 20 percent "high." Hence, it is clear that in Mycenaean times people were "moving down" from the high sites and choosing to live closer to their fields and water supply, to roads, and to the coast (Pls. 8-2, 9-1). Presumably, political conditions had stabilized to the point where they were less afraid not only of raids from neighboring villages and petty kingdoms, but also of bigger threats by land or sea from more distant points. This lessening of defensiveness in the psychological "climate" would fit neatly with the tradition that the Neleids gradually imposed centralized control on the lesser kings of the whole region and organized strong military and naval forces to perpetuate their rule and protect their subjects.

When we compare closely the distribution of sites as shown in Pocket Maps 8-13 and 8-14, it is obvious that the skeleton that was already formed by the less numerous MH settlements was fleshed out and filled in during LH times. The "great rectangle" is more visible than ever, with much heavier habitation on all four sides.

In the Soulima Valley at the northeast corner, settlement was especially heavy. Undoubtedly, the major reason is the magnificent supply of water from numerous major springs. Within the territory we have assigned to just seven LH settlements in that vicinity, present-day cultivators irrigate about 1,000 ha (over 2400 acres) of reasonably fertile farmland. The combination here of concentrated ancient and modern population and the extensive modern use of irrigation constitutes very strong inferential proof that the Mycenaeans also practiced fairly widespread and carefully regulated irrigation.

A much larger and perhaps even more intensively occupied area was the Pylos district in the southwest corner of the great rectangle. Even if the ruins of the Epano Englianos palace were unknown, one would now have to look in this area for the major administrative center. In population though not in location, the Pylos district was certainly the "heartland" of the whole region in LHIIIB. Its relative pre-eminence in earlier times is not so clear. Blegen's deep tests and trenches on and around the acropolis strongly suggest that this had been a place of some importance ever since MH times. At what point it became the "capital" of a larger than average territory cannot yet be inferred with any confidence. But, as suggested above, the impressive line of monumental tumuli constructed on the opposite ridge as early as MH times would indicate that even then this was no ordinary self-sufficient village.

Why did the Pylos district, in spite of its geometrically eccentric location, become the heartland of the whole region in the Late Bronze Age? Generally speaking, its soils are fertile loams developed on Pliocene silts, its rolling plateau country is well drained and healthful, and its water supply adequate (though in general not copious enough for modern irrigation). In agricultural potential, it would certainly have been surpassed by the Pamisos Valley and Steniklarian Plain. The eastern area was the one most coveted by the Spartans in archaic and classical times, partly no doubt because of its proximity. And it is the most densely populated agricultural area of modern Messenia (and, in fact, of modern Greece). But there are good reasons to believe that in the Bronze Age the southern valley in particular had major liabilities as well. It contained extensive perennial marshes and a much larger area that must have been seasonally inaccessible for cultivation. Communications would have been difficult for much of the year and there probably were serious health hazards as well.

Actually, the vicinity of Mt. Ithomi was always the center of Messenia in a strict geometrical sense, and perhaps also in terms of direct land communication (see Ch. 9). It is noteworthy that Messene, the federal capital of Hellenistic and Roman times, was located there. But the Ithomi area, though it has unrivaled defensive potential and is reasonably well watered, has rather limited agricultural resources. There is no hint at present that it was an unusually important center of population or political administration (or even of cult) in prehistoric times.

One can scarcely avoid the inference that a key factor in the prominence of the Pylos district during LH times (if not before) was the great sheltered Bay of Navarino, perhaps used somehow in conjunction with Osmanaga Lagoon (see Ch. 3). Navarino is the only safe and capacious harbor on the west coast of the Peloponnese. Although it is true that any good sand beach (particularly in conjunction with a protecting spit of land to the south) offered a usable moorage for ancient shallow-draft ships, the Navarino area would have been incomparably the best headquarters for a large-scale merchant fleet. We already have considerable evidence of extensive overseas trade between mainland Greece and the Ionian Islands, the head of the Adriatic, south Italy, Sicily, and still farther west. This traffic was apparently well established in early Mycenaean times – with a start, in fact, before the end of the MH period (McDonald 1967, pp. 376–80). It is likely that ships based on the east side of the Greek peninsula and in the Aegean islands had a share in the developing western trade. And political units with access to the Corinthian Gulf and to good harbors farther north on the west coast no doubt participated. But geographic, topographic, and archaeological indications strongly support the testimony of the Catalogue of Ships (*Iliad* 2) and hints in the Pylos tablets that the Pylian merchant marine was a formidable organization. There can be little doubt that most of those ships were based in the harbor of Navarino and that the nearby settlements (especially the palace) were the manufacturing centers, staging areas, and collection and distribution points for a thriving mercantile enterprise.

Outside the great rectangle, too, the distribution of LH sites can be said to correspond roughly with the MH pattern. In the north, the Alpheios-Kladheos nucleus was more intensively occupied than earlier. The present evidence is dependent in large part on chance discoveries of burials, in some cases extensive cemeteries of chamber tombs. Tholoi are conspicuously lacking, but the surviving tomb furniture leaves no doubt of local prosperity. And it is difficult to avoid the inference that Olympia, like several other Mycenaean sites that became important cult centers in later times, had already acquired some special religious significance.

There were at least a few new LH sites on and near the coast between the Alpheios and Nedha rivers. As pointed out above, we have not done sufficient work here to form the basis for any dependable generalizations about prehistoric habitation in the interior of Triphylia. Between the Nedha and Kyparissia rivers there were also some new settlements. This dissected area has been searched fairly thoroughly, and we have the quite definite impression that it was rather isolated and thinly settled in LH as well as earlier times. As mentioned earlier, the scarcity of settlements here can be interpreted as evidence that it was a border area.

The Pamisos Valley and Steniklarian Plain were certainly much more thickly settled in LH than in MH times, and the known distribution of sites presents some interesting and probably valid contrasts. There are two particularly noticeable gaps – the lower delta and the headwaters of the Pamisos River, opposite the tremendous Ayios Floros springs. In both cases the valley floor was probably too wet for agriculture. The margins of the upper (Steniklarian) valley, with its two prongs reaching toward the Arkadian Mountains, shows quite intensive use. So does most of the lower valley between Ayios Floros and the delta. In this section, and not in the delta, one would expect to find the east-west all-weather land routes (see Ch. 9). The most southerly major river crossing was probably in the vicinity of site #126, with another perhaps between sites #123 and 137. But the most used route across the valley was probably then, as later, via site # 206. No doubt there were others as well, and choice would depend in part on the season of the year and the method of travel (foot, pack animal, or wheeled vehicle).

The lower Messenian peninsula also shows a noticeable increase in settlements, especially on the west side of the Messenian Gulf. And now for the first time there is a thin string of certain sites on the opposite (Mani) coast. It is doubtful if the latter area would have been much used unless increasing population was exerting some pressure on available land. This area is in general dissected, infertile, poorly watered, and somewhat remote. Possibly the main function of these settlements was that of strategic outposts in an age of heavy ship movement and threat of external seaborne attack, but it is not even clear whether the southeast boundary of the unified kingdom enclosed this area.

To look for a moment at the coastal versus inland settlement pattern in LH times, 13 percent of the sites are on the sea and 42 percent are within easy reach of it. These are roughly the same ratios as in the case of MH sites (15 percent and 38 percent). It would thus appear that people in LH times were still oriented more to agriculture and herding in relatively protected areas than were their EH predecessors. It is indeed somewhat surprising that the site distribution does not point to a more externally oriented attitude in the later period. But we must remember that the over-all LH total is about double the MH figure, so that there were by this time roughly twice as many coastal or near coastal settlements. Furthermore, land use was becoming fairly intensive in some areas and there was no longer unlimited choice of good coastal sites. When a location for a new village was sought, it was by then probably easier to find good resources of land and fresh water in the interior. Also, calculations based on raw numbers of sites ignore relative size – a subject to which we now turn. To anticipate briefly, present evidence would indicate an average size of 1.9 ha for LH coastal settlements compared with 1.3 ha for those not within easy reach of the sea. Hence, the percentage of people living on the coast in LH times had undoubtedly risen quite sharply over that in the preceding period.

As previously mentioned, our base consists of 168 certain LH habitation sites, assuming that where cemeteries alone are known (28 instances) there must also have been corresponding villages in the immediate vicinity. Of the 140 sites that could potentially be measured, the "extent" category (H) in Register A is fairly sure for 118. We thus derive an *average size* of about 1.6 ha. Applying the usual formula, we arrive at an *average population* of about 210 inhabitants, which is slightly more than double the estimated MH average. Therefore, the minimum "certain" LH population is 168 × 210 or about 35,000. Adding the 27 probable or possible LH sites, we have an estimated total population of 41,000. This figure is surely minimal. Even if the "average size factor" is too high (as it may well be), the discrepancy between sites now known and the true total will have more than counterbalanced that error. It would be a reasonable estimate, we think, that the actual number of villages was at least 250 and that a minimum figure for the total population is 50,000.

For any sort of valid comparison with earlier prehistoric times, we must of course work from comparable data, and the safest basis is the certainly identified sites. The ratio of certain EH : MH : LH is 22 : 58 : 168, which is close to an exponential progression of 1 : 3 : 9. The estimated total population (which would be about 3,500 : 10,000 : 50,000) would suggest a ratio that climbed more steeply toward the later part of the Bronze Age. Of course, these figures must not be taken out of the context of the strong disclaimers expressed earlier. And, above all, we do not mean to imply that the Bronze Age population rise was continuous. There must have been innumerable sharp rises and dips (both local and regional) caused by epidemics, crop failures, earthquakes, agricultural or technical inventions, intra-regional conflicts, and perhaps external invasions. At present, it is not possible to see clear indications of any such "minor" events. But evidence along some of these lines may eventually be provided by closer collaboration between excavators and associated scientists.

In a gross sense, we can already detect two major rises and one horrendous plunge in the profile. The two accessions of population are, as we have seen, to be associated in a general way with MH (perhaps a gradual increase) and with LH (probably a rather steep climb toward the end of the period). The depopulation (to be discussed in a moment) seems to have occurred soon after the peak, in the twelfth century.

With the present lack of excavated settlements and consequent uncertainty about precise dating of surface pottery (especially coarse wares), there appears to be no sure index of the relative rate of change. We have mentioned above that there is already some reason to infer that the EH and MH people differed so much psychologically and in material culture that an intervening migration or invasion of new people may be indicated. But we are not aware of any reliable evidence as to whether this phenomenon was sudden or gradual or whether the numbers involved were relatively large or quite limited. Archaeologists have been prone to interpret extensive cultural shifts as evidence of major invasions that totally wiped out earlier inhabitants. But a modest number of newcomers whose culture traits became widely diffused and whose leaders gradually asserted control over earlier political entities is probably nearer the mark in most cases, including Messenia in the early second millennium B.C.

As for the second notable increase in population, the record indicates that in Messenia (as elsewhere) there probably was a peaceful transition from MH isolation to early Mycenaean dynamism. The grave goods from Peristeria suggest that innovative breezes were blowing in southwest as well as northeast Peloponnese as early as the sixteenth century B.C. And the startling number of tholos tombs (particularly in the Pylos district) tell their story of sharply increased political and economic power consolidated into fewer hands. We are at present unable to cite any firm evidence that might provide a hint whether it was already in early Mycenaean times or only toward the end that the population seems to have increased so markedly over the MH maximum. Perhaps there was a relatively rapid increase throughout Mycenaean times with no spectacular peaks. Until there is more definitive evidence, however, we favor the theory that there was a real "population explosion" during (and perhaps partly as a result of) the political consolidation under the Neleids in the thirteenth century B.C. One factor that may have had considerable impact is an inferred growth in the number of "foreign" slaves.

There has been much more excavation of Mycenaean remains in Messenia than of earlier prehistoric phases. The record was reviewed at the beginning of this chapter. Recent activity in this region is impressive when compared with that in most others in the Aegean orbit. Certainly, the evidence is far too voluminous to be summarized here, and much of it is not yet systematically published. We repeat our conviction that the regional survey strongly supports Blegen's claim that the ruins he excavated at Epano Englianos mark the political capital of a relatively large kingdom of Late Mycenaean times and that this Messenian kingdom was surely associated in Greek tradition with the dynasty of Neleus and Nestor. At the peak, its boundaries probably extended southeast to the Taygetos Mountains and northwest at least as far as the Nedha River.

Before this territory had been unified by force and diplomacy, the region presumably included a fair number of independent political units. A careful review of the location of all known tholos tombs, combined with the evidence yielded by the sizable number already excavated in western Messenia, might provide at least an estimate of the number and shifting fortunes of these "petty kingdoms." Since Professor Marinatos has excavated most of them, we prefer to await a coordinated study based on his detailed excavation notes and review of the finds. He is surely justified in regarding major habitation sites like #'s 35, 200, and 201, with single or multiple tholoi, as originally independent political capitals. They must also be reckoned among the candidates for identification with important places repeatedly chronicled in the Pylos tablets, and possibly with certain places mentioned in Homer's Catalogue (see Ch. 7). In the case of additional single tombs or concentrations of tholoi and chamber tombs that Marinatos has examined, such as #'s 8, 11, 20, 29, 32, 53, and 54, the associated habitation sites presumably lay reasonably close by but they have not yet been located.

The coordination of habitation sites with tholoi obviously needs more attention than we have given it, though it must be remembered that the identification of presumed tholos mounds is seldom completely safe before excavation. For the present, a rough estimate of the number of separate settlements in whose vicinity one or more tholos tombs have been identified is 17. And if we add tholoi that so far lack obviously related habitation sites, the number rises to about 30. Even if one were to hypothesize (as we did in *AJA* 1961) that some tholoi may have been built along major roads and relatively far from any habitation site, 17 independent petty kingdoms seems rather many. Furthermore, they would have been heavily concentrated in the south and west of the region. Except for Kakovatos, not a single tholos has been identified in the area north of the Nedha River, and few in the Pamisos Valley and Steniklarian Plain. If such tombs were the fashion everywhere in the region, it is odd that chance has not turned up a single example in important subregions where notable concentrations of chamber tombs are known.

In general, the tombs and cemeteries excavated by Kourouniotis, Marinatos, Blegen, Yalouris, Valmin, and others show that, beginning in early Mycenaean times, there was a tremendous increase in the means to acquire movable wealth of the kind the Mycenaeans treasured in life and death. This evidence combined with indications of rapidly increasing population and more intensive land use surely permits us to postulate that this was, over-all, a very prosperous period – at least as measured by the standard of living (and dying) of the upper classes. Answers to wider questions about the source of the prosperity, about the economic basis of the individual settlements and intra-regional units, about the status of the ordinary citizen, and so on can be realistically attempted only when we have much more information from excavated habitation sites. And even then there would be little hope unless this kind of question is in the forefront of the excavator's concerns.

As previously mentioned, the contents recovered from the tombs and perhaps the tomb construction as well might suggest that royal wealth was more conspicuous in earlier than in later Mycenaean times; but this kind of evidence is scarcely a sound basis for generalizing about economic conditions. Treasure from the occasional unrobbed royal tomb and items overlooked or unwanted by robbers is far too haphazard and unrepresentative an index of general prosperity. And we have already advanced the theory that the resources of the later consolidated kingdom(s) were directed toward other goals such as fortifications, palaces, roads, drainage and irrigation projects, and perhaps increasingly to big and costly wars. At any rate, we can see nothing in the excavation record that would contradict our assumption that the region enjoyed a climax of production as well as population in the thirteenth century B.C.

The Transition to the Early Iron Age. In Messenia as in the rest of Greece, the "time of troubles" in the twelfth and earlier eleventh centuries is in many ways the most obscure segment of the so-called Greek Dark Age. The problem is not entirely a lack of material evidence, since a certain amount of local LHIIIC, sub-Mycenaean, and Protogeometric ceramics (and occasional associated objects of other kinds) is gradually being recovered. But for the most part this material emanates from graves rather than stratified habitation sites, and it is extraordinarily difficult to reconstruct the historical events and cultural changes behind the material manifestations. It is now widely believed that the "Dorian Invasion" was a considerably later phenomenon, and there is no universally accepted alternative theory to explain the breakdown of the flourishing LHIIIB culture. Several explanations have been proposed involving natural catastrophes such as drought, a cold and wet climatic cycle, erosion, volcanic disturbance. These hypotheses are discussed in appropriate chapters (3, 11, 12, 16), but none is particularly convincing in the light of present evidence. We are more inclined to the view that the destruction and exodus was caused by recurrent hit-and-run attacks of sea rovers. An instructive parallel may be the abandonment of the fertile and thickly populated plains of Burgundy, because of repeated Viking invasions (Bloch 1961).

We do not yet know nearly enough about where people were living in organized communities and whether there are wide enough regional differences to postulate a predominance of Mycenaean survivors in some places and newcomers in others. But our survey does provide, for the first time, a quantitative measure of the scale (and perhaps some indication of the speed) of the disintegration and recovery in one important part of the Mycenaean world. We have already emphasized that the UMME surface search can nowhere be termed exhaustive, and in one or two areas it is scarcely more than superficial. Yet enough work has been done in Messenia to justify the confident prediction that future discoveries are unlikely to throw serious doubt on one major conclusion. All of our research so far would indicate that in the twelfth and eleventh centuries this fertile and well-watered area was occupied by scarcely more than 10 percent of the people who had lived there in the thirteenth century B.C. We think this a safe statement in spite of the caveat that invaders at a relatively lower cultural life (e.g., the Slavs of the early middle ages) may leave behind surprisingly little in the way of long-lasting material remains.

A glance at Pocket Map 8-15 tells part of the story. LHIIIC pottery has been reported from sixteen locations (three of them not certain), sub-Mycenaean from nine (five not certain), and Protogeometric from thirteen (two not certain). But at least two cautions are in order here. One is that about two-thirds of these meager data are from graves, in many cases single, isolated chance discoveries. The village sites where these people lived generally elude us. Most of them were probably extremely small, with flimsy buildings. And, secondly, ceramic attributions to these subperiods are particularly liable to error, especially in a region where not a single stratified habitation site from this era has been excavated. The 1970 and 1971 digging seasons at Nichoria (#100) show that in some places post-Mycenaean remains are stratified above LHIIIB and IIIC. There is thus reason to hope that further excavation will shed some light on the local situation immediately following the late Mycenaean peak.

Any extrapolation about population size and distribution from Pocket Map 8-15 is almost as risky as for the presently known Neolithic data; and, in fact, in at least two cases caves seem to have been used again as shelters. For whatever it is worth, we might remark that the largest group (presumably Mycenaean survivors) in the whole region during LHIIIC may have inhabited the lower Alpheios Valley around Olympia. Here several cemeteries seem to show an uninterrupted series of burials continuing from LHIIIB. On the other hand, there is comparatively less evidence of Protogeometric habitation in the north, whereas in the south one could perhaps postulate a slight increase of population in Protogeometric as compared with LHIIIC times. There was apparently a tiny concentration of Protogeometric habitation in the vicinity of the Bay of Navarino and a scattering of sites around the head of the Messenian Gulf.

A few find-spots like #'s 138 and 145 seem to represent the kind of isolated "refuge site" that one might expect survivors of a disaster to seek. But, in general, the concentrations (such as they are) appear to have been in locations relatively vulnerable to attack by sea. It would appear, therefore, that the safety factor was not uppermost in their order of priorities. Perhaps the threats had passed or the survivors had little worth stealing. In general, they were clinging to areas that had been flourishing centers a century or two before. This continuity might support the contention that the inhabitants in Protogeometric times were still, at least predominantly, descendants of the Mycenaeans. Re-use (or continuous use?) of the tholos at site #11 and transitional tomb structures at site #100 would point strongly in the same direction.

The apparent fact that the descendants of the original inhabitants either stayed in or returned to these areas might also be connected with the emphasis on olive culture (see Ch. 12). In a marginal subsistence economy like that of the Early Iron Age, olive oil may have become a much more basic food staple than it had been in Mycenaean times. The Messenians report a similar development during the long agony of the occupation and civil war in and following World War II. This seems to be the likeliest explanation for the paleobotanical record of sharply increased olive pollen in the vicinity of Osmanaga Lagoon in post-Mycenaean times. And olive culture, as Aschenbrenner emphasizes (Ch. 4), ought to be a reliable indicator of a stable population that does not expect to leave or be driven from its land.

Register B (Post-Mycenaean)

We should preface the following discussion by reiterating that our surface search and the general emphasis throughout this book has been concentrated on the Bronze Age. Thus, both the data reported in Register B and our handling of it may be rather inadequate and uneven. On the other hand, as emphasized previously, the primary interest of surface explorers and historians in previous generations was strongly in the opposite direction; and even contemporaries like Meyer, Roebuck, Valmin, and Themelis have been mainly concerned in synthesizing the post-Mycenaean documentary and archaeological evidence. Hence, if we have fairly recorded here and in Chapter 6 the evidence they published, the over-all picture should not be unduly distorted.

The question of whether the present record of settlement even approximates the actual distribution and proportion at various periods of the past is probably unanswerable. Certainly, the utmost caution is needed in drawing any conclusions from data that are admittedly incomplete and in some cases quite inadequate. Yet we believe, for example, that Pocket Maps 8-14 and 8-17 showing a total of 189 known settlements in the most densely populated prehistoric epoch (LHIIIB) versus 136 for its later counterpart (Classical-Hellenistic) do in all probability reflect the gross situation in terms of where people chose to live in the two periods. The comparative size of their towns and villages, however, is far less clear. We do not even have complete and dependable data for the extent of the pottery scattered over Classical-Hellenistic sites comparable with those given in Register A for LH settlements. It would therefore be rash to suggest over-all population statistics for the later period on the basis of the known sites. Yet one inevitably forms impressions as one ranges over the ground, and we should be most surprised if Roebuck's estimate (which was arrived at by a quite different method) of 112,000 inhabitants for Messenia south of the Nedha in late Hellenistic times does not turn out to be much too high (see Ch. 16).

The Geometric Period. (About 900–700 B.C.) The dates assigned to this period cover a reasonably long and still imperfectly known era. As is made clear in the most recent study of Greek geometric pottery (Coldstream 1968), the West Greek Protogeometric style continues until 775 or 750 B.C., and is followed almost immediately by West Greek Late Geometric (about 750–690 B.C.) "without any settled phase in between." Thus, the contents of the grave group at Salmoni (#310), for instance, are classified as West Greek Protogeometric, and the Geometric vases from the Volimidhia tombs (#20) as West Greek Late Geometric, Phase I; and both groups fall within the period under discussion.

There are relatively few cases of finds made on habitation sites, and (except for Nichoria) no Geometric settlement has yet been excavated in the whole region. Most of the evidence comes from tombs, and usually from deposits in re-used Mycenaean tombs, such as Volimidhia, Nichoria (#100), Koukounara (#35). This practice was apparently connected with the rising popularity of "hero cults." Whether or not there was an accurate, continuous tradition from Mycenaean times, it appears that from now on through Roman times (and especially in the Hellenistic period) people considered it prestigious to be buried in and near places that retained the aura of the "great old days." They could perhaps even name (accurately?) the "hero" beside whom they arranged to be buried, and they apparently wanted to be remembered with him in periodic ceremonies.

The bulk of the Geometric pottery, and especially that found in the Mycenaean tombs, seems to belong to the Late Geometric phase. This coincides roughly with the period of the First Messenian War and its aftermath, which was clearly a period of expansion both in Lakonia and Messenia (see Ch. 6). But the archaeological evidence, although very incomplete, suggests that the settlements were concentrated in the same areas, if not on the same sites, as in the Protogeometric period and earlier. Most of them apparently continued to be smaller than their Mycenaean antecedents.

Pocket Map 8-16 contains 14 certain and 5 possible Geometric sites. It is likely that much of the higher land in the interior, in particular that between the Pylos district and the Pamisos Valley and in the uplands of Triphylia, had passed out of cultivation since the end of the Mycenaean era. Too few sites are known to draw reliable conclusions, but the Olympia region (#'s 304, 315, 322, 719, 720) and Pamisos Valley (#'s 142, 539, 540) appear to have been the most exploited. There was also some residual occupation in the Pylos district (#'s 1, 20). In view of the literary traditions concerning Kresphontes' capital in the Steniklarian Plain and the concentration of warfare around Ithomi and Ampheia (see Ch. 6), we should also expect a strong nucleus at this time in the upper valley. The lack of field evidence for habitation there suggests that the archaeological record for this era is still very undependable.

The Archaic Period. (About 700–500 B.C.) There was clearly a pronounced increase in population in this period. Pocket Map 8-16 records 34 certain and 8 possible Archaic sites. This suggests that the number of communities may have more than doubled over Geometric times, and the proportion of known village sites (as opposed to cemeteries) is much higher. A good many settlements were now being founded on new sites, as is indicated by the drop in the percentage of sites where there had been prehistoric occupation (36 percent in the Archaic versus 63 percent in the Geometric period).

On the other hand, one cannot detect any major change in over-all population distribution. The concentrations previously noted in the Olympia and Pamisos areas seem to have become accentuated, particularly in the former case. In fact, it is quite safe, for archaeological as well as historical reasons, to locate a major religious (and perhaps economic) center at Olympia. Very possibly it had survived without a break through the Dark Age, since there is considerable recent evidence of its importance in Mycenaean and still earlier times. Three important shrines at sites #'s 504, 530, and 538 in the southeastern subregion were apparently new foundations of the Archaic period.

As for additional concentrations of population, one might perhaps see a minor one around the Bay of Navarino. This phenomenon could be connected with the paleobotanical evidence for heavy olive cultivation here at approximately this time (see Ch. 12). The Steniklarian Plain and Pamisos Valley (apparently the part of Messenia most closely controlled by Sparta) show continued but moderate occupation from Geometric through Archaic times. There would also seem to have been new areas of rather scattered occupation along the shores of the Messenian Gulf and in Triphylia between the Nedha and Alpheios rivers.

The Classical and Hellenistic Periods. (About 500–146 B.C.) The conventional date for the end of the Classical period in Greece (323 B.C.) is awkward in dealing with Messenia, since the most notable change can be expected to have followed the formation of the independent federal state of Messenia in 369 B.C. and the building of its capital at Messene, centrally located under Mt. Ithomi. The Mavrozoumenos bridge, the network of roads radiating from Messene, and the system of forts as well as the artillery towers of Messene itself may date from a period considerably later than 369 (see Ch. 6). And the major cultural and economic changes that resulted from independent political status may not have been fully evident until Hellenistic times. For this reason and because Classical and Hellenistic potsherds on the surface are not always easy to distinguish from each other, we have decided not to attempt, either in Pocket Map 8-17 or in the text to differentiate between the two periods. In most cases there can be no certainty that a "Hellenistic" site was not occupied earlier than 323 B.C., and most "Classical" sites presumably continued into the Hellenistic period.

The general impression is that, despite the known raids and military campaigns, this was a relatively settled and prosperous epoch. Yet we doubt Roebuck's estimate of over 100,000 population in late Hellenistic times (see Chs. 6, 11, 16). Pocket Map 8-17 records 136 known sites, more than a threefold increase over known Archaic settlements. Concentration of population continues in the richer agricultural regions – the Alpheios Valley, Triphylia, the Steniklarian Plain, and the Pamisos Valley. The most striking increase, however, is in the Pylos district, where the ratio compared with Archaic settlements is well over 4 : 1.

In general, the trend seems to be to locations on lower ground and accessible to the coast. At first glance, the percentages on coastal or near coastal versus inland sites would indicate little variation over time (i.e., 40 percent compared with 38 percent in Archaic and 36 percent in Geometric times). Yet a really striking change is clear from a glance at Pocket Maps 8-16 and 8-17. Around the Messenian Gulf there are 9 coastal settlements (four of them closely concentrated in the Kalamata vicinity) in Archaic times, whereas for the Classical-Hellenistic period there are 23. Indeed, some coastal stretches that were previously unoccupied now show what can be termed fairly heavy occupation. The situation on the western seaboard had apparently shifted even more radically. Between the mouth of the Alpheios River and the tip of the peninsula there is scarcely a single known Archaic settlement except for Navarino Bay, whereas the occupation in Classical-Hellenistic times was moderately dense considering the limited opportunities offered by the rugged topography. The increasing exploitation of coastal sites with usable harbors is in all probability to be explained by more stable political conditions that were reflected in better regulated commerce. And long-established sites with good harbors seem to have grown and flourished notably.

Another obvious and predictable development is the heavier use of the rather dissected and only moderately fertile area immediately adjacent to Mt. Ithomi. Although Ithomi was always a striking and centrally located landmark, there is as yet no evidence for a major population center in its immediate environs in prehistoric times and next to none as late as the Archaic period. In view of its strategic potential and its reputation as a sanctuary and refuge site during the Messenian wars, the dearth of archaeological evidence before the founding of Messene in late Classical times is hard to understand (and possibly accidental since a Geometric find has recently been reported).

One of the major crossings of the Steniklarian Plain in prehistoric times is now marked by the unique three-pronged Mavrozoumenos bridge about 5 km north of Messene and just northwest of Meligala (Pl. 4-1). Its lower courses date from the Hellenistic period. In medieval times and later, a major land route from Arkadia still crossed this bridge and then forked, one route traversing the pass to Kyparissia (medieval Arkadhia) and the other leading past Ithomi and on southwestward to the

Pylos area (Fig. 9-4). It is unclear whether the second route was a major one before Classical times (Ch. 9). Some light might be thrown on the history of the Messene area if we could date the foundation of the cult of Zeus on Ithomi. It must have existed at least as early as the Archaic period, when the cult places at Ayios Andhreas (#504) and Ayios Floros (#530) seem to have evolved. In any case, there is no present evidence to suggest that Ithomi was a major anchor of regional security and communications before late Classical times.

The Roman Period. (146 B.C. – 4th century A.D.) The sites known to have been occupied in the Roman period seem to reflect a decided reduction from the Classical-Hellenistic peak. Pocket Map 8-18 records 89 sites, compared with 136 in the previous period. This represents a drop of approximately one-third.

In terms of over-all population distribution, there is no clearly discernible difference between the Hellenic and the Roman periods. Coastal locations continue to be favored, and there is at least scattered occupation over all areas previously inhabitated. Perhaps the well-known Roman penchant for rural villas would explain some of the smaller inland "settlements." Yet the country squire tradition had an authentic Greek origin, as we know from accounts like those of Xenophon's estate at Skillous in the north and the farm near Messene referred to in an inscription (see Ch. 6). The bulk of the population, however, seems to have continued to concentrate in or near the main towns, especially Kyparissia and Pherai, and to a lesser extent Korone, Asine, and Mothone.

Overview of Post-Mycenaean Site Distribution

The breakdown by subregions in the accompanying tabulation reveals a general consistency in the history of known occupation from Geometric through Roman times.

	southwest	*southeast*	*center*	*north*	*total*
Geometric	3	9	2	5	19
Archaic	6	15	6	15	42
Classical-Hellenistic	26	48	19	43	136
Roman	22	31	14	22	89

After the Hellenistic period, however, the loss in population was most drastic in the north, where it approximates 50 percent. Conversely, in the southwest, where there had been much less concentration in classical-Hellenistic times, the drop seems to have been slight. And it was, of course, the southwest that retained closest contact with the outside world in medieval times.

REFERENCES

Blegen, C. W., and Kourouniotis, K. 1939. "Excavations at Pylos 1939" *AJA* 43:557–76.

Blegen, C. W., and Rawson, M. 1966. *The Palace of Nestor at Pylos in Western Messenia*, Vol. 1, 2 pts. Princeton, N.J.

Bloch, M. 1961. *Feudal Society*. Chicago.

Bolte, E. 1911. "Die Grenzlandschaften zwischen Lakonien, Messenien und Arkadien," *Verhandlungen der 51 Versammlung deutschen Philologen und Schulmänner*, pp. 13ff.

Chang, K. C., et al., eds. 1968. *Settlement Archaeology*. Palo Alto, Calif.

Choremis, A. 1968ff. "Strefi Eleias," *Deltion* 1968:171–73; *AAA* 1968:205–9.

Coldstream, N. 1968. *Greek Geometric Pottery* (London), esp. pp. 220–32 and chronological table on p. 330.

Dörpfeld, W. 1907. "Tiryns, Olympia, Pylos," *AM* 32:vi–xiv.

———. 1908. "Alt-Pylos," *AM* 33:295, 322, and Pls. XV–XVII.

———. 1913. "Alt-Pylos III. Die Lage der homerischen Burg Pylos," *AM* 38:97–139 and Pls. IV, V.

Hammond, N. G. L. 1967. "Tumulus-Burial in Albania, the Grave Circles of Mycenae, and the Indo-Europeans," *BSA* 62:77–105.

Hope Simpson, R. 1957. "Identifying a Mycenaean State," *BSA* 52:231–59.

———. 1966. "The Seven Cities Offered by Agamemnon to Achilles," *BSA* 61:113–31.

Karo, G. 1935. "Mykenische Kultur," *RE* Suppl. Vol. 6, p. 607.

Kolbe, W. 1904. "Die Grenzen Messeniens in der ersten Kaiserzeit," *AM* 29:364–78.

Kourouniotis, K. 1914. "A Tholos Tomb at Messenian Pylos," *Arch Eph* pp. 99–117.

———. 1925–26. "Concerning the Tholos Tomb of Osmanaga [Koryphasion], Pylos," *Praktika* pp. 91–92, 140–41.

Kyparissis, N. 1911. "Concerning the Trial Excavations at Kyparissia," *Praktika* pp. 247–52.

Lang, M. 1968. *The Palace of Nestor in Western Messenia*, Vol. 2. Princeton, N.J.

Marinatos, Sp. 1952ff. Annual reports in *Praktika* since 1952, in *Ergon* since 1954, in *Deltion* and elsewhere since 1960.

———. 1932–33. "The Goekoop Excavations in Kephalenia," *Arch Eph* 1932, 1ff.; 1933, 68ff.

———. 1962. "The Minoan and Mycenaean Civilization and Its Influence on the Mediterranean and on Europe," *Atti del VI Congresso Internazionale delle Scienze Preistoriche e Protostoriche*. Rome.

McDonald, W. A. 1967. *Progress into the Past: The Rediscovery of Mycenaean Civilization*. New York.

McDonald, W. A. and Hope Simpson, R. 1961. "Prehistoric Habitation in Southwestern Peloponnese," *AJA* 65:221–60.

———. 1964. "Further Explorations in Southwestern Peloponnese: 1962–63," *AJA* 68:229–45.

———. 1969. "Further Explorations in Southwestern Peloponnese: 1964–1968," *AJA* 73:123–77.

Meyer, E. 1957. *Neue Peloponnesische Wanderungen*. Bern.

Müller, K. 1909. "Alt-Pylos II. Die Funde aus den Kuppelgräbern von Kakovatos," *AM* 34:269–325, Pls. XII–XXIV.

Oikonomos, G. P. 1909. "Excavations at Messene," *Praktika* pp. 201–5.

———. 1925–26. "Excavations at Messene," *Praktika* pp. 55–66.

———. 1938. *The Work [To Ergon] of the Archaeological Society in Athens during Its First Hundred Years, 1837–1937*. Athens.

Orlandos, A. K. 1957. "Excavation at Messene," *Praktika* 1957, pp. 121–25; "Messene," *Ergon* 1957, pp. 75–80 (see these journals for reports of continuing excavation since 1957).

Papathanasopoulos, G. 1962ff. Annual reports in *Deltion*.

Renfrew, C., et al. 1965. "Obsidian in the Aegean," *BSA* 60:225–47.

Roebuck, C. A. 1941. *A History of Messenia from 369 to 146 B.C.* Private Ed.; University of Chicago Library.

———. 1945. "A Note on Messenian Economy and Population," *Classical Philology* 40:149–65.
Sackett, L. H., et al. 1966. "Prehistoric Euboea: Contributions toward a Survey," *BSA* 61:33–112.
Skias, A. N. 1909. "Excavation at Messenian Pylos," *Praktika* pp. 274–92.
———. 1911. "Topographic and Epigraphic Notes on Messenian Pharai and Vicinity," *Arch Eph* pp. 107–18.
Sophoulis, Th. 1895. *Praktika* p. 27.
Sperling, J. 1942. "Explorations in Elis, 1939," *AJA* 46:77–89 and Fig. 1.
Themelis, P. G. 1966ff. "Antiquities and Monuments of Eleia," *Deltion* 1968, 160–71; "Minoika from Olympia," *AAA* 1969, 248–56; "Early Helladic Megaron at Akovitika," *AAA* 1970:303–11.
Tod, M. N. 1905. "Notes and Inscriptions from Southwestern Messenia," *JHS* 25:32–55.
Tsountas, Ch. 1891. "A Tholos Tomb at Kambos," *Arch Eph* 189–91; *Praktika* p. 23.
Valmin (Svensson), N. 1926–27. "Two Tholos Tombs at Bodia in the Eastern Part of Triphylia," *Bull Lund* pp. 53–89, Pls. I–XVI.
———. 1927–28. "Continued Explorations in Eastern Triphylia," *Bull Lund* pp. 1–54, Pls. I–XIV.
———. 1930. *Études topographiques sur la Messénie Ancienne.* Lund.
———. 1934–35. "Rapport préliminaire de l'expédition en Messénie 1934." *Bull Lund* pp. 1–46, Fig. 2.
———. 1938. *The Swedish Messenia Expedition.* Lund.
———. 1939. *Das Adriatische Gebiet.* Lund and Leipzig.
———. 1960. "Minoische Seidlung in Messenien," *Deltion* 16:119–22.
Versakis, F. 1916. "The Sanctuary of Apollo Korynthos," *Deltion* 2:64–118, Pl. A.
Weil, R. 1882. "Messenische Grenzfelden," *AM* 7:211–22.
Wilhelm, A. 1891. "Inschriften aus Messene," *AM* 16:345–55.
Yalouris, N. 1960ff. Annual reports in *Praktika, Ergon,* and *Deltion*; especially "Trouvailles Mycéniennes et premycéniennes de la région du Sanctuaire d'Olympie," *AMCM*, Vol. 1, pp. 176–82, Pl. I–IV. Rome, 1968.

9

SETTLEMENT AND CIRCULATION: PATTERN AND SYSTEMS

by

Fred E. Lukermann

Throughout the historic period, southwest Peloponnese has been noted for its favorable environment and dense population both in relative and absolute terms. Homeric allusions to Neleid wealth and the Catalogue's citation of Nestor's ninety ships are reflected in later classical accounts of this sun-warmed paradise and its continuing allure for covetous strangers. Strabo and Pausanias, the most detailed sources for all the preceding ancient periods, take pains to contrast the relative decline of wealth and population in the Roman period as compared with the traditional accounts of the past. Yet their geographic description is still of a well-favored land and a relatively dense population among the Peloponnesian regions of their time.

Classical historians and geographers, notably Ephoros, consistently take special notice of the lure of Messenia for less favored peoples and cultures. Kresphontes' Heraklidean trickery is not unlike Neleus' earlier ways to power, and not unlike later adventurers such as de Villehardouin and Morosini in their motivations, aspirations, and deeds. In the more recent period of the nineteenth and twentieth centuries the documentation of favored environment and the seemingly inexhaustible agricultural wealth, given care and cultivation, is less epic and romantic in nature but more detailed and irrefutable in character. Both traveller and census speak to the relative prosperity and absolute abundance of rural population and productivity. Modern Messenia and southern Elis (Triphylia) are the most favored areas of rural Greece. The Pamisos Plain and its surrounding terraces are the most densely settled agricultural area of all Greece. The terraces of the west coast of the Messenian Gulf between Koroni and Petalidhi are the next highest in rural population densities; and the three areas of the plain north of Navarino Bay, the hills and plains between Agoulinitsa and the Nedha River in Triphylia, and the upper Messenian basins of Soulima and Steniklaros register only slightly lower rural densities.

Rural population densities are not necessarily indices of prosperity in the modern world but they are the most suitable analytic base (with some qualification) for evaluating previous periods and areas of reputed prosperity in medieval and classical times, if not in prehistory. For comparative purposes I have chosen two sources and periods of data from the last two centuries as a "sample" against which to evaluate the recorded past periods of greatest prosperity and population both as to the general geographic pattern and to specific areas. The periods to be matched are: the MH/LH periods as recorded in the present archaeological survey (see Ch. 8); the classical record – reaching back to the eighth century B.C. (see Chs. 6; 8); the Frankish/Venetian period of the thirteenth century until the turn of the eighteenth century A.D. (see Ch. 5); and finally, the early nineteenth century "sample" as reconstructed and qualified below.

In general, for all periods identified, I wish to compare: (1) *core areas* (settlement nuclei) of agricultural productivity and population; (2) the situation of all core areas relative to one another and to the centers of political and commercial power; (3) linkages of the flow of trade, and routes between and among the core areas and centers; and (4) the orientation of the local political and economic power within the Peloponnese and the wider Mediterranean world.

It is quite clear from a perusal of the historic sources alluded to above that a comparison of cultures and economies across time such as proposed here must take account of (i.e., subtract) technological and institutional innovations of the more recent past both in terms of specific inputs and outputs and of the more general cultural outlook and orientation. Having said that, however, it is almost impossible to deal with the latter point, other than to suggest that one must recognize that urban viewpoints are not rural viewpoints, that the local politician is not the national statesman, that immigrants and invaders are not natives. Having stated an awareness of motivational as well as behavioral limits to the comparison, the best I can do is to deal with the specifics of products, technology, institutions, and services from period to period within those qualifying constraints.

The earliest census with sufficient detail and context to serve this purpose is the Greek national census of 1928. Although not so detailed in many categories as the more recent censuses, especially as to population and settlement patterns, it may better serve comparative purposes (Ogilvie 1943). Using the 1928 census as a base minimizes as much as possible the most recent trends of *accelerated* rural depopulation, metropolitan agglomeration, and transportation improvements. Two major technological innovations are not accounted for, however. The most important technological innovation of the nineteenth century was that of the steamship and the steam railway, the second was its complement—the commercialization of a subsistence economy. Both of these changes had a pronounced effect on the agricultural economy of southwest Peloponnese in the last half of the last century. The UMME region in that period was literally "opened up" to extra-regional forces, which radically changed both agricultural practice and product in the region. The average figures of currant (raisin) production are indicative of the most radical changes in agriculture: 1830, 3,760 ha; 1891, 6,660 ha (Naval Intelligence Division, 1944–45). The impact of the market economy on other crops, though not so dramatic, must, nevertheless, be noted. The nineteenth century was a period of agricultural revolution.

Given the fact that after 1830 there was also a radical political-social change wrought in Greece, it is almost obligatory to reconstruct the settlement and communication map of the study area to the earliest possible period preceding 1830 in order to make useful historical comparisons of the type desired. Fortunately, this is possible to do in some detail for the period 1790–1815. Before that date we have some detailed travel accounts, but we lack comprehensive cartographic and census detail on the over-all settlement pattern.

It is desirable also to be able to compare on the same scale and to the same detail the population pattern of the *sample* with either the preceding or succeeding technological period to gain some sense of the rate and intensity as well as direction of population change. The source data of 1790–1815 suit this purpose insofar as settlement site, size, situation, and communication linkages are concerned relative to the 1928 base. With the preceding periods of prosperity, the thirteenth and the beginning of the eighteenth centuries, the comparison involves greater difficulties. As noted by Topping in Chapter 5, general patterns of location can be plotted, but we are unable as yet to detail size of settlement or route relationships. This is understandable, because as recently as World War II a "true" contour and drainage base map of southwest Peloponnese was unavailable. A similar difficulty is present for the communication system. Although general routes can be plotted, in no sense do we have a detailed, mapped network of routes and centers available before the late nineteenth century.

The map of the early eighteenth-century Venetian period (Pocket Map 5-9), despite inadequate information, is far superior to the reconstruction we can manage for the Frankish period of the early thirteenth century. For the latter period we have little more than the kind of information Strabo and Pausanias provide for the period of Roman occupation. The principal sources, such as the *Chronicle of Morea* and the *Assizes of Romania*, give geographic outline and a sense of a prosperous feudal landscape, but we are at a loss to describe either the relative pattern or the core areas of settlement. Because of the relative neglect of the archaeology and topography of the Peloponnese during the post-classical period (except for the monographs of Antoine Bon [1951, 1969]), we are in many ways better able to substantiate the classical and Bronze Age economies than that of the medieval period.

This rather bleak picture of "have" and "have not" information gives impetus to an attempt in the next section of this chapter to provide a theoretical framework of settlement principles, given certain underlying environmental and institutional/technological conditions within which one can partially evaluate what information we have. In addition, one can suggest further avenues and areas of research to fill in both the real and the hypotheti-

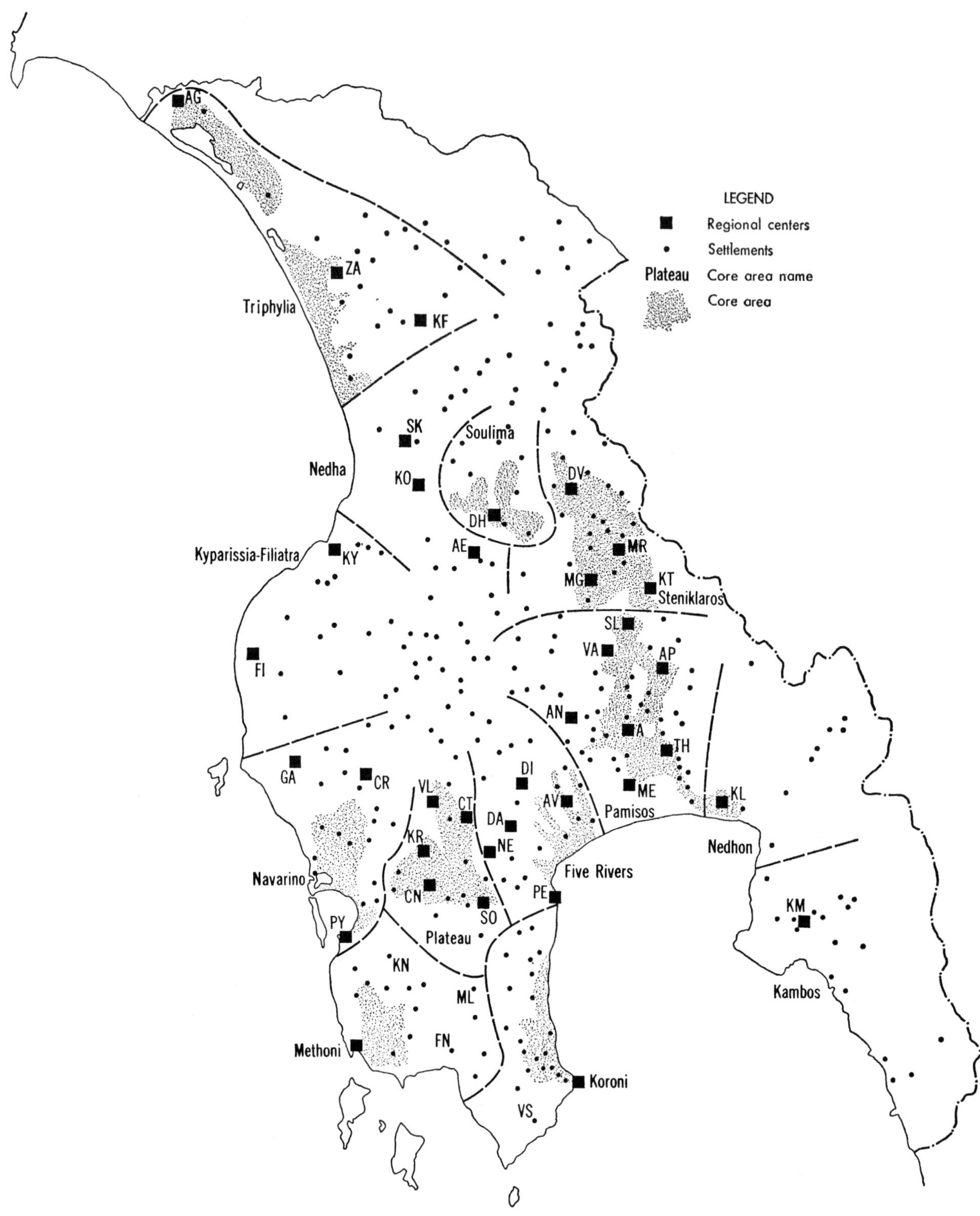

Figure 9-1. Basic settlement pattern about A.D. 1800 (place-names designated here by two letters are listed under the core areas on pp. 151–52)

cal gaps for specific periods of settlement history. Theory, however, can only provide structure and organization; it must be fed empirical data to produce more factual information. Our broadest empirical base relevant to the study area is the settlement pattern of the early 1800's (Fig. 9-1). A description of its general pattern and system are basic to the implementation of the settlement theory that follows.

The region settled about 1800 is the same as that defined in Chapter 1 – bounded by the Ionian Sea, the Gulf of Messenia, the Taygetos Mountains, and the general line of the Alpheios River. The total regional population in this period was in the range of 75,000 to 100,000 individuals. This compares with a total of 250,000 to 300,000 persons for the same general boundaries in 1928. The difference is to be accounted for in the shift within the period to a more commercialized economy, with its accompanying urbanization, and in the general increase in life expectancy, owing to improved health conditions in a relatively stable political and social situation (Naval Intelligence Division, 1944–45). Insofar as these conditions are within the context of what is meant by "modernization," they are exogenous forces to be subtracted relative to any comparison we shall make with earlier periods. The range of population size cited by Topping for about 1700 is around 45,000. The general impressions conveyed by the *Chronicle of Morea* and other medieval sources make plausible a similar range of population for the apogee of the Frankish era in the thirteenth century (see Ch. 5). Roebuck's estimate for late classical Messenia is closer to the 1800 figure (Roebuck 1945).

The general distribution of settlement around 1800 can be schematicized as follows: Settlement was nucleated and not dispersed. Characteristic village hinterlands were three to five kilometers across, although the shape of the hinterland varied considerably with the local morphology of slope and drainage. In a significant number of instances settlements were dispersed (or split) nucleations because of limited water supply and dissected land forms. That is, a village hinterland of "average" size would have two or three nuclear sites rather than one – for example, "Ano" (upper)/"Kato" (lower) pairs were a fairly common occurrence. Settlements were clustered or grouped; random or uniform patterns of villages are not discernible in a geometric sense.

Within core areas, a truncated hierarchy of one or at most two levels, as measured by size of settlement, is apparent. Core areas, in turn, are clustered or grouped, and a more complete hierarchical system of major centers and satellite "towns" becomes apparent. This differentiation in settlement size is basically tied to the route and traffic flow network and not to local site conditions. A route network is apparent at at least three levels above the smallest settlement hinterland paths: first, there is a core area network at the lowest level; there is a secondary grid level linking the largest core area centers; and there is a third level network of routes interlocking all areas into a wider regional system.

For purposes of the comparison the following "sample" system of regions and routes can be identified (see Fig. 9-1; for abbreviated designations of place-names on the map, see corresponding forms within parentheses in the list below):

A. Methoni area
   1. Major center: Methoni, port
   2. Core area: upper and lower plain
   3. Transition areas: south end Navarino Bay, Kinigou (KN) basin, Militsa (ML) Plain, Finikous (FN) lowland

B. Koroni area
   1. Koroni, port
   2. River valley and terraces, Vasilitsi (VS) to Kalamaki
   3. Finikous lowland, Militsa Plain, Likodhimo Mountain, Tsana River basin

C. Navarino area
   1. Gargaliani (GA), Chora (CR), and Pylos (PY)
   2. Romanou River valley, plain, terraces and fans north of lagoon
   3. Filiatra terraces, Aigaleon Mountain, Kremmidhia plateau, Kinigou basin

D. Central Plateau area
   1. Kremmidhia (KR), Vlachopoulo (VL), Chatzi (CT), Soulinari (SO), and Chandhrinou (CN)
   2. Dissected plateau surrounding Manglava Mountain, north flank of Likodhimo Mountain
   3. Navarino Bay, Aigaleon Mountain, Five Rivers (see E below), Likodhimo Mountain, Kinigou basin

E. Five Rivers area
   1. Neromilos (NE), Dara (DA), Dhiodhia (DI), Avramiou (AV), and Petalidhi (PE)
   2. Lower deltas and valley bottoms of the Tsana, Karia, Velika, Tiflo, Tzitzori

rivers and middle dissected plateau of the same rivers

3. Likodhimo Mountain, Central Plateau, Kondovounia Mountains, Ithomi Mountain, west Pamisos terraces

F. Pamisos area

1. Messini (ME), Andhrousa (AN), Valira (VA), Skala (SL), Arfara (AP), Aris (AR), and Thouria (TH)
2. Upper plains (Ayios Floros and Pidhima) and delta marsh (Valtos) and the surrounding terraces and ridges
3. Five Rivers, Ithomi Mountain, Skala ridge, Taygetos Mountains, and Nedhon River

G. Nedhon area

1. Kalamata (KL)
2. Nedhon River gorge, and terraces, and fan
3. Pamisos, Taygetos Mountains, and the Kambos area

H. Kambos area

1. Kambos (KM)
2. Kambos plateau
3. Nedhon, Taygetos Mountains, Mani peninsula

I. Kyparissia-Filiatra area

1. Kyparissia (KY), Filiatra (FI)
2. Coastal terraces and plain from Valta to Kyparissia
3. Navarino Bay, Aigaleon Mountain, Kyparissia River

J. Nedha area

1. Sidherokastro (SK), Aëtos (AE), Kopanaki (KO)
2. Figalia Mountains and Kyparissia River basin
3. Triphylia, Tetrayi Mountain, Soulima Valley, the Kondovounia-Aigaleon Mountains, Kyparissia area

K. Triphylia area

1. Kato Figalia (KF), Zacharo (ZA), Agoulinitsa (AG)
2. The basin of Zacharo and the coastal plain from the Nedha to the Alpheios River
3. Alpheios Valley, Minthis Mountain, Tetrayi Mountain, Nedha area

L. Soulima area

1. Dhorion (DH), Psari
2. Soulima basin
3. Figalia Mountains and Kyparissia River basin, Tetrayi Mountain, Steniklarian basin, north slopes of Kondovounia Mountains

M. Steniklaros area

1. Meligala (MG), Dhiavolitsi (DV), Meropi (MR), Katsarou (KT)
2. Steniklarian basin and surrounding hill lands
3. Soulima Valley, Tetrayi Mountain, Makriplayi Mountain, Taygetos Mountains, Skala ridge, and Ithomi-Kondovounia Mountains

The thirteen major settlement clusters identified above for about 1800 leave unidentified interstitial or transition zones of sparse population and diffused areas of no particular focus within the region as defined in Chapter 1. The Alpheios Valley, for example, is left undefined, as is the whole general mountain zone from Mt. Tetrayi to the Taygetos. Within that general boundary, areas such as the mountainous lands of the Kondovounia, Aigaleon, and Likodhimo cannot legitimately be called "core" areas of settlement inasmuch as they function primarily as barriers to the communication network. It is that route network that gives structure and organization to the settlement core areas as they relate to one another and identifies and induces, in large measure, the hierarchy of regional centers by differential size and function.

The route network, as suggested above, at its highest level links all the areas into a regional system. That system of first-order routes can be identified as follows (see Fig. 9-2):

N. West Coast routes

1. Terminals: Methoni–Agoulinitsa
2. Intersections: Pylos, Yialova, Korifasion, Gargaliani, Chora, Kyparissia
3. Linkages: all west coast areas
4. Extensions: to the Alpheios River crossing into Elis to the north and east.

   In the south the route was essentially two parallel roads from Methoni, one taking the coastal plain and lower terraces to Kyparissia via Tragana, Gargaliani, and Filiatra, the other taking the plateau route via Kinigou, Chandhrinou, Chora, and Christiani.

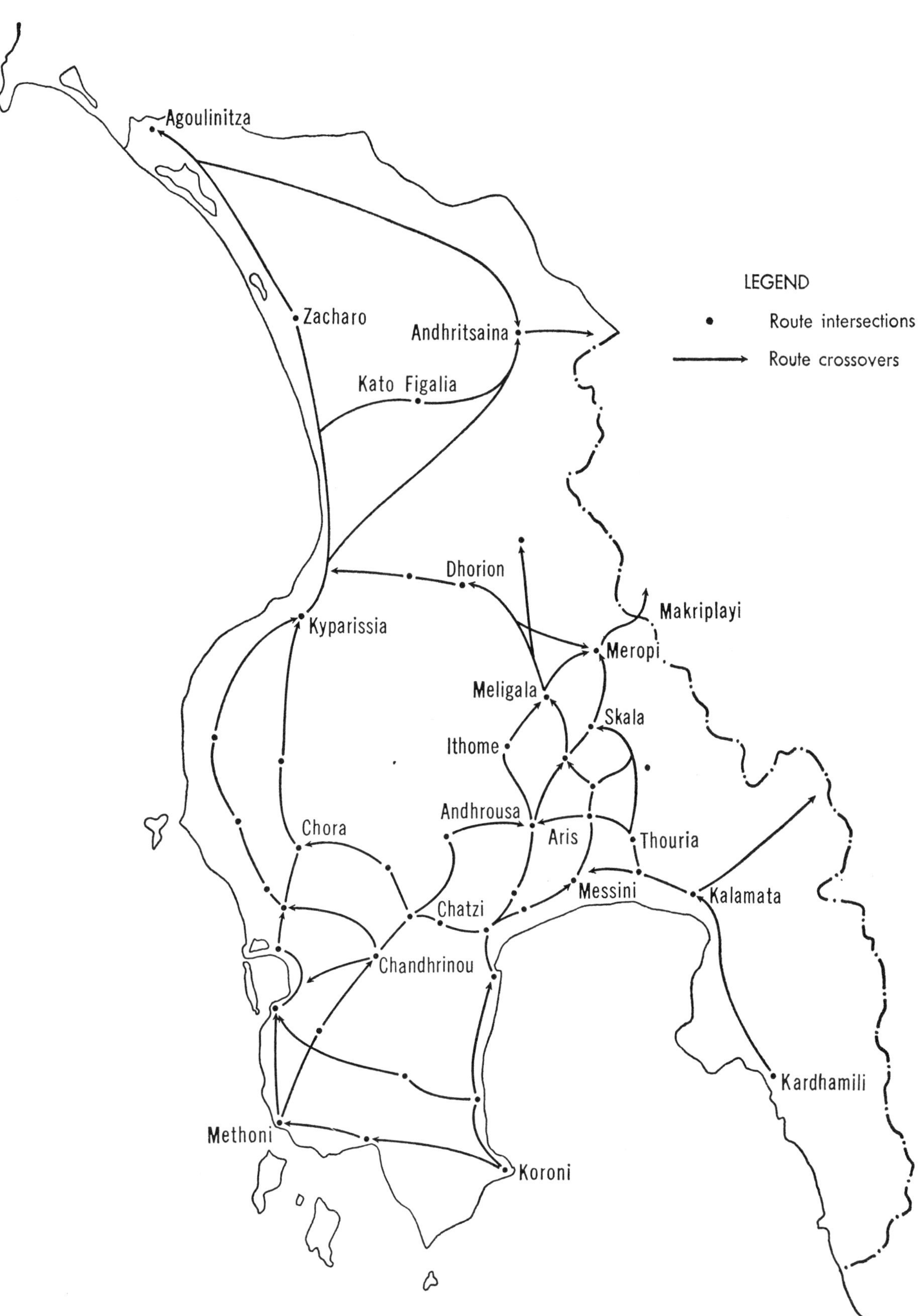

Figure 9-2. Schematic circulation system about A.D. 1800

O. West Gulf–Pamisos routes

1. Koroni–Makriplayi
2. Kastelia, Petalidhi, Rizomilo, Avramiou-Analipsis, Messini, Andhrousa, Valira, Skala, Meligala, and Meropi
3. Koroni, Five Rivers, Pamisos, and Steniklaros areas
4. To the passes of Krani, Dherveni, and Kokala into Arkadia

   In the south this route was basically a coastal road until Avramiou-Analipsis where the route divided, the western taking the ridges and dissected plateau to Andhrousa and Ithomi to Meligala, the eastern following the river terrace edges through Messini and Valira to Meligala. On reaching the Steniklarian basin at Meligala, the route divided again to circle the lowest part of that basin before ascending the passes of the Makriplayi.

P. East Gulf–Pamisos routes

1. Kardhamili–Makriplayi
2. Kalamata, Thouria-Asprochoma, Aris, Plati, Skala, and Arfara
3. Kambos, Nedhon, Pamisos, and Steniklaros areas
4. To the Mani in the south and the passes into Arkadia in the north

   In the south this was basically a coastal road until Thouria-Asprochoma; at that point a western loop went out to the Pamisos River via Aris and Plati before returning to the main inner valley route in the neighborhood of Ayios Floros at the Skala ridge intersection with route (O).

Q. Cape Crossing routes

1. Methoni–Pylos to Koroni–Kastelia
2. Militsa plain, Finikous
3. Koroni, Methoni, and Navarino Bay areas
4. Only by sea. Probably an unimportant route for internal use except during the rough winter sailing season.

R. Plateau Crossing routes

1. Chora-Korifasion-Yialova-Pylos and Methoni to Andhrousa-Messini-Kalamata
2. Chandrinou, Chatzi-Petritsi, Neromilos, Petalidhi, Avramiou-Analipsis
3. Methoni, Navarino Bay, Plateau, Five Rivers, Koroni, Steniklaros, Pamisos, and Nedhon areas
4. To Arkadia and Lakonia through the Makriplayi, Arfara, and Langadha passes. Probably the most important route insofar as it linked the greatest number of core areas with the shortest internal lines of communication. Alternative routes are either very roundabout, difficult in winter weather, or open to external incursion.

S. Kyparissia Valley Crossing route

1. Kyparissia to Makriplayi and Meligala (Kalamata)
2. Kopanaki and Dhorion
3. Triphylia, Nedha, Kyparissia-Filiatra, Soulima, Steniklaros, and Pamisos areas. An important route to the Steniklaros and Pamisos areas and to Arkadia through the port of Kyparissia, which is the best harbor between the Alpheios Valley and Navarino Bay.

T. Alpheios-Nedha Crossing routes

1. Kyparissia and Agoulinitsa to Andhritsaina
2. Kato Figalia
3. Triphylia, Nedha, Kyparissia-Filiatra areas
4. To the middle Alpheios Valley and Arkadia. This route across the Tetrayi and Nedha mountains was an arduous one and not an important internal trade link.

The general routes described above can only be appreciated on the map (Fig. 9-2). The routes were of varying strategic importance and density of traffic flow. Connected smaller segments of several routes were vastly more important than between the terminals described above. Every historic period, depending upon the particular political hegemony prevailing, offered different combinations of routes and direction and intensity of traffic. For the "sample" period around 1800 there are three important interchange and "bridge" zones that should be identified. These interchange zones are less stable historically than the route corridors described above, but are identifiable in our chosen periods of comparison. They are:

U. Plateau interchange. At two intersections, one on the west in the vicinity of Chandhrinou, one on the east in the Chatzi-Petritsi vicinity, there were important route mergers and crossovers. At Chandhrinou the main route from Methoni ran east to Petritsi, Dara, Dhiodhia, and Andhrousa. Two routes from the north side of Navarino Bay joined at Chandhrinou, one from Yialova through Pila, the other from Korifasion via Iklaina-Platanos and Kremmidhia to Chandhrinou. From the Chora area one route went to Chandhrinou and another through Vlachopoulo to Chatzi-Petritsi. From the east the main approach was from Andhrousa through Dhiodhia and Dara to Chatzi-Petritsi. The second route from Messini (Kalamata) went via Avramiou-Analipsis to Neromilos and Petritsi. A third route from Petalidhi joined the main stem at Neromilos. Turkish bridges and kalderims identify parts of the Kinigou, Pylos, and Pila routes on the west, and the Neromilos and Dara routes on the east.

V. Pamisos interchanges. In the south the Messini crossing of the Pamisos to Asprochoma is presumably of relatively recent date. It is unlikely to have been a usable all-weather road in medieval times or before. The next crossing north between Aris and Karteroli was the major and ancient crossing. The river was bridged just below the junction of the Mavrozoumenos and Pamisos rivers. On the west side routes led to Andhrousa and Ithomi and then to Meligala and Dhorion, and alternatively to Karteroli, Madhena, and Analipsis-Avramiou to the Plateau route or Petalidhi. Crossing to the east through Aris, routes led to Mikromani, Thouria, and Kalamata or alternatively Plati, Arfara-Pidhima, and Ayios Floros north to the Steniklarian Plain. On the east side of the Pamisos at Plati there was an additional crossing to the north via Valira and Skala to Meligala and the Makriplayi passes. On the west side, to the north of Andhrousa, the Mavrozoumenos was crossed at Valira going to Skala and/or Meligala. These two diagonal (X) crossings, centered on Aris and Valira, were undoubtedly of long standing. Around Aris there was a focus of fifteen villages within a radius of 5 km. in the "sample" period.

W. Steniklaros interchange. The crossings of the Steniklarian Plain had a looser focus than those in the southern plain. The center was the "open" triangle of Meligala-Meropi-Skala about 4–5 km. apart. From Meligala routes led north to Dhiavolitsi and Kato Melpia, west to Dhorion and Kyparissia, and southwest to Ithomi and Andhrousa. From Meropi routes led north to Krani, northeast to Dherveni and Megalopolis, and east to Kokala and Leondari or southeast to Katsarou and Poliani. At Skala occurred the intersection with the east Pamisos routes to Kalamata or the west Pamisos routes to Andhrousa and Messini. The "open" triangle surrounded the relatively thinly settled lowest portion of the Steniklarian Plain with the poorest drainage.

The Base Period of 1800. The period about 1800 represents a "mean" sample of a pre-steamship and railway agrarian economy. In its routes and in its core areas of settlement it represents a "full" occupation of the region at any given previous period. At times in the past, there may have been larger populations, but we cannot attest to that. We do know that there are individual sites unoccupied in 1800 that were occupied in the past, as there were routes used in earlier times that were not used in 1800; but at this scale of basic village hinterlands it is to be doubted that any core area or route corridor has been unidentified. Thus, the structure and organization (the pattern and system) of the region is presumed to be outlined in the "sample." What cannot be presumed is the internal relationships of area to area and the relative values of areas as expressed in population number and/or indices of productivity. Those values can only be assigned theoretically by including in the data an evaluation and judgment of the technological, political, and cultural orientation of the population for each historic period being considered.

From period to period, although we may be justified in describing the economy as similarly agrarian subsistence and note no change in agricultural tools, techniques, or crops nor in transportation technology, we cannot assume as much for political or cultural continuity. In 1800, the center of political power lay outside the peninsula, in Constantinople. The center lay outside in 1700 too, but Venice was not Constantinople – either in its motivation and perception, or in its direction of political or economic control. In addition to these elementary differences that must be accounted for in any comparison across time, there is the question of relict institutions and historical lag. Undoubtedly, in the sample of about 1800 there are remnants of the earlier Venetian period of more intensive urbanization and commercialization of the economy. Towns are too large in population and structures relative to their level of rural productivity and activity. Routes are physically overdeveloped and port facilities are excessive, given the amount of trade in 1800. On the other hand, the flow of goods, the operations of markets, and the movement of people is probably more circumscribed than in earlier periods of differing political and economic control. We cannot always be sure of data on these conditions, but it is necessary to make some estimates in order to implement theoretical hypotheses. These are the controlling conditions that affect both the level of interrelationships among settlement locations and the location of routes and hierarchical centers within the general core areas of settlement. In turning, then, to the theoretical framework necessary to make viable comparisons between historical periods, we shall necessarily make judgments beyond our present level of information for those periods and beyond our information for 1800.

Theoretical Considerations. General settlement theory suffers from two specific sets of unreality. The first is an assumption of an undifferentiated environment – an area of fertility but without variation of soils, slope, drainage, and so on; the second is an assumption of no time lag – that is, not only the immediate genesis of a full-scale operating economy but no relicts or lags in that economy. In this study, however, we must establish a *past* for any given point in time and must assume as *given* a highly differentiated environment for our region basically equivalent to that of our "sample" of 1800 in soil, drainage, slope, and climate. Vegetation, on the other hand, must be treated as a cultural variable with a past of human dimensions (see Chs. 10, 11, 12, 16).

Given these limitations, what can be salvaged from general settlement location theory? Basically, only three mechanisms: the concept of settlement nodality, the concept of settlement hierarchy, and the concept of interaction (communication) between settlement nodes.

From general theory, general cultural history, and specific archaeological information we know that settlement in the Middle Helladic period was basically nucleated. We know that settlements varied in size and presume that differing size was reflected in material difference in style and quality of goods and buildings (see Chs. 8, 13 for archaeological and ceramic evidence). More importantly, we must assume that increasing size of settlement was reflected not only in a spectrum of quality of goods but also in the variety (the number of kinds) of goods (see Ch. 7 for Linear B evidence).

It is generally agreed that this relationship of size with function (quality and variety of goods) in settlements is most simply explained through the cultural processes of specialization of labor and task and the exchange of goods through some market mechanism. These two processes of increased production (and quality and variety) of goods and the accompanying need of an exchange mechanism to distribute the goods are the basic operating variables of settlement location theory.

Given the need to assemble raw materials, combine special talents, and distribute the product, a premium is placed upon the tendency of producers, artisans, and consumers to congregate at central places in order to minimize costs of transportation and exchange. Places that are most central in a pattern of places have advantages of nodality, which increases their size and function relative to other places if that centrality is measured in transportation accessibility.

Thus, theoretically we have over time a process that will increasingly differentiate sites by size, function, and route intersection. A hierarchy of city, town, village, hamlet will become accentuated. An index of that hierarchy can be identified in the route network, the size of settlements, or their variety of functions. These are the general clues that we can manipulate from the past to fill in gaps in our knowledge, to outline areas for research, and to test our general reconstructions against the processes of history.

I shall say little here of the specific and inherent natural environment of the region (see Ch. 3). Nor shall I introduce assumptions that must be made of the influence of political control on the transportation system and the market mechanism. These are primary considerations which affect not only the location of settlements and routes but also their number and their place in the hierarchy. Inasmuch as we are seeking gaps in our knowledge and research as well as explanations of data we now have, it seems more judicious to introduce below what little is known of these conditions when discussing the specific historic periods rather than to speculate in a theoretical framework at this point.

The map of about A.D. 1800 (Fig. 9-1), schematicized as a hierarchical diagram of routes and centers (Fig. 9-2), will serve as the basic framework for comparisons. We cannot hope to become specific below a certain level of generalization with what is largely the still unknown past. However, similar schematic diagrams will be produced for all four periods noted at the beginning of this chapter. The reality of these schemes, if it exists, will emerge only in future work.

The MH/LH Settlement System

The archaeological record of Middle Helladic and Late Helladic sites should be read as one pattern for two primary reasons. First, the sites at this stage of discovery seem by and large to form a single pattern of demographic continuity (see Ch. 8, Pt. III). Although there is a pronounced increase in the over-all number of sites, we can establish no significant "break" in the transition from MH to LH site occupation. The pattern of the two site maps (Pocket Maps 8-13 and 8-14) is overwhelmingly overlapping. The second reason for consolidation is the difficulty of separating the "major" sites in MH and LH times from the over-all site pattern. The majority of sites are identified only by the general run of surface pottery. If evidence of a hierarchy of sites can be established through excavation, we shall undoubtedly have more material to establish both an internal chronology and more detailed demographic groupings; but at this stage we cannot safely differentiate much further on merely statistical grounds or on evidence from surficial exploration.

Using the "sample" classification of core areas, routes, and interchanges as a base, a step-by-step analysis of the MH/LH map (Fig. 9-3) indicates the following equations:

A. Methoni Core Area (8 habitation sites, 2 tombs). The area is identified in all five subareas (lower plain, upper plain, Kinigou, Militsa, and Finikous) but the distribution is uneven and gives an impression of only minor sites identified. This may be a reflection of its peripheral and exposed situation vis-à-vis other core areas. Given what we assume to be critical water, slope, soil, and drainage conditions for MH/LH settlement, further sites should be found on the northeast and eastern edges of the upper and lower plain (the zone of Pidhasos, Chomatadha, Kallithea, and Evangelismos), in the immediate Kinigou area (corner of southeast basin), and in the Lachanadha area. The castle area at Methoni should eventually reveal Bronze Age material, but the major site of the area could have been located in the upper plain cited above.

The pattern of most probable routes for the Bronze Age period points to the same general conclusions. If there was a crossing of the southern cape region, its most probable line would have been from southeast to northwest through the Kallithea area with a southwest leg to Methoni and the sea.

B. Koroni Core Area (8 habitation sites, 1 tomb). West Gulf coastal terraces between Petalidhi and Koroni are well identified in the site record for the MH/LH period. The two major subareas of Longa on the north side of the main river valley (Epis) and Falanthi-Charokopio on the south reflect characteristic environmental situations for Bronze Age sites. Three probable subareas are underrepresented – the Kaplani-Akritochori route connection to the Militsa and Finikous areas to the west, the Vasilitsi terraces on the southeast coast, and the Kastelia to Koroni margins centered on Vounaria. It is not certain that Koroni itself was the major Bronze Age site in the area. There should have been a habitation site of major proportions on the Kombi-Vounaria ridge.

The most probable route pattern suggests a coastal route from the Koroni area to Petalidhi and beyond, with two side-routes leading west to the upper plain of the Methoni area, one from the north side of the valley near Longa to the Militsa area, and one from the south side of the valley to the Kaplani vicinity, where easy passage is made to Militsa and to the coast at Finikous. This bifurcation of westward routes reflects not only the two separate but large population centers but also the drainage problem of the lower valleys of major streams in the winter wet season other than at the beach itself. The West Gulf region in total has a much larger resource base than the Methoni region. Given a more central location in the region's route pattern, it would have been an area of third or fourth rank in productivity and prosperity.

C. Navarino Core Area (22 habitation sites, 15 tombs). This, the core area of the LHIIIB palace, is obviously of the first order in environment, population, and prosperity. By all measures of any of the core areas it has the greatest accessibility (both sea and land), agricultural resource base, and distance from competing power centers, *in combination.* It is the best explored of the core areas, and it therefore biases the statistics to some degree. Nevertheless, its major environmental and locational attributes point to a major population base and politicoeconomic control center. The central area is well defined both in the palace ridge area toward Tragana and across the major valleys to the southeast around Platanos and Papoulia, but the central lowland is ill defined on the coastal side. Sites below Korifasion and on the bay and lagoon give some closure, but between Petrochori, Romanou, and the coast to the northwest there is a gap that probably should not be there on both environmental and strategic grounds. The triangle Proti-Pirgos-Tragana is also little known; yet being immediately tributary to the palace, it is potentially an important settlement area considering environmental conditions. A rational route pattern indicates that the area could not have been ignored for politico-military reasons. The subarea of the river valleys centering on the Dapia-Pila sites is separated from the central area by an environmental barrier of a high infertile ridge and deep ravines

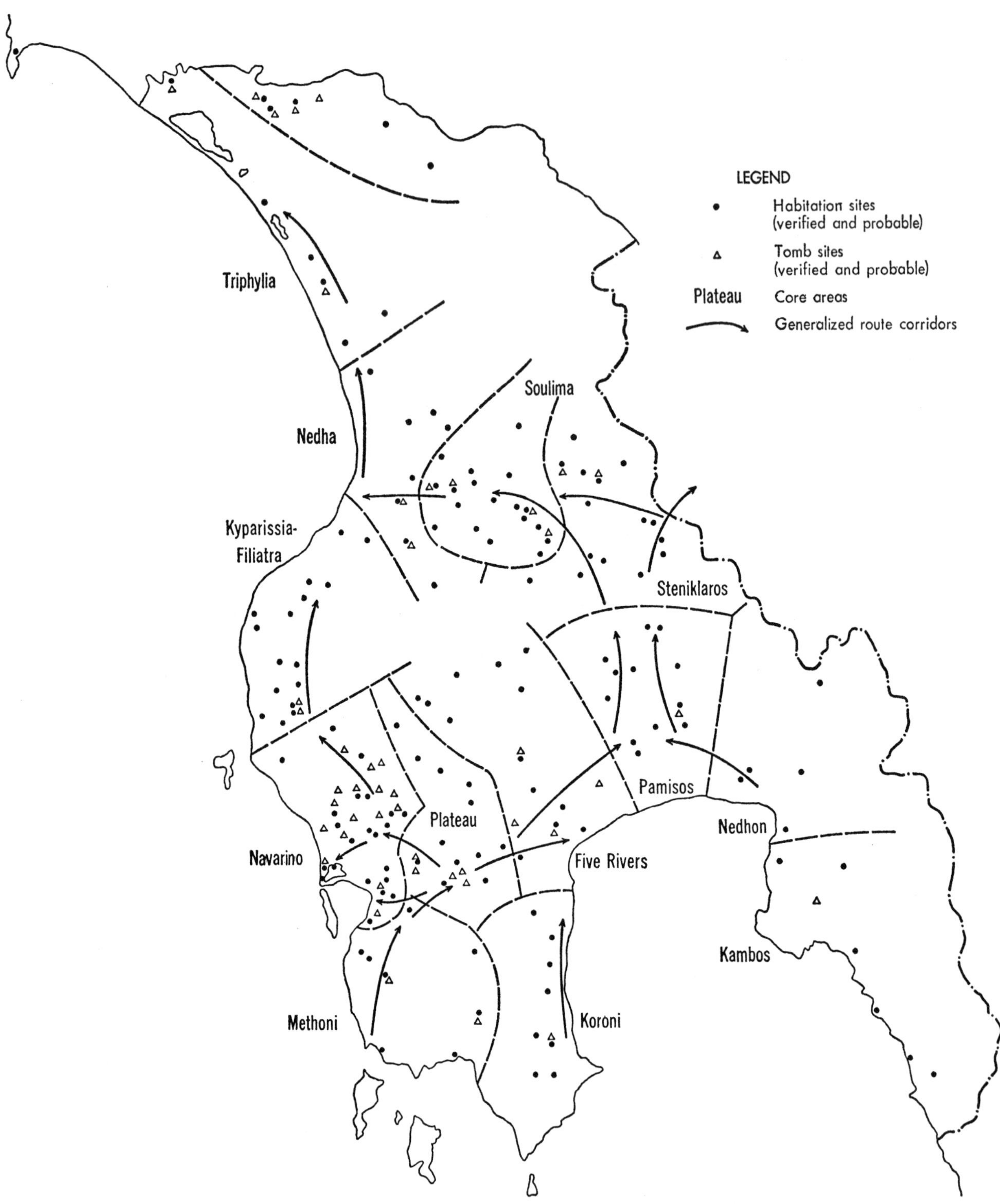

Figure 9-3. Middle Helladic–Late Helladic settlement system

between Iklaina and Yialova, which tends to curve routes from the central plateau both north and south of a direct line to the lagoon area. A similar infertile and rough arc separates the Methoni region from the Navarino Bay and from the west coast as far inland as the head of the Pilokambos escarpment between Pila and Chandhrinou-Kinigou.

The normal focus of routes for the region was centered in the Tragana-Korifasion-Romanou triangle. Routes intersected here from the coastal terraces to the northwest, from the lagoon, and from the central plateau either via Dapia-Pila or from immediately east down the Korifasion ridge from Kremmidhia and Chandhrinou. The northern inner route on the 300-m terrace at the level of Chora and Gargaliani-Valta, which extended east into the Central Plateau via either Vlachopoulo or Kremmidhia, was joined by the palace route (Chora to Korifasion) to the main coastal plain routes. There was an alternative bridge route to the northwest via Tragana, but it had steeper gradients and less fertile hinterlands. Between sea and mountain the palace commanded both corridors, but particularly it guarded the way east from the Navarino area to the fertile Gulf lands of the Pamisos, the Five Rivers, and the Koroni coastal regions.

D. Central Plateau Core Area (12 habitation sites, 5 tombs). Both the number of habitation sites and tombs is misleading. (The Koukounara area with at least ten tholos tombs excavated and presumably several habitation sites is represented by only two symbols in Pocket Map 8-14.) The settlements surround the mountainous uplift of Mt. Manglava, situated between the Aigaleon-Kondovounia Mountains to the north and Mt. Likodhimo to the south. Between the three points, flat but dissected plateau stretches for 7–8 km. To the west the plateau continues into the Navarino region toward Korifasion and Pila without serious interruption. To the east there is an escarpment averaging 100 to 150 m in height overlooking the middle stretches of the Karia and Tsana valleys of the Five Rivers area. The present pattern of known sites is admittedly uneven. More exploration is necessary in the area to the north and west of Kremmidhia-Vlachopoulo, where environmental conditions are not unlike those farther west toward Platanos and Iklaina in the Navarino area. To the northeast and east, further exploration of the Karia River boundary and the next interfluve to the Velika River should produce more evidence for relatively dense settlement, given a similar transition zone and presumed route corridor. Finally, the upper Tsana River drainage area is indistinct, even in its present route patterns. A nineteenth-century focus on the harbor at Petalidhi has been shifted to the new plateau highway, and it is difficult to judge the hinterland boundaries of settlements of the last century. The mountain flanks of the precipitous Aigaleon and Likodhimo peaks serve to define a rapidly declining population gradient on the north and south and offer no problems of definition.

The general route interchange system outlined for about 1800 is not an unlikely analogue for the Bronze Age settlement pattern. In the triangle of Chandhrinou-Koukounara-Kremmidhia, for example, we have a very heavy prehistoric focus of both habitations and tombs. From what we know of tomb siting (soil, etc.) and situation (view), this is closely correlated with major route passages. The further association with wealth and presumed politico-military power of those buried in tholos tombs indicates this area as a major focus of strategic settlement and routes for a late Bronze Age polity. Routes from Methoni, Pila, Korifasion, and Chora converge here into a corridor to the east between the mountains and at the watershed of Gulf and west coast drainage. The east side of the passage has fewer discovered sites, but it cannot have been a less important area. Two major routes are identified, directly east to Nichoria and the lower valleys of the Five Rivers at the Gulf, and northeast across the middle valley, flat interfluves to Dara, Dhiodhia, and Andhrousa on the western edge of the Pamisos interchange. The route to Petalidhi is as yet indistinct in outline. There was undoubtedly, over several historic periods, a pairing with Nichoria – the same sort of pairing or switching we have at the palace and the lagoon locations on the west coast – but there was also an independent route hinterland for the port up the Tsana Valley and to the south down the Gulf coast.

We do know that in the late middle ages and in the early modern period the mountain flanks and the escarpment and sharper ridges on the east side were covered with an oak forest that was of considerable extent and continued into the Karia and Velika upper-middle valleys (Leake 1830).

E. Five Rivers Core Area (13 habitation sites, 4 tombs). The area is only partly explored, particularly in the intricate middle river areas. The area might better be called "Fingers Core Area" because of the convolutions of ridges and hills in the zone where the rivers emerge and converge on the lower coastal plain. It is an extremely fertile area, with a more than adequate water supply. In the lower coastal margins the major problem is, in fact, drainage of the filled-in lagoons and stream deltas. The present agricultural use is intense and suggests that there are other potential ancient sites. Like the Pamisos and Navarino regions, this is probably a major area of earlier settlement, but it is difficult to explore because potential sites are obscured in presently heavily cultivated lower-valley areas.

Three foci of probable settlement can be outlined, all archaeologically established, but not as yet in sufficient depth. The Nichoria site and the lower coastal plain from Petalidhi to Analipsis is one focus. It has poor drainage areas toward the coast but on its frontal hill margins are a combination of good sites, soil, and water resources. A second focal area is the line of inner communication from the plateau at Chatzi-Petritsi across the middle river interfluves to Andhrousa on the eastern boundary. The route is partly outlined by sites #25, 26, 114, 115, but then there is a gap until #125. Two routes from site #115 are suggested by analogy with the pattern of about 1800: (a) to the north and northeast via Manesi and Trikorfo-Klima (#121) to Ithomi and the upper rivers area connecting over the back ridge with the Steniklaros via Zerbisia (#203) and the classical/medieval Mavrozoumenos bridge; and (b) Manesi to Andhrousa-Eva to the west Pamisos crossings via either Aris to the southeast or Valira to the northeast. The site in the Andhrousa area has not as yet been identified but presumably such an intervening site is necessary in this very fertile stretch of country. As in similar situations, evidence probably lurks under the heavy medieval levels on the fine acropolis of Andhrousa itself. The third focus interconnects the other two and presumes a bridge route between the inner road via Dhiodhia and the coastal roads from Nichoria and Petalidhi to Analipsis-Madhena-Karteroli. The easiest paths are up the second river valley (the Tiflo) past Avramiou to Manesi. This tends more in the right direction for presumed ancient settlement than the present engineered road via Velika-Strefi.

Two other subareas are unrepresented by significant sites, but this may be a reflection of the prehistoric settlement pattern. Nevertheless, more intensive exploration is needed. The Tsana Valley (south side) and the Petalidhi vicinity were areas of settlement focus in classical and Roman-Byzantine times. Further, the tradition of the "harbor of the Achaeans" is most likely connected with the reasonably well-protected harbor of Petalidhi in conjunction with the site at Nichoria. In the upper reaches of the Five Rivers area several sites have been identified on the flanks of the higher Kondovounia (#116–119). It is probable that these are the outer margins of settlement, but they should not be downgraded on that score. On the frontier of a culture or, if one prefers, in the "backwoods," are many important signposts for that society pointing both to the past and to the future.

F. Pamisos Core Area (12 habitation sites, 1 tomb). The number of MH/LH sites is well below the potential resource base for the region and the pattern of known sites is also incomplete. The known sites are large and have indications of both pre- and post-MH/LH occupation. The sites on the inner margins of the plain bordering on the Valtos, Pidhima, and Ayios Floros marshes may have fluctuated more than average in occupance and size. If so, the reason might be changes in the external or internal political situation or slight alternations in the over-all precipitation. Large-scale drainage channel maintenance is necessary for crop cultivation even on the margins, and that would presumably have required a supervised cooperative venture.

The critical crossing sites have been identified (#126, 128, 129, 123, and 125) in the vicinity of Karteroli-Aris and Plati. We do not know, however, the extent or density of settlement in this inner zone. Similar potential site locations extend below Messini and toward the west to the first of the five rivers below Analipsis. Between Karteroli and Lambaina on the west, the drainage divide between the Pamisos and the first of the five rivers appears to have been largely or wholly unoccupied before the medieval period. From Byzantine to modern times this has been an area of heavy and strategic occupation. If the present gap in the pattern of Bronze Age and Classical/Hellenistic times reflects the true situation, the best explanation would be that this area was one of the latest to suffer deforestation (see Ch. 16). In the north, the lack of any MH/LH sites in the Ithomi-Valira-Skala area is puzzling on two counts: its strategic route interchange function between the heavy MH/LH occupation in the Steniklarian and Pamisos basins and its preeminent settlement focus in Classical/Hellenistic and later periods. On the east side of the lower plain we can expect future discoveries in the Arfara area above Pidhima and leading to the Poliani pass, and in the Asprochoma-Antikalamos area toward the Nedhon gorge. In the plain itself, sites between Aris-Plati and Ayios Floros are to be expected on the ridge and lower hills facing into the Pamisos-Pidhima water courses.

The Pamisos region has two natural controlling foci, the Andhrousa ridge on the west and the Ellinika (Thouria) ridge on the east. These heights control the north-south route corridors, overlook the central river crossings, and behind them control the routes farther west to the plateau via Dhiodhia and farther east to Lakonia via Poliani. Both sides are naturally defensible and have served as politico-military nerve centers in later periods when land power was of paramount importance in the Peloponnese.

G. Nedhon Core Area (5 habitation sites). The pattern of known sites reflects the potential area of settlement and route probabilities. There is the possibility of further discovery immediately to the north of Kalamata in the foothills and terraces of the westward-trending Taygetos range, but it is an area of marginal importance. The Nedhon area is a transition one in two respects: it serves as an entry into the Pamisos from the Langadha pass and Lakonia and a spillover of population pressure from the Mani peninsula. The reverse, of course, is also true – it is an entry to Lakonia and a refugee-retreat to the mountains of the Mani.

The position of Kalamata is ambiguous, given a strikingly different technology than modern times and a different orientation of political power. From a west coast controlled power base it is a boundary zone, resulting in buffer zone status vis-à-vis Lakonia. One tries either to control it or to neutralize it (give it autonomy) depending on the strength of the opposing power. The latter seems to have been its status in Diokles' time as reflected in Homer's *Odyssey*. On strictly environmental terms it does not have the resource base of the Ellinika (Thouria) site, and if a superior power there controlled the Pamisos lowland, it would tend to downgrade the Kalamata site as a main urban center. Control by a sea-oriented power would tend to upgrade Kalamata, given a development of the port facilities beyond an open roadstead.

H. Kambos Core Area (6 habitation sites, 1 tomb). The general outline of sites seems to match the environmental base and presumed route pattern, although the central settlement site in the Kambos area is not as yet certainly identified. The tomb location indicates its potential focus and an accompanying site should be found. One would expect discoveries farther westward to the coast also.

The general impression is again of a buffer zone depending on a wider arena of political decisions to affect its local status. In an era of political stability, its resource base would be enhanced.

I. Kyparissia-Filiatra Core Area (16 habitation sites, 2 tombs). Sites reflect the lineal pattern of plain and terraces up to the 300-m scarp. Broken by transverse streams and the line of spring emergence, settlements appear fairly regularly both in the past and at the present time. The southern half of the strip is more fertile and site discoveries parallel this pattern. No significant gaps are apparent. Kyparissia is an important strategic lookout and commands the coastal pass, but it lacks the resource base for a major supporting hinterland.

Routes converge at the coast at Kyparissia, but other foci are only local assembly points. There was probably an interior route on the inner edge of the upper plateau (as in 1800) but other than for local traffic it presumably served largely as a strategic cutoff between the Chora area and Kyparissia.

J. Nedha Core Area (8 habitation sites, 2 tombs). The pattern of known sites is far back from the coast on mountain spurs and points of easy defense. Available water supply is a primary location focus. The general infertility of the exposed limestone mountain ridges and the similar characteristics of the lower valley terrace conglomerates narrow the available settlement base appreciably. The immediate coastal plain is fertile and water is available. However, the plain is narrow and exposed, offering few protective headlands or defensible sites. Routes are also circumscribed and basically are approaches to more fertile regions. The fertile areas of the Soulima basin and Triphylia must control the approaches through this route corridor to, and parallel to, the sea; but it can have little independence if the center of power is within the general region. If power is imposed from overseas, its only military importance would be connected with its route gateways.

The qualitative importance of the MH/LH sites seems to indicate a close and derived relationship from the Soulima Valley, inasmuch as the local site hinterlands seem incapable of sustaining either the excavated funerary wealth or the relatively impressive construction. Further exploration should extend the known site pattern into the Nedha and Kondovounia mountain areas, but it is unlikely that the present general pattern will be altered.

K. Triphylia Core Area (6 habitation sites, 2 tombs). The known sites do not reflect the resources of the region and its vaunted prosperity and fertility recorded in the ancient sources. The funerary evidence also indicates a denser settlement pattern. In the Kakovatos area in the south, potential site situations indicate that further exploration in the hill margins is needed. In the hilly interior little exploration has been attempted from an ecological basis. In the lagoon area of Kaiafa and Agoulinitsa conditions for finding Bronze Age settlements are particularly difficult, given annual silting and cyclical inundation. Nevertheless, we would expect some additional sites in the area. The pass site on the Alpheios (#303) is reasonable, as is the Samikon (#302) site on the narrowing pass formed by the westward extension of the Makistos range. Kakovatos is in the center of the agricultural area and provides the expected regional center (#300).

The relations to other settlement regions are particularly unclear. The Alpheios Valley around Olympia is a large and rich area but it is debatable whether in MH/LH times it was a neutral (in part, sanctuary) zone or a seat of political power. There is nothing to indicate it was controlled from Triphylia or Messenia. East across the Minthis range and south across the Nedha Mountains were other similar centers, but only toward the south do we have historical and mythological-traditional evidence of politico-economic relations. The evidence of the route pattern is negative. It is not developed (possibly it could not be developed) to reflect a picture of Triphylia as the center of power, or even of equal status among the identifiable areas of our total region. Until more is learned of the Bronze Age status of Olympia and Elis, it will be difficult to assess the status of Triphylia in relation to other core areas.

L. Soulima Valley Core Area (20 habitation sites, 4 tombs). The Soulima Valley is a morphological basin drained by two rivers, one on the west which drops rapidly to the coast and one on the east which provides an easy gradient to the Steniklarian basin. The known site pattern speaks for itself. This was a rich, protected area which was centrally located on an important route corridor from the sea to the even richer Steniklarian Plain.

Occupation sites are fairly obvious in the region once one has gained familiarity with Bronze Age settlement habits and has a knowledge of the water supply locations. The area is probably fairly well surveyed as to important settlement locations. The excavations at Malthi were on a boundary site in the area which is not necessarily representative of the other known sites.

Although the area seems self-contained, its position makes its relations with other areas of paramount importance. It seems unlikely to have been more than a local seat of power, certainly influencing the Kyparissia river country to the west but probably not controlling the Steniklarian Plain. Its politico-economic status in the wider regional scheme was probably as circumscribed as the mountains which physically surround it. On the other hand, it was vital for the rulers of the Steniklaros to control it, particularly if the seat of power was located either there (Steniklaros) or in the Pamisos or the Ithomi area.

M. Steniklaros Core Area (13 habitation sites, 2 tombs). The flat-bottomed Steniklarian basin is a rich and fertile area which is difficult to explore thoroughly. Its lack of obvious sites except on the very edges of the basin and the flooding and silt-depositing streams toward the center make its environmental assets difficult to describe from a stable locational viewpoint spanning several centuries. Routes within the basin could vary considerably, given shifting stream patterns. It is agriculturally rich and was heavily occupied, but exactly what it looked like as a settlement landscape is extremely difficult to reconstruct.

The entrances to the basin determine in part the settlement patterns, and in large measure the known archaeological sites reflect that fact. Three general sectors are outlined. In the north and northwest associated with debouching streams and spring exposures, six sites give evidence of a rich subregion. In the southwest, four sites only hint at the resource base and its paramount importance as a route gateway. The approach to Ithomi is now sketched in (sites #200, 204) but the route south to the east and west side routes of the Pamisos via Plati and Lambaina has not been filled in. The meeting points of these southern and western approaches is obviously at Meligala (#206), but this meant a crossing of the Mavrozoumenos to the south near Valira and also across the Skala ridge to the southeast. The third sector is probably best described as an arc from Tsoukaleïka-Katsarou (#207) in the southeast to Loutro in the northeast (#211). This northeast sector is critical inasmuch as it leaves a gap in obviously rich country between the last known site and the pattern on the northern edge of the basin beginning at Parapoungi (#213). It is in this area that the Archaic and Classical sites of Andania and Oichalia have usually been placed (see Ch. 6). If the route pattern suggested across thc Makroplayi passes is the correct one, this is an attractive assumption. The passes of Chrani, Dherveni, and Kokala, the streams, and the water supply all emerge in that northeastern quadrant. As at the present time, the open area in front of Meligala and to the southeast to the Skala ridge was probably undesirable as a settlement area because of seasonal drainage problems.

Over-all, we should expect the Steniklaros area along with the Five Rivers and west Pamisos region to increase their site numbers significantly with further exploration.

The comments and description above have been limited primarily to an ordering of data reflecting the route and settlement pattern of a base about 1800. I have refrained from linking or consolidating settlement areas beyond a few remarks which seemed significant from the core area scale and focus. If we speculate on the influence of certain political and economic orientations in the MH/LH period which differ from that of 1800, a few additional remarks are perhaps pertinent.

If, for example, political power were centered in the Navarino region, it would seem difficult for that power to sustain itself without some degree of hegemony over the Kyparissia-Filiatra, Methoni, and Central Plateau core areas also. Similarly, if political power were centered in the Five Rivers or the Pamisos region, it would seem necessary to attempt to control or neutralize the Koroni, Steniklaros, and Nedha area. If power was centered in the Steniklaros area, control of the Soulima Valley and the Pamisos Valley seems a minimal necessity, and some control over the Nedha and the Five Rivers regions would be desirable to maintain security. It is reciprocally conceivable that an outside power could control all or portions of the Triphylia, Methoni, Koroni, Nedhon, and the Kambos areas without breaking up the interchange route network which is the essential link in maintaining territorial control. Finally, it is to be doubted that any of the core areas included here for descriptive purposes could sustain themselves as fully independent states in the later Bronze Age society as we know it. Some minimal combination of core areas seems demanded for any semblance of political independence and viability.

The Classical Settlement Network

The data for my map of the classical period are derived from both archaeological and literary sources. The patterns developed are neither startling nor particularly revealing; rather, they confirm our knowledge and analysis of the Late Bonze Age (Fig. 9-4).

Although the site map of the Geometric and Archaic periods (Pocket Map 8-16) is sparse and fragmentary when compared with the MH/LH record, one can make some comments and preliminary observations. It should, for example, be noted that the areas of record are in the Navarino-Central Plateau, Five Rivers, Pamisos, and Soulima-Steniklaros core areas which were the interchange route and power control areas derived from the Late Bronze Age analysis. Two other site clusters, the Olympia-Alpheios and Kalamata-Nedhon areas, were peripheral to our derived strategic core areas. Two interpretations come to mind: first, the breakdown of centralized power after the Mycenaean Age suggests that buffer (neutral) zones gained relative influence and power; and, secondly, new areas of power emerged as technology changed, migration took place, and new and external political centers reoriented old regions of settlement. Finally, a coastal shift can be noted in the Kalamata, Koroni, and Navarino areas which predicates a changing economic and military technology. Figure 9-4 records these trends in impressive numbers.

Certainly, the greatest over-all trend (other than the filling in) is the coastward migration of settlement and power. The Nedhon, Koroni (including Petalidhi), Methoni, Navarino, and Kyparissia site clusters reorient the map from that of the Bronze Age. A second noticeable feature is the Ithomi-Skala concentration, combined with the Nedhon increase. It may reveal a shift of orientation reflected in the historic Messenian-Lakonian conflicts. Triphylia basically retains its outline, but the Olympia-Alpheios area is noticeably efflorescent, which befits its neutral (and cultural-religious) status in an age of relative prosperity and cosmopolitanism.

The archaeological site maps of this period (Pocket Maps 8-16, 8-17, 8-18) surely suggest that our Bronze Age record is still incomplete. The persistence of human habitation in areas once settled suggests that the discontinuities assumed in myth and history of the Dorian Inva-

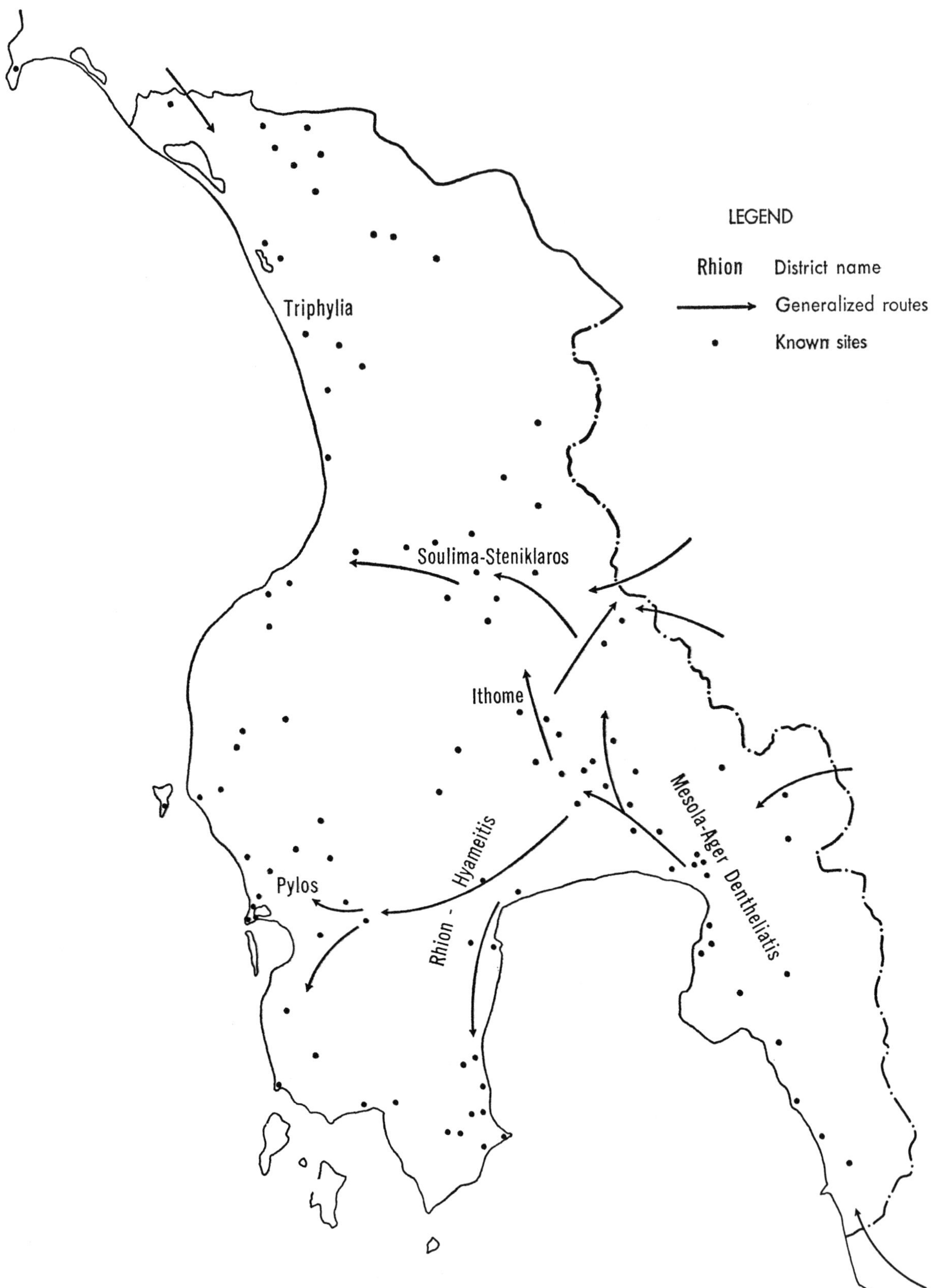

Figure 9-4. Archaic-Classical settlement system

sion, the return of the Herakleidai, and the Dark Ages that followed are not only discontinuities in settlement but breaks in the cultural and political lines of development as well. The thin line of dynastic continuity and its institutional record-keeping and patronage of the arts was broken and the ongoing act of living and subsistence was severely disrupted. That is what is primarily remembered in myth and tradition, and it is in that record that the classical age best serves our attempted reconstruction of the Late Bronze Age. But in southwest Peloponnese there are additional tales of surviving peoples (Minyae, Kaukones, and Messenians) who are incorporated in the new Dorian kingdoms (Strabo 8. 3. 16 and below).

The literary accounts of the Classical period are derived from many sources. The traditions are often confusing and contradictory, but Ephoros, Strabo, Pausanias, and their sources (including poets and dramatists who write with literary license) seem to come to some general agreements which are pertinent in our attempt to describe the gross political geography of the region. If handled with caution, this information may be useful in attempting to extract further knowledge from the archaeological site patterns analyzed above (see Chs. 6, 7, 8).

The literary sources indicate five foci of human occupance within the Alpheios-Taygetos arc during the Achaean, Dorian, and historical Spartan periods. The Homeric Catalogue (*Iliad* 2. 581–624) is the first source: outside our study arc but in part straddling it were the three regions of Lakedaimon (60 ships, 10 towns), Arkadia (60 ships, 7 towns), the Epeioi (40 ships, 4 districts). Pylos was wholly within the arc (90 ships, 9 towns), and the Seven Cities offered by Agamemnon to Achilles (*Iliad* 9. 149–153) were apparently on the border between Pylos and Lakedaimon and, therefore, presumably within the arc.

The next source from Ephoros recalled the situation at the time of the Dorian conquest which incorporated previous Mycenaean units within the arc: "When Cresphontes took Messenia he divided it into five cities; and so, since Steniklaros was situated in the centre of this country he designated it as a royal residence for himself, while as for the others Pylos, Rhion, Mesola and Hyameitis he sent kings to them after conferring on all the Messenians equal rights with the Dorians . . ." (Ephoros-Strabo 8. 4. 7).

Left aside in this division was the area of Triphylia between the Alpheios and the river of Kyparissia, then said to have been occupied by Minyae and Kaukones and later a bone of contention among Elis, Arkadia, Sparta, and Messenia. Some idea of the political status of this area vis-à-vis Kresphontes' "cities" (states?) may perhaps be inferred from the Nestorian tales of Homer (e.g., *Iliad* 11. 670–762) and the "Pylian" topographies of the *Hymn to Pythian Apollo* and the *Hymn to Hermes*.

From these sources and ancillary material, an Early Iron Age topography can be delineated, giving nodes of population and regional economies. These may be summarized as follows, starting in the northwest (see Fig. 9-4):

1. Triphylia, centered between the Nedha and the Alpheios, with its capital at Arene. Archaeological and topographic evidence points to Samikon-Kakovatos as the core area. As we have shown, ancient and modern population density patterns coincide with this center. Land use and agricultural productivity, as well as transportation routes, further suggest the validity of this focus as a stable core of population and economy.
2. Steniklaros-Soulima basins and river of Kyparissia. Kresphontes' designation of this area as his capital and earlier traditions of capital sites at Andania and sanctuaries at Oichalia and Ithomi (Messene) point to this region as a unit (Pausanias 4:2. 1–7, 3. 1–8). Ancient and modern population density, land use, and transportation routes emphasize its commanding location. In the myths (which are presumably not primarily Dorian sources since they emphasize non-Dorian elements and pre-Dorian traditions) the sequence of political power in southwest Peloponnese is first centered here, then shifts to Arene in Triphylia, and finally, under Neleus, to Pylos in the far southwest toward the end of the Mycenaean Age – then back to the Steniklaros under Kresphontes and his successors (Pausanias 3:3–10).
3. Mesola, including the Ager Dentheliatis. This is the region of the Seven Cities and the area controlled by Diokles, with its capital at Pherai (Kalamata). Its territory stretches from south of Kardhamili up to Pidhima and the lower Pamisos. The northern boundary is suggested by the account of Teleklos' conquests and his death at Limnai. Environmentally, this area is naturally bounded by the ridge of Taygetos on the east, the rugged Mani coast to the south, and the Messenian Gulf and marshes of the lower Pamisos and Pidhima on the west and north. Density of population, land use, and settlement patterns again reflect the ancient regional division.
4. Rhion-Hyameitis, including the Western Pamisos and the Petalidhi-Koroni coast. Kresphontes' divisions of Rhion and Hyameitis have not been certainly located and are quite unclear as to boundary. Presumably they included the region on the axis from Ithomi to Cape Akritas north and south, and faced on to the Messenian Gulf and the western Pamisos Plain. The literary sources give some foundation for such a region. The position of Petalidhi as the "harbor of the

Achaeans," its supposed association with the ancient place-name of Aepeia (Pausanias 4:24. 5), and the installation of the Messenian dynasty of the Aipydidai by Sparta in Hyameia after its downfall in Ithomi, point to this general region as an autonomous unit of some distinction. The tablet reference (Ch. 7) to a Rhion (*ri-jo*) and the literary reference to Kolonides (Pausanias 4:24. 8) and the sanctuary of Apollo Korynthos, plus the archaeological sites of Kafirio and Nichoria give added strength to the suggestion of a regional unity centered on the focus where the Pylos-Pherai route crossed the population pattern centered on the Pamisos Valley, the Five Rivers, and the coastal terraces south of Nichoria. Environmental patterns, population density, land use, and transportation routes all give evidence of a regional unity to this area. To the west, it was separated from Pylos by the mountain ridge and perhaps by an oak-forested plateau between the Kondovounia and Likodhimo mountains. To the east, the Messenian Gulf and the marshes of the Pamisos up to the Skala ridge and Ithomi provided definitive boundaries.

5. Pylos. There is no need to substantiate this core area in any detail. It is evident in the literary sources (Homer, Strabo, and Pausanias) and particularly evident in the archaeological record of the Englianos palace and Linear B tablets. Environmentally, it is a unit set off by itself. We lack at the moment land use and population patterns which reflect this area as a single focus of economy. In the immediate vicinity of Pylos and the bay and on the plateau some distinction is evident, but to the north along the coast to Kyparissia there is a vagueness about where the regional boundary lies.

The literary sources also contain itineraries which are suggestive of distances, times, and routes of travel. The descriptions of Strabo and Pausanias suggest, for example, in their order of description the usual routes inland around the Pamisos floodplain (that is, by Kalamata, Thouria, Ithomi, and Koroni), avoiding the direct crossing. The journey of Telemachos in the *Odyssey* is well within the time schedule for a chariot from Navarino Bay to Kalamata and from Kalamata to Sparta, whether by the Langadha or more northerly passes. It is not out of the question that the eastern part of the route was out of the Steniklaros Valley via Kokala and the vicinity of Leondari and then down the Eurotas corridor to Sparta (see Ch. 2). In the descriptions of Telemachos' return journey by sea from Pylos to Ithaka (*Odyssey* 15. 295–300) and in the itineraries of the cattle raids and the pursuit in the *Iliad*, there is additional information on the location of Nestor's Pylos. Too much can and has been made of this information alone about the topography of southwest Peloponnese; but, in conjunction with other archaeological and theoretical constructs of settlement relationships, the evidence continues to support a probable settlement center and route pattern which fit both the physical facts of environment and human motivation for settlement.

The Frankish/Venetian Settlement System

We had earlier noted the Frankish and Venetian era in the Peloponnese as a period of relative prosperity and population increase (see Ch. 5). At the present state of research it is difficult to reconstruct a detailed map with any quantitative value for population at that time, but the major outlines of settlement and centers is hinted at, and in the *Chronicle of Morea* we have some leads to the emerging political geography following the conquest.

The pattern of Frankish centers (Fig. 9-5) is not startlingly different from what we have observed so far (see Pocket Maps 5-8, 5-9). The Navarino area stands out, with the castle on the north end of the bay and Iklaina in the interior on the route from the Romanou Plain past Platanos on to the plateau at Kremmidhia. The Methoni-Kinigou-Chandhrinou route is obvious, and the Chora area is identified. Petalidhi-Koroni and the Militsa-Finikous area come in for more attention than at any point so far. Both the east and west Pamisos, including the Five Rivers area, is marked with castles and towns, as is Ithomi. The Steniklaros-Soulima area and its mountainous rims are well outlined. Triphylia is identifiable as a subregion, as is the Alpheios Valley. What appears to be a striking new emphasis in the Nedhon area from Kalamata to the Langadha pass is not actually so: the princes and castellans based in Kalamata were not able to control the Slavs of Yiannitsa, and even less so the inhabitants in the upper basin of the Nedhon.

In terms of areal subdivisions, it is instructive to compare this era with the past. Geoffrey Villehardouin, the conqueror, had landed by accident at Methoni, wintered there (1204–5), and made a perilous journey of six days – we know not by what route – to meet Boniface, king of Salonika, at Nauplia. Thence with his immediate suzerain Champlitte and about a hundred knights he proceeded to the conquest of the coasts of Achaia, Elis, and Messenia. A large Greek force was decisively beaten in the battle of Koundoura, which was fought in an olive grove probably situated in the northern Messenian Plain (autumn, 1205). As the leading sea power and virtual co-ruler of the Latin Empire of Constantinople, Venice was ceded Methoni and Koroni by the treaty of Sapientza (1209). The Villehardouin princes controlled our entire region from centers in Messenia (Kalamata and Andhrousa) and in Elis (Pondikokastro and especially Andhravidha and Clermont still farther north).

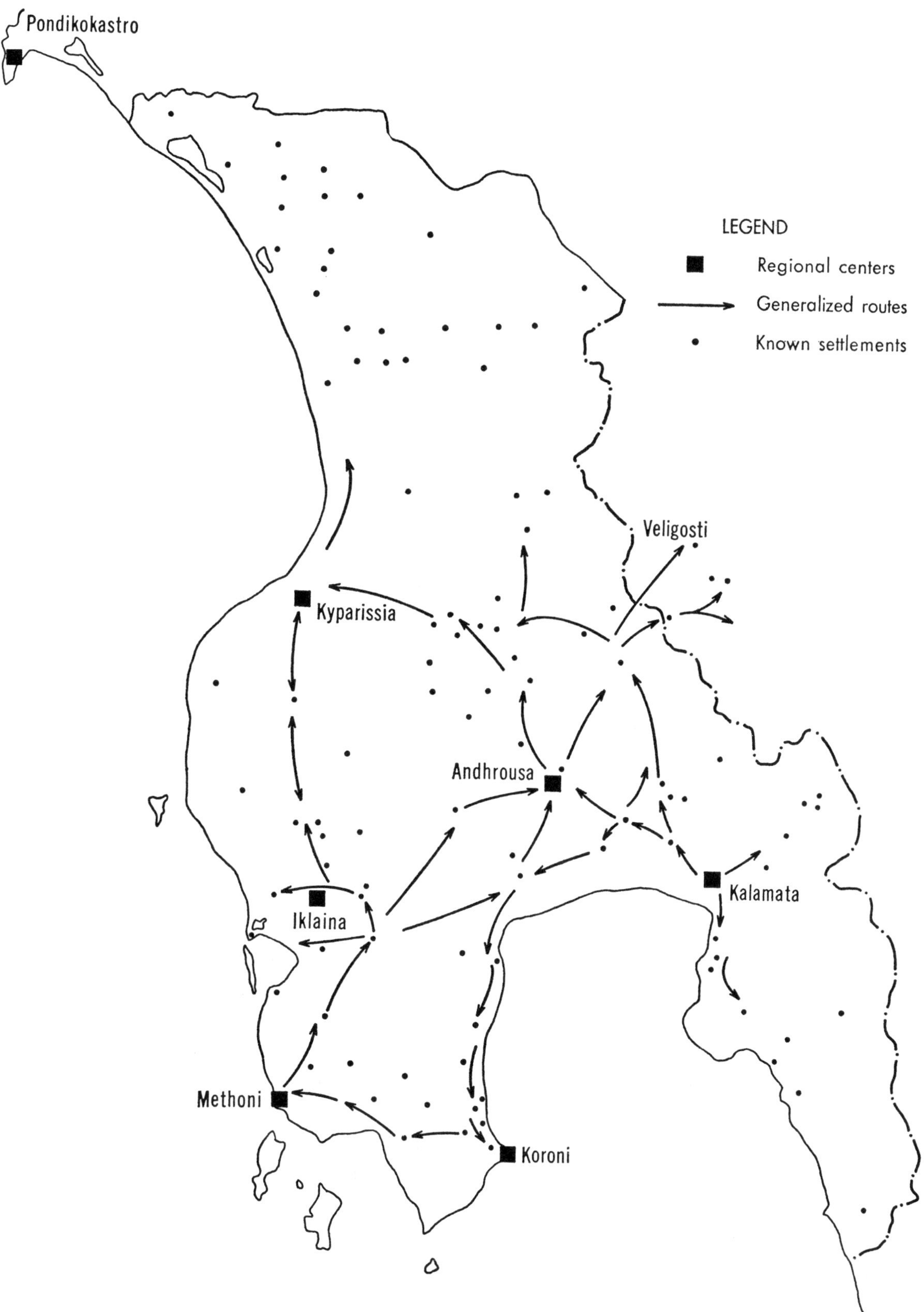

Figure 9-5. Frankish-Venetian settlement system

However, after 1278 the ultimate seat of power of Frankish Peloponnese was Naples, the capital of the Angevin kingdom (Bon, 1969). Thus, there is a change in the relative values of Kyparissia, Methoni, Koroni, Kalamata, and Pondikokastro; but the changes are not for internal reasons. The resource base within the study area remains the same – Navarino, Five Rivers–Koroni, Pamisos, and Steniklaros-Soulima. In the parade of time we have seen, thus far, rotating centers of power – Steniklaros, Arene, Pylos, Steniklaros, Ithomi, Andhrousa, Kalamata; but the bases of those shifting capitals – the settlement core areas of agricultural population and productivity – are fixed and seemingly immutable.

The Linear B Settlement Network

We have now assembled and mapped (Fig. 9-2) a detailed sample of modern settlement (about 1800) and schematic analyses of three past periods of known high population density (MH/LH [Fig. 9-3]; Classical [Fig. 9-4]; Frankish/Venetian [Fig. 9-5]). Before summarizing those analyses and their bearing on the reconstruction of the Late Bronze Age landscape one final bit of testimony should be reviewed – the Linear B tablets found at the palace site (see Ch. 7). In their present form they are not only a fragment (in time and quantity) but largely enigmatic in toponymic identity with the known archaeological source materials. Although numerous interpretations have been published on their toponymic reference, it still would be useful, I believe, to review certain parts of the Linear B corpus to see if we can distinguish for our *schematic scale* of generalization any topographic and chorographic order that later may prove useful as an underpinning for toponymic and archaeological site correlation.

Conclusions are summarized in the accompanying "map" (Fig. 9-6). In reality, it is an incomplete graph network diagram of lines and intersects (representing, respectively, "spaces" and "crossings") revealed in various selected tablets containing three or more place-names in the context of a "list" or an "order." Tablets listing only two place-names have not been used in the context of spacing, intersects, lists, or orders but only as secondary guides for interpreting "groupings." Tablets limited to one place-name have been used sparingly, as possible leads to associations of place with product, environment, or institutions, and by counting the number of occurrences with degree of importance vis-à-vis the palace.

At the province level, the tablets show that there were two primary units which were apparently referred to as "on this side" and "on that side of the mountain" (Aigaleon), relative to the palace core area. These two provincial units have, respectively, nine and seven major towns or districts (see Ch. 7). Nowhere to my knowledge are *pu-ro* or *re-u-ko-to-ro*, the two provincial capitals, specifically allocated to one of the list of nine or seven; therefore, it seems safer to assume that they were also districts. The identification of *pu-ro* and *re-u-ko-to-ro* as the two provincial capitals can be inferred from their statistical weight and their association with functions and personalities of higher order in the political, religious, and economic hierarchy. Three other place-names, *ro-u-so*, *pa-ki-ja-na,* and *ro-o-wa*, also have lesser associations with the higher order functions and functionaries.

At the district level, the ordering of names seems to be more consistent for the "this side" province. What its directional (e.g., N-S-E-W) orientation is, if any, we have few clues. The association of district or place with product or occupation has only been assumed in an "absolute" sense and not in a "relative" sense unless *multiple* statistical evidence is available. The association of a product and occupation with an environmental area has not entered into the relationships expressed by the diagram. Environmental conditions have affected the pattern of the diagram only in the general fact of gross land and sea relations and the general location of the mountain masses.

Figure 9-6 should be primarily an ordering device useful before other and more specific interpretation, but as an ordering device it should also serve the more general purpose of relating zones, regions, and core areas as the first order of topographic analysis. If general areas can be identified and linkages ascertained, we have a useful instrument for further archaeological reconnaissance which must precede further environmental, demographic, and economic reconstruction.

Two lengthy lists of place-names assigning "watches" (An 519, 654, 656, 657, and 661) and "rowers" (An 610) may be instrumental in giving basic orientation (Ventris and Chadwick 1956; Palmer 1963). The two intersecting places in the lists are *a-ke-re-wa* and *za-e-to-ro.* The assignment of these lists to given land-sea boundaries and the implied coverage of the coast from "watching" places give the diagram its first topographic correlation. Between Katakolo, north of the Alpheios mouth, and the Kambos area on the east gulf (the extremes of the UMME region and the presumable limits of the Pylian kingdom), a minimal number of watching posts giving a view of the beach margins and the ability to distinguish a small boat by eye is twenty-two places (by field observation). Twenty-one place-names are listed in the tablets, the last being *ne-do-wa-ta-de*, which many philologists assign to the Nedhon area. Between *a-ke-re-wa* and *za-e-to-ro* in the "watchers" list are three place-

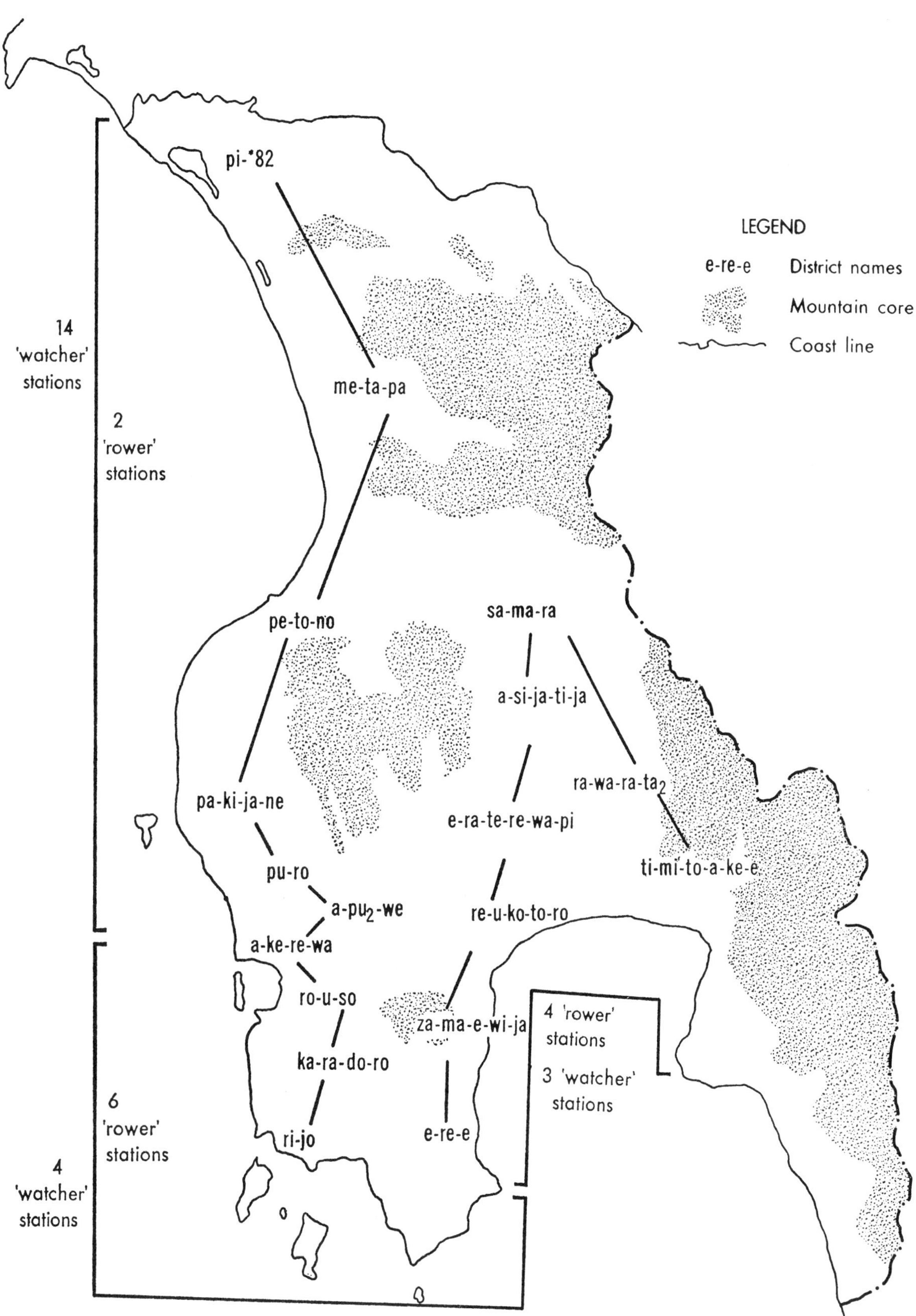

Figure 9-6. Linear B settlement network

names; between the same two names on the "rowers" list there are eight place-names. Rowing stations are not necessarily watching stations, even though presumably they are on the coast.

The other intersecting lists are place-names associated with product, function, and/or occupational attributes such as bronze, slaves, ritual sacrifices. These are uneven in number and coverage and cannot sustain an elaborate set of speculations. Certainly they cannot be the cornerstones of an analysis or a map-diagram.

Having assembled what is admittedly fragmentary evidence, caution must be used in interpretation; but certainly some tentative conclusions can be drawn. It seems reasonable to assign all or nearly all of the place-names on the tablets to our basic study area. The resulting arrangement of district names and their number are compatible with our major core areas as previously analyzed. The two provinces can fit a "this side" and "that side" allocation along the Likodhimo/Aigaleon/Kondovounia mountain axis. The districts and place-names associated with the political-religious hierarchy of the palace state and its functions tend to match the framework of known tomb and major settlement sites, with significant gaps only in the areas that are inadequately explored. Finally, the lines of linkages and the crossings of intersects do approximate the basic framework of routes we have previously formulated. Beyond that level of generalization it is probably imprudent to venture at this stage of research.

Summation

Our five schematic maps (Figs. 9-2 to 9-6) represent attempts at theorizing about the past. As *hypothetical* constructs they have their obvious limitations, but within those limitations they may be useful devices for interpreting the past. The overriding limitation of the maps is that they say nothing about individual events or places. They are intended to reflect only pattern and system and not to identify point and line. Therefore, they probably are best described and construed as organizational charts of economy, society, and polity.

The maps are intended to serve two primary objectives. The first is to help give meaning and explanation to our reconstruction of the Late Bronze Age environment. But a second and in many ways just as important an objective is to suggest certain guidelines for future archaeological exploration and excavation in the region. In technical terms, the maps are theories – they attempt to predict (or, better, retrodict) the past. But as noted, they do so in a limited way. They are at best diagrams of structure, area, and zones. They show relationships, linkages, and boundaries. To ask more is to go beyond their basic assumptions.

What has been attempted, then, is a commentary on archaeological and literary source data manipulated within a framework of settlement location theory. Our assumptions of nodality, hierarchy, and spatial interaction are just that, assumptions. The test of their appropriateness will come in future exploration and excavation that either verifies or disproves the assumptions. Naturally, we believe there is enough continuity in human social, economic, and political behavior to make logical assumptions of *general* principles of human interaction and to predict a *general* institutional structure and system that will be more or less faithfully reflected in man's settlement patterns.

REFERENCES

Bon, Antoine. 1951. *Le Péloponnèse byzantin jusqu'en 1204*. Paris.

———. 1969. *La Morée franque. Recherches historiques, topographiques et archéologiques sur la principauté d'Achaïe (1205–1430)*. 2 vols., text and album. Paris.

General Statistical Service of Greece. 1933. *Statistical Results of the Census of the Population of Greece of 15–16 May 1928*. Athens.

Leake, W. M. 1830. *Travels in Morea*. 3 vols. London.

Loy, W. G. 1970. *The Land of Nestor: A Physical Geography of the Southwest Peloponnese*. National Academy of Sciences, Office of Naval Research. Report No. 34, Washington, D.C.

Naval Intelligence Division, Great Britain. 1944–45. *Greece*. Geographical Handbook Series. Cambridge.

Ogilvie, Alan G. 1943. "Population Density in Greece," *Geographical Journal* 101:251–60.

Palmer, Leonard R. 1963. *The Interpretation of Mycenaean Greek Texts*. Oxford.

Roebuck, Carl A. 1945. "A Note on Messenian Economy and Population," *Classical Philology* 40:149–65.

Ventris, Michael, and Chadwick, John. 1956. *Documents in Mycenaean Greek*. Cambridge.

10

SOIL STUDIES

by

N. J. Yassoglou and Catherine Nobeli

In this chapter an attempt will be made to see how the data of a detailed soils map of an area surrounding one ancient site (Nichoria, #100) may be applicable to studying other archaeological sites and for discovering the basic principles of land use which were followed in the past.

Soils are anisotropic natural bodies; that is, their properties change along all three dimensions. These changes, however, are more common and more pronounced along the vertical dimension. Thus, when we observe the *soil profile* we often see that it can be divided into a number of superimposed layers which differ in color, texture, structure, and other macro- and micro-morphological properties. The causes of the vertical differentiation of the soil profiles can be divided into two broad groups: geological and pedogenetic.

The geological differentiation is inherited from the parent material on which the soil is formed. Common examples are stratification in the rock and in alluvial deposits on which the soil profile is developed.

The pedogenetic differentiation of the soil profile is the result of the soil-forming factors which alter the parent material. The accepted independent soil-forming factors are five: climate, topography, parent rock, organisms, and time (Jenny 1941, p. 2). These factors act on a parent material, each at its own rate, to form a sequence of layers which constitute and specify the soil profile. These layers are called soil horizons. The number, the properties, and the relative position of the horizons in the profile are characteristic of its history and can to a certain extent reveal the climatic, vegetational, and anthropic conditions which existed in the past.

It is possible, therefore, for an archaeologist working with a soil scientist to obtain data and derive worthwhile conclusions on a particular problem by studying the morphology of soil profiles.

The Major Soil Groups in Southwest Peloponnese

It appears that in southwest Peloponnese soil genesis has been proceeding for a long period toward the development of a characteristic profile. The profile is of an Alfisol soil, characterized by surface horizons which have lost clay and iron oxides and by underlying horizons which show an accumulation of these constituents. The reaction of the soil is slightly to moderately acid. It is the experience of the senior author that this soil profile develops in areas under oak forest and under climatic conditions similar to those existing today. Since buried profiles show genetic trends and morphology similar to more recent overlying profiles, it is logical to assume that two soil-forming factors, climate and organisms (vegetation), have not changed notably during the last few thousand years. This conclusion is also supported by Wright's (1968) findings. The influence of the other three soil-forming factors causes variations in the Alfisol profile, which can thus be differentiated in a series of lower categories with characteristic profiles. A sketch of the Alfisol profile and the geomorphological relationships of the soils is shown in Figure 10-1.

On the basis of their morphological characteristics and on their modes of genesis, the soils of southwest Peloponnese can be classified in the following four broad groups.

a. Residual Soils Formed on Consolidated Rocks (Alfisols). The typical form of these soils is red Mediterranean soil which used to be called terra rossa and which is developed on limestone or limestone conglomerate. The undisturbed profile consists of: a black surface horizon, designated as A1, rich in organic matter; an underlying yellowish-red A2 horizon, which has lost some clay and iron oxide; a dark red Bt horizon which is located below the A2 and is enriched by clay and iron oxides; and a C horizon which is transitional between the Bt and the bedrock. The soils of this group are rich in clay and are relatively shallow as compared with the soils of the other groups. The carbonates have been removed from the upper three horizons through the dissolving action of rainwater. Because of the sloping terrain, the soils of this group have gone through periods of severe erosion during which they have lost their A1, A2, and part of the Bt horizons. The present land surface, therefore, can be generally said to consist of the relics of the Bt horizon, the C horizon, and the exposed bedrock.

b. Residual Soils Formed on Tertiary Marine Marl, Clay, Sand, and Silt (Alfisols). The profile of these soils is similar to that of the previous group, although the color of the soil is not so bright. Yellowish-red colors predominate in the profiles. Another differentiating characteristic of these profiles is that carbonates, leached from the upper sections of the profiles through soil-forming processes, have accumulated in the form of concretions between the Bt horizon and the unaltered marine deposits. Depending on the slope and the density of the vegetational cover, these soils have also suffered various degrees of erosion. On sloping terrain, from which the vegetational cover has been removed by man's activities, erosion has removed the greater part of the profile. Wherever this happened, carbonate concretions and the unaltered marine deposit are exposed on the surface.

c. Older alluvial soils (Alfisols). The parent material of these soils originated from residual soils developed on the slopes of overlying hills and mountains. It consists of constituents which survived one or more cycles of soil genesis and then were carried by rainwater and deposited on the Tertiary marine deposits. There, under the cover of oak forests, a new soil profile developed similar to the profiles of the soils of group *a*. These soils, however, are characterized by cherty gravel and sand, and they lack easily weathered minerals. Their colors range from the bright red, characteristic of well-drained sites, to yellowish-brown, characteristic of imperfectly drained sites. In the latter case the profiles contain mottles and concretions of iron and manganese oxides. Polygenetic profiles are common in these soils. In other words, the alluvial materials were deposited at various times, and between each deposition enough time elapsed for soil horizons to develop. Thus, the soils show a vertical sequence of pedogenetic profiles. It is assumed that the uppermost profile has developed at least since the Late Bronze Age. Such polygenetic profiles can be seen in road cuts throughout southwest Peloponnese. At a natural cut made by erosion in the vicinity of Rizomilo one can distinguish a sequence of three or four profiles with their characteristic horizons. Of these profiles the upper and most recent one has better developed and more easily distinguished horizons, which indicates that the underlying profiles remained on the surface of the land for a shorter time than the last one. The morphological analogies, however, indicate that all profiles have been formed under similar climatic, vegetational, topographic, and geological conditions. The soils of this group are usually located on flat or gently sloping terraces. The similarity of characteristics among soils on older and on more recent terraces also indicates the continuity of the climatic and vegetational conditions.

d. Recent Alluvial Soils. These soils are found in the contemporary valleys and in the flood plains of the various streams. They seldom exceed an elevation of 50 m above sea level. In most cases the 20-m contour line separates the recent from the old alluvial soil in the coastal plains of Peloponnese. The soils of this group consist of materials eroded from the soils of all the other groups. The deposition of these materials may be considered a continuous process because the time interval between two successive depositions is so short (in terms of pedogenesis) that it does not allow the differentiation of the profile into genetic horizons. The textural variations common in these soil profiles are due to differences in the texture of the deposits. The soils of this group are agriculturally the most productive since they have not suffered any significant leaching of constituents. They have higher amounts of organic matter than the other groups, and they have structures which create favorable conditions for the penetration of the air, the balance of water, and the development of the root systems of plants. Somewhat less than 20 percent of the recent alluvial soils of southwest Peloponnese are poorly drained and severely limited for agricultural use. An important advantage of the soils of this group is their proximity to streams so they usually can be irrigated more easily than the soils of the other groups.

Soil Morphology: A Source of Information

Geology and stratigraphy have been used by archaeologists as a source of important information. Wheeler (1962), Pyddoke (1961), and Butzer (1964) discuss in detail the principles and the application of geology in archaeology. This chapter emphasizes soil as a source of information. The morphology of soil is very sensitive to environmental conditions and above all to human activities. Thus, in certain cases soil science may contribute

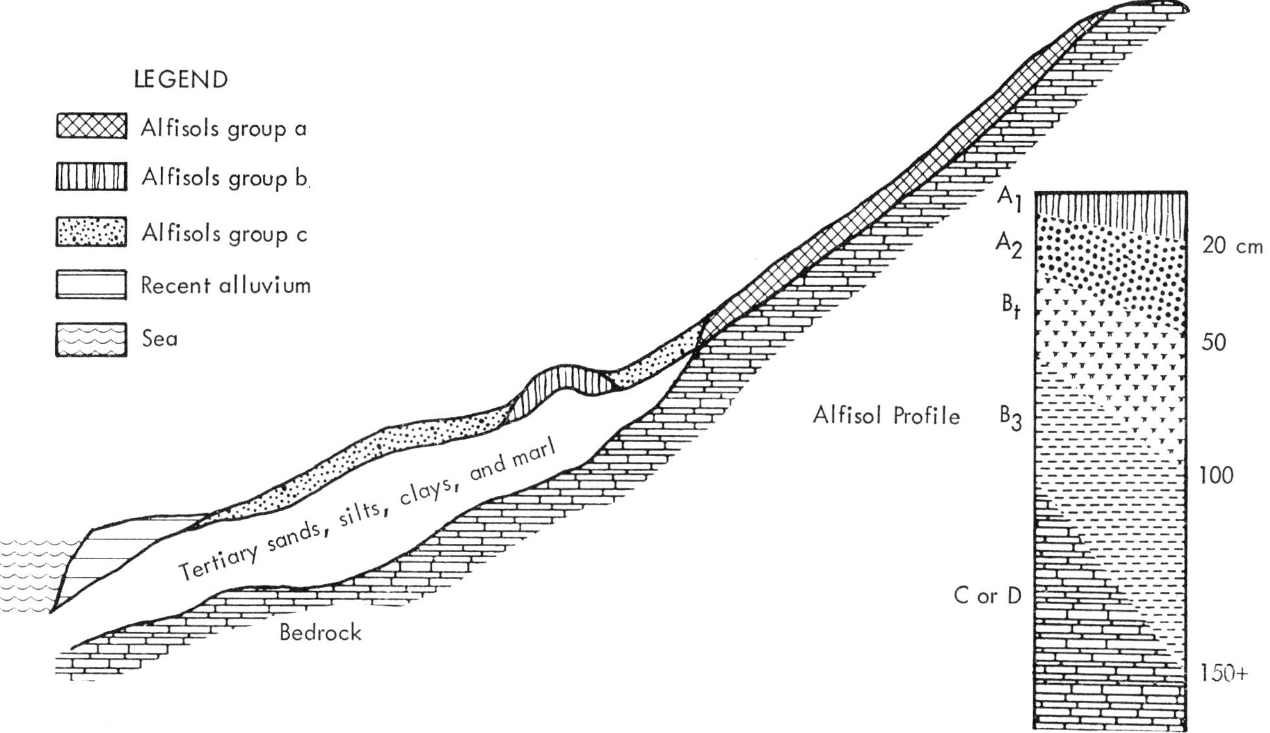

Figure 10-1. Geomorphological characteristics and profile configuration of the soils in western Peloponnese

more to the solution of archaeological problems than geological stratigraphy.

In the preceding paragraphs it was pointed out that the soils of groups *a*, *b*, and *c*, have, through pedogenetic processes, formed profiles which contain characteristic horizons. The vertical sequence of the horizons is shown in Figure 10-1. Any serious disturbance inflicted upon a soil by natural events or by man's actions will cause a visible change in the sequence and in the number of the distinguishable horizons in the profile. Thus, it is possible by studying the present morphology of the soils on a site and by comparing it with the morphology of undisturbed profiles, to obtain information about past events which have prevented the formation or caused the partial or complete destruction of the normal profiles in a particular area. The most common disturbances are the following: erosion, deposition, excavation and filling, ploughing. Erosion removes the upper horizons and in severe cases exposes the parent material or the underlying bedrock. Deposition can be either natural or result from human activity. A new deposit on the surface of the soil can be recognized in the field by an unusually thick A1 horizon, by a surface texture which cannot be related to pedogenetic processes, by the presence of carbonates on the surface of the soil which are missing from the underlying horizons, and by a color which is not expected on the surface of the particular profile in question.

As a result of ploughing, the upper horizons of the profiles are mixed and cannot be distinguished from one another. Excavation, earth filling, and other earthworks which are common in residential areas cause distinctive disturbances in soil profiles. Horizons are mixed and turned over, and their relative positions in the profiles are altered. Frequent disturbances inflicted upon the soil by man in residential areas prevent the profiles from developing pedogenetic horizons. Instead they acquire morphological and chemical characteristics which reflect man's influence on the environment.

A few examples may clarify the above statements. A detailed soils map of the Rizomilo area shows four subareas on Nichoria ridge (1, 3, 5, 7 in Fig. 10-2 and Pocket Map 10-19) where the soil shows weak development of pedogenetic horizons and contains an unusual amount of carbonates. This soil covers about 2.9 of the 5.5 ha. Surrounding these subareas are soils which have lost their carbonates and have formed profiles that belong to group *b*. The first conclusion we can reach is that the carbonate-containing soil was disturbed. This disturbance may have been erosion which removed all the pedogenetic horizons and exposed the underlying calcareous

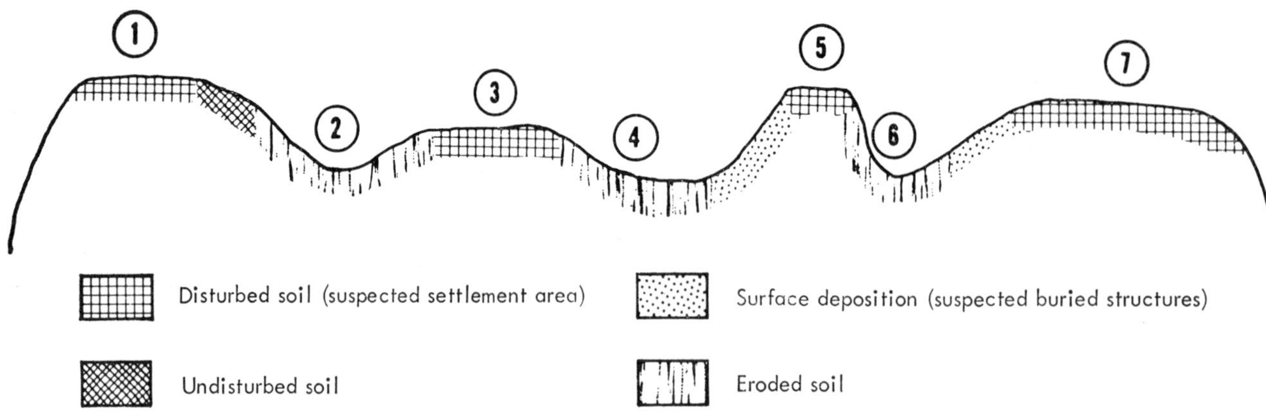

Figure 10-2. A sketch of the suggested ancient residential areas of Nichoria (see Pocket Map 10-19 for location of 1–7)

marine deposit. Or, there may have been a natural deposition of calcareous materials which buried the original profiles and pedogenetic horizons. However, the geomorphology (Fig. 10-1) excludes both possibilities. The surrounding undisturbed soils have steeper slopes than the disturbed soil and yet have not been eroded. On the slight slope of the disturbed soil one would not expect erosion to remove all the pedogenetic horizons. Natural deposition could not have taken place because these subareas are higher than the surrounding eroded areas. All of these arguments lead to the conclusion that the soil has been prevented from developing pedogenetic horizons by intensive human activity. The disturbed subareas, therefore, could have been residential. Indeed these subareas have been selected by the archaeologists for excavation. The 1969 and 1970 excavations at Nichoria revealed buried structures in areas 1, 3, 4, and 7 (see Fig. 10-2). The soils map also shows deposition of soil materials on the western and northwestern slopes around the suspected residential area (Pocket Map 10-19). The thickness of the deposition usually ranges between 0.6 and 2 m. It is therefore possible that ruins may have been buried in this area.

Another conclusion which can be derived from the soils map is that the undisturbed or slightly disturbed soils which surround the residential areas were developed under and protected by forest, most probably oak trees. It seems that the ancient residents did not destroy the forest which grew in the immediate vicinity of their settlement.

Ancient burials that were covered with soil should show polygenetic profiles at the foot of the artificial mounds. This criterion may be used to indicate whether a small mound is a natural geomorphologic feature or a hidden tomb.

In all the areas where ancient foundations were uncovered during the 1969 and 1970 excavations the soil consists of mixed material, rich in coarse sand, on which a thick dark-colored A1 horizon has developed. Generally, the soil shows minimal horizon development. The most pronounced feature is the decrease of the carbonate content in the surface layer and its accumulation in deeper parts of the profile. The development of the thick A1 horizon must be attributed to the growth of grasses, which are favored in abandoned residential areas. The weak profile development indicates that either the structures were not buried until relatively recent times or that the soil has experienced continuous disturbances.

Deeper excavations and more detailed study of the soils during the summer of 1971 have revealed strong soil profile development in some places within the residential area of the site. This development took place in the last 3,000 years. A little weaker soil development was also observed on materials which were used to cover a tomb. The morphology of these soils indicates that the deposits, which have covered structures in these two places, had not been disturbed. These two profiles are of great interest, and their detailed study has been initiated.

It must be pointed out that the general features and the morphology of the soils associated with abandoned residential areas are not always the same. Each depends on its whole environmental history. Thus, accurate predictions require experienced and detailed observations on the trends of soil genesis in each particular area of interest.

Some Thoughts on the Land Use Patterns in the Past

It was mentioned in previous sections of this chapter that the older alluvial soils have developed pedogenetic horizons, characteristic of the Alfisols, under forest vegetation and especially under oak trees.

It was also pointed out that the development and preservation of soil horizons require undisturbed conditions. It is logical to assume that the forest extended at least over all the soils which today show horizons of the Alfisol profile. Soils from which these horizons are missing may have lost them through erosion after the destruction of the forest or they may have been prevented from developing by natural or human action. It is therefore possible to obtain information about the use of land in the past for settlement or agriculture.

Again the Nichoria area provides examples. The morphological data detailed on Pocket Map 10-19, made on the basis of more than 500 field borings and observations, show that most of the hilly land on either side of the streams was forested. The bottomland along the Karia and Velika streams consists of alluvial soils with no horizon differentiation and no sign of a pre-existing undisturbed stable forest vegetation. It seems, therefore, that settlers on the site from the Bronze Age up to the eighteenth century A.D. practiced some fashion of conservation of land and of natural resources; they avoided the destruction of the forest and the cultivation of the less productive land around their settlement. Instead they farmed the alluvial soils of the bottomland even though this land was farther from their settlement than the hilly land. In using the bottomland for farming they selected the most productive soils in the area. The fertility of these soils was kept at relatively favorable levels by the deposition of new alluvium, which was and still is added from the streams. The soil structure in the bottomland was also more favorable, contributing to higher productivity. In addition, the presence of the two streams made irrigation possible.

The ancient farmer was probably aware from experience of the low productivity, the dryness during the late spring and summer months, and the erodibility of the hilly land and learned to avoid intensive clearing and farming there.

In the bottomland toward the lower end of the valley and along the coast the drainage of the soils has always been imperfect or poor. The growth of cultivated plants on these perennially wet soils must have been difficult or impossible. On the other hand, the high moisture content and the high fertility of these soils would have made them productive as permanent pasture for big animals and as a source of fodder.

Trenches dug in the bottomland showed that the streams have deposited several strata since prehistoric times. The thickness of these strata is about 1.50 m on the periphery of the bottomland and reaches 3.5 m in the middle. The depositions since the Roman era have a thickness ranging between 0.6 and 1 m. The width of the bottomland was not much different from the present, except at the lower end of the valley where a sloping Alfisol surface, covered by more recent deposits, indicates that the bottomland has become wider. This narrow opening (shown by broken lines in Pocket Map 10-19) may suggest the existence of a silted-up harbor. These speculations are based on the sherds and on the soil morphology observed at various depths. More accurate delineation of the surface of the bottomland at various times will be made on the basis of carbon 14 dating.

The earth material in the suggested harbor area has been deposited continuously and shows no trace of soil development, indicating that much of the deposition may have taken place in the sea. Outside this area the surface deposit has a thickness of 1 to 2 m and does show profile development, indicating a land surface above sea level. The present elevation of the land is about 2 to 2.5 m. Deposition of alluvium since the Bronze Age could account for the present elevation without a relative change in sea level.

The area of bottomland which could be reached within a 45-minute walk from the residential site is estimated at about 3,000 stremmata (300 ha). Under optimum conditions this area could provide food for up to 1,000 inhabitants. However, the lower part was subject to hazards such as flooding and deposition of coarse materials by the shifting streams. Three villages, Rizomilo, Karpofora, and Velika, with a combined population of 951 in 1961 now depend heavily on the productivity of this bottomland.

The gently sloping lands which are located around the ancient residential area on Nichoria were forested and probably were grazed by small animals. Northwest of the residential site there is a gently sloping limestone surface which has moderately eroded soils of group *a*. East of the limestone surface a sandy marine deposit outcrops. This area has well-preserved soils with all the characteristic horizons of the group *b*. Slopes are slightly steeper than the slopes of the limestones but still do not show any significant degree of erosion. This may mean that the area was covered by forest until recently. Protogeometric graves have been discovered in this area. The moderate erosion of the soils in the limestone area indicates some degree of early cultivation after the clearing of the forest. Thus, we could assume that these soils were used for olive groves and/or vineyards. The early settlers seem to have avoided cultivating the dry sandy and erodable soils and preferred the more productive clay loam which formed on the limestone. For the same reason we can assume that vineyards and olive trees were grown on the moderately sloping hills southwest of the residential site where an eroded soil formed on the calcareous and clayey marine silts.

Pocket Map 10-19 is a proposed land-use map for the Nichoria area in the Late Bronze Age. If suggested patterns of land use are dependable, we must admit that the ancient inhabitants had developed a sophisticated system of land appraisal and that they had accumulated considerable knowledge of the soil capability. Similar land-use patterns are found at Aristodhimion (#123). In antiquity the population was not so dense as it is now so the farmer probably had the possibility of selecting only the best land for cultivation. He did not always cultivate the nearest or the most easily accessible, however, but preferred the most productive even if it was a little farther from his village.

Another demonstration of good judgment in land use is the site of classical Megalopolis in Arkadia. The town was built on a gently sloping terrain with well-drained soils which provided solid foundations. In contrast the modern inhabitants have built on flat land. At first glance this has some geographical and planning advantages, but the soil is imperfectly drained and many basements are flooded during the winter. The population of the town frequently complains of poor health because of the wetness of the houses.

The Bronze Age settlers chose the calcareous clay loam and marine silt deposits of the Nichoria acropolis as the ground for their houses. This material provides a stable basis for foundations of buildings, and it is well drained and easy to excavate.

The above arguments support, in the opinion of the authors, the speculation that the ancient people had a surprising amount of practical knowledge of soils and that they instinctively adopted sound land conservation practices.

REFERENCES

Butzer, Karl. 1964. *Environment and Archaeology*. Chicago.

Jenny, H. 1941. *Factors of Soil Formation*. New York.

Pyddoke, Edwards. 1961. *Stratification for the Archaeologist*. Mystic, Conn.

Wheeler, Robert E. M. 1962. *Archaeology from the Earth*. Baltimore.

Wright, H. E., Jr. 1968. "Climatic change in Mycenaean Greece," *Antiquity* 42:123–27.

11
THE AGRICULTURAL ECONOMY

by

Herman J. Van Wersch

Southwest Peloponnese is a land of agricultural plenty. As has been emphasized earlier in this book, it is a favored portion of Greece with an unusually moist climate, good soils, and a comparatively high percentage of level land. The data from pollen cores and the Pylos tablets support the contention that these favorable conditions of the present existed in relatively the same state during the Late Bronze Age.

Agriculture is now the cornerstone of the economy of Messenia, and there is no doubt that it was the basis of the wealth of the kingdom of Pylos. This chapter attempts to shed more light on the ancient economy by supplying information about the present-day rural economy of Messenia. This information may serve in turn as a basis for inferences about the land-use system as well as about the general pattern of subsistence of the Late Bronze Age inhabitants of the region.

Section I reviews the agricultural economy of Messenia in the second half of the 1960's A.D., using information from official statistics and from a sample survey of farms. This section draws heavily on the results of a socioeconomic survey in four representative villages of Messenia carried out in 1966 and 1967 as part of the present writer's doctoral dissertation (Van Wersch 1969). Here and throughout the chapter the absolute figures quoted are taken from official statistical sources, and it should be emphasized that they refer to the province of Messenia only.

The present-day land-use pattern will be described in Section II. This, together with the results of a geomorphological survey, will serve as the point of departure in hypothesizing a generalized land-use pattern that corresponds to the maximum use of the land in the past.

The land-use pattern reveals only part of the agricultural economy. Therefore, in Section III, other important aspects of the rural economy will be considered in order to arrive at some preliminary formulation of the historical potential of Messenia in terms of food grain production and population.

I. The Present-day Agricultural Economy

In the twentieth century A.D. Messenia depends as much on agriculture as its almost exclusive means of subsistence as it appears to have done in the thirteenth century B.C. Obviously, agriculture has changed during the intervening period, notably because of the introduction of new crops, the improvement of farming technology (most of this in the last hundred years), and in general because of the increasing degree of integration of the regional economy into the national and the world economy.

Today Messenia is dependent upon the production, processing, and marketing of agricultural crops. Sheep and goat raising as a specialized enterprise is declining. Fishing is of little consequence, both in terms of income and employment. The agricultural processing industry operates during a small part of the year and therefore provides only seasonal employment, mostly to women.

Land Use and Production. Agricultural statistics for 1961 (NSSG 1963) show the relative importance of major crop categories for the province of Messenia. Food and feed grains – wheat, oats, maize, rice, and barley – accounted for 27.1 percent of the agricultural land. Half of this, however, was lying fallow in the tradition of alternating productive and recovery years. Wheat was by far the most important of the crops in this category. The next largest category of crops in terms of land use was olive trees with 25 percent of the agricultural land. Vine crops — currants, wine grapes, and table grapes — followed in importance with 14.5 percent. Of the land in vines, 75 percent was in currants. Vegetable and fruit crops, including figs, various nut trees, peaches, apricots, citrus, and so forth, took 9.4 percent; fodder crops, notably vetch, clover, alfalfa, and their respective fallow areas, occupied 7.1 percent of the land. The remaining 7.2 percent was in a variety of uses, such as improved pasture and industrial crops like ground nuts, flax, and cotton. In 1961, about 9 percent of the region's farmland was irrigated.

In addition to the 1,276 sq. km of agricultural land described above, the region has 930 sq. km in grazing land and 366 sq. km in forest land. The grazing land is the basis for livestock production, which focuses on sheep and goats. Cattle and work animals are usually kept on the farmland; but sheep, as a rule, are not integrated with crop production in a mixed farming operation. Most of what is statistically classified as forest land is in dense brush vegetation. Solid forest is restricted to small scattered areas in the higher parts of the Taygetos range.

Messenia's main products, in order of decreasing value, are olive oil, vegetable crops (especially potatoes, tomatoes, and watermelons), vine crops (notably currants), tree fruits (citrus and figs), wheat, sheep, and forage crops.

Population. At the time of the latest census (NSSG 1963) the population of the province of Messenia was 211,970, living in an area of 2,872 sq. km. The agricultural population was 147,564 (70 percent of total population) working 1,276 sq. km of farmland (44 percent of total land area).

Most of the population is concentrated in the lowlands and hilly areas; the mountainous parts of the region are sparsely populated. The bulk of the farmers live in villages and commute to their fields, usually dispersed throughout the village territory. In 1961, four representative villages showed an average population of 465, an average size of household of 3.1 persons, and an average age of the head of household of 54 years.

Land Tenure. Average farm size in the study villages was 3.4 ha, and the size distribution of farms was fairly even. Owner-operatorship is the nearly exclusive form of land tenure (91 percent of the farms in the sample). Farm fragmentation is a major problem. The average number of plots per farm was found to be 10.2 and average plot size less than 0.4 ha. Average travel distance between the farmer's home and his fields is about 1.3 kilometers, with often the same distance between the fields belonging to a given farmer. The fragmentation problem is a result of the owner-operatorship system and the practice of equal division of land among heirs, and it is compounded by the small size of most farms. Land changes owners chiefly by inheritance and the related institution of dowry. Sale as a means of disposing of agricultural land is rare, and demand largely exceeds supply. Even those who leave agriculture typically will not sell their land but prefer to rent it out or to give it in usufruct to relatives or other villagers.

Labor. As has been the case throughout history, labor is still the most abundant production factor in agriculture. The agricultural labor force consists mainly of family labor. Most farms employ seasonal labor during periods of peak activity, notably at harvest time. This seasonal labor is now drawn chiefly from local farmers and their dependents who feel a need to supplement the income from their own operation, which is frequently less than viable.

Women, both farmers' wives and other female members of the family, form an important part of the farm labor supply. They do most types of farm work, except plowing and heavy transport, although even this and notably the latter can be observed occasionally. Children too are sometimes seen doing light fieldwork. It appears, however, from cross-sectional observations and from interviews that both women and children are now less involved in farm work than in the past.

The number of adult family workers per hectare of cultivated land was 0.77 on the average for the villages in the study. The labor intensity of farming in Messenia is characterized by the large number of days worked per hectare of cultivated land — 109 days on the average, with a high of 170 days per hectare in the study village located in the Pamisos Plain.

Capital. The major capital items on most farms are trees and livestock. Other major items, found on a minority of farms, are irrigation equipment (wells, motor pumps, irrigation pipe), spraying pumps, tractors (mostly of the roto-cultivator type), trailers, and plastic greenhouses. Farm capital also includes a host of small items such as carts, plows, hoes, hand sprayers, and metal drums for olive oil storage.

The average number of trees per farm in 1961 was 172, of which 135 were olive trees, 28 other nonirrigated fruit trees, and 9 citrus trees. The average area in vine crops was 0.54 ha consisting of 0.16 ha in wine and in table grapes, and 0.38 ha in currants.

The accompanying tabulation lists the average number of animals per farm in 1961 (NSSG 1963). From it one immediately reads that livestock production is not a very important enterprise. In fact, interviews led to the conclusion that, in three of the four study villages, the number of animals had decreased dramatically since the early part of this century when grazing lands were more abundant, presumably because of the availability of periodically flooded valley bottoms and coastal plains that subsequently were reclaimed for crop production.

Cattle	0.4
Sheep	2.9
Goats	2.3
Hogs	0.5
Chickens	8.5
Horses	0.3
Mules	0.1
Donkeys	0.5
Beehives	0.4

In addition to the above capital items which belong to the category of investment capital, Messenian farmers use increasing amounts of working capital in the form of chemical fertilizers (taking over from organic manure, which has become scarce), herbicides, and a variety of pesticides.

Yields. Great difficulties were encountered in the collection of accurate and representative yield data. Farmers do not keep records and, moreover, are very reluctant to divulge any information that could possibly be used to extract higher taxes from them. Consequently, even present yield figures are only approximate. The accompanying tabulation summarizes these figures for selected crops (statistics for 1961–63 are from NSSG 1964; my estimate of the range of reasonable maximum and minimum values).

	1961–63	*Range*
Wheat (kg/ha)	1,140	900–2,500
Barley (kg/ha)	940	750–1,500
Olives (kg of oil/tree)	3.0	2.5–15
Currants (kg/ha)	2,170	2,500–4,000
Wine grapes (kg/ha)	3,900	3,500–7,000

Given the important fluctuations in yields between good and poor crop years, a range of yields is probably more meaningful than an average yield based on the crop results of only a few years; therefore, the second column gives my estimate of the range.

Consumption and Trade. Some information is available on per capita consumption levels of major food items. United Nations Relief and Rehabilitation Administration (UNRRA) figures for 1947, undoubtedly low as compared with the present situation because of shortages owing to the war, indicate an average annual intake per person of 175 kilograms of grain, 15 kg of olive oil, 39 kg of wine, 15 kg of potatoes, 16 kg of meat, and 40 kg of milk. My fieldwork in 1967 showed considerably higher figures. The average consumption levels of four villages representative of the region were 150–200 kg of wheat flour, 55–75 kg of olive oil, and approximately 60 kg of wine. These data represent average per capita consumption based on families of four to five persons. Bread, olive oil, wine, and cheese are the staples of the diet (see Ch. 4).

Food grains and fodder crops are almost exclusively for consumption on the farm. Currants are on the other end of the continuum, being nearly entirely destined for sale. Wine grapes on most farms are for subsistence only; in an exceptionally good year the grape surplus will be sold. Fruits and vegetables, if grown on a commercial scale – that is, outside the garden plot surrounding the home – are all marketed. Olive oil sales depend very much on the production level in a given year. In any case, domestic needs are covered first, and the remainder is sold. An average figure on the basis of several years would be a marketing percentage of 50–70, depending on the importance of olives in the village.

It is of interest to note that, despite the low intake of animal proteins and the rural population's great taste for meat, nearly all calves and lambs are marketed. The main reason is the lack of facilities to store meat and to spread the consumption of a slaughtered animal over a period of time. Exceptions to this rule are important holidays or major family events. Otherwise, farmers will buy small quantities of meat from the local butcher, who kills an animal or two on the weekend, or they will bring it from town.

The region's main export products are, in order of decreasing importance: olive oil, vegetables and fruits, dried currants, dried figs, and table olives. Dried currants and figs for overseas and European destinations are shipped through the port of Kalamata. Vegetables and fruits are moved by truck, mostly to the Athens wholesale market. Grains, wine grapes, the biggest share of most tree crops, and livestock are largely consumed within the region, much of them locally (see Pls. 12-2, 13-1, 13-2, 13-3, 13-4).

II. The Regional Land-Use Pattern Today and in Retrospect

Taking the existing geomorphology as a point of departure, then considering how it could have changed over time, and finally, interpreting landforms in terms of land use by referring to present-day land use, a generalized land-use pattern will be derived that represents the *upper limit* of agricultural possibilities available to the inhabitants in previous eras, and particularly in the Late Bronze Age.

As the basis for discussion of the present-day regional

land-use patterns, I shall refer to a land-use map constructed by interpretation of aerial photographs with the aid of field checks. The aerial photo coverage is on a scale of 1:30,000 flown by the Royal Hellenic Air Force during July and August of 1960 at 15,000 feet. The map reproduced as Pocket Map 11-20 is highly generalized. Land-use classification at the map scale is based on the leading use only, namely, the use that occupies at least 50 percent of the land in a contiguous area of a minimum size. The seven basic land-use categories distinguished on this map are as follows:

Dry crop land. This category includes all nonirrigated cultivated land and fallow land that shows evidence of recent cultivation (i.e., cultivated less than five years ago). Although all farms have part of their land in this use category, it is predominant in the western half of Messenia and in the eparchy Olympia. It is also important on the slopes of the Taygetos range south of Kardhamili.

Irrigated crop land. This land shows a marked concentration in the lowlands. This is not to say that elsewhere irrigation is not practiced on a limited scale, but as a predominant land-use category irrigation farming can only be carried on in parts of the Pamisos and Steniklarian plains, along the coast at the head of the Messenian Gulf, on the north side of the Bay of Navarino, at the mouth of the Nedha River, and in a long but narrow band along the Alpheios River.

Orchards. These consist largely of olive groves but include also significant fig plantations in the Pamisos Plain and irrigated citrus groves mostly concentrated in the vicinity of Kalamata. Olive groves are predominant in both the Pamisos and Steniklarian plains, along the eastern and most of the western shores of the Messenian Gulf, in the hilly lands and valleys surrounding the Kyparissia Mountains, in the Alpheios Valley, and in a large area at the base of the Messenian peninsula between the Bay of Navarino and the Messenian Gulf.

Vineyards. Areas specializing in vine crops are small but numerous. The following pattern can be detected: a band along the western edge of the Pamisos Plain, in the Alpheios Valley, and a concentration in the central Steniklarian Plain, the coastal zone between Longa and Koroni on the west side of the Messenian Gulf, the hinterland of Gargaliani, and a cluster of small areas along the coast north of the Bay of Navarino, along the east-west highway between Kalamata and Pylos on the Messenian peninsula, and in the southwestern corner of the peninsula.

Light brush vegetation. Light brush land – land with a light maquis or garigue that is suitable for grazing, especially of sheep – is mainly found in the southern part of the Taygetos range, over most of the Tetrayi and Minthis mountains, and on the hills between the Kyparissia Mountains and the Steniklarian Plain. Other areas of this kind are located in the Messenian peninsula and in a band running parallel to the Triphylian coast.

Dense brush vegetation. This is land with a heavy maquis that cannot be used for grazing and whose only value is in its role as a source of fuel. This land covers all of the Kyparissia Mountains and the bulk of the Taygetos range.

Forest land. This category is relatively unimportant and restricted to some of the higher parts of the Taygetos Mountains. Forests are managed by the state, but permits are given to local residents for limited cutting and grazing.

Based on his geomorphological studies in southwest Peloponnese, Loy (1970, pp. 142–43) argued that the only historically significant changes in the land took place in the major valleys. He found no appreciable change in bedrock geology nor acceptable evidence of a significant difference in climate during the past four thousand years. If these findings are correct, then the available water supply cannot have changed appreciably. Erosion has transferred some ten to fifteen centimeters of upland soil to the valley bottoms since the Late Bronze Age, but this process has been going on for several millennia at approximately the same rate.

Inferences made about the changes in vegetation cover of the area are less certain. The speculation was made by Loy (1970, p. 90) that as early as prehistoric times most of the alluvial slopes were cleared for agricultural use. The conclusion drawn from this argument is that, without enough information to be certain about details, the broad pattern that can be distinguished depicts a landscape, and by inference a land-use pattern, that is similar to the present. The most significant changes would be in the major lowland areas owing to alluviation over time and reclamation in recent history. These major areas of change are the Pamisos Valley, the bottomland of the Steniklarian Plain, and the lagoons along the west coast.

Deriving information from his geomorphological map, Loy grouped the thirteen basic geomorphic classes and arrived at five categories of relative land quality. This classification will be described briefly, with the classes ranked in order of decreasing land quality:

Class I land refers to the alluvial slopes and is described as the best agricultural land because of its high fertility, favorable natural drainage, gently sloping topography, and frequent opportunities for irrigation.

Class II land is identical with the Pliocene terrace areas of Loy's geomorphological map. This land is generally fertile and has terraceable slopes and flat valleys which in some cases can be irrigated.

Class III land includes three geomorphic categories,

hill lands, kampos, and mountain shoulders, which are characterized by moderately fertile, shallow, noncalcareous soils.

Class IV land includes another three geomorphic units, dissected kampos, rocky ridges, and ridges. Soils are rocky and rough.

Class V would have constituted the poorest agricultural potential. It consists of extremes in landforms: scarps and gorges, mountain land, beach sands, marshes, lagoons, and poorly drained alluvial and coastal plains. These areas are considered to have been too steep or too wet for farming in the Late Bronze Age.

On the basis of our knowledge about the present-day land-use pattern and with the aid of Loy's classification of relative land quality, an attempt may be made to infer a broad potential land-use pattern for the target period. This hypothesis rests heavily on the assumption that the relative importance of major land-use categories is approximately the same in the two periods. This assumption is supported by circumstantial evidence for the predominant importance of the environmental determinants of land use (Van Wersch 1969). No significant difference was found in various land-use characteristics between Messenia and the Cape Bon region in northeastern Tunisia despite substantial differences in socioeconomic structure between these regions. From this one may argue that, a fortiori, natural conditions were the major determinants of land use in prehistoric times.

Supporting evidence for the similarity of prehistoric and present-day major land use is provided by the descriptions of the diet during various periods preceding and during the Bronze Age. Hansen (1933, p. 47), Wace and Thompson (1912, pp. 53, 149, 262), Blegen (1937, p. 24), and Childe (1939, p. 57) describe the Neolithic diet, which included cereals (wheat and barley), meat from domestic animals and game, fish, pulses and tree crops such as figs, nuts, and pears. Mylonas (1934, p. 266), writing about the Early Helladic period, mentions grapes, currants, and olives in addition to the above. Most of these crops and some others, notably spices and flax, are also mentioned in the Pylos tablets. Although all items encountered in the tablets are clearly identified with the Mycenaean economy, our failure to recognize or the absence of other items from the tablets does not mean that they did not exist.

Jardé (1925) and Roebuck (1945), on the other hand, assume that the economy of classical Messenia depended almost entirely on grain and animal production. It could be argued that the two periods were sufficiently different to warrant a difference in emphasis in their respective land-use patterns. The Late Bronze Age might be generally considered a period of political stability, whereas the classical period in Messenia was characterized by a succession of threats and invasions. According to Roebuck (1941, *passim*), none of these raids was of disastrous dimensions, but the prevailing insecurity would have been bound to influence farmers' production decisions so as to minimize possible loss. Furthermore, interrupted or uncertain trade relationships may have forced the economy to become self-sufficient in its foremost staple, cereals, and to cut back its production of export crops. We have also to take into account the long period when Messenian agriculture was under a large measure of Spartan control (see Ch. 6).

Nevertheless, it is likely that Messenia in the Late Bronze Age was self-supporting in cereals because of the suitability of much of the cultivable land for grain crops and because of the strategic importance of controlling the production of what was undoubtedly the crucial staple crop. Even in today's world with widespread trade relationships, few countries are willing to depend for their strategic food supplies on other nations if they can produce them at home. Therefore, cereals probably were a more important crop in Mycenaean times than they are at present. Tree crops, and especially olives, were probably less important in the Mycenaean period; and part of Loy's class I and class II land that is now in olives might have been in grain crops at the time. One important field crop in Mycenaean days was flax, presumably used as a raw material in textile manufacturing. The Pylos tablets contain frequent references to flax, and linen textiles may have been a major export product of the Mycenaean world (McDonald 1967, p. 396). Flax now occupies only a tiny fraction of Messenia's agricultural land, but it is interesting to note that Messenia is the largest flax-producing region in Greece, with 55 percent of the national acreage in 1961.

The presence of domesticated animals such as horses, cattle, sheep, goats and pigs is well documented. Blegen (1937) and Childe (1939) accept the existence of all these species except horses during the Neolithic period, Angel (1946) during the Late Helladic (horses included), and Roebuck (1945) during the classical period. Seymour (1908) assumes that during LHIII the plow was common in Messenian agriculture, thus implying the use of draft animals, probably oxen. Most likely, these animals grazed on the natural pasture, range lands, stubble fields, and the extensive fallow lands. The floodplains and coastal lowlands must have served as grazing grounds for large animals, and during the dry season also for sheep. The steep and rocky uplands would be reserved for sheep and goats. Some of the natural pasture may have been cut to supply green fodder and hay. In case of crop failure, grains may have been cut early for feed, as is the practice today; and pigs may have been fed acorns from rather extensive oak forests (see Chs. 5, 10, 16). In view of the larger area in grazing land, especially in the lowlands and on grain fallow, the population of domesticated animals may well have been greater in the Mycenaean era than it is today.

From such hints and inferences emerges the generalized *potential* land-use pattern of Messenia that is presented in Pocket Map 11-21. Six categories are distinguished, following closely Loy's relative land quality classification. The latter are indicated in parentheses.

Our category I (Loy's land quality class I) was the best agricultural land. Vine crops probably competed with high-yielding wheat and other field crops (including flax) that require fertile soils and/or irrigation. Most garden crops were probably grown on this land, as well as some tree crops.

Category II (land quality class II) was probably dominated by tree and vine crops, with field crops in second position. Most of the expansion of olive production discussed by Wright (Ch. 12) may have taken place on these lands, at the expense of field crops.

Category III (land quality class III) comprised the largest area of agricultural land. It was probably dominated by wheat and barley, with olive and vine crops taking the scarce relatively deep soils in this class. The extensive fallow lands and stubble fields constituted an important proportion of the grazing resources.

Category IV (land quality class IV) contained the marginal cropland to which barley is best adapted. Wheat could also be grown, but yields would probably be lower and fallow periods longer than those of barley, owing to the poor quality of the land. Consequently, grazing was important both on the fallow lands and on the portion of this land category that had a natural vegetation cover.

Category V (part of land quality class V) consisted entirely of lowlands. These were unfit for cultivation because of the presumed inability of the ancient farmers to control permanent or seasonal flooding or due to the inherent infertility of the land, as in the case of sand beaches. Much of this land was used for grazing and the abundant grass cover of the wetlands made them quite suitable for large animals such as horses and cattle. It is also likely that this land supplied cut green fodder and hay for supplemental feeding to draft animals and in drought periods.

Category VI (part of land quality class V) constituted the poorest land that was covered with more or less dense shrub and forest. Economic uses may have included cutting of timber; gathering of fuel, feed (acorns), and food (honey, etc.); and hunting (deer and wild boar).

Table 11-1. Frequency Distribution of Habitation Sites by Major Mycenaean Land-Use Categories

Category	EH Sites		MH Sites		LH Sites		Geometric Sites		Archaic Sites	
	No.	%	No.	%	No.	%	No.	%	No.	%
I	7	35	10	20	29	21	2	15	6	20
II	7	35	12	24	34	25	6	46	5	17
III	6	30	19	38	53	39	5	38	17	57
IV			7	14	15	11				
V			2	4	2	1			1	3
VI					4	3			1	3
Total	20	100[a]	50	100[a]	137	100[a]	13	100[a]	30	100[a]

[a] Owing to rounding error, percentage totals may not add up to 100.

The absolute and relative importance of each of the six major land-use categories in the Late Bronze Age is indicated in the accompanying tabulation. It should be emphasized again that the areal figures represent land *potentially* available and in no sense a total acreage that we claim was actually used.

	Area (ha)	*Percentage*
I	34,000	9
II	45,750	12
III	133,000	35
IV	32,750	8
V	23,250	6
VI	113,750	30
Total	382,500	100

A comparison of the hypothesized land-use pattern with the distribution of the known habitation sites for different periods is presented in Table 11-1. It appears that land use categories I, II, and III were by far the most frequently chosen location for a habitation site. During the Middle and Late Helladic and again during the Archaic period, category III land seems to have contained the most sites. It is noteworthy that only during the Early Helladic period did category I (i.e., the best agricultural land) have as much as one-third of the known habitation sites. From Middle Helladic through Archaic times it never had more than one-fifth, which may suggest some pressure on the best land.

Nevertheless, if area in each land-use category is used as a weight, it appears that category I land had the highest density of habitation sites throughout the Bronze Age (Table 11-2), category II the second highest, and category III the next highest. From this one may conclude that, though the preferred location of a Mycenaean habitation site was on the best agricultural land, most were actually located on second- and third-quality land. Among the possible explanations for the choice of a location outside category I land are the imperative need for adequate drinking water, a reasonably defensible position, and other advantageous location factors such as control of an important crossroads.

Table 11-2. Density of Habitation Sites by Major Land-Use Category[a]

Category	EH	MH	LH	Geometric	Archaic
I	2.1	2.9	8.5	0.6	1.8
II	1.5	2.6	7.4	1.3	1.1
III	0.4	1.4	4.0	0.4	1.3
IV		2.1	4.6		
V		0.9	0.9		0.4
VI			0.3		<0.1

[a] In number of sites per 100 sq. km.

On the basis of the potential historical land-use pattern and with the aid of the description of the present-day rural economy (see also Ch. 4), an attempt will be made in this section to develop a few quantitative dimensions of an agricultural economy that may characterize Messenia in the Late Bronze Age. The reader should bear in mind, however, that because of the dearth of relevant data the following reconstruction will be highly speculative.

It has been argued above that grains on the whole, but especially barley, were more important in the Late Bronze Age than they are today. Tree and vine crops were probably less important. Modern history shows a very substantial increase in trees and vines since the late nineteenth century, chiefly in response to an increasing outside demand, which in turn was a function of the emergence of modern means of transportation and communication. Currants, figs, and olive oil were the commodities most involved in this development. Another factor that no doubt encouraged a greater emphasis on tree and vine crops was the establishment of peace and security at the end of the last century. The importance of these two factors for the evolution of the regional economy cannot be better illustrated than by the temporary effect of World War II upon the agricultural economy of Messenia. With foreign markets for its products closed and the state of war and the occupation forces constituting important instability factors, the regional economy turned to the conversion of vineyards and orchards into wheat land. At present, however, Messenia is again a net importer of grain.

Two alternative assumptions will be hazarded regarding the importance of cereals in the historical land-use pattern (Table 11-3). One assumption involves a high proportion of the cultivated land in grain crops (40 percent, or 80 percent including fallow grain land); the other posits a situation where only 30 percent of the cultivated land would be in grain crops (or 60 percent when fallow grain land is included).

As to the relative importance of wheat and barley, one can safely assume that barley was much more important in the Late Bronze Age than it is today. It was apparently used for human consumption, since it appears in the Pylos tablets as a regular ration distributed to workers (Ch. 7). The present-day ratio of wheat to barley as total quantity produced is approximately 15 : 1, but nowadays barley is almost exclusively grown for green fodder. In classical antiquity this ratio was inverted, and barley was the principal food grain (Jardé 1925, p. 124). For the purpose of quantifying historical cereals production, it will be assumed that wheat production was restricted to the best lands (categories I and II) and that

Table 11-3. Wheat and Barley Production Areas under Two Assumptions about the Importance of Cereals

Categories and Area (in Ha)	Arable Land		High Cereals Assumptions		Wheat (Ha)	Barley (Ha)	Low Cereals Assumptions		Wheat (Ha)	Barley (Ha)
	Ha	%	Ha[a]	%[b]			Ha[a]	%[b]		
I, 34,000	32,300	95	12,000	37	12,000		6,800	21	6,800	
II, 45,750	41,200	90	8,500	21	8,500		6,900	17	6,900	
III, 132,000	112,200	85	52,800	47		52,800	39,600	35		39,600
IV, 32,750	16,400	50	8,200	50		8,200	6,600	40		6,600
V, 23,250										
VI, 113,750										
Total, 382,500	202,100	53	81,500	40	20,500	61,000	59,900	30	13,700	46,200

[a] Land in cereal crops each year, excluding fallow land.
[b] Percentage of arable land.

barley was grown elsewhere, thus arriving at a ratio of barley to wheat land of about 3 : 1 (Table 11-3).

In making the above assumptions about the importance of cereals in the historical land-use pattern, fallow grain land was assumed to take up one-half of the total area devoted to grain crops. This ratio is the one found today around the Mediterranean wherever the normal biennial wheat-fallow rotation is used. This practice strikes a balance between the limited productive capacity of the land owing to rather poor soils and low, irregularly distributed rainfall on the one hand, and crop yields sufficient to sustain a population that throughout history – until a few decades ago – had probably remained fairly stable.

One may also speculate on irrigation farming in historical perspective. One would expect that the Mycenaeans had the know-how to build irrigation systems. The design and construction of the numerous tholos tombs testifies to the high level of their architectural skill. Seymour (1908) also attributes irrigation technology to Late Bronze Age farmers. It does not seem likely, however, that the irrigated area included the valley bottoms that were subject to flooding. Irrigation was presumably restricted to areas that could be watered from springs, wells, and some small streams that did not cause major flood problems. There are no indications about specific irrigation crops. This suggests supplemental irrigation of crops that can also be grown in rainfed agriculture. A few irrigations may have been given during the dry summer months to vine crops and summer or fall vegetables. Another good possibility is the occasional irrigation of orchards interplanted with annual crops to ensure good yields of both crops. A comparison of the distributions of present water resources and Late Bronze Age habitation sites (Pocket Maps 3-6 and 8-14) results in a fair correlation. About forty of the known sites are on or near a spring or small river irrigation system now in use.

III. Messenia's Agricultural Potential in Historical Perspective: Some Speculations

In the preceding section two estimates of the historical cereal area were presented. With the aid of wheat and barley yields, also assumed, a potential cereals production estimate will be hazarded.

Jardé (1925, p. 60) gives yield estimates for cereals in antiquity of 8–12 hectoliters of wheat and 16–20 hectoliters of barley per hectare. If the averages of these ranges are converted into the more common yield expression, kilograms per hectare, one obtains: 772 kg of wheat per hectare and 1,112 kg of barley per hectare. In comparing these figures with today's yields, one notes at once that not barley but wheat has the higher yield. It is known that barley nowadays outyields wheat only in a very poor natural environment – that is, on shallow rocky soil, in high altitudes, or under drought conditions. As alternatives to Jardé's estimates, the lowest average present-day yields are proposed, 900 kg of wheat and 750 kg of barley per hectare.

These are the yields of the marginal grain lands on shallow rocky soils, often on steep slopes, and at higher altitudes. These estimates are conservative considering that the Mycenaeans probably grew a good deal of wheat on land that now yields twice as much in an average year. The productivity of farming methods that are still practical on the marginal grain lands can hardly have changed from that known to the Mycenaeans. What little commercial fertilizer is applied no more than replaces the organic manure which undoubtedly was in much greater supply in the past. Soil preparation is still very superficial; seed from last year's crop is broadcast on the unprepared soil and then the farmer plows it under as well as possible. Plows are still the simple wooden type with reinforced tip, or at best a light iron plow that has a single moldboard.

Table 11-4. Potential Grain Production in Messenia under Historical Production Conditions

Grain Production	Low Cereals Assumption	High Cereals Assumption
Area in wheat (ha)	13,700	20,500
Wheat production		
Yield I[a] (kg)	10,576,000	15,826,000
Yield II[b] (kg)	12,330,000	18,450,000
Area in barley (ha)	46,200	61,000
Barley production		
Yield I[c] (kg)	51,374,000	67,832,000
Yield II[d] (kg)	34,650,000	45,750,000
Total grain production		
Yield I (kg)	83,658,000	61,950,000
Yield II (kg)	64,200,000	46,980,000

[a] Jardé's estimate, 772 kg/ha.
[b] My estimate, 900 kg/ha.
[c] Jardé's estimate, 1,112 kg/ha.
[d] My estimate, 750 kg/ha.

At this point we may venture a set of estimates on *potential* grain production under historical production conditions. The area estimates for both cereals under the high and low grain assumptions are given in Table 11-3. For yields, Jardé's estimates (yield level I) and the alternative yields proposed (yield level II) can be used. The set of production figures is derived in Table 11-4. Production estimates vary between a high of 84,000 and a low of 47,000 metric tons.

To arrive at the quantity of grain available for consumption, an allowance needs to be made for grain put aside for seed. Currently, 1 kg of seed yields 13 kg of grain.* This rate of return refers to the major wheat-producing area, the plains where modern farming techniques are being used and where fertile soils guarantee larger yields. In this light, the lower rates of return for antiquity of 7 to 1 or 6 to 1 proposed respectively by Ventris and Chadwick (1956) and by Roebuck (1945) become acceptable. Adopting, therefore, a 15 percent seed reserve, the total consumable grain production of ancient Messenia can be estimated to be within the range of 40,000 to 71,000 metric tons.

If a reasonable human consumption level of cereals can be established, a figure may be posited that would provide an indication of the potential population that could be supported by Messenian grain production. There is little doubt that cereals were the mainstay of the Mycenaean diet, as they have been throughout the history of Greece (though probably less than ever at the present day). And, as was indicated in the previous section, barley was the major cereal consumed as late as the fourth century B.C.

Roebuck (1945) adopts 1 liter as the daily consumption of flour of an adult male. In his discussion no distinction is made between grain and flour. Presumably in antiquity the whole grain would be consumed without the separation of flour and bran that is the practice today. We have reasoned that the proportion of wheat in total cereals production ranged between 23 and 40 percent, so that an average 30 percent of wheat and 70 percent of barley will be assumed for the diet. Since 1 liter of wheat weighs 0.772 kg and 1 liter of barley 0.618 kg, 1 liter of grain reflecting the relative importance of the two cereals in the diet is the equivalent of 0.654 kg. This corresponds with an annual consumption of 239 kg per male adult. To adjust this figure for the lower consumption level of female adults, children, and old people, a coefficient of 0.67 is applied. This brings the per capita grain consumption estimate to 160 kg per year.

The present upper limit of cereal consumption in rural Messenia is around 200 kg of wheat flour. The equivalent in grain of this figure is obtained by dividing it by the milling rate. Using traditional milling techniques and assuming consumer acceptance of the resulting product, which is difficult to digest, this rate can be placed between 0.8 and 0.9. Assuming an average of 0.85 and the above per capita wheat flour consumption, one obtains a grain equivalent of 235 kg. This figure appears to be more acceptable than that based on Jardé's estimate if one takes into account that in antiquity cereals were more

* Information obtained by personal communication from Mr. Vassilis Podikis, agricultural extension specialist for grain production, Kalamata, 27 February 1967.

important in the diet than today. It will therefore be proposed that the figure of 235 kg be adopted after having taken note of the high milling rate (0.85 as opposed to 0.7 today) and of the smaller body weight of Mycenaeans compared with modern Messenians.

The final factor to be considered in this context is grain consumption by animals. Even today, the principal animal feed resource is grazing land. Supplemental feeding during periods of extreme cold, exhaustion of grazing lands, or heavy labor demand on work animals consists mainly of straw and hay with occasionally, in the case of work animals, a bit of oats or barley. Sheep are never fed grain and cattle only in fattening operations, which are a recent innovation. In the absence of any information about the number of draft animals in prehistoric times, one may (for the sake of arguing the insignificance of their grain consumption) assume that Roebuck's population of work animals for classical Messenia applies to the Bronze Age. This would have included 1,000 horses, 2,100 mules, and 1,500 donkeys. On the basis of current feeding practices, one can exclude donkeys altogether as having a claim on grain feeds. In general, horses and mules receive grain in their daily ration only at those times that heavy demands are made on them, notably during the plowing season. One may posit that they receive a full grain ration of 3 kg during a maximum of 100 days per year. This would constitute a decrease in availability for human consumption of less than 1,000 metric tons of barley, 1.5 to 2.5 percent, respectively, of the two extreme production estimates. This figure is so negligible that the effect of feeding grain to animals will be disregarded.

Finally, the necessary elements have been established to produce an estimate of the number of persons that could have been supported by Messenia's grain production potential. At 235 kg of grain per capita per year and a production ranging from 40,000 to 71,000 metric tons, the population potential was between 170,000 and 300,000.

It should be well understood that these population estimates reflect a *potential* situation based on the physical capacity of the region to produce the staple food. These figures need not and, judging by the *actual* population estimates in Chapters 7, 8, and 16, do not correspond with the actual population in the Late Bronze Age. In fact, the actual population could have been much smaller, with the region exporting substantial quantities of grain in excess of consumption. Or it could well be that the Mycenaeans never fully utilized the productive capacity of their agricultural resource endowment. The latter reasoning becomes more probable in the light of the development of many regions like Messenia in the entire Mediterranean basin. Until perhaps a century ago, population had remained fairly stable while supported by a traditional economy. With the opening up of modern transportation, communication, and trade patterns and the closer integration of the region into national life and into the world economy, the age-old equilibrium was disturbed. Population increased substantially, first because of economic stimuli from outside the region, and later because of a vast and rapid improvement in health conditions. As a consequence, population grew faster than the economy on which it was based. This resulted in a strong migration movement that will no doubt continue until a new stable equilibrium is attained. On the strength of this argument one may hypothesize that Messenia reached its largest population in the twentieth century A.D., and that the terraced hill slopes that have been abandoned in recent decades reflect the maximum expansion of the region's agriculture associated with this population level.

The only other population estimate for Messenia based on the production capacity of the region was made by Roebuck (1945). His estimate is a maximum population of 112,500, of which 42 percent lived in the district under the control of the federal capital at Messene. The difference between Roebuck's and the present writer's estimates lies basically in the appreciation of the total area of Messenia, the proportion of arable land, the location of grain production, the importance of barley in the human diet, and the per capita intake of grains. Some of these differences have been discussed above, but others have not. Notable among the latter is Roebuck's location of the region's major farm production in the large plains. In this writer's judgment, the plains were still largely uncultivated because of the inability of the population to effectively control the water level. In contrast, Roebuck assigns the hill lands and mountainous areas almost entirely to use as grazing land, thus discounting the suitability for grain production of the sizable plateau lands and the rolling hill country. Moreover, the need for and the ability of the Messenians to make intensive use of the hill slopes by extensive terracing may have been underestimated by Roebuck.

An important question connected with the agricultural economy is the role of trade. The Pylos tablets testify to the existence of a lively intra-regional trade, but it is vital to try to discover what products were involved in interregional exchange and in what quantities. With its very large potential in the production of food grains and the virtual certainty that the Mycenaean population was much smaller than warranted by the productive capacity (see Ch. 16), an export surplus of grains could have been available. Although grain may have been generally in short supply in the Mycenaean world (Vermeule 1964), this may not have been the case for all of its constituent parts. Known or hypothesized Mycenaean exports included olive oil (some perfumed), wines, live animals, textiles, ceramics, and metal work including weapons. Imports seem to have consisted primarily of raw materials for metal working (copper, tin, silver, and gold) and luxury items such as dyes, spices, textiles, ceramics, amber, precious stones, carved and raw ivory (McDonald 1967, pp. 396–97).

In an essentially barter economy, imports had to be paid for by exchange of goods or services. Of agricultural products which may have figured most prominently in this exchange, surplus grain seems to be a leading possibility. Others are olive oil, flax (linen), dried figs, wine, wool and woolen textiles, cattle, horses, and perhaps honey. Much would depend on the demand for such products, both in the old and more densely populated areas to the east and in the "frontier" areas to west and north.

REFERENCES

Angel, Lawrence J. 1946. "Social Biology of Greek Culture Growth," *American Anthropologist* 48:394–533.

Blegen, Carl W. 1937. *Prosymna.* Cambridge, Mass.

Childe, V. Gordon. 1939. *The Dawn of European Civilization.* New York.

Hansen, Hazel. 1933. *Early Civilization in Thessaly.* Johns Hopkins University Studies in Archaeology No. 15. Baltimore.

Jardé, A. 1925. *Les céréales dans l'antiquité grecque.* Paris.

Loy, W. G. 1970. *The Land of Nestor: A Physical Geography of the Southwest Peloponnese.* National Academy of Sciences, Office of Naval Research, Report No. 34. Washington, D.C.

McDonald, W. A. 1967. *Progress into the Past: The Rediscovery of Mycenaean Civilization.* New York.

Mylonas, George. 1934. *Aghios Kosmas: An Early Bronze Age Settlement and Cemetery in Attica.* Princeton, N.J.

NSSG. 1963. *Results of the Census of Population and Housing of March 9, 1961*, Vol. 2, Pt. 3, *Peloponnesus, Province of Messenia.* Athens.

———. 1964. *Results of the Census of Agriculture and Livestock Production of March 19, 1961*, Vol. 1, Pt. 3, *Peloponnesus.* Athens.

Roebuck, Carl A. 1941. *A History of Messenia from 369 to 149 B.C.* Chicago.

———. 1945. "A Note on Messenian Economy and Population," *Classical Philology* 40:149–65.

Seymour, T. D. 1908. *Life in the Homeric Age.* New York.

Van Wersch, Herman J. 1969. *Land Tenure, Land Use, and Agricultural Development: A Comparative Analysis of Messenia (Greece) and the Cape Bon (Tunisia).* Unpublished doctoral dissertation, University of Minnesota.

Ventris, M., and Chadwick, J. 1956. *Documents in Mycenaean Greek.* Cambridge.

Vermeule, Emily. 1964. *Greece in the Bronze Age.* Chicago.

Wace, A. J. B., and Thompson, W. S. 1912. *Prehistoric Thessaly.* Cambridge.

12
VEGETATION HISTORY

by

H. E. Wright, Jr.

The existing vegetation of southwest Peloponnese is vastly disturbed, as a result of thousands of years of use by man. Big trees have been cut for timber, smaller trees and shrubs for fuel. Brush has been cleared for cultivation. The disturbances continue to modern time. During the Greek war of independence, dense forests in some areas were systematically destroyed by fire. The natural growth of all palatable plants has been inhibited by the grazing of sheep and goats, which avoid only the thorny or leather-leaved shrubs. In a land where the active growing season is restricted to a few months of rain in winter and spring, survival and regeneration of natural plant life under the circumstances of severe disturbance is difficult indeed. The English plant geographer Turrill (1929) gives a full account of the influence of man on the vegetation, as recorded in historical documents and inferred from the nature of the plant life.

Yet the disturbance is not uniformly severe. Areas that are easily cultivable or easily accessible have been cut, plowed, or grazed since prehistoric time, but the steep and rocky slopes of ravines, the rugged interior mountains, and the hills and mountains far from the centers of population all are covered with a vegetation that is nearly natural, so that one has a basis for reconstructing the conditions of prehistoric times.

The higher mountains still bear a solid growth of pine and fir above elevations of about 700 m (Philippson 1895, 1959; Rothmaler 1943). The pine is *Pinus nigra* (black pine), which is common throughout the Mediterranean mountains (Turrill 1929, Critchfield and Little 1966). The fir is *Abies cephalonica,* which is related to *A. alba,* the common white fir of the Balkans. As viewed along the road that crosses the Taygetos Mountains over the Langadha Pass from Kalamata to Sparta, this forest near its lower margin has patches that have been cleared and terraced so that a few olive trees could be planted, but the higher slopes of the mountains are too cold for successful growth of olives. Being far from trade routes and centers of population, and having slopes too steep or rocky for easy cultivation, the higher mountain regions have been spared extensive modification of the vegetation cover. The Taygetos is even high enough to have an upper tree line: at an elevation of about 1,800 m above sea level the pine trees give way to alpine shrubs and herbs.

The lower limit of the conifer forest is not a natural boundary in most places, because of cutting and other disturbance, but in general the conifers originally were bordered below by forest dominated by oak, including both deciduous species (*Quercus conferta, Q. brachyphylla, Q. aegilops*) and evergreen species (*Q. coccifera, Q. ilex*). Other deciduous trees also grow naturally in this belt, such as *Castanea sativa* (chestnut), *Juglans* sp. (walnut), *Arbutus unedo*, and *A. andrachne* (strawberry tree), but many of the nut trees may have been planted. The deciduous trees have not fared well through the centuries of land use, and it is rare to find any deciduous oaks in the Peloponnese, except in relatively inaccessible areas.

At elevations below the major occurrences of deciduous oak is the Mediterranean maquis, a shrubland dominated by evergreen oaks, pistachios (*Pistacia lentiscus, P. terebinthus*), wild olive (*Olea oleaster*), carob (*Ceratonia siliqua*), phillyrea (*Phillyrea media*), and strawberry tree. Dense maquis is still found on steep hillsides and ravines throughout the area, but in other places it has been cleared for cultivation or is intensively grazed and degraded. A related vegetation, termed pseudomaquis (Turrill 1929, p. 149), covers many of the interior hills and low mountains, where the climate is less mild than along the coastal region. Unlike the true maquis, which has several dominants, it is usually dominated by a single species, such as *Quercus coccifera.*

In the coastal areas of the northern part of our region, the maquis is topped by Aleppo pine (*Pinus halepensis*), with stone pine (*P. pinea*) locally along the sandy strandlines (Turrill 1929; Critchfield and Little 1966). On the west coast these species extend down the Gulf of Kyparissia as far as the Nedha River, and Aleppo pine covers the western slopes of some of the coastal mountains.

These basic vegetation zones – alpine, mountain conifer, deciduous oak, maquis, and coastal pine – are discrete enough even on aerial photographs so that they can be roughly mapped, and the Greek Forestry Service has produced such maps. A generalized version of these maps for our region (Pocket Map 11-20) indicates also the extent of cultivated land. Most of the region shown as maquis is used for grazing. The present areas of oak forest and conifer forest are small indeed.

The relation between the modern vegetation belts and the vegetation of the Late Bronze Age or any other period is difficult to determine in any detail. Because the distribution of vegetational types in the Peloponnese is controlled primarily by elevation, and secondarily by latitude and coastal influences, one might attempt a reconstruction from existing remnants, and the German plant geographer Rothmaler (1943) was bold enough to do that. Some supplementary information is furnished by historical records. For example, the tablets from Pylos refer to timber as well as to various agricultural plants, such as grains, flax, vines, olives, and figs, which must have covered an appreciable part of the landscape (Ch. 7). For later times, there is the description of oak forests on the plateau east of Pylos and pine forests on the west coast near Kaiafa by Venetian officials about 1700, who also commented on the importance of export of acorns from deciduous oak trees (Ch. 5). Another report, in 1825 by the French geographer de Boblaye, decried the intentional burning of forests by shepherds to provide pasturage for flocks, as well as the erosion caused by cultivation on slopes. But he also perceived that the record of these disturbances was held in the sediments washed into the Bay of Navarino by the streams – a quotation worth repeating from Chapter 5, because it introduces (but does not pursue) an entirely different approach to historical reconstruction – the stratigraphic approach, which had hardly even been developed in European geologic thought in those days. He states, "What a mass of human remains and of the industrial debris of all ages has not the roadstead of Navarino alone . . . swallowed up over the last thirty centuries!" He concludes that a natural upheaval could lift up the sediments and expose the record for study.

We know now that earthquake movements over a period of a few centuries are insufficient to expose the sea bottom (Ch. 3), but that there are other ways of sampling sediments and studying the "archives of history." One is the technique of historical pollen analysis, by which a core of lake or marsh sediment is studied to determine the proportions of different pollen types at successive levels. The stratigraphic succession provides a crude measure of the changing vegetation on the surrounding terrain, from which the pollen is largely derived. The following account of the vegetation history of parts of southwest Peloponnese is derived from the results of pollen analysis. It records the story of the effect of man on the vegetation. The chronology is controlled by radiocarbon dating, and the events thus documented are closely pertinent to our attempts to reconstruct the environment and the economy of the Myceneans. This geologic approach thus serves as a check on reconstructions based on travellers' accounts and other historical documents, which can rarely provide a quantitative evaluation of the vegetation cover or other aspects of the landscape.

The Technique of Pollen Analysis

Pollen grains are produced in large quantities by flowering plants and are disseminated by the wind (or by insects). The pollen that falls to the surface is generally destroyed within a few years, unless it falls onto a constantly dry or a constantly wet spot, in which case it may be preserved for thousands of years.

A constantly dry environment may be found in some desert caves. In Palestine, for example, the delicate Dead Sea Scrolls were preserved for thousands of years in desert caves because the air was so dry. Unfortunately, these are the very areas where there are relatively few plants, so this situation is not particularly favorable for pollen analysis.

Constantly wet places are more common in Greece. The best localities are small lakes or permanent marshes. The pollen grains fall on the surface, become waterlogged, and settle to the bottom, where they are buried by sediment. Although the soft protoplasm of the cell is rapidly destroyed, the cell wall resists chemical and bacteriological decomposition after burial. Further, the pollen grains have sufficiently distinctive shape and surface sculpture that they can generally be identified as to genus or even to species. A sample of lake or marsh sediment can then be treated in the laboratory to concentrate the pollen grains, for the pollen grain wall resists attack by certain chemical reagents that dissolve other organic and inorganic constituents of the sediment. After such treatment, a drop of the pollen-rich suspension is placed on a microscopic slide, and the various pollen types are identified and tallied. A count of several hundred grains is generally made, and the tallies for each type are converted to percentage of the total.

For a detailed study of the pollen succession for a particular lake or marsh, a continuous core of sediment may be taken with a specially designed steel tube about five centimeters in diameter and a meter long. At the lower end of the tube is a piston made of two laboratory rubber stoppers mounted on a threaded shaft. The piston is attached to a wire that leads out through the head of the corer. The corer is driven down through the sediment to the level at which the sampling is to start, with the piston held firmly at the bottom of the tube by an internal rod. When the desired level has been reached, the internal rod is withdrawn to the head of the sampler, the wire is held firmly at the surface of the lake, and the tube is pushed down into the sediment to cut the core. The function of the piston is to remove the hydrostatic pressure of the water above, which otherwise would prevent the core from coming easily into the tube.

The corer is then withdrawn to the surface, and the core is extruded, labeled, and wrapped for return to the laboratory. The corer can be lowered into the same hole to cut the next meter of sediment. In this way core segments through the entire sediment section can be obtained in sequence, and samples can be analyzed at regular intervals. The pollen counts for all intervals can then be compiled in a stratigraphic diagram, showing the changing pollen percentages with depth and thus time.

The Modern Pollen Rain. How dependably do the pollen counts of a sediment core reflect the vegetation of the region? After all, in paleoecology it is the past vegetation that we wish to know about, so we should try to evaluate how accurate a reconstruction can be based on pollen counts.

All plants do not produce the same amount of pollen, and the efficiency of dispersal also varies greatly. Pine, for example, produces tremendous quantities of pollen that travel a great distance in the wind. Some trees and shrubs and most herbs (especially those with brightly colored flowers) have their pollen distributed by insects, so the production is much less and the dispersal distance is also less. Many important agricultural plants in Greece, such as grape, fig, and flax, are poorly represented in pollen samples. Because of these variations in pollen production and dispersal, it is difficult to figure out just how accurately a given pollen count represents the proportions of particular plants in the vegetation cover.

The most direct way of relating the "pollen rain" to the vegetation of a region is to analyze the pollen content of soil samples in areas where the vegetation can be examined at the same time. With a scatter of surface-sample analyses from the different vegetation types of an area – including both natural vegetation and agricultural types – one has a basis for reconstructing past vegetation from pollen counts of old sediment.

So, for the situation in southwest Peloponnese, surface samples were collected from all the major vegetation regions – from the conifer forests of the Taygetos Mountains, remnant deciduous forests and maquis of the hills and steep valley slopes, the cultivated plains and plateaus of Messenia, and the area of coastal pine along the Gulf of Kyparissia. Many of the areas are extensively grazed or are cultivated in grains, vines, or olives, so the influence of agricultural plants on the modern pollen rain can be evaluated. Many of the samples consist of patches of moss on rocks. These are natural traps for dust; they dry out rapidly after rains, so the pollen that collects in them is well preserved. Other samples consist of the fine, loose plant detritus that accumulates on the soil surface under bushes or in rock crevices. Here also the preservation of pollen grains is generally good because the detritus does not stay moist long after rain.

The results of the surface-sample analyses are shown in Figure 12-1, in which the percentage for each major pollen type is shown for each sample. The samples are grouped according to the major vegetational belts. The top two samples come from the pine-fir forest of the Taygetos Mountains east of Kalamata. The high percentage of pine pollen in comparison with fir is a measure of the relative pollen production of the two trees, which are equally abundant in the nearby forest. The curve labeled *Erica* type includes the heath shrub *Erica*, which is common in the conifer forest. Other pollen types appear in very small percentages in these two samples.

The next sample (no. 31) also comes from the Taygetos Mountains, but from the west slope below the conifer forest, in the narrow belt of deciduous oak, fruit trees, and scattered olive orchards. Below this on the slopes is maquis (nos. 30 and 38) interrupted by a few olive orchards. Pine pollen in these samples is common, for it is easily blown from the pine forests of the mountains. Otherwise the pollen counts are distinguished by olive and oak.

The three samples listed for Arkadia (nos. 53, 54, 59) come from the low mountains, respectively south, east, and west of the Tripolis basin. In the latter two areas the vegetation near the sample sites includes large trees of deciduous oak, whereas no. 53 comes from a solid stand of evergreen oak shrub on the divide leading down to the basin of Sparta. The three samples from Akarnania come from mountains north of the Gulf of Patras, where

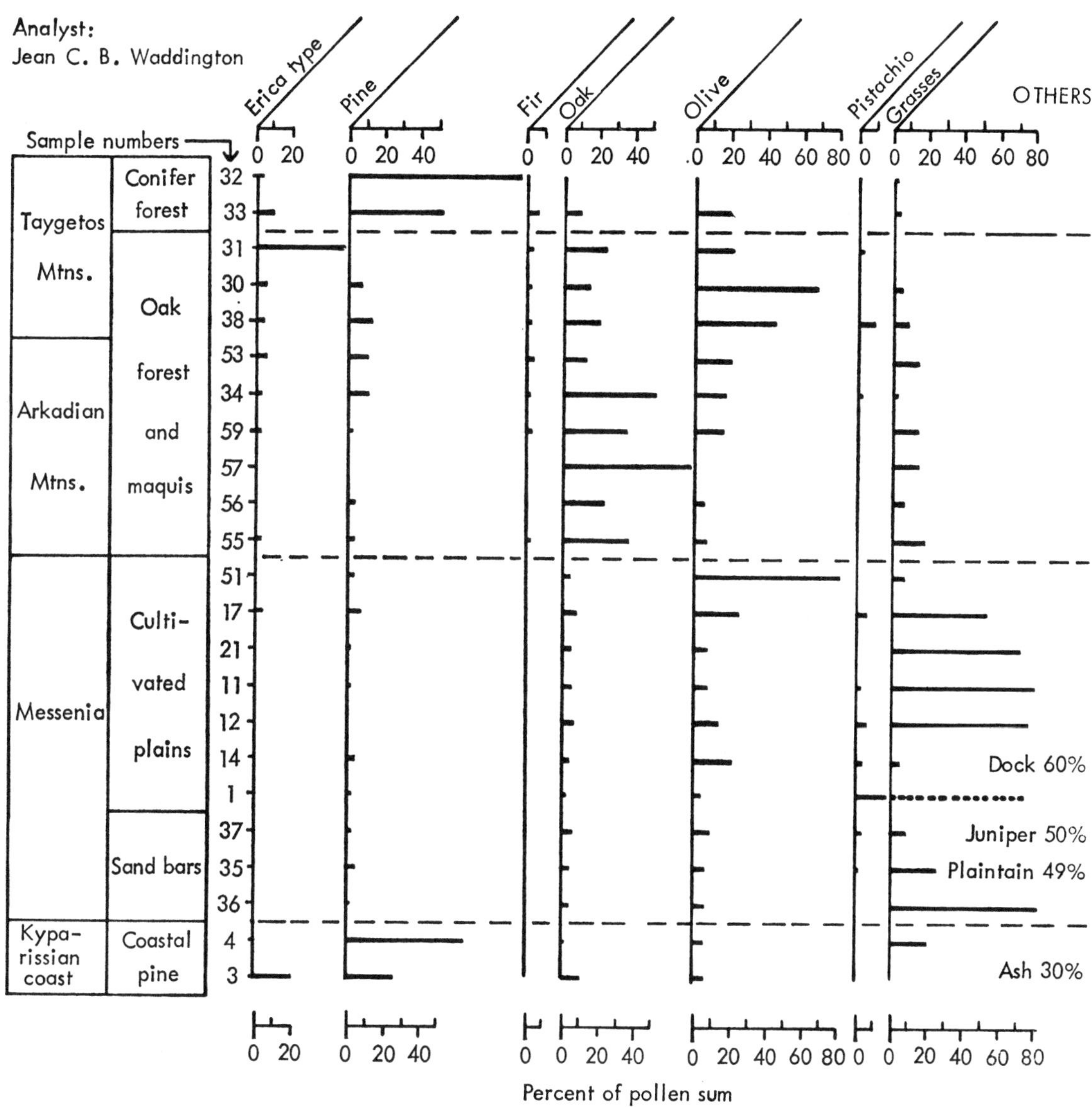

Figure 12-1. Diagram of principal pollen types in surficial plant detritus in soil samples in a transect across southwest Peloponnese. Locations of samples are shown in Pocket Map 11-20, except for those in the Arkadian Mountains. Pollen sum excludes sporadically occurring insect-pollinated types

the forest or savanna consists of deciduous oak (no. 55) or evergreen oak (nos. 56, 57), with relatively minor cultivation or grazing in the area. All six of these samples show relatively high percentages of oak pollen.

The seven samples from the Messenian plains come from localities where the natural vegetation had probably once been maquis or perhaps deciduous oak woodland, but where most of the land is now in cultivation. The dominant pollen types are grasses, olive, and oak. Cereal grains belong to the grass family, and their pollen grains are distinguishable from those of other grasses by their large size or distinctive morphology. The grass pollen grains in these samples, however, include few cereal types; the high grass-pollen percentages must therefore be attributed to weedy grasses that are common in disturbed areas. Several of the samples have very high percentages of some particular herb type, as listed on the side of the diagram – probably some local agricultural weeds. If these anomalous values are excluded from the pollen sum, the percentages of all the other types would be increased appreciably, generally by about 50 percent.

Several of this group of samples come from areas near olive groves, especially no. 51, which was taken from the heart of the huge olive plantation on the alluvial fans crossed by the road from Tripolis to Kyparissia west of the junction with the Kalamata road. But the average of less than 10 percent olive pollen in this general region of diversified agriculture provides a measure of the olive pollen representation that could be expected in sediment samples from such a region. The oak pollen, which is all of the evergreen type rather than the deciduous type, must come from the patches of maquis on steep hill slopes. The few pine pollen grains were blown from the mountains.

The three samples from the Navarino area (nos. 37, 35, 36) come from sandbars that bound Osmanaga Lagoon. Sample 37 has 56 percent pollen of juniper, which is a common plant on the sandbar. Sample 36 had many grains of chenopods, representing the abundant *Salicornia fruticosa* that grows locally around the saline shores of the lagoon. Chenopod pollen is not included in the sum on which the pollen percentages are calculated, so that the figures can be compared with those for the cores from Osmanaga Lagoon.

The two last surface samples (nos. 4, 3) come from the area of coastal pine north of the Nedha River. The values of pine pollen are conspicuously high, as well as the *Erica*-type pollen in one sample, for *Erica* is an associate of pine here as well as in the Taygetos Mountains. The modest olive percentages indicate that olive pollen is easily disseminated from distant localities, for olive orchards are not common in the region.

This surface-sample survey gives us the basis for interpreting the pollen counts from core samples. The nature of the past vegetation can thus be reconstructed and related to the influence of man or to natural factors such as climate. It is clear from the results so far, for example, that high percentages of pine and heath pollen must be attributed to conifer vegetation in the area, olive to extensive orchards, and grasses to areas of widespread cultivation.

Pollen Sites

The next job in historical pollen analysis is to find lakes or marshes in which sediment has accumulated without interruption for thousands of years, so that the record of the Bronze Age and subsequent cultural periods can be examined. Unfortunately, lakes and marshes are not common in the Peloponnese. The only two large lakes, Stimfalia south of Corinth and Lake Taka south of Tripolis, proved to have too few pollen grains to make analysis practical. Large streams bring so much silt into these lakes that the pollen concentration is greatly diluted. Furthermore, these lakes intermittently drain out through underground passageways in the adjacent limestone hills, and during periods when the lakes are drained the pollen grains are decomposed by oxidation.

Other lakes and marshes are located along the coasts, where beach bars have enclosed indentations in the coast line (Ch. 3). The lagoons behind the bars are subject to flooding from the sea by storm waves, and they are also subject to flooding from the land, because the indentations are commonly places where streams reach the sea (Pls. 5-1, 6-1). The sea waves do not carry much sediment into the lagoons, except for a little sand, but the coastal streams may deposit alluvial fans at the landward edge of the lagoon and may gradually fill it up so that it no longer holds any water. The great marshy area (the Valtos) of the lower Messenian Plain west of Kalamata is such a filled lagoon, originally formed by the long beach bar across the head of the Gulf of Messenia. It has so much alluvium in it that the pollen content is too sparse for successful analysis, as indicated by tests made at several localities.

A more productive locality is the lagoon located at the head of the Bay of Navarino north of Pylos on the west coast (Ch. 3 and Pl. 6-1). The bay itself is constricted at the mouth by the island of Sphakteria, and a broad bar has been constructed across the head of the bay to cut off Osmanaga Lagoon (Ch. 3). The lagoon is being filled by alluvium from the hills to the northeast, but the streams entering the lagoon are relatively small. The open-water area of the lagoon is more than a kilometer wide but less than a meter deep. A small gap in the beach bar admits sea waves during storms, but the relatively low salinity of the lagoon water indicates that winter stream floods constitute the principal water source. The water level falls during the summer as a result of evaporation, but the deepest part of the lagoon, near the west limit and farthest from the alluvial fan, probably has rarely gone dry, because the pollen there is well preserved.

The entire lagoon was recently trenched with canals in an effort to drain it for agriculture. A pumping station is designed to lift the water over the beach bar to the sea. The project seems doomed, however, unless provision is made for holding out the salt water that washes through the gap or over the ridge, as well as salt water that seeps through the ridge, for the floor of the lagoon is below sea level. Although the lagoonal sediment in the northern part of the lagoon extends to a greater depth, it is brown and pollen-poor. The alluvium is reddish brown when it comes from the soils on the hill slopes. If it is deposited on the land surface or in a water body that is intermittently dry, then the color is maintained and the intermittent exposure to the air causes the destruction of the pollen grains. But if the alluvium is deposited in a permanent lake in which organic detritus accumulates as well, then the chemical conditions accompanying the partial decomposition of the organic matter cause the iron minerals in the alluvial sediment to change from brown to gray. These same conditions favor the preservation of pollen grains.

Cores taken from the western part of the lagoon are much better for pollen analysis. The sharp limestone ridge on the west provides no alluvial inflow. The lagoon water there reaches its maximum depth, and the homogeneous gray color and good pollen preservation in the sediment implies a permanently wet situation. The alluvium from the northeast reached this far west in only small quantities and did not dilute the contemporaneously deposited pollen and other organic sediment to such a great extent as elsewhere. Some horizons of the sediment, however, especially in the lower part, contained relatively little pollen – probably because exceptionally large floods brought alluvial sediment all the way across the lagoon.

It is possible that in the early centuries of sedimentation the lagoon was shallower, and that the streams could bring their alluvium farther into the basin. This implies that sea level was lower than today, because it is basically sea level that controls the level of the lagoon water. This problem is discussed in Chapter 3.

The Pollen Sequence at Osmanaga Lagoon

Complete pollen analyses of two Osmanaga cores were made. The pollen stratigraphy in the two sites is essentially the same, so the pollen percentages are no accident. Such duplication of results provides greater confidence in the interpretation of the sequence.

The pollen diagrams (Fig. 12-2) are arranged with the vertical scale as depth, and thus time, and the horizontal scale as percentage of the various pollen types. Included in the pollen sum by which the percentages are calculated is the pollen of trees, shrubs, grasses, and minor herbs. Two major pollen types, namely sedges and chenopods, are excluded from the sum. Sedges make up the extensive reed patches on the west and south sides of the lagoon today, and their abundance reflects local conditions rather than the regional vegetation, which is the objective of this study. The same can be said for chenopods, including weedy types like *Salicornia fruticosa*, which grows in great profusion on the saline sandy shore areas of the lagoon. The very pronounced stratigraphic fluctuations of these two pollen types, and the lack of correspondence between correlative levels in the two cores, indicate the very local origins of most of these pollen grains. The percentages for these types are calculated on the basis of the sum of all of the other types. Radiocarbon dates noted on the diagrams are listed in Table 12-1.

Table 12-1. Radiocarbon Dates for Sediment Cores in Western Greece, Determined by Isotopes, Inc.

Sample	Depth below Water Surface (cm)	Age — No. of Years Ago	Date
Osmanaga Lagoon, core 30:			
I-1515	65–70	< 200	
I-1950	150–160	820 ± 140	1130 A.D.
I-1951	165–175	2,010 ± 140	60 B.C.
I-1952	215–225	2,820 ± 100	870 B.C.
I-1516	260–265	3,220 ± 120	1270 B.C.
I-1517	475–480	3,940 ± 270	2000 B.C.
Osmanaga Lagoon, core 15: I-834	125–157	2,205 + 250	250 B.C.
Kaiafa			
I-2864	145–155	1,680 ± 100	270 A.D.
I-2865	260–265	1,650 ± 100	300 A.D.
Voulkaria			
I-2866	389–399	3,040 ± 120	1190 B.C.
I-2867	834–840	10,900 ± 300	8960 B.C.

Pollen Zone A. The pollen sequence for the two Osmanaga cores has been subdivided into three pollen zones. Zone A is thicker in core 30 because this core is longer. The zone is dominated by pine, oak, and *Erica*-type. The preservation of the pollen is not good in this zone, perhaps because much of it was washed into the lagoons by streams rather than simply settling out of the air, and in the process it became battered and broken. If we refer back to the collection of surface-sample analyses, we see that high percentages of pine pollen can be found in the Taygetos Mountains and along the west coast north of the Nedha River. No fir pollen occurs along with the pine in the sediment core, so it is unlikely that zone A represents the inland conifer forest spread to low elevations. It seems more likely that the pine pollen represents the greater southward extent of the coastal Aleppo pine. This tree is now common in northern Peloponnese along the Gulf of Corinth and south along the west coast as far as the Nedha River, and it may thus have reached farther south in the past. Radiocarbon dates imply that the pine woodland existed until the middle part of the second millennium B.C. The dating is not very accurate; pollen-bearing samples are widely spaced at these levels, and only two relevant radiocarbon dates are available. Straight interpolation between the two dates may not be justified because the sedimentation rate may not have been constant. It seems fairly certain, however, that there was practically no pine left in this region by the Late Bronze Age.

Aleppo pine occurs today along Mediterranean coasts from Spain to Palestine (Rikli 1943). This distribution is not entirely natural, for the tree has been widely planted. But it is hard to explain its disappearance from

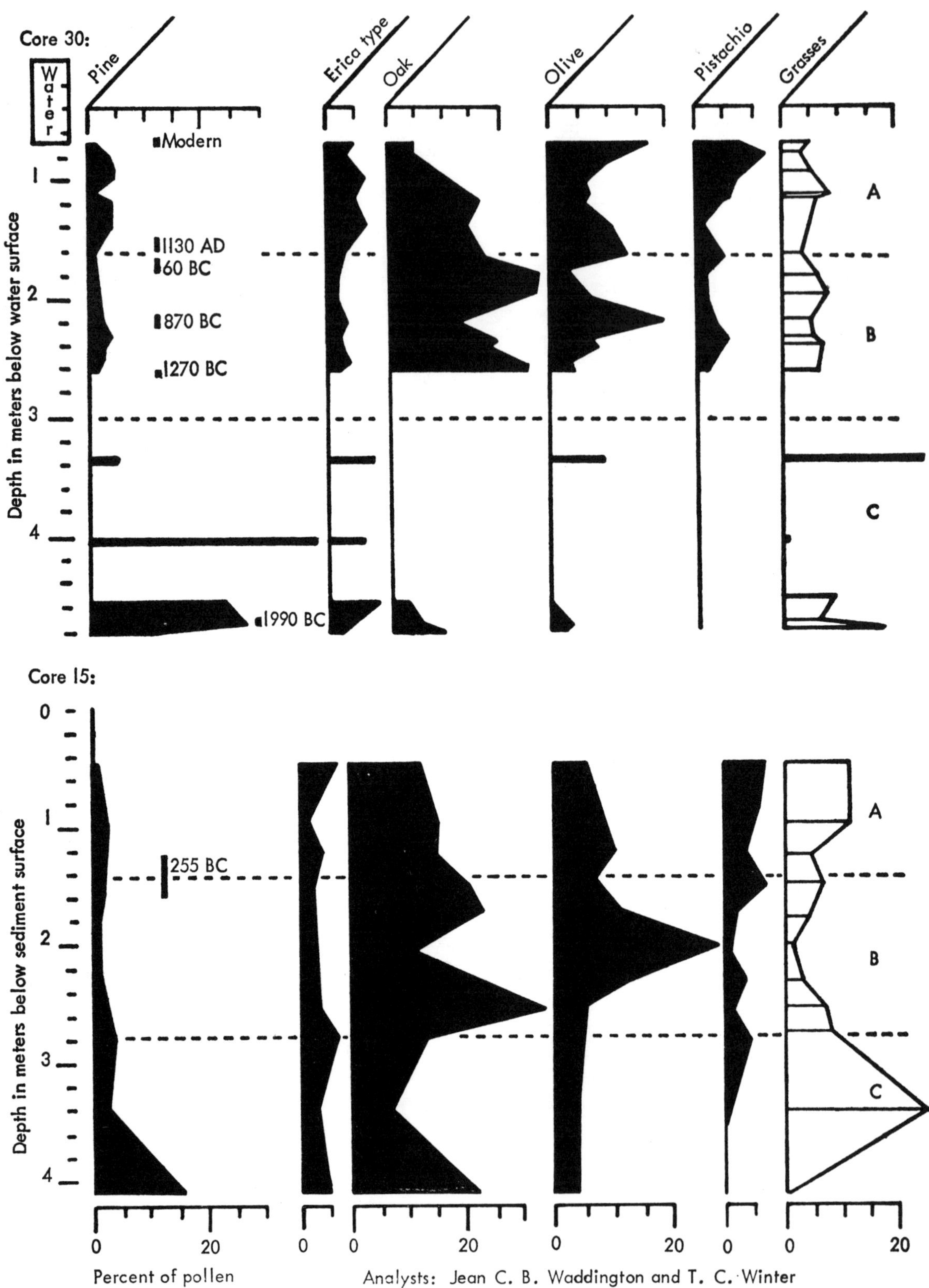

Figure 12-2. Diagrams of principal pollen types in two sediment cores from Osmanaga Lagoon. Locations of coring sites are shown on Figure 2-9 and Plate 6-1. Pollen sum excludes sedges and chenopods (not shown), which are local plants of the sandy shores

the southern part of Peloponnese by any natural factor, such as climate. Disturbance seems to be the best explanation. The removal of pine from the southwest coast apparently thus took place in the Middle Bronze Age, presumably because of a need for wood for buildings, boats, and fuel or because of forest clearance for agriculture. The Pylos tablets refer to woodcutters in this general vicinity (Ch. 7), and a case can be made that timber may have been a major export item to help pay for the copper required for the active bronze industry.

Pollen Zone B. Zone B is dominated by olive pollen in two peaks separated by a maximum of oak pollen. The pattern is nicely duplicated in the two cores, leaving little possibility that it is accidental. Pistachio pollen, essentially absent at lower levels, is common in Zone B. Pine and *Erica*-type pollen occurs in low values throughout the zone. The small percentage of pine pollen can be attributed to wind transport from the Taygetos Mountains or from areas of coastal pine farther north.

Wild olive is a minor shrub in the maquis throughout the Mediterranean region today, but cultivated olive is a major agricultural crop in the entire Mediterranean coastal region, having a gross distribution similar to that of Aleppo pine (Rikli 1943). It does not grow above about 300 m in the highlands of Peloponnese because of low temperatures. It needs a period of winter chilling to bear fruit, however, so it does not grow in tropical areas. Today cultivated olive is propagated primarily either by cuttings or by grafting on seedlings (Pansiot and Rebour 1961; see also Ch. 4). Wild trees are often domesticated by the addition of grafts from cultivated trees.

The surface sample analyses (Fig. 12-1) show modest values (generally less than 20 percent) of olive pollen in most of the agricultural areas of Messenia, where grasses and oak compose the other major pollen types. Higher percentages of olive pollen are found in the samples from the slopes of the Taygetos Mountains, where olive orchards occur but where the vegetation otherwise is heavily grazed maquis, in which wild olive is not common (Fig. 12-1, samples 30, 31, 38). Values as high as 20 percent were also found in areas many miles from any olive orchards, such as in the mountains of Arkadia (samples 34, 53, 59), indicating that olive pollen travels in quantity far from its source. The highest value (80 percent) was found in a sample (no. 51) from a vast area of olive orchards on the upper (Steniklarian) plain.

Comparison with these surface-sample counts indicates that the high value of olive pollen in zone B (more than 40 percent) must reflect extensive olive orchards rather than wild olive in the maquis. The alluvial fans and slopes bordering Osmanaga Lagoon on the north and east must have been covered with olive trees, as they are today (Ch. 11) – the topmost sample of Osmanaga sediment has 35 percent olive pollen. It can not be determined whether the olive cultivation extended farther inland or farther along the coast; analyses at other coring sites would be needed to establish a regional pattern. But the ease of pollen dispersal and the maintenance of high pollen values for probably several hundred years implies that olive was widespread in the region during the time of zone B.

Radiocarbon dates place the olive maximum at about 1100–700 B.C. This falls immediately after the end of the Mycenaean period and encompasses the time of the so-called Greek Dark Age, when the population and political importance of southwest Peloponnese was much reduced compared to both earlier and later times (Chs. 6, 8). One might expect extensive olive cultivation to mark the time of high population and a vigorous economy, such as the time of the zenith in the thirteenth century B.C. rather than the Dark Age. At the Englianos palace, only 9 km inland from Osmanaga Lagoon, the Pylos tablets refer repeatedly to olive oil (Ch. 7), and storage rooms in the palace contained large terracotta jars that were used for oil storage. Yet much, or even all, of this oil could have been tribute in kind, coming from trees growing in other parts of the kingdom.

At any rate, for Mycenaean times the diagram shows low values of olive pollen. It is possible that the oil recorded at Pylos was used only or mainly for perfumery. The tablets refer to unguent-makers, in which case the quantities may have been relatively small, and local production may have been quite limited. It is uncertain from the tablets whether olives were then used either as a basic food stuff or as a common cleaning ointment. We are told that Solon at the end of the seventh century B.C. in Attica encouraged export of olive oil rather than grain (Plutarch, *Life of Solon*, 24). Perhaps olives had really not been developed as a major food crop in Greece during Mycenaean time. It is a striking fact that there is no mention in the Homeric epics of the consumption of olives or olive oils.

An argument can be made (J. Chadwick, letter 1966) that the olive in Greece is preferentially a subsistence crop. Mature trees require relatively little care and bear fruit for many decades and even centuries. Olive fruits are nutritious, and they have sustained the Greeks through many intervals of adversity, such as during the civil war years of the 1940's (see Ch. 4). When times are good – with political stability and population growth – a more diversified agriculture can be maintained, with grains and vines favored over olives. Cultivation of those other crops, which leave a poor pollen record, may have marked the Mycenaean and classical periods. The pollen sequence for these intervals is marked by high values of oak, probably mostly the evergreen oak, which, along with pistachio, characterized the maquis of the uncultivated areas. According to this interpretation, the rise in the olive pollen curve about 1100 B.C. would mark the change to subsistence crops during the unstable years after the end of the Mycenaean period. When stability was restored and the population increased during the Archaic and classical periods, the land previously in olives may have been put into other crops. The modest rise of grass pollen for this interval may reflect the land clearance involved, for the grass pollen is apparently not that of cereal grains.

Although this explanation for the post-Mycenaean olive peak seems quite possible, other explanations must be considered. For example, it is well known that olive trees live to great age. Perhaps, when the unified kingdom disintegrated, the olive trees then existing simply persisted as mature trees for four centuries, propagating to produce countless plants all over the landscape. Yet there are several difficulties with this explanation. When an olive orchard is not maintained by annual cultivation or clearing of the weeds beneath, the area becomes overgrown with the normal shrubs of the maquis, not with olive seedlings. These shrubs may include a few wild olives, but olive does not propagate easily by seed in the wild, and other shrubs dominate. The old olive trees themselves suffer from the competition for soil moisture, and in a few years the pollen rain from the olive trees, itself probably diminished, would be swamped by the contribution from evergreen oak, pistachio, and other maquis shrubs. So this explanation may be rejected.

Other explanations might be that the radiocarbon dating is not accurate, or that the archaeological dating of the Mycenaean period is incorrect. An error in archaeological dating as large as 300 years seems unlikely. The two relevant radiocarbon dates mark the beginning and the maximum of the olive rise in core 30 (Fig. 12-2). The material dated was slightly organic sediment with no roots or other younger material. A separate analysis of a sample of the surface sediment yielded a modern date, indicating that the organic matter in the sediment contained no "dead" carbon derived from the limestones of the region. The dates therefore cannot be suspected as being too old. There is no reason to suspect laboratory error; all six dates for core 30 are at least in the correct chronological order.

It is possible that the radiocarbon time scale is not the true time scale, because the radiocarbon production in the atmosphere may not have been constant. Evidence available from tree-ring analysis and from rates of lake sedimentation indicates that serious divergence affects the time only before 500 B.C., but that short-term fluctuations in the curve may increase the possible error. In this case the 870 B.C. carbon date for the olive peak in core 30 might be corrected to 1150 or even 1200 B.C Such a date approaches more closely the Mycenaean epoch of interest. This explanation can be tested by careful radiocarbon analysis of archaeologically dated samples from Mycenaean excavations.

Pollen Zone C. The high values of oak pollen that characterize zone B are reduced in zone C. Olive has a maximum at the base of the zone in core 30 but not in core 15. Radiocarbon dates near the base do not provide much chronological detail, but they do suggest that this olive peak occurred during the first millennium after Christ, perhaps again during a time when the Peloponnese was not heavily populated (Ch. 5).

Near the top of zone C oak declines further, probably the result of progressively greater land clearance leading to modern time. Olive and pistachio pollen during the fall in oak pollen may simply indicate changing composition of the remnants of maquis in the extensively cleared terrain of modern time. The accuracy of analysis and dating for the upper part of the zone is not sufficient to relate the sequence to historic events of recent centuries.

The pollen sequence at Osmanaga Lagoon is here attributed entirely to human disturbance of the vegetation rather than to natural (climatic) factors. It thus provides no confirmation for the hypothesis of Carpenter (1966) that the fall of the Mycenaean culture was caused by the effects of climatic change on the agricultural economy – an hypothesis that is weak on other grounds as well (Wright 1968). Although the Osmanaga record is not so detailed as one might hope, it implies significant changes in the vegetation at least for the nearby section of the coastal plain. Few will deny that the vegetation of lowland Peloponnese is severely disturbed today, and the diagram shows the course of its progressive destruction and modification.

Other Pollen Sites

No paleoecological study should put all its pollen grains in one basket. Duplication of the pollen sequence in two cores at the same site, as at Osmanaga Lagoon, is the first step in the confirmation necessary to lend credence to the interpretation. But the record at Osmanaga may represent only the local situation and may not apply to the rest of our area of interest. The next step is to involve other sites, in the hope of establishing the regional similarities and differences.

Along the coast of the Gulf of Kyparissia is a continuous beach bar, extending from the peninsula at Pyrgos

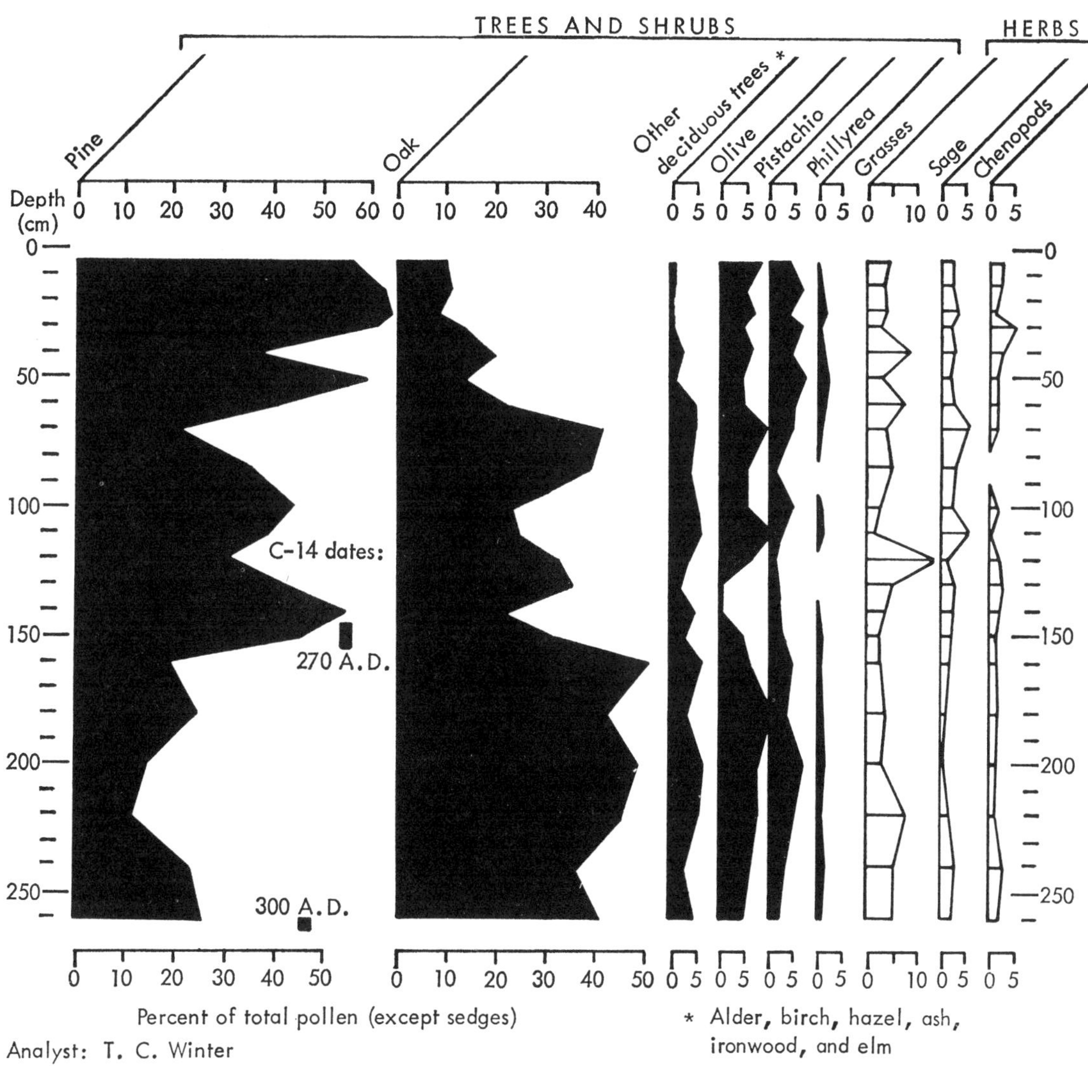

Figure 12-3. Diagram of principal pollen types for the peaty lagoonal sediments at Kaïafa (see Pocket Map 11-20 for location)

south to the headlands at Kyparissia. It is interrupted by numerous temporary gaps, which let out the floodwater streams after winter rains. The most notable interruption is the great delta of the Alpheios River, which has locally filled the long lagoon and has even pushed the beach bar seaward as a small cusp. Southward, the beach bar is partly covered with sand dunes, which are now stabilized by plantations of pine trees. Where the bar comes close to the limestone headland near the ancient mineral springs at Kaiafa, the marshy lagoon was successfully cored to a depth of almost three meters. The sediment is entirely peat.

Two radiocarbon dates at the base of the sediment indicate that the peat began to form about A.D. 300 (Table 12-1). These dates are consistent with the finding of Hellenistic buildings near the spa that are submerged by the lake (Bisbee 1937, p. 525), and with the documentary evidence that Strabo, about the time of Christ, mentions a marsh and incipient lake.

The pollen diagram for Kaiafa is distinctive only in the forms of the oak and pine curves (Fig. 12-3). In the lower part of the sequence oak pollen is dominant. After about A.D. 300, pine and oak fluctuate around the same level until near the top, where pine rises to 60 percent and oak falls to 10 percent.

The changes at Kaiafa do not provide much help in confirming the sequence at Osmanaga. Pine trees were apparently in the area from the beginning of the record, although it is possible that they had just previously been planted by the Romans and were not part of a natural distribution. The great increase in pine near the top of the diagram may also record pine plantations.

In any percentage diagram, the great increase in one component must be matched by a fall in others, so the fall in oak and *Erica*-type pollen are partly, but not entirely, a result of this relation. Exactly how the vegetation changed is uncertain. *Erica* grows in the pine woods, and one of the surface samples from the area yielded abundant *Erica*-type pollen. But *Erica* also is a component of the maquis, along with evergreen oak, so perhaps the fall of the two types reflects in part the land clearance of modern time. Olive pollen is present throughout at 10–20 percent. The coastal plain here is very narrow, and the pollen sequence may have little to do with cultivation of agricultural crops.

No additional coastal lagoons, inland lakes, or spring marshes with pollen-bearing sediment were found in Peloponnese, although attempts were made on the west coast south of Pyrgos and at Agoulinitza south of the Alpheios River, as well as in the lower Pamisos Plain between Kalamata and Messene and south toward the coastal bar, at the spring of Ayios Floros, and the large coastal marsh (now drained) south of Sparta.

With the belief that confirmatory pollen sequences would be helpful even farther away from Messenia, marshes and lakes in other parts of Greece were probed or sampled. In Attica, small coastal marshes were cored on the south coast at Anavyssos, and on the east coast at Ayios Nikolaos near Rafina and at Vlikas on the straits of Khalkis; but in all cases the sediment yielded no pollen. In Boeotia the great lake plain of Copais was also examined, in the walls of the drainage canals, but the sediment proved to be entirely mineral matter washed into the lake by the several large streams of the drainage basin. Even the spring marsh near Orchomenos in the western part of the plain had apparently been flooded by the lake sufficiently often that the sediment is essentially barren of pollen. Slightly more promising is the existing lake of Paralimni, where a marginal marsh was sampled. A core from the lake itself might yield satisfactory sediment.

In Euboea small coastal lagoons were visited near Eretria and Karystos along the west coast, but none was promising. The large interior marsh at Dystos, overgrown with reedbeds rich in mosquitoes, was cored without avail. The marsh, which seasonally contains much water, apparently drains to such a low level through limestone caverns in the edge of the basin that most of the organic matter, including pollen grains, decomposes rather than accumulates.

In western Greece north of the Gulf of Patras, several large lakes fill deep or wide valleys. The valleys were formed by crustal movements, for this is a region of active earthquakes, and the lakes result largely from segmentation of the valleys by alluvial fans of streams entering or crossing the valleys. The lakes are flooded with river sediment essentially barren of organic matter. Such lakes are either too young to have accumulated much sediment, or they are so large that wave and current action transports all the fine-grained organic sediment to the deep water, where coring could not be accomplished with the available equipment.

One lake of a different type was found on the west coast of this area, however – Lake Voulkaria. It is in a limestone sinkhole west of Bonitsa and is separated from the sea by a small ridge of limestone that rises only a few meters above sea level. The ridge has been breached by a canal. The lake is about 5 km in diameter. It is surrounded by a broad band of reeds. Large blocks of the reed mat break off and float across the lake, which is only a meter or so deep. Such floating islands provide suitable platforms for coring operations, and two cores were taken through about 8 m of lake sediments at localities about a third of the way toward the center of the lake from the west side.

The area is marked by hills now covered with maquis, dominated by shrubs of *Quercus coccifera* and *Phillyrea latifolia*, along with *Erica arborea* and *Arbutus* spp. With severe grazing, the *Quercus* and most other shrubs are cropped to very low size or even eliminated, and the unpalatable *Phlomis fruticosa* takes over the slopes. On the higher hills of the region, where the moisture is greater and the grazing pressure less, *Quercus coccifera* grows to tree size and shades out some of the maquis shrubs. It is joined by deciduous species of oak and, at higher elevations, by other deciduous trees as well, such as maple (*Acer monospessulanum*), hop hornbeam (*Ostrya carpinifolia*), and hornbeam (*Carpinus orientalis*), some of which extend upward to the tree line at an elevation of about 1,400 m. No conifers occur in the area, either in the mountains or along the coast.

The lower half of the Voulkaria pollen diagram is characterized by high pollen values of deciduous oak and grasses. Olive pollen is rare. The upper half is marked first by a rise in olive pollen to 20 percent, followed by a decrease to about 5 percent. Pollen of the maquis plants, evergreen oak (10 percent), pistachio (4 percent), and *Phillyrea* (4 percent) is more abundant than below, deciduous oak is about the same (30 percent), and pine (2 percent) is less common. Walnut, chestnut, and plane tree are consistently represented, whereas below they are absent.

A radiocarbon date (Table 12-1) at the base of the core is about 9000 B.C., but a date just below the olive rise is 1190 ± 120 B.C. Thus, just as with Osmanaga, the rise of olive pollen *follows* the Mycenaean interval, lending support to the hypothesis that olive was not introduced into Greece as a major food crop until after Mycenaean time. The same may be said for walnut, chestnut, and plane trees.

A further pollen record of the introduction of food crops comes from a small but deep lake on Mljet, an island off the Dalmatian coast 500 km northwest of Voulkaria (Beug 1961, 1967). Here the abrupt rise of olive, chestnut, and rye pollen occurs at the same level as the rise of pine, which may represent Aleppo pine planted in the area. No carbon analyses are available to date this event, but Beug correlates it with Greek colonization. The correlation is based mostly on negative evidence, however, and on the assumption that during the last 2,000 years no sediments were deposited in the lake. If sedimentation is assumed instead to have continued to the present, then the appearance of olive and nut trees is dated closer to 1000 B.C., similar to the Voulkaria and Osmanaga dates.

Summary and Conclusions

The vegetation history of southwest Peloponnese, as recorded by the pollen content of the sediments of Osmanaga Lagoon near Pylos, shows changes during the past 4,000 years that can be attributed to the activities of man. At some time during the Middle Bronze Age or early in the Late Bronze Age, pine woods disappeared from the coastal area near Pylos, probably because of woodcutting. During Mycenaean times, the land was extensively cleared for agriculture, but olive may not have been the major crop.

In the early Iron Age after the fall of the kingdom of Pylos, the region reverted to the mixed shrubland of the maquis, whose pollen rain was dominated by oak and evergreen. Then for an interval dated as about 1100 to 700 B.C. olive was widely grown in the area. Subsequent oak and olive pollen fluctuations may similarly be correlated with later cultural periods in Greek history, although neither the pollen analyses nor the radiocarbon dates are sufficient to provide much detail to the sequence.

Pollen study of a core from the lagoon at Kaiafa, 80 km north along the west coast, provides a vegetational history only since about A.D. 300. The coastal pine, which is common now along the beach ridge and also on the mountain slopes facing the sea, apparently greatly expanded a few centuries ago, perhaps as a result of planting to stabilize the sand dunes on the beach ridge.

Study of a core from Lake Voulkaria on the coast of northwestern Greece reveals a record sufficiently old to include Mycenaean time. The rise of olive pollen beginning about 1200 B.C. provides good correlation with the olive curve at Osmanaga Lagoon.

Search for other pollen sites in southwest Peloponnese, to confirm in more detail the interesting sequence at Osmanaga Lagoon, has been unsuccessful thus far, so we do not yet know how extensive geographically were the changes suggested by the Osmanaga diagram. Other coastal lagoons that have been tested in Peloponnese as well as in other parts of Greece either are too young to have sediment as early as the Bronze Age, or they have sediment unsuitable for pollen analysis. The same can be said for several inland lakes and spring marshes that were examined. Perhaps the story must remain on a speculative note – but in this respect it would not differ appreciably from much else in paleoecology and archaeology!

REFERENCES

Beug, H. J. 1961. "Beiträge zur postglazialen Floren-und Vegetationsgeschichte in Suddalmatien: Der See 'Malo Jezero' auf Mljet," *Systematisch-Geobotanischen Institut, Flora* 150:600–56. Göttingen.

———. 1967. "On the Forest History of the Dalmatian Coast," *Review of Palaeobotany and Palynology* 2:271–79.

Bisbee, H. L. 1937. "Samikon," *Hesperia* 6:525–38.

Carpenter, Rhys. 1966. *Discontinuity in Greek Civilization.* Cambridge.

Critchfield, W. B., and Little, E. L., Jr. 1966. *Geographic Distribution of the Pines of the World*: U.S. Forest Service, Misc. Publ. 991.

Pansiot, F. P., and Rebour, H. 1961. *Improvement in Olive Cultivation.* Rome, FAO Agricultural Studies No. 50.

Philippson, Alfred. 1895. "Zur Vegetationskarte des Peloponnes, 1:625,000," *Petermann's Geogr. Mitt.* 41:273–79.

———. 1959. *Die Griechischen Landschaften*, 2nd ed. Vol. 3, Pt. 2, pp. 319–523. *Der Peloponnes: Der Westen und Süden der Halbinsel.* Ed. E. Kirsten. Frankfurt.

Rikli, M. 1943. *Pflanzenkleid der Mittelmeerlande.* Berlin.

Rothmaler, Werner. 1943. "Die Waldverhaltnisse in Peloponnes,"*Intersylva* 3:329–42.

Turrill, W. B. 1929. *The Plant-Life of the Balkan Peninsula: A Phytogeographical Study.* Oxford.

Wright, H. E., Jr. 1968. "Climatic Change in Mycenaean Greece," *Antiquity* 42:123–27.

13

CERAMIC STUDIES

by

Frederick R. Matson

Pottery, roof tiles, and brick provide the most durable, though usually fragmentary, evidences of man's past activities other than those flaked from or built of stone. The ceramic record contains evidences of variation in raw materials used and their working properties, the shapes produced and decorated, the degree of firing, and the distribution of the products. In the present chapter several aspects of the wares made in MH-LH times in Messenia other than their forms and decoration will be discussed, together with the present-day pottery production of the region. The data have been obtained from the study of sherd collections, visits to archaeological sites, and extended conversations with Messenian potters as they worked.

The availability of clay has never been a problem for potters in this region. Hill slopes, valleys, and coastal areas all have workable clay deposits that have not been difficult to obtain. Transportation from the clay bed to the potter's workshop can never have been a serious problem, for no great distances were involved. It is likely that the availability of fuel for firing the ware and the nearby potential market for the products taken from the kiln were more important in determining where pottery was made than were the sources and the working properties of the clay. It may be assumed as a working hypothesis that most major towns and ports were pottery-producing areas. The strength of tradition, with sons succeeding their fathers, would also have been a stabilizing factor that could result in the clustering of pottery-producing shops in one section of town. This is still true today in Messenia, although economic factors are rapidly leading to the demise of the village potters. It was interesting and instructive to be able to visit potters at work in villages during the same field season in which one was studying the sherd collections from site surveys. These were complementary activities.

SITE SURVEYS

The sherd collections made by the UMME team during several field seasons were stored in the old and the new Kalamata museums and in the museum at Olympia. During the summer of 1963 I had the opportunity to examine over 5,000 of these sherds from 53 sites and also to visit many of the sites themselves. Thus it was possible to study the surface collections of potsherds with some appreciation of the ecological settings in which the pottery had been made, especially the clay, water, fuel resources, and transportation. Such studies have been of interest to me for some time (Matson 1965, 1966). A preliminary report on the summer's work was prepared for limited distribution in October, 1963, and was abstracted by McDonald (*AJA* 1964, pp. 243–44).

The site survey collections of Mycenaean and other wares is most valuable, but conclusions drawn from it must be used with the reserve normally accorded to materials from surface surveys. Recently ploughed fields were the most productive sites; July visitations were less satisfactory in their yield because of the vegetation cover; soil-wash exposes sherds on the steeper slopes, but certainly buries them at the lower levels; materials long exposed to weathering on rocky ground suffered surface alteration. These and other factors familiar to those making surface collections caution against quantitative conclusions based on the size and nature of the samples obtained. A return to the same sites at other times of the year and in successive years might provide the archaeologist with somewhat different sherd samplings than those obtained on the earlier visits.

A major aspect of the study of the sherds collected at the many sites visited was to use them to determine the cultural periods of their occupation. Profiles were drawn, and rim and basal diameters were determined for important pieces. A photographic record was made of selected material from each site. General comments on the technological nature of the materials were recorded on the site cards. These data have been used in suggesting cultural dates for the sites in the preliminary reports and in Chapter 8.

The technological evaluation of the sherds was another aspect of the study. Preliminary sortings were made into obvious categories such as fine and coarse ware, tempering materials used, thin- and thick-walled vessels, degree of firing, and weathering. It was surprising to note how many handles appeared in the collections. Sherds in each subgroup were examined with a 3× hand lens; several higher magnifications up to 60× were available for special problems of identification.

In general, this study sought to determine the types of clays and tempering materials used at a site for fine and for coarse wares, possible evidence of foreign wares in terms of the clays used (foreign, in this sense, might mean a site in the next valley if its soils and rocks were different), methods of manufacture, and the characteristic degree of firing. Accidental clues left in the clay when plastic but then hardened and preserved through firing for all time sometimes appeared. A few sherds characteristic of the clays and the tempering materials used were set aside for more detailed examination at a ceramic laboratory. Care was taken not to remove from the collection any sherds that were decorated or represented restorable shapes.

The fine-textured sherds, pale yellow, pink, and light red in color, constituted the most common group in the site samples, appearing in almost two-thirds of the collections. They contained few visible inclusions except occasional bits of limestone and ochre, and minute flakes of muscovite. The sites at which they occurred are concentrated in the western coastal plain from Pylos to Gargaliani, in the riverine areas of the Pamisos and the Alpheios, and in the regions of small streams draining toward the northwest corner of the Messenian Gulf. These are of course areas of concentrated Mycenaean sites, but they also are regions where fine-textured clays were deposited by river action or in marine silts. The Mycenaean potters thus had clays of good quality available near the settlements which were situated in fertile agricultural areas. This symbiotic relationship between the potters and the agriculturists is widespread. Where conditions are good for crop and animal production, clays are available which potters can work. This is especially true in water-rich areas whose soils are derived from weathered limestone.

As one handled these fine textured materials, differences could be recognized in the clays used – some sherds were soft and granular with weathered surfaces, whereas others were hard and compact with well-preserved surfaces. This variation, largely owing to the nature of the clay deposits, with differences in the plasticity and bonding strength of the clays, may in some cases serve as a clue in sorting sherds of a well-controlled collection from an excavated site if the properties of the available local clays are known. The study of the modern Messenian potters showed that within one village several sources of clay were used by different potters, and that salable vessels were produced from all of them. Hence, overly detailed sherd classifications in terms of their physical properties can be misleading in the study of a culture unless the properties of the local clays are known.

The color of the fired potsherds can often serve as a clue to the technological development and the control of temperature achieved by the potters in the period of time being studied. Fortunately, the clays of Messenia are essentially derived from the weathering and decomposition of limestones and are thus much like the clays of the Near East, where technological ceramic studies of ancient and modern pottery have been made for some years. The study of the Messenian potters at work and the examination of the color range produced in a kiln-load of pottery, brick, or tile today also serve as useful guides in the interpretation of the ancient sherds.

The variation in color of the fine textured ware if it is of a clay rich in lime will vary from low temperature light reds (about 600°–800°C) through reddish yellow (about 800°–900°C) to pale yellow (about 900°–1,050°C). At higher temperatures an olive yellow color develops, and the ware softens and becomes deformed. The color terms used here are the Soil Color Names in the Munsell Soil Color Charts (see p. 224 below). The length of firing time in the kiln as well as the temperature attained can affect the color developed by the clay, as can also the atmosphere in the kiln, especially in the final stages of the firing. If some salt is present in the clay, yellow colors will develop at lower temperatures and white ware appears. There can easily be a range of colors in one kiln load of ware since temperatures and atmosphere are far from uniform in village kilns, and there can be differences in the colors attained in successive firings. I have discussed these and other factors affecting color in another paper (Matson 1970).

The most spectacular evidence of the effect of excessive heat in a smoky atmosphere can be found in the collapsed and often fused state of the kylikes that Blegen excavated in room 9 of the main palace building (Blegen and Rawson 1966, pp. 100–2, fig. 81). Many of the vessels had melted into a slag. In the presence of a strongly reducing atmosphere such as that probably induced in the holocaust by the burning of the timbers and especially by the olive oil stored in the pithoi, a lower temperature would be required to melt the kylikes than would be needed in an oxidizing atmosphere such as a kiln firing. Similar but less extensive or informative materials might be found in a trash heap near a kiln.

In the surface collections from the many sites, the color range was about as one finds it in the modern kilns – light red through white. Few greenish sherds appeared. As a first approximation, based on surface samplings, it would appear that the firing range and the temperature distribution in the Mycenaean kilns differed little from those of the village craftsmen today. This is not surprising, for there has been little change in basic kiln design and the same fuels (except perhaps for *pirini*, the sludge from the modern olive oil and soap factories) were available – wood, brush, straw, grass, and reeds.

Some fine-textured and many sandy sherds fired to shades of red. Often they were badly abraded so that surface finishing details could not be seen. The sampling is too small to permit a useful site distribution plotting, but they appear to occur chiefly at the upland sites. These are in the regions of the red clays whose formation and distribution is discussed by Wright and Loy in Chapter 3. Many of the coarser textured wares are made from the red-firing clay, which suggests upland places of manufacture. It is tempting to think of an analogy in the Near East today. Most pottery is wheel-made from riverine clays or loess deposits, and the wares are similar to those of the Mycenaean potters in color and texture. However, utility pottery is still made in the mountain villages of Iraq, Iran, and Afghanistan for local use. It is often handmade by women in their courtyards as one of their domestic tasks. As more excavation takes place in Messenia, it would be of interest to study the red-fired pottery, especially water jars and cooking pots, and consider the possibility of their having been made in mountain villages.

The coarse-textured sherds were usually thicker in body wall, 6–12mm, in contrast to the 3–8mm walls of the fine ware. There were some thick-walled sherds of fine-textured clays, but most of them contained medium, coarse, or very coarse sand grains in the paste, in terms of Wentworth's scale of size classification that is used by sedimentary petrologists and is directly applicable for archaeologists (Shepard 1965, p. 118). Since the use of a standardized size classification is desirable, Wentworth's classification, which is based on a geometric ratio, is presented in Table 13-1 (adapted from Milner 1962, I, pp. 180, 183). Wentworth expressed the size limits or grades as fractions of millimeters. In Table 13-1 they are also presented in decimal form, since that is how grains are measured, especially in thin sections. A third column presents the American Society for Testing Materials (ASTM) sieve series numbers. If one plans to evaluate clay resources in the field, it is useful to have along a few ASTM sieves, possibly numbers 10, 20, 40, 100, and 200.

Table 13-1. Wentworth's Size Limits of Grades

Diameter (mm)	Type of Rock	A.S.T.M. Mesh
64–4	Pebble	. . .
4–2	Granule	5–8
2–1	Very coarse sand grain	10–16
1–1/2 (1–0.5)	Coarse sand grain	18–30
1/2–1/4 (0.5–0.25)	Medium sand grain	35–50
1/4–1/8 (0.25–0.125)	Fine sand grain	60–100
1/8–1/16 (0.125–0.06)	Very fine sand grain	120–200
1/16–1/256 (0.06–0.004)	Silt particle	230
1/256– (0.004–)	Clay particle	. . .

Most of the coarse and very coarse textured sherds include a range of sizes in sand grains that make it appear that a naturally sandy clay was used. It is of course possible that a very sandy and a fine-textured sticky clay were sometimes mixed together to produce the working properties that the potter desired. It is not possible to speak of this group as intentionally tempered without better knowledge of the textural variations in the local clays near a site. It should not have been difficult for a potter to procure clay of the texture desired for the ware to be made. The vessels were probably built up of coils and finished by compaction and rounding of the surfaces with the paddle and anvil. The weathered condition of the surface sherds collected at the sites makes it difficult to recognize techniques of manufacture. My nonstatistical impression is that the coarser wares tended to have gray cores, which indicate that they were fired for a short period of time, possibly in a fire pit or on an open hearth rather than in a kiln. It should by no means be assumed that all ware from Neolithic times onward in Greece was kiln-fired.

Handles occurred in significant numbers in the survey collections, probably because of their durability, and they seemed to consistently contain abundant coarse to very coarse sandy inclusions. They usually fired to a red surface color and had a gray core. They were fragments of utility ware and their study in detail might be rewarding since they were horizontal and vertical, thick and thin, strap and round. The coarser ware in the magnificent collection in the Chora museum of reconstructed vessels from the palace might serve as a guide in such a study, for there they can be associated with rim form and body shape.

Intentionally tempered pottery was made in Messenia when greater strength was needed in the plastic walls of large vessels such as pithoi, whose walls are 18–22 mm thick. The tempering material, sometimes called aplastic, would also reduce the drying shrinkage and help prevent large drying cracks from developing. Red shale in hard angular grains up to 5 mm in length was frequently used to temper pithoi and other large pieces. Such tempered ware is easy to recognize when one is sorting sherds. A pale brown to white very fine sandy inclusion, soft and often abraded, is also a characteristic aplastic. It is normally a chloritic schist, but can range from a very fine textured claystone to a fine sandstone. Pottery in which it was included has been termed "oatmeal ware" in some earlier UMME reports, but this term should be dropped. Very occasionally granules of limestone were used as aplastic, and they at times have disappeared from ware buried in acid soil, leaving holes in the sherds. Such pieces inappropriately have been termed "hole tempered." Limestone granules appear in incised ware, such as the poorly termed Adriatic ware of Middle Helladic times (Pl. 3-1), and have been recognized in sherds at sites # 51, 123, and 213.

Alternate broad bands of red shale and pale brown claystone or chloritic schist appear in road cuts in several parts of Messenia. One such exposure is near site #100 (Rizomilo:Nichoria). Another can be seen just north of the Arkadian Gate at classical Messene on the northwestern slopes of Mt. Ithomi. The red shale continues to be exposed as one drives south along the western slope toward the village of Mavromati. Samples of the shale and of the chloritic schist were collected from the beds near the Arkadian Gate for laboratory study, and will be discussed later.

Red shale inclusions were noted in sherds gathered from eighteen sites included in the survey, and the light-colored claystone/schist aplastic appeared at twenty-five sites. Fifteen of the sites had both kinds in their sherd bags. In the case of at least four sites, sherds were tempered with a mixture of the two aplastics. It is realized that the small sherd collections from many of the sites may not have included examples of coarse ware such as pithoi fragments, so the distribution found for these tempering practices gives a minimal picture that probably will be expanded as further work is done in the region. The presently available distributional data were plotted, and they showed that the sites where sherds of both types occurred centered in three areas – northwest of Navarino Bay; in the foothills near the gulf coast from Longa to Rizomilo; and in the upper Pamisos Valley – near Meligala, east and north of Zevgolatio, and near Dhiavolitsi (Fig. 13-1). In addition, red shale tempering appeared in the hills above the Pamisos Valley near Lambaina and Pidhima, and near Kambos, southeast of Kalamata. The claystone/schist tempering occurs in sherds at additional sites along a line from Rizomilo northwest toward Gargaliani, and in the Pamisos and Steniklarian valleys. The delineation of sites centering chiefly in a band from Longa-Rizomilo to Gargaliani, and in the Pamisos and Steniklarian valleys does not mean that there were no other geological occurrences of these two tempering materials. Instead, it suggests that the intentional tempering of clay in Mycenaean times for the manufacture of pithoi and some other utility wares was culturally limited to these two well-travelled zones.

For the record, the site distribution of the tempering materials is as follows. Both shale and claystone/schist were used in different wares at #'s 1, 6, 7, 51, 103, 104, 106, 112, 114, 116, 207, 208, 213, 215, 222. Red shale was used at #'s 123, 136, 146. Claystone/schist was used at #'s 15, 28, 31, 46, 122, 214.

Many of the pithoi in the palace were tempered with red shale. In room 24, one of the two magazines for the storage of olive oil directly behind the throne room, the pithoi are all still in place (Blegen and Rawson 1966, figs. 93, 102, 106). They had fractured edges on or above the shoulder area where the rims had been broken, for the necks were above the plough line of the long-buried site. (Blegen and Rawson 1966, p. 136.) Therefore it was possible to study the cores carefully, and it was found that all except pithos number 9 contained abundant shale fragments. Number 9 fired to a lighter brown and contained but a small amount of red shale. It was probably from a different workshop than that of the principal supplier of palace pithoi. Insofar as the pithoi in room 23 could be examined, it was found that they too were tempered with red shale. In addition to the pithoi, some other utility vessels in Blegen's "coarse ware" were similarly tempered with red shale or with light-colored rock fragments.

The selective use of shale and claystone/schist as tempering materials may well relate to the properties of the clays that the potters were using, if the selection had a rational rather than a traditional raison d'être. Shale is a hard angular rock, and will serve well as aplastic in clays that are fine-textured and possibly sticky. The soft claystone/schist, which breaks down with water, could have served as a binder when powdered, as well as a body stiffener when present as granules in sandy clays. Such questions might be considered while the pottery from a major excavation is being analyzed in detail. It would be useful

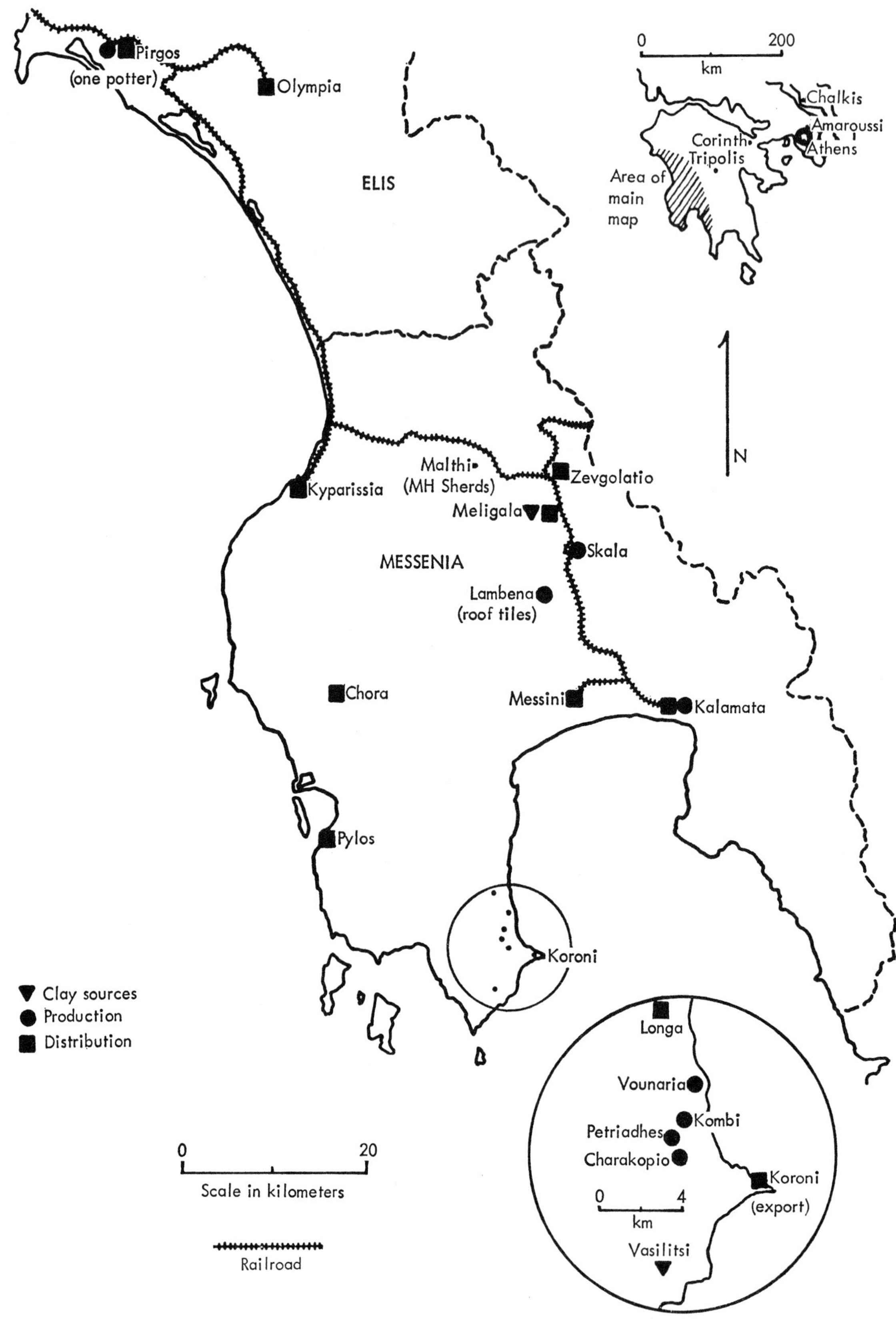

Figure 13-1. Ceramics: clay sources, production, distribution

if experiments were made mixing local clays and tempering materials, and noting the working properties while excavating the site. It would also be interesting to learn what the relationship of shapes other than pithoi (which seem always to have one or both of these aplastics included in the paste) is to the inclusion of such tempering material. My present impression is that they were used as available by the potters, and not preferentially. The alternate banding of the red and the tan outcrops also provided potters with both materials in the same area.

A few unusual pieces, probably of second millennium date, appeared in the surface collections but they are not worth detailed description in a general report. A fragment of a brazier and a rim sherd with three holes punched through it, presumably for tieing on a cover, and sherds showing evidence of techniques of manufacture will illustrate the kinds of items that occurred. Pithos fragments and roof tiles should perhaps also be included in the inventory, but their ubiquity throughout the long occupation of Messenia with little change in style and no stratigraphic ceramic sequences as yet established for such material do not at present make them useful items of study in surface collections.

The Mycenaean sites tend to be related to fertile soils, good sources of water, and low ridges or other elevations that offer defensible positions. Most of them are not far from ports or from major highways. These generalized criteria also describe areas where good workable clays might be obtained. Since pottery manufacture of necessity was a craft at or near major settlements, it is not too farfetched to suggest that one factor helping to determine the survival value of a village which later might have grown into a major Mycenaean settlement, was the availability of good clay, a clay which made possible rich crops as well as productive potters.

It is instructive to examine the map of known Mycenaean sites in terms of the physiography described by Wright and Loy, and to compare it with the present-day pottery-producing areas (Fig. 13-1). There is little correlation. At present the potters are concentrated in two areas with individual potters at two other sites. The major group is on the east shore of the Messenian Gulf between Longa and Koroni in an area of Pliocene clays washed down from the hills. The same is true for the potters at Kalamata (who get their clay from north of Messini) and the lone potter at Krestaina south of Olympia. The family of potters at Skala, south of Zevgolatio, tends to mix alluvial clay from near Lambaina, 3 km distant, with that derived from tertiary sandstones and shales in order to achieve a good workable clay, but the site of the shop was determined by its proximity to the railroad station. The limited areas of pottery manufacture today certainly do not reflect conditions in Mycenaean times. It is suggested, as a trial hypothesis, that pottery was manufactured at all Mycenaean towns built on the coastal and high inland plains with good Pliocene soils. Special wares such as kylikes and pithoi might have regional distribution. Some of the pottery excavated at the palace certainly indicates such ceramic mobility. There are interesting problems awaiting definition and field study as an active excavation program continues in Messenia.

SHERDS UNDER THE MICROSCOPE

From among the Messenian site survey sherds in the Kalamata museums, twelve were selected for laboratory study after the entire series had been examined visually and with the aid of a hand lens. The general data are summarized in notes following Table 13-2. The criteria for their selection were:

a. Geographic distribution. Material was needed for detailed microscopic study from several parts of Messenia so that a first survey could be made of possible regional mineralogical differences in the clays used and in the tempering materials that were at times added by the potters.

b. Size. Small sherds were chosen that were not unique so as not to unbalance the surface survey collections. This meant that pieces of diagnostic shape were not selected, and the sherds taken were dated by their association with the rest of the collection.

c. Mineralogical interest. Sherds containing coarse sand grains were often chosen so as to establish the range of mineral and rock inclusions that might occur in the pottery at the site. Handles, pithos fragments, and other thick sherds were considered when making the selection. Very fine textured sherds and some that appeared unusual, such as those containing abundant flakes of mica, were also chosen.

Comments on the defensive hilltop positions of the sites from which the sherds came or their location on rocky spurs from which the settlers could control the roads or passes can be found in Chapter 8. Presumably, much of the pottery was made in villages in the valleys or on the lower slopes. The ware or the clay from which it was made was brought to these higher sites. Since all of the sherds are badly eroded, there is no point in attempting to date their time of manufacture closer than MH-LH except as this may have been done for the site collections reported in Chapter 8 and listed in Table 13-2.

Malthi is the only extensively excavated MH and LH site in Messenia. It was my privilege to examine some of the sherds from the excavations with Valmin at the museum in Vasiliko in 1963. We looked particularly at the so-called "Adriatic ware" in terms of the clays used and the degree of firing that the ware received. When well fired, the clay develops a reddish yellow color (5YR 7/8), but often there is a gray core, and there are spot color differences on the exterior owing to contact with coals, other ware, and smoke or drafts during firing. There are tan claystone inclusions in many of the sherds. Two subvarieties, one possibly with slate inclusions, seem to be made from a more plastic clay, and the ware tends to be more gray in color. It was interesting to note in this collection of less than a hundred sherds that a few may have been used as scrapers, to judge by their chipped and abraded edges. From a very brief examination of the Neolithic sherds and some Late Helladic materials, it would appear that several sources of clay were used by the potters whose products were excavated at the high fortress of Malthi. Perhaps it would be more accurate to say that the wares found at the site doubtless came from several different households on the hill slopes or in the valleys, and were thus fabricated from clays derived from geologically differing origins.

Sherds from Malthi became unexpectedly available the following year in an old collection, and it was possible to obtain seven for laboratory study. They, too, were chosen to represent variations in mineral inclusions and textures, and they are included in Table 13-2.

It was my privilege to be able to spend a few days at the palace in 1963 and again to visit the site in 1964. The results of the technological study of the pottery excavated at the palace will be published elsewhere, but reference will be made in the present report to the mineralogical character of twelve sherds that were studied in the laboratory.

The preliminary examination of the sherds included:

a. Method of manufacture – finishing marks on the surfaces, alignment of particles with respect to the surfaces as seen in the cross section through each sherd; method of attachment of handle to the body; fracture pattern in kylix stems; possible coil junctures in the body walls; evidence of surface compaction with paddle and anvil.

b. Degree of firing – color indications of the firing history, such as sherds having surface oxidation with a gray core or being oxidized throughout. All color terms used in this report are those of the Munsell Soil Color Names which appear on the page opposite to the Soil Color Charts. Shepard (1965, pp. 107–13) has presented a good discussion of the Munsell method of describing the colors found on pottery. The names give an approximate indication of colors; more specific descriptions are obtained by using the Munsell system of color notation. Here, the color of each sherd will be given both by name and in the notation system. If one is familiar with the color changes that occur in the local clays as they are fired to increasingly higher temperatures under oxidizing and reducing conditions for various periods of time, a reasonable estimate can be made of the degree of firing of the pottery from the colors developed on the surface and in the core of the sherds.

c. Surface texture – sandiness of the clay, mineral or rock inclusions appearing on the surface. Examination visually, followed by use of a 7× hand lens and then by a binocular microscope, will often provide useful information.

d. Paste texture – seen on a freshly broken edge of each sherd, and also on the smooth face remaining when a slice is cut from the sherd for the preparation of the thin section. With the hand lens and under the binocular microscope one can observe the mineralogical texture, the presence and orientation of pores if the clay had been poorly worked by the potter, and the occurrence of plant inclusions such as chaff or seeds.

Petrographic thin sections were prepared by cutting a quarter-inch slice from each sherd, grinding it very smooth, cementing the smooth face to a microscope slide, grinding away the slice until only a wafer 0.04 mm thick remained, and then cementing a protective cover of glass on it. The preparation of such sections is not inexpensive, and their study is time consuming. The mineral and rock fragrants present in the sections were identified by their optical characteristics, and note was taken of their grain shape and size, abundance, and the orientation of the particles with respect to the surfaces of the sherds. The color changes in the minerals because of the kiln firing, the pore shapes, orientation and distribution, and the secondary deposition of lime in cracks or pores in the sherds from groundwater action were also observed. Almost every thin section differs slightly from all others made, and it is only the significant data in terms of the study of the pottery that is presented in Table 13-2. The thin sections are on file if they are required for comparative studies or for geological or mineralogical data. This selective approach is archaeologically more useful than is the publication of infinitely detailed reports.

The results of extended study of the thin sections have been summarized in Table 13-2. There the sherds appear grouped geographically, beginning with Rizomilo:Nichoria (#100) near the northwestern corner of the Gulf of Messenia, and continuing south along the western hills bordering the gulf to sites near Petalidhi and Longa. These are followed in Table 13-2 by the sherds from Osmanaga Lagoon just north of Navarino Bay, and by a second series which includes sherds from the east central and Pamisos and Steniklaros areas. Comments on and interpretations of the thin section evidence for each of the sections follow Table 13-2.

The minerals and rocks found in the thin sections that appear in Table 13-2 are listed in three groups: (a) the very visible tempering materials added by the potter – red shale and/or claystone, chloritic schist, or very fine

Table 13-2. Petrographic Data for Thin Sections of Messenian Site Survey Sherds[a]

Content	Site 100		Site 103				Site 106	Site 7		Site 207	Site 215		Site 222						
	P-731	P-732	P-726	P-727	P-728	P-729	P-730	P-724	P-725	P-723	P-721	P-722	P-224	P-225	P-219	P-222	P-221	P-223	P-220
Tempering materials																			
Red shale			S	M	S[b]	S[b]	M[b]		M	S[b]	C		M	C					
Claystone			C	M									C					S[b]	
With quartz					C	M			C										
With oolites			S	M															
Arenaceous chloritic schist										M[b]	C	C		M	M[b]				
Limestone													C						
Chaff											S								
Minerals and rocks in the clay matrix																			
Chlorite-oxidized	C	M	M	S			M	C	C	M	A	C	A	A	A	M	C	M	C
Muscovite	C	M	M	S	M		A	M	M	A	M	S		M	M	M	A	A	A
Biotite		M																	
Quartz	M	C	M	M	A	A	A	A	A	C	C	A	C	C	A	C	A	A	A
Quartzite		C	S		S	S	A	S	S	C	S	M	S	M	S	S	S	M	S
Chalcedony	M	C	C[c]	S	C	C[c]	C	C	M	S	M	S	C[c]	M	M	S	M	C	M
Oolitic chalcedony	S		C[c]	M	S	S[c]	M	S	S										
Auxiliary minerals and rocks																			
Red clay — very fine	M	S	M		M	M									M	M	M	S	S
Feldspars		M					M	M	S	M		S	S	S	S	S	S	M	S
Sandstone							S												
Tremolite							M												

[a] The relative frequency of occurrence of rock and mineral fragments is indicated by the letters A (abundant), C (common), M (moderate), and S (sparse). Where no letter is given, fragments were absent.

[b] Natural occurrence in the clay matrix.

[c] Tempering material.

grained sandstone; (b) the minerals usually appearing in the Messenian clays; and, (c) auxiliary mineral and rock fragments found in some of the sections.

In Table 13-2 the relative frequency of occurrence of the rock and mineral fragments in the thin sections is indicated as abundant, common, moderate, or sparse. This is a subjective indication, but it serves our purpose well in characterizing materials from site surveys. The time-consuming point counting of mineral frequencies in a section is not justified for this material. The aplastics are normally present in large-size grains in the Messenian pottery and can be recognized because the particles do not consistently grade down to finer sizes as they would in a natural deposit. However, since some crushing may occur when the potter is collecting and preparing his tempering material, it is likely that a few very fine to coarse fragments may appear in the sections. Such items are not listed in the second part of Table 13-2, for it is assumed that the listing in the first part of the table implies occasional appearance of such grains in smaller sizes as well. In the notes prepared for each of the thin sections, the Wentworth scale of grain size designation and the Munsell system of color names and notation have been used.

#100, Rizomilo:Nichoria (MH-LH)

The materials from the preliminary testing of the site in 1959 that were stored in the Olympia museum were examined in 1963. Also, two sherds had been selected from the collection of surface materials at the Kalamata museum, and they were studied. They have been assigned thin section numbers P-731 and P-732.

P-731. Wheel-turned reddish yellow (7.5YR 8/6) collar fragment of a large jar, 11–15 mm thick. It is oxidized throughout, but there is slight reduction in both surface zones that developed in the final stages of the firing. This is a soft ware – the surfaces are badly abraded, and the fractured edges are worn smooth. Red grains of iron-rich clay up to 1 mm in size appear on the surface. (Red grains appear on surfaces of most of the sherds examined at the Olympia museum.) *Thin section*: This is an exceptionally fine textured clay for the Messenian series examined. Possibly it was washed in a settling tank by the potter, as is done today, but it could be a natural water washed clay. The inclusions are less than 0.05 mm in size, usually less than 0.03 mm (in the silt particle range on the Wentworth scale). Muscovite and oxidized chlorite are common. The subrounded red clay particles present are almost all less than 1 mm in diameter. The minerals present are the same as those seen in the other inland Messenian sherds studied, except for their size. The pores are very fine and tend to parallel the surfaces except in the juncture zone where the collar had been added to the shoulder of the jar. This vessel was probably formed from Quaternary clay such as that used in the coastal villages today on the western shore of the Gulf of Messenia.

P-732. Light red (2.5YR 6/6) thin body sherd 4 mm thick from a wheel-turned vessel. It has a fine sandy texture with some very fine mica appearing on the surfaces in addition to the occasional red clay grains. *Thin section*: Medium to coarse grained inclusions up to 0.6 mm in size occur (Table 13-2). The frequency of the coarser grains would suggest that either a natural clay of this texture could be found without coarser inclusions, or, more likely, this was a more sandy portion of the washed clay taken by the potter from his clay settling tank or drying platform. It would require the sorting with respect to texture of a large number of excavated sherds to establish the characteristic textural range for the Nichoria wares and the clays used for them. The fired color as well as the presence of feldspars and biotite show that P-732 came from a geologically different clay bed than P-731. This sherd was selected because it was from a small group unusual in its thinness of vessel wall and sandy texture. The presence of a moderate amount of biotite marks this as a unique sherd in the limited series that has been studied. If locally made, it is probably formed from the Pliocene clay deposits.

#103, Kalochori:Ayios Ilias (MH-LH)

Four sherds were selected for closer study from this site because sherds were available and it is not far from #100. There may be differences in minerals in the clays used. The sherds were chosen to show the variations in the texture and the tempering materials of the Bronze Age pottery. Very pale brown claystone inclusions occur in most of the sherds examined from this site.

P-726. Handle fragment 21 mm in diameter, with plug end for insertion in the body wall. Light red (2.5YR 7/8) surface 2 mm thick. Core gray. The handle was formed by rolling a strip of clay, for pores and cracks in the cut face as well as the long axis of the mineral inclusions tend to be roughly parallel to the circumference. The inclusions seen on the surface are red shale and very pale brown claystone in grains up to 3 mm in length, lustrous white flint, lustrous red jasper, and smooth dark grains. On the saw-cut face through the handle one can see under the binocular microscope that there are two kinds of very pale brown inclusions; some are pale pink chalcedony, the others are very soft and are granular in appearance. The clay matrix is soft and has many surface imperfections. *Thin section*: The sherd was tempered with angular laminated grains of silt-textured claystone containing flakes of chlorite. There are narrow firing shrinkage cracks around the perimeter of the claystone fragments. Thin long cracks in the paste suggest, not surprisingly, that the clay was mealy in consistency. It is interesting that aplastics were added to a coarse textured clay – perhaps they were needed in the preparation of the paste for the handles, but not for the body of the vessel. There are a few angular grains of chalcedony present as large as the claystone fragments, but they are sparse; some of them are oolitic. Individual very fine oolites are common in the section.

P-727. Body sherd, 9 mm thick, with its pink (7.5YR 7/4) exterior and light red (2.5YR 7/6) interior surfaces oxidized to a depth of 1 mm. Core gray. Exterior smoothed; interior surface shows some red shale aplastic. The saw-cut face shows that the plate-like tempering material (appearing thin and elongated in cross-section) is oriented parallel to the surfaces, which indicates considerable working of the clay as the vessel walls were formed. The clay matrix is soft, smooth in texture, and has surface cracks. It has the same "feel" as P-726, but contains far fewer inclusions. *Thin section*: The clay is tempered with a mixture of granules of red shale, silt-textured claystone, and claystone containing very fine oolites of chalcedony, but the total amount of aplastic present is less than in P-726. The claystone has thin shrinkage cracks around the grains. The clay matrix contains fine sand grains in much smaller amounts than in P-726. The mineral assemblage is similar in the two sections, but there is much less mica and chlorite in P-727. The clays of the two sherds are therefore of similar but not identical origin. The strong link between the two is the presence of oolitic chalcedony, which in hand specimens would be termed red jasper.

P-728. Abraded body sherd 18 mm thick, oxidized light red (2.5YR 6/8) throughout. Probably a pithos fragment. Tempered with very pale brown (10YR 8/3) granules. The largest inclusions are at or near the surface, which suggests that some potters may have added the granules in the later stages of the vessel forming to strengthen the walls and possibly to reduce or limit surface cracking as the vessel dried. The clay matrix is soft with a gritty "feel." *Thin section*: The aplastic is a claystone containing abundant very fine quartz and oxidized chlorite. Chalcedony, some of it oolitic, is present in the matrix in grains up to 0.5 mm in size, but the dominant and abundant inclusion is very fine angular quartz. Its presence indicates that the clay would have very low shrinkage, so the addition of claystone granules, especially since they tend to be concentrated near the surfaces, must have been to strengthen the plastic vessel walls, which were being formed of what must have been a rather mealy clay.

P-729. Body sherd 9 mm thick, oxidized light red (2.5YR 7/8) throughout. Very pale brown inclusions seldom over 1 mm in size; rounded red grains up to 3 mm in diameter can be seen occasionally on the surfaces. The clay matrix is soft with a gritty "feel." *Thin section*: The tempering material is claystone containing much very fine quartz and oxidized chlorite. The grains are subrounded, and most of them are about 0.5 mm in size with little gradation to finer sizes. It is probable that the moderate amount present had been added as a dry powder by the potter to a too plastic clay paste. Chalcedony is present in grains up to 0.5 mm in size, and the abundant quartz seldom exceeds 0.2 mm. This is the same paste with the same kind (but not size) of tempering material as P-728.

The four sherds studied from #103 show that the potters used at least two different kinds of clay and associated tempering materials. The smooth and gritty "feel" of these two wares would make it possible to sort the sherds into at least these two types, and a study of the tempering materials added in terms of kinds used and distribution in the ware could provide useful data.

#106, Longa:Paliokastro (N?, MH)

The sherds found at this hilltop site situated between ravines were almost all of coarse ware, and were usually tempered with very pale brown claystone, but a few contained red shale, and some had a mixture of the two aplastics.

P-730. A fragment of an oval rope handle, 28 × 35 mm in cross section, was selected for study because it was unusual in that much mica glittered on its light red (2.5YR 6/8) coarse sandy surface. The saw-cut cross-section shows that the coarse sand grains are well distributed throughout the clay body, which has light gray zones in the central core. *Thin section*: This coarse to very coarse paste contains angular inclusions up to 2 mm in size consisting of quartzite, chalcedony (some of it oolitic), tremolite, very fine sandstone, and aggregates of muscovite. Muscovite flakes occur often along grain boundaries in the quartzite. This clay contains a mixture of mineral and rock fragments from weathered metamorphic materials as well as sedimentary deposits, both of which are probably derived from conglomerates in this region. It is unique in the series of sherds that have been studied in thin section, and would seem to have been a very sandy clay used by a potter to form handles, but perhaps not also the body of the jars.

#7, Petrochori:Osmanaga (LHIIIB)

The two sherds selected from the series collected from 59D, the old designation of the subsection of #7 (*AJA* 1964, pp. 232–33), represent the very fine textured sandy ware that is characteristic of the site and the granule-tempered cooking pots. The sherds from #7 had long been submerged in water in the Osmanaga Lagoon before its drainage in 1962.

P-724. Small flange fragment of a kylix foot that had been approximately 80 mm in diameter, reddish yellow (5YR 7/8). This is a moderately fired piece, for the central part of the core is still reddish gray (10R 6/1). The surface has a sandy texture. *Thin section*: The very fine grained inclusions, with none larger than 0.1 mm, suggest that this clay had been washed before being used. The minerals present and their frequency are much like those of the sandy clay from #103. This is not surprising, for the clay could have been derived from the western outwash slopes of the hills whose eastern slopes provided clays used at #103.

P-725. Body sherd 10 mm thick from a globular cooking pot whose diameter, judging from the curvature of the sherd, was at least 240 mm. The exterior is reddish yellow (5YR 7/8) and the core is pinkish gray (5YR 6/2). The interior surface is encrusted with black organic material. The paste is heavily tempered with very pale brown claystone and a small amount of red shale. The aplastic protrudes slightly from the very fine sandy abraded surface. *Thin section*: The paste is like that of P-724. It is tempered with granules of subrounded claystone silt-size particles of angular quartz and muscovite flakes less than 0.04 mm in size. The quartz in the claystone is far less frequent than in that seen in the two sandy sherds from #103 (P-728 and P-729). The aplastic in this case may not only help strengthen the vessel walls, as has been suggested earlier, but may also have been added to reduce surface wear and abrasion of vessels formed from this sandy clay.

#207, Katsarou:Ayios Ilias (MH?, LH)

The sherds examined from this site differed from most of those farther south in that white mica appeared abundantly on the sherd surfaces. This suggested a possibly different mineralogical regime northeast of the Pamisos Valley, so one sherd was selected for study.

P-723. Handle fragment 30 mm in diameter with a very micaceous surface. Light red (2.5YR 7/8) oxidized surface to a depth of 2 mm. The core is gray (2.5YR 5/0) and contains white angular inclusions up to 2 mm in size, as can be clearly seen on the saw-cut face. *Thin section*: The abundant inclusions seldom exceed 1 mm in size in the section, although 2-mm grains appeared in the cut face. Coarse grains of micaceous quartzite (with muscovite along many quartz grain boundaries) are common, accompanied in lesser amounts by fragments of chloritic schist and chalcedony. Muscovite flakes up to 0.5 mm in size are common in the clay matrix. The clay used was probably a naturally occurring sandy type, for there is a fairly continuous gradation in grain size in the inclusions. It is of course possible that the potter added sand to a fine grained clay when preparing the material from which to fashion the handles of his vessels. The orientation of the grains and pores with respect to the surface suggests that the handle was formed by rolling the clay.

#215, Agrilovouno:Ayios Nikolaos (MH-LH)

Two sherds, each characteristically tempered with red shale or very pale brown claystone were chosen to represent the kinds of material characteristic at this site overlooking the northwestern part of the Steniklarian Valley.

P-721. Pithos rim with a 300 mm–wide lip and 20 mm body wall, light red (2.5YR 7/8) in color, is heavily tempered with granules of red shale up to 8 mm in length. Light-colored sandy granules are also present. The cross-section cut through the sherd shows that the greatest concentration of the shale is near the surfaces. This thick piece is oxidized throughout. There are some chaff impressions on the surface that are up to 5 mm in length. *Thin section*: Angular granules of red shale are dominant; some of them are present as fine splinters, which suggests that the potter found it necessary to crush the shale before adding it to the clay. A second additive is an arenaceous chloritic schist in subrounded grains which grades into a very fine sandstone. Chaff holes, a few of them indicating by their shape the former presence of seeds in the organic additive, are well distributed in the section. Since the chaff was in small particles less than 5 mm in length, and some seeds were present in it, the possibility exists of a little dung having been added to the clay by the potter to make it more plastic. This was a common practice in the ancient Near East, and I have discussed the evidence in a preliminary fashion elsewhere (Matson 1956, p. 355; 1960, p. 68). The clay matrix is very fine textured, and the quartz and chalcedony present, together with the oxidized chlorite, were probably derived from the weathering of schists and sandstones like those seen in the tempering materials. It is interesting to note that the potter used three kinds of additive – shale, schist/sandstone and straw. His ware was well fired. This craftsman produced good ware.

P-722. Round handle, 240 mm in diameter, with plug end for insertion into the body wall. Reddish yellow (5YR 7/8) oxidized surface to a depth of 2 mm, light gray (2.5YR 7/0) core. The handle is heavily tempered with very pale brown granules. *Thin section*: The tempering material is a chloritic schist composed of very fine angular quartz grains and chlorite flakes 0.05 mm in size and finer. There is less quartz in this schist than in P-721. The matrix, however, contains more quartz and quartzite grains than does P-721. The two pastes are very similar, but that of P-722 is the sandier of the two. Possibly the potter would select a sandier clay for the forming of handles. If so, the clay would be mealier in consistency, and the addition of a claystone and some powder derived from it might increase the plasticity while maintaining the plastic strength of the clay for the preparation of handles. The addition of a little dung would have been more effective. There is a narrow void around the perimeter of many of the schist grains, and this too suggests the mealy nature of the clay.

#222, Vasiliko:Malthi (MH-LH)

As has already been mentioned, seven sherds from an old Malthi collection were available for laboratory study. They were selected for surface appearance, tempering materials, and so on to represent the range of mineralogical textures probably present at the site. They should represent materials available in the hills above the northwestern part of the Steniklarian Valley. So as to avoid repetition, in the light of the materials already presented, each will receive but brief comment.

P-224. Body sherd with attached base of a round handle, abundantly tempered with more than one kind of angular very pale brown grains. Body wall 10 mm thick, handle 24 mm in diameter. Light red (2.5YR 6/6) oxidized surface to a depth of 4 mm. Dark gray core. *Thin section*: The sherd is tempered with granules of limestone, claystone, chalcedony, and red clay lumps in which quartz grains are included. It would seem that the potter gathered gravel and used it as the aplastic. It must have come from a deposit of mixed materials washed down the slopes. The clay matrix contains medium quartz grains as well as the finer fractions of the aplastics. It is interesting that this is the only Messenian sherd in the selection that I studied which contained limestone. There are numerous pores and cracks in the paste, which is not surprising in such a coarsely tempered ware.

P-225. Flat body sherd 11 mm thick tempered with 2-mm granules of red shale and light gray claystone. Interior surface oxidized to a light red (2.5YR 6/8), but the exterior, slightly reduced, is yellow (2.5Y 8/4); the core is light gray (2.5Y 7/0). *Thin section*: The fine slivers of red shale seen in the section together with the coarser material suggest that the aplastic had either been crushed or was a natural inclusion in the clay. Subangular grains of arenaceous micaceous schist that grade into very fine sandstone also occur under the same conditions. The presence of muscovite in the claystone and the schist marks this area of pottery production as being in a somewhat different geological regime. The matrix contains a moderate amount of very fine quartz and other minerals (see Table 13-2).

P-219. Strap handle and everted rim fragment, 4–5 mm in thickness, reddish yellow (5YR 7/8) in color. Oxidized throughout. Red clay and very pale brown inclusions 1 mm in size appear on the surface. *Thin section*: Coarse red clay grains of irregular shape are probably derived from a well-developed red soil. Coarse pieces of arenaceous chloritic schist are also present; both are probably part of the base clay and are not intentionally added. A specific determination of this problem would require study of the local clays available to the ancient potters.

P-222. Kylix foot 80 mm in diameter, 10 mm thick, very pale brown (10YR 8/3) in color, not completely oxidized. Soft, abraded, very fine textured surface. *Thin section*: This kylix was made of well-washed clay, for the mineral inclusions are all less than 0.03 mm in size except for the red clay grains, which are up to 0.1 mm in diameter. There is nothing unusual in the mineral and rock fragments present. The paste resembles that of P-219, but contains much less very fine quartz.

P-221. Cup foot about 60 mm in diameter; vessel wall 8 mm thick, oxidized light red (2.5YR 6/8) throughout. Minute mica flecks can be seen on the surface. *Thin section*: This well-washed clay is rich in very fine flakes of muscovite. The very fine quartz abundantly present can be recognized in the sandy "feel" of this sherd.

P-223. Plug end of a handle inserted into the body wall. The round handle is 23 mm in diameter, the vessel wall 8 mm thick. The surface is oxidized to a reddish yellow (5YR 7/6), the core is light gray. Chalcedony fragments up to 1 mm in size appear on the surface. *Thin section*: This very fine textured sandy clay contains occasional coarse chalcedony grains but no intentional tempering material. The clay matrix is rich in very fine flakes of muscovite, but they are not apparent on the surface of the sherd, probably because of their small size. The frequency of the very fine quartz grains in the matrix is like that of P-219 and P-221.

P-220. Strap handle 5 mm thick, with surface oxidation of reddish yellow (5YR 7/8) and a light gray core. Minute mica flakes abundant on the surface. *Thin section*: The very fine quartz pattern is like that of the two preceding slides. Muscovite is strongly in evidence as individual flakes in this well-washed clay.

The Malthi pottery, to judge from the samples examined, was made from well-washed clay rich in very fine quartz. There were at least two sources, the one being micaceous. Some of the pottery was tempered, but no statement can be offered on the evidence available concerning the consistency with which the tempering materials were used, nor for what vessel forms.

The technological study of the pottery from the palace will be published elsewhere. In brief, the sixteen sherds that were thin sectioned showed close similarity to many of those just discussed. The one exception is the very fine textured pale yellow ware sherds such as those of the kylikes. They are made of a clay rich in calcite, hence the pale colors that develop when the ware is fired to high temperatures (900°–1000° C).

The detailed analysis of thin sections made of a small sampling of Messenian sherds has shown that the mineral and rock inclusions are quite consistent throughout the region but that minor variations do occur – muscovite in the upper Pamisos region, oolitic chalcedony near the Gulf of Messenia, and local variations in the claystone/schist/sandstone present. The absence of calcite is surprising, for it occurs only as an aplastic in the form of limestone in one Malthi sherd. The selective use of tempering materials from among the many kinds available, particularly with relation to the sandiness of the clay, and the possibility that at times the aplastic was concentrated at the surfaces of the vessels are of interest.

MODERN POTTERS

The potters at work today in the villages of Messenia preserve craft traditions and attitudes that are fast disappearing with the present generation. Few sons are in training to succeed their fathers. Metal vessels have been gradually encroaching on the ceramic markets; and with the use of aluminum ware in place of tinned copper, the pace has accelerated. Now very cheap plastic products are usurping the markets. I welcomed the opportunity given me by membership in UMME in 1963 to visit with the village potters as they worked, for I had done such work in other areas the preceding eight years in Iraq, Iran, Afghanistan, and the Lebanon. Since 1955 I had been talking with the potters in Amaroussi, a suburb of Athens.

For six weeks during the summer of 1963 I travelled with McDonald as he continued his archaeological and toponymic studies, and he kindly served as my interpreter. After arriving in a village where we had learned (often from potters in other towns) that pottery was still being made, we had to locate the potters. Sometimes shopkeepers who had pottery displayed for sale or small boys questioned on the streets could direct us. After introducing ourselves and being welcomed by the hospitable Greeks, McDonald carried on a conversation with the potter and sometimes with his wife or curious visitors. Since most of the potters were very voluble and wished to be helpful in providing information, the conversations followed devious routes. McDonald would translate when appropriate, and I busily took notes and often interposed questions in addition to those of the general order of data that we sought. After the discussions were well under way and the potters understood the purpose of our visit, I asked permission to see the various physical aspects of the establishment and to take pictures. Often I wandered about while the potter and McDonald were continuing their conversation and noted items about which we then asked questions. In addition to recording and photographing the normal operating procedures and equipment of the potter (and these did not vary a great deal), we tried to get information about the family history of the potters, their attitude toward their craft, their value systems and those of their customers, and methods of distributing their wares. Similar questions, when appropriate, were asked in the village shops where pottery was sold, and of the caïque captains in Koroni. It is my hope that such data will help increase our understanding of the ancient peoples who made, distributed, and used the pottery we so carefully preserve and analyze from archaeological excavations. Shape, decoration, composition, and stratigraphic changes are fundamental aspects of studies of ancient ceramics, but a better insight into the practices of man the potter and man the user of pottery must also be obtained if we are to improve our understanding of the past cultures whose ceramic remains provide tangible evidence of their ways of life.

It was not possible to remain more than an hour or two at any one potter's shop, but the information obtained was cross-checked with other potters. Since the Greeks tend to speak in a positive manner, and the hospitable potters were anxious to give answers to our questions, such checking was essential. In preparing this report I have checked the original field notes, the extended descriptions of the visits that I wrote a day or two after the events, and all of the photographs I took, as well as some of those taken by Broburg and Hope Simpson. I have tried to synthesize the data into a coherent pattern, but have also endeavored to retain some indication of the personalities and attitudes of the people involved. When costs or sale prices are mentioned in this report, they will be given in drachmas. At the time of this study, 30 drachmas were equivalent to about one United States dollar. The value of the drachma in the village economy was of course far greater than would be its dollar equivalent in Western Europe or the United States.

In the spring and summer of 1964 I was working in the Near East. During that season it was possible to return to Messenia with Professors Lukerman and Hope Simpson. The latter generously served as interpreter. As is almost always the case, I have found, the intermediary becomes actively and enthusiastically involved in the studies and makes important contributions to them.

In May and June of 1960 Hampe and Winter visited the potters of Crete, particularly the pithos makers. Their well-illustrated and sympathetically written report, the collaborative work of a classicist and a professional potter, provides much basic information for an understanding of the Aegean potters' craft today. They, too, speak of its rapid disappearance (1962, pp. ix–x). Early in July they arrived in Koroni, and spent a day with the potters in Vounaria, and another with those in Petriadhes and Kombi (1962, pp. 47–54). I am enthusiastically familiar with their work, but shall make no attempt in this report to use their data. Instead I shall emphasize those points which can augment their studies, and not discuss in detail items such as the forming of vessels on the wheel, wheel design, and kiln construction that they have so adequately presented. In their second volume (1965) they include visits with potters in other parts of Greece that they made, for the most part, in 1960.

The western shore of the Messenian Gulf from Nea Koroni south to the port of Koroni has four pottery-making villages – Vounaria, Kombi, Petriadhes and Charokopio (Fig. 13-1). This area has the greatest concentration of pottery production centers in Messenia today, so its ceramic ecology is of interest in the broader study of the region. Since olive and grape production have long flourished here, containers for oil and wine had and have a ready market – the *stámna* and *pithos* for oil, and the *vikí* for wine. The well water used for drinking is often sweetened with lime. The narrow-necked, unglazed *víka* is the vessel used for storing, cooling, and at times sweetening water; larger quantities of water are stored in pithoi. This is a region of seasonal rainfall, and possibly pithoi, in lieu of cisterns, have been useful for collecting and storing water, although I have no specific evidence on this point. The coastal land surface is a fine-textured clay that had been a seabed in Pliocene times, and is well suited to the potters' needs, so good clay is abundantly at hand. Fuel is available for the firing of the pottery in the form of prunings from the olive groves and the vineyards. Although all of the items just cited help explain why the Koroni coastal region has been a ceramic production center at least since Turkish times, they are insufficient in themselves. Probably the dominant factor is the historically important harbor of Koroni and the smaller ports along the coast. Caïques still call there for pottery, which is then sold along the Aegean and Ionian coasts. The term *Koronaïka* is used by at least some Messenians to characterize the ware of this region, as we learned north of Pylos when we were giving a ride to a former mayor of a hill town east of Korifasion. He was asked about the source of the vikes used in his village, and he said they came from Koroni. In his comments he used the general term Koronaïka, and McDonald suggested that this or a similar word would be a good one to use as a chapter heading.

There is a record of pottery production in this coastal region for over 140 years, although archaeological evidence is as yet limited to the inland hills. Koroni is known (as Asine) since the time of the First Messenian War, and it was a major medieval and Venetian fortress. Abel Blouet travelled in the vicinity of Koroni in 1829, less than a year after the French troops had landed at Petalidhi, causing the evacuation of the Turks. Blouet in the itinerary of his trip from Koroni to Petalidhi (1831, p. 17) speaks of the extensive olive groves that were in part destroyed by the Turks. He also mentions several war-ruined villages, including Petriadhes, Comus (Kombi?), and on a hill to the right of his path, Vounaria. In another itinerary (p. 15) he lists the ruins of Charokopio. Philippson travelled in Messenia in the fall of 1887 but had to stop because of the rain. He was also there in the spring of 1888, and in May and June of 1889. He comments on the great destructive earthquake of 1886, saying that south of Petalidhi, although it was the second winter after the disaster, many families were still living in tents supplied by the government (Philippson 1892, pp. 360–61). Koroni was badly destroyed, but Vounaria suffered less damage. (Could this be because Vounaria was built on hills, and so escaped the action of tidal waves?) Vounaria, however, suffered from lack of water, since the nearest source was quite a distance away. He also speaks of the manufacture at Vounaria of pottery and jugs made from the Tertiary clay deposits. The present-day potters say that there is a very old tradition of pottery-making at Vounaria, and that Turkish pottery is found in graves.

The antiquity of the pottery-making tradition in this region is of interest because in other parts of Messenia, as well as in Amaroussi (a suburb of Athens), Chalkis, and Aegina, there is a strong Siphniote tradition. A few potters came to Vounaria in the 1940's from the Aegean island of Siphnos, stayed four or five years, and then left. There may have been some repeopling of the region after the Turks left, for Philippson (1959, p. 396) reports that in 1840 Maniotes of the Mavromichalis family colonized the area near Petalidhi because of the fruitful plain and the small harbor. This would suggest that there was a low population density in the ravaged area at the time. The villages near Koroni seem best to preserve the older methods and attitudes of Messenian potters, so they will be here discussed as a separate unit.

Vounaria

The long narrow village of Vounaria, "Little Mountains," is built on coastal hills that form a geographical landmark recognizable from the distance. The potters' workshops are near the main street that traverses the hilltops in a southwesterly direction. Today the new road bypasses Vounaria, encircling it to the west at the foot of the hills next to the intensively cultivated plain. There are about fifteen potters working in Vounaria, some of whom jointly use the ten or so kilns still available in the town.

Four Vounaria pottery-making establishments were visited on July 4 and 6, 1963. Brief return visits were made to two of them on June 11, 1964, and colored prints of photographs taken the preceding year were left for all four of the establishments. (It is interesting to observe that the potters here and in the Near Eastern countries in which I have worked do not recognize foreign visitors the next year, nor do they recall the visits until they are shown and given photographs. We may conceitedly think that such visits in quiet remote villages would be remembered, but it is unusual to find a potter who quickly recognizes one later.) The methods of pottery manufacture in the four shops are similar, so they will be summarized in one presentation, followed by supplementary notes for each of the shops (here designated V-1 through V-4).

The clay is obtained locally from a pit or embankment on the potter's land, from a small mine dug into a hillside, or from a grotto north of town which supplies several of the potters. One such source is illustrated in Plate 14-1. Clay is taken by V-1's adjoining neighbor from a hillside operation that looks not unlike a dromos and tholos tomb. The roof of the entrance tunnel through the sandy clay into the hill had collapsed during the winter rains of the preceding year. The upper level of clay in the mine is sandy, with limonitic pale brown stains, and the lower clay, which begins at about the level of the hand seen in the center top of the group of people, is very fine textured, pale gray, and has to be chipped out of its bed.

The clay is mined by or delivered to the potter, who stores it in his courtyard. When some is needed, he or his assistants energetically crush it, using a bark-free bent branch from a tree as a flail (see Pl. 14-2). The assistant at V-2, having crushed some of the clay, is scraping it together to place it in a tinned container in which he will carry it to the mixing tank. The same technique of crushing clay is used in Afghanistan today.

The crushed clay is put in a pithos where it soaks in water for a few hours; here it is occasionally stirred to speed up the disintegration of the clay lumps. Plate 14-3 shows the potter of V-1 working with the clay that is being slaked. Next to the pithos full of clay is another in which two and a half kilos of water have been stored for the operation. Their bases are sunk in the ground. Behind them is a box sieve. The potters say that the pithoi they use are "over 100 years old," which of course means that they inherited them from their fathers along with much of the shop equipment. Some of the wide pithoi, whose maximum diameters are 100–122 cm, look as if they had been made for this purpose or for collecting cistern water, because their rims are finished. Others are obviously the lower portions of large broken pithoi. The sandy sludge, if any, remaining in the bottom of the pithos after the fine clay in suspension has been removed is scraped out and discarded, as can be seen in Plate 14-4 from V-2. In several parts of the Near East small pits dug into the courtyard ground are used by potters for the initial soaking of their clay. One wonders if pits and deposits of sandy clay in or near courtyards in archaeological excavations might not be the remains of clay-washing operations.

The clay, as a thick slip, is poured through a sieve box at V-2 (Pl. 14-5) into a corner of a low-walled drying platform lined with brick. The sieved slip spreads out slowly across the pan. On the second or third day, after the sun has evaporated some of the water, the assistant, using a long thin pole, walks around the edge of the platform and cuts the clay into soft slabs about 25 cm square to accelerate the drying and to control the pattern of drying cracks. In this way clay units 5–8 cm in thickness can be formed that can be easily carried to the wedging floor when sufficiently dry (after four or five days on the platform in hot weather). At V-2 a piece of canvas is spread over the plastic slabs ready for use to prevent further drying. The sandiest clay is said to be in the corner of the platform where the sieve is located. If the clay becomes too dry before it is used, it has again to be soaked in water. The size of the drying pans varies with the shop. At V-2 there are four pans adjoining one another, each about 1.5 by 3 m in size, and at V-3 there are but two pans, each about 1.5 by 2.5 m. As a rough index, it would appear that one potter with one assistant can make use of two drying pans during the summer months.

Not all potters follow this procedure. Some, as at V-1, limit the amount of water mixed with the clay, and spread the viscous mass on the wedging floor, allowing it to dry for some time in the summer heat before wedging. This can be done if the clay is originally sufficiently fine and does not contain stones and other inclusions. At several establishments in Messenia, potters mentioned finding shark's teeth from time to time in the clay when they sieved it. An encounter with such a sharp item in foot-wedged clay would be painful.

To free the clay from lumps and air voids and to distribute the water uniformly through it, the clay must be kneaded or wedged. The Vounaria potters and most of those visited in Messenia wedge their clay with their feet, working the clay out from the center of the pile into a flat circular cake perhaps 3 m in diameter, and then working it back toward a central mound again. The process may be repeated several times if necessary. This process, which takes about an hour, results in a decorative pattern (see Pl. 14-6). When two assistants are available, both may trample the clay at the same time. After the clay has been suitably worked, it is shaped into a compact mass and stored indoors under canvas or wet sacking until it is required by the potter. At that time he or his assistant forms a number of clay balls about the size of round loaves of bread (Pl. 15-1, from V-1) and places them on a bench or table where they can be conveniently reached by the potter at his wheel. The broken vika in the foreground contains water that can be used to temper the clay if necessary. Pots made that morning are beginning to dry in the corner of the room. Handles will be added the next day.

The potter's wheel is of the usual type. The large kick wheel is made of walnut in the village. One wheel seen at V-2 was built of 1 cm thick layers of walnut; the other had but three, thicker layers. The wheels at V-2 have been used "about 100 years," which should be construed as "a long while." Plates 15-2 and 15-3 show the V-3 potter forming a vika by the usual potting techniques, which are too well known to require comment here. After the vessel is finished, the basal wall zone is trimmed with a template. Two balls of wedged clay, a pile of scrap removed in finishing the vessels, and a bowl of water with which to lubricate the vessel and his hands are within his reach. Most village wheels wobble considerably as they rotate, and the potter in his many years of work has adjusted his forming techniques and rhythm patterns to the idiosyncrasies of his wheel. When foreign visitors used to the stable horizontal rotation of machined equipment try to shape vessels at the villager's wheel, they fail miserably, much to their own embarrassment and the quiet delight of the proud Greek craftsman.

The finished vessel is cut from the upper wheel with a wire, and is allowed to dry in the workshop for about 24 hours. It is then quite firm, and handles can be added (Pl. 15-4). Very plastic clay is prepared, and a series of strips are drawn from it, pinched off at the desired length, and stacked on the potter's bench. In the illustration the potter at V-4 is adding the third handle to a large stamnos. His left hand provides support for the free-flowing shape. The preformed clay strips are at his side, and the small bits pinched off as the handles are attached are tossed on the table. One of the marks of a successful potter is his skill in making handles that remain firmly fastened to the vessels and that do not crack. The wasters on the sherd pile next to a kiln will quickly give evidence on this point.

The vessels are allowed to dry outdoors in the summer sun for two or three days. In June some rains can be expected, so the ware may be kept inside when necessary, or a large canvas can be spread over the drying vessels, provided one is available as at V-4. If the drying ware cannot be protected, it has to be carried indoors.

A lump of Vounaria clay taken from the crushing platform at V-1 has been studied in the laboratory. There is a pale yellow coating of limonite on the white clay. Under the binocular microscope one can see that the clay has a fine, granular texture with very fine flakes of chlorite giving surface reflectance in a bright light much like the appearance of mica. There are pale brown concentrates of limonite and occasional spots of black organic material that can be seen on freshly fractured faces of the lump.

When a sample of the clay was placed in water, it slaked down rapidly into a sticky paste. When it was stirred in water, it quickly settled out of suspension. The sand in the clay was concentrated by washing, settling, and decanting. A portion of the dried sand was treated with dilute hydrochloric acid to remove the calcium carbonate that was abundantly present, and both samples were studied in powder mounts under the petrographic microscope. The sand consists of angular quartz and chalcedony grains characteristically 0.05 mm in size, but occasionally occurring in grains up to 0.1 mm. In the Wentworth scale these would be termed silt particles and very fine sand grains (Table 13-1). Very fine flakes of chlorite are common. Crystalline calcite is abundantly present as 0.03-mm particles, but grains twice that size are present. Calcitic foraminifera, beautifully patterned, range up to 0.4 mm in size in this clay from a Pliocene seabed. Irregular very fine to fine limonitic grains ranging in color from yellow to dark brown appear commonly. In the acid-washed sample, the calcite no longer dominates the field, and silt-size flakes of muscovite can be seen in addition to the other minerals mentioned.

Five thin sections of fired sherds taken from the kiln dumps of V-1 and V-2 were also studied. They differ in appearance from the mineral texturing described for the unfired clay in that the very fine calcite crystals are now rarely visible because of the thermal shattering and chemical disintegration that occurred when the pottery was fired; the clay matrix has lost most of its birefringence and is semi-isotropic; the chlorite is oxidized to a brown color, is slightly pleochroic, and because of the dark color caused by firing is now far more visible in the thin section; muscovite, too, shows up much more clearly; the limonitic grains have been oxidized to shades of red and probably constitute the red clay auxiliary mineral listed in Table 13-2.

The Vounaria subsurface clays mined by or for the potters from what had been seabed deposits have good working properties. The shrinkage is low, so there is little difficulty from the development of drying or firing cracks. Thus, the good clay so easily obtained in and near Vounaria is a major factor when one wishes to explain why this has been a successful pottery-manufacturing village for such a long while. Availability of fuel for firing the kilns and transportation facilities for the distribution of the finished ware are, of course, also important factors. The samples of Vounaria clay available for laboratory study were unfortunately too small to permit physical measurements and firing experiments to be carried out, but the observation of the clay preparation, vessel forming, drying and firing, together with an examination of the kiln products and of the wasters on the kiln dumps of the Vounaria potters provide ample information as to the quality of the local clays.

Some of the ware is glazed, and is therefore fired twice. First the pottery receives one standard firing. Those pieces that are glazed receive a second firing identical with the first. These are termed the *bisque* and the *glost* firings in modern pottery manufacturing terminology (Van Schoick 1963, pp. 7, 16). Because the Vounaria potters often include both unglazed and glazed ware in a single kiln load, the glazing process will be discussed before the firing practices are considered.

The processes at the several workshops differ somewhat, for there is more than one way to produce salable glazed ware. Rather than report on the slight variations in individual procedures, they will be grouped together. It is desirable to completely glaze the interiors of wine jars as well as containers for oil, pickles, cheese, yaourti, and so forth. Usually the exterior upper portion of such vessels down to the shoulder area is also glazed not only to enhance the appearance and visually define the ware, but also to make this zone impervious so that drippings on it from pouring or dipping the contents from the vessel may be wiped off easily without leaving a scummy residue.

A red clay slip often is applied to parts of the vessels before glazing. This layer is termed an *engobe* in modern ceramic practice (Van Schoick 1963, p. 14). Its function in this case is largely decorative, giving a reddish brown to red color of the 2.5YR hue to the glazed surface, whereas the glazed areas that do not carry an engobe are brownish yellow (10YR). Occasionally, white clay decorative daubs, or short parallel strokes of iron-rich clay are applied over the slip in the rim area and under the glaze. A study of four thin sections of glazed ware under the petrographic microscope showed that the engobe varied in thickness from 0.6 to 4.2 mm, and the glaze from 1.2 to 3.6 mm. Microscopically the engobe was seen to consist of a red clay that was essentially a binding material for the very fine angular sand grains 0.4 to 0.6 mm in diameter that were included in it. These grains were primarily quartz, but some chalcedony, very fine sandstone, and feldspar fragments were present. The highly siliceous engobe would help reduce the crazing of the glaze and might aid in its adherence to the body.

According to the Vounaria potters, they obtain the clay which they use as a red slip and as a component to darken the color of the glaze from the hill called Mimi near the village of Vasilitsi, which is southwest of Koroni (Fig. 13-1). The material is called *pipíni* and is of two kinds, red and yellow. Either one can be used, but a darker colored glaze is obtained with the red pipini. One day we had time to look for the sites from which the pipini was obtained. About halfway to Vasilitsi from Koroni the road, on high land following the shoreline, goes through Ayios Yeoryios. Just beyond this hamlet we had to stop because the road was blocked by the active operation of a communal thresher and binder. This was fortunate for us, because on questioning, we were directed to a gully in the cliff between the road and the sea where the potters came to collect pipini. The rocky soil exposed in the road cut and in the eroded cliff varied in color from brown to red. There were similar exposures for some distance from which materials could be obtained. A farmer from Ayios Yeoryios kindly took us to his fields on the high plateau a bit inland from the shore road and led us to a spot where potters collect the yellow (sometimes called white) pipini. He said that some people took the surface material from among the wheat stubble. Others preferred to dig down about a foot, and in one such shallow excavation we gathered our sample of the yellow pipini. Young olive trees, new grape vines, and acanthus plants border the fields.

The two samples of pipini have been tested in the laboratory and will be reported upon in detail elsewhere in terms of their physical and mineralogical properties. In brief it can be said that they are both mealy in consistency when tempered with water, but improve in workability after aging. The petrographic thin sections show that they are extremely fine textured, well-laterized soils. Small briquettes were formed from both samples of pipini and were fired for 30 min at 700°, 800°, and 1,000°C. The colors developed are shown in the accompanying tabulation.

	Red Pipini	*Yellow Pipini*
Unfired	10YR 7/4, very pale brown	10YR 8/3, very pale brown
700°C	5YR 6/8, reddish yellow	5YR 8/6, pink
800°C	5YR 6/8, reddish yellow	5YR 8/6, pink
1000°C	2.5YR 6/8, light red	5YR 8/8, reddish yellow

The red pipini develops good reddish colors with increasing firing temperature; the yellow pipini retains pale pinkish shades. It would be necessary to make an extensive field study at both the potters' shops and at the sources from which the pipini is obtained to describe in detail the relation between the materials used preferentially by the potters (which may well be influenced by social factors) and the colors of their fired products.

Pipini, after sieving, is mixed with a lead compound, *lithárgio*, to form a glaze. Formerly the lead was obtained from Lavrion, but now many of the potters buy *verníki* from a supplier in Piraeus. It is my impression that the differential cost of the Lavrion and the Piraeus materials as it fluctuates is as important for these potters (who say, "we are very poor people") as the quality of the resulting glaze. They know how to produce glazed ware of very good quality, but added costs are difficult to pass on to the customers. These village customers, in turn, are more concerned about the minimum cost of vessels that serve their function well, than they are about the perfect appearance of the glazed surface.

The standard glaze formula used by the V-2 potters is: 10 parts of lithargio; 5 parts of pipini; water. The thicker the walls of the vessel to be glazed, the more water is added to the raw glaze so that it will adhere better. If the mixture is not right, the glaze will be "sticky." On some vessels I have seen underdeveloped glazes for the firing temperature used, glazes that "crawl" in modern ceramic terminology: "A parting and contraction of the glaze on the surface of ceramic ware during drying or firing, resulting in unglazed areas bordered by coalesced glaze" (Van Schoick 1963, p. 11).

The Vounaria potters like to include in their glazes a light-weight porous stone, *pétra*, from near Sparta. It is said to come by truck from Tarapsa near Gythion. Unfortunately, my sample of this material was lost in shipment, but my impression is that it is pumice. The geologic map of Greece shows outcrops of "shales with volcanic tuffs locally" just north of Gythion, so a pumice-like material which would introduce alkaline silicates into the glaze appears to be available. The potters consider the use of this petra essential to obtain a good glossy glaze. The color is also enhanced. The V-3 potter says that when he buys verniki from Athens he can get a shinier glaze, and he uses this when making plates; but he prefers the stone from Sparta. A formula used in compounding the glaze is: 45 parts of lithargio; 20 parts of pipini; 7 parts of petra "from Sparta," plus water. In this formula the ratio of the first two ingredients remains about 2:1, as in the first formula reported. One potter said that the glaze crazes if not enough pipini is used, but if too much is added, the fired glaze is black. (The pipini helps reduce the thermal expansion of the glaze so that it agrees better with that of the body. The black color is due to the presence of excessive iron when too much pipini is used.)

The fired lead glaze is, in general, a good product in Vounaria. There is a small amount of crazing, and occasional crawling, but the glaze adheres well to the body. With growing concern for health hazards inherent in the use of lead-glazed ware, and the increasing number of aluminum and plastic vessels for sale in the shops, some of them identical copies of their ceramic predecessors, the continued production and sales of glazed ware for culinary use would seem to be limited.

The use of pipini as a red slip and as a glaze ingredient is certainly in the classical Greek tradition. In fact, one of the potters referred to the material as *mílti*. Miss Richter has ably discussed the use of *miltos* by the ancient Greek potters (1923, pp. 53–59). The nature and use of the red ochres employed by present-day potters in Greece, and the stonemasons as well, would be interesting to study in connection with ancient practices.

In 1964 Hope Simpson and I sought out the merchant on the Piraeus road who supplies potters throughout Greece with white clay from Melos which he processes into a ceramic slip paint and with the glaze verniki. We were told that the latter was not lead oxide as obtained from Lavrion but a product that he prepared. When we asked if we might see his workshop, we were politely informed that his work was an "enigma," but he readily discussed the distribution and sales pattern of his products. These data will be presented elsewhere, but pertinent to the present study is his statement that he sells to the southern Greek potters through a supplier in Patras. However, the potter at Skala ordered directly from him, for we were shown the sales slips at Skala. It is possible that the distributor in Patras repackages the 50-kg sacks of material into smaller packages which individual potters may find easier to purchase, or he may possibly accept pottery in exchange for the Melian clay and the verniki. The availability of ready cash with which to purchase the supplies needed is one of the serious problems of village potters in many Mediterranean and Near Eastern countries.

The kilns (*kamínia*) are built of sun-dried brick formed from the local surface clay – the same material as that used for the houses. They are simple cylindrical updraft kilns with conical crowns. Their general appearance can be judged from Plate 15-5 and from Hampe's illustrations of kilns at Vounaria, Kombi, and Petriadhes (Hampe 1962, Pls. 18, 20, 21). Although there are a few larger and smaller kilns, they in general have the following approximate dimensions: The interior diameter is about 3–3.5 m, and the walls are about .3 m thick. The over-all height from base of the combustion chamber to the top of the crown is about 4.5 m, but the kiln does not appear to be this tall because the firing box or combustion chamber is usually below the ground level of the working court from which the kiln is loaded, and the kiln may be built into a hill slope to facilitate the operations at the two levels (firing and loading). The lowest part of the kiln, the combustion chamber, is about 1 m in height and has a central brick pillar about 0.6 m in diameter, from the top of which supporting fired clay arms extend to underpin the hearth. Hampe illustrates the construction of this type of hearth for a Cretan kiln (Hampe 1962, Pls. 2, 3). The hearth is the floor on which the ware to be fired is stacked. It contains many flue holes so that the flames and combustion gases can rise and surround the vessels being fired. In one kiln a ring of holes each 10 cm in diameter encircled the hearth near the wall; three concentric rings of flue holes that were 5 cm in diameter were within it. There were no holes near the center of the hearth where the glazed ware tends to be placed so that ash swirling up with the flames will not settle on the molten glaze and spoil it. The firing chamber which contains the ware rises from the hearth to a height of 1.5 m. Its cylindrical brick wall is plastered with clay to protect the brick from the abrasion of the flames. The clay plastering is repaired as necessary when inspection between firings shows that large cracks have developed or some of the clay facing has spalled off. Some kilns have a thick buttressing collar of brick and clay around this wall; others have a mound of earth built around it, or the kiln itself is built into a hillside. Large sherds may be embedded in the exterior walls "to make them stronger."

The conical crown of the kiln, 2–2.5 m high, springs from the top of the firing chamber wall and is formed of overlapping brick to produce a corbelled vault. The interior is plastered in the same manner as the walls. Hampe photographed such a crown at Petriadhes (Hampe 1962, Fig. 30). The exterior of the crown is coated with a clay-straw mixture to seal cracks and improve its insulating qualities. At times a wire is tied around a cracked crown to strengthen it. At the top is a vent about 15 cm in diameter. Two similar side vents are built into the mid-slope of the crown on the axis at right angles to that of the two doors.

It was interesting to observe how the potters resolved the topographic problem of the placement at different levels on opposite sides of the kiln of the small opening at the base of the kiln (about 1 m wide and 0.6 m high) through which the fuel is introduced into the combustion chamber, and the ashes raked out, and that of the loading door (about 1 m wide and 2 m high) that opens onto the hearth so that the unfired ware can be brought in and the fired pottery unloaded. If the kiln is built into a step cut into a hillside, possibly one from which the potter's clay is being mined, the opening for fuel will be at the base of the slope, and the loading door will be on a working platform on the other side of the kiln about 1.2 m higher. If the kiln is built on fairly level ground, a trench has to be cut down to the fire door with enough room provided for the storage of the fuel needed when the kiln is being fired. In hilly Vounaria some kilns have their fuel door at the low level roadside, whereas in others it is at the level of the large flat courtyard of the potter's shop. At one establishment it was under a shed, where the fuel could be protected from rain. The loading door has to be reasonably accessible to the courtyard and the drying and storage rooms, but the potters and their assistants, often sons in training, do not mind carrying the vessels up a small slope, if necessary, to the loading door. Nor should it be too much of a logistical problem to move the fired ware from the kiln to the place where it can be loaded onto donkeys or into trucks or carts. Seldom does one see any fired ware at a potter's shop except when he is unloading the kiln. Other obvious considerations when building a kiln are the direction of the prevailing wind insofar as it affects combustion and directs both the flames that escape through the crown vents and the billowing black smoke in terms of the nearby olive groves, vineyards, and homes. Adequate drainage during heavy rains is also important. Kilns are frequently used for two or three generations, if kept in repair, in this tradition-bound family craft. Therefore, since there have been changes in the access roads, living arrangements, agricultural plot arrangements, and kinds of fuel economically available since the kilns were designed, present-day arrangements may be a bit inconvenient.

The same kiln is used for both the bisque and the glost firings. At only one shop, V-2, were there two kilns, one large and the other small, and they adjoined each other (Pl. 15-5). There were several abandoned or unused kilns in Vounaria. According to the potters, only ten kilns were actively being used in 1963, about one-third of those in use during World War I.

At V-4 the kiln had been freshly plastered early in June 1964 and had yet to be fired that year. From the central vent hole of the crown protruded a leafed twig, possibly from an olive tree, to which was attached a bulb of garlic. Over the loading door of the kiln an iron horseshoe was affixed, and scratched in the clay beneath it was *αθανιτος* [sic] *βρακος* (everlasting rock?). When asked about this, the potter's wife laughed and said that it was traditional. Hampe mentions seeing an olive branch protruding from the crown of a kiln at Petriadhes, where he was told that it was "for good" (Hampe 1962, p. 54). It is likely that this good luck symbol is related to the first firing of a kiln after it has been built or repaired. A Vounaria potter was asked about the meaning of a grotesque human head modelled over the door of a kiln I had seen at Petriadhes. It had garlic bulbs on a stem serving as ears. He said it was a "stupidity" (*koutamára*). However, he had his own way of ensuring a successful firing, for I noticed that above the sealed-up door of the combustion chamber of his cooling kiln, a large X (Christos) had piously been scratched in the soot after the firing had ended.

The potters are skilled in loading their kilns so that they effectively use the space, so that there is little damage from the simultaneous firing of unglazed and glazed ware, and so that the flames and hot gases of combustion can flow freely around the kiln load in ways that will result in quite a uniform heat distribution. Practices vary, but the following examples illustrate some of the loading techniques. Water jars (vikes) are first placed in the kiln to a depth of about 0.6 m. Above them are stamnes which, if this is their second firing, have glazed interiors and a glazed exterior shoulder and rim zone. Vikes are again used to top the load. Thus, the glazed ware is to some degree protected from the direct impingement of the flames, and may possibly be exposed to a slightly lower firing temperature. However, the fired color of the unglazed ware near the center and at the walls of the kiln is said to be about the same. The glazed ware is kept away from the wall zone, if possible, because ash rising through the larger flue holes near the walls tends to stick to the glaze. Perhaps 10 to 15 unglazed vessels out of 100 will fire to a red color (lower temperature), and these come mostly from the uppermost part of the kiln load (which of course cools the most rapidly and is the best oxidized). If the surface of the ware is pink the potters don't like it, "but on the second firing it will come out all right." This statement applies to the vessels that are to be glazed. There is no price differential when selling the red and the white pieces. The ware is usually stacked in the kiln upside down to prevent ash accumulation in the vessels, and, for the glazed ware, to maintain a thick glaze on and near the rim as well. Roof tiles are used as dividers and supports in loading the kiln, as also are large sherds from broken pieces. A kiln load of medium-sized and small vessels consists of about 700 pieces at V-3. At V-2, however, where the two potters working together with two assistants have two kilns, they report that the kiln load for the smaller kamini is about 500 vessels, but that for the larger one is about 1,000. When the kiln is ready for firing, the loading door is closed with brick and mudded up save for the triangular or arched area at the top, about 30 cm in height. This remains open, and acts as a vent, similar to the three in the crown, helping to distribute the heat more evenly.

The firing begins very slowly, which is normal good ceramic practice. Throughout the 7–10 hours of the operation, fuel is added constantly in short pieces. As one potter said, he must keep driving the firing all the time. The fuel used at Vounaria varies according to what is available and how much it costs. The generally preferred fuel is *vérga*, prunings from the vineyards, for the vine clippings burn well and do not build up a bulky mass of glowing slow-burning charcoal in the combustion chamber as would heavier wood, were it available. Brush from the hills, including branches of trees, is also used. One potter prefers the branches of the tree called *prióni*. Another frequently used fuel, when available, is carpenter's shavings from woodworking and lumber shops. At the time of our visits 20 kg of this material cost five drachmas; 60 kg were required for a firing of the large V-2 kiln. *Piríni*, the black sludge remaining after the second pressing of olives, is considered by many the best fuel for it gives good heat with little ash and reduces the length of kiln firing time. However, it is expensive (ten drachmas for 20 kg when delivered by truck), and it is difficult to dry if it has been rained upon when stored before the time of firing. One potter said that pirini was expensive, and not worth the added cost. Another said that any kind of wood would do, as long as it was in small pieces. Thus, the potters use as fuel what is available and what they can afford. Vine cuttings often require no outlay of cash, for they come from their own vineyards, or they can acquire them from friends in exchange for some fired pottery.

If one can accept the rapid replies of the potters about the length of firing time, it is: V-1, 10 hours; V-2, 7½ to 8 hours; V-3, 7 hours; V-4, 9 to 10 hours. The size of the kiln, the type of fuel used, and the reliability of the precise answers all influence the estimate of firing time. It may be significant that the two potters who used grape vine trimmings had the shorter firing periods, whereas the two who mentioned the use of brush required longer times. During the firing, black smoke billows from the vents when fresh fuel is added. Toward the end of the firing, flames, at first in dark shades but later much lighter as the temperature increases, tongue from the vent holes.

The end of the firing is determined in Vounaria by the kiln color of the pottery in the bisque firing, or by the quality of the glaze in the glost firing. Often glazed and unglazed ware are fired together. When the incandescent pottery looks "white" in the kiln, the proper temperature has been reached and the firing is finished. Judging from laboratory experiments, this will be at about 900° plus or minus 50°. When it is a glost firing, a glazed pot is placed so that it can be seen from the opening at the top of the loading door or from one of the side vent holes in the crown. A long dry reed stalk is used as a torch. It is inserted into the glazed pot somewhat like a candle to examine the nature and color of the glaze. When crawling appears in the glaze, the potter knows that the firing is almost finished. The color of the glaze and its gloss then become the determining factors. When the color of the glaze is dark (i.e., the iron is in solution and the surface is smooth and glistens in the flickering light), the firing is completed. The door to the combustion chamber is sealed up tightly, the two side vents in the crown are plugged, and some bricks are loosely placed at the top of the loading door. The potters say that if they plug up all of the openings, much pottery will break. Should it be raining, a tile or large sherd is loosely laid over the vent hole in the top of the crown, otherwise it is left open. The kiln is then allowed to cool from two to four days, depending upon its size, the exterior temperature, and the immediate need for the fired ware to supply a trucker who has come to purchase it.

A Vounaria potter fires his kiln about once a week if he has enough sun-dried pots to stock it. However, if he has enough pottery ready, fuel available, and good weather, he may fire more frequently. The demand for the ware is sufficient to absorb all of the pottery produced. There were no inventories on hand. In general, pottery is made and fired from about April into October, depending upon the weather and the time demands of the agricultural responsibilities of these potters, who usually tend some olive trees, vineyards, and fields with the help of their families. Rain causes no problem unless it occurs in the first stages of the firing.

The fired ware is sold directly to truckers, who have often placed orders well in advance. They then distribute it to small general stores in villages as far away as Chora, Tripolis, and Megalopolis, where a few pieces are displayed for sales. Some ware is taken to the quay in Koroni where the captains of the one or two caïques still actively distributing pottery throughout the Aegean world load the pieces they think they can profitably sell at other ports into the hold and onto the deck along with the the pottery they have acquired elsewhere. According to one potter in an expansive mood, the vikes (water jars) are sold as far as Athens and to the whole mainland, but the Peloponnese "eats" most of them. Their extended distribution is certainly by caïque.

Wine-filled vikia are taken by donkey west into the hills. Wheat is returned in payment. This exchange system was strongly developed in wartime but continues today because the land around Vounaria is fertile and good for raising currants. The local people do not bother to grow much wheat, but obtain what they need through exchange.

The kinds of vessels made or seen in Vounaria during our two visits will be listed with the full realization that they may not be the entire repertory of the potters, but represent the seasonal or fashionable demand. The colloquial Greek names will not be given in Greek because most of them are included in Hampe's lists (Hampe 1962, pp. 125–28; 1965, pp. 256–57). I hope in a later report on the potters of Siphnos and the mainland to include a list of terms prepared with the aid of Professors Hope Simpson and Georgacas. Space does not permit detailed discussions of shape and size, nor drawing of vessel cross-sections. Because of limitations in space, only Plate 15-6 will be included, which shows a group of vessels quickly assembled by the V-1 potter and his wife next to the kiln. Some of the pieces came from the wife's kitchen.

Víka (water jar), unglazed, about 38 cm high and 20 cm in maximum diameter. The very short small neck and 2.5-cm diameter orifice conserve the water in the hot climate and, with the two high strap handles, aid in pouring water. The handles are also of use, with a rope passed through them, for carrying a vika and for lowering the vessel by rope into a well or cistern. These vessels are made in large quantities, and many are exported by caïque to the islands and to mainland ports. They sell for about four drachmas each. The second size holds 5 okas (about 15 lbs) and the third size from 2 to 2½ okas.

Vikí (wine jar), red slip on the lower two-thirds, white slip on the shoulder, neck, and handles. The viki is glazed inside and out. It is made in two sizes and sometimes contains a very small amount of black underglaze decoration on the handles and lip, and even on the shoulder (initials and year). The large viki, which holds a little more than a kilo of wine, is slightly smaller than the vika, and has a long narrow neck 6 cm high and 2.5 cm in diameter. The two handles rise vertically from the shoulder and arch over to join the neck just below the lip, causing appreciable thickening and thus strengthening of the neck in this zone. Such a design, which certainly reduces neck breakage, is roughly reminiscent of the Late Minoan and Mycenean stirrup jars.

The *stámna* is a larger water jar that is made in two sizes; it has a much wider mouth, 8–10 cm in diameter and an inner ledge on the lip. This ledge serves to support a lid, but at least in older times helped as water was poured out to keep back sediment that had settled to the bottom. The smaller size has two handles, and the larger has three – again a design known in antiquity. The third handle, in the present case identical in shape with the other two, helps support the weight if a full vessel is lifted or suspended by rope, but it also is useful when pouring water out of the jar, the water falling over the lip on the side opposite the third handle. It was interesting to watch a large stamna being made at V-2. The apprentice, standing near the potter, rapidly turned the large lower wheel with his foot until it was spinning rapidly. Then the potter worked, with considerable strength required, to shape the vessel from the large lump of clay that he had on the upper wheel.

The *kapaklí*, a vessel made in two or more sizes for soup, resembles a Boston bean pot in shape. It has a very wide mouth, about two-thirds the width of the jar shoulder, so that soup can be dipped from the vessel. The interior and the exterior shoulder and rim areas are glazed. There is a red slip beneath the glaze on the interior of the jug, and on the exterior rim zone. Two small handles are attached to the slightly flaring rim. The larger size is about 25 cm high and 18 cm in maximum width.

Plates, flowerpots, and yaourti cups are seldom made any more in Vounaria, because there is little demand for them in the region or from the far-roaming pottery vendors, the caïque captains. Storage jars for cheese, butter, olives, and so on are sometimes made. As has been previously mentioned, pithoi were made in World War I; the *tsoukáli* (casserole) from Siphnos was copied without great success during World War II, for it cracked in use when made from the local red clay. Thus, even within a stable ceramic tradition such as that of Vounaria, slight changes owing to demand do occur.

A description of the potters' techniques, kilns, and products at Vounaria would be inadequate without some report on the men themselves. Perhaps one can best give a feeling for these Greek villagers at work by commenting on the men in each of the four shops where we spent at least an hour in conversation. Their cordial acceptance of visitors while they busily carried on their work made our study a pleasant experience.

Andreas Kanelopoulos is the potter at V-1. After we introduced ourselves, having been directed to his shop by a small boy in the village square, his wife produced chairs, and about five people joined the group, at times vigorously participating in the conversation in good Greek fashion. Andreas was about 65 years old in 1963 and had been a potter for about 40 years, but he is not the owner of the shop. Both he and his brother learned the trade from another potter as apprentices – it was not in their family tradition. One can be trained to be a potter in about a year "if he is keen." (This statement would be rejected by many potters of the eastern Mediterranean lands.) The job is attractive because a potter can earn more in a day than can a worker in the fields, but his task is harder and requires longer hours. Now it is difficult to get apprentices, for the young men are not interested in becoming potters. Andreas never drinks water directly as it comes from the spring, but only after it has stood for a while in a vika, because the pot "cleanses the water." Some potters add lime to sweeten the drinking water. Recently the government began supplying water from centrally located standpipes, thus making available good drinking water except for some traditionalists.

V-2 is on the new bypass around hilly Vounaria. It is a well-ordered establishment with two kilns, two potters, and two assistants. A radio was blaring in the workroom. Christos Kiriakakis, a very forthright man, has been a potter for 45 years; when he was about 18, he learned the trade from his father. The shop in which they were working had belonged to his father. His sister-in-law is married to his partner, Ioannis Stefanopoulos, who is also the son of a potter. The two assistants, in their twenties, were very helpful. When we asked them if they would become potters, they nervously laughed and did not give a direct answer. Perhaps they did not feel free to comment in the presence of the two "masters." The potters said that there has been no change in the methods of production nor in the shapes made in the past 45 years. Their fathers made the same shapes as they do. During World War II they had more local business than at present, for no grain was grown near Vounaria. They "exported" table wine and olive oil from their village in clay vessels to the hill towns to the west more so than they do now, in exchange for grain. After World War II they made plates and yaourti bowls by jiggering, but now the Kerameikos factory in Athens supplies most of the market, and the local potters cannot compete. Plastics are also replacing pottery. During World War I they even made pithoi and exported some of them as far as Smyrna (this statement doubtless reflects talks with the caïque captains). During World War II they could not get the good casseroles (tsoukalia) from Siphnos, so the potters made them locally of red clay, but they were not good, for they cracked easily when placed over the cooking fire. They laughed when I asked if there was much rivalry among the village potters, and said there was no more than in any other trade. Their daughters sometimes marry potters, but I got no feeling of any tradition in this matter. A young man with a job and a girl with a dowry from her parents are important economic considerations when marriage is considered. No special identification marks are placed upon his products by the potter, but each can identify the ware made by the other potters in the village. They would like to have a machine with which to temper their clay with water, but they cannot afford to buy one. The Vounaria clay is very good, much better than that at Amaroussi (the pottery-making center outside of Athens); the clay at Petriadhes is sandier. These potters think that it would be better if there were one large workshop at Vounaria for all the potters. Then they could earn more money, which they badly need.

Alexi Kiriakakis is the potter at V-3. He is 54 years old, and became a master potter in 1937, when he learned the trade by walking around and watching many potters, since he didn't know what to do for a living. His father was a potter, but not his grandfather. Alexi had an old man as his assistant to prepare the clay for the wheel.

The chief potter at V-4 is Theodoros Tsapekis, who was 38 in 1963. He began making pottery when he was 15 or 16, and assumed responsibility for the shop when his father died in 1959. Before his father's death he made plates by jiggering, but he is now discarding the plate saggars, for it is no longer profitable to produce plates. His family has been making pottery for as long as they have any record – a long, long time. There are two potters and three assistants in this shop. The local clay is sometimes better from the upper part of the clay deposits, and sometimes from the lower part. He mixes one part of white clay that he obtains nearby and nine parts of local clay. He adds the white clay to increase the strength of the ware, otherwise it may break during the firing and cooling. He covers the ware drying in the courtyard with a large piece of canvas in case of rain, and also covers his kiln with canvas if rains come during the earlier parts of the firing. He has changed the arrangements of the shop greatly since his father's death. This shop has a much more efficient appearance than the others in Vounaria and has benefited either from outside advice or from the potter's practical experience elsewhere.

These comments on the potters in the four shops in Vounaria, taken directly from their statements, indicate the range of variability in the craft tradition in this village where there is a very long history of pottery making. One hopes that young men can be encouraged to take up this craft, and that the increasing economic pressures and lack of successors do not mark the present fairly old potters as the last of their line.

Kombi

At Kombi, south of Vounaria on a side road leading to the shore (Fig. 13-1), we found but one pithos maker still at work out of the five formerly there. He is Andreas Remalos, and he practices his trade about three months out of the year, making pithoi only when he receives orders. Caïques come to the shore at Kombi to collect the fired ware. He mixes one part of the local red clay with two parts of clay from Petriadhes. A kiln load consists of 40 large and 35 small pithoi. The potter sells the former, which hold up to 150 okas, for 80–100 drachmas, and the smaller size for 60 drachmas. Andreas says that he could make a little more money if he built more pithoi, but he can't get help, the work is hard, and he is tired. He may never fire his kiln again after this year's work is done. A former potter who said that he had made pithoi for forty years reported that at one time there were 15 kaminia in Kombi, and that pithoi had been made there "for at least two hundred years." Farther up the hillside in a farmyard, we examined an empty kamini next to which were the last unsold vessels from its final firing. In addition to pithoi, there were some *trikala* (three-handled jars for the storage of water) that had an exterior slip on them. Another jar, the *limbáki*, glazed on the interior when made for the storage of cheese, was also there, as were a few stamnoi which could contain 50–100 okas. Hampe (1962, pp. 52–54) has some interesting comments on Kombi.

I had the impression that the almost defunct pottery production of this village was supplementary to that of Charokopio, a village we had no time to visit. If Charokopio could not supply the demand, a small amount of ware might still be produced at Kombi. (Petriadhes was not mentioned by Remalos, possibly because he has relatives in Charokopio.) Probably one of the major factors in the demise of Kombi as a production center was the exhaustion of the local clay supply, so that clay had to be brought in from other villages at extra cost.

Petriadhes

Petriadhes, a small village on the road from Vounaria to Koroni, is a center for pithos manufacture. There Georgios Vergis has been a potter for some 26 years, having learned the trade from his father when Georgios was 18 years old. His father as a youth had been taught by a potter in Charokopio. Pithos manufacture seems to be concentrated in the Charokopio-Petriadhes-Kombi area, with sales being primarily by caïque from the port of Koroni. Pithoi are distributed as far as Kalamata by truck.

Two clays are used in the preparation of the batch. A red clay is collected from among the rocks at the seashore, being chosen carefully to avoid including stones. It is spread on the courtyard floor and beaten with a bent stick to crush it. Occasionally sharks' teeth are found in the clay. The potter shuffles over the clay-strewn floor with his bare feet to separate the fine clay from that which requires further crushing. The red clay is then mixed with water in a *tenekés*. To this slurry is added powdered white clay in sufficient quantity – "The fine clay is like leaven in bread." The mixture is then poured through a sieve into another tenekes, and the watery mixture of the two clays is next poured for aging into a large pithos whose upper half has been broken away. There is no set proportion of the two clays used, but the potter estimates that they are approximately equal in amount. The pithoi are formed of very plastic clay in rather dark windowless cool rooms. The vessels are built up of coils of very soft clay, with one coil about 6 cm in diameter being added to each pot approximately every day (depending on the rate of drying). The potter walks around the vessel, working the coil into the body wall. "I build them like a swallow, round and around." He has to be constantly alert that the ware be sufficiently moist to avoid too rapid drying so that cracks do not develop. He likes it best when a north wind is blowing, for then his pots dry best in his damp cool rooms. It takes 20 days to form and sufficiently dry a large pithos in the shed. While the body is still plastic, external horizontal ribs are shaped into the walls – a characteristic of the pithoi of the region (Pl. 15-8). Such ribbing certainly helps to unify and strengthen the coil-built walls, as well as make the fired vessels easier to handle. Three- or four-toothed ring marks are stamped into the shoulder – the potter's marks. When the pithoi are removed from the rooms, they remain in the sunny courtyard for 3–5 days for further drying. A lead glaze is then applied to both surfaces of the rim and collar zone. Three hours later the vessels can be loaded into the kiln. Hampe (1962, pp. 50–52) provides further data on the local production of this ware.

The pithoi are stacked upside down in the kiln, doubtless to prevent the molten glaze from running too much. Forty large and thirty small vessels constitute a kiln load. The firing requires 10 hours, with local brush and reeds being used as the fuel. The fired vessels are sent by truck north to Kalamata, or south to the port of Koroni where many are loaded on caïques for distribution throughout the Aegean world. A large pithos will hold 150 kilos, and sells for 60–70 drachmas. The caïque captain will in turn sell each piece for about 100 drachmas. (Possibly our potter-informant at Kombi was overstating his price with an eye toward a possible sale when he said that he received 80–100 drachmas for each vessel.)

Laboratory tests of samples of the red and the white clay showed that the red clay required less water to render it sufficiently plastic than did the white clay, and also shrank less. In terms of the Munsell Color System, the unfired red clay was reddish yellow in color (7.5YR 6/6). When it was fired at 700°C for 30 minutes it developed to a red (2.5YR 5/8). There was a slight deepening of color at 800° and 1000°C. The unfired white clay (2.5Y 8/2) develops a reddish yellow color (5YR 7/6) when fired to 700°C for 30 minutes in an oxidizing atmosphere. There was no further color change at 800° and 1000°. The fired pithoi themselves, having been exposed to reducing conditions during parts of their firing – every time a fresh load of fuel was introduced – had a pink core (5YR 8/4) and a white surface (2.5Y 8/2). The microscopic study of two thin sections of pithos sherds from Petriadhes showed the same mineral assemblage as at Vounaria, which was to be expected. There was no visible evidence of the mixing of two clays, but very fine bits of shell up to 3 mm in length could be seen in saw-cut sections of the sherds.

The coil-built pithoi produced at Petriadhes, Kombi, and presumably at Charokopio, together with the mixing of two clays to form the paste, the ribbing of the vessels, and the use of but one firing despite the application of glaze to the collar and rim zone, indicate a relict ceramic tradition that may be closer to ancient processes than are some of the practices of the wheel-using potters at Vounaria. The exterior walls of the kilns at Petriadhes have cracked pithoi built into them, and they are further strengthened with sherds and stones (Pl. 15-7). A modeled head or mask, sometimes with garlic cloves as ears, appears over a few of the loading doors of kilns. Doubtless the relative remoteness of the pithoi makers from the larger towns, and the lack of change in the functionally well-designed pithoi over a long period of time have helped maintain a stable tradition. The need of householders for water and oil storage jars, and the effective ware distribution over great distances provided by the port of Koroni, have helped maintain the demand for pithoi. One hopes that it will continue.

DISCUSSION

Extended visits with the captains of two caïques at Koroni provided much data on the sale of Messenian pottery that will be reported upon elsewhere. The other potters in Messenia – those at Kalamata, Messini, Skala, Pirgos, and Olympia – are Siphniote in origin, and have somewhat different pottery-making traditions. The study of these potters will be included in an extensive report on the potters still working on the island of Siphnos. The major clay source for the Siphniote potters in Messenia is at Bournazi (south of Skala, Fig. 13-1). The Skala potters also obtain some clay from farther north at Meligala, a clay which they term "a bit wild." Roof tiles, too, are produced in great quantity, especially at Lambaina, Kalamata, and Kyparissia. The fired color range and the strength of roof tile and fired brick (made near Kalamata and elsewhere) can give one a first approximation of the potentialities of the local clays used, and observations of them may also be of use to archaeologists.

This report on two ceramic aspects of Messenia that are of archaeological interest – analysis of surface survey sherd collections, and study of present-day potters at work and of their products – provides a background for the analysis of the pottery now being excavated. It will also contribute to the broader study of Greek potters who are still able to earn a living as ceramic craftsmen. Their achievements, unfortunately, will soon be of historical rather than contemporary interest, and will become an item for study by industrial archaeologists.

REFERENCES

Blegen, C. W., and Rawson, M. 1966. *The Palace of Nestor at Pylos in Western Messenia.* Vol. 1, *The Buildings and Their Contents.* Princeton, N.J.

Blouet, Abel. 1831. *Expedition scientifique de Morée ordonée par le gouvernment français.* Paris.

Hampe, Roland, and Winter, Adam. 1962. *Bei Töpfern und Töpferinnen in Kreta, Messenien und Zypern.* Mainz.

———. 1965. *Bei Töpfern und Zieglern in Süditalien, Sizilien und Griechenland.* Mainz.

Institute for Geology and Subsurface Research. 1954. *Geologic Map of Greece.* 1:500,000. Athens.

Matson, Frederick R. 1956. "Techniques of the Early Bronze Age Potters at Tarsus." In *Excavations at Gözlü Kule, Tarsus,* ed. Hetty Goldman, Vol. 2, *From the Neolithic through the Bronze Age,* pp. 352–61. Princeton, N.J.

———. 1960. "Specialized Ceramic Studies and Radioactive-

Carbon Techniques." In *Prehistoric Investigations in Iraqi Kurdistan*, ed. Robert J. Braidwood and Bruce Howe, pp. 63–69. Studies in Ancient Oriental Civilization No. 31. Chicago.

———. 1965. "Ceramic Ecology: An Approach to the Study of the Early Cultures of the Near East." In *Ceramics and Man*, ed. Frederick R. Matson, pp. 202–17. Chicago.

———. 1966. "Power and Fuel Resources in the Ancient Near East," *Advancement of Science* 23:146–53.

———. 1970. "A Study of Temperatures Used in Firing Ancient Mesopotamian Pottery." In *Archaeological Chemistry*, ed. Robert H. Brill, pp. 65–78. Cambridge, Mass.

Milner, Henry B. 1962. *Sedimentary Petrography*. 2 vols. New York.

Munsell Color Company, Inc. 1954. *Munsell Soil Color Charts*. Baltimore.

Philippson, Alfred. 1892. *Der Peloponnes. Versuch einer Landeskunde auf geologischer Grundlage nach Ergebnissen eigener Reisen*. Berlin.

———. 1959. *Die griechischen Landschaften*, 2nd ed. Vol. 3, Pt. 2, pp. 319–523. *Der Peloponnes: Der Westen und Süden der Halbinsel*. Ed. E. Kirsten. Frankfurt.

Richter, Gisela M. A. 1923. *The Craft of Athenian Pottery*. New Haven.

Shepard, Anna O. 1965. *Ceramics for the Archaeologist*. Washington, D.C.

Van Schoick, Emily C., ed. 1963. *Ceramic Glossary*. American Ceramic Society, Columbus, Oh.

14

METALLURGICAL AND GEOCHEMICAL STUDIES

by

Strathmore R. B. Cooke, Eiler Henrickson, and George R. Rapp, Jr.

Within the context of Chapter 1, our efforts in this chapter are directed to the use of certain analytical methods and the disciplines of geochemistry, mineralogy, and metallurgy to elucidate the sources of the metals employed by the Late Bronze Age peoples of Greece. We shall discuss here certain historical aspects of these metals, outline the basic concept of the approach being used to trace their sources, and present some of the results so far obtained.

The earliest Greek references to metals occur in the Pylos tablets (Ventris and Chadwick 1956, ch. XI, and the Mycenaean Vocabulary) in which are identified gold (*ku-ru-so* = khrysos), silver (*a-ku-ru* = argyros), and copper or bronze (*ka-ko* = khalkos). One badly mutilated tablet from Knossos lists a metal identified as lead (*mo-ri-wo-do* = molybdos), although it may refer to tin since the somewhat superficially similar properties of lead (plumbum nigrum) and tin (plumbum candidum) led to confusion even into the Roman era. Ventris and Chadwick equate *ku-ru-so* with Hebrew and Ugaritic "harus," *a-ku-ru* with Armenian "arcanth." Dominian (1911) calls attention to the similarity of "khalkos" to the Semitic "chalak," and further states that "the classical Greek 'metallon' (a mine) probably came from the earlier Semitic 'matal.'" Lejeune (1961, p. 411) and others have pointed out that the Mycenaean names for gold, silver, and copper have no plausible Indo-European etymology, and that they are probably loanwords from Asia. Similarly, the much later Greek word for tin (kassiteros) seems to have been borrowed. Muhly (1969) discusses exhaustively the etymology of the words for copper and tin, but concludes that the Greek words for these metals are of unknown origin.

This apparent consanguinity of the Greek and Asiatic names for the metals may indicate that, at least in very early times, the metals themselves were derived from localities to the east of Greece, and that trade with western Asia was responsible for the introduction of the names and of the technology of metal working. It should not be forgotten in this connection that our own word *copper* betrays its eastern origin (ME coper, OE copor, < G kupfer < LL cuprum < L (aes) cuprum = the Cyprian metal).

By the Late Bronze Age metal working had become relatively specialized, since the tablets differentiate between copper or bronzesmiths (*ka-ke-u* = khalkeus) and goldsmiths (*ku-ru-so-wo-ko* = khryso-worgos; cf. khrysourgos). Silver, at this time a scarce metal on the mainland compared with gold, probably was worked by the goldsmith. The recovery of molds for casting metals and of innumerable metallic artifacts testifies that Mycenaean founding and smithing became skilled occupations. From the estimated quantity of *ka-ko* which was disbursed (according to the Pylos tablets something between 801 kg [1,765 lb] and 1,046 kg [2,306 lb]; Ventris and Chadwick 1956, p. 356, for the listing of smiths and their helpers), it is also evident that the technology for working this metal was well understood. Lejeune (1961, p. 411) refers to a pre-Mycenaean document in Linear A from Ayia Triadha, in which the sign *ka* is associated with a certain number of men, and speculates that this "déterminatif . . . spécifiant de quelle sorte des hommes il s'agit pourrait être l'abréviation acrophonique des noms du 'bronze' et du 'forgeron.' "

As will be documented later, it is clear that Messenia could never have been a source of lead, silver, gold, copper, or tin. The apparent absence of any word in the Pylos tablets connoting a mine or the occupation of a miner, surely a noteworthy activity in a metal-hungry civilization, independently confirms this conclusion.

The evidence against the occurrence of workable lead or lead-silver deposits in the rest of the Peloponnese is equally convincing; and on geological grounds tin and gold ores must also be unqualifiedly excluded. Although small amounts of copper occur east of the Manalon range into the Argolid, and east of the Taygetos range through southern Lakonia, the writers believe that if any of these was ever a producer it was on an extremely limited and local scale, a belief substantiated by our failure to find any but occasional minor quantities of smelting slag, possibly of a test nature. In the ancient world slag was not a commodity; it remains in situ, and attests by its quantity the extent of the smelting operation.

The inescapable conclusion to be drawn from the foregoing discussion is that practically all of the metals used in the Peloponnese during the Late Bronze Age were imported. Although the lead and silver may have come from Greece north and east of the Peloponnese or from some of the Aegean islands, and the gold from not much farther afield, the determination of the provenance of the copper and tin is an unsolved problem notwithstanding skilled scrutiny during the last several decades. This problem is peculiarly acute with respect to the tin, since no significant source is known to have existed in western Asia or the eastern Mediterranean, although noteworthy quantities occurred in central, western, and northwestern Europe. The enigma becomes even more profound when it is recalled that this metal was essential to the relatively large-scale bronze production of Mesopotamia, Egypt, Syria, Palestine, Cyprus, Anatolia, and the Aegean (all lacking in tin).

Returning to Mycenaean Greece, in view of the preceding discussion it is logical to conclude that both copper and tin were imported, either as the individual metals or as bronze itself, and probably in ingot form. Ores were normally smelted adjacent to the scene of mining operations and in those times it is doubtful if much crude or even concentrated ore was exported. The preparation of bronze from ingots of the two metals is a simple procedure; the copper is melted in a crucible, sufficient tin being added to bring the alloy to a desired compositional standard. Castings can be made from ingot bronze by simply melting it. In either process the requirements would be an adequate furnace, a crucible prepared from a refractory capable of withstanding temperatures between 1,100° and possibly 1,300°C, molds, fuel, and some way of producing either a natural air draught or an artificial air blast to attain the necessary temperature.

In melting copper or bronze, excessive loss of metal by oxidation is avoided by maintaining a thin layer of charcoal on the surface of the liquid metal. There is some oxidation of the metal, the products reacting with the material of the crucible to give a slag. Such "melting" slags are normally quite different from those produced by smelting an ore, since they contain much more copper, both chemically combined and as prills retained by the highly viscous slag. Even a simple microscopic examination permits differentiation between a melting and a smelting slag. Thus, the cupreous slags recovered thus far at the UMME excavation site at Nichoria are melting slags, irrespective of their archaeological context, although it has not yet been determined if both copper and bronze slags are represented.

It is of interest to examine the amount of fuel required to melt copper or bronze. Because wood is an indifferent metallurgical fuel, only charcoal, an excellent fuel, need be considered. Under average conditions one ton of wood produces about 400 lb of charcoal. Making reasonable assumptions concerning furnace efficiency (which undoubtedly was low), the carbon content of the charcoal, and so forth, it appears that about 5 lb of copper can be melted per pound of charcoal, or a pound of metal per pound of wood. These figures do not take into account the fuel required to bring the furnace up to working temperature, but indicate that the wood consumption for melting must have been fairly reasonable. It is doubtful if excessive deforestation was effected by the Mycenaean metallurgist; but by the same token, one can reasonably assume that there were fairly extensive fuel supplies contiguous to the rather numerous centers where the Linear B tablets document the presence of bronzesmiths.

Metal importation, of course, raises a further question, What was the nature and value of the commodities produced by the Mycenaeans which could be used in exchange? – unless, of course, the metals were "liberated" by piracy or by successful warfare against an unfortunate enemy!

Any investigation of the origins of the five metals used by the Mycenaeans is dependent upon modern techniques of scientific investigation. The development of accurate chemical analysis in the late eighteenth and the nineteenth century permitted the archaeologist, the metallurgist, and scientists in other disciplines to commence inquiries into ancient technologies. The greatest burgeoning of such effort has occurred since World War II, when radically new methods of analysis came into use, notably those employing physical methods rather than chemical. With the acquisition of a large volume of data, the powerful tool of statistical analysis can now be applied. However, the main thrust of interpretation and correlation of the data belongs primarily to the archaeologist, although he must carry on the task in close collaboration with his specialist colleagues.

Geochemistry and Provenance

To cope with his environment, to compete with his enemies, and eventually to acquire the wealth and power to establish civilizations over a period of many millennia, man learned, among other things, to utilize naturally occurring materials gathered from the inorganic world. Since the remnants of early man's legacy consist largely of the artifacts which he patiently wrought from these substances, we must consider the raw materials which he learned to recognize, to seek out, and to extract from their geological settings. First, stone for weapons and tools, then flint and obsidian, clay for household pottery and better grades of ceramics, and finally, in his long march down the centuries, the employment of metals, in particular copper and bronze, as first-class substitutes for less amenable and cruder materials. None of the foregoing substances occurs uniformly distributed at or near the surface of the earth, but each is localized by a series of geochemical events. This statement is peculiarly true of the metals, and it is to the origin of the copper and tin used in the Late Bronze Age by the Mycenaeans that this chapter is particularly directed. Geochemistry deals with the chemical reactions that result in changes in the distribution and the movement of the chemical elements on and within the earth in space and time. Any metal used by the Mycenaean civilization was derived from an ore representing the products of natural concentration under unique geochemical conditions.

Copper is sparsely distributed in most environments, and is estimated (Taylor 1964) to *average* about 55 parts per million (ppm) in the earth's crust. By comparison, iron occurs to the extent of 50,000 ppm but tin only 2 ppm.

The chemistry of copper is such that its atoms can unite with a number of different chemical elements to produce ores of widely varying composition. Each ore deposit represents a condition of stability or equilibrium between the ore minerals and the *specific* environment during formation. This is the basis for suggesting that most copper deposits may be sufficiently distinctive geochemically to possess trace impurity patterns that can be "fingerprinted." The uniqueness of an ore deposit and its trace impurities are determined by several factors, such as its geological parentage or heredity, the temperature and pressure of its formation, the environment of deposition, and the time involved in its formation.

Copper occurs in a variety of minerals and in numerous types of ore deposits. Mineralogically, copper ores can be classified into several groups: (a) "native copper" or naturally occurring metallic copper; (b) "oxidized ores," which consist of oxygen-containing compounds, such as copper oxides and copper carbonates; and (c) "reduced ores," such as sulfides and sulfosalts of copper.

With certain exceptions not germane to this discussion, copper ores are classified also as primary and secondary. Primary ores are formed at considerable depth in the crust where temperatures are much higher than at the surface. At these higher temperatures any mineral structure tends to be more open and a variety of trace metals enter the structure. Secondary ores are formed by the alteration of the primary ores. This process, the establishment of a new equilibrium, is the result of geochemical processes acting at or near the surface of the earth where atmospheric agents such as oxygen, carbon dioxide, and water are abundant. Secondary copper minerals, formed at lower temperatures, less pressure, and in less active chemical environments than the primary minerals, contain both fewer and lesser quantities of foreign elements. Rarely, the geochemical environment, either in primary or secondary deposits, favors the formation of metallic copper, which normally contains less than 0.1% impurities.

Numerous deposits of both primary and secondary ores of copper occur scattered throughout the Mediterranean, the Near East, and in more remote areas which were connected in the Bronze Age with the Mediterranean by trade routes.

The geochemistry of tin is considerably different from that of copper. The requirements for the deposition of tin ores are so specific that seldom is this element found in sufficient concentration to constitute an ore.

The Fingerprint Concept

Each geographic region has had a unique geological history. Each geochemical event in this unique geological history adds to the distinct trace element character of the final mineral assemblage. In theory, a complete trace element characterization of a mineral from an area should suffice to "fingerprint" it and thus uniquely define its place of origin. However, during smelting some of the elements from all the minerals in the furnace charge, including fluxes, will concentrate in the metal, others in the slag, and still others will volatilize and be removed with the furnace gases. This selective extraction leads to a trace element content in the metal that is different from that of the ore. In addition, the refractory lining of the furnace and the fuel (charcoal in ancient processes, although wood may have been used in very primitive smelting) may add trace elements to the metal, although under normal furnace conditions it is not expected that these will be significant.

To recognize what is chemically definitive about a particular ore and the artifacts derived from it (including slag) it is necessary to characterize the ore chemically and contrast it with ores from all other possible sources. The following highly simplified example is designed to illustrate the basic idea of what is meant by a "trace impurity fingerprint."

Consider a hypothetical specimen of native copper which has been analyzed for four trace elements: silver, mercury, gold, and lead. The basic technique consists of comparison of this analysis with the respective averages of a large number of analyses of native coppers obtained from individual metallogenetic copper provinces. The larger the number of analyses used to give the average and range, the more valid the comparison.

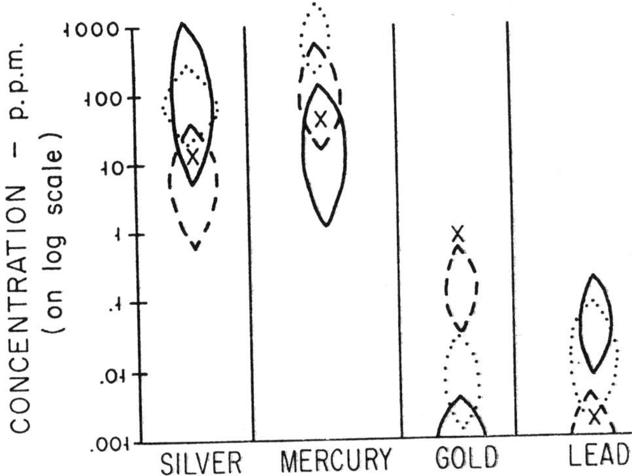

Figure 14-1. Method for fingerprint identification

In Figure 14-1 analyses of a few hundred samples of native copper from localities in Michigan (all from one metal province) are plotted to indicate the compositional range of each of the four impurity elements listed above. Chemically, the hypothetical specimen does not resemble Michigan copper. Again, comparison with analyses of native copper from Arizona (a different metallogenetic province) shows a poor match. However, when the comparison is made with analyses of native copper obtained from another metallogenetic province, Mexico, we find a reasonably close accord even though the value for gold lies a little outside the range characteristic of Mexican material. Lacking analyses of native copper from other provinces, the presumptive evidence is strong that the unknown metal was obtained in Mexico rather than in Arizona or Michigan.

Note that increasing the number of trace elements used in the fingerprint increases the reliability of the technique. If only silver and mercury had been used, it would not have been possible to determine the source of the unknown because measured values for these two trace elements fell within the range of values for both Michigan and Mexico.

To illustrate what is meant by trace impurities, the accompanying tabulation presents an analysis of Cuban native copper.

	ppm
Copper	999,900
Aluminum	10
Silicon	10
Iron	9
Potassium	6
Magnesium	4
Nickel	3
Silver	3
Chromium	3
Calcium	2
Boron	.5
Titanium	.3
Manganese	.3
Antimony	.1
Barium	.1
Cobalt	.1
Mercury	.03
Scandium	.02

A large number of analyses of ancient copper and bronze artifacts are given in the archaeological literature. In some the trace elements have been determined, but seldom to the extent shown in this tabulation.

In contrast with many other materials, metal was always a preciously conserved commodity in early civilizations; none was thrown away. The stock of metal in the hands of mankind steadily increased, because, unlike other commodities, metal can be salvaged and applied to new purposes by melting, by purification, by re-alloying, or even by simple mechanical reworking. Thus, the disentangling of the genealogy and provenance of a particular piece of metal recovered from an archaeological site presents difficulties which are not common to other materials.

Trace-Element Analysis

For many years the archaeologist has requisitioned the skills of the analytical chemist to determine the composition of various artifacts, particularly those of metal. The selection of the method or methods to be used in the analysis of an object depends upon a number of factors. Some of these are of purely analytical character, such as relative sensitivity of the method for a specific element or group of elements. Perhaps the most important single factor consists of the acquisition of an adequate sample for the analysis, and this in turn is very often governed by legitimate and understandable, but frustrating, restrictions inherent in dealing with objects of great value.

Normal chemical analyses require quantities of material measurable in appreciable fractions of a gram, the more elements to be determined the larger the quantity. However, analytical procedures have been developed recently which require either very small samples or indeed none at all, in the sense that material is not removed from the object. Of these physical methods, X-ray fluorescence is the only method which is truly nondestructive of the object, and, within certain limits defined by the ordinary X-ray equipment, can be used on both large and small artifacts. As in the case of the electron microprobe, it furnishes analyses of surfaces only. Owing to the geometry of the equipment, neutron activation analysis, thermal emission mass spectrometry, and electron microprobe analysis are limited to relatively small objects, up to about 10 cm in the first-mentioned methods, and considerably less in the other two, so that samples must be taken from artifacts where their size is prohibitive.

For any given method the response or sensitivity varies widely for different chemical elements. Most methods are subject to what is called the "matrix effect" in that the response for a given element is affected by the nature and quantity of other elements present in major amounts in the sample. No method is direct in the sense that "read out" gives the quantities of the elements present. All physical methods of analysis are comparative methods. The intensity of response of a given element in the sample undergoing analysis is compared, directly or indirectly, with the response of the same element present in known amounts in a series of standard samples which contain substantially the same levels of the major constituents.

The amount of material required for analysis by physical methods is very small compared with that for chemical procedures. One of the reasons for present-day cooperation between museums and archaeologists in the analysis of precious objects is that adequate individual samples may be taken in areas which are invisible to any but the most rigorous inspection – for example, the base, or under the toenail of a statue. A No. 80 drill, diameter 0.343 mm, must penetrate only to a depth of 1.5 mm to collect a sample of bronze weighing 10 mg. Drill holes may be filled with colored paste or plastic, or, if nondestructive testing has been used on samples removed from the specimen, they may be returned to the hole and cemented.

In the cross-comparison of artifact analyses with analyses of raw materials in the effort to trace origins, compositional inhomogeneities present as significant a problem as the remelting and re-alloying which may have taken place. There seems to be no easy solution to either problem. Analysis of several samples taken from a single artifact, when permissible, is preferable to a single analysis.

The spectroscope, in a number of modifications, has been used for over a century to analyze solids, liquids, and gases. Originally a visual method, it was placed on a sounder analytical footing with the invention of photography and with the elucidation of the characteristics of the photographic emulsion in terms of its response to light energy. Once a spectrogram has been made, a complete qualitative analysis of a single sample may be made in about 40 minutes, and if the analyst has considerable experience, the quantities of the elements present may be bracketed within certain limits, such as 0.1 to 0.01 percent, 0.01 to 0.001 percent, and so forth. A major advantage of this method is that as little as 10 mg is required for an analysis. Perhaps the chief disadvantages of emission spectrographic analysis are its limited accuracy and its limited sensitivity in trace element ranges. The authors use this technique primarily for preliminary survey work.

Perhaps more than any other method of trace-element

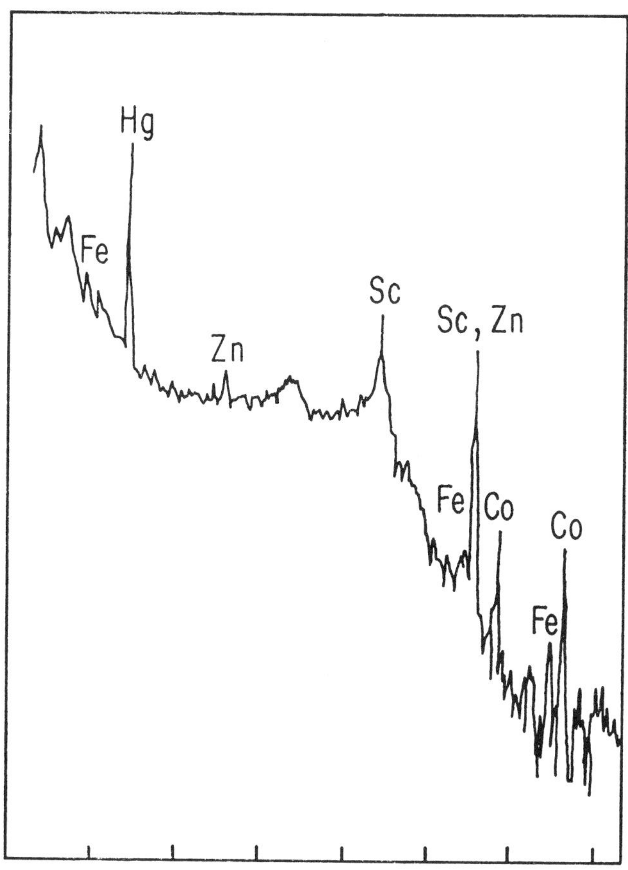

Figure 14-2. Neutron activation analysis: gamma spectrum of native copper after silver removal

determination, neutron activation analysis has been widely publicized for its capabilities. It has gained special prominence in solving archaeological problems because, in some circumstances, it may be used in a nondestructive mode; it possesses extreme sensitivity and selectivity; it is rapid; and it requires only very small samples. As with every other method, however, there are definite limitations and disadvantages as well as the much-publicized advantages. A particular drawback is the limited number of atomic reactor facilities in the world with sufficiently high flux available for such research.

The physical basis of neutron activation is simple. Let element *A* represent a trace impurity in a sample. If *A* contains an abundant isotope which has a high ability for neutron capture, then irradiation in a reactor produces significant quantities of the capture product, isotope *B*. If *B* is relatively long-lived, and if it emits a characteristic gamma ray, its presence can be determined and the quantity of element *A* originally present in the sample can be calculated. An example of a gamma spectrum of a copper sample (after the chemical removal of silver) is given in Figure 14-2. This figure shows how a gamma spectrum can be used for analysis of several trace elements.

Neutron activation analysis does not work equally well for all elements. The metal impurities that are readily determined in copper samples are: antimony, bismuth, cerium, cesium, chromium, cobalt, gold, hafnium, indium, iridium, iron, mercury, scandium, selenium, and silver.

Using the reactor facilities of the Greek Atomic Energy Commission (Democritus-Athens) and those of the Argonne National Laboratory (near Chicago), the UMME ancient metals project employs the neutron activation method for all regular trace-element analyses.

One of the most promising new tools for trace analysis is the spark-source mass spectrometer. It opens the possibility for the determination of large numbers of trace impurities, particularly some elements which are not easily determined by neutron activation analysis. Table 14-1 lists the results of some spark-source analyses.

The presence and quantity of some elements not determinable by neutron activation or by emission spectroscopy can be ascertained by this method, which will certainly aid in the expansion of the fingerprint technique and may replace other analytical methods in the future. The fact that the three samples in Table 14-1 contain mercury and silver concentrations that differ by orders of magnitude augurs well for the fingerprinting of native copper.

Table 14-1. Spark-Source Mass Spectrometric Analysis of Native Copper (ppm)[a]

Trace Element	Czechoslovakia	Alaska	Mexico
Mercury	3,000	1	30
Silver	30	1,000	300
Aluminum	10	...	10
Silicon	10	...	100
Calcium	6	2	2
Potassium	6	...	6
Tantalum	3	10	3
Iron	3	30	1
Sodium	0.4	...	0.1
Titanium	0.3	0.1	0.3
Magnesium	0.3	...	1
Scandium	0.2	...	0.2
Manganese	0.1	...	0.1

[a] Analyses made at Oak Ridge National Laboratory.

Slag

Inevitably the exhaustion of high-grade oxidized ores would force ancient metallurgists to investigate the lower-grade oxidized deposits and also the sulfides (often lying in the same deposit).

Once the high-grade material had been removed, the metallurgist would be called upon for fresh skills. Since, except for hand sorting and crude washing, the art of mineral beneficiation had not yet been devised, the metallurgist would now be required to extract metallic copper from what had become a relatively low-grade source.

Slag may be likened to an impure glass, liquid during smelting and floating on the surface of the pool of reduced metal owing to its much lower specific gravity. At present we are on shaky ground in attempting to designate the era, and to determine the ratiocination involved in the empirical discovery that combinations of certain available rocks (fluxes) form glassy substances (slags) lower in melting point than their individual constituents. The potter would already have acquired some of this information, as demonstrated by his creation of glazes and possibly by his manufacture of primitive types of glasses. Nevertheless, as witnessed by the scattered occurrence of ancient slag dumps throughout the Near and Middle East, the Copper Age metallurgist made the correct inferences and came up with a workable metallurgy.

The formation of a slag during smelting not only permits removal of undesirable impurities from low-grade ores but also tends to prevent reoxidation of the pool of liquid metal lying beneath it. Upon fairly rapid cooling, slag vitrifies and superficially then resembles obsidian, but even rapidly solidified slags may exhibit crystalline entities, and with the passage of time certain other compounds will crystallize from the solid phase.

For the following reasons, retrieval and analysis of slags possesses a number of advantages compared with attempting to locate the residuum of ore deposits for cross-comparison with metal analyses, and should complement information gathered by the other method:

a. A copper slag is a waste product, discarded at the site of manufacture, and, unless very rich in copper as a result of poor metallurgical techniques, or because it represents an intermediate product in smelting, is unlikely to be reworked or otherwise utilized.

b. Under any except most unusual conditions, ancient and modern copper smelting slags contain from 0.2 percent to over 1 percent copper. Only minor quantities of this copper occur combined as a silicate, practically all of it occurring as copper, as copper and matte (an artificial copper-iron sulfide produced by smelting copper ores containing sulfides), or as matte alone. Identification of these two constituents in a slag is easily made by established mineralographic procedures.

c. Metallic prills in a slag represent material which at the time of formation was in approximate equilibrium with the slag. This is true also of the pool of reduced metal, the goal of the metallurgist. The partition of elements peculiar to the ore should be substantially the same for the prills and for the main mass of metal.

d. Slag, a relatively stable substance, protects the enclosed prills of metal and matte from atmospheric and subsoil alteration, and accompanying selective leaching of constituents.

e. The occurrence of matte or any other artificial "mineral" entity in the slag, together with chemical and mineralogical analysis of the slag itself, is capable of providing information regarding the method of metallurgical extraction used and, quite conceivably, the type of ore treated.

f. The acquisition of sufficient quantities of material for complete analysis by the methods available presents something of a problem, particularly in respect to metals and alloys. In the case of slags, crushing and grinding, followed by any of a number of modern selective concentration procedures, should permit the acquisition of comparatively large quantities of metal and matte for examination.

Preliminary Analytical Results

Analytical work to date has concentrated on four problems: first, the analysis of a large number of copper minerals from various parts of the world to establish a basis for studies of provenance; second, an analytical survey of known or suspected tin sources; third, high-sensitivity analysis of copper and bronze artifacts; and fourth, a preliminary analytical survey of slags, volcanic materials and other substances which could throw light on the sources of Bronze Age metals and rock products.

To date, 1,150 samples of copper ore minerals from around the world have been analyzed by combinations of emission spectroscopy, neutron activation, atomic absorption, and spark-source mass spectrometry techniques. Wherever possible, samples for analysis were taken from several places in each ore body, giving a vertical as well as a lateral distribution. Most samples were obtained by our collecting them from the mines to evaluate the deposits as potential sources of metal in ancient times. Other samples were obtained from university and museum collections.

Some 310 samples either from known tin occurrences or from suspected or possible tin sources have been analyzed. A large collection of heavy sands derived from granitic rock terrains were collected on two expeditions through Persia and the Middle East in 1967 and 1968 led by Theodore Wertime and sponsored by the National Geographic Society and the Smithsonian Institution. They represent material from an area which has been represented as a provenance of Bronze Age tin. In the samples so far analyzed by neutron activation analysis, none has contained tin.

Drillings from or fragments of 443 copper or bronze artifacts have been analyzed. Recently, an additional large number of samples and analyses have been made available to us from the laboratories of the Stuttgart Group led by Dr. Junghans, from Mr. George Parker in England, from museums in Crete, Cyprus, and Turkey, and from several current excavations in addition to the one at Nichoria.

Also, 125 samples of slags, volcanic rocks, and similar materials have been studied. Only preliminary analyses of the slags have been made. Volcanic pumice and ash occurrences in the Aegean islands are being analyzed as part of an attempt to correlate volcanic materials with original sources and different periods of eruption.

Additional analyses are in progress along with computer processing and correlation studies. Preliminary results serve to increase optimism that trace analysis methods will serve archaeology in provenance studies. In the few instances where metallic artifacts are found confined to the environs of the geologic sources, the correlation coefficient is high. Trace-element distributions in ores from particular geologic regions exhibit similarities within the group that are much closer than those between groups from different geologic regions. Metal obtained from simple ore-smelting techniques retains diagnostic trace element impurity patterns. To the degree that the artifact metals have remained unmixed with metals from other sources, the technique appears valid.

Analyses of bronze occurring in different stratigraphic positions from a variety of archaeological sites seem to strengthen the hypothesis that a "tin bronze" age was preceded in many regions by an "arsenic bronze" age metallurgy. (A good discussion of the "arsenic bronze" question is given by Renfrew 1967.)

Field Examination of Potential Metal Source Areas

The authors have made fairly extensive examinations of possible source areas of Bronze Age copper in the eastern Mediterranean. We checked most of the sites in Greece and Cyprus, and some of those in Turkey which were described by or have been inferred from the writings of ancient authors or have been suggested by modern scholars.

Copper mineralization in northeastern Greece, particularly in Thrace, though more widespread than in any other part of the country, has limited potential as a major source of Bronze Age metal. Of some thirty occurrences in Macedonia and Thrace reported on the Metallogenetic Map of Greece (Zachos and Maratos 1965), sixteen in the areas around Limogardi, Antinitsa, Siaterli, Jandiki, and Hagiotheatous were visited for sample collection and on-site evalution. With modern technology the larger deposits in this region have some economic value, but their low grade and mineralogical nature throw doubt on the possibility of early exploitation.

Although no copper mineralization was observed on the extreme south eastern end of Euboea, abundant copper-bearing slags indicate early copper ore processing in this locality. Proximity to the sea and the availability of an up-canyon draft may have made this area well-suited to the smelting of imported ore.

The following four areas of copper deposits in the Peloponnese are shown on the Metallogenetic Map: (a) near Nea Epidavros; (b) the Ermioni Mine; (c) an area near the village of Tourniki, west of Argos; and (d) numerous cupriferous outcrops in central Lakonia, southeast of Sparta. Each of these localities was visited to determine the nature and extent of the deposit and to seek evidence of ancient workings. Sites *a* and *c* have been cited in the modern literature as possible sources of copper for nearby Mycenae.

With the exception of the Ermioni Mine, each of these areas has some surficial showing of secondary mineralization with minor indications of copper. However, in every location where extensive prospecting or limited mining had occurred and therefore the nature and extent of the deposit could be judged, the verdict was the same — that is, the type and extent of the deposit makes it certain that there was little or no recovery effected in the Bronze Age. Although ancient technology may have enabled extraction of small amounts of copper from such deposits (probably not more than a few pounds of metal), their contribution would have been utterly insignificant compared with other Mediterranean sources known to have been prolific and of high grade.

The Ermioni Mine is currently mining cupriferous pyrite, which is shipped abroad. The ore body is many hundreds of feet below ground with no observable surface expression, particularly in oxide copper minerals. This area must also be excluded as a potential source of Bronze Age copper.

The Metallogenic Map of Greece shows a small number of complex sulfide deposits occurring in the upper reaches of the Taygetos Mountains near the modern Kalamata-Sparta highway. Four of these sites were visited because complex sulfide ore bodies often contain copper and because these deposits would be the closest source for ancient Messenia. However, examination showed these localities to contain very small, low-grade sulfide deposits with little or no evidence of copper mineralization. The main surface expression was the occurrence of the typical gossan that results from oxidation of pyrite (an iron sulfide).

Vermeule (1964) has stated, "Even in the full Bronze Age of the Greek mainland, the new copper tools were rare for many generations, and most workers went on using obsidian or flint. Still, new things were known, imported, and justly valued: tanged or leaf-shaped dagger blades, axes, fishhooks, an occasional chisel or saw for woodworking, nails, and pins. Some Cycladic islanders in the third millennium were already prospecting and mining their mountaintop wealth: copper on Paros, silver and lead on Kouphonisi and Keos, gold on Siphnos."

It is clear from the quoted statement that Vermeule is stressing the rarity of metal over a long period of the mainland Bronze Age. However, the authors found no evidence of copper on either Paros or Antiparos, although fragments of a slag-like material, not analyzed as yet, were found on the beach at Ayios Nikolaos on Paros. Melos is similarly destitute of natural occurrences of the metal.

We visited the four major Cypriot mining areas known to the ancients: Scourriotissa, Mavrovouni, Kalavasso, and Limni. Remains of pre-Roman mining (including well-preserved mine timbers) are abundant at some of these localities. Early mine tunnels appear to have gone below the water table, well into the zone of secondary sulfide enrichment. A major feature of the Cypriot copper deposits is the current rarity, amounting almost to an absence, of an oxide zone. The significance of this is the necessity of a sophisticated metallurgy to treat sulfide ores. There is some evidence in the form of local concentrations of charcoal associated with remains of rudimentary open furnaces that roasting of sulfide ores was engaged in at an early date.

Samples of slag were found near the Late Bronze Age site at Enkomi, from which hoards of bronze objects have been recovered. Archaeologists of the Cyprus Department of Antiquities have reported evidence of copper smelting as early as Late Cypriot I (sixteenth to fifteenth centuries B.C.).

Like the Cypriot copper deposits, those of Turkey appear to be of much greater consequence to Bronze Age metallurgy than any in Greece. Locations of Hittite sites are commonly close to relatively significant copper deposits. Numerous ingots of copper have been recovered from Alaca Hüyük and ancient copper slags are widespread. Specimens of rich copper ores obtained in Turkey by the authors through Maden Tetkik Akama Enstitusu and through the Etibank Santiyesi from mines in Anatolia range from large pieces of native copper through suites of well-oxidized secondary ores to massive high-grade sulfide ores. This diversity of ore types occurring in a limited geographic area (Anatolia) may have contributed to pyrometallurgical advances brought about by trial and error. The proximity of sites containing abundant copper artifacts to potential copper sources favors correlation by trace-element fingerprinting methods.

Although discussions with government geologists pointed up the fact that there are no authenticated tin deposits in Turkey, abundant tin-bronze artifacts emphasize the availability of tin to the Anatolians. It would be premature, however, until analyses of copper and bronze artifacts and of slags have proceeded much further, to assume that all or most of the raw materials used in Greece came from eastern sources. Indeed, recent evidence points to multiple origins for early copper metallurgy.

REFERENCES

Dominian, L. 1911. "History and Geology of Ancient Goldfields in Turkey," *Transactions of the American Institute of Mining Engineers* 42:569–89.

Lejeune, M. 1961. "Les Forgerons de Pylos," *Historia* 10:409–34.

Muhly, J. D. 1969. "Copper and Tin: The Distribution of Mineral Resources and the Nature of the Metals Trade in the Bronze Age." Ph.D. thesis, Yale University.

Renfrew, C. 1967. "Cycladic Metallurgy and the Aegean Early Bronze Age," *AJA* 71:1–26.

Taylor, S. R. 1964. "The Abundance of the Chemical Elements in the Continental Crust — A New Table," *Geochimica et Cosmochimica Acta* 28:1273–85.

Ventris, M., and Chadwick, J. 1956. *Documents in Mycenaean Greek*. Cambridge.

Vermeule, E. 1964. *Greece in the Bronze Age*. Chicago.

Zachos, K., and Maratos, G. 1965. *Carte Métallogenique de la Grèce*. Institute for Geology and Subsurface Research. Athens.

15

GEOPHYSICAL EXPLORATION

by

George R. Rapp, Jr., and Eiler Henrickson

Historically, it has been the role of the geologist and geophysicist to make the final decision to "dig here" or "drill here." The geologist uses a wide variety of methods and information to predict the nature of materials and structures that lie unobservable below the surface of the earth. One of the most important sources of information is detailed observation of surface features, which often can be used to infer the nature of the subsurface geology. In this same sense the archaeologist predicts from the nature of scattered potsherds and other finds the probable occurrence of related materials at depth.

The geologist also uses sensitive electronic measuring devices to detect indirectly the presence of materials that have some physical property that contrasts with the surroundings. An important distinction between direct archaeological and geological observation of surface features on the one hand and indirect geophysical observations on the other lies in interpretation. Archaeologists infer the possible presence at depth of man-made features by finding a concentration of remnant artifacts at the surface. Field geologists make inferences about the subsurface geological configuration by projecting to depth surface features which have a limited and known range of geometrical shapes.

By contrast, the raw observational data of geophysical exploration are normally electrical impulses (recorded remotely) that indicate changes in the physical properties of materials at depth. These "black box" data must be plotted in some fashion to allow prediction of the physical nature and geometrical configuration of subsurface features. Most often the data are plotted in a manner to spotlight "anomalies," sharp discontinuities in the configuration.

Anomalies result from actual changes in the physical nature of subsurface material, or in some unfortunate instances from instrumental or human errors. Correct inferences about subsurface features from geophysical data require a broad knowledge both of the instrumentation and possible geological and archaeological configurations. An anomaly located by magnetometer observations may or may not appear in electrical resistivity measurements. The two instruments record entirely different physical conditions and are subject to different interfering phenomena. Infrared photography may be sensitive to slight physical discontinuities unrecorded by electrical or magnetic techniques.

Geological features have a limited range of geometrical shapes and physical properties. Anomalies resulting from an unexpected change in subsurface geology are ordinarily distinguishable from anomalies arising from archaeological features because the latter have the geometrical shapes and physical properties common to man-made objects. However, large contrasts in physical properties of the natural rock formations may mask the much smaller effects from buried remnants of man-made items. When an anomaly cannot be explained geologically by its shape or magnitude relative to the general background of geological features, it may qualify as a legitimate archaeological anomaly.

Geophysical Instrumentation

UMME used two geophysical techniques as part of the pre-excavation exploration in Messenia. Both the proton magnetometer and electrical resistivity meter proved useful in the surface investigations to pinpoint locations for excavation.

Several excellent descriptions of the use of the proton

magnetometer in archaeology have been published (Aitken et al. 1958; Aitken 1961; Aitken 1963; Rainey and Ralph 1966; and Ralph et al. 1968) and a journal devoted to the application of geophysics to archaeological prospecting, *Prospezioni Archeologiche*, has been founded. Only a brief review and critique of the methodology will be presented here.

The earth has a natural magnetic field generated by dynamic phenomena in the earth's fluid outer core. Every point in a magnetic field has both an intensity and a direction. In archaeological investigation only variations in field intensity are used. The strength of the earth's total magnetic field is about 0.6 gauss. It is strongly latitude-dependent but the absolute intensity is not important for archaeological work. Magnetometer exploration depends on the detection of small-scale spatial variations in the intensity of the earth's magnetic field, often amounting to no more than one gamma (1 gamma equals 10^{-5} gauss).

Unfortunately, short-term variations in intensity equal or exceed typical archaeological anomalies. These magnetic field disturbances arise in large part from solar activity; they may be worldwide or they may be localized to a region less than 10,000 sq. km. One method commonly used to correct for such extraneous variations is to return to a standard location every 10–15 minutes. From a plot of the readings taken at the standard location, corrections can be applied to all regular measurements.

The proton magnetometer consists of a small detector bottle on a staff connected by cable to a portable transistorized amplifier-display unit. This type of magnetometer makes use of the fact that a proton (hydrogen nucleus) acts as a tiny magnet. Each proton spins rapidly about an axis, giving it both magnetic and gyroscopic properties. As a magnet, a proton is constrained to become oriented in a magnetic field, but its gyroscopic spinning causes it to precess (wobble) while gradually becoming aligned with the field. The frequency of this precessing motion is exactly proportional to the intensity of the magnetic field.

The detector bottle is moved over a grid by one operator while a second monitors the instrument (Pl. 16-3). The action required is to press a start button and record the reading. Each measurement is actually a two-stage operation. A polarizing current is impressed for 3 seconds on the protons in a small bottle of methyl alcohol surrounded by a 2,000-turn coil. When the polarizing current is shut off, the protons gyrate at a frequency proportional to the magnetic field, thus inducing a voltage in the coil which is amplified and displayed by the instrument. The whole operation takes less than 5 seconds. The individual magnetometer readings are plotted on a base map. Contouring brings out the pattern of anomalies.

Archaeologically important magnetic anomalies may be caused by buried iron objects, hearths, kilns, concentrations of fired pottery, and even concentrations of top soil filling in a ditch or pit. Clays used for household pottery normally contained at least 5 percent iron oxide. Atom-sized domains of magnetic iron in the clay become aligned in the earth's magnetic field after the clay is heated above its Curie point during firing and then cooled. A piece of fired pottery thus causes a small local perturbation in the earth's magnetic field. Chemical weathering during soil formation favors the conversion of weakly magnetic α-Fe_2O_3 (hematite) to the more strongly magnetic γ-Fe_2O_3 (maghemite). Large concentrations of such material offer a magnetic contrast with normal sedimentary bedrock and subsoil.

To detect archaeologically important anomalies, magnetometer readings are taken normally at one-meter intervals on a 6×10 or 10×10 meter grid.

Electrical resistivity measurements have been used in archaeological work since shortly after World War II (see Atkinson 1952; Aitken 1961; Astrom 1967). The resistance of the ground to the flow of electric current is measured. The flow of current is often proportional to the content of water in the rock and soil because of the presence of dissolved ions in the water. Because the water-holding capacity may be an inherent property of these materials, their resistivity therefore provides a basis for detecting rocks and structures of different types in the subsurface. Unfortunately, heavy rains cause near-surface materials to become saturated with water, and summer drought (typical of Greece) causes everything to dry out extensively, so the technique is not always useful.

Large stone structures as well as voids (uncollapsed tombs, for example) have a high resistivity compared with normal soils and bedrock, which exhibit a wide variation, depending on moisture content. Under optimum conditions the geometry of most man-made structures is apparent against the normal geological background.

The technique of electrical resistivity surveying consists of using a series of four metal probes inserted into the ground at measured intervals along a surveyed traverse. A voltage is applied to the outer two probes, and the inner probes record the resultant current flow in the earth. A series of linear traverses must be made and the data for each set up, recorded, and plotted on a base map. Interpretation of results is often difficult, but features of sufficient size, such as buried walls, ditches, and tombs, can be located. The depth to which the current effectively penetrates the earth is about 1 to 1.5 times the probe spacing.

Other geophysical techniques have been tried with poor results. Tite (1961) has tested a metal detector, and Carson (1962) has described a seismic survey. The foregoing discussion of geophysical methods is intended only as background for the following presentation of UMME geophysical efforts in Messenia. Readers may check the references for a more thorough consideration of these methods.

Geophysical Investigations in Messenia

UMME geophysical surveys were undertaken by Brian Mitchell in 1966, by the authors in 1967, and by the senior author and M. J. Aitken in 1969. The magnetometer surveys were made with an LSEC proton magnetometer, and the electrical resistivity surveys with a model ER-1 of Geophysical Specialties Company in 1966 and 1967 and a Bison instrument in 1969.

At the southeast end of the Nichoria acropolis, trial trenching by William McDonald and N. Yalouris in 1959 had exposed portions of house walls. A magnetometer survey by Mitchell showed a small isolated anomaly near this location. Mitchell's resistivity traverse across this magnetic anomaly yielded no anomalous resistivity values, however. Another magnetic anomaly recorded by Mitchell in the western part of the area showed a resistivity high in five of six traverses across it.

Nichoria ridge is composed of nearly flat-lying Pliocene sediments, which consist chiefly of light brown silt, sand, and clay. At the northwest end, the ridge is capped by calcareous siltstone containing abundant fossils. Exposed a few hundred meters north of the site is a dense light gray to white limestone stratigraphically much older than the Pliocene beds and upturned during an epoch of mountain-building. This light-colored limestone provided the chief building stone for Bronze Age and later habitations on the ridge. There is no limestone formation on the ridge crest. The sharp physical difference between the porous clastic sediments and the dense limestone, which has very little iron, provides ideal contrasts for geophysical exploration.

A large mound lies just northwest of Nichoria ridge. The 1966 magnetometer survey yielded a small broad anomaly near the bottom of the gently sloping face of the mound. An electrical resistivity traverse also yielded high readings near the magnetic anomaly. Mitchell located several circular magnetic anomalies along two terraces in an area which later proved to contain several tombs. Excavation in 1969 by the Greek Archaeological Service showed these anomalies to be caused by a densely packed layer of earth roughly circular in outline lying less than 0.5 m beneath the surface. This packing may have resulted from use of the area as a floor.

Figure 15-1. Sketch showing entrance to a tholos tomb, Thouria

It is possible to increase the likelihood of correct interpretation of archaeologically related magnetic and electrical resistivity anomalies by surveying known archaeological sites and structures with a geological setting similar to the site of the anomalies. In 1967 the authors made an electrical resistivity survey across a collapsed tholos tomb (Fig. 15-1) near Thouria (#137), which may have been illicitly excavated and which now has an exposed dromos and doorway on a terraced hillside.

Two lines for electrical resistivity measurements were surveyed, line 1 on the terrace lying just above the stone lintel of the entrance to the tomb and line 2 on the next terrace up. Stakes were placed one meter apart and the normal electrical resistivity measurements were made along the two lines. Plots of the results (Fig. 15-2) show a marked increase in resistivity along line 1 as the dromos is approached. The measurements along line 2 show a decrease in resistivity above the tomb chamber, probably indicating a collapsed structure, the resistivity being less in the earth-filled center than at the walls.

The 1966 and 1967 surveys demonstrated the potential of the geophysical methods under the conditions found in Messenia and led to their extensive use in the 1969 trial season at Nichoria, where over a hundred magnetometer grids and approximately forty electrical resistivity traverses were laid out over the surface of the ridge. Forty anomalies were investigated by trenching. Thirty trenches contained significant archaeological materials (walls, graves, pits, etc.), eight anomalies marked geological phenomena (undisturbed bedrock rising to near the surface), one detected a sardine can, and

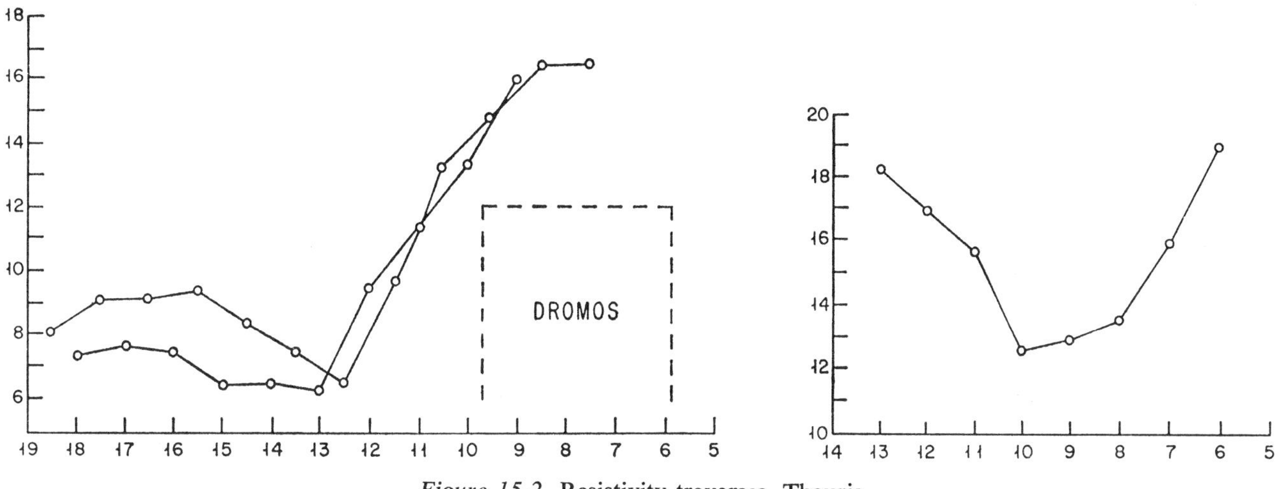

Figure 15-2. Resistivity traverses, Thouria

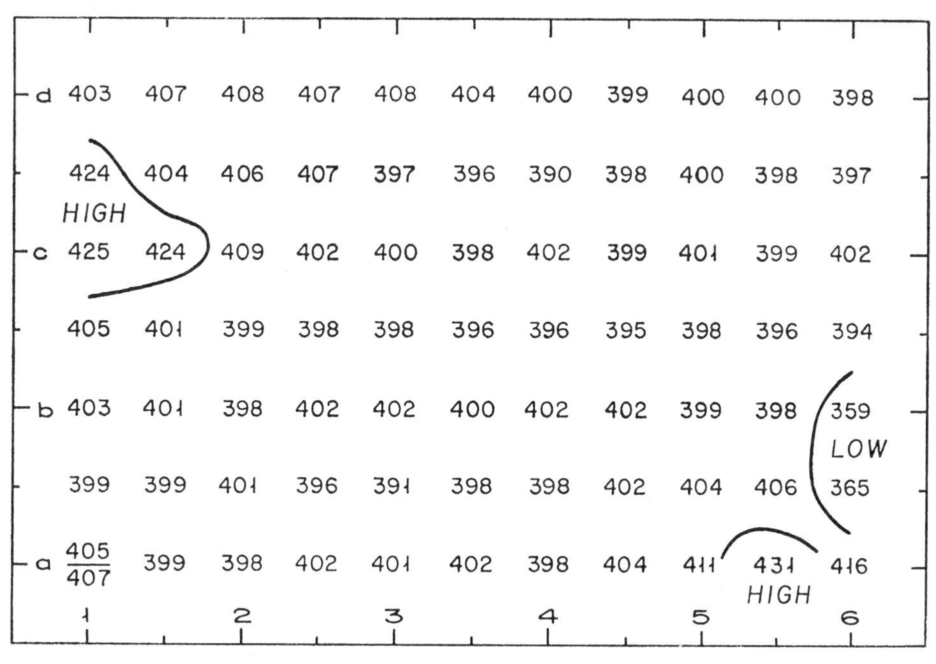

Figure 15-3. Magnetometer grid no. 15, Nichoria

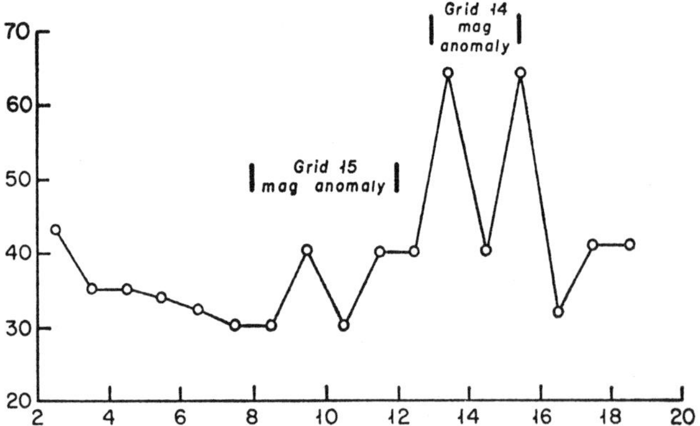

Figure 15-4. Resistivity traverse across grid no. 15, Nichoria

one excavated magnetometer anomaly remains unexplained.

The following examples will illustrate some of the results of the geophysical exploration. Figure 15-3 shows the reading from magnetometer grid No. 15, with two anomalies. Note the monotonous pattern of similar readings in the central portion of the grid, indicative of undisturbed flat-lying soil and bedrock. A low reading on the magnetometer represents a magnetic "high," so the low was of major interest. The contiguous grid No. 14 also showed a magnetic anomaly, so a single 15-m electrical resistivity traverse was run across both magnetometer grids. A plot of the data from this traverse is shown in Figure 15-4. The major magnetometer anomalies in both grids also showed up in the electrical resistivity traverse.

The grid No. 14 anomaly was close to an olive tree, so the landowner refused permission for a trial trench. However, a trial trench was sunk over the grid No. 15 anomaly. Excavation showed the anomaly was caused by a large pithos burial. The burial dates from the late Geometric Period (about 725 B.C.). Stones had been placed around and over the pithos to form a cairn about 3 m long and 1.7 m across. Inside the pithos was a male skeleton with painted terracotta vessels, bronze bowls, a bronze ring, and an iron sword.

It should be noted that there was no archaeological evidence (such as broken pottery) on the surface in this area of the ridge to indicate the potential value of excavating. Without the geophysical surveys, no trenches would have been dug there.

Figure 15-5 shows a contoured magnetometer grid that was hard to interpret precisely. It was obvious, however, that the arrangement and nature of the material below the surface were complex. The dashed lines show the outline of the trial trench dug to reveal any buried objects. Plate 16-1, taken from a hydrogen-filled balloon by Julian Whittlesley, discloses the general correspondence between the anomaly pattern and the arrangement of walls uncovered just a few inches below the surface.

Another magnetometer grid is illustrated in Figure 15-6. Note the strong anomaly at the 397 reading. A test trench was dug so that the left edge of the trench bisected the anomaly. Plate 16-2 shows the source of the subsurface magnetic disturbance, a broken pithos lying not far beneath the surface. The magnetometer grid controlling the location of the probe readings (every meter) had

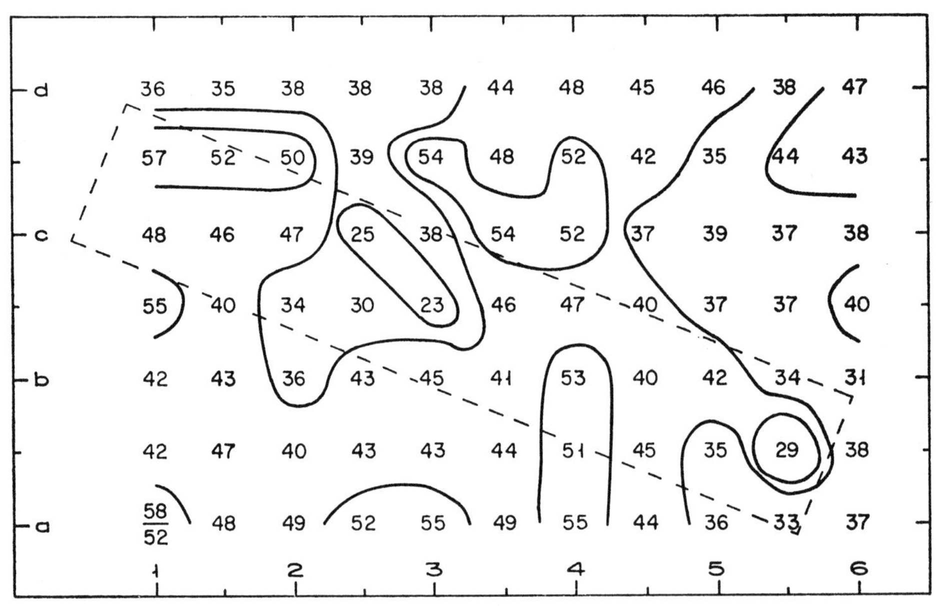

Figure 15-5. Magnetometer grid no. 9-7, Nichoria

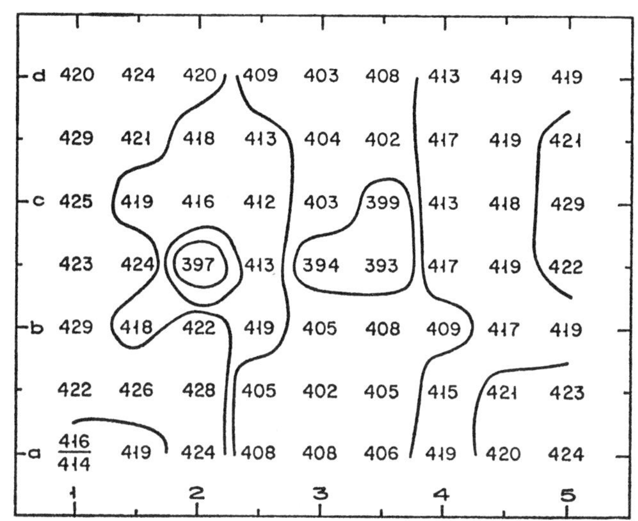

Figure 15-6. Magnetometer grid no. 6-1, Nichoria

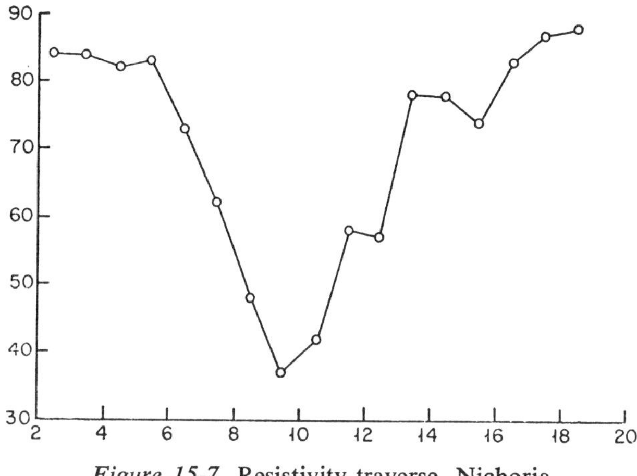

Figure 15-7. Resistivity traverse, Nichoria

positioned the probe directly over the pithos. The magnetic contrast between the fired pottery and the low-iron clay in this area was sufficient to cause a strong anomaly.

Further digging in the trench shown in Plate 16-2 revealed a Middle Bronze Age pit. To ascertain the lateral extent of this pit, a series of electrical resistivity traverses were made parallel to the edge of the trench. The plot of the data from the traverse adjacent to the trench is shown in Figure 15-7. The outline of the pit is easily seen. Undisturbed bedrock on both sides of the pit will not retain so much water as the rubbish and earth fill mixture in the pit. Thus, high resistivity readings are recorded on both sides of a resistivity low. Electrical resistivity traverses farther out from the trench showed a shallowing, then a disappearance of the Middle Bronze Age pit.

The geophysical work in Messenia has demonstrated that, under reasonably good conditions, electrical resistivity and magnetometer surveys can be a useful tool in archaeological exploration.

REFERENCES

Aitken, M. J. 1961. *Physics and Archaeology.* New York.

———. "Magnetic Location." In *Science and Archaeology,* ed. D. Brothwell and E. Higgs, pp. 555–68. London.

———; Webster, G.; and Rees, A. 1958. "Magnetic Prospecting," *Antiquity* 32:270–71.

Astrom, P. 1967. "Electrical Prospecting at Calatia, Caserta," *Estratto da Prospezioni Archeologiche* 2:81–83 and plates.

Atkinson, R. J. C. 1952. "Methods électriques de prospection en archéologie." In *La Découverte du Passé,* ed. A. Laming, pp. 57–70. Paris.

Carson, H. H. 1962. "A Seismic Survey at Harper's Ferry," *Archaeometry* 5:119–23.

Rainey, F., and Ralph, E. K. 1966. "Archaeology and Its New Technology." *Science* 153:1481–91.

Ralph, E. K.; Morrison, F.; and O'Brien, D. P. 1968. "Archaeological Surveying Utilizing a High-Sensitivity Difference Magnetometer," *Geoexploration* 6:109–22.

Tite, M. S. 1961. "Alternative Instruments for Magnetic Surveying: Comparative Tests at the Iron Age Hill-Fort at Rainsborough," *Archaeometry* 4:85–90.

16

PERSPECTIVES

by

William A. McDonald and George R. Rapp, Jr.

In Chapter 1 the question was raised whether the UMME project is really *inter*-disciplinary or *multi*-disciplinary. Now, several hundred pages later, the verdict ought to be easier. Does the foregoing text show that the various members of the team have in fact cooperated in fieldwork and interacted in writing up the results? If so, the authors of this final chapter should be able to extract from the preceding pages the raw material for a reasonably coordinated body of information about relationships between the natural environment of Messenia and its inhabitants, particularly in the Late Bronze Age.

One way to evaluate what has been accomplished is to ask ourselves how many of the specific questions posed in Chapter 1 (pp. 7, 8) we can now respond to with some confidence. We had, in fact, considered using that format for the final chapter; and we did not abandon the idea because the inadequacy of the information now in hand would still be painfully obvious. Actually, substantial progress has already been made on at least one-third of those problems; and at the end of this chapter we outline a program of further research aimed at increasing the scope and dependability of these answers as well as discovering ways to approach additional questions.

First, then, we shall attempt to sketch the "model"—that is, to describe what we have learned about the environment in which the Messenians of the Late Bronze Age found themselves and how they seem to have affected it and adapted to it. Naturally, this will not be a rounded picture. We shall omit some topics where we can at present add nothing significantly new, and concentrate instead on those aspects on which we have moved toward a somewhat clearer view. Perhaps we may be pardoned for sometimes including what might be called hunches that depend more on judgment and familiarity with the present environment than on solid new facts about the past. Where important differences of opinion occur among authors we have not attempted to gloss them over. We see no obvious order into which the topics naturally fall; all are in some sense separable, and yet almost all are interrelated.

Coastal Configurations

We shall begin with the general category that includes physical features of the coastal areas, such as swamps, lagoons, harbors, land subsidence, or rise in sea level. The high relief has changed little in the period of human occupation. Along the west coast, however, marshes and lagoons had been forming between the headlands buttressed by limestone, beginning long before our target period and continuing until the present. Some of them, like the area around Kakovatos (#300), had already filled up to form fertile arable coastal plains. Others, like Osmanaga Lagoon, were in relatively early stages of evolution. Wright has discussed the evidence in Chapter 12 (see Fig. 12-2), and we recall that Osmanaga Lagoon began to form about 2000 B.C. Incidentally, this solid fact settles a point that has long been controversial about the topography of the area at the time of the Pylos campaign in the fifth century B.C. In the Middle Bronze Age when the lagoon was forming, the surrounding area was heavily forested with pine, as is now the case around and above the lagoons in the Kaiafa vicinity farther north. The depth of water in Osmanaga Lagoon and its extent seem to have varied, since the northern area (continuously under water in modern times before a big drainage project was attempted) was apparently occupied by a prehistoric village or villages. Habitation here can be dated both in Early Helladic (presumably before the lagoon formed) and in Late Helladic times. Possibly LH people lived in this low land only seasonally, when the water level was low and the rich alluvium could be cultivated or the area used for pasture. The southwestern part must have been continually under water and could have provided good opportunities for fisheries, as in relatively modern times.

The rocky prominences of Paliokastro and Profitis Ilias to south and north respectively of the entrance to little Voïdhokilia Bay were occupied in LH times (as earlier and later); and it is natural to see in this area, particularly in site #9, the chief harbor town connected with the palace (perhaps *ro-o-wa* in the tablets). But Voïdhokilia Bay is not sufficiently large or protected to accommodate the ships of a prosperous trading kingdom like Pylos, and in Mycenaean times it was even smaller than today. If ships used this northern entrance to Osmanaga Lagoon, a channel must have been kept open between the cliff and the sand dunes. Alternatively, it is possible that the lagoon was the inner harbor but that a channel connected it with the much larger Navarino Bay to the south. A channel through the sandspit here was in use a generation ago when there were fisheries in the lagoon. Nor can we rule out the possibility that an inner harbor in Osmanaga Lagoon was connected by channel with both Voïdhokilia and Navarino bays. There is good reason to believe that slave and corvée labor was readily available for such projects.

Finally, some part or parts of Navarino Bay itself may have served as the main harbor, although the position of the known habitation sites in the immediate area poses problems for that interpretation. The same reasoning makes it quite unlikely that the main harbor lay to the north of the Navarino-Osmanaga area. Also, although there are a few beaches there, the coast is generally rocky and protection is minimal.

On the gulf coast, the marshes in the Pamisos delta (as well as those inland around the great Ayios Floros and Pidhima springs) were almost certainly more widespread and impenetrable than now: but the settlement at Akovitika (#151) shows that they were not totally uninhabitable, at least in the Early Helladic period. The existence of such early settlements as #'s 151 and 130 also proves that there has been relatively slight change in the coastline since then. Later on, in Geometric times, a sanctuary was built in the same unlikely area (#151) and it apparently continued in use right down to the Roman era. We have also pointed in Chapter 8 to several sites on the western and northern edges of the Pamisos swamps (#'s 122, 123, 124, 132) that were occupied in EH and LH times but apparently not in the interval. This phenomenon could be explained by a wetter intervening period or by the advent of people who did not know how to cope with wetland and who preferred to use drier slopes for pasturage as well as crops. At any rate, the Bronze Age inhabitants generally did not settle in the poorly drained lowlands. The known village sites occupy the lower edges of the alluvial slopes at an elevation of about 100 m in the upper (Steniklarian) plain as shown in Figure 2-3. The alluvial slope–bottomland transition zone was also a favorite site for villages in the lower (Pamisos) plain.

What useful comments can be made about harbors? It is difficult to be precise about what constituted an adequate shelter for the ships of those times. How safe is the common inference that ships really were pulled up on any convenient sandy beach? Certainly it would be difficult to unload heavy cargoes on an open roadstead without protection from strong winds and at least minimal docking facilities. The special advantages of the Navarino area seem to be clear enough, whether or not Osmanaga Lagoon was available as an inner harbor. There is, in fact, no other well-protected large natural harbor on either the west or the gulf coast of Messenia. We can probably assume that in LH times, as in later antiquity, the sailing season was practically closed in winter. This automatically imposed a special regime on shipping and trade. And the seas hereabouts can be rough at other seasons too.

In general, both the west and the gulf coasts were not as filled in and smoothed out as at present. Wright found that the lagoonal sediment in the Kaiafa area did not begin to form until Roman times and that the lagoons farther north are even younger. It is possible that some of the lagoons north of Navarino along the west coast cover earlier harbors and, if so, there may be some hope of recovering buried evidence of docking facilities. But there is a much stronger likelihood that the major harbors in the Bronze Age were those that are well known from later use.

Except for the modern artificial harbor at Kalamata, whose predecessors can scarcely be guessed at, all of these locations possess natural advantages such as protecting headlands or offshore islands. And there is some reason to believe that such protection was considerably greater in the Bronze Age. For instance, it appears that site #80, now on an island, was then at the tip of a peninsula that protected the harbor of Methoni. The possibility seems remote that river mouths formed usable harbors or that the lower stretches of some rivers were navigable for small boats in LH times, although we raised that point in connection with EH emphasis on external connections (Ch. 8).

The other candidates for important harbors on the west

coast are Pheia (#304), Kyparissia (#70), Marathoupolis (#406 – opposite Proti island and close to site #15), Methoni (#412), and Finikous (#79). On the west side of the gulf the only reasonably good harbors are at Koroni (#512) and Petalidhi (#502). The east side is generally exposed and sparsely settled, although the harbor of Kitries (#546) is known to have been heavily used in the early modern period.

We have stated in Chapter 8 that the absence of evidence so far for Bronze Age settlement at Methoni, Koroni, and Petalidhi should probably be attributed to their very intensive later utilization. The first two were famous ports of call between Western Europe and the Levant in medieval times and later, and Petalidhi should be the "port of the Achaeans" mentioned by Pausanias. Furthermore, Petalidhi may have been the major harbor for the important Bronze Age site at Nichoria (#100) that lies 3 km to the northwest. There are, however, relatively recent records of ships unloading even closer to Nichoria, at the mouth of the Karia River; and borings by Yassoglou in the bottomland near the mouth of the Karia suggest that a considerable indentation in the coastline may have once existed there (see broken lines in Pocket Map 10-19). Furthermore, it is said that there was a customhouse in relatively recent times on the unprotected coast directly south of Messini, near EH site #130.

Petalidhi-Nichoria as port and main settlement would neatly parallel Navarino–Epano Englianos, and the relationship of the Kalamata acropolis to the sea and Athens-Piraeus is comparable. We and others have emphasized the "canonical" position of major LH sites in Messenia and elsewhere as somewhat removed from the coast for the sake of safety. Yet there can be no doubt that coastal sites like Pheia, Kyparissia, and Finikous were relatively large and important; and, as just mentioned, it is not necessary to believe that the main sites in the Methoni and Koroni districts were slightly inland, rather than under the present coastal towns.

There is a widespread assumption that sea level is higher now in the east Mediterranean than in classical or Roman times. It is true that in our region one can see foundations of Greek and Roman buildings a meter or more underwater in a very few places like Pheia and Navarino Bay. However, the recent extensive work of Flemming (1969) on eustatic change of sea level and earth movements in the western Mediterranean during the last two thousand years indicates that, although most ancient sites are now lower relative to sea level, all submergence is due to earth movements and there has been no net eustatic change in the level of the Mediterranean Sea. Detailed investigations of comparable earth movements in the Peloponnese are now underway by the junior author and Professor John C. Kraft.

Communications

In the context of harbors, we should first review Lukermann's reconstruction of the road network in the Middle and Late Bronze Age (Ch. 9). There ought to be a clear correlation between land and sea routes. Lukermann does in fact find reason to posit termini of important overland communications at Kyparissia (his routes S and T), Navarino (his route R), Methoni (his routes N and Q), Koroni (his routes O and Q), and Kalamata (his route R). In addition, Petalidhi is a junction on his route O. A check of Pocket Map 8-14 shows that major concentrations of population can be made out around each of these centers, and that they provide the handiest access from the sea to most inland population concentrations.

Turning now to the pattern of land communications, Lukermann has reconstructed the Late Bronze situation on the basis of modern geographical theory that concentrates on the general process of settlement development, settlement location, and settlement interaction. The known *point* locations of prehistoric sites (Ch. 8) are compared and contrasted with what can be reconstructed from the Linear B tablets (Ch. 7), from classical antiquity (literary and topographical evidence reviewed in Ch. 6, plus site distribution discussed in Ch. 8), from medieval and early modern times (Ch. 5), and from his own observations of the existing road network. By evaluating known conditions in the past and making informed assumptions when empirical data are missing, he has constructed a settlement and circulation pattern that he describes as a set of interlocking subsystems. With sufficient data, such a construct can provide the basis for valid inferences about the relationship of size and level of functions, degrees of centrality (accessibility and nodality relative to the hinterland), level of trade, size and number of routes, and even the degree of political and institutional complexity and organization. Chapter 9 barely adumbrates what can theoretically be ascertained as this kind of study proceeds hand in hand with further site search and excavation.

Although Lukermann has included the MH with the LH data, the effect is a cumulative picture at the height of prosperity in prehistoric times. We have emphasized in Chapter 8 that site distribution would support the assumption that, generally speaking, the new LH settlements filled in a pattern already clear in MH times.

What Lukermann essentially distinguishes is a series of settlement nuclei or core areas internally connected by a secondary road network and interconnected by primary lines of communication. The fact that he includes the Triphylia core area (K) at the northwest and the Kambos area (H) at the southeast edges of our region need not imply a judgment about the actual boundaries of the kingdom of Pylos. Our present position on this question is reviewed in Chapters 1, 7, and 8. There is no point in repeating it here except to recall that there is no solid evidence that the unified kingdom ever extended north of the Nedha or south of the Nedhon River. Beginning at the south, the settlement nuclei are:

Core Area	*Main Town*
A. Methoni	Methoni? (#412)
B. Koroni	Koroni? (#512)
C. Navarino	Epano Englianos (#1)
D. Central Plateau	Koukounara (#35)
E. Five Rivers	Nichoria (#100)
F. Pamisos Valley	Thouria (#137)
G. Nedhon	Kalamata (#142)
H. Kambos (peripheral)	Kambos (#146)
I. Kyparissia-Filiatra	Kyparissia (#70)
J. Nedha	Lepreon? (#245)
K. Triphylia (peripheral)	Arene-Klidhi (#302) or Kakovatos (#300)
L. Soulima Valley	Kokla: Rachi Chani (#224)
M. Steniklaros Valley	Meligala (#206)

Lukermann then reconstructs a primary network of five "highways": a north-south coastal road connecting core areas A, C, I, J, and K; an east-west road linking core areas C, D, E, and F; a second east-west road joining core areas I, L, and M; and two north-south roads on either side of the Pamisos-Steniklaros Valley, joining core areas F and M. Thus, excluding the route on the east side of the Pamisos-Steniklaros Valley, the four remaining major routes frame the great rectangle of maximum habitation density discussed in Chapter 8 (see Fig. 9-2).

The major routes linking Messenia to neighboring regions would have been, first, the west coast route continuing to the north through Triphylia and across the Alpheios to the north into Elis, and second, routes bifurcating from the Leondari-Kokala pass (#211) at the north end of the route on the east side of the Pamisos-Steniklaros Valley and leading respectively to Arkadia and Lakonia. Outside communication by land was also provided by several routes that probably carried considerably less traffic. One led north out of the Soulima Valley into western Arkadia and eastern Triphylia. A second connected core area G (Kalamata-Pherai) to the minor core area H and on south along the east gulf coast to several passes that led over the Taygetos Mountains to Lakonia. The Langadha pass directly east of Kalamata and another behind Thouria (#137) may have provided further links with Lakonia, but how commonly they were used in the Late Bronze Age is at present unknown (Hope Simpson 1966, pp. 125–26). The most practical (though longest) route from Messenia to Lakonia was probably the northern Leondari pass (discussed above), and Fant believes (Ch. 2) that it is the only feasible candidate for wheeled traffic (e.g., Telemachos' reputed journey by chariot from Kalamata to Sparta).

There were, of course, numerous additional connecting roads, especially within core areas. The major links across the Mavrozoumenos and Pamisos rivers and wet valley bottoms in core areas F and M were (south to north) in the vicinity of Aris (#126), Plati (#135), and Meligala (#206). The existing "double" bridge near Meligala (see Pl. 4-1) has foundations dating back to Hellenistic times, and its strategic location at the confluence of two rivers draining the northwestern and northeastern parts of the Steniklarian Plain and close to the Meligala site (#206) suggests that this crossing was already in use in prehistoric times. It is also worth mentioning that the Late Bronze site near Plati now has the name Petroyefira (Stone Bridge). Although we know that the Mycenaean engineers could build monumental bridges with corbelled arches (see Ch. 2), there is at present no evidence that such bridges existed in Messenia. No doubt the safer conjecture is that these were particularly easy fording places, perhaps improved by strewing the river bottoms with heavy stones, as is still the custom.

Even in the case of rivers that are now perennial, there is of course a much heavier flow in the rainy season; and at times they must have been difficult or even impossible to cross. Most smaller streams are (and no doubt were) rushing torrents in winter and totally dry in summer. Slippery mud is another serious hazard in the wet season. When we combine the likelihood of difficult or impassable land routes with a great diminution if not cessation of seaborne traffic in winter, the necessary fluctuation in seasonal flow of goods must have required quite drastic adjustments in the economy.

South of Aris (#126) the wide swampy Pamisos delta (Valtos) was certainly a major obstacle to valley crossing. In fact, an all-weather road would have been extremely difficult to construct here. The lack of such a direct link to the east is probably reflected in the old name Nisi (island) for the large modern town of Messini on its western edge. No Late Bronze sites have been discovered in the delta area.

The easiest route connecting the approximate northeast and southwest corners of Messenia is not yet obvious. If a traveller or trader wished to go from Arkadia or Lakonia to the Navarino area, he would presumably have come into Messenia by the Leondari pass and skirted the Steniklarian Plain to Meligala. From there he might have taken the roundabout but much easier route on lower ground, crossing to the west side of the river, either at

Meligala or the Skala ridge and following the major "highway" on the west side of the valley, then swinging over on the main east-west route by Nichoria, Chandhrinou, Yialova (or the cutoff by Chatzi and Chora). To judge by what is known of practice from classical times until the last century, however, he might have chosen a shorter route involving much rougher country and difficult river crossings, skirting Mt. Ithomi and proceeding via Andhrousa across the upper part of the Five Rivers core area through Dhiodhia (formerly Loï) to Chatzi, Chora, and Navarino.

Known Late Bronze sites are scarce along this "shortcut," but the area is not yet well known and is extremely difficult to search. So far, however, there is no evidence for Bronze Age occupation at such key places as Mavromati and Andhrousa. Yet the latter site has a "canonical" prehistoric acropolis and commands a fertile area that one would certainly expect to have been cultivated in prehistoric times. The present lack of evidence may very likely be explained, as in the case of Methoni, Koroni and Petalidhi, by extremely concentrated later occupation that has totally obscured or destroyed the earlier evidence. It is relevant here to point out that we had great difficulty in getting any solid evidence for prehistoric habitation on the fine acropolises at Kyparissia and Kalamata. Whether the same reasoning might apply to Mavromati (Messene) is much less clear. There was apparently no heavy medieval use, and the extensive excavations down in the valley where the classical site was located have not turned up any prehistoric material. Yet it is difficult to believe that the great natural fortress and religious center on nearby Mt. Ithomi does not have a history going back earlier than archaic times.

There were, of course, innumerable internal linking roads (or paths) within the core areas, but we might mention one more example of a fairly major route that connected three of the southern core areas (A, B, and D). One route presumably crossed the lower peninsula joining A and B (a crucial link in later Venetian times); and a second farther north must have followed the line Mesochori (#75), Ambelokipi (#77), to Longa (#107). From this second route, somewhere in the neighborhood of the modern village of Kallithea, there was apparently a northern link with Chandrinou (#33), where it joined the main east-west route. Kallithea is a good example of a likely acropolis with good water supply (rather rare in this area) that, from both Lukermann's and McDonald–Hope Simpson's point of view, ought to have been a prehistoric site. Our failure to find evidence as yet is probably to be explained in this case by the heavy *modern* occupation over the whole hill.

What can we state or infer about the roads themselves and the kind of traffic that used them? In Chapter 2 Fant briefly describes the well-known road system in the vicinity of Mycenae in northeast Peloponnese. Its LH date is not in question and its sophisticated engineering is impressive, particularly the elaborate measures to ensure drainage and the extreme care taken to keep the grades easy by terracing along slopes. Furthermore, scenes depicted on some of the stelae from the Mycenae shaft graves strongly suggest the existence of chariots (and presumably roads to accommodate them) from the beginning of the Late Bronze Age.

On the other hand, Evans' thesis that there was a network of roads for wheeled traffic in Late Bronze Age Crete is much less sure. Several UMME colleagues spent parts of two seasons (1963, 1964) going over the ground there and checking Evans' evidence. The results are mainly negative. Although there can be no doubt that land communication was well developed at the height of Minoan prosperity and the Linear B tablets prove the use of chariots at Knossos, we were able to verify almost none of Evans' specific references to actual remains of Bronze Age roads. This could be due to the vagueness of his descriptions, to our lack of familiarity with the Cretan countryside, to the ravages of time, or even to some exaggeration by Evans. Certainly, the statement so often repeated in the handbooks (for which, as far as we can see, Evans is not really responsible) that Minoan highways were paved is unproved and cannot be true. The idea may have arisen from the paved streets within Minoan centers, or more likely from the fine stone-cobbled kalderims of medieval or early modern times that can be seen in many parts of Crete and mainland Greece. But these were narrow roads, built primarily for riders of shod horses. Such a surface would have cut to pieces the hooves of the unshod animals of Late Bronze times.

The only instance of a specific section of Minoan road referred to by Evans and still to be found (or at least seen by us) is the impressive series of *S*-curves that surmount the steep slope past the chapel of Ayia Pelayia at the eastern end of the Lasithi Plain. Fant describes the construction in detail (Ch. 2) and expresses doubt that chariots could have negotiated its sharp turns and steep grades. Its massive retaining walls give the impression of great age, but the analogy with Minoan construction is loose and nothing that we can see would prove that it was not built much later.

Coming now to Messenian "highways" in the Late Bronze Age, we have in the first place the analogy of chariot roads at Mycenae, a comparable kingdom in the general milieu of the koinê or "common" mainland culture. Any characteristic proved for one kingdom can be taken for granted to have been known (and copied if they so desired) by others. Also, the Linear B tablets show that chariots were in use at the Pylian capital (and probably up and down the coast) at the end of the thirteenth century. We can be sure, then, that there must have been at least a few roads that could accommodate this type of light, two-wheeled vehicle and that would allow travel at a fair pace. Their construction and maintenance would require a considerable amount of engineering skill and a great deal of labor, and it is not at all clear whether we should envision fairly easy chariot travel on all the major routes described above. At any rate, the best chance for vestiges of such roads to be preserved is at spots where, as in the vicinity of Mycenae and Ayia Pelayia, rough ground and sudden changes in elevation would have required particularly strong and durable construction and where later routes or other construction or cultivation have not destroyed the evidence.

The Neromilos-Kazarma area that is fully treated by Fant (Ch. 2) is the most probable that we have located so far. The highest road-line, which McDonald and Hope Simpson believe was constructed in late Mycenaean times and about which Fant is considerably more skeptical, certainly does not exhibit monumentality comparable to the Mycenae examples. Fant is particularly worried about the apparent lack of culverts to assure drainage on slopes. Yet the fact remains that the excellent surface of fine gravel over bedrock that can be seen beneath the undergrowth on the road surface has shown no deterioration whatever in the decade since we first saw it, whereas ten years easily suffices to destroy a modern paved road if poor drainage allows it to become a stream bed in winter. In any case, this road-line *is* adequately drained and, if the brush were cleared, a Land Rover could now negotiate it for several kilometers.

But how does one date a road? We can only say that the line-up of Late Bronze Age habitation sites and tombs on either side of this area proves that the road that connected them had to lie in this precise place, that chariots could have negotiated the road-line we have located and mapped, and that Late Bronze Age engineers certainly had the know-how and labor to construct it. If it served the purpose without requiring the monumentality of the roads around Mycenae, the kings of Pylos were presumably willing to settle for less.

At least one more topic should be broached in connection with communications, namely, the kind of traffic that used the roads. We have already discussed chariots and their special needs. With that exception, we have the strong impression that wheeled traffic was not common. Carts were apparently known, but their use was probably minimal, even within local areas where ground was relatively even. It is salutary to be reminded that only one wagon existed in the village of Karpofora just a generation ago. Also, the medieval and early modern cobbled kalderims that connected villages could not have been used for wheeled vehicles. They were for pedestrians, pack animals, and especially for riding horses. The latter were apparently uncommon in the Late Bronze Age.

Surely the patient donkey with his huge freight-saddle was the chief means of transport in the Late Bronze Age, as well as for many centuries before and since. Messenia is crisscrossed with hundreds of tracks that are adequate for donkey caravans, as well as for short- or long-distance movement of people and their flocks and herds. A donkey can carry a weight of about 150 kg (330 lb). Articles that are too heavy or awkward for one animal (even a mule), such as big construction timbers, could have been attached to several animals in a line and carried or dragged along the ground.

What has just been said is not meant to suggest that the network of routes outlined by Lukermann consisted mainly of goat-paths. Such tracks are the first and essential "roads," but the care expended on the quality of the road (its width, surface condition, grades, etc.) will bear a direct relation to the volume of use. The primary routes discussed above surely had some claim to permanence and perhaps even to monumentality. It may seem odd that groups like ours do so much of their prospecting for ancient habitation sites in a motor vehicle. But the truth is that the likely targets are usually on or very close to the modern road network. In spite of local and subregional changes and new modes of transportation, earthmoving, and rock cutting, this enduring *pattern* of communications is in fact a first-rate example of interaction between the natural environment and the inhabitants. There simply are *natural* routes to get most easily to the places where *humans* have always chosen to live.

Landscape and Land Use

We shall attempt now to set down our major inferences about the probable pattern of relatively undisturbed forest, scattered residual or planted groves of trees, brushland (garigue, maquis), pastureland (upland and valley), and land lying fallow or cultivated to various degrees and in various crops. We have already discussed the swamps and marshes along the west coast and in the great eastern valley. Van Wersch's careful description of modern land use and his reconstruction of the earlier pattern (Ch. 11, esp. Pocket Maps 11-20 and 11-21) are basic to this subject. Additional evidence will be drawn from several other chapters, notably 3, 4, 7, 10, and 12.

We might begin with a discussion of forestation. The key here, of course, would be Wright's pollen analyses (Ch. 12) if only they were widespread enough to reflect the vegetation history of representative subregions. Unfortunately, this is not the case, although he has tried to get usable samples from many spots where there is perennially wet ground and thus the possibility of recovering well-preserved pollen. So we must face the bad news that significant additions to present information from this vital source are unlikely. What Wright has been able to establish is that, when Osmanaga Lagoon began to form about 2000 B.C., there was a heavy pine cover in that particular area. Furthermore, although there is no indication of a major climate shift, pine pollen disappears almost completely in the course of the first half of the second millennium B.C. When we consider this relatively rapid change together with the archaeological evidence (Ch. 8), which indicates that it was in the same centuries (the Middle Bronze Age) that our region was first fairly heavily settled, it is an almost inescapable conclusion that these settlers cut and burned the pine forests in order to clear for agriculture, and secondarily to obtain timber for increased construction.

The same pollen cores show that in the sequences for the next half millennium or so there was a notable increase in grasses normally connected with cultivation, plus a modest amount of olive pollen. It would appear, then, that in the immediate Pylos district the Late Bronze landscape would have shown a countryside increasingly cleared for grain and some olive orchards, plus vines and other cultivated plants whose pollen grains are not abundantly produced or dispersed. We may also perhaps envision small stands of residual or resurgent pine. Maquis, dominated by evergreen oak, certainly survived on the steeper slopes and in less accessible areas. Deciduous oak was probably not common in this coastal area.

It is quite impossible, however, to generalize about the whole region from the situation indicated by this one very local insight. Wright's only other pollen cores that date early enough to include our target period come from Lake Voulkaria, north of the Gulf of Patras. There he finds that substantial percentages of evergreen and deciduous oak characterized the Late Bronze Age landscape. This hint may have some relevance in support of Rothmaler's thesis (1943) that scattered individual trees and small stands of oak in the modern Peloponnesian countryside constitute important residual evidence for early vegetation history. He believes that, except for the Taygetos Mountains and the coasts and wet valleys, practically all of our region was forested in oak before there was any intensive human occupation. In that case, we might visualize a Late Bronze Age landscape still characterized by considerable stretches of forest. Our estimate of the population peak in the Late Bronze Age (see Ch. 8 and later in the present chapter) suggests that the inhabitants may have needed to clear no more than 30 percent of the land that is now cultivated. And even today only 44 percent of the total area is in planted crops.

So, while the heavily populated Pylos district seems to have lost nearly all its pine, it is reasonable to assume that, if the interior was originally forested, clearing for cultivation and cutting for timber, charcoal, and firewood would by no means have totally depleted the forests in marginally cultivated or unexploited areas. We note, for example, that the Pylos tablets refer to timber-supplying areas like *ro-u-so* that are considerably closer to the palace than the Taygetos range. Indeed, good-sized groves or even forests of oak and other trees such as cypress may have existed between areas cultivated from the LH settlements; and fair numbers of big trees may have remained within cultivated areas, and even within and around the settlements themselves.

Some support is perhaps lent to this hypothesis by isolated bits of information from later times. For example, travellers in the eighteenth and early nineteenth century mention a great oak forest north and west of Neromilos toward Mt. Manklavas; we hear of large herds of pigs fattening on acorns; Kalamata was noted for its excellent leather, which was tanned with a preparation in which acorns played a crucial role; ship timbers were requisitioned from southern Messenia in classical and early modern times; and there is still an impressive total of 54 names of places or rural areas within our region that contain the root *veláni*, oak tree (Georgacas and McDonald 1969, p. 113). Furthermore, the fact that 15–20 percent of the modern countryside is listed as "forest land" (actually dense brush for the most part) suggests that at least that proportion of the land surface was either impossible to cultivate or not considered worth permanent clearing, even when population pressure was most severe in the nineteenth century.

Wright is rather wary of accepting Rothmaler's thesis, but Yassoglou and Nobeli (Ch. 10) seem to find it much more attractive. Yassoglou contends that expert study can identify existing soil profiles that developed under oak forests in climatic conditions similar to those existing at present. His intensive research in the immediate area of Nichoria (#100) has led him to believe that undisturbed or slightly disturbed soils surrounding the residential site were developed under and protected by a forest, most probably of oak. The fact that deer bones have been identified in the Nichoria excavation underlines the likelihood that these animals persisted in nearby woods; and deer are depicted on the Pylos tablets and frescoes. Also, tusks of wild boar (sometimes with holes for attachment to such articles as helmets) are frequently found at Nichoria and elsewhere. Such hints leave very little doubt that hunting still provided at least a small part of the meat diet as well as sport for nobles and perhaps for commoners.

It will require much closer collaboration between soil scientists and archaeologists, however, to provide reliable estimates of the approximate elapsed time since the forest disappeared. Thus, at Nichoria, we cannot yet prove that the forested areas coexisted with the Late Bronze Age inhabitants. It appears that the immediate area was quite intensively exploited throughout the Middle and Late Bronze Age, and the forests in the immediate vicinity may have been greatly diminished by the end of the second millennium B.C. Yassoglou believes, however, that the Early Iron Age graves to the northwest of the habitation site were dug in an area that had retained its tree cover and that was still under forest long after that date.

It has been customary to believe that, by classical times at least, the more heavily populated parts of Greece were almost totally deforested. The blame is usually put on cutting by humans for cultivation, construction, shipbuilding, charcoal and fuel, and especially on close grazing by goats. It should be remembered, however, that goats will do no damage to large trees, although by the same token large trees do not last forever, even if they are spared by man, goat, and fire. The surest indication of the potential destruction of forests in classical times will be provided by the relative pressure on the land, when and if that becomes better known. At present, classical population pressure in our region does not appear to have been so heavy as in Mycenaean times (see Ch. 8). We recall Xenophon's hunting estate in Triphylia and what seem like isolated Roman villas in a rather sparsely settled countryside such as the area north of Koroni.

In any case, the present indications of only moderate exploitation of the land by humans in the Late Bronze Age – and, by implication, no catastrophic damage by their domesticated animals, including goats – leaves open the possibility that large sections of Messenia were relatively untouched by man. To give only one example, an extensive area behind the gulf coast and stretching from Nichoria eastward to the Pamisos delta has so far yielded no evidence of habitation until the medieval period. It is our hypothesis at present that this relatively fertile area was under tree cover until long after the Bronze Age. If we are right about this and other areas, there could have been no heavy pressure on land available for cultivation in our region as a whole at any time in antiquity.

Nevertheless, Messenia certainly contained extensive areas that were marginally to intensively exploited for grazing and agriculture in late prehistoric times. What percentage of the available land surface did these areas occupy? How were they distributed? Can we infer anything more precise about the kind of soil and elevation that the farmers and herders preferred, the types and proportions of crops grown, the proportions of the various domesticated animals raised, and so on?

We may begin by making some very rough comparisons between present statistics and parallel estimates for the Late Bronze Age (Chs. 8 and 11). The present population of the region is in the range of 250,000, of whom about 70 percent or 175,000 are farmers. They cultivate about 160,000 ha or 40 percent of the land, which is close to a ratio of one rural inhabitant to one hectare. The farms are typically in several separate parcels but average 3 ha in total area, with about 33 percent in tree crops, 20 percent in vines, and the remainder in annual crops. One-half to one-quarter of the latter lies fallow in a given year. About 10 percent of the total land under cultivation is irrigated. A slightly larger percentage of the land, 172,000 ha or about 42 percent is used for grazing, although some of it is in light maquis. The population of domesticated animals is approximately as follows: 168,000 sheep, 130,000 goats, 26,000 pigs, 26,000 donkeys, 19,000 horses, 18,000 cattle, 6,000 mules (NSSG 1964).

To reach an estimate of the percentage of land cultivated in the Late Bronze Age, we shall make certain assumptions: that agricultural methods and productivity were not significantly different; that the basic crops (though not necessarily their relative proportions) were comparable; and that agricultural surpluses were a major item in the balance of trade, as they are today. In that case, the relationship between the Mycenaean population and the present agricultural population versus land cultivated would probably have been about the same. Our estimate of the minimum population (see later in this chapter) is about 50,000, most of whom were surely farmers and herders. Thus, the farmers should not have had to cultivate more than 50,000 to 60,000 ha of the better land. This would mean that only about one-third of the present acreage need have been under cultivation.

If now we take into account the possibility that agricultural methods and productivity were significantly inferior to the present, we might estimate that half or 75,000 ha were cultivated. And if we divide this maximum area among the estimated 250 settlements, the average of cultivated land per village is 375 ha. A conservative estimate of the "total land" category (L) in Register A (Appendix, p. 264) would suggest that there was an average of at least 1,500 ha per village. So we can imagine a Late Bronze Age landscape in which, typically, a maximum of 25 percent of the land surrounding a village was intensively cultivated.

When we try to go even further and suggest how the cultivated area was divided among the different crops, the picture becomes still hazier. Van Wersch reconstructs a regime where grains were more important, and trees and vines less so than today. Reducing substantially the modern percentages of trees and vines specified above and leaving room for crops like flax which was much more important in Mycenaean than modern times, there would still be ample room for the 40 percent in feed grains (including fallow) that is his higher estimate.

Before going into more detail about individual cultivated crops, we may consider how the much larger uncultivated segments may have been utilized. As argued above, a sizable amount was probably forested, although the range among villages and especially subregions must have been very large. It will be recalled that an average of over 40 percent of the territory belonging to a typical modern village is classed as "grazing land." The Late Bronze Age figure was almost surely higher, both areally and especially in quality. It is a natural inference, for example, that the manure from a larger number of animals was an important factor in maintaining soil fertility, both in permanent pastures and in fallow land.

The inhabitants of some prehistoric villages may have been basically pastoralists, though it is our impression from familiarity with the sites that the over-all proportion of families depending mainly on flocks and herds compared with those depending mainly on agriculture had dropped considerably from Middle Bronze to Late Bronze times. No doubt animals were pastured both on upland slopes where forests may have been cut down or intentionally burned for this purpose and on wet bottomlands. It is likely that villages in more mountainous and isolated areas depended especially heavily on their sheep and goats. Conversely, villages at lower altitudes and near wet bottomlands would have raised a higher percentage of cattle and horses. A preliminary examination of the animal bones from Nichoria, which was directly above a lush valley, indicates the presence of a good many surprisingly large cattle. Over-all, the percentage of large animals was almost certainly higher than is now the case. We recall Homer's account of large-scale raids on cattle and horses in Nestor's day as well as the record of Messenia's export of horses in classical times.

Some account should be taken here of the evidence in the Linear B tablets (Ventris and Chadwick 1956, pp. 195–213), although it must be fragmentary and may be misleading. Horses and donkeys do not appear in the Pylos records (though they do at Knossos); yet they must have been used for transport, both local and long distance. Cattle are rarely mentioned at Pylos, although it is clear from context that they were the main source of traction for plowing (hence the affectionate names recorded ?). Over five times as many sheep as goats (about 10,000 versus 1,800) were contributed to the palace, and the heavy preponderance of males has been shown to reflect the raising of castrated rams for wool production. A total of 540 pigs is also recorded. The only safe comparison one can draw between this information and the statistics given above for the present animal population is that the sheep-goat ratio was very different, a not unexpected situation in view of the importance of weaving woolen cloth. We shall lack really useful insights on the animal population and the meat diet in Late Bronze times, however, until excavators provide large and carefully recorded collections of bones from representative habitation sites.

Can we be any more specific about where the animals were pastured? Most of the bottomlands are now reasonably well drained and protected from damaging winter floods. Irrigation is easy and they can be used for tree crops, alfalfa, garden crops, and other relatively high-return purposes. But we must surely imagine that the use of the lower parts of these valleys was different in the Late Bronze Age. It would have been extremely risky to expose cultivated trees or even fall-planted annual crops like grain to rampaging winter floods and their coarse sedimentary load. And it is doubtful if the fine alluvial soil could have dried out soon enough to be plowed and planted in the spring. Indeed, Loy's distribution map of modern sheep raising (1970, Fig. 10) shows a major concentration precisely in the Pamisos Valley, the largest area of wet bottomland in the whole region. Although perhaps unavailable for the smaller ruminants before modern drainage projects, such areas even in semi-flooded condition may have been accessible for larger animals. If this suggestion sounds rash, we have seen herds of cattle grazing on the reeds in the lagoons on the west coast with water up to their necks and with cowherds tending them in boats.

Yassoglou believes that in the Late Bronze Age the valleys were cultivated – probably in grain; and this was Roebuck's clear assumption for classical times. Yet Loy's distribution map for modern wheat production (1970, Fig. 8) shows the Pamisos Valley to be the lowest producer in the whole region. The present practice is to grow grain, and especially barley, on the drier and less fertile slopes. Yassoglou worries about erosion if this were an ancient practice, but many of the artificial terraces seem to be very old and they would have greatly lessened this danger. And Topping mentions that the valley inland from Methoni is known to have been a major source of fodder and pasturage during the Venetian period. The main problem is to determine how much of the valley floors was perennially wet. Grain could definitely not have been grown under such conditions, although it would have flourished on the better drained alluvium and done quite well on the valley slopes. On balance, we favor the view of Van Wersch and Loy that the bottomlands in Late Helladic times served mainly as lush pasture, accessible in all seasons except perhaps in the heart of the rainy period.

As for cultivated crops, the risks of attempting a reconstruction should not be underestimated. As yet we have practically no dependable information on the proportion of the Late Bronze Age population engaged in agriculture (though it was surely high), on the efficiency of their farming methods, or on the relation between food and other agricultural products grown and consumed in the particular villages, subregions, and the total region versus what was imported or exported. And yet this topic is at the very heart of the Mycenaean economy.

In Chapter 11 Van Wersch delimits seven categories of present land use (Pocket Map 11-20), plus Loy's five geomorphic classes of land in the region (1970). Van Wersch assumes that natural conditions are the major determinants at all periods and that the environment (climate, hydrology, etc.) is relatively unchanged since the Late Bronze Age. These assumptions are strongly supported by the lack of evidence for major changes in crop type. He therefore concludes that one can reconstruct with some assurance the broad patterns of land use in our target period. Then, using what information is available about the diet and agricultural products of Late Bronze times, he estimates the relative importance of the crops grown in Messenia and their place in the land-use pattern (Pocket Map 11-21).

Without going into detail here, it should be emphasized that a comparison between the location of the land-use categories and the distribution of Late Bronze Age settlements indicates that the inhabitants lived predominantly in areas where we can expect the major crops to have been grain (wheat and barley), trees (especially olives), and vines. Van Wersch notes how often the villages are set on the approximate border between his category II (lowland mainly planted to trees and vines and often irrigated) and category III (upland where dry crops, i.e., grains, predominated). In addition, the "canonical" village would have pasture in the lower, poorly drained areas (his category V) and dry field crops, especially barley, in the higher areas with relatively poor soil (his category IV). It may be questioned, in view of our argument that land pressure was not severe, whether much of the category IV land actually needed to be cultivated in the average settlement location. His estimate of the percentage of available land in the above categories is: category III, 35 percent; category II, 12 percent; category IV, 8 percent; category V, 6 percent.

Van Wersch's reconstruction of the "normalized" agricultural landscape can be usefully compared with the intensive study by Yassoglou of the probable situation in one Late Bronze Age community, Nichoria (#100). Yassoglou's 500 borings form a picture of this sort (Pocket Map 10-19): poorly drained bottomland toward the sea in pasture for large animals; upper valley bottomland cultivated in grain; gentle slopes of marine sandy silt around the valley mostly in forest, with perhaps some grazing by small animals; limestone surfaces to the northwest and calcareous clay loam to the southeast of settlement cultivated for trees and vines. Although, as already mentioned, Yassoglou believes that grain was grown in the better-drained bottomland, he does not rule out the higher slopes, especially for barley.

Van Wersch suggests that two of the major modern crops, olives and vines, may have played a considerably less important role in the agricultural economy of the Late Bronze Age. There can be little doubt that he is right in the case of viticulture. As we have noticed, about 20 percent of the cultivated area of the typical farm is today planted in vines, and dried currants are one of the major exports. In an economy where grapes are used only for table use and wine, it is extremely unlikely that anything approaching this percentage of land would be in vines, even if wine was exported in considerable quantity (and we have as yet no solid evidence that it was).

Olives present a more difficult problem; but again it is extremely unlikely that 33 percent of the cultivated land was devoted to them, as in the modern economy. There was a large oil-storage area in the palace at Epano Englianos (as well as a separate building for wine), and the Linear B tablets suggest that there was a palace industry concentrating on the production of fine-quality scented oils. Although the bulk of this commodity may well have been exported, no huge quantities of oil would have been required. Unfortunately, little is known as yet about the scale of production and consumption of olives and oil in Mycenaean times. We need far more evidence about production from such sources as pollen analysis and about dietary habits from careful excavation of habitation sites. If the main use of the common false-necked amphora was for oil in transit, one gets the impression that volume was considerable.

Wright's evidence from the pollen (Ch. 12) and his tentative inferences are intriguing, but the questions he raises must remain unanswered for the present. It may be true that around Osmanaga Lagoon and also around

Lake Voulkaria in the north olive production was much higher in the Early Iron Age than at the peak of Mycenaean prosperity. But this situation might reflect purely local phenomena rather than a major shift in the agricultural regime of our region and beyond. To adduce Homer's failure to mention olives or olive oil as a food is only to compound the problem. The omission could be fortuitous, or the minor role of oil in the diet could reflect conditions in either the Late Bronze or Early Iron Age. In the olive context, too, Aschenbrenner's evidence about the biennially alternating rhythm of modern production has interesting implications for storage, market speculation, and distribution.

As to grain production, Van Wersch's high and low estimates (Ch. 11) for the yield from potentially available land indicate that the region could have supported 170,000 to 300,000 inhabitants, allowing 235 kg per capita per year. He does not, of course, make any claim that this potentiality was fully exploited, but he suggests that grain, especially wheat, could have been the major item in agricultural surplus to balance imports. In addition, we have Roebuck's calculation (1945), based on some rather uncertain epigraphical evidence from Hellenistic times, that all-out grain production in eastern Messenia (including poorly drained bottomlands) might have supported about 112,000 inhabitants. One more hint is relevant, i.e., reference (Ch. 6) to average production of 164 *medimni* (246 bu) of barley by Messenian serfs working 9,000 (or possibly 12,000) "lots" for their Spartan masters. Reckoning only the half of this production which the serfs retained and using Van Wersch's calculation for individual intake, this amount of grain would have fed 110,000 to 150,000 persons. Although such totals are probably exaggerated (see later discussion), it appears likely that barley and wheat, in varying proportions in different epochs, played a considerably larger role in the farming regime at certain times in the past than they now do. The potential of surplus grain production was clearly a major factor in the economy of ancient Messenia.

Two crops known to have been important in the Late Bronze Age economy require special mention, although our research on their cultivation is still incomplete. The Linear B tablets show that figs, presumably dried, were then a far more basic item of local diet (most are now exported) and that the weaving of linen cloth from flax was an important industry, presumably with an export potential. Both figs and flax have at present a special status in Messenia and there is some reason to think that quite restricted areas within the region are specially adapted by nature for their successful cultivation. This is in contradistinction to the staple crops mentioned above, which will grow reasonably well almost anywhere within the Mediterranean range of soil, climate, elevation, and water supply.

Kalamata is now a major center for the processing, packaging, and export of figs, and figs are an important cash crop for some farmers. The commercial groves are concentrated parallel to the coast in an arc from Kalamata to Petalidhi. Aschenbrenner (Ch. 4) has an account of their cultivation, and he reports that they have not done well when tried in villages just a few kilometers inland from Karpofora. We need to learn more of their tolerances, especially to poorer soil and higher elevations. It would appear that fig culture was either considerably more diffused throughout the region in Mycenaean times, or that the favored area(s) must have been devoted to a notable degree to this one crop. If the latter supposition were to prove true, it would be the first dependable indication that the region had an important *internal* exchange of special products.

The case of flax is equally intriguing, and we are equally uninformed as yet on details. To the casual eye, it is certainly not now a major crop; yet Messenia is by far the biggest producer in Greece (55 percent of the total acreage in 1961). Loy's map of modern flax distribution (1970, Fig. 9) shows a sparse but fairly even pattern. Slight concentrations occur in the Soulima Valley, in the Finikous-Lachanadha Valley, and south of Mt. Likodhimo. There is notably little flax in Triphylia, the Pamisos Valley, the foothills of Taygetos, and on the eastern side of the gulf. Modern distribution may therefore have a definite connection with the situation reflected in the Linear B tablets, where it appears that flax production was concentrated in the "hither" (western) part of the kingdom. It is possible, indeed, that western Messenia produced six times as much flax as the "further" (eastern) province. *Ro-o-wa* was one of the centers and we are inclined to identify it as the main port below the palace. Heavy flax production in the lowlands around Navarino Bay would seem to make sense in terms both of natural advantages and of the linen industry centered at the palace. This could be at least a partial explanation, too, for the apparent scarcity of olive orchards here at the Mycenaean levels of Wright's pollen cores.

The information in the tablets leaves open the possibility that heavy concentration on flax may be a hallmark of Late Bronze Age Messenia. If so, has there been a continuous tradition until the present? As with figs, there may be special requirements that Messenia (or areas within it) meet particularly well. Like tobacco, flax has the reputation of being hard on soil, requiring special natural fertility or artificial fertilization. It will not do well on poorly drained heavy clays or highly calcareous soils. Abundant moisture and cool weather are also factors in good yields. But perhaps even more important is the necessity for a plentiful supply of running water when the "retting" or soaking process is carried out after harvest in midsummer. Even in Messenia, a particularly fortunate part of Greece in terms of big springs and some perennial rivers, this requirement would drastically narrow the range of communities that qualify as flax producers – or at least as flax processers. Of course, the processing could theoretically have been done at quite different centers from where the flax was grown.

Climate and Water Supply

We can be brief in reviewing the available evidence on climate and water supply. Loy and Wright (Ch. 3) make a strong and convincing case for the essential verdict of "no change." This does not mean, of course, that there have been no minor alternations of dry and wet, hot and cold years, or somewhat longer periods. The Mediterranean climate, though apparently remarkably stable over the past four thousand years, is never totally static. We have seen, just over the last generation, years in which one crop or another was almost a total failure because of a slightly prolonged drought or unseasonal rains. Farmers here, as everywhere, are aware of their vulnerability to the weather, and their age-old religious practices and beliefs bear witness to the fact.

This negative evidence shows that we should be wary of any sweeping theories, like Carpenter's (1966) and Bell's (1971), that temporary climatic shifts may have produced disasters of sufficient magnitude to depopulate the whole region. It is difficult indeed to see in the Pylos tablets any justification for the claim that a fearful drought occurred about that time. Instead, the evidence seems to indicate that we can postulate with fair confidence the essential continuity of conditions like soil, climate, and water supply that are the basic determinants in agricultural regimes. There have certainly been changes since the Late Bronze Age in kinds and proportions of crops, in breeds of animals, in agricultural practices and equipment, in pestilences, and in dietary preference; but we can be reasonably sure that none of them was caused by cataclysmic changes in the natural environment. Perhaps the most serious threat of this kind is damaging earthquakes (Galanopoulos 1964), but here, too, our region seems to have been comparatively favored.

It is a natural transition to turn from hydrology to irrigation. Loy and Wright (Ch. 3) feel that there is no physical reason that the farmers of Late Bronze times could not have irrigated valleys and lower slopes with essentially the same simple but effective methods now in use. Topping documents the use of irrigation in Crete and Euboea as far back as the fifteenth century B.C. We know of no positive archaeological evidence that irrigation was in fact practiced in Messenia during the Late Bronze Age, but in Chapter 8 the authors point to the heavy concentration of prehistoric population in areas such as the Soulima Valley where irrigation agriculture is surely the main reason for intensive modern population (see category N in Register A for information on land now irrigated). The Late Bronze Age farmers may very well have used irrigation as intensively as the modern – that is, for about 10 percent of total land cultivated. The idea would seem to be natural enough in areas where water is plentiful, and the Pliocene silts when simply furrowed with a hoe act as efficient channels. Hence, one would not expect any monumental constructions, as in parts of the Near East and Meso-America, that may leave identifiable traces centuries later. Even if the advantages of irrigation did not become spontaneously obvious to the Late Bronze cultivators, their constant contacts with the Near East would have acquainted them with the practice there.

Regarding water supply for general purposes, the data supplied in category K in Register A make it clear that most prehistoric sites were located close to adequate sources. We assume that the springs and rivers produced at least their present amounts. Actually, it is reasonable to believe that, if we are correct about the extent of forest cover, the flow would have been somewhat greater on the average; and (a much more crucial point) it would have been somewhat better distributed through the year, owing to less runoff and proportionately greater infiltration of the groundwater.

There are, however, Late Bronze habitation sites that now have no available springs (and presumably never did) and that would seem to have depended solely on water from rivers that are now dry for several summer months. If these sources failed regularly, we must assume that wells were dug somewhere near the village. The most likely place would have been in or near the stream bed itself, and there are modern parallels for this practice. In that case, we could scarcely expect any evidence to survive. In fact, there is little archaeological evidence in mainland Greece for Late Bronze Age wells. But again, this seems such an obvious idea that it is difficult to believe they did not dig shallow wells when and if the need arose.

There were and are, of course, habitation sites where water is not easy to get, even from wells. Aschenbrenner (Ch. 4) has vividly described a marginal water supply of this sort and the difficult adjustment that it necessitates. He has also referred to the networks of piped water systems, often operating by gravity only, that are now making life much easier and more pleasant for villagers in large areas where water was previously a scarce commodity in the long dry season. In this connection we note that the Epano Englianos palace was apparently supplied by a dug channel from a spring at a slightly higher elevation about a kilometer distant. Hence, the know-how for such projects did exist, and their use elsewhere cannot be totally ruled out. It would have been relatively easy, for example, to bring water by channel from water-rich higher sites like Vrises (#72) to Kyparissia (#70), which has no good local supply. Yet one doubts that ordinary villages shared with royalty such labor-consuming amenities.

It can be assumed that the trip to the nearest perennial river for washing clothes, which is as old as Homer's description of Odysseus' meeting with Nausicaa and as recent as Aschenbrenner's observation in 1969, was a regular feature of life in many villages. And it is an intriguing idea that the kind of seasonal transhumance that Aschenbrenner reports from a poorly watered village on high ground to a nearby river valley may have been an annual occurrence in the summer. More attention needs to be directed toward this possibility in future surface search and in excavation.

Metallurgy

It is no great surprise that Cooke, Henrickson, and Rapp conclude (Ch. 14) that Messenia has never had local resources in the metals that were so vital for use and prestige to the people of the Late Bronze Age. They have also field-checked various spots in other parts of the Greek peninsula and islands where reports have circulated in archaeological publications that metals, particularly copper, might have been mined in prehistoric times. Almost without exception their preliminary judgment has been negative. To pinpoint the sources of Bronze Age copper and tin, they have collected samples of ores, slags, and artifacts and have embarked on a program of trace-element analysis.

The UMME copper-tin project is a large one, and the major part of the job lies in the future. But it is good to have some rumors already laid to rest and to know that a concerted effort with the latest analytical techniques holds considerable promise for identifying the sources with whom the Late Bronze Age people in Messenia and elsewhere in Greece traded to obtain copper and tin. In addition, their related research on ancient bronzes and slags should reveal new evidence about ancient bronze technology.

Meanwhile, there are implications one can already mention. We can be sure that there was no occupation labeled "miner" in our region and no skewing of the settlement pattern owing to mining activity. Lack of smelting means less consumption of fuel, but we should not lose sight of the 400 bronzesmiths who must have been melting imported ingots for the manufacture of weapons and implements. Adequate fuel supply may have been a factor in their scattered location. Their numbers seem excessive in relation to the total estimated population and this leaves open the possibility that a surplus of processed metal goods was produced. If so, they would have helped pay for the labor of digging and smelting the ores elsewhere.

We may also ponder why Messenia was engaged in this kind of activity on what seems to have been a fairly large scale. Perhaps a relatively good supply of fuel was one reason, but the existence of a large Pylian "merchant marine" and the location of the source of supplies may provide a more basic clue. If at least some of the shipping depots for copper and tin ingots were in the west Mediterranean and/or at the head of the Adriatic Sea, the use of Pylian ships in their transport and of Pylian smiths for the manufacture of finished goods would become understandable.

Ceramics

Matson's research (Ch. 13) has contributed to a better understanding of various aspects of this crucial craft, and some of his evidence applies well beyond the boundaries of our region. It appears that, unlike metallurgy, pottery making was carried on by local village craftsmen, using mainly local materials and producing for local markets. The present situation, where manufacture is concentrated in the villages immediately north of Koroni, seems quite different. Yet there may have been parallels in the Late Bronze Age. Clays are not equally good everywhere, and easy access to transportation routes would be important if wider markets were sought. The impressive concentration of unused pottery stored in certain rooms of the Epano Englianos palace could be interpreted as a surplus meant for a wider market, either within or outside of the kingdom. And there were certainly imported wares in use in ordinary villages as well as in the larger centers. Matson has recognized sherds from our surface collections that appear to be of island clay, a situation that is paralleled by the modern sale in our region of highly heat-resistant casseroles from the island of Siphnos. We might also note the appearance in the Nichoria excavation of pottery that seems to be from Crete, the Cyclades, and northeast Peloponnese. Minoan imports are particularly noticeable along the west coast and in the Alpheios district (e.g., #'s 313, 316). Spectrographic analysis can now certify broad attributions, and the kind of detailed analytical research Matson reports will perhaps make possible distinctions even among local clays.

Trade

It will require a great deal of excavation with this kind of evidence in mind before we are in a position to make dependable statements about intra-regional and external trade in southwest Peloponnese. There is no purpose in repeating here statements about Mycenaean trade in general (McDonald 1967). The basic local fact that we must face is that Messenia could not have been economically self-sufficient. Very considerable quantities of metal, especially copper, tin, and later iron, had to be procured from outside and paid for directly or indirectly in goods or services. In addition, we can identify imports such as pottery (for contents or intrinsic desirability), amber, obsidian, ivory, and other luxury goods in raw or manufactured form. There is no evidence that the region needed to import any basic foodstuffs.

We can already form some theories about the major agricultural and manufactured surpluses. Van Wersch believes that grain could have been the leading export (Ch. 11). Olive oil, most of it perhaps scented, is another possibility, although Wright's evidence (Ch. 12) may throw some doubt on the volume of this commodity. Another possibility is timber, although its transportation from the interior would have posed problems. Other possible agricultural surpluses that deserve attention are wine, dried figs, honey, linseed oil (from flax), horses, and cattle.

As for manufactured items, one might infer from the Pylos tablets that there may have been an exportable surplus of woolen and linen cloth and of bronze implements and weapons; also, pottery for its own sake, not simply as a container, cannot be excluded. The situation in regard to possible slave trade is unclear. The major services that might have been supplied by our region would certainly include shipping by the large merchant marine and perhaps know-how such as metallurgy.

Settlement Distribution

From its inception, our archaeological fieldwork in Messenia was focused on locating as many as possible of the actual sites which the inhabitants chose for their villages and towns. The settlements belonging to the Late Bronze Age have been of particular concern because of their special connection with the Epano Englianos palace and the wide-ranging royal bureaucracy that the Pylos tablets prove was centered there. But we have also sought to identify the habitation pattern at all periods of antiquity before and after the target phase. We soon realized that we needed to enlist colleagues from other disciplines to assist in the search, and especially to help us understand the emerging pattern over time and space. This whole book describes the stage we have reached in that joint enterprise.

Chapter 1 describes the organization of the project. Part I of Chapter 8 reports what was already known and what we and others discovered about the location, duration, and function of ancient settlements. Registers A and B (Appendix, pp. 264–321) represent a concise statement of the cultural and environmental data that we have collected for each site. Part III of Chapter 8 draws inferences from the Registers (and other chapters as well) about the characteristics of each successive phase, as well as indications of stability and discontinuity over time. We shall not repeat these conclusions here, even in summary. Readers will find them easier to follow by using the distribution maps (Pocket Maps 8-11 to 8-18) as overlays to compare with one another, with the pattern of medieval and modern settlement distribution (Pocket Maps 1-1, 5-8, 5-9), and with the base maps of geomorphology, soils, hydrology, land use, and communications.

Comparison of the maps should also provide a useful test of the validity of our interpretations. We are fully aware of the tentative nature of some of them. In particular, there are no doubt gaps in the discovered sites themselves, perhaps serious enough in some cases to skew the inferred pattern. We realize also that settlements already located may assume disproportionate importance in relation to the original situation, and this principle applies with at least equal validity to excavated versus unexcavated sites. But we feel fairly confident that, at least in the target period, the known sites are so numerous that, even if a fairly large number of additional discoveries are eventually made, the *pattern* of distribution will not be seriously affected.

If the decade of our involvement in this region had accomplished nothing else, it would have proved its worth in underlining the potential value of systematic, large-scale site distribution studies to field archaeology in Greece. The results have underlined the relative abundance of evidence still available and constitute, in the words of one highly respected scholar (Finley 1970, p. 20), a "sobering experience" to counter the "illusion of grandeur" that can be generated by concentration on a few important sites (most of them royal capitals) that may seem to reveal as much of the story as is worth the effort to recover.

The work that is reported, particularly in Chapter 8, has also been a sobering experience for the proponents. We have emphasized repeatedly that our results should not be taken as complete and authoritative. Much can still be done in surface search, and even more in the digestion, discussion, and interpretation of the data.

Population

We come finally to a central problem closely connected with the size and distribution of sites, the size of the population in prehistoric Messenia. Cautious colleagues have advised us that it would be wiser at present to avoid specific numbers, even the most general estimates. But it may be years before we or others have much more relevant information about this or other regions of the Greek peninsula in prehistoric times, and it seems to us that in the meantime we have an obligation to make available to interested scholars the present state of our thinking. After all, the basis for estimates on population in classical Greece (or parts of it) rests on quite different yet generally "soft" data; yet who would wish that Beloch, Gomme, and others had avoided such a controversial area of scholarship? Population data form an essential basis for any attempt at reconstructing ancient economic history, and the recovery of evidence bearing on economic history is a central aim of prehistoric archaeologists. To quote Grahame Clark (1957, p. 244), "The question of the density of population at different periods has been stressed because of its immense importance as a measure of economic progress, and although the difficulties in the way of reaching even approximately accurate answers are formidable it is certain that we cannot afford to let slip any opportunity of gaining information on this point."

Readers should assess what follows in the light of explanatory remarks made in Part II of Chapter 8 on the background of categories H and O in Register A and discussion in Part III of each of the major periods. Every component used in arriving at the estimate of total population is less than firm, and most of them will probably remain uncertain no matter how they are refined in future research. The calculations rest basically on the sizes of known sites. At present we must depend on a somewhat arbitrary estimate of the area that is scattered with broken pottery, although sometimes soil color (indicating prolonged and intensive human disturbance) and the outside physical limits (such as a hilltop) provide further information. It is also our experience at Nichoria (#100) and at a few other places where we had the opportunity to test out the magnetometer, that this or other electronic and physical devices could be of significant help in establishing the limits of habitation sites (see Ch. 15). Of course, the most useful check on estimates from surface indications would be a wide-ranging program of limited excavation.

The second major input is the estimated relationship of site area to site population. As tests and extensive excavation of prehistoric sites in Messenia develop together, a reasonably firm basis should emerge for *local* predictions. At present, however, there is practically no dependable evidence from Messenian excavations. Unfortunately, in the case of the one site that has been fully dug to date, the fortified hilltop village of Malthi, stratigraphic uncertainty detracts from its usefulness in this record. We are unaware of any usable general or individual estimates for over-all village size and population anywhere in prehistoric Greece, so we are treading virgin ground.

Estimates of varying precision do exist, of course, for ancient populations in other parts of the world, notably the Near East and Meso-America. The methods used are relevant to our task, but the particular equations of estimated population versus village area naturally reflect quite diverse situations (available land, water, climatic conditions, agricultural regime, nonagricultural economic bases, architectural and familial traditions, etc.). For instance, the equation of 200 persons per hectare used by Adams for the Diyala Basin (see the description of the project in Ch. 1) would be inappropriate in our situation. Almost equally inappropriate to adopt uncritically would be estimates such as J. C. Russell's (1958) averaged 100–150 persons per hectare in his monumental synthesis concerning late ancient and medieval population within the whole range of the Roman Empire.

For our work in ancient Messenia we can make a start by using statistics from *modern* villages in the same area and by checking these figures against what little is known at present about the use of space within areas of excavated prehistoric villages. The calculation (Table 8-1) for 11 villages is admittedly the barest beginning. The results show an *average* of 112 persons per hectare. The task is a tricky one, however, even for the existing situation. We know from experience that published statistics can be unreliable, particularly in terms of the specific village areas. We have used aerial photographs for calculating area, and where scattered cloud or vegetation cover does not obscure the whole extent, this is certainly the most accurate approach presently available. But serious problems remain, such as calculating the exact scale on aerial photographs and the inclusion of houses that are unoccupied but still standing. Even for the modern analogue the only satisfactory solution is a large-scale field project. It should be possible in the near future to make more accurate estimates, but in the meantime we must assume that this tentative equation is reasonably dependable.

A more difficult calculation is the relationship of the modern usage to that of the past. It would be preferable to make judgments using village conditions in 1800 or even more recently, before the modernization of this part of Greece had begun. One can see today great differences between bustling towns on a highway or railroad and isolated mountain villages; but even the latter have been affected by modern trends. Perhaps an archaeological and document-related program aimed at checking this kind of development over time might provide some dependable data.

For the equation here used we have increased the modern equation of 112 persons per hectare to 130 per hectare of village area for prehistoric times, and even this figure should probably be considered minimal. The rationale rests on a strong impression that prehistoric villages in Messenia and generally throughout Greece were somewhat more densely populated than nowdays. The published plans of partially excavated sites can probably be said to bear out this judgment. But archaeologists in Greece have not usually assigned high priority to such tricky questions as how many families of what size occupied even the fractions of villages that they cleared. And there is as yet no hint that anyone has distinguished trends in such matters within periods or even contrasts between the major divisions of the Bronze Age. The concept of "settlement archaeology" has not yet gained recognition in Greek prehistoric archaeology.

When we apply our formula of 130 persons per hectare to the known Messenian sites from different periods, we face further problems of calculating area (method discussed above) and of estimating what percentage of the villages existing in a given period have been discovered so far. Also, many sites undoubtedly were not *continuously* occupied for the total duration of the period(s) assigned to them. Again, simply to make the first assault on the problem, we offer what we hope are informed conjectures. But even when additional sites are found and firmer calculations become possible about the length of occupation, the whole story can never be known.

It remains to enumerate briefly our estimates and to compare them with the sparse documentary evidence (equally imprecise, in general) for Late Bronze, classical, medieval, and early modern times. For Early Bronze, it might have been wiser to state simply that the regional population was undoubtedly much smaller than in later prehistoric times. Certainly, it is in the EH era that the proportion of unlocated to presently known sites is likely to change most radically. The suggested range of 3,000–4,000 inhabitants as a minimum over-all estimate could prove to be low. There can be no doubt, however, that the regional population total increased considerably in the Middle Bronze period. Present indications are that the number of sites approximately tripled and that the size also increased. The evidence is therefore definitely firmer for placing the MH population in the range of 10,000 inhabitants.

The number and size of villages again increased substantially in the Late Bronze Age, but at present we are not sure whether the change was gradual or primarily a phenomenon of the fourteenth and especially the thirteenth centuries. We estimate that, by the latter century, the number of villages had approximately tripled and the average size doubled since MH times. We estimate the number of villages at 250 *minimum*, and the *minimum over-all population* at 50,000.

Chadwick (Ch. 7) has also estimated total population for the kingdom centered at Epano Englianos at the end of the thirteenth century, and he is equally unsure of the margin of error in his figures. By a complex calculation concerning the labor force and tax exemptions in the Linear B tablets, he envisages something like 100 towns of "reasonable size" (i.e. between 800 and 1,200), yielding a total population of 80,000 to 120,000. The little villages, whose existence Chadwick also mentions, would add several thousand to the mean of 100,000.

The estimates in Chapters 7 and 8 might seem far enough apart to throw doubt on both. And yet reflection on the two minimums – 50,000 and 80,000, respectively – would suggest that they are not necessarily so contradictory. At worst, they could be defended by the argument that there is no other region in the Aegean orbit where estimates of prehistoric population could be made with anything approaching this kind of "accuracy."

Chadwick's calculation that there may have been up to 100 towns with populations in the range of 800 to 1,200 is not supported by our field observations. If any confidence is to be placed in estimates of inhabited area, Register A will show that relatively few sites had more than 400–500 inhabitants. Even in the case of the acropolis of Nichoria (#100), which Chadwick believes may be the capital of the "Further Province," our present opinion is that it could not have accommodated more than about 600–800 inhabitants; and it was a very large town by local standards. If Chadwick's figures are substantially correct, more of the "place-names" in the tablets may have to be viewed as names of subdistricts or economic nuclei, somewhat in Lukermann's terms (Ch. 9); and our estimate of the proportion of known settlements to the original total would need rather drastic revision.

Hope Simpson (Ch. 6) and Van Wersch (Ch. 11) have already expressed skepticism about Roebuck's estimate of a population in the range of 112,000 for the federal state of Messene *only* in late classical times. There is no doubt about the *potential* of the region to support a large population with an agricultural regime based on cereals. We simply reiterate that the archaeological evidence strongly suggests that the ancient inhabitants never came close to exploiting the full potential. And what is known about the inhibiting factors on population growth in medieval and early modern times seems to us generally applicable to earlier periods. We shall not press the argument further, but we call attention to the tendency of classical authors and many who use their work to accept and propound inflated population estimates. This credulity may stem from idealizing the greatness and glory of the classical past, illustrated perhaps by the uncritical use of the English word *city* (Greek *polis*) to refer to places that were in some cases not much more than hamlets. A recent study suggests that the population of the capitals (i.e., the largest centers) of classical city-states, excluding Athens, ranged in size from about 20,000 down to about 200, with almost half of them having 750 or less (Pounds 1969). Roebuck's is a courageous attempt to get at the kind of historical evidence most needed to probe new aspects of the classical world, but it fails to make use of what is known about more recent population statistics and about modern land use (e.g., recently improved land) in the same area.

It is an instructive experience to turn to Topping's review (Ch. 5) of what can be reconstructed about the population of this region between Roman and modern times. Figures are fragmentary until the sixteenth century, but there is no reason to think that totals ever exceeded those mentioned below. In the census made early in the reign of Suleiman the Magnificent (1520–66), when economic conditions seem to have been reasonably good, the whole Peloponnese had 50,941 "hearths" (families), something in the range of 200,000–250,000 souls. Assigning about one-fifth to Messenia, it would have had a total of about 45,000 inhabitants, somewhat below our estimated minimum for the Late Bronze Age peak. In another census of about 1702, southwest Peloponnese had, according to Topping's reckoning, 44,737 inhabitants. In 1715 it was approaching 60,000. Even in 1820, on the eve of the revolution, the estimated population for the whole Peloponnese is 440,000, giving our region barely 90,000 inhabitants; the French census in 1829 reveals a drop to less than 60,000. In 1851 the official figure for our whole region is slightly under 100,000, and by 1861 it had risen to about 120,000. At that time Messenia had the highest density of rural population (except for the islands) in the whole kingdom of Greece.

In the above perspective, our estimate for Late Bronze Age Messenia emerges as a not unreasonable beginning in the process of reconstructing one of the vital factors in the early economic history of the region. The peak population of about 250,000 in the twentieth century approaches maximum pressure on the productive land, as calculated by Van Wersch. This level was attained only in the context of greatly expanded foreign trade and relative freedom from the epidemics, piratical raids, ruthless exploitation by outside powers, and the direct or indirect effects of war that characterize so much of Topping's narrative. Although there is reason to believe that conditions were somewhat better in Mycenaean and late classical times, neither general considerations nor the present archaeological record can support inflated estimates of 100,000 and more inhabitants.

UNFINISHED BUSINESS

We turn, finally, from a summary of the present status of our research to look ahead at the directions in which the momentum already generated should take us during the next decade. The regional investigations reported above have placed the specific site chosen for excavation, Nichoria (#100), in a broadly defined physical, cultural, and chronological setting. The excavation, in turn, provides the opportunity to work out for this particular settlement and its immediate environs a minutely detailed reconstruction of as much of the physical and man-made environment as is possible.

The evolving regional reconstruction described in this book reflects the varied interests and competencies of individual UMME members. Some aspects of the model, such as those concerned with settlement patterns, communication networks, land use, and agricultural products, are sufficiently developed and documented to be reasonably secure in outline if not in all desirable detail. On the other hand, further information on the internal organization and hierarchy of settlements as well as a better understanding of most cultural aspects must await intensive excavation of selected habitation sites such as Nichoria.

What sort of historical-anthropological-archaeological model do we want to construct for Nichoria? Our specific aims and mode of operation are summarized in Figure 1-1. However, a complete history of occupation, with a description and analysis of the changing nature of the site and its inhabitants in all periods of use, would require total excavation of most of the six hectares on the ridgetop; and, unfortunately, few expeditions have the time and resources necessary for an undertaking of that magnitude. The approach has to be more selective.

In the first place, we are carrying out extensive areal investigation and mapping to ascertain in detail the nature and extent of the local area controlled by this prehistoric town. A significant share of our effort is concentrated on the recovery and study of remains of agricultural, mineral, and small-animal products. Associated investigations of building materials and construction techniques, provenience studies of pottery and metals, nature of craft industries, character of special facilities (e.g., for storage), topography, and so forth should provide additional input for the model.

Artifacts are the durable remains of man's technology. They reveal the need for weapons, interest in ornaments, use of tools and pottery, and style in houses and tombs. Most reconstructions are biased by this heavy input of data about manufactured items. By concentrating a greater percentage of attention on the physical, geographical, climatological, agricultural, and botanical setting, we hope to make the total environment, rather than the technology, the central theme in our reconstruction of the various phases of habitation on this site.

Excavation provides dangers as well as opportunities. Any model of the prehistoric past is based on the accumulated evidence of limited investigations. And history inferred from the results of archaeological excavations is inevitably biased by the "chance" importance given to certain sites (or parts of sites) simply because they were dug. *An extensive, well-published excavation of a site may endow the site with an importance well out of proportion to its ancient role.*

Possibly the time will come when *regional* excavation programs can be undertaken in coordination with exploration. Test sites would be selected to provide a maximum of the demographic, architectural, land-use, metallurgical, and ceramic information that is needed to develop detailed and dependable regional models. For example, one might test a limited number of suspected one-phase sites in a study of the dispersion and the diffusion rates of certain pottery styles. This type of evidence is badly needed, especially in more peripheral or "provincial" areas, to refine the pottery-based time lines that are so important in archaeology. A stratigraphic unit in archaeology, as distinct from a stratigraphic unit in geology, is a body of lithologic and artifact material deposited during a specific time interval. It is a time unit whose upper and lower contacts are time parallel, whereas a stratigraphic unit in geology does not have to be time parallel. A "time period" in archaeology defined by a pottery chronology adopted from one or more sites and used at others is not time parallel but transgressive; the departure from parallel depends primarily on diffusion rates (historical lag) but also is affected by taxonomic decisions.

The need for absolute dates and parallel time lines remains a problem for prehistoric archaeology. Intensive microscopic study of cores and vertical sections from excavation sites and nearby undisturbed areas such as lagoons might uncover the micro-volcanic ash beds that must have formed from the eruptions of Santorini. Such marker beds would provide time-parallel lines to anchor studies of diffusion rate.

Even without digging there are possibilities for acquiring more information for our regional model. The successful use of geophysical and remote-sensing methods in archaeological exploration and surveying suggests that these techniques might find wider application in prehistoric studies. A combination of geophysical methods could be used to delineate more accurately the size and shape of ancient habitation sites. Ideal physiographic and geologic conditions would allow recovery of geophysical data sufficient to indicate the outline of buildings, roadways, ditches, and similar man-made features.

We should perhaps insert here a word of caution about the use of maps to record information on site size and site distribution. Since history is an "incompletely observable box," the descriptions and analyses of what is seen (or measured) must be rendered in a way that adduces the unseen. The plotting on a map of sites located by field search presents hazards. The location of "unfound" or destroyed (completely eroded) sites can be predicated in part, as shown in Chapter 9. However, users should be wary of some kinds of pattern analysis and correlation from the map data because we cannot specify *on the map* our inferences and evaluation concerning the unseen.

We may now describe in somewhat greater detail a few of the lines of research that may place the Nichoria site in clearer relation to its local situation and to the larger regional setting. One such project is a search for harbor facilities. The recent work of Yassoglou (Ch. 10) in the area where the Karia River reaches the sea suggests that this location might have provided a small sheltered harbor for Bronze Age Nichoria. From geological considerations it is reasonable to assume that the dashed lines of Pocket Map 10-19 represent the inner edge of a lagoon rather than the "coastline." If the coastline had such a shape, then longshore winds would have closed off the area to form a lagoon. An adequate sand supply is now available at this location and the direction of longshore drift noted during recent summer months is east northeast.

Wright and Loy (Ch. 3) have noted that sea level had stabilized enough by 2000 B.C. for a sandbar to form Osmanaga Lagoon at the north end of Navarino Bay. The barrier beach formed across the small bay at the mouth of the Karia may have completely enclosed the lagoonal area, but it is more likely that a narrow channel remained open (see Fig. 16-1). The lagoon might then have served

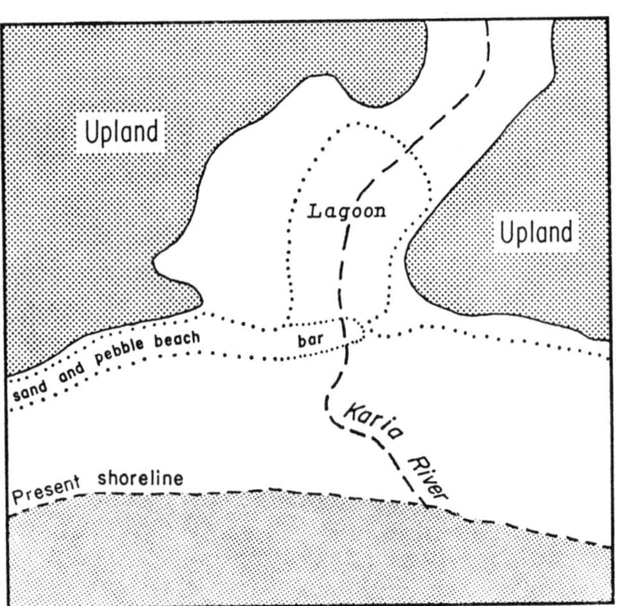

Figure 16-1. Lagoon. The dotted lines indicate a reasonable shoreline configuration for the Karia drainage during the Late Bronze Age. The proposed lagoon would have provided a safe harbor for small ships. (See shoreline on Pocket Map 10-19.)

as a protected harbor at some period in history (or prehistory) before it silted up with mud. Geophysical exploration might reveal remains of Bronze Age docking facilities. More extensive soil borings might also provide evidence for a reconstruction of the Holocene events attendant on the filling in of the lagoon, although Wright's work indicates that little vertical differentiation can be established in the muds that filled in the lagoons at the mouths of other Messenian rivers.

With the information uncovered at Nichoria as a base for comparison, a dozen or so representative sites should be studied in more detail by surface methods to record their complete physical setting – distance to water supply, extent of water resources, topographic setting, settlement plan (by geophysical methods), relation to road network, modern habitation, and land use (see Loy 1970, Pt. III). A detailed study of the nature of the sites chosen by the ancient inhabitants for their villages is feasible when the results of both a systematic regional survey (of the type reported in Ch. 8) and an extensive excavation are available as a framework. Categories D, E, I, J, K, and P of Register A provide the basis for much further research.

On the excavation site itself and its environs, maps will be prepared to record (1) the present distribution of plant species, (2) additional detail on soils (supplementing that recorded in Fig. 10-2 and Pocket Map 10-19), (3) the topographic profile of the Nichoria ridge throughout its habitation, and (4) maps of the limestone outcrop used for building construction and of the clays used for ceramics.

Intensive use should be made of photogrammetry to record the locational and structural parameters of materials removed by excavation or likely to disintegrate in time. Written descriptions, sketches, and measurements made by excavators should be only a supplement to basic recording by precise photogrammetric and surveying methods that will allow future researchers to reconstruct the complete geometry of the finds or recover additional information not apparent or not of immediate interest to the excavator. Flemming (1969), in his excellent work on archaeological evidence for eustatic change of sea level in the western Mediterranean, makes a telling point in regard to the use of "archaeological" labeling or identification of structures (with limited supporting measurement or description) rather than photographs or accurate maps compiled from careful engineering surveys. For later scholars, a recorded opinion that a number of limestone blocks represents the remains of a mole, or a warehouse wall, or a dock facility, is of scant (or misleading) value compared with accurate plans or photographs.

A strength-of-materials study of modern mud brick from the Nichoria area should help to determine structural properties that would in turn indicate its limits as a building material, that is, its load-bearing capacity. This could provide a basis for suggesting whether or not, for example, Bronze Age builders were able to construct three-story buildings with timbers supporting the upper floors and roof but not the upper walls. A companion physical analysis, particularly the quantitative distribution of grain sizes in the mud brick, might provide more dependable criteria for distinguishing ancient mud brick from the surrounding soil.

Much has been made in archaeological literature of the possible destruction of palaces and other buildings by natural disasters, particularly earthquakes. We know that the Peloponnese is rocked by a *major* earthquake as often as every fifty years (Galanopoulos 1964). In 1947, for example, approximately 350 buildings were destroyed in the eparchy of Pylia by a strong quake, and in 1899 the town of Kyparissia lost 250 buildings. Possibly one cause for the temporary or permanent abandonment of a site was severe or total destruction of buildings during an earthquake. Careful analysis of the relationships among structures, comparative chronology, building materials, and the condition and scatter of the rubble might reveal positive evidence for such destruction.

A thorough mapping of alignments and grades of all roadways and especially trails that were in use before the modern road-building effort (i.e., before 1930) should clarify not only the pattern of local circulation and communication but also the relationships of this community to its neighbors. When this pattern is coordinated with the mapping of all surviving surface evidence for ancient occupation and use of the land surrounding the Nichoria hilltop, a much clearer picture should emerge of local shifts of population both during and following the Bronze Age. It may then be possible to gain a better understanding of river crossings, points of contact with the coast, seasonal transhumance, shifting preferences for "high" versus "low" sites for permanent occupation, and so on.

The raw materials from every excavation provide the basis for innumerable special studies. Every piece of slag, fragment of a metal artifact, stone implement, sherd, bit of plaster contains in its chemistry and structure a number of clues to its origin and manufacture. But such materials must be intelligently selected and documented by the excavator before they receive the attention of the specialist. Seeds, teeth of small animals, shells, volcanic ash, and other fine-grained materials are of potential importance to a complete reconstruction of an ancient environment.

The use of statistics in archaeology to define clusters, populations, or types is just beginning. David Clarke (1968) has described numerous statistical methods of evaluating archaeological data. These data are by nature fragmentary. Better sampling techniques followed by statistical methods to determine degree of similarity (typology), degree of correlation, and other relationships are needed. Data storage, retrieval, and manipulation (statistical) where large numbers of items or parameters are involved are best handled by computers. To date the UMME effort has used computer storage and analysis primarily in the ancient metals project (Ch. 14) where a large data base is essential for correlation studies. However, efforts are now under way to extend computer technology to manage the mass of materials such as potsherds and building stone that are produced by a large-scale excavation.

New areas of interdisciplinary study are constantly evolving. As this chapter was being written, Drew et al. (1971) reported means of differentiating between domestic animals and their wild counterparts on the basis of structural differences in their bones. Their research, using techniques commonly employed in mineralogy, was based on bone material from two sites in Anatolia of the sixth and seventh millennia B.C. It can confidently be predicted that archaeological efforts in the future will be increasingly interdisciplinary in scope.

The stress on the man-in-his-environment theme throughout this book might suggest that we view such broadly based studies as a relatively recent phenomenon. It may be recalled, however, that in Chapter 1 we emphasized that its roots go back to the early nineteenth century and even further. So it is fitting that we close this chapter by quoting in translation a few paragraphs from a truly insightful field study of ancient man-in-his-environment published by Émile de Boblaye in 1833.

"Man's action – given his weakness and recent origin – has doubtless not been able to produce on the surface of the globe changes comparable in magnitude to those of the powerful and prolonged action of other natural agents. Nevertheless, being unceasingly directed toward a few constant ends, man's action is not without importance as a single physical agent. Moreover, if we consider its effects, however feeble they may be, as manifesting for the first time the action of intelligence and will in the geognostic products of the globe's surface, we shall judge them worthy of our entire attention. The era of thought is a new era, which begins with the appearance of man; its character is of a new order, more durable even than the character of preceding epochs. While all the creatures that have preceded him have left only their remains, man, through indestructible monuments, will transmit forever not only the proofs of his existence but even the elements of his history. The catastrophes which have overturned the globe have permitted the impressions of the most fragile leaves and insects to subsist. Our mountains, our seas, our continents can therefore once again change their shape without annihilating the remains and the imprint of the diverse human races, and the most delicate products of their industry.

"In Greece a numerous population, crowded on its shores and in its narrow valleys, has for more than thirty centuries been heaping up the debris of its generations and their works on the mainland, and above all in the seas surrounding it. At the same time this population, with the help of forces multiplied by industry and a constant direction, has been modifying the surface it inhabits.

"The loose surface layer, disturbed for so many centuries by cultivation, has become a veritable product of man. Everywhere where the soil is virgin there prevails in the parts composing it a certain order of succession. Cultivation ceaselessly destroys this order, making a homogeneous whole of the surface layers. Only by this characteristic can one distinguish the soil worked by the plow from the virgin soil of some of our forests. In Greece the debris from pottery and the remains of men and domestic animals are so abundant in the topsoil that one can regard the ceramic debris as a constituent part of the soil and the animal remains as one of its characteristic fossils.

"Cultivation of such duration has brought about the denuding of the elevated parts. We have seen the industrious people of Mani struggle against this scourge, especially in the district of Zarnata, by building terraces that hold on the sides of steep slopes whatever remains of the soil. . . .

"Man found in fire a powerful auxiliary to hasten the destruction of vegetation in elevated regions. This barbarous custom, no doubt proscribed when Greece was more civilized but practiced for many centuries, consists in burning down the forests and thickets of the mountains. We have seen shepherds on Mt. Lykaion burn down forests of chestnuts, the creation of centuries, to provide pasture for goats, or sow a little barley on ground soon stripped. Today, when the forests are no more, they fall upon bushes that still cover part of the mountains. They keep burning them at certain intervals, to provide new shoots for the flocks. It takes little time this way to destroy the layers of soil completely; the dry and friable earth is carried away by the winter rains, and only the completely bare rock remains. Such is the state of the mountains of a large part of Greece, especially of Argolis, Attica and Laconia, where the richest vegetation has failed to resist man's destructive action.

"We might say there is no place where fire has not passed a hundred times: the surface of the rocks bears witness to this everywhere. Having become dull and friable, the limestone rocks break off into scales or crooked slabs. In the schist mountains of Lykovouno the hyaline quartzes have become milky and cracked, and the schists reddish on their surface.

"The immediate result of the destruction of these forests and of the soil is the drying up of the springs and wells of the valleys. Thus we have heard the Albanians of the valleys of Kelly and Angelokastro in the Argolid complain about the disappearance of the water since the time when their ancestors came to settle there. But instead of correcting the evil, they are content to anathematize the dried-up sources, as they fill them up with stones. A still more disastrous effect is the increase in the violence and the products of the torrents, which devastate a large part of the lower plains.

"The earliest historical tradition shows that the establishment of man in Peloponnesus was a lengthy conquest over the animals which frequented its forests and mountains. Lions and bears disappeared first, and for the last two thousand years they have existed only in the Pindus. More fortunate investigations than ours will reveal in the caves of Greece, apart from animals of extinct species, the bones of these large carnivores joined with those of man and some coarse remains of his industry – as in the caves of southern France – and on top the ossified deposits which have been in process of formation for more than three thousand years, composed of the bones of various representatives of the human race, of domestic animals, of the lynx and the wolf, the only carnivores which still dispute the possession of the mountains with the shepherds.

"To these general phenomena we should add the local but indestructible changes which man has brought to the soil of Greece. These include: crypts, subterranean tombs cut into the rock, and enormous quarries excavated in orderly fashion, whether open to the sky or with underground galleries. Wherever we encountered the various sorts of Tertiary limestone that the ancients called poros or *Conchylites lapis*, the beds of it were almost entirely removed. We may cite Aegina, Megara, Corinth, the quarries near Elafonisi, Methone, etc., as the sites where we have seen the destructive action of man on the Tertiary terrain more greatly impressed. His structures, too, can be looked upon as geological features that are nearly ineffaceable. The cyclopean monuments have traversed thirty centuries on ground unceasingly shaken by earthquakes, and do not bear any traces of destruction other than those due to the hand of man.

"But it is above all in reflecting on the huge number of monuments of human industry that have been buried in the seas of Greece since the historical era began that we can conceive a lofty idea of the indestructible testimonies that man has left of his works. What a mass of human bones and of the remains of the industry of all the ages has not the roadstead of Navarino alone – unlucky place to be sure in the history of our forefathers – swallowed up over the last thirty centuries! It is nearly the same with the Gulf of Lepanto, that of Athens and of the entire Mediterranean, where thousands of buildings are lost every century, where deposits of marl, sand, and limestone preserve them and establish their order of succession. Let a phenomenon of upheaval bring to light a portion of the bottom of these seas, not by heaping up scoria around an igneous vent, as volcanic phenomena do, but by lifting up a part of the earth's crust. Then, instead of a few bones, or a few fragile plants or shells preserved intact in the midst of ancient deposits – analogous moreover to those which are formed in our days – we shall find in the bones of the various races, in the badges and all the products of their industry, veritable archives for the history of the human species."

REFERENCES

Bell, Barbara. 1971. "The Dark Ages in Ancient History," *American Journal of Archaeology* 75:1–26, esp. p. 6.

de Boblaye, Émile le Puillon. 1833. *Expédition scientifique de Morée. Section des sciences physiques*, Vol. 2, pp. 372–75.

Carpenter, Rhys. 1966. *Discontinuity in Greek Civilization.* Cambridge.

Clarke, David. 1968. *Analytical Archaeology*. London.
Clark, Grahame. 1957. *Archaeology and Society*. London.
Drew, Isabella; Perkins, D.; and Daly, P. 1971. "Prehistoric Domestication of Animals: Effects on Bone Structure," *Science* 171:280–82.
Finley, M. I. 1970. *Early Greece: The Bronze and Archaic Ages*. London.
Flemming, N. C. 1969. *Archaeological Evidence for Eustatic Change of Sea Level and Earth Movements in the Western Mediterranean during the Last 2000 Years*. Geological Society of America, special paper 109.
Galanopoulos, Angelos. 1964. "Seismic Geography of the Peloponnese," in *Peloponnisiaki Protochronia*, pp. 44–53. Athens.
Georgacas, D. J., and McDonald, W. A. 1969. *The Place Names of Southwestern Peloponnesus*. Athens and Minneapolis.
Hope Simpson, R. 1966. "The Seven Cities Offered by Agamemnon to Achilles," *BSA* 61:113–31.
Loy, W. G. 1970. *The Land of Nestor: A Physical Geography of the Southwest Peloponnese*. National Academy of Sciences, Office of Naval Research. Report No. 34. Washington, D.C.
McDonald, W. A. 1967. *Progress into the Past: The Rediscovery of Mycenaean Civilization*. New York.
NSSG. 1964. *Results of the Census of Agriculture-Livestock of March 1961*. Vol. 1, Sec. 3, *Peloponnese*. Athens.
Pounds, Norman J. G. 1969. "The Urbanization of the Classical World," *Annals of the Association of American Geographers* 59:135–57.
Roebuck, C. A. 1945. "A Note on Messenian Economy and Population," *Classical Philology* 40:149–65.
Rothmaler, W. 1943. "Die Waldverhaltnisse im Peloponnes," *Intersylva* 3:323–42.
Russell, J. C. 1958. "Late Ancient and Medieval Population," *Transactions of the American Philosophical Society* NS. 48 (Pt. 3):1–152.
Ventris, M., and Chadwick, J. 1956. *Documents in Mycenaean Greek*. Cambridge.

APPENDIX

NOTE: See Chapter 8, pages 123–28, for explanation of the categories of detailed information on individual sites summarized in Registers A and B under headings A through P.

REGISTER A. Prehistoric Habitation Sites

A Number	B Name	C Bibliography	D Location	E Physical Description	F Archaeological Description	G Analysis of Pottery	H Extent
1 (42)	Chóra: Áno Englianós (Mycenaean [and Homeric?] Pylos)	Preliminary reports *AJA* 1939, 1952ff.; 1961, 237–38; 1969, 147–48; Blegen and Rawson 1966; Lang 1968	3 km SW along main highway	Low hill on long high ridge oriented NE-SW	HAB-CEM. 3 tholos tombs NE (100 m), SW (150 m), and S (1 km); cemetery of chamber tombs partially excavated to W (300 m); ruins of palace occupying SW half of acropolis; lower town to SW, W, and NW (extent unclear)	EH? MH LHI–II–IIIA–IIIB G (medium)	Whole settlement at least 325 NE-SW × 200 m; acropolis 170 × 90 m reserved for palace and related bldgs. in IIIB (minimum 6.5 ha)
2 (42A)	Pisáski: Choúrou and Mavroudhiá	*AJA* 1961, 238–39; Blegen and Rawson 1966, 17–19	500 m N-NE; 3 km S of #1	Low hill	CEM. 2 probable tholos tombs; chamber tomb and small PG tholos E of highway in same vicinity	EH? LHIIIB–IIIC PG (sparse)	
3 (55)	Korifásion: Pórtes	*AJA* 1939, 559; *AJA* 1961, 242	700 m W-SW; main highway bisects it	Low mound	HAB. Heavy blocks reported under surface; artifacts of stone, obsidian, flint	MH? LHIIIA–IIIB C; H (medium)	120 m E-W × 80 (1 ha)
4 (56)	Korifásion: Belérbeï	*Praktika* 1909, 289; *Praktika* 1960, 197; *AJA* 1939, 559; *AJA* 1961, 242	1 km S	Low hill forming N extension of long ridge	HAB. Probable graves to S and E	LHIIIA?–IIIB (medium)	200 m N-S × 150 (3 ha)
5 (57)	Korifásion: Charatsári	*Praktika* 1925–26, 140–41; *AJA* 1939, 557; *AJA* 1961, 242; *Hesperia* 1954, 158–62	800 m S-SW	Very low mound	CEM. Tholos tomb; dug into level ground with steeply descending dromos; 6 m diameter	Late MH LHI	
6 (59)	Petrochóri: Profítis Ilías	*AJA* 1961, 243–44	1½ km S; immed. NW of Voïdhokilia Bay; chapel on summit	Flat top of low rocky headland S of chapel hill	HAB. Possible EH cemetery on E shoulder ca. 500 m NE; chert, obsidian, bone, house foundations?	N?; EH; MH? (medium)	100 m E-W × 60 (0.6 ha)
7 (59 A–E)	Petrochóri: Osmánaga	*AJA* 1964, 232–33; *AJA* 1969, 149–50; Pritchett 1965, 6–11	1½ km S-SE; in N section of lagoon bed	Flat area	HAB. Bone, roof tiles, foreign stones in spoil banks of drainage ditches	EH; MH? LHIIIB PG (sherds noted in 5 spots) (medium)	At least 1,750 m E-W × 600 m (seems too large for continuous site and too concentrated for separate ones)
8 (60)	Petrochóri: Voïdhokiliá	*Ergon* 1956, 90–93; *AJA* 1961, 243	1½ km S; at S end of headland N of entrance to bay	Low promontory	CEM. Tholos tomb	LHIIIB	
9 (61)	Petrochóri: Paliókastro (classical Koryphasion; *ro-o-wa* of Pylos tablets?)	*Ergon* 1958, 148–50; *AJA* 1961, 243	2 km S-SW	Low narrow flat N end of headland immed. S of entrance to little bay	HAB-CEM. LH, C, H town on headland; PG grave group from SE slope; large H cemetery on sandspit to E; R bldg. at SE foot	LHIIIA–IIIB PG C; H; R	200 m N-S × 70 (LH area probably smaller) (1.4 ha)
10 (62)	Petrochóri: Cave of Nestor	*AJA* 1961, 243; *AJA* 1964, 32	2½ km S-SW	Large cave in steep N face of acropolis at medium height	HAB. (at least in N)	N; EH; MH LHIII C	

REGISTER A

I Communications	J Strategic Features	K Water Supply	L Land: Total	M Land: Percentage Cultivated	N Land: Irrigated	O Population	P Special Features
Mainline (land); 9 km N of best port in region	Fairly well protected except to NE; wide view over productive countryside and harbor	Fair spring 1 km NE	2.8 km radius; 2,463 ha	95	48 ha	800 min. (from archaeological clues *only*)	Discovered 1939; excavated in 1952–66; administrative center of large kingdom in LHIIIB; local capital from late in MH through LHIIIA; some protection from NW winds
Mainline (land); 6 km from sea							Chamber tomb and tholos excavated by Taylour 1958–59; probably extension of cemetery area belonging to #1
Mainline (land); 3 km from sea	On road from harbor to palace		2 km radius; 1,256 ha	95	40 ha	130	Possibly small manufacturing center
Near mainline (land); excellent (sea)		Fair spring 50 m E	2 km radius; 1,256 ha	95		390	Tested by Marinatos; badly eroded
3 km from sea							Excavated by Kourouniotis; review of pottery suggests this earliest known tholos in region; connected with #1?
Secondary (land); excellent (sea)	Strong defensive position commanding entrance to little bay					78?	Typical EH site
Secondary (land); excellent (sea)			2 km radius; 1,963 ha	90 (result of extensive modern drainage project)	15 ha		Apparently N part of lagoon bed above water level at times between Early Bronze and Early Iron Age
							Excavated by Marinatos
Secondary (land); excellent (sea)	Strong defensive position—probably main harbor town for palace		0.3 m radius; 28 ha	see #7	see #7	182	Tested by Marinatos
Secondary (land); excellent (sea)	Spacious natural shelter		see #7	see #7	see #7	Half dozen families	Tested by Blegen and Theocharis; possibly shrine in LH and later

REGISTER A

A Number	B Name	C Bibliography	D Location	E Physical Description	F Archaeological Description	G Analysis of Pottery	H Extent
11 (46)	Tragána: Viglítsa	*Praktika* 1909, 274, 292; *Arch Eph* 1912, 268; Valmin 1930, 147; *Ergon* 1955, 88–91; *AJA* 1961, 240; Desborough 1964, 281–83	700 m SW	SW end of medium ridge	CEM. 2 tholoi ca. 20 m apart	MH? LHIIIA–IIIB SM?; PG H	
12 (45)	Tragána: Voroúlia	*Ergon* 1956, 90; *AJA* 1961, 239	800 m N-NE	High steep slope to E immed. below road	HAB. (only one bldg. sure)	MH LH I–II–III?	
13 (44)	Tragána: Kapouréïka	*AJA* 1961, 239	2 km N	Low ploughed-down mound beside road	CEM. Multiple burial mound; frags. of pithoi and stone slabs	MH (pithoi only)	
14 (43)	Lévki: Kaldámou	*AJA* 1961, 239	ca. 2 km S-SE; scattered ca. 700 m along track leading NE from main road to Ambelófito	On crest of high ridge	CEM. At least 6 multiple burial mounds (10–25 m diam.; 2–5 m high); broken pithoi; stone slabs	MH (pithoi mainly)	
15 (38)	Gargaliáni: Kánalos	*AJA* 1961, 236–37	3 km W-SW	SW end and SE slopes of low spur projecting into extensive coastal plain	HAB. CEM? Possible tholos (certainly burial mound) ca. 400 m SE; fortifications (prehistoric?); C or H dressed blocks (some in situ); obsidian; tiles	MH LHI?–II?–IIIA–IIIB C; H; R? (medium)	170 m NE-SW × 110 (1.9 ha)
16 (37C)	Gargaliáni: Koutsovéri	*AJA* 1969, 146–47	3 km NW; immed. E of highway	Medium hill (outcrop of escarpment); chapel on top	HAB	LH (sparse)	150 m WNW-SSE × 120 (1.8 ha)
17 (39A)	Flóka: Pánitsa	*AJA* 1969, 147	1 km N-NW; immed. SW of spring supplying Gargaliani	Low hill	HAB?	Inconclusive but probably LH (very sparse except for modern)	
18 (39)	Pírgos: Tsoúka	*AJA* 1961, 237	1½ km SW	Top of long ridge	CEM. Mound ca. 12 m diam. and 5 m high; prob. multiple burial	MH? (scarce)	
19 (40)	Ambelófito: Lagoú	*AJA* 1961, 237	1 km N-NE; ca. 100 m E of highway	Flat area near edge of high spur overlooking Chora to S	HAB	MH? LHIIIB (sparse)	100 m × 100
20 (41)	Chóra: Volimídhia (*pa-ki-ja-si* of Pylos tablets?)	*Ergon* and *Praktika* 1952ff.; *AJA* 1961, 237; 1969, 147 and bibliography there	800 m N-NE; E part of cemetery cut by road	At foot of Aigaleon Mts. on easy slope to S-SW	CEM. Ca. 30 chamber tombs excavated	N?; MH (late) LHI–II–IIIA–IIIB H; R	

REGISTER A

I Communications	J Strategic Features	K Water Supply	L Land: Total	M Land: Percentage Cultivated	N Land: Irrigated	O Population	P Special Features
2 km from sea							Excavated by Skias, Kourouniotis, Marinatos; related settlement unclear; very important for transition from Bronze to Iron Age
Secondary (land); 2½ km to sea			2.3 m radius; 1,662 ha	90	24 ha	?	Excavated by Marinatos
3 km to sea							Probably related to #1
3½ km to sea							Probably related to #1
Mainline? (land); fair (sea); 2 km	Close to excellent land	Small spring immed. S	3.3 km radius; 3,421 ha	80	18 ha	247	
Mainline? (land); fair (sea); 3 km	Strong defensive position	River and copious spring ca. 1½ km N	2.4 km radius; 1,810 ha	65		234	
Secondary? (land); 8 km to sea		Fair spring at NE foot	4.1 km radius; 5,081 ha	80			Fairly recent occupation has probably obscured ancient evidence
7 km to sea							Second smaller artificial mound ca. 200 m NE
Near mainline? (land); 9 km to sea		Small spring ca. 200 m N	3.6 km radius; 4,071 ha	90		130	Since discovery in 1953, intensive cultivation has completely obscured surface pottery
11 km to sea		Copious spring ca. 300 m NNE	3.4 km radius; 3,632 ha	90	10 ha	Relatively large; extensive re-use of tombs may suggest special cult significance	Extensive excavation by Marinatos; no habitation site identified but must have been nearer than #1 (ca. 4 km)

REGISTER A

A Number	B Name	C Bibliography	D Location	E Physical Description	F Archaeological Description	G Analysis of Pottery	H Extent
21 (41A)	Chóra: Áyios Ioánnis	*Praktika* 1954, 305–8; *AJA* 1969, 147	Contiguous to SW; just W of church of Ayios Ioannis	Low hillside sloping to E	CEM. 5 chamber tombs identified; 2 excavated; large R bath	LHIIIB–IIIC? R	
22 (41B)	Metaxádha: Kalópsana	*AJA* 1969, 147	1 km S-SW; 300 m W of bridge	High spur extending E from Aigaleon Mts. into narrow valley	HAB. CEM? Habitation on upper S and SE terraces; chance finds (some said to come from graves) include 2 bronze double axes (in Chora museum), sword, beads, bones	MH? LHIII (and earlier in LH?) (medium)	200 m NW-SE × 150 (3 ha)
23 (69D)	Metamórfosis: Áyia Sotíra	*AJA* 1969, 152	500 m N; chapel immed. W of road	Dissected area N and W of chapel	HAB?	LH? (very sparse) Large M site	Unclear
24 (69C)	Vlachópoulo: Stamáti Ráchi	*AJA* 1969, 152	2 km N-NW; immed. E of road	High hill	HAB on and near top	MH LH (sparse)	110 m NNW-SSE × 60 (0.6 ha)
25 (69B)	Vlachópoulo: Agriliá	*Praktika* 1964, 89–92; *Ergon* 1964, 84–85; *BCH* 1965, 734; *AJA* 1969, 152	2½ km E-NE	High hill	HAB-CEM. Habitation on top and upper W and S slopes; tholos ca. 700 m W of site looking toward Vlachopoulo (a second probable)	MH? LHIIIA–IIIB (sparse) tholos LHIIIA	120 m NNE-SSW × 80 (1 ha)
26 (69A)	Chatzí: Barbéri	*Deltion* 1967, 207; *AJA* 1969, 151–52	1 km W-NW; immed. W of road	Low hill	HAB. Top and SSE terraces	MH? LHIIIB C; M (medium)	150 m NW-SE × 120 (1.8 ha)
27 (69)	Mesopótamos: Velevoúni	*AJA* 1961, 245; 1969, 151; *Deltion* 1967, 207	Contiguous to NW	Low hill	HAB-CEM. Top and upper S slope; foreign stones; tholos or burial mound ca. 700 m N-NW and on opposite (W) side of highway	LHIIIB H (sparse)	150 m NE-SW × 70 (0.9 ha)
28 (68)	Mesopótamos: Chília Choriá	*Ergon* 1966, 105; *AJA* 1961, 245	2 km W-NW; ca. 250 m N of highway and contiguous to new village (settled from Soulinari)	Flat terrain near height of land	HAB-CEM. Burial mound on N side of highway dated R by Marinatos	MH? LHI?–IIIB R (medium)	100 m N-S × 50 (min.) (0.5 ha)
29 (68A)	Soulinári: Tourlidhítsa	*Ergon* 1966, 107–10; *Praktika* 1966, 129–32; *AJA* 1969, 151	2½ km NW	Small distinct mound	CEM. Small tholos; bronze razor and knife	LHIIB–IIIA	
30 (70)	Milióti: Áyios Ilías	*AJA* 1961, 246	1 km NW; on crest of medium ridge	Large mound (at least partially artificial)	CEM. Multiple burial ca. 20 m diam. and 4.5 m high; frags. of pithoi and stone slabs	MH?	

REGISTER A

I Communications	J Strategic Features	K Water Supply	L Land: Total	M Land: Percentage Cultivated	N Land: Irrigated	O Population	P Special Features
8 km to sea							Excavated by Marinatos; may suggest related habitation site between it and #20
Secondary (land); 14 km to sea	Defensible but isolated	Fair spring ca. 400 m E-NE; river ca. 300 m E	4.3 km radius; 5,809 ha	50	8 ha	390	
Mainline (land); 13 km to sea		Copious spring under chapel; small spring 300 m NW; third spring in village	3.1 km radius; 3,019 ha	70	20 ha		
Mainline (land); 14 km to sea		Copious spring ca. 500 m E	3.5 km radius; 3,848 ha	85	5 ha	78	
Mainline (land); 12 km to sea		Very copious spring at NW foot	3.2 km radius; 3,217 ha	85	10 ha	130	Tholos excavated by Marinatos
Mainline (land); 11 km to sea		2 small springs at NE foot	3.4 km radius; 3,632 ha	85		234	
Mainline (land); 10 km to sea	Central position near height of land in fertile plateau country	Streams on S and N sides with springs in beds	2.5 km radius; 1,963 ha	90	3 ha	117	Tholos illicitly excavated; H lamp, tearbottle, and sherds (not found by us) presumably from near LH habitation site
Mainline (land); 9 km to sea	On height of land ca. midway between Pylos and Messenian Gulf; ruined Turkish khan on opposite (N) side of old roadway (kalderim) suggests posting stop		2.3 km radius; 1,662 ha	80		65	
10 km to sea							Excavated by Marinatos; related habitation unclear
10 km to sea							Illicitly excavated

REGISTER A

A Number	B Name	C Bibliography	D Location	E Physical Description	F Archaeological Description	G Analysis of Pottery	H Extent
31 (75B)	Romíri: Ávisos	*AJA* 1964, 233–34	1½ km NW	Medium spur	HAB	MH? LHIII (medium)	80 m E-W × 50 (min.) (0.4 ha)
32 (67A)	Chandhrinoú: Kissós	*Ergon* 1966, 105–7; *Praktika* 1966, 121–28; *AJA* 1969, 151	1 km E-NE	Artificial mound	CEM. Multiple burials in slab-lined cists and pithoi; scanty and poor contents (bronze knife)	LHIIIA–IIIB	
33 (67)	Chandhrinoú: Platánia	*AJA* 1961, 245; *Deltion* 1964, 149; *Deltion* 1968, 156; *AJA* 1969, 151; *Deltion* 1969, 145	Within village beside spring	Very low mound (now almost effaced)	HAB-CEM. Cache of 30 N celts found ca. 700 m NW at spot called Kotronakia; small tholos at spot called Yenitsari had LH pottery scattered around but none inside; small circular mound (within village) containing bones said to have been destroyed	N LHIIIB A C	80 m E-W × 50 (min.) (0.4 ha)
34 (65B)	Káto Kremmídhia: Fourtzóvrisi	*JHS Arch Reports* 1960–61, 11; *AJA* 1964, 233	900 m E-SE	See category F	HAB? CEM. Habitation site prob. on one or more knolls surrounding springs; artificial mound (18 m diam.; 4 m high) ca. 400 m to W; another ca. 150 m S; C tombs	LH C (sparse)	Unclear
35 (65)	Koukounára: Kataráchi (possibly the *a-pu₂* of the Pylos tablets)	*Praktika* 1954, 311; 1960, 195–57; 1961, 174–76; 1963, 114–18; *Ergon* 1958, 150–52; 1959, 117–25; 1960, 145–46; 1961, 169–71; 1963, 81–85; *AJA* 1961, 244; 1969, 150	800 m NE	Low hill in deep gorge of Potami tou Arapi	HAB-CEM. Apsidal "megaron"; 7 tholoi excavated in neighborhood and others known; tombs built LHI–IIB	MH LHI–IIA–IIB G; H (sparse)	120 m N-S × 70 (min.) (0.8 ha)
36 (65A)	Stenosiá: Londaríti	*Praktika* 1961, 174–76; 1962, 90; *Ergon* 1961, 171; *AJA* 1969, 150 (see also #35)	800 m SE; on S side of gorge	Dissected plateau country	HAB-CEM. Large building with bathtubs, etc.; multiple burial mound (3.6 m diam.); 3 tholoi	LHI–II–IIIA–IIIB–IIIC	
37 (66)	Chandhrinoú: Koubé	*AJA* 1961, 245	1½ km W; 100 m NW of highway	Relatively flat area sloping to W	HAB-CEM. Low artificial burial mound ca. 40 m NW; higher one ca. 150 m SE (across highway)	LHIIIB (sparse)	130 m E-W × 80 (1 ha)
38 (66A)	Kinigoú: Avarinítsa	*AJA* 1964, 233; 1969, 150–51	3½ km N; ca. 200 m W of road	Medium spur; site of small, recently abandoned village	HAB. CEM? Artificial mound ca. 500 m E of road	LH R? (sparse)	100 m NW-SE × 50 (0.5 ha)
39 (58C)	Píla: Elítsa	*AJA* 1969, 149	300 m S; across deep gully	Medium ridge	HAB. Foreign stones	LH (sparse)	100 m E-W × 50 (0.5 ha)
40 (58B)	Píla: Kokkinórachi	*AJA* 1969, 149	800 m N; overlooking Arapi ravine to N	Low ridge	HAB	MH? LH (sparse)	80 m NW-SE × 40 (0.3 ha)
41 (58A)	Píla: Vígles	*AJA* 1969, 149	1 km W-NW	E end of medium ridge	HAB-CEM. Habitation on summit and W slope; multiple burial mound (MH?) ca. 120 m W-NW	EH?; MH? LHIIIB (medium)	200 m E-W × 125 (min.) (2.5 ha)

REGISTER A

I Communications	J Strategic Features	K Water Supply	L Land: Total	M Land: Percentage Cultivated	N Land: Irrigated	O Population	P Special Features
Isolated (land); 9 km to sea		Fair spring at E foot; poor spring on W flank	3.1 km radius; 3,019 ha	50	20 ha	52	
8 km to sea							Excavated by Marinatos
Mainline (land); 7 km to sea		Copious spring immed. E	2.4 km radius; 1,810 ha	85	64 ha	52 (min.)	Tholos excavated by Choremis
Mainline (land); 8 km to sea		2 fair springs in immed. area	3.1 km radius; 3,019 ha	90			
Mainline (land); 6 km to sea	Strong defensive position	Fair spring at E foot; stream immed. adjacent	2.6 km radius; 1,385 ha	95	32 ha	104 (min.)	Excavated by Marinatos; possibly at least 1 additional habitation site in vicinity; this general area had astonishing number of "royal" burials
Secondary (land); 5 km to sea						Obviously heavily populated area but data lacking for estimate	Excavated by Marinatos; widely separated and more than 1 habitation complex almost certain
Mainline (land); 4 km to sea	Biggest water source in area; aqueduct to modern Pylos since Turkish times	Copious spring ca. 300 m E	2.3 km radius; 1,662 ha	95	32 ha	130	
Secondary (land); 8 km to sea		Stream near S foot; poorly watered area	3.4 km radius; 3,632 ha	70		65	
Mainline (land); excellent (sea), 2 km			2.2 km radius; 1,520 ha	70	See #41–42	65	
Secondary (land); 2 km to sea		Poor spring at SW foot	0.8 km radius; 201 ha	95	See #41–42	39	
Mainline (land); excellent (sea), 1½ km	Near W end of major E-W highway	Above well-watered valley	1.2 km radius; 452 ha	90	65 ha	325	

A Number	B Name	C Bibliography	D Location	E Physical Description	F Archaeological Description	G Analysis of Pottery	H Extent
42 (58)	Yiálova: Paliochóri	*AJA* 1961, 242	500 m NE	W end of high ridge; between two fertile valleys	HAB. CEM? Two possible burial mounds 500 m E and on parallel ridge to N; habitation on summit and upper W slope	LHIIIB (heavy)	150 m N-S × 120 (min.); sparse pottery over additional 300 m N-S × 120 (1.8 ha)
43 (64)	Schinólakka: Kokkiniá	*AJA* 1961, 244	Contiguous to NE	Low ridge	HAB. Pithoi, gems, bronze tweezers (prob. from cemetery) reported 200 m S	MH? LHIIIA?–IIIB (medium)	125 m E-W × 100 (1.3 ha)
44 (63)	Pýlos: Vígla	*AJA* 1939, 559; 1961, 244	1½ km E-NE; between highway and cliffs above Navarino Bay; 700 m SW of road junction (Midhén) of Kyparissia-Methoni and Pylos-Kalamata highways	Low mound (partially fallen over cliff)	HAB-CEM. Two tholos tombs just NE of Midhen; 2 N celts from beside highway ca. halfway between Vigla and Pylos	N LHIII	50 × 50 m (0.3 ha)
45 (72E)	Pýlos: Áyios Nektários	*AJA* 1969, 154	1½ km S-SE; immed. S of sharp loop in Pylos-Methoni highway	Low hill	HAB. Possibly ancient wall	LH H? (sparse)	120 m WNW-SSE × 60 (0.7 ha)
46 (52)	Íklaina: Tragánes	*Ergon* 1954, 42; *Praktika* 1954, 308–11; *AJA* 1961, 241	1½ km W-NW	W end of low spur	HAB. Foundations of substantial bldg. above ground showed pebble floors, fresco frags.; LHIII animal figurine	MH LHII?–III M (heavy)	200 m N-S × 150 (3 ha)
47 (53)	Íklaina: Gouvítses	*AJA* 1961, 241	2 km W-NW	Eroded slope	HAB?	LH? (very sparse)	
48 (51)	Plátanos: Kritharítses	*AJA* 1961, 241	500 m W-SW; on S side of Platanos-Korifasion road; second mound at Alí Chóza ca. 1200 m W-SW	2 low mounds	CEM. Probable MH multiple burial mounds; bones, pottery, frags. of pithoi	MH? LH?	
49 (51A)	Plátanos: Lambrópoulou Piyí	*AJA* 1964, 232	1 km W	Flank of low hill in ravine	HAB	LH (sparse)	(small)
50 (54)	Íklaina: Panayía	*AJA* 1961, 241	1 km NE; chapel at E end	Low hill	HAB. CEM? Possible grave(s) on W slope where slab exposed and local reports of antiquities	MH? LHIII (sparse)	200 m E-W × 70 (1.4 ha)
51 (50A)	Plátanos: Merzíni	*AJA* 1964, 232	800 m E-SE	Low mound on SW slope	HAB	MH LHIIIB (heavy)	150 m E-W × 120 (1.8 ha)

REGISTER A

I Communica- tions	J Strategic Features	K Water Supply	L Land: Total	M Land: Percentage Cultivated	N Land: Irrigated	O Population	P Special Features
Mainline (land); excel-lent (sea), 1 km	Strong defen-sive position on main E-W highway over-looking Nava-rino Bay	Yianouzaga River (perennial) and copious springs close to NW foot	1.4 km radi-us; 616 ha	75	180 ha	234	Local rumors of tombs
Close to main-line (land); 3 km to sea		Fair spring 500 m E	2.1 km radi-us; 1,385 ha	90		169	
Near mainline (land); high above bay (sea)	Excellent lookout over S entrance to bay		1.9 km radi-us; 1,134 ha	45		39	
Secondary (land); fair (sea), 1½ km		Poorly watered area	1.7 km radi-us; 908 ha	25		91	
Secondary (land); 5 km to sea		Fair spring below W edge	2.1 km radi-us; 1,385 ha	90		390	Trial excavation by Marinatos
Secondary (land); 5 km to sea							
6 km to sea							
7 km to sea		Copious spring at N foot	1.4 km radi-us; 616 ha	90			
Secondary (land); fair (sea), 6 km			1.7 km radi-us; 908 ha	95		182	
Secondary (land); 7 km to sea		Copious spring 200 m S	2.1 km radi-us; 1,385 ha	90		234	

REGISTER A

A Number	B Name	C Bibliography	D Location	E Physical Description	F Archaeological Description	G Analysis of Pottery	H Extent
52 (50)	Papoúlia: Áyios Ioánnis	*Ergon* 1954, 42–43, Fig. 55; *AJA* 1961, 240; *Deltion* 1967, 207	1 km W; on N side of Platanos-Papoulia road	Artificial mound	CEM. Multiple burial mound; empty chamber in center of stone core; burials in pithoi facing outward around edge	MH LHIIIC	
53 (49)	Papoúlia	*Praktika* 1954, 311–16; *AJA* 1961, 240; 1964, 239	Within village and contiguous to W	On low hill	CEM. HAB? 4 small, badly destroyed tholoi; traces of habitation site reported	LHIII A (sparse)	
54 (48)	Mirsinochóri: Roútsi	*Ergon* 1956, 91–96; *AJA* 1961, 240 and bibliography cited there	1½ km NE	Medium plateau	CEM. 2 excavated tholoi; 1 relatively undisturbed; rich contents; 3 additional artificial mounds to N and W	LHII–IIIA H	
55 (42B)	Mirsinochóri: Váïes	*Deltion* 1964, 150–51; *AJA* 1969, 148–49	2 km W; on top of high ridge opposite (E of) palace (across deep ravine)	High ridge	HAB. Test excavation revealed only surface sherds	LH	
56 (47)	Chóra: Koukoúyera	*AJA* 1961, 240	2 km S	Top of high ridge and immed. N of ravine	CEM. Artificial mound ca. 25 m in diam. and 7 m high; probable tholos tomb	LH	
57 (37)	Gargaliáni: Órdhines	*AJA* 1961, 236	4½ km NW; S side of ravine overlooking sea	Medium hill	HAB	EH; MH? LHIII (sparse)	200 m N-S × 100 (2 ha)
58 (37A)	Válta: Áyios Pandeleïmonas	*AJA* 1969, 145	Contiguous to SW	High hill with church at S edge and village behind	HAB-CEM. LH tomb apparently destroyed ca. 200 m S; frag. of N celt	N? LH C?; H (sparse)	150 m NW-SE × 120 (1.8 ha)
59 (37B)	Válta: Kastráki	*AJA* 1969, 145–46	500 m SW; immed. S of bridge on Valta-Gargaliani road	Medium ridge oriented NE-SW	HAB-CEM. Probably two knolls are MH multiple burial mounds; probable tholos immed. N of road; foreign stones	MH LHIII (medium)	120 m NE-SW × 70 (min.) (0.8 ha)
60 (22P)	Válta: Áyia Paraskeví	*AJA* 1969, 136	2½ km NW	Low spur with house on summit and chapel ca. 200 m E-NE	HAB	MH LHIII (sparse)	120 m ENE-WSW × 100 (1.2 ha)
61 (22N)	Filiatrá: Kastráki	*AJA* 1969, 135–36	5½ km SE	Medium spur; immed. W of bridge over Evangelistra River	HAB-CEM. Artificial mound ca. 150 m NE with rifled slab graves (probably H or R)	LH H?; R? (sparse)	150 m NW-SE × 120; top and NE slopes (1.8 ha)

REGISTER A

I Communications	J Strategic Features	K Water Supply	L Land: Total	M Land: Percentage Cultivated	N Land: Irrigated	O Population	P Special Features
8 km to sea							See p. 135 of Ch. 8; excavated by Marinatos; LHIIIC sealstone found at Afanolax ca. 300 m NE of mound
Secondary (land); 8 km to sea							Excavated by Marinatos
9 km to sea							Excavated by Marinatos
Secondary (land); 8 km to sea	Good lookout toward E for palace		1.9 km radius; 1,134 ha	90			Tested by Papathanasopoulos, who suggests small village, army post, or private estate here
9 km							Magnificent view in all directions
Isolated (land); fair (sea)	Good coastal lookout	Copious spring along highway ca. 600 m E; Langouvardhos River (perennial) immed. to N	1.7 km radius; 908 ha	95		260	Typical of several W coast sites at river mouths
Secondary (land); 4 km to sea	Strong defensive position controlling some good land and prob. interior land route	Dhipotamo River (perennial) at S foot; modern village pipes water from spring 2 km E	1.6 km radius; 804 ha	50		234	
Secondary (land); 4 km to sea		Dhipotamo River (perennial) ca. 50 m E	1.9 km radius; 1,134 ha	50		104	
Secondary (land); 3 km to sea		Stream ca. 700 m N; farmers depend on wells	2.5 km radius; 1,963 ha	65		156	
Secondary? (on probable line of route of penetration from coast to Valta area); 4 km to sea		Spring-fed river at E foot	2.1 km radius; 1,385 ha	55		234	

A Number	B Name	C Bibliography	D Location	E Physical Description	F Archaeological Description	G Analysis of Pottery	H Extent
62 (22M)	Korovilḗïka	*AJA* 1969, 135	Contiguous to E	Flat E edge of medium limestone spur	HAB	LH (sparse)	75 m N-S × 50 (0.4 ha)
63 (22L)	Filiatrá: Áyios Christóforos	*AJA* 1969, 135	3 km SE; on both sides of road at W edge of escarpment and just above chapel	Low knoll on S side of road; terraced slope to N	HAB	MH LHIIIA?–IIIB (heavy)	300 m N-S × 150 (4.5 ha)
64 (22K)	Filiatrá: Áyios Ioánnis	*AJA* 1969, 135	1½ km N-NW; cut thru by Filiatra-Kyparissia highway at sharp loop	NW edge of low escarpment above coastal plain; chapel on E side of highway	HAB. Blade of obsidian	MH? LH (medium)	210 m NNW-SSE × 130 (2.7 ha)
65 (22F)	Filiatrá: Stómio	*AJA* 1969, 133–34	3 km N-NW; at mouth of Filiatra River	Very low mound on cliff at S side of river and overlooking sea	HAB. Many foreign stones	LH (sparse)	125 m diam. (1.2 ha)
66 (22J)	Chalazóni: Paliochóri	*AJA* 1969, 135	400 m SW	Low hill	HAB. Several chips of obsidian	LH (very sparse)	80 m E-W × 50; on W slopes (0.4 ha)
67 (22H)	Farakládha: Dhési	*AJA* 1969, 134–35	1½ km E-SE; on N side of deep ravine	Level plateau	HAB? Possible Paleolithic scraper found on opposite (S) side of ravine; good caves in N face of ravine	LH? (extremely sparse)	
68 (22E)	Armenioí: Mána	*AJA* 1969, 133	1 km S-SE	Sloping ground above spring	HAB	LHIII (sparse)	Small
69 (22G)	Spiliá: Príndzipa	*AJA* 1969, 134	800 m N-NW; just NE of side-road from Kyparissia highway	Low rise	HAB	LH? C?; H	70 m NE-SW × 30 (0.2 ha)
70 (22)	Kyparissía: Kástro ([*ku*]-*pa-ri-so* of Pylos tablets?; Homeric Kyparisseeis?; M Arkadhiá)	*Praktika* 1911, 247–52; *Klio* 1923, 14; *Bull Lund* 1928/29, 34–35, 141; 1929/30, 1–5; Roebuck 1941, 24–25; *AJA* 1961, 232; 1969, 133; *Deltion* 1961–62, 96–98; 1967, 206; 1968, 156–58	E edge of town	Top and W foot of high hill forming NW spur of Ayia Varvara Mts.	HAB. Obsidian and flint artifacts; A head; C wall foundations on acropolis; H and R bldgs., R agora (?), architectural frags., inscriptions, H and R graves, coins, reservoir (?) in lower town; ancient harbor works (?)	MH LHI?–III A C; H; R; M	150 N-S × 65 (acropolis); unknown for lower town (1 ha plus)

REGISTER A

I Communications	J Strategic Features	K Water Supply	L Land: Total	M Land: Percentage Cultivated	N Land: Irrigated	O Population	P Special Features
Secondary (land); 4 km to sea	Controls E end of pass thru escarpment from Filiatra to Valta	Fair spring ca. 100 m S	2.1 km radius; 1,385 ha	40		52	
Secondary (land); 3 km to sea	Tremendous view to W; controls route from coast in vicinity of Filiatra into interior	Poor spring ca. 100 m W	2.2 km radius; 1,520 ha	60		585	
Mainline; 2 km to sea		Local farmers depend entirely on wells	1.9 km radius; 1,134 ha	95	12 ha	351	
Isolated (land); fair (sea)	River mouth possibly usable as harbor; good coastal lookout	Poor spring halfway down N side (near cave)	1.7 km radius; 908 ha	95	24 ha	156	
Secondary (land); 3½ km to sea		Stream below N edge; local residents depend on wells	2.9 km radius; 2,642 ha	80	73 ha	52	
Isolated (land); 3½ km to sea		Copious spring immed. to S in ravine	2.3 km radius; 1,662 ha	95	201 ha		Likely Paleolithic site
4 km to sea		Fair spring immed. to N; another ca. 400 m farther N	3.4 km radius; 3,632 ha	60	99 ha		
3 km to sea		Small spring immed. to SW	2.2 km radius; 1,520 ha	95	62 ha	26	
Crossroads (land); good (sea)	Strong defensive position controlling N-S land traffic and W end of major E-W route into interior; one of few fairly sheltered spots on W coast	Possibly brought from #72 (as today)	2.8 km radius; 2,463 ha	65	217 ha	130 (min.)	Excavation (R only) by Yalouris and Papathanasopoulos

REGISTER A

A Number	B Name	C Bibliography	D Location	E Physical Description	F Archaeological Description	G Analysis of Pottery	H Extent
71 (23G)	Kyparissía: Rízes	*Praktika* 1965, 111	About halfway (6 km) along side road between Kyparissia and Peristeria (#200)	Low hill in open field	CEM. Pithos burial	"PG or rather SM"	
72 (22C)	Vríses: Palió-frigas	*AJA* 1969, 133	800 m W-SW; on S side of road from Kyparissia	Medium spur projecting N	HAB	MH? LH? (sparse)	100 m E-W × 90 (mainly W slope) (0.9 ha)
73 (36A)	Flesiádha: Misoráchi	*AJA* 1969, 145	700 m N-NE; 1 km W of Palio Loutro	Low isolated ridge	HAB	LH (medium)	150 m WSW ESE × 80 (W end of ridge) (1.2 ha)
74 (72B)	Palioneró: Áyios Konstandínos	*AJA* 1969, 153	Contiguous to SW	High spur projecting W; directly above chapel on side road to Mesochori from Pylos-Methoni highway	HAB	MH LH (sparse)	60 m E-W × 50 (0.3 ha)
75 (72A)	Mesochóri: Koutsovéri	*AJA* 1969, 152–53	300 m SE; immed. N of road to Pidhasos	Low hill	HAB	LH (sparse) M (heavy)	100 m × 100 (top and upper S slopes) (1 ha)
76 (72)	Mesochóri: Gdhití Ráchi	*AJA* 1961, 247; 1969, 152	1 km SE; on edge of deep gully	Low artificial mound; 15 m diam.; 2 m high	CEM? Multiple burials?	MH (sparse)	
77 (72C)	Káto Ambelókipi: Astrapokaï-méno	*AJA* 1969, 153	Contiguous to NW	High spur above village	HAB	LH (sparse) M	150 m E-W × 50; mainly SW slopes (0.8 ha)
78 (73A)	Exochikón: Áyios Nikólaos	*Deltion* 1965, 208; *AJA* 1969, 154	1.5 km W-SW; 250 m W of Kaplani-Lachanadha road	High ridge	HAB-CEM. Destroyed tholos ca. 7-8 m diam. on lower Mistofolaka ridge	MH LHIIIB N summit and E-NE slopes (medium)	100 m N-S × 80 (0.8 ha)
79 (73)	Finikous: Ayianálipsi (*ka-ra-do-ro* of Pylos tablets?)	Valmin 1930, 155–57; *BCH* 1959, 641; *AJA* 1961, 247; *Deltion* 1967, 207	200 m S-SW; chapel on summit	Medium hill; partially eroded by sea	HAB. CEM? Chert; walls exposed in cliff above sea; foreign stones; possible burial mound 500 m NE; late G tomb; probable ruined tholos 1 km E on coast; R habitation 500 m W	EH; MH LHI?–II?–IIIA–IIIB G C; H; R (medium)	180 m N-S × 140 (2.5 ha)
80 (72D)	Methóni: Nisakoúli	*AAA* 1969, 10–14; 1969, 153–54; *Deltion* 1969, 145	2 km S-SE; SE side of bay ca. 350 m N of cliff on mainland	Round heavily eroded islet (ca. 60 m diam.) of medium height	HAB. MH building and altar (?)	MH LH R?; M? (heavy but much worn)	60 m × 60 (min.) (0.4 ha)

REGISTER A

I Communications	J Strategic Features	K Water Supply	L Land: Total	M Land: Percentage Cultivated	N Land: Irrigated	O Population	P Special Features
4 km to sea							Chance find reported by Marinatos
Secondary (land); 4 km to sea		2 copious springs bracket site	3.5 km radius; 3,848 ha	55	65 ha	117	
Isolated (land); 16 km to sea		Very copious spring at N foot; headwaters of Karia River (see #100)	3.5 km radius; 3,848 ha	40	35 ha	156	Ruins of recent village at E end of ridge
Secondary (land); 3 km to sea		Fair spring at SW foot	2.1 km radius; 1,385 ha	35		39	
Secondary (land); 4 km to sea		M cisterns suggest water scarce	4.1 km radius; 5,027 ha	65		130	
5 km to sea							
Secondary (land); 9 km to sea	Strong defensive position on height of land with very extensive view	Very copious spring 500 m NE; copious spring 300 m NW	5.0 km radius; 7,854 ha	85	12 ha	104	Only good water in large area; supplies several villages
Isolated (?); 5 km to sea	Excellent view in all directions	Fair spring on lower E slope	5.0 km radius; 7,854 ha	85		104	
Secondary (land); excellent (sea)	Good acropolis above relatively sheltered beach	Fair spring 600 m W	3.2 km radius; 3,217 ha	85	10 ha	325	
If present island was end of peninsula, excellent protection (sea)			3.3 km radius; 3,421 ha (on mainland opposite)	80		52	First reported by Choremis and trial excavation followed

REGISTER A

A Number	B Name	C Bibliography	D Location	E Physical Description	F Archaeological Description	G Analysis of Pottery	H Extent
100 (76)	Rizómilo: Nichória (*re-u-ko-to-ro* or *ti-mi-to-a-ke-e* of Pylos tablets?)	*Deltion* 1960, 108; 1961–62, 95–96; 1968, 156–59; *AJA* 1961, 248–49; 1964, 234; 1969, 156; *BCH* 1961, 697; 1962, 725; *AAA* 1968, 205–9; Loy (1970) 125–36	300 m SW	High ridge oriented NW-SE	HAB-CEM. Bronze Age habitation proved over major portion (80%) of hilltop; considerable PG and G habitation; several M bldgs. at NW and SE ends; 6 tholoi excavated and others probable below NW end; PG cemetery 500 m N; chamber tombs 200 m W, 200 m N, and 500 m SE; C-R remains in vicinity	Few EH sherds reused by MH inhabitants MH; LHI–II–IIIA–IIIB–IIIC SM; PG; G; A C; H; R; M (medium to sparse on surface)	Ridge top ca. 500 m NW-SE × avg. of 100; (ca. 4 ha probably built over in LH)
101 (71)	Nerómilos: Viglítsa	*AJA* 1961, 246	1 km W-SW; at lower (E) end of sudden change of height in Kalamata-Pylos highway	Low artificial mound	CEM. Almost certain tholos (no pottery visible) 33 m diam. and 5 m high	LH	
102 (75E)	Péra: Kárkano	*AJA* 1969, 155	1 km N-NE; large cement basin and channel for water from spring at E foot	High hill	HAB	MH? LH (sparse)	150 m NE-SW × 120 (S and SE slopes) (1.8 ha)
103 (75A)	Kalochóri: Áyios Ilías	*AJA* 1964, 233	1½ km N; immed. N of Kalochori-Paniperi road	High spur projecting N over deep gorge	HAB. Remains of fortifications on E flank	MH LHIII (medium)	120 m N-S × 90 (top and E slope) (1.1 ha)
104 (75D)	Mathía: Pirgáki	*AJA* 1964, 234	400 m N-NE; on N side of road to coast	Medium hill high above coastal plain	HAB?	MH? LH?	50 m × 50 (0.3 ha)
105 (75F)	Vígla: Áyios Ilías	*AJA* 1969, 155–56	300 m W	High ridge; chapel on E end	HAB	LHIIIB (medium)	200 m E-W × 80 (E top and E slopes) (1.6 ha)
106 (75C)	Longá: Paliókastro	*AJA* 1964, 234	1 km S-SW	High steep hill between ravines; cave on S side	HAB. Obsidian, chert	N?; MH (sparse)	Unclear
107 (75)	Longá: Kafirió	*JHS Arch Reports* 1960–61, 11; *AJA* 1961, 248	1 km S-SW	High spur projecting E over coastal plain	HAB. CEM? Probable tholos under chapel of Ayios Ilias 500 m NW; H and R bldgs. with mosaics reported in lower ground toward village	MH? LHIII PG; G?; A? C; H; R (medium)	180 m E-W × 100 (mainly N and E slopes) (1.8 ha)

REGISTER A

I Communications	J Strategic Features	K Water Supply	L Land: Total	M Land: Percentage Cultivated	N Land: Irrigated	O Population	P Special Features
Crossroads (land); well-protected harbor at Petalidhi ca. 4 km SE; ca. 2 km to nearest point on coast	Commands pass on southern highway between W and E Messenia; very strong defensive position; exceptionally wide view	Copious spring 800 m NW; Karia (Skarias) River immed. to E with perennial flow (12,420 lpm flow); Velika River 1½ km farther E with perennial flow	3.1 km radius; 3,019 ha	80	376 ha	520 (595 total in 2 modern villages bracketing site)	Acropolis tested by Yalouris and McDonald (1959); salvage excavations in cemeteries by Yalouris, Papathanasopoulos, Choremis, Karayeorya 1960ff.; excavation of acropolis by UMME 1969ff.
Mainline (land); 6 km to sea							
Secondary (land); 5 km to sea		Copious spring at E foot	3.5 km radius; 3,848 ha	85	25 ha	234	
Isolated (land); 7 km to sea	Natural fortress with extensive view to N and W	Perennial stream in gorge below	2.5 km radius; 1,963 ha	85	3 ha	143	
Isolated (land); 3 km to sea	Excellent lookout to NE, E, and SE		3.9 km radius; 4,778 ha	70	16 ha	39	
Isolated (land); 1 km to sea	Magnificent view to coast far below	Streams to N and S have some water in early summer; nearest village depends on well	2.4 km radius; 1,810 ha	80		208	
Very isolated (land); 2 km to sea		Small spring at S foot	2.4 km radius; 1,810 ha	80			
Mainline (land); good (sea), 1 km		Small spring on E slope; copious spring 3½ km W and higher	2.8 km radius; 2,463 ha	85		234	Tested by Yalouris and McDonald (1959) and shown to be very badly eroded

A Number	B Name	C Bibliography	D Location	E Physical Description	F Archaeological Description	G Analysis of Pottery	H Extent
108 (74B)	Falánthi: Panória	*AJA* 1969, 155	200 m NW; at sharp bend in road just above (E of) spring of Ayia Pelayia	Low ridge	HAB	LH (sparse; much recent material)	100 m N-S × 60 (0.6 ha)
109 (74)	Charokopió: Demotic School	*Ergon* 1958, 154; *AJA* 1961, 247; 1964, 233	300 m NW; immed. S of school bldg.	Top of low hill	HAB-CEM. Tholos 120 m N illicitly dug and partially destroyed; probable tholos 1 km N (outskirts of Petriadhes); R bath and funeral stele near Kandirogli to W	LHIIIB C; H; R (sparse)	ca. 150 m E-W × 100 (min.) (1.5 ha)
110 (74A)	Áyios Isídhoros: Lioftákia	*AJA* 1969, 154–55	1½ km S	S edge of low ridge; on edge of fertile country to N	HAB? Foreign stones	LH? (sparse)	100 m × 100 (1 ha max.)
111 (74C)	Chrisokellariá: Áyios Athanásios	*AJA* 1969, 155	100 m NW; on and above site of school bldg.	Medium hill	HAB	LH C?; H? (medium)	150 m N-NE × 100 (top and S-SW terraces) (1.5 ha)
112 (76B)	Velíka: Skordhákis	*AJA* 1964, 234	1½ km SE; on E bank of Velika River and 500 m from mouth	Very low hill (10 m a.s.l.)	HAB	MH LHIII C?; H? (sparse)	120 m N-S × 70 (0.8 ha)
113 (76A)	Velíka: Kókora Troúpa	*AJA* 1964, 234	1½ km NW; in cliff on E bank of Velika River where it emerges from narrow gorge	Medium sized cave	HAB. Animal bones	N LHIIIC	
114 (76D)	Dára: Viglítsa	*AJA* 1964, 234–35	600 m SE; 100 m W of Rizomilo-Dara road	Medium hill	HAB. Frags. of obsidian	MH LH (medium)	150 m E-W × 100 (1.5 ha)
115 (76F)	Stréfi: Garalavoúni (or Galaravoúni)	*Deltion* 1965, 207; *AJA* 1969, 156	1 km N-NW; 100 m NE of Strefi-Dhiodhia track	Low hill; artificial mound near SE edge	HAB-CEM. Collapsed tholos ca. 8 m diam. at SE edge of hill; obsidian; marble statue base of R times (chance find in or near village)	EH LHIIIA–IIIB R (medium)	150 m NW-SE × 100 (toward NW end of hill and 100 m from tholos) (1.5 ha)
116 (34)	Maryéli: Koutsovéri	*AJA* 1961, 235; *Deltion* 1969, 143	500 m N-NW	High hill in sheltered valley	HAB. Tremendous stone piles (some probably foreign); H lamps reported from spot called Farmá Ráchi	MH LH? H (medium)	150 m × 150 (rounded top) max. (2.2 ha)
117 (36)	Flesiádha: Koufiéro	*AJA* 1961, 235–36; 1969, 145	1 km E-NE	Large cave (40 m × 9) ca. 100 m above stream; facing NW to Palio Loutro across gorge	HAB. Frags. of worked chert	N LHII?–IIIA–IIIB (sparse)	

REGISTER A

I Communications	J Strategic Features	K Water Supply	L Land: Total	M Land: Percentage Cultivated	N Land: Irrigated	O Population	P Special Features
Secondary (land); 3 km to sea		Good spring at W foot	3.1 km radius; 3,019 ha	90		78	
Secondary (land); fair (sea), 2 km	Center of extremely fertile area (now almost entirely in vines)		2.3 km radius; 1,662 ha	95		195	Bronze cauldron (in Kalamata museum) salvaged from tholos and sword reportedly found; Marinatos later cleared remains of structure; pithos frags. and rim of bronze vessel 0.235 diam. from probable tholos
Isolated (land); fair (sea), 2 km		Two springs in stream bed immed. to S (one supplies Koroni)	2.3 km radius; 1,662 ha	95		130	
Isolated (land); 3 km to sea	Spectacular view down to S, E, and N	Fair springs 150 m SW and 300 m S	3.0 km radius; 2,827 ha	70	10 ha	195	
Isolated? (land); fair (sea)		Perennial river	2.0 km radius; 1,257 ha	95	30 ha	104	
Very isolated (land); 3 km to sea		Perennial river	2.7 km radius; 2,290 ha	95			
Secondary (land); 7 km to sea		Small springs immed. NE and 100 m E	3.9 km radius; 4,778 ha	90	17 ha	195	
Mainline? (land); 11 km to sea	Highest point in fertile plateau	Fair spring 200 m SW	4.5 km radius; 6,362 ha	90	20 ha	195	Pottery quality suggests close connections with major centers
Isolated? (land); 17 km to sea		Fair spring 300 m S-SE	4.3 km radius; 4,301 ha	60		286	
Isolated (land); 17 km to sea		Spring-fed river immed. below					Quite possibly a sanctuary in LH (modern chapel of Ayii Anaryiri inside)

REGISTER A

A Number	B Name	C Bibliography	D Location	E Physical Description	F Archaeological Description	G Analysis of Pottery	H Extent
118 (35)	Chalvátsou: Kástro	*AJA* 1961, 235	2 km S-SE; immed. E of Aristomenis-Chalvatsou road	High hill	HAB	MH? LH? M (sparse prehistoric)	300 m N-S × 150 (prehistoric on SW terraces; M on top and slopes) (4.5 ha)
119 (35A)	Dhraïna: Koutsovéri	*AJA* 1969, 144	1 km N-NW; immed. W of Draina-Koromilea road	Medium spur projecting W over valley	HAB. Frags. of worked obsidian and chert	MH LHIII (and earlier?) (medium)	120 m NW × 80 (flat top and upper S slopes) (1.0 ha)
120 (35B)	Manganiakó: Paliámbela	*AJA* 1969, 144–45	400 m NE	Three low knolls	HAB. Foundations of ancient bldgs. in several spots	LHIII (heavy)	200 m NE-SW × 130 (top and upper E slopes) (2.6 ha)
121 (76G)	Tríkorfo: Kakó Kataráchi	*AJA* 1969, 157	2 km S-SW; immed. S of water channel	Low hill	HAB. Foreign stones	LHIII (and earlier?) C (medium)	150 m NE-SW × 120 (top and SE terraces) (1.8 ha)
122 (77B)	Lámbaina: Tourkokívouro	*AJA* 1964, 235–36; 1969, 157–58; *Deltion* 1964, 153–54	1 km E-SE; immed. NE of tile factory on E side of highway	Low rolling ground	HAB? CEM. Slab grave	EH LH G	
123 (77A[1])	Aristodhímion: Paliámbeles	*AJA* 1964, 235; Loy (1970) 116–25	500 m SE; immed. above (W of) road to Plati	Low terrace sloping SE over valley alluvium	HAB. Burial mound called Tourkoskotoméno ca. 200 m SE; M architectural frags. in area to S	LHIIIB M (heavy)	90 m E-W × 30 (min.) (0.3 ha)
124 (77A[2])	Aristodhímion: Glikorízi	see #123	700 m SE; immed. below (E of) road to Plati	Low mound	HAB. CEM? Probable cemetery in vicinity of modern cemetery ca. 100 m NE of village	EH (bricks in ruined bldg. on mound made of local clay and full of sherds)	120 m E-W × 70 (max.) (0.8 ha)
125 (77C)	Éva: Nekrotafíon	*AJA* 1964, 236	300 m E-SE; 100 m W of modern cemetery	Medium spur projecting E over valley	HAB. Roof tiles	MH LHIII C (sparse)	150 m E-W × 100 (1.5 ha)
126 (77E)	Áris: Mesovoúni	*AJA* 1969, 158	1.8 km SE; 800 m E of Pamisos River and immed. E of intersection of road and railroad	Low hill	HAB	MH? LHII?–IIIA–IIIB (sparse)	200 m E-W × 80 (center and E) (1.6 ha)
127 (77D)	Vournázi: Baroutospiliá	*AJA* 1969, 158	ca. 3 km N of Andhrousa at point where Liyidhi gorge widens	Cave in NE face of cliff; some rock falls; present dimensions 200 m wide × 6 m high × 10 m deep	HAB. Obsidian	N C	

REGISTER A

I Communications	J Strategic Features	K Water Supply	L Land: Total	M Land: Percentage Cultivated	N Land: Irrigated	O Population	P Special Features
Isolated (land); 18 km to sea		Small spring on W slope; copious spring S of Chalvatsou; river in valley to W	3.9 km radius; 4,778 ha	55	45 ha	585 (max.)	
Secondary (land); 18 km to sea		Several small springs in valley to S	3.5 km radius; 3,848 ha	60	25 ha	130	
Secondary (land); 18 km to sea	Fine view down toward gulf to SE	Good spring 400 m SW	4.0 km radius; 5,027 ha	60	5 ha	338	
Secondary (land); 15 km to sea		Copious spring 200 m NW (supplies (Trikorfo)	4.2 km radius; 5,542 ha	85	15 ha	234	
Mainline (land); 14 km to sea			3.7 km radius; 4,301 ha				Being used as clay pit for tile factory; trial excavation by Papathanasopoulos established stratification
Mainline (land); 13 km to sea	At W end of probable ford over Pamisos	Spring 250 m E-NE (50 lpm); swamp further E (738 lpm)	1.9 km radius; 1,134 ha	95	18 ha	39 (min.), 100 (max.)	Slightly higher above river than #124
see #123	see #123	see #123	see #123	see #123			
Mainline (land); 10 km to sea		Small spring 500 m E	3.9 km radius; 4,778 ha	90	14 ha	195	
Mainline (land); 7 km to sea	Best location for town controlling river ford on southernmost route across Pamisos Valley	Perennial river	2.7 km radius; 2,290 ha	95		208	
14 km to sea							

REGISTER A

A Number	B Name	C Bibliography	D Location	E Physical Description	F Archaeological Description	G Analysis of Pottery	H Extent
128 (77)	Karteróli: Áyios Konstandínos	Valmin 1930, 64; *BSA* 1957, 246; 1966, 124; *AJA* 1961, 249–50	500 m E-NE; near intersection of Karteroli-Piperitsa road with main highway	Several medium hills NW and NE of intersection	HAB? CEM. Extensive cemetery of chamber tombs (9 certain and 4 probable) on slopes of hills, especially that with chapel of Ayios Konstandinos; habitation probable on Rachi Papoulia NE of intersection	LHIIIA–IIIB	Unclear
129 (77F)	Mavrományti: Panayiá	*AJA* 1969, 158	500 m NE	Low ridge immed. W of highway leading N from Messini	HAB	EH LH (medium)	90 m E-W × 50 (0.5 ha)
130 (76C)	Messíni: Méxa	*AJA* 1964, 234	4 km S-SW; 400 m N of old customhouse (Bouka) on W side of road to sea	Low hill; ca. 500 m from present coast	HAB	EH? (sparse)	70 m E-W × 40 (0.3 ha)
131 (76E)	Mádhena: Áyios Konstandínos	*Deltion* 1965, 207; *AJA* 1969, 156	Contiguous to S	See category F	HAB? CEM. Destroyed chamber tomb along track S of village; habitation site probably on ridge above; R bath?	LHIIIC R (sparse)	
132 (78D)	Áyios Flóros: Kamária	*AJA* 1969, 159	600 m N-NW; 200 m W of Kalamata-Megalopolis highway	Low hill crowned with chapel of Panayia	HAB. Chert fragments	EH LHIIIB H? (medium)	150 m N-S × 100 (max.) (1.5 ha)
133 (78E)	Tsoukaléïka	*AJA* 1961, 255; 1969, 159–60; Valmin 1930, 71–74; Roebuck 1941, 4, 13; *Deltion* 1965, 207	Immed. NE of village	Very high isolated hill	CEM? Grave group said to come from vicinity	PG	
134 (78C)	Áyios Flóros	*AJA* 1964, 236–37	Contiguous to E	Medium knoll	HAB	MH? LH? (sparse)	150 m E-W × 80 (1.2 ha)
135 (78A)	Platí: Petroyéfira	*AJA* 1961, 255; 1964, 236	1 km W-SW; immed. E of bridge over Pamisos	Low hill (cut through by road)	HAB	LHIII (sparse)	Unclear
136 (78B)	Pídhima: Áyios Ioánnis	Valmin 1930, 53; *AJA* 1964, 236	700 m S; on W side of road and SW of chapel of Ayios Ioannis	Low terrace within 100 m of main spring and barely above level of present marsh	HAB. Frags. of obsidian	LHI–II–III (medium) A? C (heavy on E side of road) M (on sheltered site high above reservoir)	250 m E-W × 160 (4 ha)

REGISTER A

I Communications	J Strategic Features	K Water Supply	L Land: Total	M Land: Percentage Cultivated	N Land: Irrigated	O Population	P Special Features
Mainline (land); 6 km to sea			2.4 km radius; 1,810 ha	95			
Mainline (land); 5 km to sea			2.3 km radius; 1,662 ha	95		65	
Isolated (land); fair (sea)			1.8 km radius; 1,018 ha	95			
Mainline? (land); 4 km to sea		Small spring in valley to S	4.1 km radius; 5,081 ha	95			Contents saved from chamber tomb now in Kalamata museum
Mainline? (land); 17 km to sea	Dominating greatest water source in Messenia	Tremendous springs just to SE	3.5 km radius; 3,848 ha	75		195 (max.)	Probably most of land too wet for cultivation
							Vases chance find; Valmin later conceded fortifications probably modern
Mainline (land); 16 km to sea		Tremendous springs form source of Pamisos River; mean flow at 4.8 m^3/sec.	3.1 km radius; 3,019 ha	75		156	
Mainline (land); 13 km to sea	Probably river crossing here (ruins of previous bridge)	Fair spring immed. S; perennial river	3.3 km radius; 3,421 ha	95			
Mainline? (land); 13 km to sea	Fine water source supplies modern Kalamata	Mean flow 1.2 m^3/sec.	4.2 km radius; 5,542 ha	70		520	

REGISTER A

A Number	B Name	C Bibliography	D Location	E Physical Description	F Archaeological Description	G Analysis of Pottery	H Extent
137 (78)	Áithaia: Elliniká	*Bull Lund* 1928/29, 1–31; Valmin 1930, 56–62; Roebuck 1941, 30–31; Frazer III 424–25; Hope Simpson 1957, 234–35; 1966, 121–24; *AJA* 1961, 250–51; 1964, 239; 1969, 158–59; *Deltion* 1965, 207	800 m N-NE	High ridge; exceeds 1 km N-S and parallel to highway	HAB-CEM. LH habitation on S top and SW slopes; EH on SW terrace; C on N top; 26 LH chamber tombs on E slopes at center; tholos ca. 600 m to SW; 2 possible tholos mounds across Xeropotamos gorge to E; well-preserved fortification and terrace walls (probably early H); inscriptions, cistern, temple	EH; MH LHIIIA–IIIB–IIIC? PG; G?; A? C; H; R (medium)	400 m N-S × 150 (LH) (6 ha); 90 m N-S × 70 (EH)
138 (79E)	Artemísia: Vólimnos	*BCH* 1959, 641; *AJA* 1961, 255; Hope Simpson 1966, 121	5 km W-NW (guide needed); chapel of Panayia	High terraces below chapel	HAB. Bronze harpy from C vase	LH?; SM? PG; G; A C; H (heavy)	200 m N-S × 100 (max.) (2 ha)
139 (79B)	Thouría: Áyios Athanásios	*AJA* 1969, 160	800 m E; 200 m NE of chapel of Ayios Athanasios	Low knoll (barn on summit)	HAB. CEM? Frags. of obsidian; probable cemetery 500 m SW near concrete cistern	MH? LH?	100 m N-S × 60 (0.6 ha)
140 (79C)	Perivolákia: Sóla (ancient Kalamai?)	*AM* 1894, 360–63; *Arch Eph* 1911, 117; Roebuck 1941, 122–24; *BSA* 1966, 119; Hope Simpson 1966, 118–19; *AJA* 1969, 160	300 m N	Medium hill	HAB. On SW slope at spot called Marmara squared blocks and inscriptions	LHIII H?; R (sparse)	100 m NNE-SSW × 80 (0.8 ha)
141 (79A)	Kalamáta: Toúrles	*AJA* 1961, 251; 1964, 237; 1969, 160	Contiguous to NE; 500 m E-NE of Kastro and immed. N of Sparta road	Medium hill	HAB. House foundations	EH? LHIII C (medium)	200 m NE-SW × 100 (summit and SE terraces) (2 ha)
142 (79)	Kalamáta: Kástro (Homeric Pherai)	*Arch Eph* 1911, 107–18; Valmin 1930, 45–55; *BCH* 1959, 632–36; *AJA* 1961, 251; 1964, 237; *Deltion* 1961–62, 96; 1968, 156	Within city (NE sector)	Medium hill; fine flat-topped acropolis; heavily built over in later periods	HAB-CEM. Archaic inscriptions in Nedhon gorge; traces of ancient walls in Kastro; heavy foundations of H bldgs. excavated under plateia S of Kastro; section of city walls (4th c. B.C.?) N of Kastro; late R grave; lamps, terracotta statuettes, vases, reliefs of A through R (mainly from graves?)	LHIIIA–IIIB G; A C; H; R; M (sparse)	
143 (79D)	Vérga: Kastráki	*AJA* 1969, 160	Contiguous to NW	Medium ridge across gully from village (whole area high above gulf)	HAB	LH (heavy)	100 m × 100 (W terraces) (1 ha)
144 (80A)	Mikrá Mandínia: Áyios Yeóryios	*AJA* 1961, 255; 1969, 160–61	500 m NW	Medium hill with chapel of Áyios Yeóryios	HAB? C roof tiles around chapel and on W facing terraces to N and E	LH? C (sparse)	120 m E-W × 80 (0.7 ha)
145 (80)	Pigádhia: Kokkinochómata	Hope Simpson 1957, 240; *AJA* 1961, 251	ca. 4.5 km W	Collapsed cave	HAB? CEM? Human bones	N?; EH? MH? LHI–II–IIIA–IIIB–IIIC SM? PG?	

REGISTER A

I Communications	J Strategic Features	K Water Supply	L Land: Total	M Land: Percentage Cultivated	N Land: Irrigated	O Population	P Special Features
Mainline (land); 8 km to sea	Large but defensible acropolis; road to pass through Taygetos Mts. skirts N end of acropolis	2 small springs on W slopes; river to E	2.8 km radius; 2,463 ha	90		780 (LH)	
Very isolated (land); 13 km to sea		Well near chapel	5.0 km radius; 7,854 ha	5		260	Probable refuge site and shrine
Mainline (land); 7 km to sea		Fair spring near cemetery(?)	3.4 km radius; 3,632 ha	85		78	
Isolated (land); 5 km to sea	Superb view to Kalamata area	Fair spring 400 m SE	5.0 km radius; 7,854 ha	20		104	Inscriptions support Kalamai equation
Mainline (land); excellent (sea), 3 km			2.6 km radius; 2,124 ha	80		260	
Mainline (land); excellent (sea), 2½ km distant	Controls approach to fertile Pamisos Valley from sea		2.6 km radius; 2,124 ha	80			
Close to mainline (land); excellent (sea), 1 km	Secluded lookout over Kalamata area and gulf	Good spring in gully to E	3.0 km radius; 2,827 ha	35		130	
Secondary (land); fair (sea), 1 km		Good spring 500 m SE	3.0 km radius; 2,827 ha	65		91	
Isolated (land); 7 km to sea			5.0 km radius; 7,854 ha	30	5 ha		

REGISTER A

A Number	B Name	C Bibliography	D Location	E Physical Description	F Archaeological Description	G Analysis of Pottery	H Extent
146 (81)	Kámbos: Zarnáta	*Arch Eph* 1891, 189–91; Roebuck 1941, 31; *BSA* 1957, 236–39; 1958, 239; 1966, 114; *AJA* 1961, 251; *Deltion* 1967, 206–7	600 m W; highway to Kardhamili winds around it	High hill	HAB? CEM. Tholos tomb 8.50 m in diam. excavated on E slope below highway; H walls on acropolis above highway; inscriptions; R head; caves at spot called Koutalas ca. 3½ km SW said to have N pottery	N? LHII–IIIA–IIIB C; H; R; M	Location of LH habitation unclear but presumably centered on acropolis
147 (82)	Kardhamíli: Kástro (Homeric and later Kardamyle)	*Bull Lund* 1928/29, 42–44; Valmin 1930, 198; Roebuck 1941, 31; Hope Simpson 1957, 234–46; 1966, 114; *BCH* 1959, 639; *AJA* 1961, 251; *Deltion* 1965, 208; 1967, 206	800 m NE	High flat-topped acropolis	HAB-CEM. Rock-cut tombs; walls (C or earlier), stairs, roof, tiles; A or C architectural fragments; coins, lamps, statuettes	N?; EH?; MH? LH SM; A C; H; R; M	300 m E-W × 200 (max.) (6 ha)
148 (83)	Stoúpa: Lévtro	Valmin 1930, 203; Hope Simpson 1957, 232; *BSA* 1957, 234; *BCH* 1959, 640; *Deltion* 1960, 108; *AJA* 1961, 251	400 m E-SE	Medium flat-topped acropolis	HAB-CEM. At N foot chamber tomb apparently destroyed; antiquities of C and later toward sea and village; numerous R mosaics in vicinity	MH? LH C; H; R; M	250 E-W × 200 (max. on summit) (5 ha)
149 (83A)	Áyios Dhimítrios: Vígla	*AJA* 1964, 237; Hope Simpson 1966, 113	Contiguous to S	Easy terraces sloping down to low cliffs above sea	HAB	LHIII (sparse)	200 m N-S × 100 (2 ha)
150 (84)	Koutífari: Svína (ancient Thalamai)	*BSA* 1904–5, 124–36; Hope Simpson 1957, 232–33; *BCH* 1959, 641; *Deltion* 1960, 107–8	Contiguous to E	Terraces above village	HAB. C walls; head of terracotta statuette (7th c. B.C.?); A marble head; handle of bronze vase; silver earrings	LH PG?; G?; A C; H; R	Unclear
151	Kalamáta: Akovítika	*BCH* 1959, 639–40; *AAA* 1969, 352–57; *AM* 1968, 175–85	ca. 4 km WNW; on E bank of Pamisos and ca. 800 m from coast	Flat marshy delta; very little above present sea level; water 0.5 m below surface and area much disturbed by recent drainage and irrigation project	HAB. Well-preserved foundations of two major and several minor EH bldgs.; only 200 m SE foundations of large rectangular bldg. with peristyle, probably shrine of Poseidon; destroyed end of 7th c. B.C. and rebuilt; bronze workshop; Doric capital; G horse; A statuettes; C bronze statuettes	EH G; A C; H; R (EH pottery and small finds very sparse)	Unclear; this discovery proves coastline has changed little since 3rd millennium B.C.
200 (22B)	Mírou: Peristeriá	*JHS Arch Reports* 1960, 5; *Ergon* 1964, 85–90; 1965, 84–92; *Praktika* 1965, 109–20; *BCH* 1965, 734; *Deltion* 1966, 166–68; *AJA* 1969, 133	1 km N	High spur overlooking Kyparissia River to N	HAB-CEM. 2 tholos tombs apparently within settlement; rich burial(s) associated; MH tumulus with pithos burials 500 m W	MH LHI–II–IIIA–IIIB C; H; R	
201 (22A)	Mouriatádha: Ellinikó (Lolling's candidate for Homeric Dorion)	*Praktika* 1960, 201–6; *Ergon* 1960, 149–52; *Deltion* 1960, 116–17; *AJA* 1969, 133; Lolling 1889, 99, in Müller's *Handbook*, Vol. III	1 km E	Medium spur	HAB-CEM. Ruined fortification wall in Cyclopean style; large bldg. on crest may be megaron; "temple" on S slope; tholos 200 m E	LHIIIB–IIIC	

REGISTER A

I Communications	J Strategic Features	K Water Supply	L Land: Total	M Land: Percentage Cultivated	N Land: Irrigated	O Population	P Special Features
Secondary (land); 5 km to sea			5.0 km radius; 7,854 ha	50	25 ha		Tholos excavated by Tsountas (seals, beads, ivory, steatite, lead figurines)
Secondary (land); fair (sea)		River immed. N	3.6 km radius; 4,071 ha	65	35 ha	720 (max.)	Unusually retentive name
Secondary (land); fair (sea)		Critical now (grain does not mature)	3.4 km radius; 3,632 hs	90		650 (max.)	
Secondary (land); fair (sea)		Fair spring at water's edge in village	2.9 km radius; 2,647 ha	70		260	
2 km to sea		2 springs	3.6 km radius; 4,071 ha	40			
Isolated (land); probably excellent (sea)	Protection of delta marshes?	Perennial river	Marshy area difficult or impossible to cultivate				Plan of major EH bldgs. reminiscent of House of Tiles at Lerna; excavated by Themelis and Karayeorya
Mainline (land); 5 km to sea	Strong defensive position; controlling major E-W route	Copious spring at foot of hill; perennial river	3.4 km radius; 3,632 ha	75	20 ha		Excavated by Marinatos
Mainline (land); 7 km to sea			3.6 km radius; 4,071 ha	45	60 ha		Excavated by Marinatos

REGISTER A

A Number	B Name	C Bibliography	D Location	E Physical Description	F Archaeological Description	G Analysis of Pottery	H Extent
202 (22D)	Sellás: Nekrotafíon	*AJA* 1969, 133	500 m SW; cemetery along road above village	W end of high spur	HAB	MH LH? (medium)	150 m E-W × 80 (top and upper S terraces) (1.2 ha)
203 (28B)	Konchílion: Kástro	*AJA* 1969, 141–42	300 m W-SW	High hill	HAB. Thick wall (probably ancient) enclosing oval area in higher E part; recent (Turkish?) fort at NE end; traces of bldg. (probably ancient) in SW of enclosure	MH LHIII (medium)	150 m NNE-SSW × 70 (1.5 ha)
204 (28C)	Neochóri: Koúnoura	*AJA* 1969, 142	700 m SW; 200 m S of Neochori-Zerbisia road	Low slopes immed. above (S of) stream	HAB	LHIII (sparse)	150 m E-W × 100 (1.5 ha)
205 (32D)	Steníklaros: Káto Ráchi	*AJA* 1969, 144	1½ km SE; on S side of Steniklaros-Magoula road; 200 m E of ruined chapel	Low hill at E end of cluster of hills	HAB	LH (medium)	100 m × 100 (max.) on hilltop (1 ha)
206 (32C)	Meligalá: Áyios Ilías	*AJA* 1969, 143–44	Within town; on site of church of Ayios Ilias (clock tower)	Highest (NW) part of medium isolated hill	HAB. Wall foundations (probably ancient)	MH LHIII (and earlier?) (medium)	80 m E-W × 50 (min.) top(?) and SW slope (0.4 ha)
207 (32B)	Katsaroú: Áyios Ilías	*AJA* 1964, 232	1½ km W-SW; NE of junction of Katsarou side road with Kalamata-Megalopolis highway; chapel of Ayios Ilias on summit	Medium isolated hill	HAB	MH? LH (sparse)	
208 (32A)	Siámou: Paliochóri	*AJA* 1964, 231–32; 1969, 143	400 m N	Low hill	HAB. Terrace walls on W could be ancient	MH? LHIII (sparse)	50 m × 50 (0.3 ha)
209 (32)	Loutró: Karatsádhes	*AJA* 1961, 235; Valmin 1930, 39; *RE* Suppl. VI, 607	800 m E; immed. N of Xerias River	Very low mound(?) ca. 200 m diam.	CEM. HAB? Slab-lined cist and pithos burials	EH?; MH? LH?	
210 (33A)	Kalívia: Páno Chorió	*Deltion* 1967, 206; *AJA* 1969, 144	300 m E	High hill	HAB-CEM. 100 m S of village destroyed chamber (?) tomb from which LHIII piriform jar, alabastron, electrum beads, gold leaf; possible tholos 200 m SW (chapel of Ayios Ilias); R and Venetian coins said to come from acropolis	LHIIIB (and earlier?) R?; M? (heavy)	180 m N-S × 120 (top and upper W terraces) (2.2 ha)

REGISTER A

I Communications	J Strategic Features	K Water Supply	L Land: Total	M Land: Percentage Cultivated	N Land: Irrigated	O Population	P Special Features
Secondary? (land); 12 km to sea	Commands difficult route linking Kyparissia River valley with interior to S and E	Copious springs 500 m NE	5.0 km radius; 7,854 ha	50	181 ha	156	Both pottery and location suggest "provincial" status
Secondary? (land); 20 km to sea		Fair spring 300 m E-NE	4.2 km radius; 5,542 ha	45	20 ha	195	
Secondary (land); 22 km to sea		2 small springs in streambed	3.0 km radius; 2,827 ha	85		195	
Secondary (land); 24 km to sea	Possible river crossing	Small spring 900 m W-NW; Mavrozoumenos River flows around site (300 m E)	2.6 km radius; 2,124 ha	90	120 ha	130	
Mainline (land); 24 km to sea	Commands S end of upper Pamisos Valley and major ancient and modern crossing of Mavrozoumenos River	River 1 km W	2.7 km radius; 2,290 ha	90		52 (min.)	
Mainline (land); 22 km to sea	Controlled N-S traffic on E side of Pamisos Valley		4.9 km radius; 5,027 ha	80			Site first identified by Hood (1961)
Secondary (land); 24 km to sea		Small spring at NW foot; another 1 km NW	3.1 km radius; 3,019 ha	65		39	
Secondary (land); 26 km to sea		River immed. to S	4.2 km radius; 5,542 ha	85			
Secondary (land); 24 km to sea		Good spring 500 m to N; small spring immed. to S	3.7 km radius; 4,301 ha	70		286	Salvage by ephorate

REGISTER A

A Number	B Name	C Bibliography	D Location	E Physical Description	F Archaeological Description	G Analysis of Pottery	H Extent
211 (33)	Loutró: Kók-kala (C Ampheia?)	Valmin 1939, 42; 1930, 74–78; *AJA* 1961, 235	ca. 5 km E	High hill	HAB? Valmin reports prehistoric walls, G(?) sherds, N celts, obsidian	N?; EH? LH? G?	
212 (29)	Políchni: Áyios Taxíarchos (classical Andania?)	*Bull Lund* 1928/29, 34; Valmin 1930, 92, 93, 97; *AJA* 1961, 234	400 m N; ruins of M convent on summit	High hill	HAB. C sherds in Kalamata museum said to come from here; inscriptions	MH? LHI–III C (medium)	250 m NNW-SSE × 100 (2.5 ha)
213 (31B)	Parapoúngi: Áyios Yeóryios	*AJA* 1964, 231; Loy 1970, 106–15	400 m NE; N of railroad and S of chapel of Ayios Yeoryios	S terraces of high spur (225 m above plain)	HAB. Obsidian	MH LHIII (medium)	100 m N-S × 60 (0.6 ha)
214 (31C)	Dhiavolítsi: Loútses	*Deltion* 1964, 154; *AJA* 1964, 231; 1969, 143	800 m W-SW	Low hill	HAB-CEM. Chamber tomb destroyed by construction near railroad station 800 m E-NE	MH? LHIIIB M (medium)	Unclear
215 (31A)	Agrilóvouno: Áyios Nikólaos	*AJA* 1964, 231	Contiguous to N	High hill; chapel of Ayios Nikolaos on summit	HAB. Foreign stones; column base (not in situ)	MH LHIIIB (medium)	190 m N-S × 40 (top); probably also upper S and E slopes (0.8 ha min.)
216 (31)	Káto Mélpia: Krebení	*AJA* 1964, 234–35	400 m N; chapel of Ayios Dhimitrios at E edge	High steep terraces facing SW toward village and plain	HAB. C-H ruins including terrace walls, stairways, door jambs and threshold blocks, loomweights; Frankish fort above (N)	MH? LHIIIA?–IIIB–IIIC A? C; H (heavy, but mainly C)	600 m E-W × 300 (prehistoric probably much less) (9 ha max.)
217 (30)	Mándhra: Chazná	*RE* Suppl. VI, 607; *AJA* 1961, 234; 1969, 142	200 m W-SW	Low ridge	HAB-CEM. Ruined tholos (ca. 13 m diam.) 20 m SW of church of Ayios Yeoryios	EH?; MH? LH (sparse)	100 m E-W × 50 (min.); pottery found on N slopes only, but top may have been included (0.5 ha)
218 (28D)	Míla: Profítis Ilías	*AJA* 1969, 142	700 m N-NE; chapel of Ayios Ilias on summit	High spur projecting E	HAB	LH (sparse)	100 m E-W × 80 (max.) (0.8 ha)
219 (28E)	Kástro: Kástro tou Míla (M Chateauneuf?)	*AJA* 1969, 142	200 m N	High hill	HAB. Frankish fort	MH? LH M (prehistoric sparse)	100 m × 100 (min.) (1 ha)
220 (28)	Vasilikó: Xerovrísi	Valmin 1926–27, 88, 89; 1927–28, 171–224; *AJA* 1961, 234	1½ km S-SE; immed. N of railroad	Rolling country sloping S	CEM. One tholos with side chamber excavated; possible tholoi reported 150 m SE and 250 m SW	LHI–II	

REGISTER A

I Communications	J Strategic Features	K Water Supply	L Land: Total	M Land: Percentage Cultivated	N Land: Irrigated	O Population	P Special Features
Mainline (land); 27 km to sea	Controls major Leondari pass between Messenia and Lakonia						
Mainline (land); 21 km to sea	Controls (with #219) E end of pass from Steniklaros Valley to Soulima and Kyparissia River valley	Good springs	3.9 km radius; 4,778 ha	85	105 ha	325	
Secondary? (land); 26 km to sea		Copious (720 lpm) spring 200 m W; fair (11 lpm) spring 100 m E	4.3 km radius; 5,809 ha	65	7 ha	78	So-called Adriatic ware very prominent in surface collections
Secondary (land); 25 km to sea		Copious spring 900 m E-NE	2.4 km radius; 1,810 ha	95	10 ha		Salvage of tomb contents by ephorate
Secondary (land); 22 km to sea	Commands access to NW extension of Pamisos Valley	Small spring on S flank	2.1 km radius; 1,385 ha	85		104	
Isolated (land); 21 km to sea		Magnificent spring immed. to W	3.7 km radius; 4,301 ha	60	312 ha	1,170 (probably much too high for prehistoric)	
Isolated (land); 20 km to sea		Two good springs 800 m S	3.0 km radius; 2,827 ha	60	20 ha	65	
Secondary (land); 19 km to sea		Good spring 700 m S-SW; two small springs closer to NW and SE	2.9 km radius; 2,642 ha	65		104	
Mainline (land); 20 km to sea	Commands (with #212) E end of pass from Steniklaros Valley to Soulima and Kyparissia River valley	Small spring 1 km SE	2.4 km radius; 1,810 ha	85		130	
Mainline (land); 20 km to sea							Excavated by Valmin

REGISTER A

A Number	B Name	C Bibliography	D Location	E Physical Description	F Archaeological Description	G Analysis of Pottery	H Extent
221 (28A)	Vasilikó: Veïzi	*AJA* 1969, 141	800 m S	Low ridge	HAB. Worked flint	MH? LH? (sparse)	
222 (27)	Vasilikó: Málthi (Homeric Dorion?)	*Bull Lund* 1926–27, 60–89; 1927–28, 171–224; 1933–34, 9–12; 1934–35, 1–42; Valmin 1938, *passim*; 1953, 29–46; *AJA* 1961, 233–34; *AJA* 1969, 141	1½ km W-NW	High hill at N end of ridge projecting into Soulima Valley	HAB-CEM. Upper area fortified in MH; habitation area inside fortifications completely excavated; two tholoi at S-SW foot (one uncollapsed)	N?; EH?; MH LHI–II–IIIA–IIIB (tholos 2 may have LHIIIC)	140 m N-S × 80 (1.1 ha)
223 (27A)	Málthi: Goúves	*Op Ath* I 1953, 29–46; II 1955, 66–74; *Deltion* 1960, 119–22; *AJA* 1969, 141	3½ km N-NE; only 100 m W of foot of hill #222	Low hill	HAB. Small area excavated showed closely spaced houses, stone reliefs	LHIIIB G?	200 m N-S × 150 (max.) (3 ha)
224 (27B)	Kókla: Ráchi Cháni	*Deltion* 1964, 154–55; *AJA* 1969, 141	Contiguous to N	Low hill (bisected by cut for new highway)	HAB-CEM. Large cemetery of simple cist graves from H and R times	EH; MH LH H; R (medium)	100 m × 100 (min. in LH) (1 ha)
225 (26B)	Aëtós: Palió-kastro	*AJA* 1969, 140	1 km E; immed. W of Aetos-Dhrosopiyi track	High hill crowned with M fort	HAB. Venetian coin	MH LH M (heavy)	100 m NW-SE × 80 (upper N and NE terraces) (0.8 ha)
226 (26)	Aëtós: Áyios Dhimítrios (A)	*Bull Lund* 1925–26, 57; Valmin 1930, 104, 117; *AJA* 1961, 233; *Deltion* 1964, 155	Within village	High terraces S and E of church of Ayios Dhimitrios	HAB? Terrace wall 60 m S of church could be prehistoric; C H R architectural frags.; R bldg.	LH? C; H; R	
227 (26A)	Aëtós: Áyios Dhimítrios (B)	*AJA* 1969, 140	1 km NW	Eminence toward N end of medium N-S ridge	HAB	MH? LH	80 m NNW-SSE × 50 (0.4 ha)
228 (24C)	Aëtós: Mourloú	*AJA* 1969, 140	4 km N-NE; 700 m S of main highway on W side of Aetos side-road	Low hill	HAB. Frags. of chert	MH LHIIIA?–IIIB	120 m ENE-WSW × 100 (1.5 ha)
229 (24B)	Káto Kopanáki: Chalíkia	*AJA* 1969, 140	1 km SW; marked by water tower	Medium ridge	HAB. Tiles	LH R	70 m NW-SE × 40 (upper NE slopes) (0.3 ha)

REGISTER A

I Communications	J Strategic Features	K Water Supply	L Land: Total	M Land: Percentage Cultivated	N Land: Irrigated	O Population	P Special Features
Secondary (land); 18 km to sea		Good spring immed. W	2.0 km radius; 1,257 ha	65			
Mainline (land); 17 km to sea	Commanding position on E-W route through Soulima Valley	Very copious (3,888 lpm) spring 1 km NW; good spring 1,100 m E; Klesouraïko River 1 km N	1.0 km radius; 314 ha	80	222 ha	143 (min.)	Very well-known site from Valmin's exploration and excavation
Mainline (land); 17 km to sea		see #222	1.1 km radius; 380 ha	70	31 ha	390 (max.)	This was probably lower town connected with #222 in LH times; excavated by Valmin
Mainline (land); 16 km to sea	Magnificent Kokla spring must be that mentioned by Pausanias (4. 33. 7) and called Achaia; a natural resting place on E-W highway from Steniklaros Valley to W coast	see #222	2.4 km radius; 1,810 ha	80	145 ha	130	This site or #223 has at least as good a claim as #222 to be Homeric Dorion; salvage by Yalouris
Secondary (land); 15 km to sea	Strong defensive position with wide view to NE and SE	Good spring 800 m SE	2.3 km radius; 1,662 ha	70	107 ha	104	
Secondary (land); 14 km to sea		Copious spring at NW edge of village	2.2 km radius; 1,520 ha	60	114 ha		
Secondary (land); 13 km to sea		Good spring 2½ km S and higher (channel now runs under W flank of site)	2.0 km radius; 1,256 ha	80	90 ha	52	
Mainline (land); 14 km to sea		Four small springs within 500 m S and SW	2.7 km radius; 2,290 ha	90		195	
Mainline (land); 11 km to sea		Good spring at SW foot; copious spring 800 m NE (source of Kyparissia River)	2.5 km radius; 1,963 ha	80	34 ha	39	Approximately on height of land in valley between Steniklaros Plain and west coast

REGISTER A

A Number	B Name	C Bibliography	D Location	E Physical Description	F Archaeological Description	G Analysis of Pottery	H Extent
230 (23C)	Artíki: Ráchi Gortsiá	*AJA* 1969, 136–37	300 m W-NW	Medium hill (high up on S flank of Kyparissia Valley)	HAB	MH? LH	90 m × 90 (max.) (0.8 ha)
231 (24A)	Dhórion: Kóndra	*AJA* 1969, 139–40	2½ km N-NE; immed. W of Dhorion-Psari road above chapel of Ayios Konstandinos	High hill	HAB. Possible ancient fortifications	MH? LHIII H? (medium)	160 m NE-SW × 110 on summit; may have included E and SE slopes (1.8 ha)
232 (25)	Chrisochóri: Panayía	Valmin 1930, 103–4; *AJA* 1961, 233	1 km NE; chapel of Panayia in area called Klisakoukia	High terraces descending to SW	HAB?	LH? H? (sparse)	Unclear
233 (24)	Áno Kopanáki: Stilári	*Bull Lund* 1927–28, 31; Valmin 1930, 79–81, 101–3; Roebuck 1941, 39ff.; *AJA* 1961, 233	1 km E-NE	Medium hill; few modern houses on summit	HAB. CEM? Valmin records tholos on S slope; fine H fortifications on N edge of summit; LHIII terracotta figurine	MH? LHII–III C; H; R? (medium)	75 m × 75 on summit; probably S slopes inhabited (0.4 ha)
234 (23)	Áno Kopanáki: Akoúrthi	*Bull Lund* 1927–28, 31–54; Valmin 1930, 79–81; *AJA* 1961, 233	1½ km W; between highway and railroad line	Medium plateau	CEM. 3 tholoi (2 excavated) within 75-m radius	LHII–III C	
235 (23A)	Káto Kopanáki: Paradámi	*AJA* 1969, 136	2 km W; immed. N of main highway just W of junction of sideroad from Artiki	High hill sloping to W	HAB? R or M roof tiles	LH? R? M (sparse)	Unclear
236 (23D)	Kamári: Goúva	*AJA* 1969, 137–38	1½ km S	High N-S ridge on skyline ca. 1 km W of Kopanaki-Kamari road	HAB-CEM. Illicitly excavated tholos contiguous to S; foreign stones; ruined M? chapel	LHIII M (medium)	120 m N-S × 100; mainly upper slope (1.2 ha)
237 (23B)	Kamári: Mesovoúni	*AJA* 1969, 136	300 m E-NE	Medium hill	HAB	MH LHIIIA–IIIB (heavy)	130 m NNE-SSW × 70 (min.); probably upper S slopes as well as summit (1.6 ha)
238 (23F)	Áno Kopanáki: Báfano	*AJA* 1969, 139	2 km N; immed. W of Kopanaki-Kefalovrisi road	Low spur toward S end of high ridge	HAB	LH (medium)	130 m N-S × 70 (terraces descending to E) (0.9 ha)

REGISTER A

I Communications	J Strategic Features	K Water Supply	L Land: Total	M Land: Percentage Cultivated	N Land: Irrigated	O Population	P Special Features
Isolated (land); 9 km to sea	Lookout site over whole central valley	Good spring 300 m SE	3.3 km radius; 3,421 ha	45	32 ha	104	
Secondary (land); 15 km to sea	Commanding location	Copious spring at E foot	3.9 km radius; 4,778 ha	80	226 ha	234	
Isolated (land); 15 km to sea	Fine position for lookout to S	Good spring under chapel	4.7 km radius; 6,940 ha	65	52 ha		
Mainline (land); 11 km to sea	H fortifications stress commanding position on E-W land route where route N to Figalia intersects		2.2 km radius; 1,520 ha	95		52 (min.)	
Mainline (land); 10 km to sea							Excavated by Valmin
Mainline (land); 9 km to sea	Excellent command of E-W communications near height of land	Small spring on N slope	2.0 km radius; 1,257 ha	90			
Isolated (land); 9 km to sea			1.7 km radius; 908 ha	90		156	
Secondary (land); 8 km to sea	Commands small valley to S and pass to N	Good springs close to NW and NE foot	2.6 km radius; 2,124 ha	90	22 ha	208 (min.)	
Secondary (land); 13 km to sea	Good view over valley to S	Good spring 700 m NE; small spring 600 m E	2.8 km radius; 2,246 ha	90		117	

REGISTER A

A Number	B Name	C Bibliography	D Location	E Physical Description	F Archaeological Description	G Analysis of Pottery	H Extent
239 (23E)	Glikorízi: Áyios Ilías	*Deltion* 1968, 160; *AJA* 1969, 139	1½ km W-SW; 1½ km E-SE of Kakkava	High hill at S end of lower ridge	HAB. Foundations (some possibly ancient) and modern tiles on summit (chapel of Ayios Ilias?); N axe reported from nearby spot called Petrádha	N? LHIIIB (medium)	180 m NE-SW × 120 (S and SE part of summit and upper SE terraces) (2.2 ha)
240 (21F)	Kefalóvrisi: Tsoukedhá	*AJA* 1969, 131	1½ km W-NW; 300 m W of track to Avlon	Medium hill	HAB. Frag. of obsidian	MH? LH (sparse)	120 m NW-SE × 80 (min.) mainly on S and E slopes (1 ha)
241 (21E)	Sidherókastro: Sfakoúlia	Valmin 1930, 82; *AJA* 1969, 131	1½ km N-NE; 700 m N of nearest point on Sidherokastro-Avlon road	Medium spur extending S into valley from higher ridge	HAB. Valmin's report of C sherds, statuettes, bronze axe seems to refer to different site	MH LHIIIB (medium)	250 m NNW-SSE × 100 (summit and upper W and S terraces) (2.5 ha)
242 (21D)	Vanádha: Kastrí	*AJA* 1969, 131	600 m NW; above (S of) Vanadha-Agaliani road	Low hill at higher W end of long high ridge	HAB. Foreign stones; frags. of obsidian; possible cist grave toward W edge	MH? LHIII (and earlier?) (sparse)	100 m × 100 (summit and upper SE slopes) (1 ha)
243 (21C)	Fónissa: Áspra Lithária	*AJA* 1969, 130–31	800 m SW; 2½ km from coast	High spur; projecting N above Nedha Valley	HAB. Foreign stones	MH LH (medium)	100 m N-S × 60 (mainly W slopes) (0.6 ha)
244 (21A)	Tholó: Áyios Dhimítrios	*AJA* 1969, 130	500 m E-NE; 200 m E of chapel of Ayios Dhimitrios and 50 m S of Tholo-Lepreon road	Low knoll or mound	HAB. Roof tiles	LHIII C (sparse)	60 m × 60 (later settlement larger) (0.4 ha)
245 (21)	Lépreon: Áyios Dhimítrios	Sperling 1942, 86; Meyer 1957, 63; *AJA* 1961, 231–32; Frazer III 474	Contiguous to S; chapel of Ayios Dhimitrios at NE end	High spur overhanging valley	HAB. C-H architectural blocks, house foundations, water system, fortifications?, temple?	N? EH; MH LHII–IIIA–IIIB A C; H; R? (heavy)	150 m N-S × 100 (acropolis only; C settlement much larger) (1.5 ha)
246 (21B)	Yannitsochóri: Áyios Yeóryios	*AJA* 1969, 130	Contiguous to NW; site of church of Ayios Yeoryios; on N side of Nedha River	Low mound	HAB. Several frags. of obsidian	EH (sparse)	60 m × 60 (0.4 ha)

REGISTER A

I Communications	J Strategic Features	K Water Supply	L Land: Total	M Land: Percentage Cultivated	N Land: Irrigated	O Population	P Special Features
Secondary (land); 5 km to sea	Magnificent view over W end of Kyparissia Valley	Copious spring 700 m W-NW; good spring 500 m N; small spring 500 m NW (both latter in bed of stream)	2.7 km radius; 2,290 ha	75	80 ha	286	
Isolated (land); 8 km to sea	Commands E part of Avlon Valley and looks S through pass to Kyparissia Valley	Copious spring 1½ km E-SE; small springs at SW foot, 700 m E and 1 km SW	3.6 km radius; 4,071 ha	45	21 ha	130	
Isolated (land); 7 km to sea	Dominates W part of Avlon Valley and pass to S toward Kyparissia	Fair spring 300 m NE; small spring 500 m SE	3.0 km radius; 2,827 ha	60		325	
Isolated (land); 5 km to sea	Commanding view in all directions (especially through gorge toward Kyparissia)	Fair spring 800 m SE	4.0 km radius; 5,027 ha	45		130	
Secondary (land); fair (sea), 2½ km		Fair spring 700 m NE; second spring 1½ km E	3.2 km radius; 3,217 ha	60	99 ha	78	Seems to have replaced EH settlement (#246) that was on opposite side of river, somewhat lower and nearer sea
Mainline (land); fair (sea), 1½ km		Several fair springs close to village; Tholo River	3.4 km radius; 3,632 ha	75		52	
Secondary (land); 6 km to sea	Dominates traffic through valley	Copious springs; river immed. SW	3.5 km radius; 3,845 ha	40	80 ha	195	
Mainline (land); fair (sea), 1½ km	Situation at river mouth	Nedha River	2.2 km radius; 1,520 ha	70		52	See comments on #243

REGISTER A

A Number	B Name	C Bibliography	D Location	E Physical Description	F Archaeological Description	G Analysis of Pottery	H Extent
300 (20)	Kakóvatos: Néstora (no longer tenable as Pylos of LH IIIB period)	Dörpfeld 1907 I–XVI; 1908, 295–317; 1913, 97–139; Müller 1909, 269–328; McDonald 1942, 538–45; Sperling 1942, 81–82; Meyer, *Museum Helveticum* 1951, 119–36; Meyer 1957, 61f., 78f.; *AJA* 1961, 230–31; *AJA* 1969, 130	1½ km E-NE	Medium spur above coastal plain	HAB-CEM. Large rough blocks from fortifications on acropolis; foreign stones of buildings in lower town to NW; 3 LHI–II tholoi excavated ca. 400 m NE of acropolis; C settlement closer to sea	MH LHI–II–IIIA?–IIIB C; H; R (medium)	200 m E-W × 90 (small acropolis; lower town on NW slopes) (1.8 ha)
301 (19A)	Zacháro: Kaïména Alónia	*AJA* 1964, 231	400 m NW	Medium ridge	HAB	LHIIIB (sparse)	Unclear (small)
302 (19)	Káto Samikón: Klidhí (probably Homeric Arene and Tomb of Iardanos)	Dörpfeld 1908, 320–22; 1913, 111–14; Sperling 1942, 82, 87; Meyer 1957, 75–76; *Deltion* 1965, 6–40, 185–86; *AJA* 1961, 230; 1969, 130	1½ km S-SW; immed. W of coastal highway	Low ridge; cut through by railroad; mound below N end	HAB-CEM. Tumulus 50 m diam. with multiple burials; large rough blocks on acropolis	EH; MH LHI–II–IIIA–IIIB (medium)	300 m NW-SE × 50 (max.) (1.5 ha)
303 (12)	Epitálion: Áyios Yeóryios (probably Homeric Thryon; classical Epitalion)	Meyer 1957, 49, 50, 60; *AJA* 1961, 227–28; 1969, 129; *Deltion* 1966, 171–72; 1967, 210–11; 1968, 165–71, Fig. 1; *AAA* 1968, 201–4; *Arch Eph* 1969, 16–17; *AMCM* 178	1½ km NW; between highway and railroad; N of side road to Epitalion	Cluster of 4 medium hills (chapel of Ayios Yeoryios on SW summit; Tou Varkou to Vouno at SE) at W end of E-W ridge on S side of Alpheios Valley	HAB-CEM. Cemeteries on E slope of Tou Varkou to Vouno and S slope of Ayios Yeoryios; settlements probably connected with both; LH and H houses; late C wall; male figurine showing Minoan influence; R dyeworks; R milestone	MH LHI–II–IIIA–IIIB–IIIC C; H; R (medium)	200 m NW-SE × 150 (3 ha)
304 (1)	Áyios Andhréas: Pondikókastro (C Pheia; P. is M name for acropolis)	Sperling 1942, 82; *Arch Eph* 1957, 31–43; *Deltion* 1960, 126; 1968, 162; *AJA* 1961, 224	Contiguous to E; 300 m from coast	N end of medium ridge	HAB. Early Cycladic figurines; large C H R site between acropolis and coast; architectural pieces, amphorae, etc.	N; EH; MH LHI–II–IIIA–IIIB SM; PG; G; A C; H; R; M (heavy)	215 m N-S × 75 (min.) (1.6 ha)
305 (2)	Skafidhiá: Anemómilo	Sperling 1942, 85; *AJA* 1961, 225; *Deltion* 1968, 162; 1969, 148	700 m SW	Low ridge	HAB. House foundations; numerous frags. of obsidian; H statue and R tombs from spot called Lavrion	EH LH? H; R (sparse)	100 m E-W × 50 (SW slopes) (0.5 ha)
306 (3)	Áyios Ioánnis: Sodhiótissa	*AJA* 1961, 225	1 km W; 150 m N of monastery of Panayia Sodhiotissa	Low ridge	HAB. Worked chert	EH? LH (sparse)	50 m × 50 (S slope) (0.25 ha)

REGISTER A

I Communica-tions	J Strategic Features	K Water Supply	L Land: Total	M Land: Percentage Cultivated	N Land: Irrigated	O Population	P Special Features
Mainline (land); fair (sea), 2 km	Commanded N-S land traffic		3.5 km radius; 3,848 ha	80	small (5 ha?)	234	Very important contents of LHII period from tholoi excavated by Dörpfeld
Mainline (land); fair (sea), 2 km		Small spring at S foot	3.7 km radius; 4,301 ha	80			
Mainline (land); fair? (sea), 1 km	Controlled N-S land traffic; there was probably a lookout above, on heights of Ano Samikon		3.9 km radius; 4,778 ha	40	5 ha	195	Burial tumulus excavated by Yalouris; LMIa imports
Mainline (land); fair (sea), 2 km	Controls both pass to E (railroad) and narrow coastal strip to W (new highway); presumed ford(s) of Alpheios River directly N	Perennial Alpheios River	4.4 km radius; 6,082 ha	75	10 ha	390	Site suggested in *AJA* 1961, 228, for habitation connected with these cemeteries now unlikely as result of excavation and study by Themelis
Secondary? (land); excellent (sea)	Defensible acropolis near good harbor; if Pylian territory ever reached this far, tenable anchor for control of Alpheios mouth (N side)	Small spring at W foot	1.5 km radius; 707 ha	90		208	Underwater exploration of partially submerged later town by Yalouris and colleagues
Secondary? (land); fair (sea)	Good lookout site in all directions		2.8 km radius; 2,463 ha	95		65	
Secondary? (land); fair (sea), 1 km			4 km radius; 5,026 ha	95		32	

REGISTER A

A Number	B Name	C Bibliography	D Location	E Physical Description	F Archaeological Description	G Analysis of Pottery	H Extent
307 (4)	Varvássaina: Vromonéri	*AJA* 1961, 225–26; *Deltion* 1967, 209; 1968, 161; 1969, 148	1 km W-NW; 500 m N of Pirgos-Olympia highway	High ridge	HAB. H pottery at spot called Marathia	MH? LH H (medium)	200 m N-S × 50 (1 ha)
308 (5)	Salmóni: Palió-pirgo	*Deltion* 1960, 126; 1968, 171; *AJA* 1961, 226 and references cited there	700 m S; immed. N of railroad	Medium ridge	HAB. CEM? 2 pithos burials reported from vicinity; C or H roof tiles; cut blocks	MH? C H	Unclear
309 (4A)	Stréfi	*Deltion* 1961–62, 107; 1969, 150–52; *AJA* 1969, 128	200 m N-NW		CEM. 2 chamber tombs; EHII pottery and 4 H tombs (near new railroad bridge)	EH LHIIIB H	
310 (5A)	Salmóni: Vam-vákia	*Deltion* 1960, 126; *AJA* 1969, 128	1 km W		CEM. Pithos burial	PG	
311 (15)	Makrísia: Kaniá	*Ergon* 1954, 41; *AJA* 1961, 229; 1969, 130	2 km W-NW	Medium spur; cemetery on SE slope	HAB-CEM. 2 LHIII A-B chamber tombs (plus at least 2 unopened)	EH; MH LHIIIA–IIIB	
312 (14)	Makrísia: Áyios Ilías (tomb of hero Alisios?; ancient Skillous?)	Meyer 1957, 47–48, 65; *AAA* I 1968, 126–27; *AJA* 1961, 229; 1969, 129; *Deltion* 1968, 284–92	500 m W; church and convent of Ayios Ilias on summit	High hill	HAB-CEM. LHI cist grave within destroyed tumulus; worked flint and chert; clay and stone "whorls," bronze knives and brooch; LMIa imports	MH LHI–IIIB SM? C?; H; R? (medium)	100 m E-W × 80 (0.8 ha)
313 (16)	Makrísia: Yerakovoúni	Meyer 1957, 47; *AJA* 1961, 229	2 km E-NE; 400 m S of track from Makrisia to river ferry	High hill	HAB-CEM. LHII burial mound (cf. #302); LHI vases, C sherds, and roof tiles at Raza (not far E of Sklava spring)	MH? LHI–II–III C (sparse)	80 m N-S × 50 (higher area to NW); pottery also scattered over 50 m × 50 lower area to N (0.7 ha)
314 (16A)	Babés: Arnoka-táracho	*Praktika* 1956, 186–92; *BCH* 1958, 570; *Deltion* 1966, 171; 1968, 284–92; 1969, 148; *AJA* 1969, 130; *AMCM* 177	1½ km W	High hill	CEM? Mycenaean dagger; small late 6th-c. temple (Zeus? Artemis Daidaleia?); later town on NE slopes; G figurine; H pithos burial; LHII tomb	LH G; A C; H; R	
315 (8)	Olýmpia: Áltis (classical sanctuary)	*AM* 1906, 205–18; 1908, 185–92; 1962, 3ff.; *Alt-Olympia* I, 73–102; *Deltion* 1967, 209; 1969, 148; *AAA* 1969, 248–56; *AJA* 1969, 128	900 m S-SE	Flat ground near confluence of Kladheos and Alpheios rivers	HAB-CEM. MH apsidal houses; pithos burials; LH terracotta statuettes; bronze statuette of adorant type; EH-LH pottery in stadium area	EH; MH LH G; A C; H; R; M	
316 (6A)	Flóka	*Deltion* 1963, 103; 1968, 171; *AJA* 1969, 128; *AAA* 1969, 248–56	Near dam on the Alpheios ca. 2 m SW		CEM. Destroyed LHIIIB tomb; female terracotta figurine showing Minoan influence; at nearby Panoukla H graves	LHIIIB C; H	
317 (7)	Olýmpia: Dhroúva	*BCH* 1959, 655; *AJA* 1961, 226	700 m SW (within partially abandoned village of Dhrouva)	S end of high ridge overlooking confluence of Alpheios and Kladheos rivers	HAB. Abundant obsidian	LHIIIB (heavy)	150 m E-W × 100 (1.5 ha)

REGISTER A

I Communications	J Strategic Features	K Water Supply	L Land: Total	M Land: Percentage Cultivated	N Land: Irrigated	O Population	P Special Features
Secondary (land); 8 km to sea	Near point where Alpheios Valley widens toward W	Small spring at S edge	4.8 km radius; 7,238 ha	80		130	
Secondary (land); 9 km to sea	Overlooks Alpheios Valley to S		3.4 km radius; 3,632 ha	75			Little evidence of prehistoric habitation; theory that Homeric Thryon here is untenable
Secondary (land); 11 km to sea							Salvage by ephorate
8 km to sea							Salvage by ephorate
Secondary (land); 8 km to sea		Selinounda River ca. 500 m to E	2.5 km radius; 1,963 ha	80	Considerable		Salvage by ephorate; recent EH and MH evidence indicates prehistoric settlement as well as cemetery
Secondary (land); 7 km to sea	Strong defensive position with control of Alpheios crossing opposite Olympia	Good spring 700 m NE	3.0 km radius; 2,827 ha	90		104	Salvage by ephorate and study by Themelis
Secondary (land); 10 km to sea	Near Alpheios crossing	Good spring 600 m NE; small spring at NW edge; Alpheios River 700 m N	2.3 km radius; 1,662 ha	70		91	Apparently 2 distinct concentrations; Raza area cemetery?; excavation and study by Themelis
Secondary? (land); 11 km to sea							Excavated by Yalouris
Mainline (land); 11 km to sea	Commands river crossing	Perennial rivers	1.0 km radius; 314 ha	75			German Archaeological School excavating here since 1870's; until recently sparse evidence for LH habitation but now incontrovertible; possibly an important shrine in LH or even before
Secondary (land); 10 km to sea							Salvage by ephorate
Secondary (land); 11 km to sea	Commands confluence of rivers	Perennial rivers	1.5 km radius; 707 ha	85		195	Yalouris tested the site

REGISTER A

A Number	B Name	C Bibliography	D Location	E Physical Description	F Archaeological Description	G Analysis of Pottery	H Extent
318 (7A)	Plátanos: Tómbrino and Rénia	*Deltion* 1960, 126; 1964, 177; 1967, 209; *AJA* 1969, 128	SE edge		CEM. 3 pillaged LHIIIB-C chamber tombs; necklaces of gold and glass paste; late A vase frag.; numerous H and R tombs nearby at place called Kamari	LHIIIB–IIIC A? H; R	
319 (7B)	Máyira	*Deltion* 1966, 170; 1969, 149; *AJA* 1969, 128; *AAA* 1969, 248–56	S of village		CEM. MH burial tumulus; late Mycenaean remains at place called Kioúpia; low mound containing H cist grave, R? pithos burials, H and LH pottery at spot called Kouveli or Vamvakia 200 m S	MH LHIII C; H; R?	
320 (6)	Ladzóï: Etiá	*AJA* 1961, 226	1 km N; 500 m W of ruined chapel of Ayios Ioannis	Medium hill	HAB. Bronze double axe; worked chert; foreign stones; roof tiles	LHIIIB (earlier?) C; H (medium)	100 m NE-SW × 60 (0.6 ha)
321 (8A)	Olýmpia: New Museum	*Deltion* 1960, 125–26; 1961–62, 105; 1964, 174–77; 1965, 209; 1969, 149; *AJA* 1969, 128–29; *AMCM* 178	500 m E-SE; at NW foot of hill of Kronos	Slope and valley floor	HAB-CEM. Jewelry and metal objects, house walls, and paved hearth (?) in excavation for museum basement; 13 LHIIIB chamber tombs in slope above; more ruined Mycenaean tombs still farther E; ruins of Mycenaean and pre-Mycenaean houses on summit of Hill of Kronos	EH; MH LHII–IIIB	
322 (8B)	Olýmpia: railroad station	*Deltion* 1960, 126; 1963, 103; *AJA* 1969, 129	N outskirts	N bank of Kladheos River	CEM?	MH LH G; A	
323 (9)	Miráka: Oinomáos (ancient Pisa?)	*AM* 1908, 318–20; 1913, 137; *Alt-Olympia* I 273–75; II *Beil.* 23–24; Sperling (1942) 83; *AJA* 1961, 226–27	800 m SW; immed. N of Olympia-Tripolis highway	High conical hill	HAB-CEM. R cemetery of Frangonisi 500 m E and beside highway	MH LH? C; H; R	80 m E-W × 60 (0.5 ha)
324 (9A)	Miráka: Réma (or Lakoúla); other prehistoric finds at Chandákia, Samakiá, and at Goúva or Perivóli	*Deltion* 1964, 178–79; 1966, 171; 1968, 160; *AJA* 1969, 129	"Around Miraka"		CEM? LHI sword and spearhead and LHIIIB alabastron; C sculpture; late R stele	LHI–IIIA–IIIB–IIIC C; R	
325 (9B)	Kládheos: Stravokéfalo	*Deltion* 1963, 103; *AJA* 1969, 129; *AMCM* 178	"Near Kladheos"; on right bank of Kladheos River		CEM. 7 chamber tombs of large Mycenaean cemetery uncovered and partially destroyed during road construction; necklaces of glass paste, diadems (one found intact on cranium), terracotta figurines, metal artifacts, vases of LHIIIA–B	LHIIIA–IIIB H; R	
326 (9C)	Kládheos: Trípes	*Deltion* 1964, 177; *AJA* 1969, 129	2 km N on right bank of Kladheos River		CEM. 10 chamber tombs of Mycenaean cemetery; objects of bronze, gold, ivory; many LHIIIA–C vases	LHIIIA–IIIB–IIIC	
327 (9D)	Kavkaniá: Fengaráki (or Marmarosikiá or Vathiá Lákka)	*Deltion* 1960, 126; 1964, 178; *AJA* 1969, 129	On border between land of Kafkania and Kladheos	Hill slope	CEM. Cist graves covered with stone slabs; faience beads	LH H; R	

REGISTER A

I Communications	J Strategic Features	K Water Supply	L Land: Total	M Land: Percentage Cultivated	N Land: Irrigated	O Population	P Special Features
Secondary? (land); 14 km to sea							Salvage by ephorate
Secondary (land); 16 km to sea							
Secondary? (land); 15 km to sea	On N-S route via Lestenitsa Valley leading to interior of Elis	Fair spring below NE foot	5.0 km radius; 10,936 ha	70		78	
Mainline (land); 12 km to sea		Kladheos River immed. to W	1.0 km radius; 314 ha	85			Salvage by ephorate
Mainline (land); 12 km to sea							Salvage by ephorate
Secondary (land); 13 km to sea		Fair spring 800 m NE; Alpheios River 700 m S	2.9 km radius; 2,642 ha	60		65	Some excavation on hilltop by Dörpfeld; excavation of cemetery by ephorate
Secondary (land); 14 km to sea							Salvage by ephorate
Secondary (land); 16 km to sea							Salvage by ephorate
Secondary (land); 18 km to sea							Salvage by ephorate
Secondary (land); 16 km to sea							Salvage by ephorate

REGISTER A

A Number	B Name	C Bibliography	D Location	E Physical Description	F Archaeological Description	G Analysis of Pottery	H Extent
328 (9E)	Kavkaniá: Agrilítses	*Deltion* 1967, 209; *AJA* 1969, 129	Contiguous to S		HAB? Large quantities of potsherds	MH LH	
329 (10)	Áspra Spítia: Toúrla	Sperling 1942, 86; *AJA* 1961, 227	ca. 3 km SE; overlooking confluence of Erymanthos and Alpheios rivers	Medium hill at S end of ridge	HAB. Roof tiles	EH?; MH? LH? C; H (sparse for prehistoric)	200 m E-W × 150 (max.) (3 ha)
330 (11)	Trípes: Palió-kastro	Meyer 1957, 106; *BCH* 1956, 522–46; *AJA* 1961, 227	Above village	High hill	HAB-CEM. Chamber tombs	LH C	
331 (17)	Dhiásela: Koutsochéra	*Ergon* 1954, 87–88; *BCH* 1957, 574–79; 1958, 574–78; *AJA* 1961, 229–30	2½ km N-NW; 300 m NE of chapel of Ayios Athanasios	Low hill	HAB-CEM. 3 chamber tombs on lower S slope; 2 possible tholoi on crest; roof tiles; foundations of houses and fortifications (probably classical)	LHIIIA?–IIIB–IIIC SM? C	130 m E-W × 100 (top and upper S slope) (1.3 ha)
332 (18)	Tripití: Kástro (ancient Stylangion?; M Ísova ca. 2 km N-NW)	Sperling 1942, 81; Meyer 1957, 40, 41, 69; *Praktika* 1955, 244; *AJA* 1961, 230	1 km W-SW	Medium hill	HAB. Abundant later blocks, column drums, roof tiles; silver and bronze coins; metal and terracotta objects	MH? LH? C; H; R; M	150 m E-W × 50 (much larger C site spread over several hills) (0.8 ha)

REGISTER A

I Communications	J Strategic Features	K Water Supply	L Land: Total	M Land: Percentage Cultivated	N Land: Irrigated	O Population	P Special Features
Secondary (land); 16 km to sea							Salvage by ephorate
Secondary? (land); 19 km to sea	Controls N end of important river crossing	Small spring 800 m NW; perennial rivers	4.5 km radius; 6,362 ha	70		390	Apparently excavation on hilltop and local rumors of "treasure" discovered
Mainline? (land); 29 km to sea	Controlled important routes		5.0 km radius; 7,854 ha	40			
Secondary? (land); 16 km to sea	Controlled possible river crossing	Kovitsa River 800 m W; Alpheios River ca. 2 km N	5.0 km radius; 7,854 ha	70	159 ha	169	Salvage and excavation by ephorate
Secondary? (land); 17 km to sea	Controlled possible river crossing	2 good springs ca. 2 km N-NW	4.5 km radius; 6,362 ha	80		104	

REGISTER B. Post-Mycenaean Habitation Sites

A Number	B Name	C Bibliography	D Location	E Physical Description
400	Romanoú: Viglítsa	*Praktika* 1909, 289; Valmin 1930, 146–48; *BCH* 1962, 726, 728; *Deltion* 1961–62, 92	Large area N of Navarino Bay and near W coast; generally E of villages of Petrochori and Romanou	Generally flat or slightly rolling
401	Yiálova: Dhivári	*JHS Arch Reports* 1960–61, 11; 1967–68, 10–11; *Deltion* 1965, 208; 1966, 164–65; Pritchett 1965, 6–29; *AAA* 1968, 189–93	700 m W	Narrow sandspit between Yialova and Paliokastro; separates Bay of Navarino and Osmanaga Lagoon
402	Píla	*Deltion* 1965, 208		
403	Tragána: Tsopáni Ráchi (or Ríkia)	*Deltion* 1961–62, 98–99; 1963, 91–94; 1966, 184–97	W of Tragana and 500 m from sea	Flat coastal plain
404	Sfaktiría (island): Maránou	*Deltion* 1964, 151	NE side of island	Little bay where oil reservoirs are located
405	Plátanos: Palió Loutró	*AJA* 1964, 232	Ca. 1,200 m SE	Hollow with good spring and heavy undergrowth
406	Marathoúpolis: Dhialiskári (ancient Erana?)	Valmin 1930, 136–40; *Praktika* 1960, 193–94; *Ergon* 1960, 141–45	2 km along coast	Flat terrain
407	Próti [island] (classical Prokonnesos; M Kástro Tis Vourliás)	*Bull Lund* 1928/29, 45–48; Valmin 1930, 141ff. and Fig. 26; Roebuck 1941, 23, 29, 39ff.	Ca. 1 km off Gargaliani coastal plain	Rocky island ca. 4 km N-S, 1 km maximum width and narrowing toward S
408	Ayía Kiriakí (ancient Erana?)	Valmin 1930, 136; *Praktika* 1960, 193–94; *BCH* 1960, 718	On coast	Flat coastal plain
409	Kyparissia [vicinity]	*BCH* 1959, 649	3 km S of Kyparissia on road to Filiatra	Coastal plain
410	Christíani	*Bull Lund* 1928/29, 35–36, 142ff.; Valmin 1930, 132; *BCH* 1958, 286; Stikas 1951	12 km S of Kyparissia	Small inland valley; copious springs
412	Methóni (ancient Methoni or Mothoni; medieval Mothon or Modon)	*Bull Lund* 1928/29, 37; Valmin 1930, 152–54; *JHS* 1905, 33–36; Roebuck 1941, 29; *BSA* 1957, 252–55; 1966, 125; *Deltion* 1961–62, 94; 1963, 93–94; *AJA* 1961, 254; 1969, 154; *Arch Reports* 1962–63, 18	On W coast below Pylos	Fair harbor protected by islands; well-preserved Venetian castle immed. to N
413	Neroulá	*BCH* 1959, 641	In village	
414	Methóni: Áyios Vasílios	UMME surface search	Chapel of Ayios Vasilios ca. 2 km NNE of Methoni; site 600 m NW of chapel	Open field
415	Methóni: Áyios Ilías	*JHS* 1905, 34; Valmin 1930, 154	Near shore E of Methoni	
416	Finíki: Palioliní	*Deltion* 1960, 108	4 km E of Methoni	

REGISTER B

F Archaeological Description	G Analysis of Pottery	H Extent	I Miscellaneous
HAB-CEM. C and H statuettes, coins; R graves; bronze lebes used as cover for pithos burial of A times; column of M period	A C; H; R; M	Scattered concentrations	
HAB-CEM. Extensive H cemetery with stone-lined cist graves and tile-covered graves; evidence of pyres; coins, figurines, glass, jewelry, frags. of woven material; remains of houses and public bldgs. with column drums and capitals; monument bases ranging A-R; R bldgs. and mosaics at W end below Paliokastro and Venetian (?) mole; M aqueduct S of H settlement	A C; H; R	200 m E-W × 75 (min.)	55 graves in H cemetery excavated by Yalouris
CEM. Archaic pithos burial with 3 iron swords, bronze vases, ring	A		
CEM. Low tumulus; large stele base; 3 slab-lined cist graves, many skeletons; 2 graves with wooden coffins; gold diadems, silver vase, 3 glass vases, bronze and silver coins; many terracotta vases; lamps; bronze implements	H (end 3rd c. and beginning 2nd c. B.C.)		Excavated by Papathanasopoulos
HAB?	H; R; M		Well (difficult to date); exploration by ephorate
HAB. Well-preserved foundations of large bldg. (R bath?)	R		
HAB-CEM. Rock-cut cist graves; modern house on ancient foundations; R (?) public bldg. (bath?); mosaic; columns; circular structure; H inscription (now in Gargaliani)	H; R		Exploration by Valmin
HAB. H fortress at S end with well-preserved walls, especially along W side; round tower at NE between fort and little NE harbor; roof tiles; inscriptions "Euploia" on rock	Late C? H	200 m N-S × ca. 140 (fortress only)	
HAB. Unfluted M columns; early Christian basilica; late R bath	R; M		Excavation by Pallas does not support Erana equation
HAB? Fine H bronze female bust; terracotta antefix in form of female head	H?		
HAB. Large M church of Ayia Sotira; C architectural blocks and frags. of public bldg. (bath?); inscriptions; H grave	C?; H?; R?; M		No solid evidence for settlement before M period; earlier material may be from elsewhere
HAB-CEM. Cist graves with C and late A pottery; column drums; R mosaic; ancient mole?; R (?) blocks and architectural frags. in Venetian fortifications; lower courses in SW sector claimed to be H or R; H and R coins, tombs, inscriptions; C or H cemetery 1½ km N with rock-cut tombs	A C; H; R; M		This may have been main LH site in area but only one Mycenaean button reported; exploration by Papathanasopoulos; for Valmin's claim that Palia Methoni has prehistoric remains, see *AJA* 1961, 254, and *JHS* 1905, 34
HAB. Walls of H bldg.	H		
HAB. Roof tiles, cement floor, frags. of large basin; possibly ruins of villa	R		
HAB? Mosaics reported	R?		
CEM. 2 R graves with vases, iron axe, and knife	R		

REGISTER B

A Number	B Name	C Bibliography	D Location	E Physical Description
417	Grízi: Paliókastro	*Bull Lund* 1928/29, 41–42, 148ff.; Valmin 1930, 157–58	Straddles valley leading inland; ca. 2 km N of Grizi and 500 m from coast	High hill
419	Tsapí	Valmin 1930, 155–56	6 km NW of Akritas (tip of peninsula) on W coast	Very small coastal plain at mouth of stream
420	Sapiéntza [island] (one of ancient Oinoussai group)	Valmin 1930, 160	Near small port and lighthouse on E side	
421	Venétiko [island] (ancient Theganousa)	Valmin 1930, 160–61	Island off S tip of Messenian peninsula; site on N side	
422	Schiza [island] (one of ancient Oinoussai group)	Valmin 1930, 160	N and E sides	
500	Polistári: Pólenes	UMME surface search	About 700 m SW; immed. E of small spring (Polenes)	Sloping ground
501	Polistári	UMME surface search	About 500 m S of Polistari above (W of) track to Kastania	Big artificial mound on hillock
502	Petalídhi (ancient Koroni)	*Bull Lund* 1928/29, 37–39; *JHS* 1905, 40, 41; Valmin 1930, 176–79; Hope Simpson 1957, 249, 251; 1966, 124; *JHS Arch Reports* 1960–61, 11; *Deltion* 1966, 163	Modern village on W coast of Messenian Gulf; acropolis immed. to W	Fairly well-protected harbor with excellent spring 10 m from sea; big and imposing acropolis with fine spring still higher at Tzanes (perhaps Plataniston mentioned by Pausanias as 20 stades from ancient Asine, i.e., modern Koroni)
503	Panipéri	UMME surface search	N of copious spring of Goulia	Open fields
504	Áyios Andhréas (temple of Apollo Korynthos)	*Deltion* 1916, 65–118; *Bull Lund* 1928/29, 39–40, 146ff.; Valmin 1930, 173–75; *BSA* 1966, 125, 131	Around chapel of Ayios Andhreas and across Longa road to N	Gentle slope toward sea (E) about 1 km distant
505	Koróni: Áyia Triádha	Valmin 1930, 171; 1938, 469–75; *Deltion* 1966, 163; 1967, 206 and Pl. 145a	250 m N of church of Ayia Triadha and 350 m inland	
507	Kastélia-Vounária (ancient Kolonides?)	*JHS* 1905, 37–40; Valmin 1930, 171–73; *JHS Arch Reports* 1960–61, 11; *BSA* 1966, 125	500 m E; immed. above sea	2 eminences (Ayios Ilias and Goulas)
508	Potamiá (formerly Kandírogli): Koulé	Valmin 1930, 169; *JHS Arch Reports* 1960, 11	Vicinity of Potamia (1 km W of Charokopio)	
509	Charokopió: Gargaroú	UMME surface search; *JHS Arch Reports* 1960–61, 11	Between Charokopio and Kombi	Ridge overlooking sea
510	Chrisokellariá (formerly Saratsá): tou Dhiós i Layinítsa	Valmin 1930, 162	600 m SW; on N slope of Mt. Tsarnaoura	Little terrace

REGISTER B

F Archaeological Description	G Analysis of Pottery	H Extent	I Miscellaneous
HAB. Fortress with ancient foundations on W; 2 cisterns of H or R period; H and R coins; H inscriptions; R bath in plain	H; R		Guards entrance to defile on route to Koroni on E coast
HAB. Roof tiles; foundations of large bldg. (storehouse?)	R; M		
HAB? Cisterns (?)	R		
HAB-CEM. Large R bath; R house walls; graves reported by Valmin	H?; R; M		Evidence of ancient salt production reported; we saw very little recognizable R material and nothing earlier
HAB	H; R		
HAB?	H; R?	Very small	
CEM. Stone slabs, apparently covering of cist graves	R		
HAB-CEM. C or H fortifications of acropolis at least 2 km long; very numerous frags. of architecture, sculpture of H-R times; coins; inscriptions; aqueduct; mosaics; graves; bath; should be important prehistoric site (perhaps harbor of Nichoria (#100) but no ceramic evidence)	C; H; R	Large	Perhaps Pausanias' "harbor of Achaeans" — best port on W side of gulf above Koroni
HAB	R?; M	Medium	
SHRINE. Versakis excavated foundations of 4 "temples" and several other bldgs. of A, C, H, R, M date; inscriptions identifying site; peribolos (?) wall; bothros; bronze and terracotta statuettes; H and R bldgs. with mosaics reported below (E of) acropolis of Kafirio about 1 km SW; R cemetery immed. above (E of) Longa-Adhriani road opposite Kafirio	A C; H; R		Shrine excavated by Versakis
HAB. Large R (Trajanic?) bldg. with mosaics (largest depicts Dionysos carrying off Ariadne; now in Kalamata museum)	R		Bldg. partly cleared by Valmin
CEM. Inscriptions, coins, statuettes, graves of C and H period and later	C; H; R; M		Must be settlement in immed. vicinity; cf. modern ceramic industry here (Ch. 13)
HAB. Small R bath; large R bldg. (bath?) by stream; unfluted column drums; marble statue (head previously found)	R		Spring (walled in) said to be most important in area
HAB. Inscribed tombstone reported from vicinity	C; H	Small	
HAB? H roof tiles	H	Small	Possibly fortress on route across peninsula to Koroni; Valmin records second fortress (?) in similar position about 1 km farther N

REGISTER B

A Number	B Name	C Bibliography	D Location	E Physical Description
512	Koróni: Boúrgo (ancient Asine; medieval Coron; Mycenaean and later district or town called Rhion?)	*JHS* 1905, 32, 36, 37, and extensive bibliography cited there; *Bull Lund* 1928/29, 44–45; Valmin 1930, 165–68; Roebuck 1941, 21; *BSA* 1957, 249; 1966, 125; *AJA* 1961, 254; 1969, 155; *Deltion* 1969, 142	At SE edge of town	Fine acropolis with lower extension projecting into sea and forming best natural harbor on Messenian Gulf
513	Koróni: Zánga	Valmin 1930, 169; *JHS* 1905, 36	Ca. 2 km SW of Koroni; near shore on road to Vasilitsi	
514	Koróni: Kaminákia	*AJA* 1969, 155	Along Koroni-Vasilitsi road; near shore	
515	Livadháki: Faneroméni	Valmin 1930, 168	7 km SW of Koroni; near church of Faneromeni just N of Livadhaki	Small coastal plain
517	Nerómilos: Panayítsa	*AJA* 1961, 246	1 km S; immed. S of Pylos-Kalamata highway; chapel on top	Low hill
518	Dhiódhia: Áyios Ioánnis	*Deltion* 1965, 207	600 m NW	Hill overlooking village
519	Dhrosiá (formerly Zaïmogli)	Valmin 1930, 180	5 km NW of Velika	
520	Ellinoekklisiá	*BCH* 1959, 640	In village	
522	Kaloyerórachi: Samarína	Valmin 1930, 63; Hope Simpson 1957, 246; *AJA* 1961, 254–55	Just W of and below road	Small valley
523	Lámbaina	UMME surface search	Immed. above (N of) village and spring	Hill with good view E to Pamisos Valley
524	Platí	UMME surface search	Ca. 200 m S of railroad station	Low hill
525	Bálira	UMME surface search	Ca. 100 m W; on W bank of Balira River and beside bridge	Lowest terraces above river
526	Moní Voulkánou	UMME surface search	Ca. 1 km S of monastery; near small spring	Hillock
528	Ithómi: Moní Voulkánou	*Deltion* 1965, 207	Ca. 4 km ESE of Mavromati (ancient Messene)	Terrace on lower mountain slope
529	Mavromáti (ancient Messene)	*Praktika* 1895, 27; 1909, 64, 201–5; 1925–26, 15, 55–66; 1957, 121–25; 1958, 177–83; 1959, 162–73; 1960, 210–27; 1962, 99–112; 1963, 122–29; 1964, 96–101; Roebuck 1941, 3, 39ff.; Valmin 1930, 67–69; *Deltion* 1960, 108–9; 1963, 95–97; 1966, 164; 1967, 206; 1969, 143–44; *AJA* 1961, 255; *Ergon* 1969, 97–132	At S base of Mt. Ithomi	Center of city in hollow to S of steep acropolis of Ithomi; copious spring in modern village on N rim of hollow
530	Áyios Flóros (temple of Pamisos)	Valmin 1938, Pt. II; Roebuck 1941, 17, 37	On N outskirts of Áyios Flóros	Low swampy ground

REGISTER B

F Archaeological Description	G Analysis of Pottery	H Extent	I Miscellaneous
HAB-CEM. Ancient blocks in Venetian fortifications; H and R coins, architectural frags., R statue, inscriptions, cistern, rock-cut tombs, traces of roads	A C; H; R	Large	Natural spot for major prehistoric site in this district but no ceramic evidence at present
HAB. Inscriptions	C; H	Small	
HAB. Loomweights, amphora, and tile frags.	C		
HAB. Mosaics and walls of R bath; R aqueduct; R coins	R	Small	
HAB? Thick deposit (*apothetis*?) of A pottery; walls reported below surface	A		
HAB? Foundations of large rectangular bldg.; large quantity of pottery brought to Kalamata museum; probably from temple *apothetis*	C; H		This town (formerly Loï) was important point on M (and earlier?) shortcut across peninsula (Ch. 9)
HAB. Remains of R bath	R		
HAB. R and M bldgs.; frag. of relief sculpture	R; M		
HAB? Fine early M church; C or H blocks in lower courses may be from ancient Messene; tombs	C?; H?; M		
HAB	C?; H	Small	
HAB?	C?; H	Small	
HAB?	C?; H	Small	
HAB	C?; H	Small	
HAB? Relief sculpture of R date and H statue base (built into walls)	H?; R?		This area very important in M times; earlier material might come from Mavromati
HAB. Early G ithyphallic figurine; well-preserved agora with public bldgs. in and around it; many inscriptions, statues, architectural members; water system; magnificent and well-preserved fortifications with elaborate subsidiary system of flanking forts	G C; H; R	Huge area within walls	Major rallying point and religious center for all Messenia (from at least A times); Ithomi and Acrocorinth best natural fortresses in Peloponnese; subsidiary forts W and N guarded route from Pylos to Meligala; major administrative center in H and R; no evidence for earlier habitation; excavated by Sophoulis, Oikonomos, and Orlandos
SHRINE. Ramp and temple foundations; votive deposits	A C; H; R		Temple mentioned by Pausanias

REGISTER B

A Number	B Name	C Bibliography	D Location	E Physical Description
532	Ámfia	*BCH* 1959, 640		
533	Sperchóyia (formerly Kourtsaoúsi)	Valmin 1930, 63	Ca. 2 km SE of modern Thouria	Gardens of village
534	Thouría (modern)	UMME surface search	200 m W of Thouria; under bridge on Thouria-Mikromani road	In stream banks
535	Polianí: Palióchora	*BCH* 1959, 640		High upland
537	Yiánnitsa (ancient Kalamai?)	*AM* 1894, 365–67, 481–85; *Bull Lund* 1928/29, 31; Valmin 1930, 40, 48, 54, 188, 208; Roebuck 1941, 122–24; Hope Simpson 1957, 242; 1966, 119–21	Crowned by chapel of Ayiï Taxiarchi	Steep limestone acropolis
540	Ayíon Pándon [Kalamata]: Péra Kalamítsi (Pausanias' *Alsos Karneion*?)	*Deltion* 1965, 207	About 1 km E of Ayion Pandon	
542	Faraí (formerly Yiannitsánika): Tímiova	*Deltion* 1965, 207	"Near Timiova"	Cave
543	Almirós	*BSA* 1957, 240	Just S of great spring on shore	
545	Avía: Palióchora (Homeric Hire? classical Abia?)	Valmin 1930, 181; Anapliotis 1956, 9–12; *BSA* 1957, 240; *Deltion* 1966, 163	On SW outskirts of Avia	Promontory with M ruins (Kastro)
546	Kitriés	Valmin 1930, 182; *BSA* 1903–4, 163	On coast W of productive Kambos Valley	South side of valley just above village
548	Brínda: Áyios Ilías (temple of Artemis Limnatis?)	Valmin 1930, 187; Valmin 1939, 44; Hope Simpson 1966, 115–16	Ca. 5 km NE of Kambos	Acropolis 100 m above Sandava gorge (ancient Choireios)
549	Áyios Nikólaos (formerly Selinítsa)	UMME surface search	Ca. 100 m E of Ayios Nikolaos; near round tower	Stony fields on low rocky plateau
601	Palió Neró: Vounáki (ancient Avlon?)	Valmin 1930, 108; Valmin 1933–34, 11; Roebuck 1941, 25–26, 65; *AJA* 1961, 253; *BSA* 1966, 127	2½ km N; between highway and railroad	Medium conical hill
602	Áyios Ilías (vicinity of Lepreon): Nekrotafíon	*Deltion* 1965, 210	At SW edge of village	High hill at N end of a lofty ridge
604	Kástro tou Míla: Chamouzá	*AJA* 1969, 142	500 m S on road to Neochori	Lower E slopes on both sides of road
605	Vasilikó: Filákion	Valmin 1939, 59–76; Roebuck 1941, 12; *CP* 1945, 151	400 m E of hut 15 on railroad line	
606	Kalívia	UMME surface search	Ca. 1½ km S	
607	Konstandíni: Áyios Athanásios [Dhivári] (ancient Andania?; M Isári)	*Bull Lund* 1928/29, 32–34; Valmin 1930, 92–98 and s.v. Andania; Roebuck 1941, 7–10	1,300 m N of Kalliröi station	

REGISTER B

F Archaeological Description	G Analysis of Pottery	H Extent	I Miscellaneous
HAB? R portrait head	R		
HAB. Wall blocks; marble statue found in river	C?; H?; R; M		
CEM? Curved and flat roof tiles	H		
HAB? Lamp, bronze disks, tearbottles in Kalamata museum	C; H		
HAB. Remains of fortifications and house walls; probably 4th c. or 3rd c. B.C. (no prehistoric evidence); traces of carriage road	C; H	150 m N-S × 80	Guards W end of route across Mt. Taygetos
HAB-CEM. Cover tile from public bldg. (temple?); pithos burial with G bronze horseman and 4 pins	G; A		Well close by to NE (cf. that mentioned by Pausanias)
SHRINE. Terracotta "religious" statuettes of austere style	A? C		
HAB? CEM?	C		
HAB? CEM. Wall of squared and sawn blocks just SW of chapel that is ca. 50 m E of Kastro (site of Asklepieion?); tomb ca. 100 m ENE of Kastro with R sarcophagos (now in Kalamata museum); glass jug and lamp; inscription	H?; R; M		
HAB? Columns and tesellated pavement (of villa?)	R		Fair small harbor
HAB. Inscriptions; imposing polygonal fortifications on acropolis	C; H; R; M	About 150 m E-W × 100	Superb command of gorge marking traditional Messenia-Lakonia border
HAB	H?; R	Ca. 100 m diameter	
HAB. Fortress (?) on top; roof tiles; cistern	C?; H; R	100 m N-S × 80	Controls land traffic along coast; fort rather than town?; no ceramic evidence of prehistoric occupation
HAB. Pithos and part of Doric column capital; C lamp and inscribed grave stele; terracotta water channel of R times	A C; H; R (heavy)	At least 300 m N-S × 100; summit and terraces	Tremendous view; should be an important town (perhaps named in historical sources)
HAB. Roof tiles	C; H (heavy)	250 m NE-SW × 150	Small spring below road and 200 m NE; should have been major site to judge from position and extent
Ruins of guardhouse (?)	A C?		
HAB?	H?	Small	
HAB. R bath (?); inscriptions (including famous regulations of mystery cult, *IG* V, 1; 1432–33); ruins of public bldgs.; aqueduct; architectural frags.; tombs; H and R coins; tiles; large M church of Ayios Vasilios	C; H; R	Large	Abundant spring (walled in); see #212 for prehistoric remains at nearby Polichni

REGISTER B

A Number	B Name	C Bibliography	D Location	E Physical Description
608	Dhesíla: Ellinikó (ancient Ampheia?)	Valmin 1930, 75–90; Hiller and Lattermann, *Hira und Andania* 31–37; Roebuck 1941, 8, 9	On ridge about 2 km E of Dhesila and N of railway	
609	Trífa (ancient Andania?)	*Praktika* 1900, 17; Valmin 1930, 75–90; 1939, 76–77; Roebuck 1941, 8, 9; *Deltion* 1968, 156	Within village	At foot of N slope bounding Steniklarian Plain
610	Steníklaros: Áyios Yeóryios or Chalásmata	*Bull Lund* 1928/29, 31–32; Valmin 1930, 83; *AJA* 1964, 239	300 m NE	Open flat fields
611	Kakalétri: Áyios Athanásios (ancient Eira?)	Valmin 1930, 118–19; Hiller and Lattermann, *Hira und Andania* 1911, 13ff.; Philippson 357; Roebuck 1941, 11–12		
614	Tzorotá	Hiller and Lattermann, *Hira und Andania*, 37–38; Valmin 1930, 78; Roebuck 1941, 11, 39ff.	At N edge of Steniklarian Plain	
700	Kalídhona: Giftókastro	Dörpfeld 1913, 124–25; Sperling 1942, 82	Just S of Kalidhona	Precipitous hill
701	Vrestós (ancient Pteleai?)	*Praktika* 1955, 243–44; Meyer 1957, 55–58, 71–73; *Deltion* 1968, 162	10 minutes E of Vrestos	
703	Kaïáfa	*Hesperia* 1937, 525–38; Dörpfeld 1908, 320–22; Sperling 1942, 81; *JHS* 1956, 17; Meyer 1957, 78	In lagoon near modern spa	Submerged now
704	Kombothékra: Psilolithária (temple of Artemis Limnatis)	Dörpfeld 1908, 323–26	Ca. 5 km N of Kombothekra	Promontory at end of ridge stretching E from Kaïafa
705	Platiána (ancient Epion or Tympaneai?)	Dörpfeld 1913, 124; Sperling 1942, 85; Meyer 1957, 22–36 and bibliography cited there	S of Platiana and higher	Steep hill
707	Káto Samikón: Kástro (ancient Samikon)	Dörpfeld 1908, 322; *Hesperia* 1937, 525–38; Sperling 1942, 85; Meyer 1957, 34f., 68, 76f.; *Deltion* 1964, 178; 1965, 210; 1969, 148; Philippson 1892, 261–62; Partsch 1890, 10, 14–15	On W spur of Mt. Smerna	Very high and precipitous hill
708	Gríllos (formerly Moúndriza) (ancient Hypana?)	*Praktika* 1955, 243; *BCH* 1956, 290; 1958, 568; 1959, 658; Meyer 1957, 43–44, 61	S of Grillos on slope of Mt. Smerna	Series of 3 eminences
709	Skilloundía (formerly Mázi) (ancient Skillous?)	*AJA* 1940, 539; *BCH* 64–65 (1940–41) 245–46; Sperling 1942, 83; Meyer 1957, 45–48, 68–69; *Praktika* 1960, 174–76; *Ergon* 1960, 135–40; *Deltion* 1965, 210; 1967, 209	Short distance W of Skilloundia	Hill
710	Skilloundía: Kaliváki	*Deltion* 1964, 179	2 km N	
712	Platiána: Karína	*Deltion* 1960, 126	Above Platiana	

REGISTER B

F Archaeological Description	G Analysis of Pottery	H Extent	I Miscellaneous
HAB?	H		Perhaps fort rather than town
HAB? R mosaic with hunting scene	R		Mosaic excavated by A. Likakis; weak candidate for Andania (cf. Ch. 6)
HAB. Late inscription with "Asklepios" under holy table in chapel of Ayios Yeoryios	R; M		Relatively good spring
HAB. Remains of two forts (A and H)	A C; H		Cf. Ch. 6
Square tower	H?		Tower guarding route from Messenia to Arkadia
HAB? Fortifications (ancient?) and foundations of bldgs.	C?; H?	Small	Perhaps fortress rather than settlement
HAB. Fortifications (4th c. B.C.); roof tiles; theater; cemetery at W foot; grave stele (1st c. B.C.); C H M coins	A C; H; R; M	500 m N-S × 200	Large and well-preserved site
HAB? Long straight foundations of large squared blocks, probably C or H (roadway? settlement?); frags. of C roof tiles of public bldg.	C; H		Dörpfeld suggested temple of Poseidon
SHRINE. Doric peripteron; scale and finds comparable to Metroon at Olympia; A and H figurines; identifying inscription on mirror	A C; H		Brief excavation by Dörpfeld
HAB. Fortification wall (probably H) well preserved with towers, gates; perhaps some earlier sections; agora, theater; residential area in E and S; cisterns; H or R inscription on E saddle (cemetery?)	C; H; R	680 m E-W × 30	Surveyed and examined by Meyer; large and very well preserved site
HAB. Main fortifications C; one section possibly A; chance finds in area include inscribed H stele, C lamp (one diagnostic Mycenaean sherd)	A? C; H; R	Ca. 180 m E-W × 100	Strong position guarding narrow coastal road; carefully studied by Bisbee
HAB. Ruins of walls and bldgs.; also at Áyios Ilías ca. 500 m N of Moundriza foundations of C bldg. 14.50 × 10 m (temple?); at nearby Xilókastro H coins, A-C vases, terracotta female bust	A C; H; R	300–400 m × 100–150	
SHRINE. A bronze statuette; inscription; numerous frags. of pediment sculpture representing gigantomachy; ruins of large Doric temple (4th c. B.C.?) probably that of Athena Skillountia mentioned by Strabo; C pottery at nearby Réthi	A C; H; R		Chance discovery of marble statue led to minor excavation by Stavropoulos and more thorough examination by Yalouris
CEM? Bronze hydria	C		
HAB. Over life-size hand of R statue; foundations of bldgs. (300 m distant at Pteri)	R		

REGISTER B

A Number	B Name	C Bibliography	D Location	E Physical Description
713	Kréstaina	*Deltion* 1965, 210		
714	Ladhikoú	*Deltion* 1961–62, 107; *BCH* 1962, 742	N of Ladhikou on S bank of Alpheios River	
715	Epitálion: Samakiá (ancient Epitalion)	*JHS Arch Reports* 1960–61, 14; Meyer 1957, 49f., 60f., 69; *AJA* 1961, 228, Fig. 3	400 m NE	High ground overlooking Alpheios Valley to N and narrow coastal plain to SW
717	Pírgos (ancient Letrinoi?)	Sperling 1942, 85; *Deltion* 1968, 152; Philippson-Kirsten 1959, 347	Within modern town and toward sea	
718	Stréfi	Sperling 1942, 85; *Deltion* 1965, 209; 1968, 160, 171–73	S of Strefi	
719	Makrísia: Lachnídhia	*Deltion* 1965, 210		
720	Áyios Ilías	*JHS* 1954, 157	Opposite Olympia	
722	Salmóni: Áyios Ilías	*Deltion* 1963, 104		
723	Miráka: Frangonísi (ancient Pisa?)	*BCH* 1959, 656; *Deltion* 1966, 171; 1967, 212; 1968, 164; 1969, 147	4 km E of Olympia on N side of Tripolis highway	Slope to S and Alpheios Valley (now cut into by gravel pit)
724	Kréstaina: Tsamá	Meyer 1957, 48–49	2½ km from Krestaina on W bank of Selinous River	Isolated hill
727	Makrísia: Skála	*AJA* 1961, 229	3 km NW	Hill overlooking Alpheios Valley
728	Angóna	*BCH* 1955, 253	3 km W of Olympia (on "sacred way") opposite Makrisia	
729	Kamboúlis	*Praktika* 1954, 293; *JHS* 1954, 156; *Deltion* 1968, 288–94	3 km SW of Olympia on left bank of Alpheios River	Valley
730	Loúvrou: Stavropódhi	Sperling 1942, 83	On N side of Alpheios, opposite Frixa	Hill
732	Fríxa (formerly Fanári): Paliofánaro (ancient Phrixa?)	Sperling 1942, 84	500 m N of Frixa	High hill overlooking Alpheios to N
733	Kavkaniá: Paliochórafa and Ayía Marína	*Deltion* 1963, 103		
734	Pournári: Dhragáta	Sperling 1942, 85	NW of Pournari	Side hill
735	Pournári: Fakístra (ancient Herakleia?)	Sperling 1942, 85	Contiguous to S	

REGISTER B

F Archaeological Description	G Analysis of Pottery	H Extent	I Miscellaneous
CEM? R lekythos and lamp; statuette of kouros (at Ayios Ioannis)	R		
CEM. Large H cemetery with stone-built graves; vases and bronze comb; large tumulus nearby may be prehistoric	H		
HAB. Wall foundations; roof tiles; terracotta perirrhanterion	A C; H; R	350 m E-W × 150 (max.)	Explored by Yalouris
CEM. Tile-covered graves; R tombs at spot called Vlisídhi	C; H; R		
HAB-CEM. Pithos burial with 2 skeletons and vases; C cist graves; bronze hydrias	C; H		
CEM? Bronze statuette of bull and tripod foot of G period	G		
SHRINE. Temple 20.05 m long; frags. of painted terracotta sima; G bird and animal figurines; R and M objects	G; A C; H; R; M		
HAB-CEM. Good walls of A period; R tombs	A R		
HAB-CEM. Large R cemetery; C graves; walls of A and C bldgs.	A C; H; R		Excavated by Yalouris and Papathanasopoulos
HAB. Foundations of building(s) (temple?)	C; H		
HAB	C		Site of considerable extent reported by Yalouris
HAB. Large C bldg. with interesting architectural frags.	C		
SHRINE? Very large *apothetis* of shrine (probably temple of female deity) with pottery, statuettes, and bronze jewelry	A C		Salvage by ephorate
HAB	C	Small	
HAB. Traces of fortifications	C; H		
HAB. CEM? 2 bronze covers of mirrors of 4th c. B.C.; bldg. foundations	C; H; R		
HAB	A? C		
HAB. Roof tiles	C		

Conversion Table of Original (1961–69) and Revised System of Numbering Individual Prehistoric Sites

Original	Revised	Original	Revised	Original	Revised	Original	Revised
1	304	22N	61	40	19	72B	74
2	305	22P	60	41	20	72C	77
3	306	23	234	41A	21	72D	80
4	307	23A	235	41B	22	72E	45
4A	309	23B	237	42	1	73	79
5	308	23C	230	42A	2	73A	78
5A	310	23D	236	42B	55	74	109
6	320	23E	239	43	14	74A	110
6A	316	23F	238	44	13	74B	108
7	317	23G	71	45	12	74C	111
7A	318	24	233	46	11	75	107
7B	319	24A	231	47	56	75A	103
8	315	24B	229	48	54	75B	31
8A	321	24C	228	49	53	75C	106
8B	322	25	232	50	52	75D	104
9	323	26	226	50A	51	75E	102
9A	324	26A	227	51	48	75F	105
9B	325	26B	225	51A	49	76	100
9C	326	27	222	52	46	76A	113
9D	327	27A	223	53	47	76B	112
9E	328	27B	224	54	50	76C	130
10	329	28	220	55	3	76D	114
11	330	28A	221	56	4	76E	131
12	303	28B	203	57	5	76F	115
14	312	28C	204	58	42	76G	121
15	311	28D	218	58A	41	77	128
16	313	28E	219	58B	40	77A	123
16A	314	29	212	58C	39		124
17	331	30	217	59	6	77B	122
18	332	31	216	59 A-E	7	77C	125
19	302	31A	215	60	8	77D	127
19A	301	31B	213	61	9	77E	126
20	300	31C	214	62	10	77F	129
21	245	32	209	63	44	78	137
21A	244	32A	208	64	43	78A	135
21B	246	32B	207	65	35	78B	136
21C	243	32C	206	65A	36	78C	134
21D	242	32D	205	65B	34	78D	132
21E	241	33	211	66	37	78E	133
21F	240	33A	210	66A	38	79	142
22	70	34	116	67	33	79A	141
22A	201	35	118	67A	32	79B	139
22B	200	35A	119	68	28	79C	140
22C	72	35B	120	68A	29	79D	143
22D	202	36	117	69	27	79E	138
22E	68	36A	73	69A	26	80	145
22F	65	37	57	69B	25	80A	144
22G	69	37A	58	69C	24	81	146
22H	67	37B	59	69D	23	82	147
22J	66	37C	16	70	30	83	148
22K	64	38	15	71	101	83A	149
22L	63	39	18	72	76	84	150
22M	62	39A	17	72A	75		

PLATES

Plate 1-1. Stereo photography (pair). K25 Ic 1970 (Nichoria). Compare Figure 2-12.

Plate 1-2. LH tholos interior, Kambos (#146)

Plate 1-3. LH tholos entrance, Thouria (#137)

Plate 1-4. MH multiple burial mound, Kaldamou (#14)

Plate 2-1. LH chamber tomb entrance, Thouria (#137)

Plate 2-2. Neolithic pottery

Plate 2-4. LH tholos dromos, Malthi (#222)

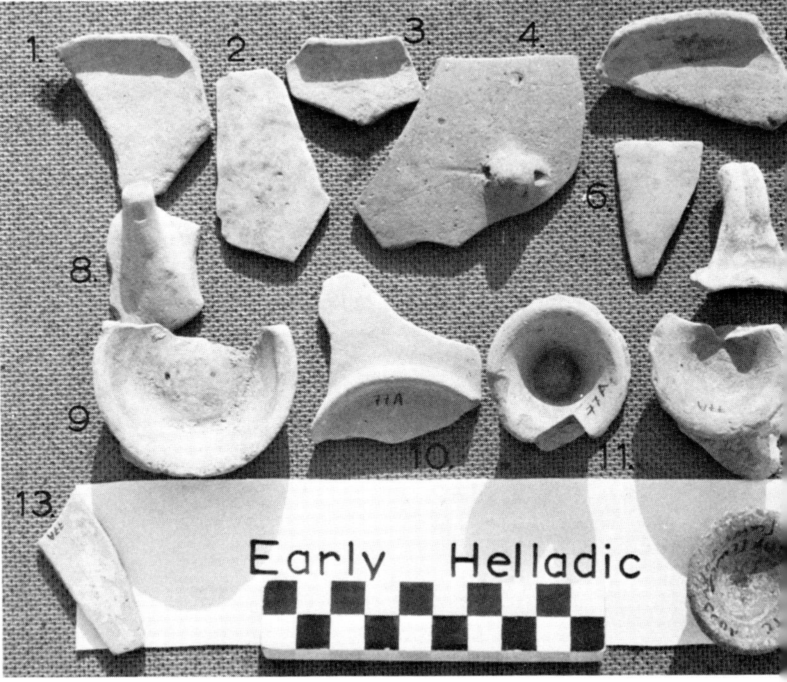

Plate 2-3. Early Helladic pottery

Plate 2-5. Middle Helladic pottery

Plate 3-1. "Adriatic" ware

Plate 3-2. Yiannitsa kalderimi

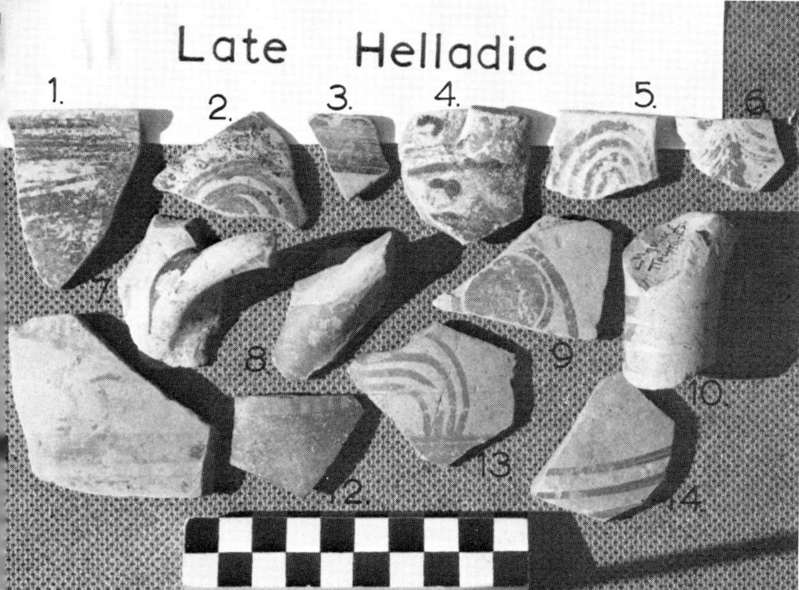

Plate 3-3. Late Helladic pottery

Plate 3-4. Road between Neromilos and Kazarma

Plate 4-1. Mavrozoumenos bridge

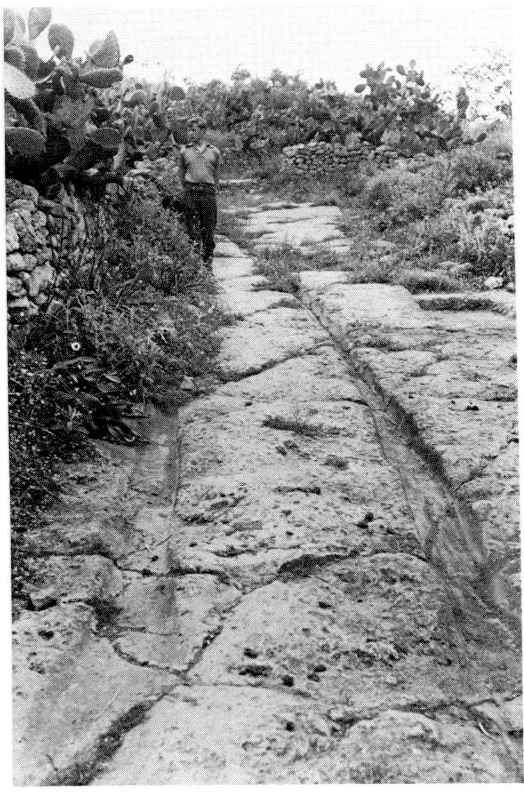

Plate 4-2. Wheel ruts, Thouria

Plate 4-3. Nichoria kalderimi

Plate 5-1. Samikon and lagoon to north

Plate 5-2. Voïdhokilia Bay and Osmanaga Lagoon

Plate 6-1. Voïdhokilia Bay and Osmanaga Lagoon from the southwest

Plate 6-2. Paliokastro and Neolithic "Cave of Nestor" (#10)

Plate 7-1. EH mound, Yanitsochori (#246)

Plate 7-2. EH-LH acropolis, Finikous (#79)

Plate 7-3. EH-LH acropolis, Klidhi (#302)

Plate 7-4. MH-LH acropolis, Malthi (#222)

Plate 8-1. MH-LH acropolis, Konchilion (#203)

Plate 8-2. MH?-LH acropolis, Leftro (#148)

Plate 8-3. MH-LH acropolis, Kyparissia (#70)

Plate 9-1. LH acropolis, Kalamata (#142)

Plate 9-2. Classical acropolis of Eira

Plate 9-3. Tower and curtain wall, Messene (#529)

Plate 9-4. Ashlar wall, Thouria (#137)

Plate 10-1. Medieval acropolis, Yiannitsa

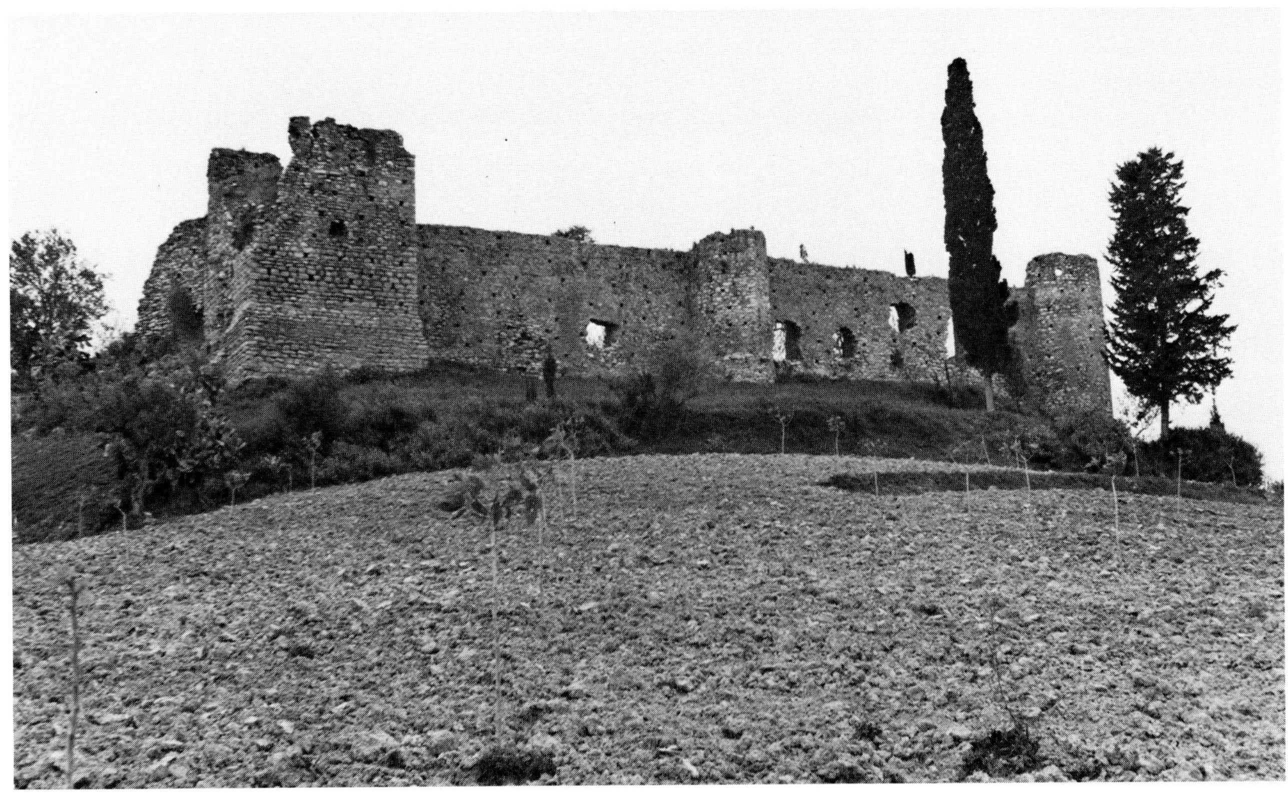

Plate 10-2. Medieval acropolis, Andhrousa

Plate 11-1. Medieval fortress, Koroni (#512)

Plate 11-2. Medieval church, Samarina

Plate 12-1. Karpofora from the air

Plate 12-2. Near Malthi: harvesting wheat with olives interplanted

Plate 13-1. Kalochori: in foreground rocky slope for grazing; in middle ground terraced fields for grain, vineyards, and fruit trees

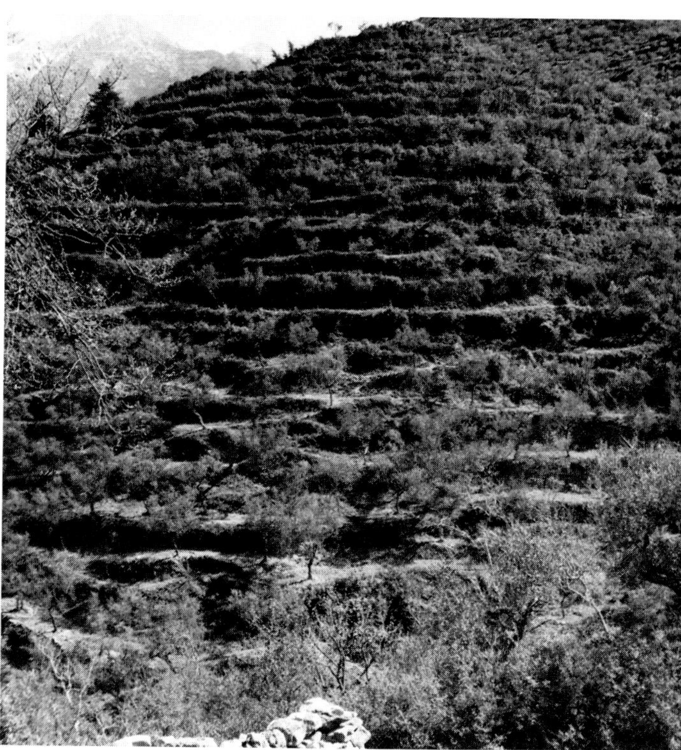

Plate 13-2. Exochori: terraced mountainside above village; now exclusively in olives (formerly interplanted with grain)

Plate 13-3. Exochori: rocky hill above village, formerly in grain but now grazed; scattered almond trees

Plate 13-4. Pilokambos: mainly currants with some olives and irrigated field crops; Bay of Navarino in background

Plate 14-1. Clay pit, Vounaria

Plate 14-2. Crushing clay

Plate 14-3. Slaking clay

Plate 14-4. Removing sludge

Plate 14-5. Pouring slip through sieve

Plate 14-6. Kneaded or wedged clay

Plate 15-1. Forming ball of clay

Plate 15-2. Throwing vika on wheel (earlier stage)

Plate 15-3. Throwing vika on wheel (later stage)

Plate 15-4. Applying handles

Plate 15-5. Pottery kilns, Vounaria

Plate 15-6. Pots of various shapes

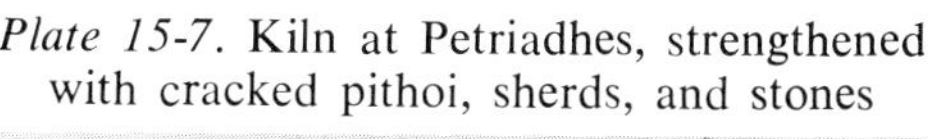

Plate 15-7. Kiln at Petriadhes, strengthened with cracked pithoi, sherds, and stones

Plate 15-8. Horizontally ribbed pithoi

Plate 16-1. Trench dug to reveal the source of magnetometer anomalies (Fig. 15-5)

Plate 16-2. Trench revealing a buried pithos to be the source of magnetometer anomaly (Fig. 15-6)

Plate 16-3. Magnetometer survey of Osmanaga Lagoon

KEYS TO POCKET MAP 1-1

Alphabetical Key to Pocket Map 1-1, Modern Towns and Villages

NOTE: Left-hand number indicates location within each eparchy; capital letter and right-hand number indicate grid coordinates.

Commune Capitals in Eparchy of Elis

Achladhiní 47 I 24
Áspra Spítia 1 I 21
Áyios Ilías (Letrínon) 44 A 23
Áyios Ioánnis 23 B 23
Áyios Yeóryios 36 C 23
Chelidhóni 43 G 23
Dhoúka 46 H 24
Flóka 5 F 22
Granitséïka 28 B 23
Iráklia 34 F 23
Kámena 10 H 22
Katákolo 6 A 22
Kavkonía 32 F 23
Kládheos 25 G 23
Kolíri 30 D 23
Korakochóri 18 A 23
Koskiná 11 G 22
Kriónero 45 G 24
Lála 40 H 23
Landzóï 39 E 23
Lánthi 38 E 23
Lastéïka 33 C 23
Levendochóri 29 A 23
Linariá 7 H 22
Loúvro 4 I 22
Máyira 15 G 22
Miráka 2 G 22
Mirtiá 41 B 23
Mouriá 8 H 22
Nemoúta 37 I 23
Olympia 3 G 22
Palió Varvásena 24 E 23
Pelópion 21 F 23
Pévkes 17 H 23
Pírgos 16 C 22
Plátanos 13 F 22
Pournári 31 F 23
Prásino 42 C 23
Salmóni 12 E 22
Skafidhiá 35 A 23
Skourochóri 26 B 23
Smíla 22 E 23
Stréfi 14 E 22
Varvásena 19 D 23
Vasiláki 9 I 22
Vitinéïka 27 B 23
Xirókambos 20 J 23

Commune Capitals in Eparchy of Olympia

Agrídhi 60 E 21
Alfioúsa 64 E 22
Alifíra 39 K 20
Amigdhaliés 26 K 19
Andhrítsaina 20 L 18
Anemochóri 55 E 21
Anílio 14 H 18
Aríni 27 H 19
Áyios Ilías 5 H 17
Dhafnoúla 53 K 21
Dhiásela 49 I 20
Dhragóyi 7 K 17
Epitálion 63 D 22
Fanári 25 K 19
Figalía 2 J 16
Fríxa 61 H 21
Gréka 44 H 20
Gríllos 50 G 20
Kakóvatos 15 G 18
Kalídhona 17 H 18
Kalivákia 62 H 21
Kallithéa 43 J 20
Káto Figalía 11 I 17
Káto Samikó 42 F 20
Koufópoulo 19 K 18
Koumouthékra 36 H 19
Kréstena 54 G 21
Krionéri 16 J 18
Krouní 48 F 20
Ladhikoú 56 F 21
Lépreon 9 H 17
Linístena 12 K 18
Livadháki 38 J 19
Mákistos 35 H 19
Makrísia 58 F 21
Mátesi 37 L 19
Miléa 31 H 19
Mínthi 28 I 19
Mirónia 22 J 18
Neochóri 8 G 17
Perivólia 6 K 17
Petrálona 10 J 17
Plátanos 40 I 20
Ploutochóri 59 H 21
Prasidháki 4 H 17
Ráches 51 E 21
Rodhiná 23 H 19
Róvia 24 L 19
Samikó 47 F 20
Schíni 18 H 18
Sékoula 52 K 21
Sikiés 34 K 19
Skilloundía 57 H 21
Sméma 41 H 20
Stómio 3 J 17
Taxiárchai 13 I 18
Thisóa 32 M 19
Trípes 33 I 19
Tripití 46 I 20
Vrestó 29 J 19
Vrína 45 G 20
Xirochóri 30 G 19
Yiannitsochóri 1 H 16
Zacháro 21 G 18

Commune Capitals in Eparchy of Triphylia

Aëtós 37 J 13
Agalianí 60 H 15
Agriliá 51 J 14
Ambelióna 74 L 17
Ambelófito 2 H 9
Amfithéa 49 K 14
Áno Dhórion 56 K 15
Áno Kopanáki 47 J 14
Armeniï 29 G 12
Artíki 41 I 13
Avlón 63 J 16
Áyios Sóstis 76 L 17
Chalazóni 22 G 12
Chalkiá 61 K 15
Chóra 3 H 9
Chrisochóri 59 K 15
Christiánou 13 H 11
Dhórion 46 K 14
Dhrosopiyí 35 K 13
Elaía 66 H 16
Exochikó 23 F 12
Farakládha 25 G 12
Filiatrá 14 F 11
Flesiás 11 I 10
Flóka 6 G 9
Gargaliáni 5 G 9
Glikorízi 50 I 14
Kakalétri 71 L 17
Kalítsena 67 J 16
Kaló Neró 48 H 14
Kaloyerési 24 J 12
Kamári 52 I 14
Kariés 69 H 16
Kefalóvrisi 57 J 15
Kókla 44 K 14
Koúvela 65 K 16
Krionéri 33 J 13
Kyparissia 40 H 13
Landzounátou 19 J 11
Lévki 1 G 9
Likoudhési 18 I 11
Máli 16 H 11
Málthi 34 K 13
Marathópoli 4 F 9
Metaxádha 9 I 10
Mírou 42 I 13
Monastíri 32 J 13
Mouriatádha 38 H 13
Mouzáki 8 H 10
Nédha 73 M 17
Palió Loutró 12 I 10
Perdhikonéri 20 H 12
Pétra 72 L 17
Pírgos 7 H 9
Platánia 68 J 16
Pláti 15 G 11
Polithéa 36 J 13
Pródhromos 62 H 16
Psári 54 K 15
Ráches 45 H 14
Raftópoulo 21 I 12
Rodhiá 28 I 12
Selá 27 I 12
Sidherókastro 55 I 15
Sírrizo 64 L 16
Sitochóri 53 J 15
Skliroú 75 L 17
Spiliá 26 G 12
Stásimo 70 L 16
Stasió 30 G 12
Tripília 17 J 11
Válta 10 G 10
Vanádha 58 I 15
Vasilikó 43 K 13
Vríses 39 H 13
Xirókambos 31 H 12

Commune Capitals in Eparchy of Messini

Agriliá 21 M 10
Agrilóvouno 71 L 14
Amfithéa 18 M 10
Análipsi 2 M 8
Andhroúsa 25 L 10
Andhanía 64 M 14
Áno Mélpia 80 L 15
Áno Voútena 34 I 11
Anthoúsa 47 M 12
Aristodhímion 33 M 11
Aristoménis 16 J 9
Arsinóï 39 L 11
Avramioú 4 L 8
Dhasochóri 79 M 15
Dhesíla 74 M 14
Dhiavolítsi 73 M 14
Dhiódhia 15 K 9
Dhraïna 30 K 11
Ellinoklisiá 32 L 11
Éva 26 M 10
Fília 68 N 14
Ichalía 61 M 13
Iléktra 72 L 14
Kalamará 24 M 10
Kalívia 59 N 13
Kalliróï 65 L 14
Kaloyerórachi 27 L 10
Karnásion 77 M 15
Karteróli 12 M 9
Káto Mélpia 78 L 15
Katsaroú 50 N 12
Kefalinoú 44 K 12
Kefalóvrisi 35 J 11
Kendrikó 69 M 14
Klíma 31 K 11
Konstandíni 70 L 14
Koromiléa 38 L 11
Koutífari 22 J 10
Lámbaina 37 M 11
Levkochóra 6 L 9
Likótrafo 7 M 9
Loutró 62 M 13
Mádhena 5 M 9
Magoúla 56 M 13
Málta 67 M 14
Mándhra 76 L 15
Mandzári 63 M 14
Mánesi 17 K 9
Manganiakó 36 K 11
Mavromáti (Ithómis) 42 L 12
Mavromáti (Pamísou) 10 M 9
Meligalá 52 M 13
Merópi 58 M 13
Messíni 9 M 9
Míla 53 K 13
Neochóri (Aristoménous) 3 L 8
Neochóri (Ithómis) 51 L 13
Paliókastro 40 J 11

Parapoúngi 75 M 14
Péfko 48 O 12
Pilalístra 11 M 9
Piperítsa 13 M 9
Platanóvrisi 23 J 10
Políchni 66 L 14
Polílofos 19 L 10
Poulítsi 28 J 10
Rematiá 49 K 12
Siámou 54 N 13
Skála 43 M 12
Soláki 55 M 13
Spitáli 14 M 9
Steníklaros 57 L 13
Stréfi 8 K 9
Tríkorfo 29 K 10
Tríodhos 20 M 10
Tsoukaléïka 46 M 12
Valíra 41 M 11
Velíka 1 L 8
Zerbísia 45 K 12
Zevgolatió 60 M 13

Commune Capitals in Eparchy of Pylia

Achladhochóri 31 L 6
Adhrianí 22 K 5
Akritochóri 4 K 3
Ambelókipi 26 J 5
Chandhrinoú 35 J 7
Charavyí 42 K 7
Charokopió 7 L 3
Chatzí 52 J 8
Chrisokelariá 3 K 3
Chomatádha 19 I 5
Dára 56 K 8
Dhrosiá 55 K 8
Evangelismós 13 I 4
Falánthi 11 L 4
Finikoús 5 J 3
Glifádha 48 I 8
Iámia 6 K 3
Íklena 45 H 7
Kainoúryio Chorió 16 H 5
Kakórema 25 L 5
Kallithéa 20 J 5
Kalochóri 38 K 7
Kapláni 8 K 4
Karpofóra 47 L 8
Kastánia 37 K 7
Kinigoú 24 I 5
Kókkino 29 K 6
Kómbi 12 L 4
Korifásion 46 H 8
Koróni 2 M 3
Koukounára 39 I 7
Kourtáki 57 J 9
Kremmídhia 43 I 7
Lachanádha 10 J 4
Likísa 28 K 6
Longá 23 L 5
Maniáki 62 I 9
Maryéli 64 J 9
Mathía 30 K 6
Mesochóri 17 H 5
Mesopótamos 40 J 7
Metamórfosi 60 I 9
Methóni 9 H 4
Milióti 61 J 9
Milítsa 21 J 5
Mirsinochóri 53 H 8
Néa Koróni 15 L 4
Nerómilos 51 K 8
Panipéri 41 K 7
Papaflésa 63 J 9
Papoúlia 50 I 8
Pelekanádha 59 K 9
Petalídhi 36 L 7
Petrítsi 49 J 8
Pídhasos 18 I 5
Píla 34 I 6
Pylos 27 H 6
Romanoú 44 G 7
Romíri 32 K 6
Soulinári 33 J 6
Vasilítsi 1 L 2
Vlachópoulo 54 J 8
Vlási 58 J 9
Vounária 14 L 4

Commune Capitals in Eparchy of Kalamata

Ágrilos 53 O 11
Aíthaia 41 N 10
Alagonía 48 R 10
Alónia 50 M 10
Altomirá 27 Q 7
Ámmos 45 M 10
Andikálamos 35 N 9
Anemómilos 52 M 11
Áno Ámfia 46 O 10
Ánthia 47 N 10
Arfará 58 N 11
Ariochóri 51 N 10
Áris 42 M 10
Artemisía 43 Q 10
Asپróchoma 33 O 9
Aspropouliá 49 N 10
Avía 24 P 7
Áyios Flóros 60 N 11
Áyios Nikólaos 7 R 4
Áyios Níkon 1 S 2
Elaiochóri 32 Q 9
Exochóri 17 R 5
Faraí 30 P 8
Kalamáta 31 O 8
Kámbos 22 Q 6
Kardhamíli 16 R 5
Kariovoúni 12 S 5
Karvéli 38 Q 9
Kastanéa 13 S 5
Káto Dholí 21 P 6
Káto Vérga 29 P 8
Kéndro 23 R 7
Ladhá 40 Q 10
Langádha 3 S 3
Léïka 34 O 9
Mikrí Mandínia 26 P 7
Mikrománi 37 N 9
Miléa 9 T 4
Nédhousa 56 Q 11
Neochóri 11 R 4
Nomitsí 5 S 3
Pídhima 55 N 11
Pigádhia 28 R 8
Pírgos 10 S 4
Piyés 44 R 10
Platí 54 M 11
Plátsa 6 S 3
Polianí 59 P 11
Proástio 14 R 5
Prosílio 19 R 6
Rínglia 8 S 4
Saïdhóna 15 R 5
Sotiriánika 25 Q 7
Sperchóyia 36 N 9
Stamatinoú 61 N 11
Stavropiyí 20 Q 6
Thalámai 4 S 3
Thouría 39 N 9
Trachíla 2 S 3
Tséria 18 R 6
Velanidhiá 57 O 11
Vromóvrisi 62 N 12

Numerical Key to Pocket Map 1-1, Modern Towns and Villages

Commune Capitals in Eparchy of Elis

1 Áspra Spítia
2 Miráka
3 Olympia
4 Loúvro
5 Flóka
6 Katákolo
7 Linariá
8 Mouriá
9 Vasiláki
10 Kámena
11 Koskiná
12 Salmóni
13 Plátanos
14 Stréfi
15 Máyira
16 Pírgos
17 Pévkes
18 Korakochóri
19 Varvásena
20 Xirókambos
21 Pelópion
22 Smíla
23 Áyios Ioánnis
24 Palio Varvásena
25 Kládheos
26 Skourochóri
27 Vitinéïka
28 Granitséïka
29 Levendochóri
30 Kolíri
31 Pournári
32 Kavkonía
33 Lastéïka
34 Iráklia
35 Skafidhiá
36 Áyios Yeóryios
37 Nemoúta
38 Lánthi
39 Landzóï
40 Lála
41 Mirtiá
42 Prásino
43 Chelidhóni
44 Áyios Ilías (Letrínon)
45 Kriónero
46 Dhoúka
47 Achladhiní

Commune Capitals in Eparchy of Olympia

1 Yiannitsochóri
2 Figalía
3 Stómio
4 Prasidháki
5 Áyios Ilías
6 Perivólia
7 Dhragóyi
8 Neochóri
9 Lépreon
10 Petrálona
11 Káto Figalía
12 Linístena
13 Taxiárchai
14 Anílio
15 Kakóvatos
16 Krionéri
17 Kalídhona
18 Schíni
19 Koufópoulo
20 Andhrítsaina
21 Zacháro
22 Mirónia
23 Rodhiná
24 Róvia
25 Fanári
26 Amigdhaliés
27 Aríni
28 Mínthi
29 Vrestó
30 Xirochóri
31 Miléa
32 Thisóa
33 Trípes
34 Sikiés
35 Mákistos
36 Koumouthékra
37 Mátesi
38 Livadháki
39 Alifíra
40 Plátanos
41 Smérna
42 Káto Samikó
43 Kallithéa
44 Gréka
45 Vrína
46 Tripití
47 Samikó
48 Krouní
49 Dhiásela
50 Gríllos
51 Ráches
52 Sékoula
53 Dhafnoúla
54 Kréstena
55 Anemochóri
56 Ladhikoú
57 Skilloundía
58 Makrísia
59 Ploutochóri
60 Agrídhi
61 Fríxa
62 Kalivákia
63 Epitálion
64 Alfioúsa

Commune Capitals in Eparchy of Triphylia

1 Lévki
2 Ambelófito
3 Chóra
4 Marathópoli
5 Gargaliáni
6 Flóka
7 Pírgos
8 Mouzáki
9 Metaxádha
10 Válta
11 Flesiás
12 Palió Loutró
13 Christiánou
14 Filiatrá
15 Pláti
16 Máli
17 Tripília
18 Likoudhési
19 Landzounátou
20 Perdhikonéri
21 Raftópoulo
22 Chalazóni
23 Exochikó
24 Kaloyerési
25 Farakládha
26 Spiliá
27 Selá
28 Rodhiá
29 Armeniï
30 Stasió
31 Xirókambos
32 Monastíri
33 Krionéri
34 Málthi
35 Dhrosopiyí
36 Polithéa
37 Aëtós
38 Mouriatádha
39 Vríses
40 Kyparissia
41 Artíki
42 Mírou
43 Vasilikó
44 Kókla
45 Ráches
46 Dhórion
47 Áno Kopanáki
48 Kaló Neró
49 Amfithéa
50 Glikorízi
51 Agriliá
52 Kamári
53 Sitochóri
54 Psári
55 Sidherókastro
56 Áno Dhórion
57 Kefalóvrisi
58 Vanádha
59 Chrisochóri
60 Agalianí
61 Chalkiá
62 Pródhromos
63 Avlón
64 Sírrizo
65 Koúvela
66 Elaía
67 Kalítsena
68 Platánia
69 Kariés
70 Stásimo
71 Kakalétri
72 Pétra
73 Nédha
74 Ambelióna
75 Skliroú
76 Áyios Sóstis

Commune Capitals in Eparchy of Messini

1 Velíka
2 Análipsi
3 Neochóri (Aristoménous)
4 Avramioú
5 Mádhena
6 Levkochóra
7 Likótrafo
8 Stréfi
9 Messíni
10 Mavromáti (Pamísou)
11 Pilalístra
12 Karteróli
13 Piperítsa
14 Spitáli
15 Dhiódhia
16 Aristoménis
17 Mánesi
18 Amfithéa
19 Polílofos
20 Tríodhos
21 Agriliá
22 Koutífari
23 Platanóvrisi
24 Kalamará
25 Andhroúsa
26 Éva
27 Kaloyerórachi
28 Poulítsi
29 Tríkorfo
30 Dhraïna
31 Klíma
32 Ellinoklisiá
33 Aristodhímion
34 Áno Voútena
35 Kefalóvrisi
36 Manganiakó
37 Lámbaina
38 Koromiléa
39 Arsinóï
40 Paliókastro
41 Valíra
42 Mavromáti (Ithómis)
43 Skála
44 Kefalinoú
45 Zerbísia
46 Tsoukaléïka
47 Anthoúsa
48 Péfko
49 Rematiá
50 Katsaroú
51 Neochóri (Ithómis)
52 Meligalá
53 Míla
54 Siámou
55 Soláki
56 Magoúla
57 Steníklaros
58 Merópi
59 Kalívia
60 Zevgolatió
61 Ichalía
62 Loutró
63 Mandzári
64 Andhánia
65 Kalliróï
66 Políchni
67 Málta
68 Fília
69 Kendrikó
70 Konstandíni

Numerical Key to Pocket Map 1-1. (continued)

71 Agrilóvouno	76 Mándhra
72 Iléktra	77 Karnásion
73 Dhiavolítsi	78 Káto Mélpia
74 Dhesíla	79 Dhasochóri
75 Parapoúngi	80 Áno Mélpia

Commune Capitals in Eparchy of Pylia

1 Vasilítsi	30 Mathía
2 Koróni	31 Achladhochóri
3 Chrisokelariá	32 Romíri
4 Akritochóri	33 Soulinári
5 Finikoús	34 Píla
6 Iámia	35 Chandhrinoú
7 Charokopió	36 Petalídhi
8 Kapláni	37 Kastánia
9 Methóni	38 Kalochóri
10 Lachanádha	39 Koukounára
11 Falánthi	40 Mesopótamos
12 Kómbi	41 Panipéri
13 Evangelismós	42 Charavyí
14 Vounária	43 Kremmídhia
15 Néa Koróni	44 Romanoú
16 Kainoúryio Chorió	45 Íklena
17 Mesochóri	46 Korifásion
18 Pídhasos	47 Karpofóra
19 Chomatádha	48 Glifádha
20 Kallithéa	49 Petrítsi
21 Milítsa	50 Papoúlia
22 Adhrianí	51 Nerómilos
23 Longá	52 Chatzí
24 Kinigoú	53 Mirsinochóri
25 Kakórema	54 Vlachópoulo
26 Ambelókipi	55 Dhrosiá
27 Pylos	56 Dára
28 Likísa	57 Kourtáki
29 Kókkino	58 Vlási

59 Pelekanádha	62 Maniáki
60 Metamórfosi	63 Papaflésa
61 Milióti	64 Maryéli

Commune Capitals in Eparchy of Kalamata

1 Áyios Níkon	32 Elaiochóri
2 Trachíla	33 Aspróchoma
3 Langádha	34 Léïka
4 Thalámai	35 Andikálamos
5 Nomitsí	36 Sperchóyia
6 Plátsa	37 Mikrománi
7 Áyios Nikólaos	38 Karvéli
8 Rínglia	39 Thouría
9 Miléa	40 Ladhá
10 Pírgos	41 Aíthaia
11 Neochóri	42 Áris
12 Kariovoúni	43 Artemisía
13 Kastanéa	44 Piyés
14 Proástio	45 Ámmos
15 Saïdhóna	46 Áno Ámfia
16 Kardhamíli	47 Ánthia
17 Exochóri	48 Alagonía
18 Tséria	49 Aspropouliá
19 Prosílio	50 Alónia
20 Stavropiyí	51 Ariochóri
21 Káto Dholí	52 Anemómilos
22 Kámbos	53 Ágrilos
23 Kéndro	54 Platí
24 Avía	55 Pídhima
25 Sotiriánika	56 Nédhousa
26 Mikrí Mandínia	57 Velanidhiá
27 Altomirá	58 Arfará
28 Pigádhia	59 Polianí
29 Káto Vérga	60 Áyios Flóros
30 Faraí	61 Stamatinoú
31 Kalamáta	62 Vromóvrisi

INDEX

INDEX

Index

Index

DF 261 M45 M56 c.1

THE MINNESOTA MESSENIA EXPEDITION.

(21 CHARTS IN BACK POCKET)